I0887429

Church in Crisis

CHURCH IN CRISIS

The Enlightenment and Its Impact upon Today's Church

Martin R. Tripole, S.J.

Sapientia Press
of Ave Maria University

Copyright © 2012 by Sapientia Press of Ave Maria University, Ave Maria, Florida. All rights reserved.

No part of this publication may be reproduced or transmitted in any form or means, electronic or mechanical, including photography, recording, or any other information storage or retrieval system, without permission in writing from the publisher.

Requests for permission to make copies of any part of the work should be directed to:

Sapientia Press
of Ave Maria University
5050 Ave Maria Blvd.
Ave Maria, FL 34142
888-343-8607

Cover Design: Eloise Anagnost

Cover Image: *The Storm on the Sea of Galilee*, 1633 (oil on canvas)
by Rembrandt Harmensz. van Rijn (1606–69)
© Isabella Stewart Gardner Museum, Boston, MA, USA
The Bridgeman Art Library

Printed in the United States of America.

Library of Congress Control Number: 2012933238

ISBN: 978-1-932589-61-0

To my sisters Nina and Genevieve,

to the Sisters of the Order of the Visitation
of Holy Mary in Philadelphia,

to Sister Francis Cecilia English, S.S.J.,

to Barbara,

and to all whose prayers made possible
the publication of this work,
this book is dedicated.

Table of Contents

Preface

FOR SOME TIME I have been troubled by the serious crisis that exists in the Church. *Webster's Third New International Dictionary* defines the word "crisis" in several ways, but significant for our discussion regarding the Church would be the following: "the point of time when it is decided whether an affair or course of action shall proceed, be modified, or terminate; decisive moment; turning point"; or perhaps, "a psychological or social condition characterized by unusual instability caused by excessive stress and either endangering or felt to endanger the continuity of the individual or his group; *especially* such a social condition requiring the transformation of existing cultural patterns and values."

All of these seem to apply to our contemporary experience of the Church. Perhaps we might synthesize the above by saying that the Church is at a point of such conflict and division regarding what it is and what its course of action should be that many serious questions have to be investigated: What are the conflicts at issue, what are the origins of the problem, how did matters get so divisive, and what can be done to correct the problem? Resolving these issues would be decisive in that it would bring unity and peace to the Church even as it would determine the direction the Church might take for years to come.

Surely involved in such a discussion would be the question as to whether or not the Church should continue as it has for centuries, or needs to redirect its course, even as it proceeds to its predetermined destiny to become the new Jerusalem of the Kingdom of heaven. Are there better ways to get to that destiny, or are those of the past satisfactory? Knowing previous history that has led to the present crisis situation will be very helpful in addressing the nature of the problem and signaling a course of action.

The thesis of this publication is that crisis in the Church in America, though most acutely felt since the recent breakout of the sex-abuse problems, has been going on for centuries, and is the result of the growing dominance of the eighteenth-century Enlightenment mentality that supports the primacy of reason over revelation and faith in the pursuit of knowledge of the truth. The origins of the Enlightenment mentality can be traced to William of Ockham in the fourteenth century, who is the first major figure to give the argument for the separation of reason from faith its justification. While the Enlightenment has had much positive effect on the Western world, I would argue that its negative impact has been even greater. The origin and growing dominance of the Enlightenment mentality are discussed in chapters 3 through 5.

I argue that evidence for the growing pervasiveness of the Enlightenment mentality may be found from its effects in various areas of life, especially in the breakdown in the acceptance of the Church and its teachings. The loss of the authority of the Church and of fidelity to its teachings may be seen in copious statistical data available today documenting the rationalistic orientation of contemporary American Catholics, especially as seen among today's youth. Such statistical data is presented in chapters 1 and 2.

But the Enlightenment mentality does not simply begin and end with the Church; rather, the Church is part of a larger Enlightenment movement in the Western world, whose effects are slowly overpowering life in the Church and leading good Catholics off the proper course. Special areas where the Enlightenment mentality shows its dominance in America are to be found in Catholic higher education, the social apostolate, the misguided movement known as separation of church and state, and the recent sex-abuse crisis. All of these issues are treated in chapters 6 through 9.

I argue, finally, in chapters 10 and 11, that the only way to correct the problems caused by the Enlightenment is to restore the primacy of faith and revelation over reason, as argued especially by Pope John Paul II in *Fides et Ratio*. It is critical that this primacy be restored, not only to preserve the unity of the Church, as argued by Paul in the Letter to the Ephesians, but especially for the success of Christ's redemptive mission for the world as presented in John's Gospel.

This book is directed primarily toward overcoming the divisions that are impairing unity within the Catholic Church and impeding Christ's saving mission for the world. Our ability to overcome the present crisis will take a lot of soul-searching on the part of the disparate factions within the Catholic Church, so as to put the unity of the Church and the success of Christ's mission ahead of their own particular agendas. But this work is directed also to all the members of the disparate groups within the total Christian community, urging them as well to foster unity in the one true

Church of Christ for the success of Christ's saving mission for the world. This goal is so important to all true Christians that it supersedes the values to be derived from fostering any of our particular agendas.

I owe a supreme debt of gratitude to all those who have made this work possible, especially Dr. Matthew Levering, Professor of Theology at Dayton University, who was enthusiastic about the project from the beginning; Diane Eriksen, Managing Editor of Sapientia Press, and the staff of the press, for their patience, kindness, and expertise in composing the final pages of this document; and Joseph Pearce, Editor-in-Chief of Sapientia Press, for his gracious support of me and this publication. I also wish especially to thank my sister, Nina M. Koehler, for her gracious subvention toward this project.

PART ONE

DATA OF IMPENDING CRISIS

CHAPTER ONE

Catholic Attitudes and Practices: Statistical Data

THOUGH PROBABLY over half of the American Catholic population was unaware of how much had gone awry in the life of the Church before the beginning of the sex-abuse scandal in 2002, deeply committed Catholics knew full well that the Church had been in a state of turmoil for some time. Describing this turmoil and its causes, and suggesting ways to restore harmony to the life of the Church, is what we are about in this study.

Our initial step is to examine statistical data about Catholic attitudes and practices regarding principles central to the life of the Church. Theoretically, if such data indicated an increasing identification of American Catholics with the Church's life and its teachings, we would have to look elsewhere for reasons for unrest.

But as it is, what we shall see is a growing disaffection with the Church on the part of many Catholics. We must consider over the long haul why this disaffection is occurring, and whether it is critically undermining a unity essential to the life of the Church. We will also discover in the course of the two chapters in part 1 the existence of one major group strikingly different from the disaffected. This group will give us our major signal as to what is necessary for overcoming the crisis in the Church.

Far more data are presented in part 1 than the average person will want to read, and so the reader should always feel free to stop at any point and move to the conclusion to part 1 that appears at the end of chapter 2 (see pp. 132–34).

The purpose of presenting so much data is to drive home the extent of the problem: merely summarizing the drift of the data, as other studies have done, would not prove nearly so convincing. The quantity of evidence presented here covering every area of Catholic life and conviction is designed to show that, from whatever independent sources the surveys are taken and regarding whatever issue one might wish to investigate, the results are nearly always the same: the problem of disaffection is there, and it is pervasive. The person, then, who takes the time to travel through the surveys presented in these pages will understand how pervasive the problem is, and feel less free to conclude that the author simply has a pessimistic bent that is clouding his objectivity. No, the situation is really bad, and the vast data amassed here will prove it.

Loss of Catholic and Christian Identity

There are a growing number of Catholics and Christians who are abandoning their specific ecclesial community for other Christian denominations. But perhaps even more disturbing are the large numbers who are abandoning Christianity entirely.

According to the Gallup Organization, "in 1948, when Gallup began tracking religious identification, the percentage who were Christian was 91%." That figure in 2008 "stands at 77%," its lowest point. Gallup's data show that it is the "group of non-Catholic Christians" that has "dropped the most over the decades." Protestants who stood at 69% in 1948 are at 55% in 2008 (having fallen below 60% for the first time in 1979), whereas Catholics, who were 22% of the U.S. population in 1948, remain at that level in 2008.[1]

While the Christian community has continued to decrease in size, the percentage of those saying they have no religious identity has continued to rise. "In 1948, 2% of Americans interviewed by Gallup volunteered that they had 'no religion.' The number stayed at that range until about 1970." Today the percentage stands at 12%, its highest point so far. As to the reasons for this decline, Gallup cites two social scientists from the National Opinion Research Corporation (NORC), Tom W. Smith and Seokho Kim: "In sum, an array of social forces from cohort turnover, to immigration, to reduced retention rates, indicate that the Protestant share of the population will continue to shrink and they will soon lose their majority position in American society."[2]

Gallup data showing the gravity of the decline in Christianity are confirmed by other data prompting Jon Meacham, former editor of *Newsweek*, to write an article in 2009 entitled "The End of Christian America." In it,

---

[1] Frank Newport, "This Easter, Smaller Percentage of Americans Are Christian," Gallup Poll, April 10, 2009, www.gallup.com/poll/117409/easter-smaller-percentage-americans-christian.aspx.

[2] Ibid., 4.

he quotes R. Albert Mohler, Jr., president of the Southern Baptist Theological Seminary:

> A remarkable culture-shift has taken place around us . . . . The most basic contours of American culture have been radically altered. The so-called Judeo-Christian consensus of the last millennium has given way to a post-modern, post-Christian, post-Western cultural crisis which threatens the very heart of our culture.

Meacham adds that "the Christian God" is not dead, but "he is less of a force in American politics and culture than at any other time in recent memory." Mohler argues:

> What we are seeing now is the evidence of a pattern that began a very long time ago of intellectual and cultural and political changes in thought and mind. The conditions have changed. Hard to pinpoint where, but whatever came after the Enlightenment was going to be very different than what came before.[3]

Meacham and Mohler's conclusions are based on data from contemporary studies of religious and Christian demographics.

U.S. Religious Landscape Survey and **Faith in Flux**

Pew Forum conducted a nationwide survey from May 8 to August 13, 2007, of more than thirty-five thousand adults in the United States. Their U.S. Religious Landscape Survey found that the number of adults unaffiliated with any particular religion today is 16.1%, compared with only 7.3% who were "unaffiliated with any particular religion as a child."[4] The survey also found that 28% of U.S. adults "have left the faith in which they were raised in favor of another religion—or no religion at all," though if the changes within Protestantism were also included, the figure rose to "roughly 44%."[5]

In April 2009, the Pew Research Center published a new survey, *Faith in Flux*, intended as a "follow-up" to the above U.S. Religious Landscape Survey, with an "in-depth analysis of about eight-in-ten of those who now have a different religious affiliation than the one in which they were raised."[6]

---

[3] Jon Meacham, "The End of Christian America," *Newsweek*, April 13, 2009, 34.

[4] Pew Forum on Religion & Public Life, *U.S. Religious Landscape Survey Report 1: Religious Affiliation: Diverse and Dynamic* (Washington, DC: Pew Research Center, February 2008), 23, www.religions.pewforum.org.

[5] Ibid., 5.

[6] Pew Forum on Religion & Public Life, *Faith in Flux: Changes in Religious Affiliation in the U.S.* (April 2009), 2, www.pewforum.org.

Some surprising findings occurred; for example, whereas the Landscape Survey found 44% of Americans changed religious affiliations from the ones in which they were raised, the new survey found that among the 56% who currently belong to the religious tradition of their youth, 16% said "there was a time in their life when they had a different faith than they have now." The new survey finds, because of margins of error, that a more accurate figure would be anywhere from 47% to 59% of U.S. adults who "have changed religious affiliation at least once," and concludes that "roughly half of the U.S. adult population has changed religion at some point in their life."[7]

The data from these two surveys regarding membership in the Catholic Church are particularly disturbing. From the Landscape Survey:

> Catholicism has lost more people to other religions or to no religion at all than any other single religious group. These losses, however, have been offset . . . mostly by the significant number of Catholics who have immigrated to the U.S. in recent decades, primarily from Latin America.[8] . . . The group that has experienced the greatest net loss by far is the Catholic Church. Overall, 31.4% of U.S. adults say that they were raised Catholic. Today, however, only 23.9% of adults identify with the Catholic Church, a net loss of 7.5 percentage points.[9] . . . Overall, 2.6% of the U.S. adult population has switched their affiliation to Catholic after being raised in another faith or in no faith at all. But nearly four times as many people (10.1% of the adult population overall) were raised in the Catholic Church but have since left for another faith or for no faith at all.[10]

Additional data regarding loss of Catholic identity from the *Faith in Flux* survey indicate:

- Almost a third of those who were raised Catholic have left the Church, including 15% who became Protestant and 14% who became unaffiliated.[11]
- Most of these left the Church before they reached the age of 18.[12]

---

[7] Ibid., 3.

[8] Pew Forum, *Landscape Survey Report 1*, 19.

[9] Ibid., 23. Since the total U.S. adult population (18 years and older) in 2008 was estimated to be about 228,182,000 (see p. 3 of the American Religious Identification Survey (ARIS) 2008 report, (note 19 below), the 31.4% of U.S. adults who said they were raised Catholic equaled about 71,600,000, and the 23.9% identified with the Catholic Church equaled about 54,500,000.

[10] Pew Forum, *Landscape Survey Report 1*, 25.

[11] Pew Forum, *Faith in Flux*, 21.

[12] Ibid.

- A high percentage of Catholics attended worship services weekly as children, but among the presently unaffiliated, that attendance dropped from 74% to 44% while they were teens, and to 2% now as adults; among those who became Protestant, the percentage dropped from 79% when they were children, to 60% when they became teens, and is now 63% as Protestants; among those still Catholic, the figures go from 86% when they were children to 69% when they became teens, and is now 42% as adults.[13]

Two points to note here: all were raised as rather faithful Catholics, but a large drop-off in weekly service attendance occurred as teenagers; and those who are now Protestant are far more churchgoing as Protestants than those who are still Catholics (63% to 42%). This may imply a lack of real commitment to their faith as children; it would also seem to indicate a greater commitment of former Catholics to their newfound faith than of Catholics who endured in their faith as Catholics.

So how strong was the faith of the Catholics as children? The figures are revealing: "While 46% of lifelong Catholics report having had very strong faith as children, only 35% of Catholic converts to Protestantism and 30% of those who have become unaffiliated say the same." It was by their teenage years that the faith of all three groups declined: only 12% of the now unaffiliated said their faith was "very strong" as teens and their percentage remains the same as adults. Those still Catholic today fell to 34% with "very strong" faith as teens, then returned to 46% as adults. What is remarkable, however, is that among those who are now Protestant, 35% had "very strong" faith as children, and while that figure fell to 22% as teens, it rose to 71% as adults, more than double the percentage as children![14] Clearly many of these former Catholics found something in Protestantism they had not found as children that led them to a "very strong" faith today.

What was it about Catholicism that turned them away from the Church, and what was it about Protestantism that awoke them to a strong Christian faith?

According to the survey, the majority of those who are now unaffiliated left the Catholic Church because they "stopped believing in Catholicism's teachings overall (65%)," or were dissatisfied "with Catholic teachings about abortion and homosexuality (56%)," and "almost half (48%) cite dissatisfaction with church teachings about birth control." Among those who became Protestant, "50% say they stopped believing in Catholicism's teachings, 23% say they differed with the Catholic Church on issues such

[13] Ibid., 22.
[14] Ibid., 23.

as abortion and homosexuality, and only 16% say they were unhappy with Catholic teachings on birth control."[15] Clearly these three issues were more detrimental to the Catholic faith of those who became unaffiliated than with those who turned Protestant.

But the most common reason for leaving the Catholic Church among those who became Protestant (71%) was because "their spiritual needs were not being met." Another 70% said "they found another religion they liked more." Other reasons given for becoming Protestant: "dissatisfaction with teachings about the Bible," "married a non-Catholic," "dissatisfaction with the priests at their parish," and "unhappiness with the Catholic Church's treatment of women." Less than a third among the Protestants (21%) and those now unaffiliated (27%) felt the "clergy sexual abuse scandal played a role."[16]

Perhaps much can be learned about how to retain Church membership from the reasons lapsed Catholics gave for joining their current religion (including the unaffiliated). Reasons given by those who became Protestant include: "enjoying the religious services and the style of worship of their new faith" (81%); "feeling called by God to join their current faith" (62%); "attracted by a particular minister or pastor" (30%); "because a member [of the new religion] invited them" (30%); "because they married a member of their current religion" (28%).[17] Perhaps less helpful are reasons given among those who became unaffiliated: "just do not believe in God or the teachings of most religions" (42%); "just have not found the right religion yet" (33%).[18]

One might conclude from the data given in these two Pew studies that it would be difficult to retain or win back many Catholics who leave the Catholic Church because of personal conflict with immutable moral teachings of the Church such as those regarding abortion; on the other hand, the Church could probably do a better job of making the wisdom of its position convincing. But there are probably ways of making life in the Church more attractive to those who leave because of the lack of appeal of some aspects of the spiritual life of the Church, especially regarding Sunday services, or because of the failure to have an inviting social environment in the ecclesial community.

American Religious Identification Survey

The directors of the American Religious Identification Survey (ARIS) produced their third and latest study in March 2009 tracking "changes in the

[15] Ibid.
[16] Ibid., 25–26.
[17] Ibid., 28.
[18] Ibid., 29.

religious loyalties of the U.S. adult population within the 48 contiguous states from 1990 to 2008."[19]

The study confirms many of the points we noted in the Pew studies. For example, according to ARIS, as the number of self-identified Christians in the American population goes down, the number of "Nones" ("no stated religious preference, atheist, or agnostic") goes up (though the connection, if any, between the two is not yet clear).

In 1990, according to ARIS, 86.2% of Americans self-identified as Christian; in 2008, the percentage was 76%, an astounding loss of 10.2% in only eighteen years. Even more astounding is the fact that almost all of the loss—9.5%—occurred between the 1990 and the 2001 studies. Moreover, the fact that a far smaller loss occurred between the second and third studies was due largely to outside forces: "the influence of the heavy immigration primarily from Latin America in recent years." Barry Kosmin and Ariela Keysar support the findings of the two Pew studies in concluding that "Americans are slowly becoming less Christian," and that the challenge to Christianity is not coming from other religions but "from a rejection of all organized religions."[20]

To illustrate this last point: The number of Christians who identified themselves as "unspecified" grew from 8,073,000 in 1990 to 16,834,000 in 2008. The self-identified "non-denominational Christians" numbered 194,000 in 1990; in 2008 they numbered 8,032,000![21] Concomitantly, the percentage of "Nones" was 8.2% in 1990, but rose to almost double—14.1%—in 2001, and in 2008 to a new high of 15%. By hard numbers, the count is even more ominous: the "Nones" numbered 14,331,000 in 1990, but rose to more than double that amount—an astounding 34,169,000—in 2008, with the largest increase having occurred in the 1990s, to 29,481,000. According to ARIS, by 2008, "one in five adults does not identify with a religion of any kind compared with one in ten in 1990."[22] The "Nones" represent the "most significant influence on American religious geography over time": they have "increased in numbers and proportion in every state . . . . No other religious bloc has kept such a pace."[23] Moreover, only 69.5% of Americans now even believe in a personal God, the traditional foundation of all Christian religions![24]

---

19 Barry A. Kosmin and Ariela Keysar, *American Religious Identification Survey (ARIS 2008): Summary Report* (Hartford, CT: Trinity College, March 2009), 2, www.americanreligionsurvey-aris.org.

20 Kosmin and Keysar, *ARIS 2008*, 3.

21 Ibid., 5.

22 Ibid., 3.

23 Ibid., 17.

24 Ibid., 8.

Regarding Catholics: they numbered 46,004,000 in 1990, and grew to 57,199,000 self-identifiers in 2008, a gain of 11,195,000 Catholics, but this, again, was due largely to immigration. Catholics now account for 25.1% of the adult American population, but this is a loss of 1.1% since 1990.[25] Catholics have "lost ground within every ethnic group between 1990 and 2008": they have lost 6% of the "White non-Hispanic" population, and 7% of the "Hispanic."[26] Consistent with the Pew studies, ARIS indicates that the number of "Nones" among former Catholics grows. ARIS notes: "If the Hispanic population, which is the most Catholic, had not expanded then the Catholic population share nationally would have significantly eroded. One feature of the white population today is in fact the large number of ex-Catholics, who are now found among the Nones and have helped that group grow."[27]

How Many Catholics Are Still Going to Church?

One of the surest indications of the health of the Church is evidenced by how often Catholics attend Mass, since "the liturgy is the summit toward which the activity of the Church is directed" and "the fountain from which all her power flows."[28] "Frequency of Mass attendance is a strong indicator of the general importance of Catholicism in a person's life and of his or her level of commitment to living out the faith."[29] We therefore need to examine data regarding Catholic Mass attendance: Are Catholics going to Church?

George Gallup, Jr., estimated in 1987 that there were anywhere from 11 million to 16.5 million inactive or unchurched Catholics.[30] If the second

---

[25] Ibid.

[26] Ibid., 14.

[27] Ibid., 15.

[28] Paul VI, *Sacrosanctum Concilium* (Constitution on the Sacred Liturgy), par. 10, in Walter M. Abbott, S.J., gen. ed., *The Documents of Vatican II* (New York: Guild, 1966).

[29] Center for Applied Research in the Apostolate (CARA), *Sacraments Today: Belief and Practice among U.S. Catholics* (Washington, DC: Georgetown University, April 2008), 2.

[30] George Gallup, Jr., and Jim Castelli, *The American Catholic People: Their Beliefs, Practices, and Values* (Garden City, NY: Doubleday, 1987), 162–63. Gallup has defined "unchurched" in different ways. In a 2002 publication, he claims to have defined "unchurched" in a 1978 survey as "those who answered 'no' to either one or both of the following questions: 'Do you happen to be a member of a church or synagogue' or 'Apart from weddings, funerals, or special holidays, such as Christmas, Easter, or Yom Kippur, have you attended the church or synagogue of your choice in the past six months, or not?' " (George Gallup, Jr., " 'Unchurched' on the Rise?," Gallup Tuesday Briefing, March 26, 2002, www.gallup.com/poll/5521/unchurched-Rise.aspx). But in his 1987 publication, he defines unchurched as "those who were not members of a church and who had not attended church in the

figure was the more accurate, about one in four Catholics was not practicing the faith. A 2008 report by the Center for Applied Research in the Apostolate (CARA) seems to indicate that number has increased: whereas the report found in 2002 that 25% of Catholics "rarely or never" attended Mass, in 2008 that percentage increased to 32%.[31] George Barna reports in 2006 that the unchurched are 76 million adults or "one-third of the adult population (34%)" who have "not attended any type of church service or activity, other than a special event such as a funeral or wedding, during the past six months," and that "denominationally, the largest share of unchurched adults is made up of lapsed Catholics: almost three out of every ten unchurched people (29%) associate with Catholicism."[32] In other words, according to Barna, about 22 million unchurched adult Americans are lapsed Catholics.

Bryan T. Froehle and Mary L. Gautier reported in 2000 that the Catholic population in the United States had grown "106 percent since 1950, from 28,769,878 to 59,181,907." On the other hand, Mass attendance had "declined by about half during this period."[33] The real percentage of decline is probably steeper. We know that in the 1950s, about 75% of Catholics went to Mass every week,[34] and that as late as 1972, a majority of 54.9% of Catholics continued to attend church weekly or more often.[35]

It is not clear how many Catholics attend today. A wide disparity of figures has been reported: Philip Lawler reports a 1997 survey showing a 57%

---

past six months except for weddings, funerals or special holidays like Christmas, Easter, or Yom Kippur." In any case, in the 1987 publication, he claims to have found 11 million Catholics unchurched in 1978. In 1985, using the definition "those who have attended church or synagogue less than two times in the past year," he found "24 percent of American Catholics—about 16.5 million people—are unchurched" (pp. 162–63).

31 CARA, *Sacraments Today*, 20.

32 Barna Group, "Spirituality May Be Hot in America, But 76 Million Adults Never Attend Church," Barna Update, March 20, 2006, www.barna.org.

33 Bryan T. Froehle and Mary L. Gautier, *Catholicism USA: A Portrait of the Catholic Church in the United States* (Maryknoll, NY: Orbis, 2000), 49–50 and n. 9 (207). The 2010 *Official Catholic Directory* lists 68,503,456 Catholics in the United States, representing 22% of the total American population of 310,252,317 (p. 2065).

34 James D. Davidson et al., *Search for Common Ground: What Unites and Divides Catholic Americans* (Huntington, IN: Our Sunday Visitor, 1997), 18. In 1958, 75% of American Catholics said they attended Mass at least once a week. William V. D'Antonio, James D. Davidson, Dean R. Hoge, and Ruth A. Wallace, *American Catholic Laity in a Changing Church* (Kansas City, MO: Sheed & Ward, 1989), 44.

35 National Opinion Research Center (NORC), General Social Survey (GSS) Cumulative Data File, 1972–2004 (Roper Center for Public Opinion Research, University of Connecticut), sda.berkeley.edu/.

weekly Mass attendance.[36] A Zogby poll conducted in 2006 has 56% attending weekly or daily Mass.[37] William A. Donohue reported in 1995 that 51.8% of Catholics attended weekly Mass,[38] Andrew Greeley said 50% in 1987,[39] the Knights of Columbus reported 44% of Catholics attended religious services at least once a week in 2008,[40] and the Pew Landscape Survey in the same year reported 42% of Catholics attend religious services at least once a week.[41] The 2007 Baylor Religion Survey reports 41% of Roman Catholics attend Church weekly.[42]

All of these figures seem inflated. More realistic figures for weekly Catholic Church attendance may be the *New York Times* (37% in 1995),[43] the Gallup Center (37% in 2009),[44] George Gallup, Jr., (36% in 2002),[45]

---

36 Philip F. Lawler, "A Principle Rejected," *Catholic World Report* 7 (March 1997): 45. The survey was taken by the Roper Center for Public Opinion Research of one thousand Catholic Americans in late January and early February 1997.

37 Zogby International, "National Survey of Catholic Adults," telephone survey of 1,901 Catholics in March 2006, posted on the web page of the *Philadelphia Inquirer*, June 2, 2006, www.philly.com (site discontinued). The data in Zogby polls will consistently deviate from the findings in most other polls in our study.

38 William A. Donohue, "Catholic League's Survey of American Catholics," *Catalyst* 22 (June 1995): 6. The survey was taken of eight hundred Catholics 18 and older in February 1995 by Fabrizio, McLaughlin, and Associates.

39 Michael Hout and Andrew M. Greeley, "The Center Doesn't Hold: Church Attendance in the United States, 1940–1984," *American Sociological Review* 52 (June 1987): 333, 335. So far as I know, Greeley never changed this figure.

40 Knights of Columbus, "Moral Issues and Catholic Values," October 2008, 17, www.kofc.org/un/cmf/resources/Communications/documents/moralissues.pdf. The telephone survey with 813 Catholics in the contiguous United States was conducted by the Marist College Institute for Public Opinion, September 24–October 3, 2008.

41 Pew Forum on Religion & Public Life, *U.S. Religious Landscape Survey Report 2: Religious Beliefs and Practices: Diverse and Politically Relevant* (Washington, DC: Pew Research Center, June 2008), 36, www.religions.pewforum.org.

42 Rodney Stark, *What Americans Really Believe: New Findings from the Baylor Surveys of Religion* (Waco, TX: Baylor University Press, 2008), 19.

43 As reported by David Masci in "Catholic Church in the U.S.," *CQ Researcher* 5 (September 8, 1995): 780.

44 Mohamed Younis, "Muslim Americans Exemplify Diversity, Potential," March 2, 2009, 4, www.muslimwestfacts.com.

45 In response to the question "How often do you attend church or synagogue?" Survey results are "based on cumulative sample of 25,000 persons, 18 and older, interviewed in national Gallup surveys between 1992 and 2001" (George H. Gallup, Jr., *Religion in America 2002* [Princeton: Princeton Religion Research Center, n.d.], 36).

In 1996, Gallup reported that 34% of Catholics attended Mass weekly, based on a telephone survey made in 1995 asking the above question of 1,098 Catholics (George Gallup, Jr., *Religion in America 1996* [Princeton: Princeton Religion Research Center, 1996], 30). Gallup often presents a much higher rate for Catholic Church attendance based on asking "Did you, yourself, happen to attend church

James D. Davidson (35% in 1997),[46] Froehle and Gautier (34% in 2000),[47] the *National Catholic Reporter* (*NCR*/Gallup Poll) (34% in 2005),[48] the Baylor Religion Survey (32.8% in 2006),[49] Kirk Hadaway (28% in 1993),[50] Mark Chaves and James Cavendish (26.7% in 1994),[51] a 1994 Notre Dame study (26.6%),[52] and the General Social Survey (GSS) (26.5% in 2008).[53] CARA, which has done repeated surveys on this question, may be the most accurate at 23% (in 2008).[54] CARA also reports the

---

or synagogue in the last seven days, or not?" Answers to this question always produce higher figures. For example, when Catholics were asked that question in the 1995 survey, the result was 47% (p. 29).

Though the question about weekly church attendance might seem to provide the more accurate data, Gallup seems to think otherwise, that asking about attendance "in the last seven days" may reflect "*usual* church attendance," whereas asking about weekly church attendance may be more difficult to recall or be affected by occasional breaks, such as illnesses or vacations (Frank Newport, "Estimating Americans' Worship Behavior: Survey-based estimates have value," Gallup Poll, January 3, 2006, www.gallup.com).

46 Davidson, *Common Ground*, 183. Davidson's data are mainly a product of a national telephone poll of 1,058 Catholics 18 or older between May 8 and July 5, 1995, but also include interviews with Catholics and focus groups, and questionnaires sent to Catholics from the summer of 1993 to September 1994. The Mass attendance percentage is the average of his weekly or more attendance percentages of parish members (58%) versus nonmembers (13%).

47 Froehle and Gautier, *Catholicism USA*, 24.

48 Mary L. Gautier, "Lay Catholics firmly committed to parish life," *National Catholic Reporter* (*NCR*), September 30, 2005, 20.

49 Baylor Institute for Studies of Religion, *American Piety in the 21st Century: New Insights to the Depth and Complexity of Religion in the US*, The Baylor Religion Survey (Waco, TX: Baylor ISR, 2006), 14, www.isreligion.org; hereafter, Baylor Religion Survey 2006. The study was conducted by the Gallup Organization from October 8 to December 12, 2005.

50 C. Kirk Hadaway, Penny Long Marler, and Mark Chaves, "What the Polls Don't Show: A Closer Look at U.S. Church Attendance," *American Sociological Review* 58 (December 1993): 746. Hadaway argues that polls that estimate church attendance at much higher percentages are based on self-reported Catholic data that are exaggerated. His report is based on actual counts at Mass. He concludes that the "true rate" is probably "closer to 25 percent" (p. 747).

51 Mark Chaves and James C. Cavendish, "More Evidence on U.S. Catholic Church Attendance," *Journal for the Scientific Study of Religion* 33, no. 4 (1994): 380. Their study, like Hadaway's, is based on "count-based church attendance data" (p. 377), which lead to a figure "approximately half the self-reported rate" (p. 380).

52 Kenneth C. Jones, *Index of Leading Catholic Indicators: The Church Since Vatican II* (St. Louis, MO: Oriens, 2003), 76.

53 National Opinion Research Center (NORC), General Social Survey (GSS) Cumulative Data File, 1972–2008, sda.berkeley.edu. This represents more than a 50% decline from 1972's percentage of 54.9%.

54 CARA's figure is most interesting. The CARA survey from September 2004 based on a random-sample telephone poll, reported in "Self-reported Mass Attendance of

results of other surveys, including Barna (55% in 2006); Gallup (45% in 2004); CARA telephone polls (35% in 2005); Hadaway and Marler (25% in 2005); Hadaway et al. (24% in 1998); and Presser and Stinson (26% in 1998), using other methods such as "head counts and time diaries."[55]

Thus the figures range from a high of 57% to a low of 23%. This averages to 37.1%, which may be one way of drawing a conclusion. The Philadelphia Archdiocese counted people in the pews one Sunday in October 1997 and found only 31%.[56] Since the percentage Hadaway proffers (28%), and the 26.7% that Chaves reports, as well as the Presser and Stinson percentage (26%), seem to be based on more accurate sampling methods, I am inclined to think a figure around 27% might be closest to the truth. If so, this represents a loss of nearly 50% in the last fifty years. At that rate, the Church in America should be just about out of existence in 2060.

The sociologist Pierre Hegy gives another good indication of how steep and how quickly the drop has taken place. He reports that in 1963, 71% of Catholics still attended Mass every week, but, as we saw, by 1972, the percentage was down to 55%, a loss of 16 percentage points in nine years. By 1990, the figure was down to 40.5%, a loss of another 14.5 percentage points in just eighteen years.[57]

It is important to note that this falling off in church attendance is not unique among Catholics, at least according to the GSS, which indicates that, while 29.9% of the total American adult population attended weekly or more than weekly religious services in the 1970s, the percentage was down to 27% in the 1990s, down to 25.6% in the 2000s,[58] and to 25.5% in 2008.[59] But George Gallup, Jr., is much more positive: he reports in 2002 that to the question "How often do you attend church or synagogue?"

U.S. Catholics Unchanged during Last Five Years," January 2005, p. 1, gave 31% as the weekly attendance figure. In the Executive Summary of its latest study, *Sacraments Today*, CARA reports 23% of Catholics attend Mass weekly, based on a February 2008 survey of 1,007 self-identified adult Catholics using Knowledge Networks procedure, which uses a system where responses are self-administered from on-screen questions on computers or television. Such surveys have been found to be more accurate, consistently showing "lower levels of Mass attendance than what is exhibited typically in CARA's telephone calls" (ibid., 160).

[55] CARA, *Sacraments Today*, 160.

[56] Lou Baldwin, "The Archdiocese Takes Roll," *Catholic Standard and Times*, July 9, 1998, 3.

[57] Pierre Hegy, " 'The End of American Catholicism?'—Another Look," *America* 168 (May 1, 1993): 4. Hegy uses data from William C. McCready and Andrew Greeley for 1963 and 1972 statistics, and the GSS data thereafter.

[58] University of California, Berkeley, "Quick Table: GSS 1972–2006 Cumulative Datafile," sda.berkeley.edu/.

[59] GSS Cumulative Data File 1972–2008, sda.berkeley.edu/.

a national average of 32% said at least once a week (34% for Protestants); and to the question "Did you, yourself, happen to attend church or synagogue in the last seven days, or not?" the national average for weekly church attendance was 41%, though down from a high of 49% in the late 1950s.[60]

Gallup has kept a watch on Catholic Mass attendance since 1958. At that time, he reported that 74% of Catholics answered they had attended church in the past seven days. Since then, the numbers have been in decline. By 1985, the percentage had dropped to 53%, a drop of 21% in twenty-seven years. He notes the drop occurred in stages: nine points in the first decade to 1968, thirteen points during the next decade to 1978, and relative stability from 1978 to 1985.[61] As already noted, Gallup reports a further drop of six points to 47% in 1995.

Gallup has been conducting valuable surveys for *NCR* regarding American Catholic adult (18 and over) attitudes and practices every six years since 1987 (each was conducted shortly after the Easter celebration in 1987, 1993, 1999, and 2005). According to these surveys, 44% of Catholics attended Mass at least once a week in 1987, and in 1993, 43%. Significant decline occurs by the 1999 survey when only 37% said they attended at least once a week.[62] As indicated earlier, the percentage at weekly Mass attendance according to the 2005 survey is 34%.

A Gallup poll conducted December 17–19, 2004, provides an invaluable benchmark for the drop-off in Catholic Mass attendance. In that survey of 1,002 national adults, 34% of the total American population of 18-year-olds and older said they attended church weekly. Catholics were not singled out in this survey, though as we saw in the NCR/Gallup survey of 2005, Catholics attended Mass weekly or more at the same rate. In spite of that similarity, Gallup added this notation in his 2004 survey: "Catholics are less likely to attend church than Protestants."[63] Where do the data to support this notation come from? Apparently from three different Gallup surveys.

In a survey Gallup conducted in November 2003 to the alternate question—did you happen to attend church in the last seven days—47% of Protestants responded yes, but only 40% of Catholics did.[64] When that

---

60 Gallup, *Religion in America 2002*, 36, 32, 30.

61 Gallup, *American Catholic*, 26.

62 William V. D'Antonio, James D. Davidson, Dean R. Hoge, and Katherine Meyer, *American Catholics: Gender, Generation, and Commitment* (Walnut Creek, CA: AltaMira, 2001), 22.

63 Frank Newport, "Update: Americans and Religion," Gallup Poll, December 23, 2004, www.gallup.com.

64 George H. Gallup, Jr., "Catholics Trail Protestants in Church Attendance," Gallup Poll, December 16, 2003, www.gallup.com.

same question was asked again in late 2004, 51% of Protestants said yes, but only 45% of Catholics.[65] But in interviews conducted 2002–2005, when asked, "How often do you attend church or synagogue—at least once a week, almost every week, about once a month, seldom, or never?" similar results occurred: 45% of Catholics said weekly/almost weekly, but many Protestant groups, including Church of Christ (68%), Pentecostals (65%), Southern Baptists (60%), other Baptists (56%), and nondenominational Protestants (54%) excelled the Catholics, while Methodists (44%), Presbyterians (44%), Lutherans (43%), and Episcopalians (32%) did not.[66]

Since Catholics are obliged by Church law to attend Mass every Sunday while Protestants are not, such a finding is distressing, if not astounding. Gallup notes that, while Catholics had traditionally excelled Protestants in rate of church attendance (in 1971, 57% of Catholics said they had gone to church in the past week versus 37% of Protestants),[67] a reversal occurred "for the first time in nearly a half-century of Gallup Poll data collections" in March 2002, shortly after the outbreak of the sex-abuse scandal, and Protestant attendance has "remained higher than that of Catholics since then."[68]

How Important Is Religion to Catholics?

CARA asked Catholics in February 2008, "How important is your Catholic faith in your daily life?" The responses were somewhat disappointing: Only 14% said it was the "most important part" of their lives, down 3% from 2001. On the other hand, 27% considered it "among the most important parts" of their lives, giving a total of 41% for high importance,[69] which is encouraging. Only 19% considered it not important.

A recent Gallup report is important in that it makes clear that today's disparity between Catholic and Protestant attitudes and behavior cannot be blamed entirely on the recent sex-abuse scandal.

Gallup has been investigating American religiosity since 1941 by conducting what he calls an Index of Leading Religious Indicators, based on answers to several questions measuring religious beliefs and practices. In 2004 a perfect score on the Index was 1,000; the average score, drawn from surveys of American adults conducted throughout that year, was 648. That is the second lowest average score since Gallup began this survey. There are

---

65 Linda Lyons, "Protestants vs. Catholics: Who's Got Religion?: Catholics Lag behind Protestants," Gallup Poll, January 25, 2005, www.gallup.com.

66 Frank Newport, "Mormons, Evangelical Protestants, Baptists Top Church Attendance List: Jews and Episcopalians Least Likely to Attend on Regular Basis," Gallup Poll, April 14, 2006, www.gallup.com.

67 Ibid., 3.

68 Gallup, "Catholics Trail Protestants."

69 CARA, *Sacraments Today*, 102.

two remarkable points about this score: First is how much higher the score was among Protestants when taken alone: 690 (no *average* score has been that high since the early 1970s). Second, what is even more remarkable is how much the average score on the Index is brought down by the score for Catholics: 609. The disparity is called by the author of the report "a fairly substantial gap."[70]

The fact is that Catholics lagged behind Protestants on all but one item in the index survey: church membership. This was not always so. Gallup notes that in 1952, when Protestants and Catholics were asked, "How important is your religion to you?" 83% of Catholics and 76% of Protestants said "very important." However, in the 1994 survey, long before the sex scandals, Catholics were trailing Protestants on whether religion was "very important" in their lives by 65% to 51%. In the 2004 survey, when asked how important religion is to their lives, 69% of Protestants said "very important," while only 52% of Catholics did.[71] Pew Landscape Survey indicates only 56% of Catholics in 2007 found religion very important in their lives, while the average among Protestant groups was 70%.[72] As to whether "religion can answer most of today's problems" in society, 69% of

---

[70] Lyons, "Protestants vs. Catholics"; cf. Linda Lyons, "Religiosity Measure Shows Stalled Recovery," Gallup Poll, January 11, 2005, www.gallup.com.

[71] Lyons, "Protestants vs. Catholics." This finding is confirmed by a Barna 1991 survey: when asked to rank the importance of the following in their lives—family, health, having close friends, free time, time, religion, career, living comfortably, the Bible, and money—the Bible and religion came in fourth and fifth as "very important" for Protestants (73% and 70%, respectively), but ninth and sixth for Catholics (38% and 59%, respectively). Family and health were first and second for both groups (D'Antonio et al., *American Catholics*, 39).

In the January 2006 study of the same survey, Barna notes that 62% of all American adults claimed they were "deeply spiritual." Yet, when asked to "identify their single, most important priority in their life these days," family again ranked at the top by 51%. Faith came in second, but was chosen by only 16% of all adults. Noteworthy is the fact that "Protestants were more than three times as likely as Catholics to prioritize faith (24% versus 7%)" (Barna Group, "Americans Reveal Their Top Priority in Life," Barna Update, March 6, 2006, www.barna.org).

In the same January 2006 survey, Barna uncovered a most revealing finding regarding commitment: when asking, "Overall, how committed are you to the Christian faith?" 58% of Protestants chose "absolutely committed," while only 43% of Catholics did (*State of the Church: 2006* [Barna Group, April 2006]). Nevertheless, on the part of both Protestants and Catholics, there may be a deep yearning for commitment: in a 2008 study, Barna found 84% of Protestants said it would be "very desirable" to "have a close personal relationship with God" as opposed to 76% for Catholics, and 75% of Protestants said it would be "very desirable" to be "deeply committed to the Christian faith" as opposed to 59% among Catholics (Barna Group, "Survey Reveals the Life Christians Desire," Barna Update, July 21, 2008, www.barna.org).

[72] Pew Forum, *Landscape Survey Report* 2, 23.

Protestants but only 52% of Catholics said yes in the 2004 Gallup survey; in 1994, Catholics already trailed Protestants 71% to 51%.

Finally, in 2004, 60% of Protestants professed a "great deal or quite a lot of confidence in the church or organized religion," but only 53% of Catholics did. In this case, does the difference reflect Catholic disillusionment with the Church due to the sex-abuse scandal? Not entirely, because once again, Catholics lagged behind Protestants even in the 1994 survey, 63% to 59%.

Gallup draws this remarkable conclusion in early 2005:

> Importance of religion is a key measurement that explains the overall lower Index score for Catholics. . . . By a considerable margin, the gap shows that religion is less important for Catholics than Protestants. This wasn't always true. . . . Self-identification as 'Catholic' is often a cultural rather than a religious declaration, particularly for those who consider themselves 'lapsed' Catholics.[73]

What exactly does it mean to Catholics to be Catholic? One would expect that worshiping God at Mass would be considered central to Catholic identity for Catholics, but the data show otherwise.

CARA reports that 68% of Catholics agree "somewhat" or "strongly" that "I can be a good Catholic without going to Mass every Sunday" (34% agree "strongly").[74] When Gallup asked if they would mind not having a Sunday Mass but only Communion because of the shortage of priests, 70% of Catholics said they would not mind, at least if done only occasionally.[75] Gallup asked Catholics: "Can you be a good Catholic without going to church every Sunday?" In 1987, 70% said yes; in 1993, 73%; in 1999, 77%; and in 2005, 76%. Gallup notes that post-Vatican II Catholics were "most likely" to say yes. As we saw, according to Gallup, the percentage of Catholics who went to church every week dropped from 44% in 1987 to 34% in 2005.[76] It seems legitimate to correlate the data of the two surveys: the decrease in Mass attendance is related to the fact that the importance of Mass attendance for Catholic identity has decreased, so that now, only a quarter of the Catholic population considers weekly participation at the Sunday liturgy important to being a good Catholic.[77]

---

[73] Lyons, "Protestants vs. Catholics."

[74] CARA, *Sacraments Today*, 96.

[75] D'Antonio et al., *The American Catholic Laity*, 174.

[76] James D. Davidson, "Generations Have Different Views of the Church," *National Catholic Reporter* (*NCR*), October 29, 1999, 13; Dean R. Hoge, "Center of Catholic identity," *NCR*, September 30, 2005, 11, 14.

[77] Zogby data are often high, and may conflict with Gallup here. Zogby reports that 84% of Catholics in a March 2006 telephone survey said it was "important" for a Catholic to attend Mass every week (Zogby, "National survey of Catholic adults").

This brings to the fore the question: What, then, do the 76% in Gallup's survey consider important to Catholic identity? We will be considering that question later.

A Right-Left Split

Evidence of crisis in the Church is also indicated by data showing deep division over fundamental moral and ecclesial issues. The disturbing fact is that almost any moral issue disputed in American society today is equally disputed within the Church. And on most issues, there is little difference between how Americans in general and Catholics in particular think and act.

Moral Issues

The most hotly contested moral issue in America today is abortion. Senators fight contentiously over nominations to the Supreme Court not primarily over whether the nominees are qualified for the position but on the basis of how they would vote on overturning *Roe v. Wade*. Although most Americans don't realize it, any type of deliberate, direct abortion in the United States, from the moment of conception to the moment of birth, is legal today for any reason at all for a woman of any age, young or old. Such abortions are called "abortion on demand." The so-called "right" to an abortion for American women on the basis of a constitutional "right to privacy" was totally fabricated by the Supreme Court in 1973 in its *Roe v. Wade* and *Doe v. Bolton* decisions. (More on decisions of the modern Supreme Court in chapter 8 [see pp. 353–89].)

There is no moral issue over which the Catholic Church has more vigorously contended than the woman's "right" to an abortion. The Church has strongly condemned any abortion directly and deliberately incurred for whatever reason.[78] It will be useful, therefore, to examine data on Catholic views on abortion to see how much American Catholics identify with the Church on this teaching, and whether there is evidence of erosion of support in recent years. Unfortunately, Catholic views on this issue are "complex and often inconsistent."[79]

---

[78] Most Catholics are unaware that the Church permits indirect abortion, that is, when not directly willed but resulting indirectly from a good action directly intended, as, for example, the indirect result of the removal of a cancerous uterus. This distinction is never clarified when surveys are taken regarding Catholic views on abortion. To some extent, this clouds the clarity of data when Catholics are asked if they approve of abortion or of abortion "under certain circumstances." This should always be remembered when examining Catholic views on abortion.

[79] Gallup, *American Catholic*, 93.

Abortion

"Abortion easily ranks as one of the most controversial social issues in American society." So says George Gallup, Jr.[80] It is estimated that about 3,700 procured abortions occur every day, and 1.21 million a year (2005), in the United States; and 115,000 a day, and 42 million a year, worldwide. Fifty-two percent of abortions in the United States occur among women younger than 25 years of age, 18% among teenagers. Fifty-four percent say they were using some form of contraceptive when they became pregnant, and "93% of all abortions occur for social reasons (i.e. the child is unwanted or inconvenient)." It is estimated that "43% of all [American] women will have at least 1 abortion by the time they are 45 years old."[81]

Among the general American public, the abortion industry has grown remarkably over the years since its legalization in 1973. The pro-choice organization of Planned Parenthood of America—the Alan Guttmacher Institute—estimates that in the first full year (1974) after abortion's legalization, the number of procured abortions in the United States was 898,600, at a rate of 19.3 per 1,000 women aged 15–44. By the following year (1975), the number had already grown to 1,034,200, at a rate of 21.7. The greatest number of abortions is estimated to have occurred in 1990: 1,608,600, at a rate of 27.4.[82] Every year thereafter until 2005, with the exception of a slight rise in 1996, the numbers have steadily declined, so that in 2005, the number of abortions was 1,206,200 at a rate of 19.4 abortions per 1,000 women, the lowest number of yearly abortions since 1976.[83] The total number of surgical abortions in the United States since 1973 is estimated at

---

80 Ibid., 91.

81 All of the above data are to be found in the Center for Bio-Ethical Reform, "Abortion Facts" (drawn from the Alan Guttmacher Institute and Planned Parenthood's *Family Planning Perspectives*), accessed October 3, 2010, www.abortionno.org/Resources/fastfacts.html; and the Guttmacher Institute, "Facts on Induced Abortion in the United States," May 2010, www.guttmacher.org/pubs/fb_induced_abortion.html. Guttmacher Institute estimates there are about 42 million abortions worldwide each year.

82 National Right to Life, "Abortion in the United States: Statistics and Trends," using the Alan Guttmacher Institute figures, accessed October 3, 2010, www.nrlc.org/Factsheets/FS03_AbortionInThe_US.pdf. The highest rate per 1,000 women ages 15–44, however, occurred in 1980 when the rate was 29.5.

83 Ibid. On January 26, 2010, however, the Guttmacher Institute reported that "For the first time in more than a decade, the nation's teen pregnancy rate rose 3% in 2006, reflecting increases in teen birth and abortion rates of 4% and 1%, respectively." The implications of this rise have yet to be determined, but even the Guttmacher Institute's senior public policy associate, Heather Boonstra, found the reversal "deeply troubling," but only because she saw it as a consequence of "abstinence-only-until-marriage programs, which received major funding boosts under the Bush administration" and which "do not work." Media Center, "Following Decade-Long Decline, U.S. Teen Pregnancy Rate Increases as Both Births and

49,915,603, as of 2007,[84] with California by far the highest at 280,180 (1996).[85] According to Randall K. O'Bannon, director of education and research at National Right to Life, "The world was appropriately horrified and shocked when we lost about a couple thousand people on Sept. 11. . . . What we're talking about here is that sort of loss multiplied dramatically."[86]

It is noteworthy that "pregnancy rates for women under age 25, including teenagers, in the United States declined in 2004 compared to 1990. . . . Nearly 38 percent of pregnancies in 2004 were to women under age 25, down from nearly 43 percent in 1990. The proportion of pregnancies among teens under age 20 dropped from 15 percent in 1990 to 12 percent in 2004."[87] "Declines [in teenage pregnancies] also took place among all racial and ethnic groups and in every state in 2000."[88] The recent rise of the birth rates between 2005 and 2006 "follows a 14-year downward trend in which the teen birth rate fell by 34 percent from its recent peak of 61.8 births per 1,000 in 1991."[89]

What might explain this prolonged period of reduction?

According to Lawrence Finer and Stanley Henshaw, "Reasons for changes . . . are hard to determine . . . . Abortion may decline because fewer women experience unintended pregnancies, or because fewer women faced with unintended pregnancies end these pregnancies by abortion."[90] According to Jacqueline Darroch and Susheela Singh: "It appears that increased abstinence

---

Abortions Rise," accessed January 27, 2010, www.guttmacher.org/media/nr/2010/01/26/index.html.

[84] National Right to Life cites Guttmacher figures, estimating the total number of legal abortions performed in the United States from 1973 through 2009 to be 52,008,665. A reversal in the downward trend of the total number of abortions in the United States has also recently been noted. According to the Guttmacher Institute, a 1% rise in the abortion rate occurred between 2005 and 2008, with the hard numbers climbing from 1,206,200 at a rate of 19.4 abortions per 1,000 women in 2005, to 1,212,400 abortions at a rate of 19.6 abortions per 1,000 women in 2008. The significance, if any, of this reversal of the downward trend has yet to be determined (Rachel K. Jones and Kathryn Kooistra, "Abortion Incidence and Access to Services in the United States, 2008," *Perspectives on Sexual and Reproductive Health* 43 (March 2011): 43.

[85] Abortion Statistics," accessed October 3, 2010, www.abortiontv.com/.

[86] Michael Foust, "Tragic: U.S. passed 47 million mark for abortions in 2005," *Baptist Press News,* January 20, 2005, www.bpnews.net.

[87] National Center for Health Statistics, "Pregnancy Rate Drops for U.S. Women Under Age 25," Centers for Disease Control and Prevention (CDC), April 14, 2008, www.cdc.gov.

[88] "Abortion Statistics," accessed October 3, 2010, www.abortiontv.com.

[89] National Center for Health Statistics, "Teen Birth, Rate Rises for First Time in 15 Years," CDC, December 5, 2007, www.cdc.gov.

[90] Lawrence B. Finer and Stanley K. Henshaw, "Estimates of U.S. Abortion Incidence in 2001 and 2002," May 18, 2005, 4, www.guttmacher.org. Significant is the fact

among women accounted for approximately one-quarter of the drop in the U.S. teenage pregnancy rate between 1988 and 1995," and trends in more effective contraceptive use were also a "significant" factor.[91] The Guttmacher Institute supports these points: "Between 1995 and 2002, 86% of the decline in the U.S. teenage pregnancy rate was due to improved contraceptive use; 14% was due to teens' delaying sex."[92]

Numerous factors are reported at ReligiousTolerance.org, such as "a change in the U.S. culture which makes abortion less acceptable to women," and increased contraceptive use.[93] Frederica Mathewes-Green gives four reasons for a decline: "a social movement to encourage teenagers to postpone sexual relations until marriage, increased professionalism and sensitivity in the nation's pro-life pregnancy care centers, growth in state laws fostering a fully informed abortion decision, and a decline in the number of doctors who perform abortions."[94]

Other reasons given: National Right to Life argues that pro-life educational literature now makes it possible for more and more women to "see for themselves in sonograms and hearing on fetal heartbeat stethoscopes—that abortion stops a beating heart and ends the lives of children with hands, feet, and face."[95] Kate Michaelman of NARAL Pro-Choice America argues that new state restrictions on abortion since 1995 "make it very difficult for women to effectuate and act on their choice."[96]

More recently, there seems to be a growing acceptance of the reality of abortion as murder. A Google search of the National Right to Life web pages indicates "another reason to be encouraged arises from the growing percentage of respondents describing abortion as 'murder.' " The account then lists a *Time* /CNN poll of Americans of August 1994 showing that "43% thought that abortion was murder"; a University of Virginia poll of

---

that, while the overall rate of abortion declined after 1990, abortions "increased among poor women and women on Medicaid" (ibid.).

91 Jacqueline E. Darroch and Susheela Singh, *Why Is Teenage Pregnancy Declining? The Roles of Abstinence, Sexual Activity and Contraceptive Use* (Occasional Report No. 1), December 1999, 12, www.guttmacher.org.

92 Guttmacher Institute, *40 Years, 4 Defining Achievements: Advancing Sexual and Reproductive Health Worldwide through Research, Policy Analysis and Public Education* (2007 Annual Report), 6–7, www.guttmacher.org.

93 B. A. Robinson, "Abortion Statistics: U.S. Abortion Ratio by Year," www.religioustolerance.org/abo_decr3.htm.

94 Frederica Mathewes-Green, "Embryonic Trend: How Do We Explain the Drop in Abortions?," *Policy Review* 73 (Summer 1995), www.policyreview.org.

95 National Right to Life Committee, "A Closer Look: Factors Involved in Abortion Decline," January 2008, www.nrlc.org.

96 Jarret Murphy, "Abortion Battles at the Crossroads," January 22, 2003, www.cbsnews.com.

January 1996 indicating 48% thought abortion was murder; a CNN/*USA Today*/Gallup poll of January 1998 indicating the same percentage; "a CBS/New York Times poll of January 1998 listing 50% holding that 'abortion is the same thing as murdering a child' "; and finally, a "Los Angeles Times poll of June 2000" with 57% agreeing that "abortion is murder."[97]

Some recent polls also seem to indicate the number of people favoring life is increasing: According to CNN/*USA Today*/Gallup polls in July 1996, 36% of adults nationwide described themselves as pro-life and 53% as pro-choice, but in a poll of January 6–8, 2006, while the pro-choice percentage remained the same, 42% were pro-life.[98] A Zogby poll of April 15–17, 2004, found 49% of Americans considered themselves pro-life, while 45% were pro-choice.[99] The Knights of Columbus poll in 2008 found 50% of Americans considered themselves pro-choice and 44% as pro-life.[100] A Fox News/Opinion Dynamics poll of May 12–13, 2009, recorded 49% of registered voters nationwide who said they were more pro-life, while 43% were pro-choice.[101]

In May 2009, Gallup reported a remarkable finding: for the first time since Gallup began asking in 1995, a majority of 51% of Americans are calling themselves pro-life, and only 42% pro-choice. According to Gallup, "the new results . . . represent a significant shift from a year ago, when 50% were pro-choice and 44% pro-life. Prior to now, the highest percentage identifying as pro-life was 46%, in both August 2001 and May 2002."[102]

Gallup finds comparable changes regarding views on the legality of abortion. In contrast to the previous four years when there was a "strong tilt" in favor of "unrestricted abortion," about as many Americans say in May 2009 that abortion "should be illegal in all circumstances (23%) as say it should be legal under any circumstances (22%)." When including qualifying views, Gallup finds that while 41% in May 2008 held that abortion

---

97 Wanda Franz, Ph.D., "Public Opinion and the Morality of Abortion," January 28, 2006, www.nrlc.org/news/2002/NRL06/pres.html.

98 Gallup Organization, "Abortion," January 26, 2006, Gallup Poll, www.gallup.com/poll/1576/abortion.aspx. Forty-four percent were pro-life in a Gallup May 2005 poll when asked about being pro-choice or pro-life after having been asked other questions on abortion.

99 Zogby International, www.priestsforlife.org/statistics/zogby04-04.pdf.

100 Knights of Columbus, "Moral Issues and Catholic Values," 19.

101 "Abortion and Birth Control," accessed May 18, 2009, www.foxnews.com/projects/pdf/051809_issues_web.pdf.

102 Lydia Saad, "More Americans 'Pro-Life' Than 'Pro-Choice' for First Time," May 15, 2009, www.gallup.com. The results are based on telephone interviews with 1,015 adults, 18 and older, conducted May 7–10, 2009. Gallup reports in May 2010 the percentage who identify themselves as pro-life is 47%, while the percentage pro-choice is 45%; Gallup Organization, "Abortion," accessed October 6, 2010, www.gallup.com/poll/1576/abortion.aspx#1.

should be legal under any or most circumstances, in May 2009 only 37% held those views; and whereas 57% thought abortion should be legal only in a few circumstances or illegal in all circumstances in May 2008, the percentage in May 2009 is 60%.[103]

Gallup questions how much recent politics is playing a role in these polls; for example, its polls show that all of the above changes are due to movement toward a "pro-life" position among Republicans and independents who lean Republican, but "no change in the views of Democrats and Democratic leaners." And regarding gender polls, "this is the first time in nine years . . . that significantly more men and women are pro-life than pro-choice" (49% vs. 44% for women; 54% vs. 39% for men); furthermore, men jumped from 46% to 54% in just one year, and women from 43% to 49% in the same period. Gallup offers this interesting observation:

> With the first pro-choice president in eight years already making changes to the nation's policies on funding abortion overseas, expressing his support for the Freedom of Choice Act, and moving toward rescinding federal job protections for medical workers who refuse to participate in abortion procedures, Americans—and, in particular, Republicans—seem to be taking a step back from the pro-choice position. However, the retreat is evident among political moderates as well as conservatives.
>
> It is possible that, through his abortion policies, [Barack] Obama has pushed the public's understanding of what it means to be "pro-choice" slightly to the left, politically. While Democrats may support that, as they generally support everything Obama is doing as president, it may be driving others in the opposite direction.[104]

While the above data seem to indicate the public's understanding is turning more "pro-life," other data seem not to support that reading. According to Catholic News Service (CNS), abortion numbers seem suddenly to be increasing: "Abortion clinics across the U.S. were reporting increased traffic in the past several months. . . . Planned Parenthood clinics in some states reported record-high numbers of abortions in the last half of 2008, following years of a national decline in the numbers." CNS quotes

---

103 Ibid. Confirmation of Gallup's findings may be found in a national survey by the Pew Research Center for the People & the Press, conducted March 31–April 21, 2009, among 1,521 adults reached on landlines and cell phones, reporting that the percentage saying abortion should be legal in all or most cases had declined from 54% in August 2008 to 46% in April 2009, the slippage coming entirely from those saying abortion should be legal in most cases; the percentage saying abortion should be illegal in all or most cases had risen to 44%, up from 41% in August 2007(Pew Research Center for the People & the Press, "Public Takes Conservative Turn on Gun Control, Abortion," April 30, 2009, pewresearch.org.)

104 Saad, "More Americans 'Pro-Life,' " 6.

sources suggesting the cause is the recent meltdown in the economy: "A National Network of Abortion Funds spokeswoman confirmed that calls from women seeking funds for abortions quadrupled in the past year. . . . There is anecdotal evidence to suggest that some of this increase is attributable to the economy." The article suggests that baby booms occurred after World War II and in 2007 when there was economic prosperity, whereas there were "dramatic declines" in U.S. fertility during the depression of the 1930s and the energy crisis of the 1970s.[105]

This kind of thinking relating fertility and abortion to the rise and fall of the economy provided a basis for pro-Obama Catholics in the 2008 election to support Barack Obama as a pro-life candidate who would build up the economy and provide universal health care and other social benefits, thereby reducing the number of abortions even while supporting pro-abortion legislation. Thus Douglas M. Kmiec, chair and professor of constitutional law at Pepperdine University, argued that Catholics could reduce abortions by supporting "Obama's call to reduce the need for abortion, through education, contraception, improved adoption services, and support for a woman to carry her pregnancy to term."[106]

Tide Moving toward Limiting Right to Abortion

Gallup reports "a majority of Americans [favor]fairly strict limits on abortion, saying it should be legal in only a few or no circumstances."[107] A Harris poll of October 16–23, 2007, confirms that, when asked if they favored permitting a woman to have an abortion only in "some circumstances," 52% of adults said yes.[108] Another 42% even favored laws making it more difficult to get an abortion. Only 25% favored abortion "in all circumstances" (abortion on demand).[109]

Davidson argues that American attitudes on abortion "have been quite stable since the 1970s" when "54–55 percent of Americans believed abortion 'should be legal only under certain circumstances,' " and that, over the years, that position has "fluctuated between 48 and 61 percent, with no overall trend."[110]

---

105 Chaz Muth, "Bad Economy Seen as Cause for Reports of Increased Abortions," Catholic News Service, April 6, 2009, ncronline.org/news/justice/bad-economy-linked-increased-abortions.

106 Douglas Kmiec, "Finding Common Ground on Life Issues," *National Catholic Reporter*, June 1, 2009, ncronline.org.

107 Lydia Saad, "Abortion Views Reviewed as Alito Vote Nears," Gallup Poll, January 20, 2006, www.gallup.com. The Gallup data is based on a November 2005 poll.

108 "Abortion and Birth Control," www.pollingreport.com/abortion2.htm.

109 Ibid.

110 James D. Davidson, "What Catholics believe about abortion and the death penalty," *NCR*, September 30, 2005, 18.

But the tide appears to be changing to a greater percentage favoring a narrowing of the circumstances under which a right to an abortion should be permitted. The Knights of Columbus report that only 8% support abortion on demand, and that 92% would restrict abortions in some way: 13% would never permit abortion, 32% would permit abortion during the first three or six months of pregnancy, and an additional 47% only for the three exceptions of rape, incest, or to save the life of the mother.[111] While a Zogby survey of January 20–23, 2006, showed that 43% oppose abortions except for the same three exceptions and a "52% majority favor abortion in most circumstances," this was "down markedly from [the] 1990s": "What's striking to me is that the numbers were radically different ten years ago," says Zogby. "Ten years ago, maybe just seven or eight years ago, pro-choice forces were in the ascendancy and posted pro-choice numbers in the area of 65% to 68%."[112]

Further evidence of the tide changing toward stricter limits on abortion: The only time abortion advocates are in the majority in the 2008 GSS is in the very small percentage of cases that include "if there is a strong chance of serious defect in the baby" (73.7% support in 2008), "if the woman's health is seriously endangered by the pregnancy" (88.6% in 2008), or if the woman "became pregnant as a result of rape" (75.6% in 2008).[113] The same three cases where a majority rules in support of abortion appear to be found also in the 2006 Baylor Religion Survey: only 27.1% felt abortions were always wrong when the "baby may have a serious defect," 14.1% when the "woman's health is in danger," and 23.5% when a pregnancy results from rape.[114]

A Pew Research Center poll of July 13–17, 2005, found that 63% said that abortion should either never be permitted, be "under stricter limits than it is now," or be "against the law except in cases of rape, incest, and to save the woman's life," while only 35% said it should be generally available.[115] The GSS of 2008 reports only 21.8% say abortion should always be legal, a whopping 70% say it should be legal "sometimes," while 8.2% want it never to be legal.[116] A CNN/Opinion Research Corporation Poll of

---

[111] Knights of Columbus, "Moral Issues and Catholic Values," 19–20.

[112] Zogby, "Support for Abortion in Sharp Decline," Interactive Poll, January 23, 2006, www.zogby.com.

[113] GSS Cumulative Data File 1972–2008, sda.berkeley.edu/. Unfortunately, although in 2004 the first two of these were at their lowest since 1972, they rose 1.5% and 3.2%, respectively, in 2008.

[114] Baylor Religion Survey 2006, table 9, 32.

[115] Pew Research Center for the People & the Press, "Abortion, the Court and the Public," October 3, 2005, people-press.org/commentary/?analysisid=119.

[116] GSS Cumulative Data File 1972–2008, sda.berkeley.edu/.

April 9–11, 2010, showed a majority of Americans favoring limits on abortion: When asked, "Do you think abortion should be legal under any circumstances, 21% said yes, but a large majority of 78% said it should be legal only under certain circumstances (56%) or illegal in all circumstances (22%).[117] In a *Los Angeles Times*/Bloomberg poll of October 19–22, 2007, 50% wanted abortion to be illegal without exception (10%) or illegal except in cases of rape, incest, and to save the mother's life (40%).[118] In a Pew Research Center Survey of August 11–17 and 20–27, 2009, only 16% thought that abortion should be legal in all cases.[119]

Further nuanced questioning regarding restrictions according to trimesters in a survey of January 10–12, 2003, indicated that during the first three months of pregnancy, 66% versus 29% felt abortions "should generally be legal," but in the second three months, only 25% versus 68% felt abortions should be legal, and in the last three months, 10% versus 84% felt the same.[120] And in a Gallup poll of May 19–21, 2003, the majority felt abortions should be legal in the last three months of pregnancy only when the woman's life was in danger (75% vs. 22%), when the child would be born with a life-threatening illness (48% vs. 47%), or when the pregnancy was caused by rape or incest (59% vs. 39%).[121]

A National Conference of Catholic Bishops poll of January 1998 found 53% of Americans saying abortion should either not be allowed or be permitted only in cases of rape, incest, and to save the life of the mother.[122] A CBS News poll conducted July–August 2005 indicated that 68% of Americans took a pro-life stand, including 5% who would never allow abortion, 15% who would permit legal abortions "only to save the woman's life," 15% who wanted "greater restrictions on abortion," and 33% who would permit legal abortions "only in cases of rape, incest, or to save the woman's life." Only 28% favored abortion on demand.[123] According to Lawrence B. Finer et al, only 4.5% of women have abortions for reasons of health or rape, meaning that, according to the above CBS poll, 68% of Americans

---

[117] CNN/Opinion Research Corporation Poll, April 9–11, 2010, www.pollingreport.com/abortion2.htm.

[118] "Abortion and Birth Control," October 23, 2007, www.pollingreport.com/abortion2.htm.

[119] Pew Research Center Survey, August 11–17 and 20–27, 2009, www.pollingreport.com/abortion2.htm.

[120] CNN/USA Today/Gallup Poll, www.pollingreport.com/abortion2.htm, accessed October 4, 2010.

[121] Gallup, "Abortion," www.gallup.com/poll/1576/abortion.aspx#1.

[122] Randall K. O'Bannon, "Support for Pro-Life Policies and Legislation Growing," www.nrlc.org/news/1998/NRL2.98/randy298.html.

[123] Pennsylvania Pro-Life Federation, "2005 Abortion Polls Show Americans Support Abortion Restrictions!" *LifeLines* 25 (Winter 2006): 2.

are opposed to over 95% of the reasons women have abortions.[124] There is probably another important development (in addition to the possibility of the Obama effect that Gallup noted) explaining this new interest in restricting cases of legal abortion, which we will consider shortly.

However, even though the mood may be swinging toward a desire for greater restrictions on abortion, polls are not always encouraging: A Gallup survey of January 9–12, 2006, shows that while 38% of Americans want to see abortion laws in this country made more strict, 59% want them to remain the same or be made less strict.[125] And an ABC News/*Washington Post* poll of December 15–18, 2005, showed a majority of 57% favored abortion in all or most cases, while only 40% favored abortion being illegal in all or most cases.[126] A possible factor in these discrepancies is that data often vary depending on how pollsters phrase their questions.

Apparent Contradiction in Public Views on Abortion

Most polls indicate an apparent contradiction in people's views on abortion: on the one hand, they are tending toward a desire to limit the circumstances under which abortion might be permitted; on the other hand, they don't want to overturn *Roe v. Wade*, which permits unlimited abortion.

When most Americans are asked if they want to reverse the 1973 Supreme Court decisions that legalized abortion on demand, the answer is no. For example, an ABC News/*Washington Post* poll of April 22–25, 2010, indicated that only 38% want to overturn *Roe v. Wade*, and 59% do not;[127] Pew reports 65% do not.[128] A CNN Opinion Poll of adults nationwide of May 14–17, 2009, showed only 30% of Americans would like to see *Roe v. Wade* completely overturned, while 68% would not.[129]

How to explain these conflicting data? The answer may be that most Americans are not aware of the unlimited scope of the 1973 decisions and support Roe because they feel it legalizes some option for abortion (the 2006 Baylor Religion Survey indicates that only 12.2% of Americans believe that abortion "is wrong in all circumstances"[130]). This was probably the case

---

[124] Lawrence B. Finer, Lori F. Frohwirth, Lindsay A. Dauphinee, Susheela Singh and Ann M. Moore, "Reasons U.S. Women Have Abortions: Quantitative and Qualitative Perspectives," *Perspectives on Sexual and Reproductive Health* 37 (2005): 114.

[125] Gallup Poll, January 9–12, 2006, www.pollingreport.com/abortion2.htm.

[126] Ibid.

[127] ABC News/*Washington Post* Poll, April 22–25, 2010, www.pollingreport.com/abortion2/htm.

[128] Pew Forum on Religion & Public Life, "Abortion and Rights of Terror Suspects Top Court Issues," August 3, 2005, www.pewforum.org/Abortion/Abortion-and-Rights-of-Terror-Suspects-Top-Court-Issues.aspx.

[129] "Abortion and Birth Control," www.pollingreport.com/abortion2.htm.

[130] Baylor Religion Survey 2006, 31.

when a Quinnipiac University poll asked July 8–13, 2008, if registered voters nationwide agreed or disagreed with the *Roe* decision that established a woman's right to an abortion, and 63% said they agreed, and only 33% said they disagreed.[131] The problem may also be that Americans feel caught in a quandary: they want permission for abortion only in certain circumstances, and they don't know how else to retain that permission apart from maintaining *Roe v. Wade*. The apparent contradiction may also be due to the fact that Americans in general are hesitant to disagree with the Supreme Court, and are reluctant to appear to be intolerant of opposing views.

Abortion among Catholics

As we noted above, Gallup, in a survey of May 7–10, 2009, found a majority of Americans identifying themselves as "pro-life" for the first time since Gallup began asking about this issue in 1995. Other remarkable "pro-life" changes, all in one year: an eight-point "pro-life" gain among Protestants (from 51% in May 2008 to 59% in May 2009) and a seven-point gain among Catholics (from 45% in May 2008 to 52% in May 2009). But a contradiction similar to the one discussed above for all Americans is reflected in Catholic thinking about abortion: When asked by Pew Research, March 8–12, 2006, if they supported South Dakota's abortion ban becoming the law of the nation, banning all abortions except to save the life of the mother, only 34% of Catholics supported the ban, while 54% opposed it.[132] Yet in a survey by the Pew Research Center, February 1–5, 2006, that forced a choice as to whether abortion was "morally acceptable, morally wrong, or not a moral issue," 57% of Catholics said "morally wrong," only 9% said it was "morally acceptable," and a surprising 21% said it was "not a moral issue."[133] Such data seem to confirm a popular disconnect between Catholics' personal views on abortion and their views of a public morality on abortion.

GSS data show remarkable though distressing stability on Catholic views on the public morality of abortion. Among Catholics in 1977, 31.5% supported abortion on demand; in 2006, the percentage rose to 35.9%, and in 2008, 37.7%. Those who opposed abortion on demand in 1977 were 66.5%; in 2006, the percentage dropped to 64.1%, and in

131 "Abortion and Birth Control," www.pollingreport.com/abortion2.htm.

132 Pew Research Center for the People & the Press, "Less Opposition to Gay Marriage, Adoption and Military Service," March 22, 2006, www.people-press.org. When the same question was asked of all Americans in a Harris poll of April 2006, 44% said they would support the law in their state and 52% opposed it (Harris Poll no. 35).

133 Pew Research Center, "Sex, Drugs and the 1040: A Barometer of Modern Morals," March 28, 2006, 7, pewresearch.org.

2008, to 62.3%.[134] Though these percentages may provide some comfort in that the rejection of Church teaching is not higher, the figures inevitably mean that about a third of American Catholics are not in agreement with the Church on this issue.

Gallup polled Catholics from May 2002 to May 2004 on the moral acceptability of abortion, and found that 37% found it "morally acceptable."[135] Gallup also discovered that Catholic views on abortion do not differ markedly from the Protestant, though Catholics are slightly more liberal: In an aggregate poll of surveys from May 2004 to June 2005, Gallup found that 20% of Protestants and 23% of Catholics felt that abortion should be legal regardless of the circumstances, while 22% of Protestants and 20% of Catholics felt it should always be illegal.[136] In aggregated data from Gallup's 2006–2008 Values and Beliefs Survey, Gallup reports 40% of Catholics found abortion "morally acceptable," while 41% of non-Catholics did.[137] The Pew Landscape Survey of 2007 reflects the tone of these findings: while 48% of Catholics said that abortion should be legal in all or most cases, only 45% of Protestants did; and while 45% of Catholics thought abortion should be illegal in all or most cases, 49% of Protestants did.[138] The Pew Forum in July 2005 found 31% of white Catholics saying abortion should be "generally available."[139] A Roper survey of Catholics in 1997 found that only a significant minority of 36% either strongly or mildly agreed that "abortion is never justified."[140]

Donohue reported in 1995 that 22.5% of Catholics opposed abortion under any circumstances, and that another 40.3% felt that in "*a few*" instances, the choice would best be left to the individual. This means that 62.8% of the respondents were opposed to abortion at least "in most instances."[141] GSS data show, however, that in 2008, 82.6% of Catholics held that abortion should be available if the woman's health is seriously endangered, down from 86% in a 1972–1975 study.[142] Kenneth Wald's data

---

134 GSS Cumulative Data File 1972–2008, sda.berkeley.edu/.

135 Frank Newport, "U.S. Catholics Vary Widely on Moral Issues," Gallup Poll, April 8, 2005, www.gallup.com.

136 Frank Newport and Lydia Saad, "Religion, Politics Inform Americans' Views on Abortion: Churchgoing Frequency is Associated with Strength of Anti-Abortion Views," Gallup Poll News Service, April 3, 2006, www.gallup.com.

137 Frank Newport, "Catholics Similar to Mainstream on Abortion, Stem Cells: Catholics Actually More Liberal on Some Issues," Gallup Poll, March 30, 2009, www.gallup.com.

138 Pew Forum, *Landscape Survey Report* 2, 90.

139 Pew Forum, "Abortion and Rights of Terror."

140 Lawler, "Principle Rejected," 45.

141 Donohue, "Catholic League Survey," 9.

142 According to the Church, such abortions are permissible only if indirect.

are also high: he reports that, unlike evangelical and African-American Protestants who strongly favor the "pro-life" position, and Jews and secular Americans who favor "pro-choice," Roman Catholics (and mainline Protestants) are "in the middle": 44% of Catholics either want abortion never to be permitted (9%) or permitted only in the three exceptional cases (35%), while 56% either favor abortion on demand (40%) or with few limitations (16%).[143] Pew reports that 11% of white Catholics never want abortion permitted, but 32% want it illegal except in the three usual cases.[144] And in 2009, the Pew Forum on Religion & Public Life reported that 48% of Catholics wanted abortion legal in all cases (16%) or in most cases (32%).[145]

Thus the figures range from as high as 56% in 2000 to as low as 31% in 2005 for Catholic acceptance of abortion either on demand or with limited circumstances. Even if the most conservative figure is the most accurate, and this is likely since most polls show that Catholic attitudes toward abortion have recently become more restrictive, it still means that at least a third of Catholics does not accept the official teaching of the Church on abortion. Moreover, if Wald's 2005 figure is accurate, a 40% Catholic approval of abortion on demand is distressingly high. Distressing also is the fact that the data regarding Catholic women who have had abortions are high, though apparently not as high as among Protestants: According to the Guttmacher Institute's six-page fact sheets, 28% of women obtaining abortions identified themselves as Catholics, while 37% said they were Protestant.[146] Even worse are the percentages given by the Center for Bio-Ethical Reform: 37.4% for Protestant women, 31.3% for Catholics.[147] Wald estimates that 30% of the women receiving abortions are Catholics, slightly more than the Catholic proportion of the American population.[148] All of this seems to indicate that the official teaching of the Church, at least on this issue, has minimal impact upon Catholics. Their judgments are being formed on the basis of some other standard(s).

---

143 Kenneth D. Wald, *Religion and Politics in the United States*, 4th ed. (Lanham, MD: Rowman & Littlefield, 2003), 171. The figures are taken from the American National Election Studies survey done in 2000 by the Center for Political Studies at the University of Michigan.

144 Pew Forum, "Abortion and Rights of Terror."

145 Pew Forum on Religion & Public Life, "Abortion Views by Religious Affiliation," January 15, 2009, www.pewforum.org/Abortion/Abortion-Views-by-Religious-Affiliation.aspx.

146 Guttmacher Institute, "Facts on Induced Abortion," 2.

147 Center for Bio-Ethical Reform, accessed October 6, 2010, www.abortionno.org/Resources/fastfacts.html. Yet the Center indicates that the Guttmacher Institute is their source of data.

148 Wald, *Religion and Politics*, 293n8. Wald is citing from a 1988 publication.

Erosion in Catholic Support for Church Teaching on Abortion

Though GSS data showed Catholic stability on this issue, surveys taken by Gallup indicate significant erosion in complete acceptance of Church teaching on abortion in the last twenty years.

In 1987, Gallup found that 39% of Catholics thought you could be a good Catholic without obeying the Church's teaching on abortion. In 1993, however, George Gallup, Jr., indicates in one publication that that figure rose to 62%,[149] although in the survey taken for *NCR* in 1993, he reports 56% held that position.[150] In the *NCR*/Gallup survey for 1999, the figure declines to 53%, but in 2005 rises to 58%. Such a finding forces us to raise the question again: What is considered important to being a good Catholic, if three-fourths of American Catholics think weekly Mass attendance is not, and nearly two-thirds consider supporting a moral position taught so emphatically by the Church is not?

In the 1993 survey, Gallup also reports that 58% of Catholics said the Church should relax its standards forbidding abortion[151]—this in contrast to a 1977 Gallup Catholic Press Association study, made four years after *Roe v. Wade*, reporting only 44% had taken that stand.[152] As a result, more than half of America's Catholics today, according to Gallup, not only don't see accepting the Church's teaching on abortion as important to being a good Catholic, but also represent a growing movement away from accepting the teaching.

Catholics seem to be conflicted on whether there are absolute moral standards of right and wrong. Zogby reports in March 2006 that 29% of Catholics felt the decision on whether it is right or wrong to have an abortion should be left to the individual, while another 47% felt the decision should be jointly made by the individual and the Church.[153] This seems to indicate that many feel that judgment on this issue is ultimately subjective and relative.

But Catholics seem ultimately confused. The Pew Landscape Survey of 2007, on the one hand, found that a surprisingly high number of Catholics were absolutists: when asked whether or not they agreed with this statement, "There are clear and absolute standards for what is right and wrong," 78% agreed and only 19% disagreed. On the other hand, when asked what

---

[149] Gallup, *Religion in America 1996*, 44.

[150] William V. D'Antonio, "The American Catholic Laity in 1999," *NCR*, October 29, 1999, 2.

[151] Gallup, *Religion in America 1996*, 44. Remarkably, Donohue's 1995 survey indicates that 63.6% of Catholics do *not* want the Church to change its position on abortion (Donohue, "Catholic League's Survey," 8–9).

[152] Gallup, *American Catholic*, 51.

[153] Zogby, "National survey of Catholic adults."

influenced them most in deciding questions of right and wrong, 57% said practical experience and common sense; only 22% looked to religious teachings and beliefs, 10% to philosophy and reason, and 7% to scientific information.[154] It seems doubtful that practical experience, common sense, and scientific information could be adequate resources for perceiving absolute standards. In any case, one can only conclude there has been a significant erosion of identification with the Church and its teachings as a guide to moral truth.

In 1988, Gallup found that Catholics were more likely than in 1977 to support legal abortion "in the case of rape, incest, severe risk to the mother's physical health, the chance that a baby will be born deformed and when the mother cannot afford to have the child." In 1988, 77% believed in legal abortion to save the life of the mother, 71% when there is severe threat to the mother's physical health, and 71% in the case of rape or incest, but also "for the first time, a majority of Catholics (57 percent) said in 1988 that abortion should be legal when there is a risk that the baby will be born deformed; 40 percent held this view in 1977 and 41 percent in 1979." Among the five reasons cited for having an abortion—life of mother, physical health, rape/incest, deformed fetus, and can't afford—only in the last case where the mother was not able to afford to have a child was the support for abortion below 50% in 1988, but even then, it had gone up to 35% as opposed to 15% in 1977.[155]

Even more evidence of the erosion of Catholic support for the Church's position on abortion is provided in a series of studies Gallup has made since shortly after the Supreme Court decisions of 1973.

In March 1974, Gallup asked Catholics if they favored the Court's decision in *Roe v. Wade* legalizing abortion during the first three months: 32% said they favored the decision, 61% said they opposed it—nearly a two-thirds majority. In February of 1979, when Catholics were asked if abortions should be legal under all circumstances (which the 1973 Supreme Court decisions had approved, though most Catholics were unaware of it), legal under certain circumstances, or always illegal, 17% said always legal, 52% said legal in certain circumstances, and 25% said always illegal. From May 30 to June 2 of 1991, the same question was asked: the figures were 28%, 52%, and 19%, respectively. Finally, in January of 1998, to the same question, the figures are 23%, 57%, and 19%, respectively,[156] the only

---

[154] Pew Forum, *Landscape Survey Report* 2, 62.

[155] George Gallup, Jr., and Jim Castelli, *The People's Religion: American Faith in the 90's* (New York: Macmillan, 1989), 177–78.

[156] George Gallup, ed., *International Gallup Polls: Public Opinion 1972–77* (Wilmington, DE: Scholarly Resources, 1978), 249; *Public Opinion 1979* (1980), 134; *1991* (1992), 119; *1998* (1999), 159.

percentage increasing there among those who accepted that abortion should be legal under certain circumstances.

What we see here is a marked erosion of conformity with the Church's teaching on abortion: whereas it is difficult, because of the variation in questioning, to compare the 1974 data with the data gathered thereafter, we do see that in 1979, 17% of Catholics favored abortion on demand, while by 1991, 28% favored it. Though the acceptability of abortion on demand declined to 23% in 1998, accommodation with the idea of having an abortion nevertheless increased: the 52% in 1979 and 1991 favoring legalizing abortion in certain circumstances rose to 57% in 1998, and those who considered abortion always illegal dropped 6% from 1979 to 1998.[157]

The 1998 figures compared to the 1991 figures may indicate that the erosion process was at least temporarily reversed, in view of the fact that the percentage favoring legalized abortion on demand dropped by 5% in 1998. If so, what might have caused such a drop at that time? We also saw earlier a 3% drop from 1993 to 1999 among those saying you could be a good Catholic without obeying the Church's teaching on abortion (56% to 53%), implying perhaps a temporary reversal of the erosion process here as well (temporary, in view of the fact that the figure rose to 58% in 2005). Other data we saw earlier indicate some increase in the number of those favoring a pro-life stand. That such a reversion occurred is possible, and may be explained to some extent against the background of an event that happened in the '90s that began to awaken people to the evils of abortion.

Partial-Birth Abortion

By November 1992, the issue of "partial-birth" abortion came to national attention: the procedure by which a doctor, as late as the third trimester, though usually in the fifth and sixth months of pregnancy when the fetus may already be viable, inserts forceps into the womb, grabs a leg of the unborn baby, and pulls the baby out of the birth canal except for the top of the head. The doctor then jams scissors into the baby's skull, making the opening wide enough so that a tube may be inserted to suck out the baby's brains and make the skull collapse. The dead baby is then removed from the womb. Thus the baby is aborted while both partially in the mother's

---

[157] Though the precise "circumstances" for permitting an abortion were not stated in the poll, we know from Gallup's 1988 poll, discussed above, that the majority of all American Catholics supported abortion in the first trimester if the woman's life or health was in danger, and for rape, incest, and serious deformity of the baby. In the second trimester, a majority of *all* Americans supported abortion only to save the life of the mother. Gallup survey of 1990, in James R. Kelly, "Abortion: What Americans *Really* Think and the Catholic Challenge," *America* 165 (November 2, 1991): 311.

womb and partially born, and the legal technicalities preventing this from being prosecuted as infanticide, which is what it really is, are satisfied.

Public consciousness was raised against such a horrific procedure, and most people were outraged when told the process was legal. The National Right to Life Committee rightly takes some credit for the change in public opinion, due to its campaign, begun in 1995, to stop partial-birth abortions by emphasizing "the humanity of the unborn child." Pictures disseminated of "fully formed arms and legs and bodies" of partially born infants demonstrated they could no longer be considered a "blob of tissue" and stressed the "fundamental immorality of abortion." This action probably contributed to the downward trend in abortions.[158]

Gallup polling since 1995, when Congress first introduced the Partial-Birth Abortion Ban Act, has always indicated that a majority of Americans support a ban. In a survey of October 24–26, 2003, 68% of Americans supported legislation to ban partial-birth abortions except to save the life of the mother; 25% opposed it.[159] In a survey of May 10–13, 2007, Gallup found 72% of Americans wanted late-term abortions to be illegal; only 22% wanted it legal. Pew Research found in its survey of August 1–18, 2007, that 75% of Americans wanted partial-birth abortions to be illegal; only 17% wanted it legal. In an ABC News/*Washington Post* of July 17–21, 2007, 55% approved of banning the procedure except when a woman's life is at risk; 43% disapproved.[160]

When Gallup asked in 1998 if Catholics would vote for a law to make "partial-birth" abortions illegal in the last six months of pregnancy except to save the life of the mother, 61% said they would, while 36% said they would not.[161]

One could argue, then, that as a result of the public consciousness by 1995 of the "partial-birth" method of abortion many people turned against the idea of legal abortion without limits, and moved to legalize it only in certain cases. A reversal of the slide toward accepting an unlimited right to abortion probably occurs here, but not enough to turn people totally against legalizing abortion. This might, then, explain the drop of 5% in the approval of legalizing all abortions between Gallup's 1991 and 1998 surveys, and the corresponding increase of 5% approval of abortion under limited circumstances. This may also explain the reversal between 1993 and 1999 against the possibility of being a good Catholic while not obeying the Church's teaching on abortion.

---

158 O'Bannon, "Support for Pro-Life."

159 Lydia Saad, "Americans Agree with Banning 'Partial-Birth Abortion,'" Gallup Poll, November 6, 2003, www.gallup.com.

160 "Abortion and Birth Control," www.pollingreport.com/abortion2.htm.

161 Gallup, *Public Opinion 1998.*

The data allow us at least to conclude that significant erosion has occurred in Catholic acceptance of abortion on demand, and that in itself is already an advance. Still, when one adds the total percentage of Catholics favoring legalizing abortion at least in limited circumstances in 1991 and again in 1998, one arrives at 80% each year. This is far more than the 69% total Catholic approval in 1979, and at a cost to the percentage wanting abortion illegal in all circumstances—25% in 1979 to 19% in 1993 and 1998. Thus what we see in the 1998 figures is a reversal in Catholics' degree of comfort with the idea of legal abortion on demand, but at the cost of greater support for abortion in limited circumstances.

American Catholics are unfortunately caught between their love affair with the freedom to choose and their realization of the horrible reality of what may be chosen. This is the conflict also reflected in the admission of many who, while they accept that abortion is murder, are unwilling to impose that view on others by making all abortions illegal.

Repeated attempts to make partial-birth abortions illegal except to save the life of the mother were made by the United States Congress, but, largely because of Catholic congressional opposition, never passed with sufficient votes to overturn President Bill Clinton's two vetoes. Finally, President George W. Bush signed the Partial-Birth Abortion Ban Act into law November 5, 2003, after the Senate passed the act October 21, 2003, by a vote of 64–34, nearly three weeks after the House passed the same bill October 2 by a 281–42 vote. The act was, however, declared unconstitutional by federal district judges in San Francisco (June 1, 2004), New York (August 26, 2004), and Lincoln, Nebraska (September 8, 2004), for failing to include an exception, as required by *Doe v. Bolton*, for when the woman's health is in danger.

On April 18, 2007, by a 5–4 decision, the Supreme Court overturned the lower court decisions, and upheld the federal ban on partial-birth abortion. Justice Anthony Kennedy, who wrote the decision, said that the 2003 Partial-Birth Abortion Ban Act, despite the fact that it does not contain an exception allowing the procedure to preserve a woman's health, does not violate a woman's constitutional right to an abortion: it is uncertain the procedure is ever necessary to preserve a woman's health; there are other medical options available; the State has an "interest in promoting respect for human life at all stages in the pregnancy"; "physicians are not entitled to ignore regulations that direct them to use reasonable alternative procedures"; and the "law need not give abortion doctors unfettered choice in the course of their medical practice."[162]

[162] Justice Kennedy, writing the majority opinion of the Court, in *Gonzales v. Carhart* et al., Slip Opinion, No. 05–380, October Term 2006, April 18, 2007; Associated Press, "Top Court Upholds Abortion Ban," April 18, 2007, www.msnbc.msn.com.

On July 17, 2007, presidential candidate Barack Obama, speaking at a Planned Parenthood conference in Washington, DC, strongly criticized the Court's decision, and said if he became president, he would appoint justices with "empathy":

> We need somebody who's got the heart, the empathy, to recognize what it's like to be a young teenage mom. The empathy to understand what it's like to be poor, or African-American, or gay, or disabled, or old. And that's the criteria by which I'm going to be selecting my judges.[163]

Perhaps even more importantly, Obama said, in answer to a question after his talk, "Well, the first thing I'd do as president is, is [sic] sign the Freedom of Choice Act. That's the first thing that I'd do."[164]

The origins of the Freedom of Choice Act (FOCA) go back at least to 1989 when the bill was first introduced into the Senate at a time when there was fear that *Roe v. Wade* might be overturned. Since then, FOCA has repeatedly been reintroduced as a bill, most recently in 2007. FOCA's "main goal was to create a fundamental right to abortion for all women, which would criminalize any government action that limited, or impeded access."[165] While the exact ramifications of the bill remain unclear, pro-life advocates understand it to mean that taxpayers would be forced to fund abortions, and all restrictions of any kind—federal, state, or local—to a woman's so-called right to have an abortion would be outlawed, even to the extent of forcing Catholic doctors and hospitals to perform abortions against their will or face fines or closure.

FOCA was never reintroduced in the 111th Congress which convened in January 2009. However, one of its chief proponents, Rep. Jerrold Nadler [D–NY], has promised that it will be introduced 'sooner rather than later' and President Obama has promised his Administration's support for this radical legislation."[166] More recently, Obama has backed away from giving the proposed bill executive priority.

---

163 Mark Murray, "Obama on judges, Supreme Court," July 17, 2007, firstread.msnbc.msn.com.

164 "Barack Obama before Planned Parenthood Action Fund, July 17, 2007," transcribed by Laura Echevarria, a spokesperson for National Right to Life, www.lauraechevarria.com.

165 Osayi Osar-Empokae, "History of the Freedom of Choice Act," April 23, 2010, www.aul.org/2010/04/history-of-the-freedom-of-choice-act/, 1.

166 Ibid., 2.

President Obama was elected in November 2008 by a majority of 69.5 million Americans, or 53% of those who voted.[167] Catholics voted 54–45%, Protestants voted 45–54%, for Obama.[168]

Homosexuality

The acceptance of homosexuality or same-sex relationships as a way of life is in flux in American society. Though opponents of same-sex marriage still seem generally to be in the majority, the gap between the percentages for and against is narrowing.

The Knights of Columbus reported in 2008 that "70% of Americans do not support same-sex marriage, including 38% who advocate no legal recognition and 32% who favor civil unions."[169] The GSS continues to show a high percentage of adults opposing same-sex relationships, but the percentages are declining. Thus, according to the 2008 survey, 52.4% of Americans thought that same-sex relationships are always wrong (56.2% in 2006), 3.1% almost always wrong (4.9% in 2006), 6.7% sometimes wrong (same percentage in 2006), and 37.8% not wrong at all (32.3% in 2006).[170] The 2006 Baylor Religion Survey shows 57% of Americans hold that gay marriage is "always wrong."[171] A Gallup poll of adults May 7–9, 2009, showed 57% of Americans opposed to legalizing same-sex marriage (68% in 1996), while 40% were in favor (27% in 1996).[172] Conversely, a *Times* poll of 808 likely voters conducted July 31–August 4, 2008, showed Americans evenly divided: 47% supporting and 47% opposing legalized gay marriages.[173]

On the other hand, a growing number of states are legalizing same-sex marriage, often by a court decision overruling the will of the people. A court decision allowing same-sex marriage had done just that in California on May 15, 2008, arguing that the state's existing voter-approved law defining marriage as only between opposite sexes was unconstitutional. But a Proposition 8 referendum to amend the state constitution, eliminating the right of same-sex couples to marry, was placed on the November 2008 ballot and passed. The California Supreme Court upheld the right of the people to alter the

[167] CNN Politics, Election Center 2008, www.cnn.com.

[168] Pew Forum on Religion & Public Life, "How the Faithful Voted," November 10, 2008, pewforum.org.

[169] Knights of Columbus, "Moral Issues and Catholic Values," 28.

[170] GSS Cumulative Data File 1972–2008, sda.berkeley.edu/.

[171] Baylor Religion Survey 2006, 32.

[172] Jeffrey M. Jones, "Majority of Americans Continue to Oppose Gay Marriage," May 27, 2009, www.gallup.com.

[173] *Times* Poll, "Should gay and lesbian couples be allowed to marry, giving them full legal rights of married couples, or not?", PollingReport.com.

constitution and upheld the ban on May 26, 2009. On August 4, 2010, a federal judge in San Francisco struck down the ban, and as of March 2011, the United States Ninth Circuit Court of Appeals is staying the ban until it decides on its constitutionality.[174] As of June 8, 2009, six states are recognizing same-sex marriages: Massachusetts, Connecticut, Iowa, Vermont, Maine, and New Hampshire,[175] but more are sure to follow.

State constitutional amendments to ban same-sex marriages were overwhelmingly passed in all three states that proposed the ban—California, Florida, and Arizona—in the November 2008 elections: in California, Proposition 8 passed by 52% to 48%; in Florida, Proposition 2 passed, 62% to 38%; in Arizona, Proposition 102 passed, 56% to 44%[176] (the ban had been narrowly defeated in Arizona in a 2006 referendum).[177] As a result, as of this writing, twenty-nine states have now amended their constitutions to ban same-sex marriage, twenty-six of them doing so since Massachusetts became the first state to legalize such marriage following a 4–3 majority ruling by the state's Supreme Court on November 18, 2003.[178]

Among Catholics, some data provide encouraging signs of support for the teaching of the Church. According to Greeley, 71% of American Catholics in the 1970s thought that homosexuality was always wrong; in the mid-1980s, the figure was 69%.[179] Both figures indicate strong support for the teaching of the Church at that time. In 1994, Greeley stated that about two-thirds of American Catholics continue to hold that position, a figure that has remained constant as well for Protestants.[180] The 2008 Knights of Columbus poll shows that 68% of Catholics do not support same-sex marriage.[181] A Zogby poll of 2006 indicated that 58% of Catholics hold that sexual relations between same-sex adults are always

---

174 "California's Proposition 8 (Same-Sex Marriage)," August 17, 2010, www.topics.nytimes.com/top/reference/timestopics/subjects/c/californias_proposition_8.

175 Abby Goodnough, "New Hampshire Legalizes Same-Sex Marriage," *New York Times*, June 3, 2009, www.nytimes.com.

176 CNN Politics, "Ballot Measures," Election Center 2008, www.cnn.com/ELECTIONS/2008/results/ballot.measures/.

177 Pew Forum on Religion & Public Life, "States with Voter-Approved Constitutional Bans on Same-Sex Marriage, 1998–2008," November 13, 2008, pewforum.org/Gay-Marriage-and-Homosexuality/States-with-Voter-Approved-Constitutional-Bans-on-Same-Sex-Marriage-1998-2008.aspx.

178 Ibid. Three states had already passed a ban on gay marriage before 2003: Alaska (1998), Nebraska (2000), and Nevada (2002).

179 Andrew M. Greeley, *American Catholics Since the Council: An Unauthorized Report* (Chicago: Thomas More, 1985), 82. The figures are from the GSS 1972–75 and 1982–85 data.

180 Andrew M. Greeley, *Sex: The Catholic Experience* (Chicago: Thomas More, 1994), 112.

181 Knights of Columbus, "Moral Issues and Catholic Values," 28.

wrong.[182] A Zogby poll of 2005 indicated that 61% of Catholics hold that homosexual behavior is against the natural law.[183]

In the three state ballot initiatives in November 2008 regarding same-sex marriages, the Catholic vote seems generally to have played a major role. In California, 60% of Catholics voted for the ban (66% of Protestants did as well);[184] in Florida, 66% to 34% of Catholics supported the ban;[185] in Arizona, the "exit polling found that Protestants generally supported the measure but that Catholics were fairly evenly divided."[186]

But other current data show quite a different situation among Catholics and considerable variance from the general public: according to the GSS, 70.5% of Catholics thought that having homosexual relations in 1973 was always wrong—roughly the same percentage as the general public in 2006—but only 49.1% of Catholics held that position in 2008; and whereas only 10.1% of Catholics in 1973 felt that homosexual activity was not wrong at all, that figure rose to about a third of the Catholic population—37.2%—in 2008, the highest percentage yet.[187] Pew reports that in February 2006, 43% of Catholics found homosexual behavior "morally" wrong and only 13% morally acceptable, but a surprising 39% considered such activity not a moral issue at all.[188]

Donohue's report indicates that a majority of Catholics—55.8%—hold that the Church should not abandon its teaching on homosexuality, but nearly a third—31.5%—thought it should.[189] According to Gallup, Catholic acceptance of homosexuality has gradually increased since the '70s. He reports that while in 1977, 44% of Catholics supported legalizing homosexual relations between consenting adults, that percentage rose to a majority of 51% in 1985,[190] and to 54% in 1989.[191] In 1993 he reports

---

182 Zogby, "National survey of Catholic adults."

183 Le Moyne College/Zogby International Contemporary Catholic Trends Poll, March 7–10, 2005, www.lemoyne.edu/centersofexcellence/catholictrends/tabid/547/Default.aspx.

184 Public Policy Institute of California, "Just the Facts," www.ppic.org.

185 Linda Reeves, "Catholics play major role in passage of marriage amendment," November 11, 2008, www.thefloridacatholic.org/iv/catholics-play-major-role-in-passage-of-marriage-amendment?searchPhrase=amendment2'sapprovalaidedby Catholic.

186 Associated Press, "Age, religion factors in Ariz. marriage vote," November 5, 2008, www.azcentral.com.

187 GSS Cumulative Data File 1972–2008, sda.berkeley.edu/.

188 Pew, "Sex, Drugs," 9.

189 Donohue, "Catholic League's Survey," 8.

190 Gallup, *American Catholic*, 64.

191 Based on a survey taken October 12–15, 1989, as reported in George Gallup, Jr., ed., *Gallup Poll: Public Opinion 1989* (Wilmington, DE: Scholarly Resources, 1990). It is striking to note that in 1989, the percentage of support among Protestants was only

that 47% of Catholics believe people who engage in homosexual acts are still good Catholics, and that 44% disagree that homosexual behavior is always wrong.[192] In a 2002–2004 survey of Catholics, Gallup found 48% saying homosexual behavior is "morally acceptable," more than non-Catholics did (39%).[193]

In 2006, Pew found that 50% of Americans said that homosexual behavior is never justified.[194] In 2007, the Pew Landscape Survey asked Americans if homosexuality as a "way of life" should be "accepted" or "discouraged by society," and only 40% said it should be discouraged, while 50% said it should be accepted. But among Catholics, the number who said it should be accepted was even higher—58%—and only 30% said it should be discouraged.[195] Thus, Pew supports other surveys showing Catholics to be more open to a homosexual lifestyle than the average American.

In 2005, Zogby found only 39% of Catholics saying same-sex couples should be allowed legally to marry (although only 29% thought the sacrament of marriage should be made available to them).[196] The Pew Research Forum found in July 2006 that only 38% of white Catholics favored gay marriage, an increase of three points since August 2004, but a hefty 63% favored civil unions, an increase of three points over August 2004.[197] This seems to indicate that Catholics are accepting a compromise position on gay marriage issues whereby marriage is kept sacred, but civil liaisons are not.

Moral authority on this issue is also sliding to the individual: in 1987, 32% of Catholics thought morality on a Catholic engaging in homosexual behavior should be decided by Church leaders, as opposed to 39% who thought it should be decided by the individual; in 1999, the corresponding figures were 20% and 49%.[198]

An astonishing Pew poll of October 6, 2010 shows that "For the first time in 15 years of Pew Research Center polling, fewer than half [of Americans] oppose same-sex marriage." According to Pew, in 2009, 37% favored

---

42%. We note again that Protestants are often significantly more supportive of Catholic teaching than Catholics.

192 Gallup, *Religion in America 1996*, 44. Gallup is sometimes inconsistent: in a Gallup poll in 1994, he reports from a survey taken in August 1993 that only 35% said you could engage in homosexual activity and still be a good Catholic, and that 49% disagreed that homosexuality is always wrong.

193 Newport, "U.S. Catholics Vary Widely."

194 Pew Forum on Religion & Public Life, "Attitudes Toward Homosexuality in African Countries," November 14, 2006, pewresearch.org.

195 Pew Forum, *Landscape Survey Report 2*, 92.

196 Le Moyne College/Zogby poll, March 7–10, 2005.

197 Pew Forum on Religion & Public Life, "Pragmatic Americans Liberal and Conservative on Social Issues," August 3, 2006, pewforum.org.

198 D'Antonio, *American Catholics*, 76.

legalizing same-sex marriages, but 54% were opposed; in 2010, "42% favor same-sex marriage while 48% are opposed." Pew indicates that the shift in position is "broad-based," but states, "Notably, pluralities of white mainline Protestants and white Catholics now favor allowing gays and lesbians to marry legally—the first time this has occurred in Pew Research Center surveys." There is a shift also among all Catholics and all Protestants, though the shift is much greater among all Catholics than it is among all Protestants: Protestant percentages in 2010 are 31% in favor of same-sex marriages versus a majority that is still opposed—59%—compared in 2009 to 27% versus 64%; whereas percentages among all Catholics in 2010 show a plurality now in favor for the first time—46%—and 42% opposed, compared in 2009 to 42% favorable versus 45% opposed. The tide is indeed shifting, though more quickly among Catholics. [199]

UNIQUE SIGNIFICANCE OF CLOSENESS TO THE CHURCH

One factor we did not take into consideration when presenting the above data were the variations that occur in the findings depending on the relative degree of one's closeness to the Church or participation in religious activity. The principle we are setting forth at this point is a simple one: the closer one's life is to the Church, to religious influence, or to religious activity, the more this closeness tends to affect one's character, dispositions, and actions, and sometimes, markedly so.

We have yet to speak about the difference in Mass attendance between many younger and older Catholics in today's Church, but we will do so in chapter 2 (see pp. 77–134), and note there that there can be a considerable difference. One of the reasons for this difference is the fact that there is a greater tendency in the pre-Vatican II generation of Catholics to identify with the institutional Church than there is among Vatican II and post-Vatican II Catholics. But this is only one of many subsets showing the effect of closeness to the Church on Catholic attitudes and practices. Other examples of the effect of closeness: A major portion of CARA's study entitled *Sacraments Today* is devoted to measuring the effect of frequent Mass attendance on Catholic beliefs and attitudes. The study reports that Catholics who attend Mass weekly or more often find all seven sacraments "somewhat" or "very" meaningful to them by higher percentages than those who attend less often.[200] By way of summary, the report states:

---

[199] Pew Forum on Religion & Public Life, "Support for Same-Sex Marriage Edges Upward," 1, 4, October 6, 2010, pewforum.org/Gay-Marriage-and-Homosexuality/Support-For-Same-Sex-Marriage-Edges-Upward.aspx. Data are results of two surveys, the first conducted July 21–August 5, 2020, among 3,003 adults, and the second August 25–September 6, 2010, among 3,509 adults.

[200] CARA, *Sacraments Today*, 32.

> Frequency of Mass attendance is a strong indicator of the general importance of Catholicism in a person's life and of his or her level of commitment to living out the faith. Consequently, analyzing survey responses according to frequency of attendance consistently reveals strong differences among Catholics. In general, the more frequently one attends Mass, the more frequently he or she participates in other Church or religious activities, the greater his or her knowledge about the Catholic faith, the greater his or her awareness of current events in the Church, and the greater his or her adherence to Church teachings.[201]

NCR /Gallup found striking differences when comparing Mass attendance figures of registered parish Catholics to nonregistered Catholics. In the 2005 survey, 48% of the former said they attended Mass weekly compared to only 7% of the latter. In addition, "registered Catholics are more committed to the church, . . . they are more likely to be married, and they are more likely to have been married in the church" (82% vs. 51%).[202] Davidson also compares Mass attendance figures between parish members and nonmembers, and finds 58% of parishioners attended "once a week or more," while only 13% of nonmembers did.[203] CARA found that 96% of weekly Mass attendees are registered with a parish, as compared to 85% registered for those who attend less than weekly but at least once a month, and 37% registered for those who attend a few times a year or less often.[204] In these cases, a willingness to identify with the institutional Church as a registered member apparently correlates with a desire to participate more fully and on a regular basis in the life of the Church.

NCR /Gallup has consistently conducted an extremely valuable study of the overall effects on one's Catholic life from being "highly committed" to the "institutional church." High commitment is measured on the basis of high scores in three areas: stated importance of the Catholic Church to one's own life (most important or among the most important), attendance at Mass at least once a week, and admission that one would not leave the Catholic Church. In 2005, the survey found only 21% of Catholics with a high level of commitment, 64% medium, and 15% low. What is already significant about these numbers is that those highly committed have gradually decreased from 27% in 1987 to barely one out of five today, undoubtedly related to the fact that weekly church attendance has also decreased from 44% in 1987 to 34% in 2005.

---

201 Ibid., 113–14.
202 Gautier, "Lay Catholics," 20.
203 Davidson, *Common Ground*, 183.
204 CARA, *Sacraments Today*, 22.

Other important findings: those highly committed "tended to have more Catholic education," tended to "assign more moral authority to church leaders and less to the consciences of individuals" regarding matters such as sex outside of marriage (39% vs. 21% overall), had more stringent requirements on what it takes to be a good Catholic (49% considered weekly Mass attendance unnecessary vs. 76% for the total sample), and tended to "express fewer criticisms of the church or of church leadership." In almost every case of issues involving controversy in the Church today, the highly committed are more supportive of the hierarchy and the teaching of the Church. *NCR* concludes, "Catholics with strong church commitment have stronger loyalty to church leaders, more obedience to church authority, and less criticism of the church leadership."[205]

Nevertheless, these statistics are not so encouraging when read in reverse: even among the pre-Vatican II Catholic group, which had the highest percentage of commitment, only a minority was highly committed (42%), only a minority (39%) gave the final word regarding the acceptability of sex outside of marriage to church authority, and only about half thought attending Mass every week necessary to being a good Catholic. Even in the CARA study, among those who attended Mass weekly or more, only 36% strongly agreed that in deciding moral issues, they would look to the Catholic Church for forming their conscience.[206]

Effects of Closeness to the Church on Moral and Ecclesial Views

The Roper Center for Public Opinion Research shows some effect of weekly Mass attendance on Catholic views on abortion: while 36% of Catholics strongly or mildly agreed that abortion is never justified, among weekly Mass attendees, the percentage rose to 46%.[207] Gallup surveys strongly illustrate the wide disparity of views on abortion between weekly church attendees and nonattendees: in aggregate figures from four polls taken from May 2004 to June 2005, Gallup found that only 9% of Christians who attend church weekly felt abortion should be legal under any circumstances while 39% felt it should always be illegal, whereas among those Christians who seldom or never attended church, 29% felt it should always be legal and only 11% felt it should always be illegal.[208]

What is also interesting is how much the weekly church attendees with similar convictions on abortion tend to aggregate toward the same political

205 Dean R. Hoge, "Attitudes of Catholics highly committed to the church," *NCR*, September 30, 2005, 12, 14.

206 CARA, *Sacraments Today*, 97.

207 Lawler, "Principle Rejected," 45.

208 Newport and Saad, "Religion, Politics."

party: only 4% of Republican weekly church attendees think that abortion should be legal in all circumstances, while nearly half (47%) felt it should always be illegal; among Democratic weekly church attendees, however, 17% felt it should always be legal and only 26% felt it should always be illegal.[209]

At least seven studies have been made that are useful in examining the effect of closeness to the Church on Catholic attitudes regarding contemporary moral and ecclesial issues.

1. ***NCR*/Gallup surveys.** An important survey measuring these differences is the NCR/Gallup survey of 2005. What does the survey show regarding the effects of religious commitment? "Weekly Mass attenders and people who pray on a daily basis are more pro-life . . . than Catholics who go to church and pray less often. . . . Prayer and Mass attendance foster a consistent life ethic . . . . The consistent life ethic is a compelling theological construct and religious commitment fosters it, at least to some degree."[210]

   Gallup's 2002–2004 survey of Catholic moral views reveals a striking confirmation of the effect of closeness to the Church. According to this survey, while 54% of Catholics who seldom or never attend church find abortion "morally acceptable," only 34% of those who attend nearly every week or monthly do, and only 20% of weekly church attendees do. And when dividing Catholics according to weekly Mass attendance, Gallup found that 63% of those who seldom or never attend church find homosexual behavior "morally acceptable," but only 45% held that view among those who attend nearly every week or month, and only 35% agreed among those who attend weekly.[211]

   The *NCR*/Gallup survey of 1999 noted that those who "attend Mass weekly or more are relatively more likely to support church leaders as the locus of moral authority" than the individual. Among the total Catholic population, 20% of Catholics gave final moral authority to church leaders, but among weekly or more Mass attendees, the percentage rose to 33%; those giving the individual final moral authority declined from 47% to 31%. *NCR* notes, however, that even among Mass attendees, there was a decline from 41% in 1987 of those giving final moral authority to Church leaders to 33% in 1999. Thus, notes *NCR*, even among "the church's most committed Catholics," support for church leaders is in decline.[212] When the same 1999 survey broke

---

209 Ibid.

210 Davidson, "What Catholics Believe," 18–19.

211 Newport, "U.S. Catholics Vary Widely."

212 William V. D'Antonio, "Trends in U.S. Roman Catholic attitudes, beliefs, behavior," *NCR*, October 29, 1999, 8.

down those interviewed into parishioners and nonparishioners, 26% of parishioners made Church leaders the locus of moral authority regarding the choice of abortion, but only 8% of the nonparishioners did. When asked if one could be a good Catholic without obeying the Church's teaching on abortion, 50% of the parishioners said yes, but 61% of the nonparishioners did.[213]

None of the figures in any of these three surveys is especially encouraging, though our point is that in a comparison, weekly or more Mass attendees as well as parishioners are more supportive of the Church than those who are not, even though the support there is also in decline.

2. **James Davidson's *Search for Common Ground.*** Confirmation of much of the above is found in a valuable study by Davidson. Following a theory of generations held by Karl Mannheim, Davidson argues three principles: that "persons are shaped and molded during their adolescence in ways that forever impact their behavior and attitudes"; that persons are largely shaped by the "collective understanding of the world" shared by people "during the same time period and in a similar geographical area"; and that persons "belonging to a particular generation, or birth cohort, have a shared vision of the world."[214] Davidson sets up three cohorts: pre-Vatican II, Vatican II, and post-Vatican II Catholics, and finds there are remarkable differences among the three regarding matters such as acceptance of traditional beliefs and practices, views toward sexual and reproductive ethics, the social teachings of the Church, and commitment to the Church.

   Davidson's findings show that pre-Vatican II Catholics are the most institutionally oriented. They identify with the Church and with God through his presence in the Church. For these Catholics, "a Catholic identity, participation in the sacraments, acceptance of Church teachings, and overall commitment to the Church are essential to relating with God," because "involvement with the Church and relating to God" are "deeply interconnected."

   The second cohort, Vatican II Catholics, were conflicted: in some ways less institutionalized and less committed than the pre-Vatican II Catholics, in other ways similarly related to the Church as pre-Vatican II Catholics.

   The largest variation occurs between the first two cohorts and the post-Vatican II Catholics:

---

213 Ibid., 6.

214 Davidson, *Common Ground*, 112.

> The post-Vatican II generation is the least committed to the institutional Church. When asked about the essentials of being a "good Catholic," concern with whether an individual is a "good person" dominated their responses. When asked outright whether a "good Catholic" needs to attend Mass regularly and accept various Church teachings, these young Catholics answered no.

When asked if a life-cycle understanding of religious orientation, supported by so many pollsters, meant that this generation might reflect the views of the pre-Vatican II Church at a later stage, Davidson said: "It is very unlikely that Vatican II parishioners will someday reflect the faith and morals of pre-Vatican II Catholics, and that post-Vatican II parishioners will ever embrace the religious sensibilities of their parents and grandparents."[215]

The clear differences in the generations is immediately evident from data such as these: regarding the Church's teaching on abortion, while 51% of the pre-Vatican II Catholics hold that abortion is "always morally wrong," only 36% of Vatican II Catholics and 31% of post-Vatican II Catholics do. Moreover, only 20% of the pre-Vatican II Catholics hold that the morality of abortion may be left "up to the individual," while 34% and 28% of the other two groups do.[216]

Davidson also stresses the effects of parish membership on Catholic attitudes and practices. The difference in closeness to the Catholic Church between the twenty million American Catholics who are not members of a parish[217] and those who are is remarkable. Some of the findings: Pre-Vatican II Catholics have high levels of religiosity, great identification with parishes, and tend to be "the most committed parishioners";[218] "young Catholics" are "less committed to the Church . . . than their parents and grandparents."[219] "The post-Vatican II generation is almost two and a half times more likely to be without a parish than the pre-Vatican II generation."[220] Catholics who have parish membership are much more likely to accept traditional Catholic beliefs and practices and sexual teachings,[221] to agree on the importance of major doctrines such as the Trinity (79% vs. 53%) and the Resurrection (92% vs. 68%), to agree "that the Catholic Church is the one true church [and] that the pope is the

[215] Ibid., 138.
[216] Ibid., 131.
[217] Ibid., 195.
[218] Ibid., 206.
[219] Ibid., 204.
[220] Ibid., 185.
[221] Ibid., 181.

Vicar of Christ," and much less likely to agree that one can be a good Catholic without going to Mass (57% vs. 81%).[222]

Davidson examines the reasons why some Catholics are without parishes and finds certain governing factors operative: (1) one's upbringing, (2) major life course experiences, and (3) personal conceptions of self and self-interest. A brief sketch of some of his findings:

- (1): The greater "the religiosity of one's family" when one is a child and the greater one's religiosity as a child, the greater likelihood of the adult being a member of a parish: "Parents who rear their children in a religious atmosphere tend to produce adults who have strong attachments to the parish; and those who don't tend to produce adults who distance themselves from the institutional church."[223] Thus the importance of the religious upbringing of the child cannot be exaggerated for adult closeness to the Church. "The more Catholic schooling, the less likely one is to be unaffiliated later in life. . . . Those who had mostly lay teachers are much more likely than those who had priests or nuns to be unaffiliated (41 vs. 26 percent)."[224]
- (2): "If one's spouse is Catholic, only 19 percent are unaffiliated. If one's spouse is not Catholic, 50 percent are unaffiliated . . . . This growing phenomenon of mixed-faith households and the accompanying difficulties of reconciling conflicting demands seem to contribute to a growing number of couples simply dropping out—withdrawing from any organized religious activity at all."[225]
- (3): "Self-concepts and self-interests also are very important determinants of parish membership. If one thinks one's parish is a very important part of one's life and/or thinks of oneself as very religious, he/she is much more likely to join and maintain membership in a parish. . . . Persons with little or no Catholic identity and little or no stake in the Church are most likely to be without parishes. . . . While 31 percent of all Catholics are non-members, only 12 percent of the highly committed are not affiliated with parishes."[226]

---

[222] Ibid., 184–85.
[223] Ibid., 187.
[224] Ibid., 187, 189.
[225] Ibid., 189, 192.
[226] Ibid., 193–94. Recall above in Gallup's 1985 study, 24% of American Catholics were unchurched.

Davidson concludes: "In general, parishioners are more religiously active and more likely to agree with Church teachings than non-parishioners are. Catholics without parishes are less active in the Church, more inclined to disagree with specific Church teachings, and more willing to embrace ideas that are incompatible with Canon Law."[227]

Davidson also stresses the importance of closeness to God to one's relationship to the Church. "If one has had a close personal relation to God over the course of one's life, one is much less likely to be unaffiliated (24 percent) than if one has not (55 percent)."[228] For Davidson, "closeness to God increases commitment to the Church" and a readiness "to agree with the Church's traditional concepts" of faith and morals.[229] But commitment to the Church is also a reflection of how meaningful a role the Church plays in one's life: "The more parishioners identify with the Church and the more they feel the Church meets their social and religious needs, the more they are likely to embrace the Church's worldview."[230] Because of "declining levels of childhood religiosity, closeness to God and commitment to the Church," Davidson warns, "Unless steps are taken, these trends portend a future of dwindling faithfulness among young Catholics, diminishing awareness of God's presence in the lives of Catholic adults, further erosion of Catholic identity, and a declining sense that the Church is worth supporting. These trends, in turn, signal a continuation of recent tendencies to disagree with traditional faith and morals and to embrace religious ideas that are incompatible with Church teachings."[231]

3. **Notre Dame Study of Catholic Parish Life.** The Notre Dame Study of Catholic Parish Life was released March 1986. It was a uniquely valuable study for two reasons: it examined the differences in attitudes of Catholics based on their degree of "participation at different levels" in the life of the Church, and it surveyed "the attitudes of different parish communities." Thus it was able to determine if attitudes depended on degree of "church involvement" as well as on the collective mentality of a specific parish.

   The study determined that the views of Catholics are strongly influenced by the culture of the parish to which they belong. The study concluded that " 'the Catholic viewpoint' is not well tapped by descriptions

[227] Davidson, *Common Ground*, 200.
[228] Ibid., 192–93.
[229] Ibid., 205.
[230] Ibid., 206.
[231] Ibid., 204.

that rely on national survey data alone," as most surveys do, because Catholics "soak up the ideas they hear around them. . . . All this is to emphasize that parishioners who spend a goodly share of their religious and social life in a particular parish are more likely to be exposed to the ideas of different but fellow parishioners than they are exposed to the ideas of Catholic parishioners from elsewhere in their own age group or occupation." The study stressed, therefore, that the parish to which one belongs is more important than "generational, educational, age and income differences" in determining a Catholic's viewpoint:[232] "We understand less about American Catholics by lumping them together as Catholics than we do by examining them within St. Mary's or Christ the King or whatever the local parish."[233]

Thus the first reason why the study is of so much interest to us is because it stressed that membership in an immediate, strong, and truly Catholic environment can do much to counteract the influences made upon a person by the general cultural or social environment. Or to put it in other words, the erosion process going on in society regarding the acceptance of traditional values can be stemmed if there is a countercultural influence coming from the immediate environment in which a person lives.

But this study points out as well that the closer one's level of identification with Catholic parish life, the more likely one will identify with its principles. The Notre Dame study began in 1981 by selecting 36 representative parishes from 1,100 Catholic parishes from different regions and demographic groups in the United States. The data are based on four groups representative of those increasingly involved in the life of the parish: a scientific sample of 2,667 parishioners randomly selected, 212 volunteers "identified as the most-influential unpaid leaders in the parishes," 89 staff members who, apart from the pastors, are "identified as the most-influential paid staff in the parishes," and 35 pastors.[234]

When asked if "abortion is always acceptable" (equivalent to abortion on demand), 1% of parishioners and 1% of volunteers said yes, and 0 percentages were measured for the staff and pastors[235] (note that in the contemporary GSS study of 1982–1985, 37% of Catholics

[232] David C. Leege and Msgr. Joseph Gremillion, "Notre Dame Study of Catholic Parish Life: Pastors and People: Viewpoints on Church Policies and Positions," *Origins* 15 (April 24, 1986): 741.

[233] Ibid., 734.

[234] Ibid., 734–35.

[235] Ibid., 744. All the Notre Dame percentages are from this page.

approved of abortion on demand,[236] and Gallup reported in 1984 that 27% of Catholics favored abortion on demand[237]). When asked if "abortion is acceptable under most circumstances," the percentages in the Notre Dame study were 5% for parishioners, 1% for volunteers, 3% for staff, and 0% for pastors. When asked if abortion was "acceptable under certain extreme circumstances, like a threat to the mother's life, rape or incest," the percentages were 69% for parishioners, 53% for volunteers, but 45% for staff, and only 23% for pastors. Finally, in the Notre Dame study, when asked if "abortion is never acceptable," 26% of parishioners, 46% of volunteers, 52% of staff, and 77% of pastors agreed (in the Gallup study of 1985, 25% of Catholics held that abortion should always be illegal[238]).

In every instance, the Notre Dame study shows those closest to the life of the Church sometimes to some extent, sometimes to a large extent, and sometimes enormously supportive of the Church's teaching, and generally the greater the closeness to the Church, the greater the support. The significance of this finding for the life of the Church cannot be exaggerated, for it clearly shows how great an influence upon the minds and hearts of Catholics the Church can make, if it maintains a close identity with its members.

Finally, it is noteworthy that in the Notre Dame study all four parish groups ranked the view that the Church should remain strong in its opposition to abortion at the top or in second place among issues to be supported, representing a resounding advocacy for the teaching of the Church, whereas in a contemporary 1984 Gallup survey, 59% of Catholics favored a constitutional amendment allowing legal abortion in the case of rape and incest.[239]

On the downside: even in the Notre Dame study, even among those closest to the Church, support for the Church is not total. The Notre Dame Study was forced to note that "active parishioners do not generally accept the church's teaching on contraception"; they "feel comfortable with selecting which of the church's teachings they will espouse and which they will reject," and often reflect an assimilation into the "prevailing American cultural values or social problems."[240]

4. **William Donohue's *Catalyst* study.** Donohue's survey discussed earlier distinguishes between the attitudes and behavior of those who are

---

236 GSS Cumulative Data File 1972–2004, sda.berkeley.edu/.

237 Gallup, *American Catholic*, 93.

238 Ibid., 96.

239 Ibid., 98.

240 Leege and Gremillion, "Notre Dame Study," 736.

regular Mass attendees and those who are not. The former group is more supportive of the Church's teaching. According to Donohue, 69.5% of the regular Mass attendees do not think the Church should change its position on abortion, but among those who do not go to Church, only 42.2% hold that position. Also, 72.3% of the regular Mass attendees are opposed to abortions "in most instances," while only 31.3% hold that position among the non-attendees.[241]

5. **Parish Evaluation Project.** A study conducted by Thomas Sweetser, S.J., of the Parish Evaluation Project, also dealing with parishioners, finds that 58% think abortion is always wrong—a higher percentage than all participants in parish life in the Notre Dame study except for priests. Sweetser finds that this number has remained constant since the 1980s.[242]

6. **Pew Landscape Survey.** The Landscape Survey is particularly valuable because it shows the effects of closeness to one's religious tradition in general, and not simply among Catholics. This effect is evidenced in two important areas of moral choice: abortion and homosexuality.

   Regarding abortion, the study reported: "Views on abortion not only differ among religious traditions but also within them. Religious beliefs and practices significantly influence views on abortion, with those exhibiting high levels of religious commitment (on measures such as frequency of attendance at religious services, frequency of prayer or importance of religion in one's life) much more likely to oppose legalized abortion than their less-committed peers."[243]

   Regarding Catholics, the survey reported that among those who attend church weekly or more, 58% said that abortion should be illegal in all or most cases, while only 35% agreed among all other Catholics; among those who said that religion is very important to their lives versus all other Catholics, the percentages were 56% and 31%; and among those who said they pray at least daily versus all others, the percentages were 51% to 35%.[244]

   Regarding homosexuality, the study reported: "Views on homosexuality follow similar patterns as views on abortion, for the general public as well as for religious traditions."[245] Regarding Catholics, the survey reported that among those who attended services weekly or

241 Donohue, "Catholic League's Survey," 9–10.

242 Thomas P. Sweetser, S.J., "The Parish: What Has Changed, What Remains?" *America* 174 (February 17, 1996): 6.

243 Pew Forum, *Landscape Survey Report 2*, 90.

244 Ibid., 91.

245 Ibid., 92.

more, 37% said that homosexuality should be discouraged by society, as opposed to 25% among all other Catholics; among those for whom religion is very important versus all others, the percentages were 35% versus 23%; and among those who pray at least daily, the percentages were 33% versus 26%.[246]

What these percentages show is that, even among those closest to the Church and religious life, the figures are not especially high, probably due to the increasing influence of the surrounding culture that discourages support for traditional values; nevertheless, the figures indicate that being closer to the Church and to religious activity influences Catholics as well as those of other religious traditions to remain more faithful to the traditional teachings on these moral issues than others do.

7. **Knights of Columbus national survey.** In its survey on "Moral Issues and Catholic Values," the Knights of Columbus repeatedly noted the effects of closeness to the Church:

    - 59% of practicing Catholics ("those who practice their faith regularly")[247] identify themselves as pro-life, while only 29% of nonpracticing Catholics do.[248]
    - 21% of practicing Catholics would never permit abortion, while 11% of nonpracticing Catholics would.[249]
    - 28% of practicing Catholics would permit abortions either any time, during the first three months, or during the first six months, while 53% of nonpracticing Catholics would.[250]
    - 25% of practicing Catholics support legalizing same-sex marriages, while 46% of nonpracticing Catholics do. Thirty-seven percent of practicing Catholics support no legal recognition of same-sex couples, not even civil unions, while 22% of nonpracticing Catholics do.[251]

All of these studies, to be sure, indicate a growing Catholic trend toward permissiveness, but less so among Catholics who experience some degree of closeness to the Church. The data thus seem to indicate that the trend toward permissiveness can be largely counteracted and perhaps even thwarted by a greater experience of union with the Church.

---

[246] Ibid., 94.
[247] Knights of Columbus, "Moral Issues and Catholic Values," 6.
[248] Ibid., 22.
[249] Ibid., 23.
[250] Ibid.
[251] Ibid., 28.

Influence of Cultural Currents on Moral Judgments

Catholics who do not experience this closeness to the Church tend much more to reflect the mood of the nation rather than influencing it. That mood is often generated today by politicians, vocal homosexual interest groups, and the dominantly liberal media, including the television and film industry, all maintaining a drumbeat calling for tolerance of left-wing moral attitudes.

How public opinion can be affected by influential currents of the day may be reflected in the results of other Pew Research surveys: In June 1996, only 27% of the nation supported the legalization of gay marriage, but by July 2003, that number had grown to 38%. Then sharp opposition to that position occurred in late 2003 and early 2004, sparked to a large extent by a backlash over the legalization of same-sex marriage in Massachusetts on November 18, 2003. By February 2004, when it was widely reported that the Massachusetts Supreme Court had legalized same-sex marriage, the percentage of support dropped to 30 and even to 29% in August of that year. Afterward, as the media attention waned, the trend toward tolerance set in again, and in the Pew poll of March 8–12, 2006, 39% of the nation was in favor of legalized same-sex marriage.[252] As we saw, in the GSS 2008 survey, that percentage had risen to 44.5%.[253]

Support of same-sex civil unions has notably increased: in October 2003, 45% of Americans favored same-sex civil unions; by November 2006, that number had risen to 54%.[254] Since the issue of morality is increasingly being marginalized, civil unions are probably considered an acceptable pragmatic compromise for those who are reluctant to change the centuries-old understanding of marriage, and civil unions usually provide benefits similar to those provided by marriage.

Figures against gay marriage represent the same swing: whereas in July 2003, 30% of the nation strongly opposed gay marriage, 42% held that position in February 2004, again apparently reflecting the acrimonious debates around the Massachusetts Supreme Court decision. But in the March 2006 poll, the trend back toward permissiveness is reflected in the fact that only 28% strongly opposed gay marriage, an even smaller percentage than before the debates began.[255]

Zogby data reflect this same temporary reversal: In the Fall of 2003, 39% of Catholics supported legal marriage for same-sex couples and 29%

---

252 Pew, "Less Opposition," 1, 4.

253 GSS Cumulative Data File 1972–2008, sda.berkeley.edu/.

254 Pew Forum on Religion & Public Life, "Support for Civil Unions vs. Gay Marriage," accessed November 15, 2006, pewresearch.org.

255 Pew, "Less Opposition," 1, 4.

supported sacramental marriage. But by Spring 2004, the percentages had fallen to 33% and 20%, respectively. By Spring 2005, however, the percentages were exactly the same as in Fall 2003.[256]

Gallup data 2003–2004 reflect a similar temporary reversal while indicating that over the long haul the trend is decidedly toward permissiveness. Depending on the question, those favoring homosexual relations are sometimes still clearly in the minority, at other times clearly in the majority; for example, whereas only 34% of Americans felt that homosexuality should be considered an acceptable alternative lifestyle in 1982, that figure had risen to 54% in May 2003. Already by July of that year, the figure sharply reversed to 46%, lower than it had been since February of 1999. But by May of 2004, the figure returned to a clear majority of 54%, where it still stood May 2006. But in the same May 2006 poll, a slight majority of Americans—51%—still found the homosexual lifestyle morally wrong, with 44% finding it morally acceptable.[257]

Interestingly enough, a later temporary reversal is tabulated when Gallup sought answers to the question "Do you think marriages between homosexuals should or should not be recognized by the law as valid, with the same rights as traditional marriages?" Only 27% of the American people in March of 1996 said yes, while 68% were opposed, but by May 2004, the percentage favoring had risen to 42%, while those opposed dropped to 55%. But a dip in support for the validity of homosexual marriage is recorded in the August 2005 poll, when only 37% were in favor, and 59% were opposed. In May 2006, the percentage favoring had increased to 39%, while the percentage opposed remained roughly the same (58%). As usual, when weekly church attendance is factored in, a wholly different set of percentages appear: according to Gallup, "Highly religious Americans—defined as those who attend their churches or other places of worship weekly—are widely opposed to sanctioning gay marriages (77% say they should not be valid) while a majority of those who seldom or never attend church (51%) say they should be valid."[258]

As we saw in Gallup's May 2009 poll, a clear majority of Americans (57%) are opposed to gay marriage. Apart from the issue of gay marriage,

---

256 Le Moyne College/Zogby poll, March 7–10, 2005. This dip in 2004 was not represented in Catholic support for civil unions: In Fall 2003, 56% supported such unions, which Zogby states "provide the same legal rights and protections as marriage without being called 'marriage.'" The percentage rose to 62% in Spring 2004 and remained there in Spring 2005.

257 Lydia Saad, "Americans at Odds Over Gay Rights," Gallup Poll, May 31, 2006, www.gallup.com.

258 Lydia Saad, "Americans Still Oppose Gay Marriage," Gallup Poll, May 22, 2006, www.gallup.com.

however, the trend at the present time is in the direction of gay rights, perhaps as part of a conciliatory mood toward the strongly vocal minority pushing gay rights. Gallup's 2009 poll shows 56% of U.S. adults support the legality of gay or lesbian relationships between consenting adults (a relationship that traditional morality considers immoral); 67% say such partners should have health insurance and other employee benefits; 67% favor hate-crime laws to cover crimes committed against them; and 69% believe gays and lesbians should be allowed to teach children.[259]

Where do Catholics stand? The data indicate they have become even more permissive than the national average. Pew shows that in July 2003, 19% of Catholics strongly opposed gay marriage, but that 35% did so in February 2004. By March 2006, Catholic strong opposition dropped back to the 19% figure, while the national strong opposition percentage stood at 28%. Among all Protestants, strong opposition was at 36%—almost twice that of Catholics. A majority of evangelical Protestants, whose opposition bounced up by 10 percentage points in February 2004, remained as strongly opposed in March 2006 as they were July 2003—at 56%—once again making them the strongest supporters of the Catholic Church on moral issues.[260]

We have already discussed the Pew Forum on Religion & Public Life's poll of October 6, 2010, where the dramatic shift is noted toward the acceptance of same-sex marriage by the American public in general. According to the poll, there is also a plurality of Catholics for the first time supporting the legalization of same-sex marriage—46% versus 42%. The poll goes on to point out, however, the differences that occur when weekly church attendance is taken into consideration.

The poll noted that 42% of Americans in October 2010 favor legally sanctioned same-sex marriage, while 48% are opposed. Among those who attend weekly church services, however, the gap in percentages is much greater: 24% in favor, 68% opposed. Support for same-sex marriage seems to come primarily from those who attend church services only monthly or yearly—49% in favor, 40% opposed—or seldom or never—59% in favor, 29% opposed.

Separate Protestant groups are also polled regarding church attendance: (1) white evangelicals: those who attend weekly: 14% in favor, 81% opposed; those who attend less: 31% in favor, 61% opposed; (2) white mainliners: those who attend weekly: 35% in favor, 57% opposed; those who attend less: 53% in favor, 33% opposed; (3) black protestant: those who attend weekly: 22% in favor, 69% opposed; those who attend less: 37% in favor, 52% opposed. In every case except one (white mainliners), whether one attends

---

259 Jones, "Majority of Americans Continue to Oppose Gay Marriage."
260 Pew, "Less Opposition," 4.

church weekly or not, the majority is opposed to same-sex marriage, but the opposition is significantly greater among those who attend church weekly.

Percentages are strikingly different among white Catholics,[261] depending on whether or not they attend church weekly: among those who attend weekly, 34% are in favor, 55% are opposed; but among those who attend less, 59% are in favor, 31% are opposed. Thus, while closeness to the church is important among all Christian religious groups regarding one's position on same-sex marriage, its significance is especially noteworthy among Catholics: a majority of Catholics support the teaching of the Church on this issue only when they attend church weekly.[262]

Conclusion on Abortion

Significant data indicate an erosion of support for the teaching of the Church on abortion, with a large percentage of Catholics today holding that abortion is acceptable under conditions the Church finds unacceptable. A reversal seems to be occurring regarding abortion on demand, in spite of continued support for *Roe v. Wade*, especially among younger Catholics who seem to be more conscious of the evil of abortion and wish to narrow its use to limited circumstances. The erosion of support for the Church is considerably less among those who practice their faith or are parishioners, especially if they are regular Mass attendees and more closely involved in the life of the Church and religious activities. In general, closeness to the life of the Church seems to create greater support for Church teaching, though not complete support. It is there that the Church needs to work—to create more highly committed Catholics who will stand in support of the Church and its teachings in the continuing struggle to counteract the increasing secularization of our society.

Conclusion on Homosexuality

The trend is decidedly toward tolerance of homosexual behavior. The movement is also clearly underway toward private moral decision-making on this issue, where less weight is given to the objective moral standards taught by the Church and more weight given to subjective standards decided by the individual. Those closer to the Church, however, are more likely to support the Church's teaching, as on the abortion issue, especially if they are parishioners or weekly Mass attendees. Commitment seems once again generally to retard the erosion process. The same conclusions follow here as with reversing the tide with abortion.

---

[261] Percentages for Hispanic Catholics are 42% in favor, 43% opposed, with no polling given regarding church attendance.

[262] Pew Forum, "Support for Same-Sex Marriage," 4.

Birth Control

According to Gallup, "The subject on which there is the greatest disagreement [by Catholics] is the Church's ban on artificial means of birth control."[263] Gallup reports that just after the promulgation of Paul VI's condemnation of all artificial methods of birth control in his July 1968 encyclical *Humanae Vitae*, already "54 percent of the American Catholic laity who had heard about the encyclical opposed it, [and] 28 percent favored it."[264]

According to Gallup, 58% of Catholics in 1971 said a good Catholic could ignore *Humanae Vitae*. By 1977, 73% rejected it.[265] In 1993, despite the fact that John Paul II continued to oppose artificial methods of birth control, a Gallup survey reported that 73% of Catholics said one could be a good Catholic without obeying the Church's teaching on birth control,[266] although in another report apparently of the same survey, Gallup reports that 89% of Catholics held that view.[267] In his 1999 *NCR* survey, he reports a 72% figure holding that view,[268] and in 2005, 75%.[269] In the 1999 survey, even among parishioners, 67% said you can be a good Catholic and practice birth control.[270] In 1997, 73% of Catholics said they disagreed with the position "It is morally wrong to use artificial methods of birth control."[271]

Greeley reports as well that just over half of American Catholics rejected the encyclical when it was issued. But in 1985, he reported that nine out of ten rejected it, and that six out of ten Catholic women of childbearing age were using some form of contraceptive.[272] Donohue reports that in February 1995, 58.4% of Catholics agreed that the Catholic Church should abandon its opposition to artificial birth control, and only 33.8% disagreed.[273] Zogby found in 2006 that 70% of Catholics felt the Church should permit the use of artificial birth control.[274] Lawler reports in 1997 that 57% of Catholics strongly disagreed with the Church's teaching on contraception, and 16% "mildly disagreed," giving a total of 73% disagreeing with this teaching of the Church.[275]

---

263 Gallup, *American Catholic*, 50.
264 D'Antonio, *American Catholic Laity*, 51.
265 Gallup, *American Catholic*, 50.
266 D'Antonio, *American Catholic Laity*, 174.
267 George Gallup, Jr., and D. Michael Lindsay, *Surveying the Religious Landscape: Trends in U.S. Beliefs* (Harrisburg, PA: Morehouse, 1999), 85.
268 D'Antonio, *American Catholic in 1999*, 2.
269 Hoge, "Center of Catholic Identity," 11.
270 D'Antonio, *American Catholic in 1999*, 6.
271 Lawler, "Principle Rejected," 45.
272 Greeley, *American Catholics*, 83–84; Greeley, *Sex*, 112.
273 Donohue, "Catholic League's Survey," 8.
274 Zogby, "National Survey of Catholic adults."
275 Lawler, "Principle Rejected," 44–45.

Even among the Church's more faithful members, the erosion process is in an advanced stage on this issue. In the NCR/Gallup survey of 1999, 67% of parishioners said you could be a good Catholic without obeying *Humanae Vitae*, while 83% of nonparishioners did.[276] According to the Roper poll, only 30% of Catholics who attend Mass at least once a week "recognize contraception as morally wrong."[277] Among parishioners in Sweetser's poll, ever since the 1970s, "only 9 percent consider birth control for married couples wrong."[278] And the American bishops reported at their Fall 2006 semiannual meeting in Baltimore, MD, that "Catholics use birth control to the same extent as other Americans," and that only 4% use natural family planning, "the type of birth control backed by the church."[279]

Davidson notes that only 9% of Catholics hold that artificial methods of birth control are always wrong, and 81% say the decision should be left to the individual.[280] In the 1999 *NCR*/Gallup study, 61% of those polled said it should be left to the individual, though among Mass attendees the figure is considerably lower at 45%.[281] The Notre Dame study reports that opposition to the Church's teaching on this issue is generally "very strong." Pastors are often unwilling to bring up the issue in their homilies either because they fear a negative reaction, or because they know the teaching has been widely rejected or become irrelevant to the lives of their congregations.

Gallup feels that it was with this teaching that the Church "clearly established the pattern that [Catholics] accept church teaching only when it makes sense in terms of their own situations and their own consciences." As a result, Catholics did not simply turn a deaf ear to the teaching on birth control; rather, the Church "lost much of its credibility on everything related to sex. . . . When it comes to sex, church leaders are preaching to an audience that is simply not paying any attention."[282]

But support for the Church may now be coming from an unexpected source. As a more conservative mind-set has been growing in the United States, Protestant anti-abortion organizations have become more cognizant of the inevitable linkage of abortion to the contraceptive mentality that separates sex from procreation. Once again, the Catholic Church finds its biggest support among Protestant evangelicals. R. Albert Mohler, Jr., the president of the Southern Baptist Theological Seminary, was recently cited in the *New*

---

276 D'Antonio, "Trends in U.S.," 6.
277 Lawler, "Principle Rejected," 45.
278 Sweetser, "Parish," 6.
279 Neela Banerjee, "U.S. Bishops Adopt Guidelines on Gays," *New York Times*, November 15, 2006, www.nytimes.com.
280 Davidson, *Common Ground*, 47.
281 D'Antonio, *American Catholic in 1999*, 3–4.
282 Gallup, *American Catholic*, 183.

York Times Magazine addressing the onset of a "contra-contraception" movement: "The effective separation of sex from procreation may be one of the most important defining marks of our age—and one of the most ominous. This awareness is spreading among American evangelicals, and it threatens to set loose a firestorm. . . . A growing number of evangelicals are rethinking the issue of birth control—and facing the hard questions posed by reproductive technologies."[283]

Premarital Sex

American attitudes toward sex before marriage have become increasingly liberal in the last twenty-five years, and Catholics are showing the effects of it in their lives: "Premarital sex and homosexuality have become more acceptable in the culture at large, and this probably affects the views of many Catholics."[284]

According to Gallup, whereas 68% of Americans in 1969 said premarital sex was morally wrong, only 38% held that position in 2001. Baylor found only 31.5% of Americans holding premarital sex as "always wrong," and only 24.7% feeling the same about "cohabitation."[285] Pew in 2006 found that 35% of Americans found sex between unmarried adults morally wrong, 22% as morally acceptable, and 37% as not a moral issue.[286] According to the 2008 GSS, 22.6% of Americans found premarital sex always wrong (down from 25.6% in 2006), while 54.8% found it not wrong at all (up from 45.7% in 2006).[287]

Hegy and the GSS data show the growing permissiveness on this matter more so among Catholics than among Protestants. In 1963, 75% of Catholics and 64% of Protestants thought premarital sex was always wrong, but in the period from 1972 to 1975, only 38% of Protestants held that premarital sex was always wrong, and the figure dropped to 34% by 1988–1990. But the Catholic percentage in 1972–1975, according to the GSS data, was at 32%—in twelve years having already dropped from 11 points higher than the Protestant percentage to 6 percentage points below—and in 1988–1990 dropped to 18%, 16 percentage points below the Protestant percentage at that time. In 2008, Catholics dropped to 14.1% holding premarital sex as always wrong—a drop of nearly 61% in

---

283 Russell Shorto, "Contra-Contraception," *New York Times Magazine*, May 7, 2006.

284 Christina Michaelson, assistant professor of psychology at Le Moyne College, cited in "Majority of Catholics approve of same-sex civil unions but not same-sex marriage," Zogby International Poll, May 11, 2005, www.zogby.com/news/ReadNews.cfm?ID=992.

285 Baylor Religion Survey 2006, 32.

286 Pew, "Sex, Drugs," 13.

287 GSS Cumulative Data File 1972–2008, sda.berkeley.edu/.

forty-five years—while the Protestant percentage remained at 33%, a drop of 31% in the same period, but more than twice the percentage of Catholics. On the other hand, the Protestants who held that premarital sex was "not wrong at all" in 1972 amounted to 24% and increased to 35% in 1988–1990. But the percentage of Catholics who held premarital sex was not wrong at all in 1972 was at 21%—3 percentage points less than the Protestants—but increased to 44% in 1988–1990, 9 percentage points higher than the Protestants.[288] In 2008, GSS data showed that nearly two-thirds of Catholics—64.2%—hold that premarital sex is not wrong at all, while the Protestant percentage has risen to 43.8%. Notable is the fact that considerable change occurred in both groups between 2006 and 2008: in 2006, the Catholic percentage was at 51.5%; the Protestant percentage still at 34%.[289]

George Gallup's figures on Catholics are hardly less discouraging. According to him, in 1969, 72% of Catholics thought that premarital sex was morally wrong, but by 1985, only 33% held that position. That represents a drop of 39% in sixteen years. In 1985, Catholics approved of premarital sex by 58%, Protestants by only 46%. Therefore, Catholics went from disapproving slightly more (by 2%) than Protestants in 1969 to approving by 12% more than Protestants in 1985. According to Gallup, Catholics were even more approving (by 6%) of premarital sex in 1985 than the American population as a whole, and represent "the most permissive major Christian denomination in the nation."[290]

What about data regarding actual practice? Greeley uses GSS data showing that Catholics are less likely to be chaste than Protestants: In 1991, only about 35% of single American Catholics said they had had no sexual relations in the past year, as opposed to 41% to 44% among various Protestant groups. Moreover, among those Catholics who were not chaste, more than 37% had had sex once a week or more, as opposed to 27% to 34% among various Protestant groups. Greeley concludes: "Catholics are more likely to engage in single sex and, once they engage in it, to do so more frequently [than Protestants] because they are less likely to think that it is always wrong"[291]

Hoge comments: "Here again we see changing attitudes, but there is more change among Catholics than among Protestants. . . . Catholics are leading the trend, showing more tolerance than Protestants. This figure could be reproduced on other attitudes regarding sex, although usually

[288] GSS data, and Hegy, "End of American Catholicism?," 6.

[289] GSS Cumulative Data File 1972–2008, sda.berkeley.edu/.

[290] Gallup, *American Catholic*, 51, 183.

[291] Andrew M. Greeley, "Sex and the Single Catholic: The Decline of an Ethic," *America* 167 (November 7, 1992): 344.

without the divergence between Protestants and Catholics."[292] Hegy agrees: "Increasingly it seems that conservative Protestants are closer to Rome than are young Catholics—or even the majority of Catholics."[293] Greeley sees these figures indicating "the catastrophic collapse of the old Catholic sexual ethic."[294]

Extramarital Sex

According to GSS, 74% of Catholics in 1972–1975 held that extramarital sex (adultery) was always wrong, and the percentage only decreased to 71% in 1982–1985. Nevertheless, the percentage among Protestants in 1982–1985 is significantly higher at 77%. Greeley asserted in 1994 that there is no erosion regarding extramarital sex, that Catholics still support the teaching of the Church by substantial majorities on this issue: "Three-quarters of Catholic Americans think that extramarital sex is always wrong, a proportion which is the same as that of Americans who are not Catholic and which has not changed since the early 1960s."[295] Baylor confirms Greeley among the American public in general where 72.6% find extra-marital sex "always wrong."[296] GSS indicates that in 2008, 84.9% of Catholics said extramarital sex was always wrong, but the percentage had climbed to 89.2% among Protestants.[297] Among Catholics, Pew Research's figures are even higher: in 2006, 85% of Catholics said sexual behavior between married people was morally wrong, and 88% of the total American population agreed.[298]

Gallup, however, reported in 1993 that only 48% of American Catholics held that "sex outside of marriage is always wrong."[299] In 1987 he reported that one out of three Catholics refused to say extramarital sex was always wrong.[300] In 1999, a subjective element is noted: 46% held that the final moral authority on extramarital sex should be the individual (a 4% increase over 1987).[301]

---

292 Dean R. Hoge, "Catholic Generations Polarized on Gender and Sex," *America* 179 (November 21, 1998): 17.

293 Hegy, "End of American Catholicism?," 6.

294 Greeley, "Sex and the Single Catholic," 344.

295 Greeley, *Sex*, 111.

296 Baylor Religion Survey 2006, 32.

297 GSS Cumulative Data File 1972–2008, sda.berkeley.edu/.

298 Pew, "Sex, Drugs," 8.

299 *Gallup Poll: Public Opinion 1998*, 146. It is difficult to explain the large discrepancy here between the GSS and Pew Research's data, and Gallup's data. Perhaps the confusion is regarding the meaning of Gallup's "sex outside of marriage." The expression is ambiguous, to say the least.

300 Gallup, *American Catholic*, 183.

301 D'Antonio, "Generational Differences," table 9, *NCR*, October 29, 1999, 8.

Divorce and Remarriage

The data here show little sympathy across the board for the teaching of the Church. Greeley speaks of a "drastic decline" in the acceptance of the Church's position on divorce and remarriage. According to him, whereas in 1963 over half the American Catholics disapproved of divorce, in 1985 "only little more than a tenth believe that remarriage after divorce is impossible."[302]

According to Gallup, in 1987, 57% said you could be a good Catholic and not obey the Church's teaching regarding divorce and remarriage; in 1993, 62% held that position; in 1999, 65%; in 2005, 66%. Parishioners agreed in 1999 by 62%, nonparishioners by 71%, that one could be a good Catholic without obeying the Church's teaching on divorce and remarriage.[303] In the twelve-year period from 1987 to 1999, there was an increase of 14 percentage points to a total of 45% of American Catholics who felt that the individual should have the final say on getting remarried after divorce without an annulment, but among regular Mass attendees, only 29% agreed.[304] When Gallup asked in 1993 if divorced Catholics should be permitted to remarry in the Church, 78% said yes, and only 19% disagreed.[305] In the Notre Dame study, views were mixed: while the majority of parishioners and staff agreed that the Church should liberalize its position on divorce, the majority of the volunteers and even more of the pastors did not.[306] Conclusion: The institutional Church and the sacrament of marriage are becoming irrelevant to Catholics, even among the more committed and faithful members, though the process of erosion among them is less marked.

Hoge concludes that these data indicate that the "center of Catholic identity" is losing its traditional boundaries which are "now fairly vague and porous, and they are slowly becoming more so over time."[307] This seems to be a gentle way of saying the meaning of Catholic identity is losing its focus on teachings and principles that have traditionally defined what it means to be a Catholic. A kind of "common sense" approach has invaded Catholicism, carried over from extra-ecclesial social attitudes. The "what" of Catholicism is giving way to the "why," and answers rooted in esoteric spiritual principles no longer resonate. Metaphysics is being abandoned. Davidson has aptly

---

302 Greeley, *American Catholics*, 84.

303 D'Antonio, *American Catholic in 1999*, 2.

304 "Final Moral Authority," table 3; "Locus of Moral Authority," table 5, *NCR*, October 29, 1999, 3–4.

305 George H. Gallup, Jr., ed., *Gallup Poll 1993* (Wilmington, DE: Scholarly Sources, 1994), 144. Gallup repeats the 78% figure in his 1999 book: Gallup and Lindsay, *Religious Landscape*, 83.

306 Leege and Gremillion, "Notre Dame Study," 743.

307 Hoge, "Center of Catholic identity," 14.

concluded that in sexual and reproductive matters, "consequentialism" has taken its place where "there is nothing intrinsically right or wrong about sexual and reproductive acts. Rather, their rightness or wrongness depends on the circumstances and their consequences for the persons involved. From this point of view, it is up to individuals to decide whether their actions are right or wrong."[308]

Ecclesial Issues

We now examine data regarding two controversial ecclesial issues: women priests and married priests.

Women Priests

Various data indicate gradual erosion in support for the Church's teaching on the inadmissibility of women priests.

According to Greeley, in 1974, only 29% of American Catholics thought that women should be allowed to be ordained priests. That number rose to 36% in 1977, to 40% in 1979, and to 44% in 1982.[309] The Notre Dame study in 1985 shows no majority support for women priests among any of the four groups studied—parishioners, volunteers, staff, or pastors.[310]

Gallup reports that, whereas in 1974 only 29% supported women priests, by 1985, Catholics were evenly divided on the issue, with 47% in favor and 47% opposed.[311] But in 1993, there was a "dramatic jump to 64 percent" support.[312] In a *New York Times*/CBS News poll of April 21–23, 1994, 59% of Catholics favored ordaining women.[313] Donohue's survey, where figures tend to be conservative, indicates that in 1995, 55% of Catholics supported women priests, but this is the average between those who attend Mass regularly, where the figure is 48.6%, and those who never go to Church, where 71% support it.[314] According to Davidson, 57% of parishioners in 1995 supported women priests.[315] But according to Sweetser, only 42% of parishioners supported women priests in 1996, but this figure is up 13% over 1992.[316] In an early 1997 survey, 58% of Catholics said they mildly or strongly disagreed with the position that women cannot be ordained to the priesthood.[317] In 1999 when asked if

308 Davidson, *Common Ground*, 47.
309 Greeley, *American Catholics*, 182.
310 Leege and Gremillion, "Notre Dame Study," 743.
311 Gallup, *American Catholic*, 56.
312 D'Antonio et al., *American Catholics*, 108.
313 Masci, "Catholic Church in U.S.," 780.
314 Donohue, "Catholic League's Survey," 6.
315 Davidson, *Common Ground*, 45.
316 Sweetser, "Parish," 6.
317 Lawler, "Principle Rejected," 45.

they supported ordaining celibate women, 62% of Catholics said yes, with 68% among those 18–38 years old, but only 47% among those 59 and older. Even 56% of parishioners supported ordaining women priests, although 80% of nonparishioners supported it.[318]

The 2005 *NCR*/Gallup survey continues to show that 62% of Catholics support women's ordination, but the major support is coming from those less close to the Church: only 40% of those at a high level of commitment to the Church support it, but 81% of those at a low level.[319]

An Associated Press poll taken at the time of John Paul II's death found that 60% of American Catholics said women should be allowed to become priests.[320] A Zogby poll of March 2006 indicates that almost 62% of Catholics agree that a woman who felt called to the priesthood should be ordained.[321] And the 2008 GSS reports that 54.2% of Catholics agree somewhat or strongly that it would be good if women were allowed to be priests.[322]

Support Increases Simultaneously with Vatican Opposition

The above survey data make it clear that there has been increasing support for the ordination of women from 1974 to the present, though probably less support among those closer to the Church. Majority votes in favor did not occur until the early 1990s. It might be valuable to correlate that data with the increasing opposition by the Vatican to the ordination of women during this same period.

The first clear statement of opposition is contained in Paul VI's letter of November 30, 1975, pointing out to the Anglican Archbishop of Canterbury, Donald Coggan, that for the Catholic Church, "it is not admissible to ordain women to the priesthood."[323] The Pope later commissioned the Congregation for the Doctrine of the Faith to study the matter of women's ordination at length and draw up a position paper on the issue. That declaration, *Inter Insigniores*, dated October 15, 1976, and released the following January, was authorized by the Pope, and contains the most extensive presentation to that date of the views of the Vatican on this issue.[324]

318 D'Antonio, "Trends in U.S.," 8, 6.

319 Hoge, "Attitudes of Catholics," 12.

320 Associated Press, "Poll: New pope should push for change: Most Americans want priests to be able to marry, AP survey finds," April 4, 2005, www.msnbc.msn.com.

321 Le Moyne College/Zogby poll.

322 GSS Cumulative Data File 1972–2008, sda.berkeley.edu/.

323 Cited by John Paul II in his *Ordinatio Sacerdotalis* (Apostolic Letter on Ordination and Women), *Origins* 24 (June 9, 1994): 49.

324 Congregation for the Doctrine of the Faith, *Inter Insigniores* (Declaration on the Question of Admission of Women to the Ministerial Priesthood), October 15, 1976.

In 1988, in his apostolic letter *Mulieris Dignitatem*, John Paul II presents his most extensive theological treatment of women's ordination and supports *Inter Insigniores*.[325] Nevertheless, when the Anglican Church decided in 1993 to allow women priests, renewed discussions arose among Catholic theologians in the United States over whether the Catholic Church should follow suit. It was at this time that popular majority views in favor of women's ordination were recorded for the first time.

John Paul felt the need to clarify that the issue was not "open to debate." So he wrote the brief apostolic letter *Ordinatio Sacerdotalis*, dated May 22, 1994, declaring in no uncertain terms "that the church has no authority whatsoever to confer priestly ordination on women and that this judgment is to be definitively held by all the church's faithful."[326] It was rumored that the Pope wanted to declare the teaching infallible but had been discouraged from doing so by many members of the American hierarchy fearing uproar in their dioceses. While the hierarchy may have prevailed, the apostolic letter is tantamount to a declaration of dogma, as the above citation makes clear.

Nevertheless, public discussion continued, leading the Congregation for the Doctrine of the Faith, in an effort to overcome any lingering doubt, to publish a statement dated October 28, 1995, declaring that the teaching as stated in *Ordinatio Sacerdotalis* "requires definitive assent," that it "has been set forth infallibly by the ordinary and universal magisterium," and that it is "to be held always, everywhere and by all as belonging to the deposit of the faith." The statement, added Cardinal Joseph Ratzinger, then prefect of the congregation, was approved by the Pope as definitive.[327] By that statement, the Vatican intended to make clear that the teaching was to be infallibly held as dogma.[328]

Our point in itemizing the documentation here is to show that the Vatican had increasingly been clarifying its stand in opposition to the ordination of women from 1975 on, and especially in the late '80s and early '90s. Yet the above surveys show an increasing rejection of the Church's position, from 29% in 1974 to as much as 62% in 2005 (following Gallup), indicating that Vatican teaching either increased the opposition or simply held no sway against opposing currents.

---

325 John Paul II, *Mulieris Dignitatem* (On the Dignity and Vocation of Women), August 15, 1988.

326 Pope John Paul II, *Ordinatio Sacerdotalis*, 51.

327 Congregation for the Doctrine of the Faith, "Response to 'Dubium,'" *Origins* 25 (November 30, 1995): 401, 403.

328 There followed much discussion over whether the teaching had in fact been infallibly proclaimed, in spite of the congregation's declaration. Cf. Ladislaus Orsy, S.J., "The Congregation's 'Response': Its Authority and Meaning," *America* 173 (December 9, 1995): 4–5; and in the same issue, Francis A. Sullivan, S.J., "Guideposts from Catholic Tradition," 5–6.

Married Priests

Views on this issue are unlike those above, in that moral or theological truth is not at issue, but only Church policy. Nevertheless, since the Roman Catholic Church has strongly indicated its unwillingness to deviate, except in unusual cases, from requiring celibacy for ordination to the ministerial priesthood, those who support a universal voluntary married clergy represent a viewpoint at odds with the official mind of the Church.

According to George Gallup, Jr., there "has been a steady increase in support for a married priesthood."[329] He reports that in 1971 49% favored it, but in 1973, a majority of 57% already supported it. By 1983, Gallup says that "62% of Americans who practiced the Catholic faith favored allowing priests to marry," and that in 1993, the number reached 75%.[330] Gallup's figures in the *NCR* surveys are slightly different: 63% in 1987 thought "it would be a good thing to allow married men to be ordained"; the figure rose to 72% in 1993, remained at 71% in 1999, and stood at 75% in 2005. Moreover, in 2005 when Catholics were asked if priests who got married should be allowed to return to active ministry, 81% of respondents agreed.[331]

In a *New York Times*/CBS Poll of April 21–23, 1994, 64% of Catholics favored letting priests marry.[332] Donohue reports that 66.5% said the Church should ordain married men, and even 53.2% of weekly Mass attendees were willing to accept it.[333] Davidson tells us that 49% of Catholics favored married priests in 1974, but the number rose to 76% in 1993.[334] According to Sweetser, 61% of parishioners in 1996 favored it.[335] In sum: solid and growing majorities from 1973 on, even among those closest to the Church.

Participation in the Sacraments

CARA reports the somewhat shocking statistic in 2008 that only 38% of Catholics agree "strongly" that "sacraments are essential to my faith" (61% agree "somewhat" or "strongly"). But among weekly or more than weekly Mass attendees, where percentages are normally more supportive of the Church and its teachings, the percentage of Catholics who "strongly" agree rises to 83%. Among those who attend Mass infrequently, only 14% agree

---

329 Gallup, *American Catholic*, 55.

330 Gallup and Lindsay, *Religious Landscape*, 86–87.

331 D'Antonio et al., *American Catholics*, 108; James D. Davidson, "Belief in church as mediator slips," *NCR*, September 30, 2005, 21.

332 Masci, "Catholic Church in U.S.," 780.

333 Donohue, "Catholic League's Survey," 8.

334 Davidson, *Common Ground*, 26.

335 Sweetser, "Parish," 6.

"strongly."[336] What greater evidence could one need to show the effect of closeness to the Church on Catholic attitudes and convictions?

Still, Greeley, based on the theology of David Tracy, argues in *The Catholic Myth* that the Catholic religious imagination is "sacramental," meaning that Catholics see the world and all that is in it as a creation of God that reveals in various ways God's presence; the world is thus the sacrament of the presence of God.[337] That insight is apt. One might conclude that Catholics carry this sacramental understanding of the world into a deeper awareness of the importance of the sacramental life of the Church, but the opposite appears to be true.

In fact, there appears to be an inverse ratio between the two. The more deeply modern Catholics find God present in creation, the less likely they seem to understand the need for the sacramental life of the Church. The logic seems to be that if God is present in the world—if grace-filled moments can be experienced in creation—why bother setting up special instruments of grace within the Church? Thus the analogical sacramental understanding of the whole of creation that Greeley prizes so highly in Catholics seems to be detracting from a sacramental understanding of life in the Church. Is there statistical data to substantiate this? I think there is.

There is no doubt that, among those who go to Mass, a strong awareness of the sacramental understanding of life in the Church is present. Reception of the Eucharist has increased enormously. At Mass on any given Sunday, almost everyone goes to Communion. Davidson notes that "seventy-seven percent of all parishioners who are highly committed to the Church . . . participate regularly in traditional practices such as Mass attendance, receiving Holy Communion, and saying the rosary."[338] And 87% of Catholics in a poll taken in 2000 said participation in the Eucharist was an important aspect of being Catholic.[339] CARA found that 64% of all Catholics said the Eucharist was "very" meaningful to them, and even higher percentages said the same about marriage (71%) and baptism (72%).[340] This seems to indicate that attachment to the sacraments is still important to the mind-set of faithful Catholics.

As we saw, CARA's percentages are especially high for those who are close to the Church, and we have already discussed the positive effect of participation in weekly Mass. Indeed, similar positive effect is shown by closeness to Catholic education: "Respondents who attended a Catholic

336 CARA, *Sacraments Today*, 96–97.

337 Andrew M. Greeley, *The Catholic Myth: The Behavior and Beliefs of American Catholics* (New York: Scribner's, 1990), 45.

338 Davidson, *Common Ground*, 63.

339 Froehle and Gautier, 27.

340 CARA, *Sacraments Today*, 31.

elementary or middle school are more likely than those who did not to say all seven sacraments are 'very' meaningful to them. . . . Respondents who attended a Catholic high school are more likely than those who did not to say all seven sacraments are 'very' meaningful to them. . . . Those who have had more personal experience of a sacrament are more likely to select it as being most meaningful."[341]

Nevertheless, studies show that "participation in the sacramental life of the Church has declined somewhat in a number of areas compared to rates at mid-century."[342] So is the sacramental mind-set of Catholics as a whole thriving, or is this only true for faithful Catholics?

A decline in the appreciation of the sacramental life of the Church is painfully obvious in the starkly reduced Mass attendance figures seen earlier. In addition, Froehle and Gautier report that "the number of sacramental marriages as a proportion of all marriages [in the United States] has also been decreasing"—from 20% in 1970 to 13% in 1990—even though Catholics continue to constitute about 23% of the total American population. Such data lead our authors to suggest that "Catholics are less likely to marry in the Church than in the past."[343] In view of the fact that in the *NCR*/Gallup 2005 survey, an average of 68.2% of Catholics said you can be a good Catholic without marrying in the Church, and another 79% said you could be a good Catholic without attending Mass every week,[344] how much of a sense of the sacramental life of the Church can really be present in Catholics today?

But let us assume for the sake of argumentation that "attachment to the sacraments" was still important to Catholics' self-understanding when they were asked in Gallup's 1999 survey, "As a Catholic, how important is each of the following to you?" Eighty percent of the time, among a forced choice of six elements, the Catholics who responded with "very important to me" chose "sacraments, such as the Eucharist and marriage" as their number one choice, with "spiritual and personal growth" a close second (76%). In third place, at 71%, was "Church involvement in activities directed toward social justice and helping the poor."[345]

In the *NCR*/Gallup 2005 survey, however, a notable change occurs. For some unexplained reason, when the pollsters forced a choice this time among twelve elements of Catholicism, they separated "Church involvement in activities directed toward social justice" from "helping the poor." This opened up the survey to a fascinating but crucial change from the

---

341 Ibid., 32, 34.

342 Froehle and Gautier, 22, 27.

343 Ibid., 24.

344 D'Antonio, "Generational Differences," 15.

345 D'Antonio et al., *American Catholics*, 46.

1999 results: the number one choice for "very important" was a tie at 84% for "helping the poor" and "belief in Jesus' resurrection from the dead," an element not listed in 1999. "The sacraments, such as the Eucharist," which had been first choice as recently as six years earlier, came in third at 76%. So while aid to the poor increased by a large 13% to tie for first place, and to a higher percentage than the first place that had been given to sacramental life in 1999, the value of the sacramental life of the Church declined 4 percentage points to third place in the rankings. The previously third-ranked "Church involvement in activities directed toward social justice," now separated from "helping the poor," fell into a minority ranking and tied for sixth at 47% with "teachings that oppose same-sex marriage."[346]

What are we to make of such alterations in the ranking of these elements in so short a time? The pollster simply notes the obvious without drawing a conclusion: "In past studies the sacraments were usually in first place ahead of helping the poor (or charity toward the poor). . . . Here helping the poor and belief in the Resurrection came out ahead. Nevertheless, we consider it noteworthy that helping the poor is held in such central importance by American Catholics." The author concludes that, in view of the fact that Church moral teachings (elements not listed in the 1999 survey) came in last, "basic creedal beliefs such as Jesus' resurrection and the nature of the sacraments" are distinguished by most Catholics from "most specific moral teachings about sexuality or the death penalty," such as "celibate priesthood, the death penalty, abortion and same-sex marriage," and that the latter are considered "as more optional than essential . . . as less than central to their Catholicity."[347]

That such moral teaching should hold such low concern for Catholics is already a distressing matter. But what is especially noteworthy is that "helping the poor" is considered so very important as to tie for first place with "belief in Jesus' resurrection from the dead" in the 2005 survey, but the Church's involvement in activities directed toward social justice—basically the same principle as "helping the poor"—falls to sixth place. The difference in the two is obviously the involvement of the Church in the lower element. So what made Church social justice activity drop so low in so short a time when separated from helping the poor, while the latter rose so high when separated from the former as to become equal in importance to "belief in Jesus' resurrection from the dead"? The pollster fails to take note of the fact that concern for the poor, while it is "held in such central importance by American Catholics," is not a specifically Catholic activity, nor is it directly related to the Church's sacramental life.

346 Hoge, "Center of Catholic Identity," 11.
347 Ibid.

What, then, does its rise to such prominence mean? Such realignment can only indicate a downgrading of the importance of the institutional Church to the Catholic mind-set, and the upgrading of benevolent social action as a value independent of its relationship to the institutional Church. Though the pollster takes consolation in the fact that belief in Jesus' resurrection tied for first and the importance of the sacraments came in third, he fails to take cognizance of the remarkable fact that a secular, noble, but not specifically Catholic activity—"helping the poor"—has been ranked by Catholics *in their lives as Catholics* in a tie for first place of importance over the importance of the sacramental life of the Church. So much for the importance of the sacramentality of the Church versus that of the world.

That this is the significance to be drawn from the primacy given to "helping the poor" over the importance of the sacramental life of the Church may be confirmed by directly viewing these results in relation to another important finding in this survey: When Catholics were asked whether "how a person lives is more important than whether he or she is a Catholic," 88% agreed. The pollster rightly takes this to mean that "the vast majority of Catholics take more seriously a person's behavior than his or her professed creed or church membership."[348] But another more specific conclusion may also be drawn: that for most Catholics today, what they share with other Catholics in their life in the institutional Church—including membership in Christ's Body, participation in the divine life through the sacraments, and belief in the truths revealed to them by their faith—is of less importance to them than what they share with other human beings simply as human beings. Life in the institutional Church is in the process of being reduced to ritual and formality, while life in the world is being understood as meaningful social action.

The significance of this data should also be considered in the light of other important findings. For example, we have seen that a high percentage of Catholics—76%—consider "the sacraments, such as the Eucharist" as "very important" to their lives as Catholics. But if this is the case, then 24% of Catholics do not rate the Eucharist as "very important." We are also told in this same survey that 36% say one can be a good Catholic "without believing that the bread and wine become the body and blood of Christ in the Mass."[349] That's 12% more than the 24%. So how is it that 12% are able to accept that one need not view the Eucharist as the body and blood of Christ to be a good Catholic and at the same time consider the Eucharist as "very important" to their lives as Catholics? Do we see the inroads of

[348] Ibid., 14.
[349] Ibid., 11

relativism here—that what is important to me as a Catholic need not necessarily be important to you as a Catholic?

Zogby data on this same issue are also disconcerting: Zogby reports that 84% of Catholics consider it "important" for "a Catholic to attend Mass every week," which means that 16% do not. Zogby also reports that only 58% of Catholics hold that the bread and wine "actually become" the body and blood of Christ at Mass, which means that 42% do not hold this position. This seems to indicate that many Catholics believe it is important to attend Mass every week, even though they do not accept transubstantiation of the elements of bread and wine. Such anomalies can only be explained by a latent relativism in Catholics that lacks conviction regarding the objective truth of the sacraments. That Catholics are flabby in their faith convictions is supported by another disconcerting finding: when Catholics were asked if "Catholicism contains a greater share of truth than other religions do," only 56% agreed, including only 43% of those 26 or younger. The pollster rightly concludes: "about half of American Catholics are uncertain about the greater truth of Catholicism."[350]

Sacrament of Reconciliation

Perhaps we should take consolation in the continuing frequent reception of the Eucharist by large numbers of Catholics. But what about the sacrament of Reconciliation, the sacrament that prepares for participation in the Eucharist?

It is the least appreciated among the seven sacraments. CARA reports only 39% of Catholics found the sacrament "very" meaningful, although 66% found the sacrament "very" or "somewhat" meaningful. But, as usual, the percentages rise considerably with closeness to the Church: among those who attend Mass weekly or more, 90% found the sacrament "very" or "somewhat" meaningful. Moreover, among respondents who had children, 77% felt it was "somewhat" or "very" important for their children to receive First Reconciliation, whereas the percentage was 95% for weekly or more than weekly Mass attendees.[351]

Zogby reports in 2006 that 35% of Catholics stated they went to confession once or more in the last month, but that 65% said they had not gone at all during that time.[352] We find curious data on confession in the 1986 study conducted by George Gallup, Jr. He reports that in 1971, 24% of Catholics

---

350 Hoge, "Center of Catholic Identity," 14. In Zogby's survey, however, 81% held that the "Catholic Church is the one true church," with even 76% of those 18–35 years old agreeing (Zogby, "National Survey of Catholic Adults"). That is a surprisingly high figure for that age group.

351 CARA, *Sacraments Today*, 31–32, 37.

352 Zogby, "National Survey of Catholic Adults."

said they had gone to confession in the last eight weeks. In 1977, 18% said they had gone to confession in the past month, and, finally, in 1986, 23% said that. Gallup sees the upswing in the last finding as most positive, and argues against the common conception that participation in confession has decreased in recent years. What is more, he finds participation for those under 30 increasing: from 12% in 1977 to 14% in 1986. These figures, says Gallup, are part of a general pattern of greater participation in religious activity from 1977 to 1986, such as reading the Bible and praying the rosary.[353]

But as we shall see in chapter 2, when we examine the downward trend of sacramental activity among the youth, long-range data are not encouraging. As Davidson sees it: "Only about one-fifth of today's Catholics go to private confession, a far cry from the hordes of people waiting for confession in the 1940s and '50s."[354]

Lack of Commitment to the Institutional Church

A growing number of scholars are stressing the importance of commitment—that is, personal identification with Christ in his Church—as essential to the future of the Christian religion if it is to survive as a distinct religious phenomenon. Studies contend that the survival of the Protestant and Catholic churches is threatened by the fact that their members are losing or have already lost a sense of the importance of a spiritual life related to membership in a specific church. Other data, such as Hoge's study on the confluence of secular humanism and Protestant and Catholic thinking, confirm the existence of a threat to the uniqueness of the Catholic Church.

Are all religions equally good? Answers to that question reveal much about how one relates to one's own religious community. Data from a Gallup December 1999 survey showed that 82% of Americans held that other religions were equally as good as theirs, while only 16% felt their religion was "the best path to God."[355]

The Pew Landscape Survey reports that 70% of Americans who have a religious affiliation say that "many religions can lead to eternal life"; the percentages who hold that position are higher among mainline Protestants (83%) and Catholics (79%) than among other religious groups.[356] This may explain the fact that only 23% of Catholics say they are "very strong" in their faith.[357] Would it not make it much more difficult to make a

---

353 Gallup, *American Catholic*, 30–34.
354 Davidson, *Common Ground*, 26.
355 Newport, "Americans Remain Very Religious."
356 Pew Forum, *Landscape Survey Report 2*, 58.
357 *Gallup Poll 1993*, 148.

commitment to a Christian faith experience if it is only one of many possible routes to eternal life?

According to the 1993 Gallup survey, Catholics "routinely disagree with what are supposedly inviolable Church teachings."[358] That is apparently why Catholics are routinely leaving decisions about core Catholic teachings, such as the importance of attendance at Sunday Mass, abortion, marriage, birth control, divorce and remarriage, to individual judgment. Only a minority say the Church's teaching on such issues as same-sex marriage, social justice, or abortion, is "very important" to them.[359] When the 2008 GSS asked Catholics if the Pope, under certain conditions, is infallible on matters of faith and morals—a dogmatic teaching held by the Catholic Church—only 17.2% said it was "certainly true," whereas a combined 50.1% either said they were uncertain, or that it was probably false, or certainly false.[360] Even though the Vatican has decreed that women cannot be ordained as priests, a majority of Catholics state it would be "a good thing" if celibate (61%) or married (54%) women were allowed to be ordained.[361] A *USA Today* /CNN/Gallup poll taken at the time of John Paul II's death found a majority of Catholics felt the next pope should allow priests to marry (7 to 4 ratio), allow Catholics to use birth control (4 to 1 ratio), and make Church doctrine on stem-cell research less strict.[362] The Pew Landscape Survey found a majority of 57% of Catholics felt that the Church should "adjust to new circumstances" or "adopt modern beliefs/practices" rather than preserve traditional beliefs and practices.[363] There appears to be no conviction regarding the underlying principles motivating Church teaching on these issues.

In a poll of August 3–5, 1993, 85% of Catholics said they would more likely follow their own conscience, versus 9% who said they would more likely follow papal teaching on difficult moral questions.[364] In the Landscape Survey, only 22% of Catholics said they would "look for guidance" to religious teachings and beliefs.[365] Gallup is correct in concluding that Catholics have "little regard for the authority of the Church" when making decisions on moral issues.[366]

All in all, the data show that there is a greater tendency to support the teaching of the Church among more committed Catholics, and that even

---

358 Ibid.

359 Hoge, "Center of Catholic Identity," 11.

360 GSS Cumulative Data File 1972–2008, sda.berkeley.edu/.

361 Davidson, "Belief in church," 21.

362 Susan Page, "Survey reveals affection, respect for John Paul," April 3, 2005, usatoday.com.

363 Pew Forum, *Landscape Survey Report 2*, 60.

364 Masci, "Catholic Church in U.S.," 780.

365 Pew Forum, *Landscape Survey Report 2*, 62.

366 *Gallop Poll 1993*, 148.

when erosion occurs among them, commitment tends to slow the process. Clearly, if the Church wishes to survive in any meaningful way, it needs to restore Catholic understanding of the importance of commitment to Christ and his Church as the heart of the Christian faith experience.

CHAPTER TWO

Catholic Attitudes and Practices: Trends among Youth

IN OUR FIRST chapter on the Church, we included statistical data regarding the frequency of Mass attendance among Catholics, and Catholic attitudes toward important teachings of the Church. We saw that, when Catholics are divided between those who are nominal Catholics and those who identify more closely with the Church, the rate of Mass attendance, participation in the sacraments, and support for the Church's moral and ecclesial teachings are generally higher in the latter group. We ended by stressing the importance of commitment to Jesus Christ and the life of the Church for the survival of the Christian community.

The purpose of this chapter is to revisit the above studies, as well as to examine several other studies, focusing on data showing the attitudes and beliefs of a group whose role in the Church is so important it merits special consideration: Catholic youth. We do this for two reasons. First, obviously, unless the Church maintains a close relationship to its youth, the Church will eventually cease to exist. But secondly, Catholic young people often represent a block whose attitudes and practices so differ from the rest of Catholics that it is important to highlight and analyze the bases for those differences.

How important is religion to youth? The data are conflicting.

Gallup reported in November 2006 on aggregated data gathered over the previous four years. According to that summary, 72% of Americans 65 or older said religion was very important in their lives, 60% of those 50–64 agreed, 57% of those 30–49 agreed, but only a minority of 47% of those 18 to 29 agreed. Inverse ratios answered that religion was not very important in their lives, ranging from 22% for those 18–29 to 9% for those 65 and older.[1]

[1] Frank Newport, "Religion Most Important to Blacks, Women, and Older Americans," Gallup Poll, November 29, 2006, 3, www.gallup.com/poll/25585.

The Pew Landscape Survey shows the percentages of those who find religion important in their lives are the same or slightly lower for Catholics: 45% of Catholics 18–29 years old say religion is very important to their lives, while the percentages increased to 54% for those 30–49, 57% for those 50–64, and 72% for those 65 and older.[2] Again, only among Catholic youth is there a minority who rate religion as very important to their lives.

Less than half (43%) of America's teens (13–17 years old) in a Gallup survey of March 1990 saw "having a deep religious faith" as "very important." Moreover, when asked in the same survey to rank the importance of faith on a scale with eight other values, seven outranked faith, with "having personal peace and happiness" highest at 92% and "having lots of money" in seventh place at 44% (only "being famous" at 16% ranked lower in importance than having faith). Yet a surprisingly high number of teens (79%) in 1992 saw themselves as "a religious person." As usual, Protestants outstrip Catholics: in the 1992 survey, 23% of Protestant youth described themselves as strongly religious, while only 14% of Catholic youth did.[3] Could it be that a significant group of young people see themselves as religious persons even though they don't consider having a deep religious faith very important to their lives? What, then, does it mean to be a "religious person"?

Recent sociological studies indicate that while most American youth claim affiliation with a religious group or tradition—77% of Gallup's teens in 1995 stated a Protestant or Catholic preference[4]—the number of those who say they have no religious affiliation appears to have climbed to a new level.

The Cooperative Institutional Research Program run by the Higher Education Research Institute (HERI) of the Graduate School of Education & Information Studies at the University of California, Los Angeles, has conducted an annual national survey of incoming college freshmen since 1966. The surveys show that in 1966, 6.6% indicated they had no religious affiliation. That number increased to 15.4% in 1971, decreased to 7.6% in 1981 and 1982, and rose to 14% in 1995 and 1996, 17.6% in 2003, 19.1% in 2006, a new high of 23% in 2010.[5] Gallup reported in 2004 that 16% of those 18–29 years old did not identify with a religion.[6] Christian Smith finds, moreover, that the "*number of American adolescents within the Christian*

---

2 Pew Forum, *Landscape Survey Report 2*, 24.

3 George H. Gallup, Jr., *The Spiritual Life of Young Americans: Approaching the Year 2000* (Princeton, NJ: George H. Gallup International Institute, 1999), 40–42.

4 Ibid., 44.

5 John H. Pryor and Sylvia Hurtado, et al., *The American Freshman: Forty Year Trends, 1966–2006* (University of California, Los Angeles: HERI, April 2007), 46–47; John H. Pryor and Sylvia Hurtado, et al., *The American Freshman: National Norms Fall 2010* (Los Angeles: HERI, University of California, 2010), 23.

6 Newport, "Update: Americans and Religion."

tradition has been gradually declining over the last two and one-half decades," while the number of those claiming to belong to other religious traditions has increased slightly. The latter trend, Smith argues, may be due to an increase "in religious tolerance and relativism among American youth."[7]

Pryor and Hurtado's figures for the trend in freshman religious participation are not encouraging: whereas in 1997, 85.4% of college freshmen indicated they had attended religious services "frequently" or "occasionally" during senior year in high school, in 2010 the figure, though still high, fell to 74.8%.[8] Even more sobering data come from Gallup and Smith: Gallup reported in 1998 that 49% of teens (ages 13–17) attended "religious services" in "the last seven days,"[9] while Smith records average adolescent weekly attendance of eighth, tenth, and twelfth graders at only 38% in 1995, with "a slight but noticeable decline" in attendance among twelfth graders from 1976 to 1996.[10] Smith reports, moreover, that about half of the adolescents said of themselves that they "are not religiously active" and attend church services "only rarely or never."[11]

Greeley doesn't see a problem with attendance percentages among Catholic youth. He holds that the post-Vatican II Catholic generation is not any less faithful to the Church than previous generations were when they were young: they are not "any less loyal, any less committed, any less devout than their predecessors."[12] But the data do not substantiate his claim.

Rather, the data indicate a continuous and somewhat drastic drop in weekly church attendance from the 1950s to today, but the drop is especially prevalent among young adult Catholics.

According to Hegy, the late sociologist Joseph H. Fichter, S.J., reported in the 1950s "that 93% of those less than 20 years old . . . attended Mass every Sunday." And Hegy reports GSS data showing that 40.4% of Catholics fewer than 25 years of age attended Church in 1972 "nearly every week or more often."[13] GSS data for 2008, however, indicate 22.1% of Catholics ages 18–29 attend Mass every week.[14]

---

7 Christian Smith, Melinda Lundquist Denton, Robert Faris, and Mark Regnerus, "Mapping American Adolescent Religious Participation," *Journal for the Scientific Study of Religion* 41 (2002): 609 (emphasis in original). The authors draw data from the Monitoring the Future survey, 1996; the National Longitudinal Survey of Adolescent Health, 1995; and the Princeton Survey of Parents and Youth, 1998.

8 Pryor and Hurtado, *American Freshman: Forty Year Trends*, 55; Pryor and Hurtado, *American Freshman: National Norms 2010*, 25.

9 Gallup, *Spiritual Life*, 8.

10 Smith et al., "Mapping American," 601–2.

11 Ibid., 609.

12 Greeley, *Catholic Myth*, 257.

13 Hegy, "End of American Catholicism?," 5.

14 GSS Cumulative Data File 1972–2008, sda.berkeley.edu/.

Fichter noted in 1992 a "downward curve" in "all the measurable norms of devotional Catholicism" since Vatican II, including weekly Mass attendance as well as acceptance of Church teachings on "premarital and extramarital sex relations, birth control, and abortion," and pointed out that the "changes found in the general Catholic population over the decades are showing up now in surveys of Catholic high school students."[15]

The data clearly show growing disaffection with the Church among younger Catholics, even greater than that among the rest of the Catholic population. As we reported in chapter 1, the *NCR*/Gallup Survey repeatedly checks on the percentage of Catholics who rate as "highly committed" to "the institutional church." The survey measures such commitment on the basis of how the sample of laypersons scores in three areas: the importance of the Catholic Church to their own lives (the Church must be either the most important or among the most important parts of their lives), attendance at Mass must be at least once a week, and a self-ranking of one or two on a scale of seven, where "one" indicates they would never leave the Catholic Church and "seven" that they might do so.

As we saw in the 2005 *NCR*/Gallup survey, Gallup found only 21% of Catholics "highly committed." But when these were divided into demographic groups, "Catholics highly committed to the church are concentrated in certain demographic categories. The most important fact is that they are older. Of persons 64 or older, 42 percent scored as high-commitment; of persons 44 to 63, 19 percent; of persons 26 to 43, 18 percent; of persons 25 or younger, none."[16] Thus, without the pre-Vatican II Catholics, the percentage of high commitment to the institutional Church would be reduced to 12.3%.

In the 2008 Center for Applied Research in the Apostolate (CARA) study, 31% of pre-Vatican II Catholics "strongly" agreed that "I can be a good Catholic without going to Mass every Sunday," while 38% of "Millennial" Catholics strongly agreed (defined in the study as adults "born after 1981" and "currently in their mid-20s and younger").[17] In the *NCR*/Gallup 2005 study, 76% of pre- through post-Vatican II Catholics said one can be a good Catholic without attending weekly Mass, but 95% of "Millennial" Catholics agreed![18] Though the two studies are not of equal groups,[19] clearly

---

[15] Joseph H. Fichter, S.J., "Foreword," in Patrick H. McNamara, *Conscience First, Tradition Second: A Study of Young American Catholics* (Albany, NY: State University of New York, 1992), xiv.

[16] Hoge, "Attitudes of Catholics" 12.

[17] CARA, *Sacraments Today*, 99, 2.

[18] Davidson, "Belief in Church," 21.

[19] The "Millennials" in the *NCR*/Gallup survey include 18- to 26-year-olds, those in the CARA study 20- to 26-year-olds. The *NCR*/Gallup data are based on those who agreed, CARA on those who strongly agreed.

weekly Mass attendance has lost its importance among many, if not most, Catholic youth.

What adds to the ominous nature of this downward trend are the percentages regarding weekly churchgoing habits among Catholic youth. Though so-called pre-Vatican II Catholics—those born 1940 and before, ages 65 and older—declined from 64% to 60% in weekly or more than weekly Mass attendance from the 1999 survey to the 2005 *NCR*/Gallup survey, the biggest reasons for the overall drop in these six years occurred because of a decline in attendance among so-called Vatican II Catholics—born between 1941 and 1960, ages 45–64—and post-Vatican II Catholics—those born after 1960, ages 18–44: the former dropped from 42% to 35% from 1999 to 2005, and the latter from 27% to 20.5% during the same period. But the cause of the drop in the latter group can be determined more precisely since, for the first time, the post-Vatican II Catholics are divided by the study into two groups: the "Gen X Catholics"—those born between 1961 and 1978, ages 27–44—and the "Millennials"—born between 1979 and 1987, ages 18–26. The drop in the post-Vatican II group was not caused by the "Gen X Catholics" who dropped only from 27% to 26%,[20] but by the low percentage among the "Millennials," among whom only 15% attended Mass weekly or more in 2005.[21] According to the Pew Landscape Survey, the explanation for the low 42% Mass attendance among Catholics today is found in the decline in attendance especially among Catholic youth: "Nearly two-thirds of Catholics over age 65 (62%) say they go to church every week, compared with only about a third of Catholics under age 30 (34%)."[22]

The 2005 *NCR*/Gallup poll supports the trend shown in the GSS study. Though the 1990 GSS figure of 13.2% for weekly Mass attendance for the under-25 age group seemed extreme at the time, this poll indicates, as we saw, that only 15% of today's "Millennials" attend Mass weekly. This is even significantly below the 26% figure for the group immediately above them, the "Gen Xers" (27–44 years old).[23] Since the average percentage of

---

20 In a survey conducted in 1997, 31.5% of Catholics 20–39 years old attended Mass once a week or more in the past year. In 2006, these people are 29–48 years old, mostly "Gen X Catholics." Dean R. Hoge, William D. Dinges, Mary Johnson, S.N.D. de N., Juan L. Gonzales, Jr., *Young Adult Catholics: Religion in the Culture of Choice* (Notre Dame, IN: University of Notre Dame, 2001), 51.

21 William V. D'Antonio, "Generational Differences," *National Catholic Reporter*, September 30, 2005, 13, 15. Of course, those born between 1982 and 1987 were not included in the 1999 survey.

22 Pew Forum, *Landscape Survey Report 2*, 37. Pew reports similar, "though somewhat less pronounced, generational differences" among Protestants.

23 This in sharp contrast to Zogby's finding that 46% of Catholics ages 18 to 35 said they attended Mass weekly in March 2006; David O'Reilly, "A faith in flux," June 4, 2006, www.philly.com.

participation of these two groups that together constitute today's post-Vatican II Catholics is 20.5%, which is 9.5% below the figure for post-Vatican II Catholics in the first *NCR*/Gallup Poll survey of 1987, one gets further confirmation here of a drastic decline in Catholic church attendance among America's younger generation, which proves Greeley wrong.[24] Pew's Landscape Survey figures are only slightly better: 34% of Catholics ages 18–29 attended worship services weekly in 2007, while 36% of those 30–49 do, 42% of those 50–64 do, and 62% of those 65 or older do.[25]

Such a precipitous drop-off, especially among younger people, should set off alarms: What will happen if the drop-off rate continues at the same pace for the next few years? Such a serious decline inevitably leads one also to ask what caused such decline, beginning in the immediate post-Vatican II period and continuing unabated, and whether further reductions may be prevented? More on these points later.

One may with due reason wonder whether by 2015 any young people will be going to weekly Sunday Mass. Yet many, like Gallup, Hoge, and Greeley, assert that there is a religious cycle in life, meaning that young people typically go through a crisis of faith, expressed by a drop-off in weekly church attendance in their late teens and twenties, but return to the faith later, especially after marriage with children, and therefore low figures of church attendance among youth need not cause alarm.[26] Gallup supports this position with data from 2000–2001 surveys that found that 54% of youth 13–15 years old said they attended church or synagogue in the past seven days while only 32% of those 18–29 did, but the figure rises to 44% among those 50–64 years old, and 60% for those 75 and older.[27] But using these data to support the religious cycle theory fails to take into account that those in the latter two groups belong to pre-Vatican II Catholics, whose loyalty to the Church was strong even in their youth, and the Vatican II Catholics, who experienced vestiges of that same spirit of loyalty.

Moreover, if the religious cycle theory is valid, how does one explain the 93% of weekly Mass attendance among youth under 20 years of age in the 1950s, or even the still relatively high 40% attendance of youth under 25 in the early 1970s? Did youth not have crises then?[28] Hegy, disagreeing

---

[24] D'Antonio, "Generational Differences," 15.

[25] Pew Forum, *Landscape Survey Report 2*, 38.

[26] Hout and Greeley, "The Center Doesn't Hold," 331–32; Greeley, *American Catholics*, 73–76, 174.

[27] Cf. George Gallup, Jr., "Religion and Values: The Religiosity Cycle," Gallup Poll, June 4, 2002, www.gallup.com.

[28] Greeley seems to say they didn't. He admits that in the studies he made on Catholics in the early '60s, "there was much less of a life-cycle correlation with church attendance." He attributes the change to the fact that by the '90s more young people were living away from their families (Greeley, *Catholic Myth*, 259).

with Greeley's conclusion, argues that we cannot any longer "entertain the possibility of a return for the young. The exodus is too massive and the returnees too few" to warrant this conclusion.[29] Davidson agrees: "Rather than becoming more attached to the church over time (as the age argument would suggest), young Catholics continue to question the importance of the church and some of its norms as they move into their middle years. The Vatican II generation, in turn, is not adopting the pre-Vatican II generation's commitment to the church as it ages."[30]

A possible explanation for the lack of evidence of a life cycle in the 1950s and 1960s is the fact that youth at that time still held to the teaching of the Church that weekly Sunday Mass attendance was necessary for salvation, whereas many young people today no longer accept that teaching. There is undoubtedly merit to the argument that the more rigorously held view would have had compelling influence on Mass attendance.

However, while this explanation may help to explain the difference in mentality between the youth of the '50s and today's, it does not eviscerate the fear that the statistics regarding the low Mass attendance of today's youth are an ominous foreboding of what is to come. In Hegy's presentation, the ratio of general Catholic attendance at Mass in 1972 versus the under-25 Catholic population was 61% to 40.4%; eighteen years later, in 1990, it was 40.5% to 13.2%. One notes that the percentage for the under-25-year-olds in 1972 was almost the same as the percentage for the whole Catholic population in 1990. If the Mass attendance figure for the under 25-year-olds in 1972—40.4%—is about the same figure as the total Catholic Mass-attending population today, then those under 25 years old in 1972 did not return to Mass attendance in any significant way some 30 years later. Does this, then, mean that the much smaller percentage of 13.2% of the under-25-year-old Mass attendees in 1990 and the 15% of the "Millennial" Mass attendees of 2005 will drop as well, so that, as a result, there will be far fewer Catholics attending Mass in some 30 years than there are today?

On the other hand, other data may indicate merit to Hoge's and Greeley's argument. As we saw, 13.2% of Hegy's under-25 group attended Mass nearly every week or more often in 1990, and *NCR*/Gallup's 2005 survey shows 26% of today's "Gen Xers" attend weekly or more. Hegy's under-25 age group of 1990 is now 33–39 years old, which makes them a significant group within today's "Gen Xers." Does the increase of percentage points indicate some kind of a bounce back? Perhaps so. To support this thesis, Gallup presents data indicating that in 1990, 57% of those 18–29 years old said they

[29] Hegy, "End of American Catholicism?," 5.
[30] Davidson, "Generations have different views," 13.

were members of a church or synagogue, while 63% of people 30–49 years old claimed church membership, and 74% of people 50 or older did.[31] If this thesis is correct, does it mean that today's "Millennials" might bounce back to about 30% in another fifteen years? Thirty percent is hardly a consoling figure, but it is better than 15%.[32]

Perhaps some consolation may be found in Gallup's 1995 survey where the data showed Catholic teenagers (13–17 years old) attending church more often than their parents, though I find these data hard to believe. According to Gallup, 50% of Catholic teenagers said they attended church in the last seven days, whereas 47% of the general Catholic population did.[33] (A 1997 survey put the figure for the teens at 51%.)[34] Does this indicate some kind of a turnaround in religious participation in the younger generation? On the other hand, as we noted earlier, this question about the last seven days may be less helpful, since what one does in any given week does not necessarily tell us anything about one's overall behavior. There is also reason to be discouraged by Gallup's finding that, "whereas 80% of Protestant teens say they go to church because they want to, just 54% of Catholic teens make the same claim."[35]

Altogether, data from these surveys about young people's weekly Mass attendance give mixed signals, some rather encouraging, but most rather ominous. Even more ominous data about Catholic youth beliefs and attitudes follow in other studies presented in this chapter. Such data should awaken interested Catholics to the implications for the future life of the Christian faith. Figures that indicate erosion of interest in weekly Mass worship are at least a warning that cannot be ignored. Such data indicate impending crisis, if not already present crisis, in the Church, and should lead to investigation regarding the causes of such a drop-off, so that measures might be taken to implement course correction. Some suggestions for such correction follow in the study by Smith and Denton, which we will shortly consider.

---

31 Gallup, *Spiritual Life*, 47.

32 To be fair, we should report that the survey done in 1995 for the Catholic League found that 29.6% of young people attended Mass once a week or more (Donohue, "Catholic League's Survey," 6). Donohue's population of young people includes 18- to 25-year-olds, while Hegy's includes only those under 25.

33 Gallup, *Religion in America 1996*, 29, 70.

34 Gallup, *Spiritual Life*, 8. Somewhat supportive of Gallup's data are Smith's 1995 data, according to which about 40% of Catholic adolescents attend Mass weekly (Smith et al., "Mapping American," 602). Unfortunately, I find no survey where Gallup asks Catholic teenagers if they attend Mass weekly. The question about weekly Mass attendance always presents lower percentages than when respondents are asked about attendance in the last seven days.

35 Ibid., 10.

Youth and a Trend toward Life

Perhaps one somewhat bright spot is the new attitude of young people toward abortion. Data regarding young people reported in 1995 showed increased moral sensitivity on the issue:

> A recent CBS/*New York Times* poll found that . . . the age group most likely to voice that opinion [that abortion was murder] was 18 to 29. In 1990, a series of focus groups was conducted by researchers for the Center for Population Options, exploring teens' attitudes toward abortion. To the authors' evident dismay, "In response to the question, 'What first comes into your head when you hear the word "abortion"?' participants—regardless of race, sex, or residence—most often responded with 'murder,' 'killing a baby' or 'death.'. . . Comments focused on the 'innocence' of the baby, regardless of the circumstances."[36]

Further evidence of a trend toward life among young people:

- A Pace University/Rock the Vote survey of first-time voters, defined as "voters who registered after the 2000 presidential election," indicated they supported Kerry, a pro-choice candidate, over Bush, the pro-life candidate, in a head-to-head race in 2004 by a margin of 50% to 40%. Yet the survey also indicated that 54% of these voters were pro-life, meaning they felt abortion should either be illegal in all cases, or legal "only in the most extreme cases, such as to save the life of the mother, incest, or rape," while only 44% were pro-choice, meaning they supported legal abortion "generally" or "in many circumstances."[37]
- A survey of high school seniors of the class of 2006 was conducted by Hamilton College. The poll indicates, according to the survey directors, an "inconsistent conservative leaning pattern." The students appear to be torn between their desire to be tolerant of all views, and their own judgment about the morality of abortion: on the one hand, 62% said they want the Supreme Court to preserve *Roe v. Wade*, which has led to the legalization of abortion on demand, but on the other hand, 66.8% of them said "they believe abortion is always or usually 'morally wrong.'" The only cases where the majority thought a woman should have the legal right to an abortion were when the pregnancy

[36] Mathewes-Green, "Embryonic Trend," 2.

[37] Duncan Currie, "First-Time Voters for Life: What a Pace Poll suggests about new registrants and abortion rights," *Weekly Standard*, August 20, 2004, www.crosswalk.com/new/commentary/1280491/. About 95% of abortions are done as a form of birth control, 3% due to health problems of the mother, and 1% because of rape or incest. Central Illinois Right to Life, accessed October 10, 2010, www.abortiontv.com/Misc/AbortionStatitistics.htm#WhyAbortionsArePerformed.

seriously threatened the woman's health or if the pregnancy was the result of rape. Over 70% of female seniors said they would not consider having an abortion if they became pregnant in high school, and 69.3% of male seniors said they would not want a high school partner to have an abortion. The pollsters concluded that the seniors' views on abortion were "influenced by strong pro-life sentiments": 47.2% of the seniors identified themselves as more sympathetic to pro-life, while 47.5% indicated they were more pro-choice.[38]

- A Gallup poll of teens aged 13–17 conducted January 23–February 20, 2003, revealed an astonishing turn away from abortion. According to the poll, 33% of those asked thought abortion should be illegal under all circumstances, and another 45% thought it should be legal only under certain circumstances. Only 21% of the youth thought abortion should always be legal. The study concludes that abortion will remain "an extremely contentious issue in the years to come."[39]
- Lifesitenews reports that about 400,000 people attended the 38th annual March for Life in Washington, DC, on January 24, 2011. According to the web site, this was the largest attendance ever, surpassing the record crowd of 2010.[40] The first march of 20,000 was held in 1974. An estimated 40,000 people attended the 7th annual Walk for Life West Coast in San Francisco on January 22, 2011, "a record-breaking figure."[41] Noteworthy was the large participation by young people at the most recent walks. One young woman stated on EWTN's presentation of the San Francisco walk in 2007 what is probably a major reason for the pro-life trend among today's youth: that a third of the babies conceived after 1973 never survived abortion, and that she and many of her peers were grateful to their mothers, who, though they could legally have murdered their children, allowed them to survive.[42]

---

[38] Hamilton College National Youth Poll: "Hot Button Issues Poll: Guns, Gays and Abortion," January 2006, www.hamilton.edu/news/polls/HotButtonFinalReport.pdf.

[39] Josephine Mazzuca, "Current Teen Views on Abortion," Gallup Poll, March 11, 2003, www.gallup.com; results also reported in Hal Marcovitz, "Gallup Youth Survey: Major Issues and Trends," *Teens & Sex* (Broomall, PA: Mason Crest, 2004), 38.

[40] John-Henry Westen, "400,000 March for Life in DC with great joy," January 26, 2011, www.lifesitenews.com/home/print_article/news/28200/.]

[41] Stephanie Samuel, "West Coast Pro-Life March Draws 40,000 in San Francisco," www.christianpost.com/news/west-coast-pro-life-march-draws-40000-in-san-francisco-48619/.

[42] The figure may actually be closer to 21%: The total number of births in the United States from 1974–2007 is about 129,024,000 (U.S. Census Bureau, "Live Births, Deaths, Marriages, and Divorces 1960–2007," 2011 Statistical Abstract, Table 78, www.census.gov/compendia/statab/2011/tables/), while the total number of abortions in those same years is about 38,248,027 (*World Almanac and Book of Facts*

Yet data are not always consistent. HERI's College Senior Survey (CSS), when compared with its Freshman Survey of the same cohort of students, has provided since the 1990s valuable "longitudinal data on students' cognitive and affective growth during college."[43] The results of the 2009 CSS survey show that, at college entry, 29.8% of the students said they were liberal or far left; in 2009 they were 39% liberal. That leftist drift is evident in their answer to the unnuanced question if "abortion should be legal": 51.6% said at college entry that they "agreed somewhat" or "agreed strongly," whereas at the end of college, 63.8% held those positions.[44] In the 2009 survey, 53.9% of the graduating seniors had also taken the freshman survey. It will be interesting to note if this leftist trend continues.

When it comes to data to support the Church's teaching on abortion, however, the evidence of support from America's Catholic youth as a whole is not clear. According to the 2008 GSS, 35.1% of Catholic youth 18–35 years old support abortion on demand, a slight increase of .3% over 2006, while 64.9% oppose abortion on demand. While that represents a minority of Catholic youth, it still means that well over a third do not support the Church's teaching, although fewer than the percentage among Catholics in general—37.7%. A high percentage support the extremely small percentage of cases where abortion is committed in the case of rape (83.7% support), defect of the child (80.1% support), or serious danger to the mother's health (91.9% support). In the area of the most common reasons for abortion, however, percentages are always in the minority: for example, the woman is married and wants no more children (41.4%), or can't afford the child (45.9%).

It may be possible now to pinpoint which subgroup within the Catholic population is contributing the most to the erosion of support for the Church's teaching on abortion. Evidence is provided in the *NCR*/Gallup 2005 survey, which for the first time correlates generational views on obedience to the Church's teaching on abortion with being a good Catholic: Among pre-Vatican II Catholics, only 44% said this teaching was not important to being a good Catholic, but among Vatican II Catholics, the percentage had already risen to 56%. Among post-Vatican II Catholics, the percentage was slightly higher at 59%. But among the "Millennials," the

2011, "Number, Ratio, and Rate of Legal Abortions in the U.S., 1970–2006," 175; and Centers for Disease Control and Prevention, Morbidity and Morality Weekly Report (MMWR), "Abortion Surveillance—United States, 2007," Abstract, 1). Abortion figures are somewhat higher in the Alan Guttmacher Institute estimates, presented earlier.

43 Ray Franke, Sylvia Ruiz, Jessica Sharkness, Linda DeAngelo, and John Pryor, Findings from the 2009 Administration of the College Senior Survey (CSS): National Aggregates (Los Angeles: HERI, University of California, Los Angeles, February 2010), 1.

44 Ibid., 33.

percentage rose to a whopping 89%,[45] indicating that it is especially the younger Catholics who no longer see obedience to Church teaching on abortion as integral to what it means to be a good Catholic. This percentage is astounding, in view of the centrality the Church has given to this teaching. Such data also inevitably provoke the question: If this mentality continues, what will be left of the Church's teaching on abortion for Catholic generations of the future, if the religious cycle theory is not valid?

William Dinges's Survey of Catholic Youth

A survey of 20- to 39-year-old Catholics, conducted by William Dinges of the Catholic University of America, produced somewhat encouraging findings about attitudes among Catholics of that age when Mass attendance was factored into the study, but some discouraging findings when Mass attendance was not a factor.

When asked, "How essential is each of these elements to *your* vision of what the Catholic faith is?" the highest ranking went to "belief that God is present in the sacraments." This ranking was chosen by 80% of the weekly Mass attendees, as well as by 58% of those who attend Mass rarely or never, both of whom ranked this belief as most essential. However, Mass attendees ranked in second place at 74% "belief that Christ is really present in the Eucharist," and in third place at 67% "charitable efforts toward helping the poor"; among nonattendees, tied for second at 49% was "charitable efforts toward helping the poor" and "devotion to Mary the Mother of God"; ranked fourth at 41% was "belief that Christ is really present in the Eucharist."

When considering the importance to Catholics of the sacramental life of the Church, one rejoices at the high priority given to it by both Mass attendees and nonattendees, but one cannot ignore the astounding fact that among nonattendees, belief in Christ's presence in the Eucharist is ranked of lesser significance to one's faith as a Catholic than devotion to Mary or charity toward the poor. One is also encouraged by the priority given to the sacramental life of the Church over service to the poor by both Mass attendees and non-attendees. But Dinges raises a serious question: How genuine can this priority be, in view of the fact that young people show so little evidence of the importance of the sacramental life within the total context of their lives?

> Although this "sacramental imagination" appears to rank high in Catholic identity, the question of its durability remains uncertain. It is not obvious how the coherence or common understanding of the Catholic "sacramental imagination" will be sustained, given that many

[45] Davidson, "What Catholics Believe," 18.

> young adults do not have a shared historical experience or lack a significant web of Catholic social relationships and overlapping memberships that might function as "plausibility structures." Their low rate of Mass attendance does not augur well in this regard. It is also not obvious that the "sacramental imagination" will continue to have any necessary connection with Catholic institution identity, per se. The cultural influences of contemporary American society weigh heavily here.[46]

Evidence that the "sacramental imagination" is already on the wane among young Catholics appears evident in the CARA study, which breaks down by generations how many Catholics agree that "sacraments are essential to my faith." While 58% of pre-Vatican II Catholics "strongly" agreed with this statement, only 39% of Vatican II Catholics did, only 31% of post-Vatican II Catholics, and only 32% of "Millennials." Thus, according to this survey, only about a third of our young people have a strong appreciation today for the sacramental life of the Church.[47] And without a strong Catholic social context within which that sacramental life can be nurtured, one must seriously question its ability to endure.

CARA and Closeness to the Church

Once again, when closeness to the Church is factored into the CARA study regarding the reception of the Eucharist, remarkable differences are evident among all generations of Catholics, but especially among the young.

When asked how important the reception of the Eucharist is to their sense of what it means to be a Catholic, 84% of pre-Vatican II Catholics who attend Mass at least once a month said "very" important, while only 27% of those who attend a few times a year or less often said the same. Among Vatican II Catholics, the corresponding percentages were 77% and 25%; among post-Vatican II Catholics, 79% and 29%; among "Millennials," 91% and 28%. Thus CARA's astounding conclusion: "Among those attending Mass at least once a month, Millennial Generation Catholics are most likely to say that receiving the Eucharist is 'very' important to their sense of what it means to be Catholic."[48] The question arises: Why so much appreciation for the Eucharist among "Millennials" who attend Mass at least once a month, whereas only 32% of all "Millennials" agreed strongly that sacraments are essential to their faith? One can only conclude to the tremendous power of the Eucharist in the lives of young people who more frequently attend Mass.

---

[46] William Dinges, Dean R. Hoge, Mary Johnson, Juan L. Gonzales, Jr., "A Faith Loosely Held: The institutional allegiance of young Catholics," *Commonweal* 125 (July 17, 1998): 15.

[47] CARA, *Sacraments Today*, 99.

[48] Ibid., 107.

Youth on Birth Control, Premarital Sex, and Extramarital Sex

Regarding youth's position on birth control: Davidson finds in 1997 that only 20% of pre-Vatican II Catholics find birth control "always morally wrong," but among Vatican II Catholics and post-Vatican II Catholics, the percentages are virtually nonexistent: 6% and 4%, respectively. As to the locus of authority for deciding the morality of birth control, 65% of pre-Vatican II Catholics, but 87% of Vatican II Catholics and 90% of post-Vatican II Catholics are willing to leave the decision "up to the individual,"[49] another reflection of the influence of relativism.

In the 1999 *NCR*/Gallup study, 61% of Catholics said it should be left to the individual, though among Mass attendees, the percentage was considerably lower at 45%.[50] By 2005, 77% of "Millennials" felt that the final decision whether to obey the teaching of the Church should be left to the individual, while only 10% said the decision belonged to Church leaders. Even a plurality of pre-Vatican II Catholics were willing to leave the final decision to individuals as opposed to Church leaders, 46% to 20%. (A third, separate option leaving the decision to a combination of the individual and church leaders was included in the 2005 survey).[51] The Notre Dame Study had already learned in 1986 that among young people, Church teaching on birth control was "often seen as irrelevant to their lives."[52] Indeed, anyone who lectures on *Humanae Vitae* knows that most students have not even heard of its teaching and reject it when they do.

Regarding premarital sex: as we saw in chapter 1, Gallup found in 1969 that 68% of Americans said premarital sex was morally wrong, but by 2001, that percentage had dropped to 38%. What we did not record there, however, was Gallup's finding that the main reason for the "remarkable" drop occurs among the young: 59% of adults over 65 continued to hold to the immorality of premarital sex in a 1996 poll, while only 25% of those 18–29 years old did.[53] Even among those under 35 among Sweetser's parishioners, only about 30% consider premarital sex wrong, whereas 60% of those 55 and older do.[54]

According to Davidson, it is the pre-Vatican II Catholics who remain most sympathetic to Church teaching: 55% say premarital sex is "always morally wrong," as opposed to only 26% among Vatican II Catholics and

49 Davidson, *Common Ground*, 124, 131.

50 D'Antonio et al., "American Catholic Laity in 1999," 3–4.

51 D'Antonio, "Generational Differences," 15.

52 Leege and Gremillion, "Notre Dame Study," 738.

53 Gallup and Lindsay, *Religious Landscape*, 101–2; George Gallup, Jr., "Religion and Values," Gallup Tuesday Briefing, February 19, 2002, www.gallup.com.

54 Sweetser, "Parish," 6.

20% among post-Vatican II Catholics; also, only 37% of pre-Vatican II Catholics, as opposed to 65% of Vatican II Catholics and 71% of post-Vatican II Catholics, leave the decision on its morality "up to the individual."[55] According to Zogby, only 25% of Catholics 18–35 years old feel that the Church alone should have the final say on sex outside of marriage.[56]

Hegy's data are extremely discouraging regarding younger Catholics' views on premarital sex, because the data show them breaking away significantly from Church teaching on this issue: Only 14% of Catholics under 30 held that premarital sex was always wrong in 1972, but by 1988–1990, the percentage of the under-30 group holding that position had dropped to a mere 7%, while those holding premarital sex was not wrong at all in that age group climbed from 36% in 1972 to 56% by 1988–1990. Only 6% of those 30–39 years old in 1988–1990 held premarital sex was always wrong, a decrease of 28% for that age bracket since 1972, while the number in that same age bracket who held that premarital sex is "not wrong at all" stood at a majority of 57% in 1988–1990, an increase of 33% since 1972. Even those 40–49 years old in 1988–1990 stood at 46% holding premarital sex was not wrong at all, an increase of 33% in that same age bracket from 1972.[57]

Finally, regarding extramarital sex: in 1999, Gallup reported that 46% of Catholics thought the final moral authority on the issue should be the individual; however, among those 18–38 years old, the percentage who felt that way was 54%.[58]

Importance of Catholic High School Attendance

Gallup reports that in 1990 only 39% of Catholic teens 13–17 years old held that it is "very important to have a deep religious faith," even though 53% said they "attend church regularly." Such data obviously raise the question: Why is a "deep religious faith" not very important to 14% of Catholic youth who "attend church regularly"? By contrast, 50% of Protestant teens said it was very important to have a deep religious faith, and 58% attended church regularly. This continuingly poor ranking of Catholic teens by comparison with Protestant teens can only be viewed as troubling and in need of investigation.

---

[55] Davidson, *Common Ground*, 131.

[56] O'Reilly, "A Faith in Flux."

[57] Hegy, "End of American Catholicism?," 6.

[58] D'Antonio, "Generational Differences." Incidentally, in the 2005 *NCR*/Gallup survey, pre-Vatican II Catholics supported women's ordination by 53%, but 60% of Vatican II Catholics did, and 69% of post-Vatican II Catholics—further indication of the growing disaffection for the Church's teaching, but especially among younger Catholics.

But it is important to note that among those Catholic teens Gallup interviewed, only 10% attended a parochial school.[59] Would parochial school attendance have made the percentages different? Data are conflicting.

The *NCR*/Gallup 2005 survey seems to indicate that it would. The survey found "the strongest effects" on the positive side because of "measures of attachment to the church":

> Those who attended a Catholic high school are more likely than those who did not to say they would never leave the Catholic church. They are more likely to say that the Catholic church is quite important or among the most important parts of their life. They are more likely to say they pray regularly and they are more likely to be high commitment Catholics on our scale of commitment to the church. . . . They are somewhat more satisfied with the church as it exists today and more accepting of some of the measures many dioceses are adopting to address the shortage of priests.[60]

Unfortunately the survey did not measure the effect of a Catholic education on rate of Mass attendance or on views regarding the importance of a deep religious faith.

Growing Acceptance of the Homosexual Agenda?

The gay community has very patiently been pushing its agenda for the last forty years, and that patience seems to have paid off, especially among young people. Gallup reports in a survey in 1979 that 54% of teens 13–18 years old "opposed gays holding jobs" in major professions, such as "salespersons, soldiers, college professors, high school teachers, elementary school teachers, clergymen, and physicians." But Gallup concluded, as a result of a 1990 Gallup Youth survey, that "attitudes had definitely changed" when 64% of teens questioned responded: "Homosexuality should be considered an acceptable lifestyle."[61]

As we saw in chapter 1, Gallup found in 2006 that a slight majority of Americans—51%—still found the homosexual lifestyle morally wrong, while 44% found it acceptable. But when the 44% is broken down, it includes only 32% of seniors, but 54% of those fewer than 40 years of age.[62]

In the 2006 Hamilton College poll of American high school students in general, while one in four supported a constitutional amendment to

---

[59] Gallup, *Spiritual Life*, 42–43.

[60] Mary L. Gautier, "Does Catholic education make a difference?" *National Catholic Reporter*, September 30, 2005, 23.

[61] Hal Marcovitz, "Gallup Youth Survey: Major Issues and Trends," *Teens & Gay Issues* (Broomall, PA: Mason Crest, 2005), 12.

[62] Saad, "Americans at Odds Over Gay Rights."

ban same-sex marriages, three-quarters favored legal recognition of same-sex relationships, whether in marriage or civil unions. A 2003 Gallup Poll assessment of the views of people ages 18–29 found 53% supporting the legality of marriage between homosexual couples while 45% did not, whereas only 32% of older Americans approved of legal homosexual marriages and 64% did not.[63] And in the 2009 HERI CSS longitudinal study, 59.3% of the students at college entry "agreed somewhat" or "agreed strongly" that "same-sex couples should have the right to legal marital status," while at the end of college, 72.8% held those positions. In line with that, at college entry, 23.8% of the students "agreed somewhat" or "agreed strongly" that "it is important to have laws prohibiting homosexual relationships"; at the end of college, 14.9% held those positions.[64]

D'Antonio reported in 1996 that surveys in recent years "suggest that Catholics are becoming more tolerant on the matter" of homosexuality, but that tolerance shows up most of all among the young. D'Antonio reports a survey of young Catholics (ages 18–29) in 1981 indicating that 77% of them held that homosexual relations were "almost always or always wrong." But in a 1992 survey, where those young Catholics would now be 29–40 years old, 45% of all Catholics said that homosexual relations "in a committed relationship can be morally acceptable."[65]

Davidson reported in 1997 that continued support for the Church's teaching regarding homosexual relationships comes mainly from pre-Vatican II Catholics who continue by 66% to hold that homosexual relations are "always morally wrong," while only 42% of Vatican II Catholics, and 47% of post-Vatican II Catholics agree, averaging out to 51.6% of the total Catholic population.

As to whether the matter should be left to individual judgment, however, only 32% of pre-Vatican II Catholics would agree, but 53% and 49%, respectively, of the Vatican II and post-Vatican II Catholics agree.[66] The trend toward individual judgment is cross-generational, though markedly so among youth: in the pre-Vatican II generation in 1987, 46% gave the final authority on the morality of homosexual behavior to Church leaders versus 18% to the individual, but in 1999, the corresponding figures were 35% versus 36%; among post-Vatican II Catholics in 1987, 26% gave final authority to Church leaders versus 47% to the individual, but in 1999, the

---

63 Joseph Carroll, "Gallup Poll Assesses Views of Young Americans," Gallup Poll, November 5, 2003, www.gallup.com.

64 Franke et al., *Findings from the 2009 Administration of the College Senior Survey*, 33.

65 All data as reported in William V. D'Antonio, James D. Davidson, Dean R. Hoge, and Ruth A. Wallace, *Laity American and Catholic: Transforming the Church* (Kansas City, MO: Sheed and Ward, 1996), 56.

66 Davidson, *Common Ground*, 131.

corresponding percentages were 13% and 56%.[67] What kind of judgment would individual Catholics make? In Zogby's March 2006 poll, only a minority of 47% of Catholics 18–35 years old held that same-sex relationships are "always wrong."[68]

The Pew Forum on Religion & Public Life did extensive polling from July to September, 2010, on generational differences in the American population over the legality of same-sex marriage, as well as among white Catholics. The poll was conducted among 6,512 adults living in the continental United States, 18 years of age or older. Regarding the American population as a whole, as we saw in chapter 1, 42% of Americans now favor same-sex marriage while 48% are opposed. But, as the report states, "substantial age and generational differences in opinions" exist.

Among the Millennials (born after 1980), 53% now favor same-sex marriage versus 39% opposed (in 2004, only a minority of 44% were in favor). Among Gen Xers (born 1965 to 1980), 48% now favor same-sex marriage, while 43% are opposed (in 2004, only 40% were in favor, though in 2001, 49% were in favor. This is the only group that had a higher favorable percentage before 2010). Among Baby Boomers (born 1946 to 1964), 38% are in favor, 52% are opposed (though in 2004, 30% were in favor). Finally, among the Silent Generation (born 1928 to 1945), 29% are in favor, 59% are opposed (in 2001 21% were in favor). Thus, today, less than a third of the Silent Generation support same-sex marriage, while among the Millennials, more than half support it.

Among white Catholics in general, as we saw, 46% now support same-sex marriage, and 42% are opposed. The poll breaks Catholics into only two age groups, those 50 and older and those 18–49 years old. Among those 50 and older, 39% favor same-sex marriage, and 48% are opposed; among 18- to 49-year-olds, 58% support same-sex marriage, while 33% are opposed—thus, a 19% gap in favorable ratings between the younger and the older white Catholics. Among white Protestant evangelicals 50 and older, 15% support same-sex marriage, and 78% are opposed; among those 18–49 years old, 26% support same-sex marriage, while 69% are opposed. Among white Protestant mainliners, 44% of those 50 and older favor same-sex marriage and 43% are opposed; 54% of those 18–49 years old are in favor, while 34% are opposed.[69]

These figures speak for themselves: (1) the views of the Catholic Church's youth reflect those of the youth of America much more so than the views of Protestant youth, though it is the more conservative Protestant youth (the

---

[67] D'Antonio et al., *American Catholics*, 76.

[68] Zogby, "National survey of Catholic adults."

[69] Pew Forum, "Support for Same-Sex Marriage," 1–4.

evangelicals) who are less inclined to reflect the youth of America than the mainline youth. This would seem to reflect Protestant evangelical youths' greater closeness to their church. Still, even the mainline youth are not as supportive of same-sex marriage as are Catholic youth; (2) the Catholic Church's youth are even more supportive of same-sex marriage than America's youth as a whole, thus making Catholic youth the most supportive of same-sex marriage of any Christian group polled; (3) the Catholic Church is clearly losing support for its position on same-sex marriage among its youth, and the trend can only be expected to continue, as secular society continues to inculcate its views on morality throughout the American culture.

The matter of the acceptability of homosexual relations is clearly one of those instances where age conditions one's response considerably. Hoge states the pattern is always the same: "Catholics over 50 are more traditional and more averse to these practices than those under 50. Catholics under 50 are tolerant and individualistic, and the two young age groups (18–29 and 30–49) are similar in attitudes. There is a single large age gap in Catholic attitudes at about age 50."[70] The 2008 GSS confirms this: when Catholics were asked, "Is homosexual sex wrong?" 76.7% of Catholics 50 and older said it "was always or almost always wrong," while 65% of those 39–49 agreed, and only 54% of those 18–29 agreed. Such data seem clearly to indicate the direction in which support for Church teaching is going, especially because of the young.

What, then, do we make of the results of this other GSS 2008 survey of Catholic generational differences on the morality of homosexual relationships? According to this survey, when asked to express their position on the morality of homosexual relationships, 81.1% of Catholics 50 years of age or older said such relationships were "always or almost always wrong," 66.7% of those 39–49 said the same, and 60.5% of those 18–29 years old agreed.[71] While a greater tolerance of homosexual relationships is indicated in the poll among the young, nevertheless, the percentage of those who find such relationships immoral has notably increased among all three generations. Is there a turnaround here somewhat comparable to the recent turnaround in support for the pro-life movement, occurring since the beginning of the Obama presidency?

McNamara's Study of High School Seniors

In contrast to Gallup's data on the positive effects of Catholic parochial education come valuable, sobering data provided in sociologist Patrick McNamara's study of the Catholic attitudes of two thousand upper middle-class

[70] Hoge, "Catholic Generations," 17.
[71] GSS Cumulative File, 1972–2008, sda.berkeley.edu/.

graduating seniors at one Catholic high school in the southwestern United States from 1977 to 1989.

The findings are troubling regarding both Catholic student practices and attitudes: "Church attendance, importance of religion, and degree of religious conviction, all show downward trends." According to McNamara, whereas about 75% of the seniors went to church weekly through 1981, less than half went to church in 1988 and 1989. "Seniors saying religion is 'very important' in their lives fell to decade-low percentages in 1986 and 1987." Doctrinal conviction was extremely low: only about 20% of the seniors of 1988 and 1989 were "convinced" about Church teachings.[72]

McNamara finds as a dominant trait among all the graduates what he calls the "post-Vatican II ascendancy of the 'individual conscience' over what one believes and practices."[73] This selective Catholicism is based on a "relativizing" or "subjectivism" of conscience: "a kind of 'tuning in' to oneself and one's experiences, legitimated religiously by the assumption that God expects us to follow our own consciences and that these promptings transcend the rules and regulations of any institution, including one's church."[74] The students exhibit "little loyalty to the institutional Church, with fewer than half active in a Catholic parish or attending Church with any regularity."[75] Even among those who do attend church weekly, only 15.4% made Church teaching the guide to conscience formation, while a whopping 80.3% listen to themselves as the ultimate authority.

McNamara argues students are becoming assimilated with Protestants in their views on sexuality where the emphasis is "on primacy of personal conscience": "seniors were not prepared to acquiesce in traditional teaching on sexual morality. Their own experiences and insights, as they interpreted and discussed them in peer contexts, effectively rule out for most any favorable consideration of the Church's traditional teachings."[76]

Other findings: Before 1983, 39.5% of the seniors found premarital sex immoral, but after 1983, only 29.5% thought so; however, among those in the total sample who felt that religion was "very important," nearly half (49.5%) said premarital sex was immoral, compared to only 11.2% among those who said religion was unimportant; among those who attended church weekly, 42.4% found premarital sex immoral, but only 14.9% felt so among those who attended a few times a year; among those who were members of a religious group, 48.9% said premarital sex was immoral, but only 31.8% said so among those in no religious group;

[72] McNamara, *Conscience First*, 68–69.
[73] Ibid., 102.
[74] Ibid., 103.
[75] Ibid., 61–62.
[76] Ibid., 157.

among those who found religion very important, 24.4% thought more sexual freedom a good thing, whereas among those for whom religion was unimportant, 53.7% felt so. Among those who found abortion acceptable if the fetus is deformed, only 8.1% claimed a "high" degree of religious conviction, compared to 20.3% among those without much religious conviction; only 7.7% of weekly church attendees found such an abortion acceptable, but 23.5% agreed among those who went a few times a year; among weekly church attendees, 31.8% planned future participation in a parish, while only 4.4% planned it among those who attended a few times a year. Such data overwhelmingly substantiate the positive effects of closeness to the Church and deep religious conviction for maintaining support for Church teaching, and the dire consequences for the Church of that lack of closeness.[77]

McNamara got fifty-four of the original senior interviewees of 1977 to resubmit to a questionnaire again in 1987 to see how their views might have changed since graduation. The results were not encouraging. He found the alumni were "not unlike well-educated young Americans nationally, whether Catholic or mainline Protestant," still "liberal" on personal and moral issues. He found they had subjected most of traditional Catholicism to a test to determine what is "irrelevant, senseless, or even harmful," and what is "liberating, fulfilling, and comforting." Elements that failed the test were discarded. Gone was any sense of "owing loyalty to an institution as such." Religious commitment was not a primary value. The Church as an institution was accepted as a guide to thought, only when it supported the "humanistic" values the students already embraced.

Still, McNamara argues that there are capable institutions and teachers who are able to harness the "reservoir of social idealism" latent in these Catholics and turn it into "spiritually and intellectually resonant experiences expressed in meaningful symbolic and liturgical forms."[78] The words might sound more inspiring than the reality.

HEGY'S "END OF AMERICAN CATHOLICISM?"

Davidson's and McNamara's pessimistic findings seem to be in line with Hegy's, who argues that younger Catholics will not return to the Mass attendance practices of their elders.

In his 1993 article, Hegy repeats the question originally asked by Greeley and McCready in 1972: "Are we experiencing 'The End of American Catholicism?'" In 1972, the two authors concluded that such great changes were occurring among those under 30 that Catholic life would

[77] Ibid., 176, 179, 180–82, 184, 190–91, 196.
[78] Ibid., 152–54, 162.

become indistinguishable from Protestant life. Hegy reaffirms this prediction, but in a new way.

He shows that Protestants are often more supportive of Catholic teaching than Catholics, especially when younger Catholics are compared to younger Protestants: 34% of Catholics under 25 attend church several times a month or more, whereas 40% of Protestants under 25 do; Catholics under 30 are more likely to accept the legality of abortion than Protestants of the same age.[79]

The fact that the Catholic perspective is increasingly becoming the same or even more liberal than the Protestant perspective leads Hegy to conclude, in answer to his question whether we are coming to the end of American Catholicism, that we are indeed, if we mean by American Catholicism those elements in the past that distinguished it from Protestantism, such as Mass attendance, sacramental life, and obedience to Church authority. The Church of tomorrow, says Hegy, will emphasize more general principles, such as empowerment through the Scriptures, daily life in imitation of Jesus, and life in the power of the Spirit. The whole "people of God," rather than a selected few, will be empowered to bring the "transcendent" into everyday life. Religion, then, says Hegy, will increasingly become a "social movement—like feminism, liberation theology and the fight for social justice." The "conservative-liberal dichotomy" will be overcome, as well as the Protestant-Catholic differential; these will be replaced by "the praxis of liberation theology, the commitment to social justice for all and the end of limiting gender roles in church and society."[80]

I would argue that if the Catholic Church of the future became, as he predicts, merely a social movement, the Catholic Church would not simply cease to exist as a church distinguishable from Protestantism. It would simply cease to exist.

"Are You Spiritual, but Not Religious?"

Kirk Cameron, a star of the once-popular ABC television series *Growing Pains*, is known for having ended the seven-year run of that series in 1992 by the fact that he went from being, in his own words, a "staunch atheist" to a "biblical Christian" at the age of 16, and would no longer tolerate what he considered to be non-Christian plot developments of the program's producers. He has since devoted much of his career to furthering on TV and films fundamentalist Christian apologetics. By all accounts he is a deeply committed Christian.[81]

---

[79] Hegy, "'End of American Catholicism?,'" 5–7.

[80] Ibid., 8–9.

[81] Cf. Martin Bashir, "Kirk Cameron, From Sitcom Star to Evangelist," March 17, 2006, abcnews.go.com/Nightline.

Yet, in an early 2006 TV appearance on the Larry King Show of a panel of performers from the *Growing Pains* series, when King addressed Cameron saying, "You're a very religious person, aren't you?" Cameron quickly responded, "I'm not religious, I'm spiritual." Unfortunately, King did not ask Cameron to clarify his distinction. It appears, however, to be a distinction recently come into vogue and apparently used by many young people today, though its roots in America, according to Robert C. Fuller, go back "as far as the colonial era." [82] Fuller asserts that today "it is likely that perhaps one in every five persons (roughly half of all the unchurched) could describe themselves in this way."[83] According to Gallup, while 54% of Americans describe themselves as "religious," 30% say they are "spiritual, but not religious."[84]

May one legitimately distinguish being "spiritual" from being "religious"? Is it appropriate to ask "are you spiritual, but not religious?" Though their meanings may seem obvious, the terms appear to be used today in so many different ways and by such a broad spectrum of people that it is almost impossible to come up with clear definitions.

Hoge's explanation is perhaps the simplest: he says "the catchall formula, 'I'm spiritual but not religious'" is a distinction especially used by young Catholics to "distinguish between personal faith and adherence to the rules of the church."[85] Brian J. Zinnbauer, professor of psychology at Bowling Green State University, tells us that "no single perspective on religion dominates postmodern culture, but rather multiple perspectives exist simultaneously." His study showed that only a small group of people from his sample (19%) claimed to be "spiritual not religious," and that this group was distinguished from the "religious and spiritual" group in that the former

> was less likely to evaluate religiousness positively, less likely to engage in traditional forms of worship such as church attendance and prayer, less likely to hold orthodox or traditional Christian beliefs, more likely to be independent from others, more likely to engage in group experiences related to spiritual growth, more likely to be agnostic, more likely to characterize religiousness and spirituality as different and nonoverlapping, more likely to hold nontraditional "new age" beliefs, and more likely to have had mystical experiences.[86]

---

[82] Robert C. Fuller, *Spiritual, but not Religious: Understanding Unchurched America* (New York: Oxford University Press, 2001), 5.

[83] Ibid.

[84] Frank Newport, "Americans Remain Very Religious, But Not Necessarily in Conventional Ways," Gallup Poll, December 24, 1999, www.gallup.com.

[85] Hoge, "Attitudes of Catholics," 12.

[86] Brian J. Zinnbauer, Kenneth I. Pargament, et al., "Religion and Spirituality: Unfuzzying the Fuzzy," *Journal for the Scientific Study of Religion* 36 (December 1997): 549–64, at 562, 555, and 561.

Christian Smith presents an explanation of the "spiritual but not religious" group. He calls them "seekers," and describes them as

> people who have an interest in spiritual matters but who are not devoted to one particular historical faith or denomination and in fact may be hostile to traditional or organized religion per se. Such spiritual seekers are reported to be exploring the world's storehouse of faiths and spiritualities for a variety of meaning systems and practices with which to experiment in order to find some that work for them, that meet their needs. They are dispositionally open to a multiplicity of truths, willing eclectically and selectively to mix and match traditionally distinct religious beliefs and practices, and suspicious of commitment to a single religious congregation. They tend to eschew religious proselytizing as paternalistic and coercive. And they operate, whether self-consciously or not, as religious and spiritual consumers by defining themselves as individual seekers, the authoritative judges of truth and relevance in faith according to how things subjectively feel to them. Such consuming seekers are not religiously rooted or settled but are spiritual nomads on a perpetual quest for greater insight and more authentic and fulfilling experiences.[87]

In view of the above statistics that indicate a disappointingly low percentage of young people who attend religious services and, in the case of Catholics, accept the teachings of the Church on critical moral questions, one might conclude that young people today are no longer interested in religion or spirituality. There are significant studies, however, indicating that the religion-spirituality issue among youth is complicated, and conclusions positive or negative depend ultimately on how one defines these terms.

HERI Study of Spiritual Life of College Students

The Higher Education Research Institute (HERI) of the University of California, Los Angeles, conducted a seven-year project, directed by its co-principal investigators Alexander W. Astin and Helen S. Astin, entitled "Spirituality in Higher Education: College Students' Search for Meaning and Purpose." The project's purpose is "to examine the spiritual development of undergraduate students during their college years" so as to enhance an understanding "of the role that spirituality plays in students' lives and to identify strategies that institutions can use to enhance students' spiritual development."[88]

---

87 Christian Smith with Melinda Lundquist Denton, *Soul Searching: The Religious and Spiritual Lives of American Teenagers* (New York: Oxford University Press, 2005), 73.

88 From the opening nonpaginated page of Alexander W. Astin and Helen S. Astin, Spirituality in Higher Education, The Spiritual Life of College Students: A

The project never defines "spirituality," but defines "spiritual development" in a sense which it admits is "very broad": "how students make meaning of their education and their lives, how they develop a sense of purpose, and the value and belief dilemmas that they experience."[89] Whether or not the students exhibit "spirituality" in their lives is based on whether the students rate as "very important" or "essential" to their lives "several key life goals,"[90] such as "believing in the sacredness of life, seeking out opportunities to grow spiritually, and believing that we are all spiritual beings."[91] On HERI's spirituality page, further elements of spirituality are delineated: it is described as "a universal impulse and reality" that "points to our interiors, our subjective life," and is "reflected in the values and ideals that we hold most dear, our sense of who we are and where we come from, our beliefs about why we are here—the meaning and purpose we see in our lives—and our connectedness to each other and to the world around us."[92] This broad definition proves to be very helpful for finding high levels of growth in student spirituality.

Being "religious" is also never defined, but is described as including such characteristics as "following religious teachings in everyday life," "finding religion to be personally helpful," "attending religious services," "praying," "reading sacred texts," and standing in "opposition to such things as casual sex and abortion."[93]

The first phase of the project got under way in the fall of 2000 with an initial pilot study "based on a sample of 3,680 undergraduates attending 46 diverse colleges and universities across the country," including public, private nonsectarian, Catholic, and other religious institutions. Its purpose was to explore "the trends, patterns, and principles of spirituality and religiousness among college students, and how the college experience both

---

National Study of College Students' Search for Meaning and Purpose (Los Angeles: HERI, University of California, Los Angeles, Fall 2004). The final results of this study have now appeared in book form, too late to be referenced in this work: Alexander W. Astin, Helen S. Astin, and Jennifer A. Lindholm, *Cultivating the Spirit: How College Can Enhance Students' Inner Lives* (San Francisco: Jossey-Bass, 2011).

89 HERI, "Spiritual Changes in Students during the Undergraduate Years: New Longitudinal Study Shows Growth in Spiritual Qualities from Freshman to Junior Years," *Spirituality in Higher Education* (Los Angeles: Graduate School of Education & Information Studies, UCLA, December 18, 2007), 5, www.spirituality.ucla.edu.

90 HERI, "Students Experience Spiritual Growth during College: UCLA Study Reveals Significant Changes in Undergraduates' Values & Beliefs," *Spirituality in Higher Education* (Los Angeles: Graduate School of Education & Information Studies, UCLA, December 18, 2007), 1, www.spirituality.ucla.edu.

91 HERI, *Spiritual Life of College Students*, 8.

92 HERI, *Spirituality in Higher Education* brochure, under "What is Spirituality?," www.spirituality.ucla.edu/docs/spirituality-brochure.pdf.

93 HERI, *Spiritual Life of College Students*, 8.

influences and is influenced by spiritual development." The students' views were canvassed in their freshman year, Fall 2000, and again in their junior year, Spring 2003.[94]

The results of the pilot study are informative. In the face of so much evidence today that seems to indicate young people have lost interest in the spiritual or at least the religious, it is surprising to find that the study concludes with a glowing report on the spiritual and religious lives of college students:

> There is a high level of spiritual engagement and commitment among college students, with more than half placing a high value on "integrating spirituality" in their lives (58%), 77% saying "we are all spiritual beings," and 71% indicating they "gain spiritual strength by trusting in a higher power." Substantial numbers of students, upwards of 84%, have had what is called a spiritual experience at least occasionally (e.g., witnessing the beauty and harmony of nature, listening to beautiful music). Regarding perspectives on religion, among the third-year college students surveyed, three in four report that they pray, that religion is personally helpful to them, and that they discuss religion and spirituality with friends.[95]

Other data presented are frequently impressive: The study found that 21% of the students qualified not simply as "spiritual" but as "highly spiritual,"[96] and only 17% as "having little or no spiritual focus."[97] The students often rate themselves as spiritual: 73% said they had had a "spiritual" experience while "witnessing the beauty and harmony of nature"[98] and 64% from "listening to beautiful music";[99] 51% believed "to a great extent" "in the sacredness of life"[100] and 41% had "to a great extent" an "interest in spirituality";[101] 39% rated themselves "above average" in having a quality of "spirituality."[102]

But the data sometimes provide curious, apparently conflicting combinations that raise questions of meaning: for example, while 27% were

---

94 HERI, *Spirituality in Higher Education: A National Study of College Students' Search for Meaning and Purpose: Summary of Selected Findings (2000–2003)* (Los Angeles: HERI, Graduate School of Education & Information Studies, UCLA, October 2004), 1–2, www.spirituality.ucla.edu.

95 Ibid., 2.

96 Ibid., 9.

97 Ibid., 10.

98 Ibid., 3.

99 Ibid.

100 Ibid.

101 Ibid.

102 Ibid., 4.

103 Ibid., 5.

indifferent as to whether or not a "Supreme Being"[103] existed, only 12% did not consider themselves to be on "a spiritual quest."[104] Does this mean that 15% felt they were on a spiritual quest yet were indifferent to the question of God's existence? This, moreover, raises the larger question as to whether a more precise definition of "spiritual" was needed. From the characteristics as provided above, being spiritual seems to be broadly equated with openness to any kind of uplifting experience such as "becoming a more loving person (84%)"[105] or "developing a meaningful philosophy of life (52%)."[106] The study reports, for example, that the "ultimate spiritual quest" most often chosen by students is to "become a better person (30%),"[107] while only 14% choose "to know what God requires of me."[108]

The study shows the students distinguishing being "spiritual" and "religious" and placing greater value on the spiritual: "Seven in ten agree that most people can grow spiritually without being religious, and 88% say that non-religious people can lead lives that are just as moral as religious believers."[109] This disengagement of spirituality from religion may be the product of how the students' experiences developed in college. One of the most dramatic discoveries in the study was that "over half (52%) of the sample reported attending religious services frequently the year before they entered college, but less than one-third (29%) attend frequently by their junior year. Furthermore, only 9% report that their 'religiousness' is much stronger since entering college, and only 13% say their spirituality is much stronger."[110]

One of the reasons for the decline in the importance of religion and for the fact that their spirituality did not grow much stronger may well have been the fact that, while 75% of the students reported they were "searching for meaning and purpose in life"[111] during their college years, 56% said that "their professors *never* provide opportunities to discuss the meaning and purpose of life,"[112] and 62% said that "professors *never* encourage

---

104 Ibid., 6.

105 Ibid., 4.

106 Ibid.

107 Ibid.

108 Ibid., 5.

109 Ibid.

110 Ibid., 7. This in contrast to a report from a study of March 13–27, 2006, of 1,200 telephone interviews with college students done at Harvard, indicating that 25% of students say "they have become more spiritual since entering college," while only 7% say they have become "less spiritual." "Redefining Political Attitudes and Activism: A Poll by Harvard's Institute of Politics," April 11, 2006, 5, www.iop.harvard.edu.

111 Ibid., 4.

112 Ibid., 6; emphasis in original.

discussions of spiritual or religious matters."[113] Fully 53% reported that the "classroom has had no impact" on their spiritual or religious lives.[114]

Nevertheless, the pilot study seems to indicate a high level of interest in what the Institute considers to be "spiritual" among young people in higher education today, but a growing alienation from organized religion. What is troubling, however, is that what is meant by "spiritual" seems often to have little to do with a personal Supreme Being considered fundamental to Christianity, if not most other religions. Is it enough to be "spiritual" simply to have lofty goals or experiences? Finally, the college experience seems to have had a negative impact on the students' basic desire to grow in a search for God or for any liaison with a religious community, thanks perhaps to the lack of interest in such matters by university personnel.

So much for the pilot study.

The HERI project called "the first longitudinal study of students' spiritual growth" formally got underway Fall 2004 with a survey using a revised version of the pilot study and given to 112,232 incoming freshmen at 236 colleges and universities throughout the country. The survey was completed Spring 2007 with a subsample of 14,527 of those same students in their junior year from 136 institutions.

The results of the survey were released December 2008. They confirm what was found in the pilot study, namely, the considerable interest among the students in what the study calls "spiritual qualities." The study also affirms that growth occurred in spirituality as the students progressed from their freshman to their junior years. One project leader, Co-Principal Investigator UCLA Emeritus Professor Alexander W. Astin, summarized the results of the study, saying that it shows that "many students are emerging from the collegiate experience with a desire to find spiritual meaning and perspective in their everyday lives . . . . The data [also] suggest that college is influencing students in positive ways that will better prepare them for leadership roles in our global society."[115]

The growth in "spirituality" is evidenced in the longitudinal study, for example, in the fact that the number of students rating "integrating spirituality into my life" as "very important" or "essential" among their "life goals" increased from 41.8% in their freshman year in 2004 to 50.4% in 2007, and those similarly rating "developing a meaningful philosophy of life" increased from 41.2% to 55.4%. Those emphasizing the humanitarian dimension of spirituality also decidedly increased: those rating "helping others in difficulty" as "very important" or "essential" increased from

113 Ibid.; emphasis in original.

114 Ibid.

115 HERI, "Spiritual Changes in Students," 1.

62.1% to 74.3%, and those giving similar ratings for "improving the human condition" grew from 53.4% to 63.8%.[116]

All of this made the surveyors happy, as it probably should. But do these figures represent real growth in spirituality? That is the question. Clearly by the understanding of spirituality the project proposes, they do, but not by any standard of spirituality where a relationship with God is determinative. Thus, the results of the project are largely dependent on an understanding of "spirituality" that is decidedly psychological and humanistic, if not secularist.

By the project's understanding of being "religious," however, the results were quite the opposite: participation in religious observance showed a "steep decline": "The rate of frequent attendance drops from 43.7 percent in high school to 25.4 percent in college, and the rate of non-attendance nearly doubles, from 20.2 percent to 37.5 percent."[117] Thus, the project shows that the so-called growth in "spirituality" is not supportive of growth in a relationship to a religious community or to public expressions of religious worship. In spite of this, one professor is quoted as concluding from the data that "student interest in spirituality and religion is at a level not seen since perhaps the 1950's," and "colleges need to support the growing interest and activities of our students"![118]

Perhaps this lack of religious connectedness is related to the fact that the political orientation of the students "toward socio-cultural issues" becomes increasingly liberal: the percentage identifying themselves as "liberal/far left" climbed from 28.6% in 2004 to 34.3% in 2007.[119] This may help to explain why the students are increasingly willing to accept propositions traditionally supported by liberals, such as "most people can grow spiritually without being religious," which increased from 62.8% in 2004 to 74.8% in 2007, and "it doesn't matter what I believe as long as I lead a moral life," which increased from 51.1% to 57.8%.[120] Same-sex marriage becomes more acceptable (53.8% to 66.1%), as well as the legalization of abortion (51.9% to 59.7%), and casual sex among people who "like each other" (44.7% to 51.5%). Laws prohibiting homosexual relationships were rejected 68.4% in 2004 and 78.6% in 2007.[121] All of this implies, of course, a growing base of relativism in the students' philosophy of life.

A total of twenty religious preference groups made up the study, the Roman Catholics at 28% representing the largest group. Unfortunately, the data were not broken down according to the various groups at the conclusion

116 Ibid., 1–2.

117 HERI, "Students Experience Spiritual Growth," 2.

118 Ibid.

119 Ibid.

120 HERI, "Spiritual Changes in Students," 2.

121 Ibid., 4.

of the study. Less than encouraging statements, however, are made in 2004 regarding the Catholics who were included in the study. According to the study, the groups separated into

> two clear-cut clusters of religious preferences. The first—involving Mormons, 7th Day Adventists, Baptists, and "other Christians"—is strongly spiritual, religious, and religiously-socially conservative and expresses very little religious skepticism. . . . The second group—involving Unitarians, Buddhists, Hindus, Episcopalians, Jewish students, and members of the Eastern Orthodox Church—tends to score low on religiousness, high on Religious Skepticism, and high on Ecumenical Worldview, Ethic of Caring, and Charitable involvement. . . . Students choosing Roman Catholic as their religious preference tend to score below the overall average on four measures: Religious Commitment, Religious Engagement, Religious/Social Conservatism, and Religious Skepticism.[122]

Negative Impact of College on Catholic Students

HERI conducted another study, reported in March 2003, based on "a 1997 national survey of incoming freshmen" and a "near-identical survey of graduating seniors in 2001" from thirty-eight Catholic institutions, tracking attitudes, practices, and changes among Catholic students during their college years. The report, commissioned by *Catholic World Report* and the Cardinal Newman Society, a higher education watchdog group, provides "hard data that confirms the failure of many Catholic colleges to tend to their students' spiritual needs."[123] Some of the findings:

While 38% of the Catholic students arrived in 1997 saying that "abortion should be legal," 52% held that position as graduating seniors; supporting casual sex between newly formed friends, 28% of freshmen, but 48% of seniors; saying same-sex marriage should be legalized, 52% of freshmen, 70% of seniors; attending a religious service frequently in 1997, 68% of freshmen, only 43% of seniors. Only 16% of seniors reported much stronger religious beliefs and convictions since freshman year, and while 14% as freshmen reported no hours spent weekly in prayer or mediation, 26% made that report as seniors. Finally, 9% of the Catholic students left their faith by graduation.[124]

Patrick J. Reilly, president of the Cardinal Newman Society, argues that "Catholic colleges should be helping students move *closer* to Christ, and certainly doing a better job of moving students toward the Catholic faith than

---

122 HERI, *Spiritual Life of College Students*, 17, 22.

123 Patrick J. Reilly, "Are Catholic Colleges Leading Students Astray?," *Catholic World Report*, 13 (March 2003): 38, cns.winxweb.com/Portals/0/docs/UCLAStudy.pdf.

124 Ibid., 42.

secular colleges do," but concluded in 2003 that "the HERI data show that Catholic colleges are not significantly different from the secular schools in terms of their effect on students' beliefs and conduct. . . . The sad fact is the HERI survey results show *increasing* dissent and *declining* morality among students during their four years of a Catholic college education."[125]

Further discouraging data result from a national survey of 251 current students and 255 recent graduates or attendees under 30 years of age at Catholic colleges and universities in the United States, conducted by QEV Analytics for the Cardinal Newman Society in May and June 2008 and released in October 2008. The Executive Summary of the survey, entitled "Behaviors and Beliefs of Current and Recent Students at U.S. Catholic Colleges,"[126] reports that most of the students surveyed

> reject traditional Catholic teachings on key moral issues, and significant numbers have engaged in premarital sexual activity, regular viewing of pornography, and substance abuse—even though most of the respondents were Catholic while attending college, and just under half were "sacramentally-active Catholics" (attending Mass at least weekly and receiving the Sacrament of Reconciliation at least annually).
>
> Most respondents say that the experience of attending a Catholic institution made no difference in their support for the Catholic Church or its teaching or their participation in Catholic Sacraments.[127]

Some of the data to substantiate this summary:

- "46% of current and recent students . . . said they engaged in sex outside of marriage."
- "60% agreed strongly or somewhat that premarital sex is not a sin."
- "57% agreed strongly or somewhat that same-sex 'marriage' should be legal" (down sharply from the 70% of graduating seniors in 2001 as reported in the above-mentioned March 2003 HERI study of Catholic higher education).
- "60% agree strongly or somewhat that abortion should be legal" (an increase of 8% over the same 2001 graduating seniors).[128]

---

125 Ibid., 41, 43.

126 Steven Wagner, "Behaviors and Beliefs of Current and Recent Students at U.S. Catholic Colleges," *Studies in Catholic Higher Education* (Cardinal Newman Society, Center for the Study of Catholic Higher Education, October 2008), www.CatholicHigherEd.org.

127 Wagner, "Behaviors and Beliefs," 1.

128 Ibid., passim.

When the data are broken down to separate the three different groups, the study notes that "significant behavioral and attitudinal differences are found between sacramentally-active Catholics and inactive Catholics and non-Catholics."[129] However, the differences are not always great: for example, the study found only a 4% difference regarding those who engaged in sex outside of marriage between inactive Catholics while in college and those who were sacramentally active in college (45% compared to 41%).[130]

The differences between the inactive Catholics and the sacramentally active regarding acceptance of Catholic teaching range from meager to significant:

- While 53% of current students identified as Catholics agreed strongly or somewhat that abortion should be legal, 50% of the sacramentally active Catholics during their last year at college did as well.
- While 55% of current Catholics "agree strongly or somewhat that premarital sex with someone you really care about is not a sin," 53% of sacramentally active Catholics agreed as well.
- While 53% of current Catholics "agree strongly or somewhat that same-sex marriage should be legal," only 48% of sacramentally active Catholics agreed.
- While 57% of current Catholics held it was not moral to have "sex with someone of the same sex," 62% of sacramentally active Catholics agreed.
- While 69% of current Catholics held it was not moral to have an abortion, 72% of sacramentally active Catholics agreed.
- While 47% of current Catholics students said being at a Catholic college had no impact upon their support for Catholic teachings, and 11% said it had even a negative impact, 51% of the sacramentally active Catholics said the experience had had a positive impact, while 10% said it had a negative impact.
- While 47% of current Catholic students while in college felt that being at a Catholic college had no impact on their participation in sacraments, 51% of the sacramentally active Catholics felt it did.[131]

---

129 Ibid, 1. Some breakdown of the data regarding the students surveyed: 65% of the students considered themselves Catholic while attending college, but only 48% were sacramentally active Catholics during their last year at college; 58% consider themselves Catholic today as well as when they were students; 6% were Catholic in college but not now; and 29% were not Catholic in their last year of college and are not Catholic today.

130 Ibid., 5.

131 Ibid., 6, 7, 9.

While one might have expected the data to be worse, one must nevertheless conclude that being at a Catholic college is not having the effect it should have in increasing Catholic students' relationship to Christ and his Church in their attitudes and behavior, nor is it having the impact it should upon their acceptance of the teachings of the Church. Closeness to the Church continues generally to have a positive effect upon their views and the quality of their Catholic life, but the effect seems to be diminishing.

National Study of Youth and Religion

Evidence of the sorry state of spirituality among Catholic pre-college young people today is found in the wide-ranging National Study of Youth and Religion report on the spirituality of American teenagers (13–17 years old), presented in Christian Smith's *Soul Searching*, which he claims is "the largest, most comprehensive and detailed study of American teenage religion and spirituality conducted to date."[132]

The study's findings, regarding 3,370 teenagers of all persuasions surveyed from 2001 to 2004, are sometimes encouraging. Smith found that, contrary to what many such as Greeley have asserted, today's teenagers are not rebellious: "Few teenagers today are rejecting or reacting against the adult religion into which they are being socialized";[133] rather, "the vast majority" of them "are *exceedingly conventional* in their religious identity and practices."[134] The study also found "40 percent of all surveyed U.S. teens report attending religious services once a week or more."[135] The study showed that "religion is a significant presence in the lives of many U.S. teens today," that "most have not dropped out of the religious congregations in which they were raised," that "very few U.S. youth" subscribe to or are interested in the "spiritual but not religious" mentality, and that the "vast majority of contemporary teenagers living in the United States identify themselves as Christians." In a way that seems to contradict the findings of Gallup in the *NCR*/Gallup surveys, Smith also argues that generational gaps are "superficial compared with and far outweighed by the generational continuities."[136] Teenagers are in fact the way they are because they are a reflection of their parents: though peers are still important to the shaping of teens' views, the "single most important social influence on the religious and spiritual lives of adolescents is their parents."[137] Of major importance is the conclusion the authors made about how the religious

---

[132] Smith et al., *Soul Searching*, 7.
[133] Ibid., 70.
[134] Ibid., 120.
[135] Ibid., 37.
[136] Ibid., 264.
[137] Ibid., 261.

spirit found in these students needs the input of religious communities if it is to be maintained: communities that "prioritize ministry to youth" will be "much more likely to draw youth into their religious lives and to foster religious and spiritual maturity in their young members" than communities that invest little in their youth.[138]

There is much that is not encouraging, indeed depressing, in the survey, some of which we shall discuss in the chapter on social justice. Smith reports that teens who are Christian are part of a significant movement among Christians whose views and practices make them "only tenuously Christian." Religion, moreover, does not play a serious role in their lives: they are "*incredibly inarticulate* about their faith," and consider it of marginal value.[139] Nor does Christianity challenge them to countercultural action. In contrast to the HERI pilot study, which found "a high level of spiritual engagement and commitment among college students," Smith does not find pre-college teens "spiritual seekers."[140] This may be because what HERI often calls "spiritual" Smith understands as interests associated with more positive adolescent life outcomes.

A major conclusion of Smith's study is that, though teens say they are Christian, their dominant religion is really not Christian in a sense that has anything to do with the origins and history of Christianity and its fundamental dogmas; it is what he calls a "Moralistic Therapeutic Deism," where the "central goal of life is to be happy and to feel good about oneself," and which features a benign God who created human beings and watches over them from afar, "wants people to be good, nice, and fair to each other," is not called upon except when needed, and sends "good people" to "heaven when they die."[141]

Smith devotes an entire chapter to the nearly one-quarter of all U.S. teens who are Catholic. As gloomy as his findings are on teens in general, the picture gets even worse when Smith concentrates on Catholics. Smith's study shows Catholic teenagers to be "consistently scoring lower on most measures of religiosity" than other teens: "Compared both to official Catholic norms of faithfulness and to other types of Christian teens in the United States, contemporary U.S. Catholic teens are faring rather badly. On most measures of religious faith, experience, and practice, Catholic teens as a whole show up as fairly weak."[142]

According to the study, 40% of Catholic teens go to church once a week or more, exactly the same as the national average. While this is encourag-

[138] Ibid., 260–62.
[139] Ibid., 171, 131, 161.
[140] Ibid., 78.
[141] Ibid., 162–63.
[142] Ibid., 216.

ing, the opposite figure is not: 32% go a few times a year or never.[143] While 41% felt religion was extremely or very important in shaping their daily lives, fully a quarter of them felt distant from God.[144] And while 41% said they had made a personal commitment to live life for God, only Jewish youth ranked lower on this scale among religious traditions.[145] Further, 63% never or only a little talked about their faith openly at school (86% of the Catholic students surveyed attended public school),[146] a figure excelled only by Jewish students by 1%.[147]

The majority of the Catholics teens interviewed "tended to be rather religiously and spiritually indifferent, uninformed, and disengaged."[148] Smith finds three reasons for this: First, the late twentieth-century "upward mobility and mainstream acculturation" of Catholics makes them now "among the best-educated, occupationally privileged, and most affluent Americans." Such social and economic changes have had the consequence of "weakening American Catholics' religious identity and commitment," of which Catholic teenagers are a reflection. Second, the relative religious laxity of their teenagers reflects the "relative religious laxity" of Catholic parents, in terms of "their lower levels of church attendance" and of "importance of faith" to their lives.[149] Third, the "relatively low institutional priority that youth evangelization, formation, and ministry" have at the diocesan and parish levels in today's Catholic Church has had its effect. Smith notes that today "only 5 percent of the staff of today's nearly 8,000 Catholic schools consists of priests, nuns, and religious brothers," while the 95% of lay Catholic school teachers' "theological knowledge and commitments" are "sometimes quite thin."[150]

Thus Smith shows that the loss of the rich Catholic heritage in faith and culture, absent from the lives of uncommitted Catholic families, is having a deleterious effect on the level of life of today's Catholic teenagers. To correct this bleak situation, Smith concludes that the Church will have to "invest a great deal more attention, creativity, and institutional resources

---

143 Ibid., 37.

144 Ibid., 40.

145 Ibid., 45.

146 bid., 289.

147 Ibid., 59.

148 Ibid., 195.

149 It may be worth noting here that Davidson finds "Millennials" less religiously illiterate than pre-Vatican II Catholics: "Religious illiteracy is highest among pre-Vatican IICatholics, 59 percent of whom say they cannot explain the faith to others," whereas only "47 percent of Millennials feel that way." James D. Davidson, "Challenging assumptions about young Catholics," *NCR*, September 30, 2005, 22. At least that is how the 47% of the "Millennials" say they feel.

150 Smith et al., *Soul Searching*, 207–17.

into its young members."[151] But is there much likelihood of this? Is the Christian community committed enough to the Christian well-being of its youth to address the crisis of faith that looms so ominously on the future horizons of the life of the Church?

The New Faithful?

In contrast to the discouraging data presented by Smith in *Soul Searching*, concrete evidence of a new spiritual and religious movement among young people is being stressed in recent publications such as that of Colleen Carroll's *The New Faithful*.[152]

Carroll interviewed mostly Gen X (born between 1965 and 1983) Catholics, Protestants, and Orthodox Christians, and found what she calls "a phenomenon that has gone largely unnoticed in the secular media and even within the church," a "revitalization of American Christianity and culture" evident all across the nation, coming from a "grassroots movement," a "small but committed core of young Christians . . . intentionally embracing organized religion and traditional morality."[153]

Carroll briefly outlines these Christians' spiritual journey. It begins with deep dissatisfaction with what the world considers success, which many of them have often already tasted deeply, and with the relativism of postmodernism that leaves them yearning for a "more authentic" spirituality.[154] Rebelling against their elders, as well as "repulsed by the sexual license, moral confusion, and social chaos they see around them," many younger Catholics, says Carroll, are "embracing conventional morality and an orthodox faith that gives meaning to their countercultural choices."[155]

In calling them orthodox, Carroll means they accept a "transcendent moral authority as revealed in the Scriptures, a commitment to regular worship and prayer, a belief in absolute truth, and a recognition of objective standards of personal and public morality." Being orthodox means accepting all the teachings of the Apostles' Creed.[156] The searches of these new faithful lead them to commit to "a transcendent God who knows them personally, has a plan for their lives, and wills their cooperation."[157] While their approach involves a profound rejection of popular, secular culture, at the same time it allows them to take advantage of the culture in the most ironic

---

151 Ibid., 217.

152 Colleen Carroll, *The New Faithful: Why Young Adults Are Embracing Christian Orthodoxy* (Chicago: Loyola, 2002).

153 Ibid., 13, 4.

154 Ibid., 17.

155 Ibid., 124.

156 Ibid., 13–14.

157 Ibid., 18.

of ways, such as promoting a Christian rock festival in the summer of 2001 that drew fifty thousand Christian music fans to the beat of "Jesus Rocks" and to the tune of millions of dollars in music and video sales.[158]

In a revealing interview with Zenit News, Carroll describes the new faithful as youth coming from various Christian backgrounds, though mostly Catholic and evangelical, nearly all of whom have reached a critical point in their lives "that forced them to decide if they would make following Christ the central concern of their lives": "These young adults have chosen to take Christianity seriously, and have decided that embracing Christian orthodoxy is the way to do that. Their faith commitments have led them to make countercultural decisions about everything from who [sic] and how they date to which careers they pursue and which political causes they embrace."

Most of the Catholics in the group, she pointed out, having received little or no training in their faith as children, have "taken it upon themselves to learn the faith and study Church teaching." They identify themselves as "religious" rather than "spiritual but not religious," and have rejected "a society saturated with moral relativism and dominated by the idea that they should 'do whatever feels good.' " They love Church traditions and history, the rosary, confession, Eucharistic adoration and evangelization. They want to follow the pope (at that time John Paul II) in "defending the truth in season and out of season," and "crave stability" for themselves as well as their children.[159]

Carroll found that, though the movement still constituted "a fairly modest segment of the population," many of them are bright "rising stars" and "educated professionals" who could have "a disproportionate amount of cultural influence" as the movement grows. She warns, however, that they could be "tempted to fall into extremes of either isolation from the culture or capitulation to it," and hopes that they will continue to strive to be "in the world, but not of the world."[160]

It should be noted that Davidson and Hoge dispute the existence of this new movement: "Colleen Carroll (The New Faithful) has argued that young Catholics are turning in a more traditional direction. We have found no evidence of such a trend in our previous studies, and the present survey indicates that youngest ('millennial') Catholics are similar to—not markedly different from—the post-Vatican II generation."[161] In fairness to Carroll, however, it should be noted that she claims the trend is still a "grassroots movement" and

158 Ibid., 255.

159 Zenit News Agency, "Generation X and the Turn to Christian Orthodoxy," April 29, 2003, 1–5, www.zenit.org/article-7128?=english.

160 Ibid., cf. also Carroll, *New Faithful*, 24.

161 James D. Davidson and Dean R. Hoge, "Catholics After the Scandal," *Commonweal* 131 (November 19, 2004): 18–19.

a "small but committed core of young Christians." Is the group a sign of what is to come, but still too small to appear on the radar screens of sociologists?

God on the Quad

Confirmation of Carroll's position appears to be coming from other studies such as *God on the Quad*, presenting a movement toward orthodoxy on religious college campuses. The journalist Naomi Schaefer Riley has published the results of her visits to twenty colleges and universities, including the Mormon Brigham Young University, the fundamentalist Bob Jones University, the Catholic Thomas Aquinas College, the Ave Maria School of Law, and the University of Notre Dame, as well as the Jewish Yeshiva University and the Evangelical Wheaton College, and finds them "all training grounds for the new Missionary Generation" that happily combines training in the liberal arts with religious instruction and fervor.[162]

Riley notes that typically "formal religious practice and adherence to traditional moral codes drop off among undergraduates," and among the "relatively few students" who continue to be involved in "faith groups," many call themselves "spiritual, not religious."[163] Not so among the twenty religious colleges Riley visited in 2001 and 2002, where, according to Riley, the majority of the students are from Red America, reject the relativism of secular schools and the "spiritual but not religious" dichotomy, and are "determined to change the culture of Blue America from the inside out." In a way reminiscent of Carroll's report, Riley's work argues that the students are dedicated to the Scriptures and to traditional religious and moral values, spurn the dissolute life of many of their peers, and are joining the military and professional careers that "will transform the broader secular culture" of America.[164] Schools that are dedicated to promoting different religions are supporting their interests, eager to supply them with "the tools to succeed in the secular world and the strength to do so without compromising their faith." Again, like Carroll, Riley argues that only the future will show whether the graduates of these institutions do go on to change the secular environment of America, or, overcome by the secular, choose to retreat into their own worlds.[165]

Not all is promising in Riley's presentation. While experiencing the atmosphere at Brigham Young as intensely dedicated to religious and moral values, she finds life at Notre Dame "at a crossroads. Will it become more secular or more Catholic?"[166] A desire to preserve high academic standards

---

162 Naomi Schaefer Riley, *God on the Quad: How Religious Colleges and the Missionary Generation Are Changing America* (New York: St. Martin's, 2005), book jacket, 263.

163 Ibid., 2.

164 Ibid., 4–6.

165 Ibid., 9–10.

166 Ibid., 54.

among its faculty may be cutting into Notre Dame's chances of maintaining a 50% plus Catholic faculty of high quality due to a shortage of such faculty. Professors complain of lack of knowledge of Catholic doctrine and "promiscuous" sexual behavior among the students.[167] Life in the single-sex dorms supposedly follows the "in loco parentis" model, but rules are lax: visiting hours are "some of the most liberal at religious colleges."[168] On the positive side, the university continues to maintain its stand against supporting abortion clinics and officially recognized homosexual student groups.

Yet claims that the university was sliding more and more toward secularism were raised when the new president, the Reverend John I. Jenkins, C.S.C., presented his closing statement resolving the controversy over the campus's annual presentation of the left-wing *The Vagina Monologues*. The President concluded that since Notre Dame is "a Catholic *university*" "committed to a wide-open, unconstrained search for truth," with "nothing to fear from engaging the wider culture," performances of the play could continue.[169] John M. D'Arcy, then bishop of the diocese of Fort Wayne–South Bend (within whose jurisdiction Notre Dame resides), said on his diocesan web page that he was "deeply saddened" by Jenkins's decision to continue to allow the university's sponsorship of the play,[170] which D'Arcy said "depicts in an approving way" sexual actions which are "a crime in both civil and church law" as well as "serious sin in Christian moral teaching."[171] David Solomon, a professor at Notre Dame, charged that Jenkins's decision was "one more step in a long process of secularization . . . proceeding apace" on the campus.[172] In March 2008, Bishop D'Arcy again wrote a pastoral statement criticizing Jenkins's continuing decision to permit the performance of the play on campus, arguing that the president's arguments justifying his decision are "deficient," that such performances are "pornographic and spiritually harmful," and "not consistent with the identity of a Catholic university."[173]

167 Ibid., 56–59.

168 Ibid., 172.

169 John I. Jenkins, C.S.C., "Closing Statement on Academic Freedom and Catholic Character," April 5, 2006, president.nd.edu/events-and-communications/communications/statements-on-academic-freedom/closing-statement/.

170 Bishop D'Arcy, "Statement on Vagina Monologues," April 5, 2006, www.diocesefwsb.org.

171 Bishop D'Arcy, "Concerning the 'Vagina Monologues,'" February 2006, www.diocesefwsb.org.

172 David Solomon, "A President's Retreat," *Wall Street Journal*, April 14, 2006, opinionjournal.com.

173 Bishop D'Arcy statement, "The decision to allow performances of 'The Vagina Monologues' at the University of Notre Dame," March 1, 2008, www.diocesefwsb.org/2008/03/the-vagina-monologues-2008.

More recently, a flair-up occurred over the fact that Notre Dame invited President Barack Obama to receive an honorary doctor of law degree and to be the keynote speaker at the commencement ceremonies on May 17, 2009. Bishop D'Arcy refused to attend the ceremony, in view of Obama's "long-stated unwillingness to hold human life as sacred" and support for the "direct destruction of innocent human life."[174] The bishop's decision reflected the statement by the U.S. Catholic bishops in 2004: "The Catholic community and Catholic institutions should *not honor* those who act in defiance of our fundamental moral principles. They should not be given awards, honors or platforms which would suggest support for their actions."[175] Eighty-three U.S. Catholic bishops "expressed disapproval" of Notre Dame's invitation.[176] Persons who supported Notre Dame's decision argued that the university was respecting the office of the President and not necessarily any of the President's views; those who called for Obama to be disinvited argued that the university's actions were in defiance of the bishops' 2004 statement, and a further indication of the secularization of Catholic education.

An atmosphere far different from Notre Dame's prevails at the three-hundred-student Catholic conservative Thomas Aquinas College of southern California, founded in 1971, where "it's not unusual to find fifty students at mass during the day"[177] and where the spirit of Catholicism envelopes the life of the campus. Ninety percent of the students "in this monastic and homogeneous community" are Catholic and half of the remaining convert to Catholicism during their time there: proselytizing is part of the life of the students.[178] Seven percent of the school's graduates have found a religious vocation, and those who marry tend to marry alumni of the school. Dormitory life is single-sex, with no visiting hours ever. No demonstrations of affection are allowed on campus, drinking is rarely permitted, and no TVs are allowed in rooms. "Most of students' free time is spent studying and praying."[179] Students debate at high levels of intellectual discussion day and night at this Great Books school (the average SAT score is 1300), and when it comes to belief in Christianity, says one student, "there are no doubters here."[180]

Riley finds that, with "certain exceptions," "religious campuses are devoid of the alcohol, drugs, sexual activity, and violence that plague many secular

174 "Concerning President Barack Obama speaking at Notre Dame graduation, receiving honorary law degree," March 29, 2009, www.diocesefwsb.org.

175 United States Conference of Catholic Bishops, "Catholics in Political Life," June 2004, usccb.org/bishops.

176 "List of Bishops Opposing the Notre Dame Invitation and Award to President Obama," May 6, 2009, www.lifesitenews.com.

177 Riley, *God on the Quad*, 76–77.

178 Ibid., 82.

179 Ibid., 87.

180 Ibid., 89.

universities."[181] She finds that religious campuses "have no problem acting in loco parentis,"[182] though she admits she does not have in mind Jesuit schools when she says this. In fact, she admits that Jesuit schools are "further along the liberal side" and that Jesuits "have historically been more open to secularizing trends."[183] She identifies Fordham University as "one of the more liberal Catholic universities,"[184] and notes that "A certain gleeful subversiveness has overtaken the faculty and students at many of these schools" that "see the current pope [John Paul II] as far too conservative."[185]

Riley notes that students in religious schools "represent the most spiritually interested and morally serious element of the school." At the same time, she sees "temptations pulling religious college students in a more secular, less distinctive direction." She finds the influence of "postmodernism . . . threatening to undermine the very idea that there is religious truth." She finds "secular understandings of the purpose of community service" tempting schools to reject the religious "motive for engaging in service" as being "backward" and "explicit proselytizing." She urges schools to engage in "cultural discernment" so as to help their students know how to interact with the secular world: "If religious college leaders can navigate between the dangers of secularization and isolation, these schools can more effectively transmit their ideas to a larger American audience."[186]

Riley sees religious schools as the "vanguard of a more conservative generation" eager to "enhance the ethical core of American life." She seems to accept, however, that such dedication is more representative of the "most seriously religious colleges" that "have an evangelical mission."[187] Indeed, one of the weaknesses in her conclusions, it would seem, is that she paints religious institutions with too broad of a brush. Her findings appear to reflect a "missionary generation" found largely in conservative evangelical and Catholic institutions and not in religious institutions in general, the more liberal of which would contain at the most pockets of such a mission spirit, engulfed already in a wider sea of secularism.

Religion on Campus

A 2001 work entitled *Religion on Campus* attempts to "test" the veracity of so-called "secularization theories," which hold that secularization has

---

[181] Ibid., 170.
[182] Ibid., 171.
[183] Ibid., 75, 55.
[184] Ibid., 182.
[185] Ibid., 75.
[186] Ibid., 259–60.
[187] Ibid., 261–62.

taken over and religion has declined in its presence and influence on America's campuses.[188]

The three authors, after visiting widely scattered institutions across the country, find the basis for such secularization theories totally lacking. Their positive conclusion, however, may have been predetermined by the fact that in their study they applied a broadened concept of religiosity and a narrowed understanding of secularization. Based on their reworked criteria, any religious or spiritual element present on a campus satisfied their standard of religiosity. As a result, their study leads them to conclude, not that the contemporary campus has become secularized, but just the opposite, that "both the practice and the study of religion are thriving and supported by campus cultures."[189]

Secularist theories, the authors argue, do not really reflect the growth of secularization on campuses, but the confusion that has been generated by the presence of "new appearances" or "new shapes" of religion. These have created a new "atmosphere of religious diversity, tolerance, and choice" that has been mistaken for secularity. These changes are erroneously judged when compared with past structures that once represented religious presence, such as ties with religious denominations. Rather than seeing the changes as elements in a process of secularization or "marginalization of religion," say the authors, the changes more clearly "add up to the declericalizing, de-denominationalizing, and, in some cases, de-Christianizing of campuses."[190] Why these three movements do not add up to increased secularization may be lost on persons more concerned about retaining a vibrant Christian life on the campus.

Each author visited one or more of four universities, each representing a distinctive religious or secular tradition. An attempt was made to keep all institutions anonymous. "West University" stands for a public state university representing the "secular" model; "East University" is the pseudonym for an eastern Roman Catholic institution; "North College" represents a Lutheran liberal arts college in the north; and "South University" is the pseudonym for a formerly African-American institution now defined as nondenominational with Presbyterian roots. Though each institution was chosen to represent the cadre of schools within four distinct traditions, the authors give no indication as to how they chose the schools or whether the schools are in fact representative. They also readily admit that "wide differences may exist among schools of each type."[191]

---

[188] Conrad Cherry, Betty A. DeBerg, and Amanda Porterfield, *Religion on Campus* (Chapel Hill, NC: University of North Carolina), 2001.

[189] Ibid., book jacket.

[190] Ibid.

[191] Ibid., 6–7.

"West University" is represented as providing a "healthy supply" of "well-designed and well-publicized religious groups and activities." Remarkably, in view of the secular nature of the institution, the university was found to have an "ethos . . . dominated by Christianity." Yet the author who visited the institution is forced to admit that the university's program cannot be accurately described as a "success" because so few students take advantage of the thirty religious organizations represented on the campus. Notable for our purposes is that the students tend to describe themselves as "spiritual, not religious."[192]

The author who visited "South University" found a "pervasive religious atmosphere" on this campus as well. But since the students largely "hailed from Baptist and Pentecostal backgrounds," was this not to be expected? These students also call themselves "spiritual, but not religious," and take courses on "world religions, religious factors in society and literature, and African American spirituality," designed to expand their "spiritual horizons and experiences." The author submits that "virtually every public event became a worship service," and that "African American evangelicalism . . . dominated the religious scene." However, since there has been no department of religion on the campus since 1975, there are few courses on religion as such, and little opportunity for the study of religion in depth.[193]

The "ethos" of the "North College" is also "overwhelmingly Christian," and nearly half of the students are Lutheran. About 23% of the student body regularly attends religious services in the Lutheran tradition. "Sacred music" defines much of the ethos of the college and is "the source of much of its religious identity."[194] Virtually all religion courses are in biblical and Christian studies. Since a mission requirement in the college is to foster "biblical and theological literacy," a course is required of every student in each of those two areas, although the contents of the courses are flexible, with "diverse approaches" to the Bible permitted "from a variety of angles," including feminism and American culture.[195]

Most revealing for our purposes is the ethos of "East University," in this case a Jesuit university. The author of this visit, herself not a Catholic, presents the ethos of the campus as decidedly Catholic and permeating much of the life of the institution. At the same time, she describes the ethos of the institution as "more humanistic than that of more conservative Catholic schools" that more closely identify with "upholding the sacred authority of the church in the midst of a perceived onslaught of religious declension."

192 Ibid., 76–80.
193 Ibid., 140–42.
194 This can only be St. Olaf's College of Northfield, MN.
195 Cherry et al., 270–74.

East's Catholic ethos, as described by the author, has a curious admixture of "various forms of Catholic belief" that allow "significant" religious diversity. The author finds the role of religion on the campus to be conflicted and undirected, with varying forces pulling the school in opposite directions, secular as well as religious. She finds that it is the emphasis on academics rather than religious direction that brings unity to the campus, so that, as one administrator put it to her, "university" is the noun and "Catholic" the adjective. In fact, the school's commitment to academic excellence has paid off, in that the school is now ranked as "among the highest" in the country.[196]

On the negative side, the ambiance of religious commitment on the Jesuit campus appears to be low. One theology professor told the author regarding the students' relationship to Catholicism that "we are living in the pluperfect tense," and "theology is in desperate straits here." Whereas at one time the purpose of the school was, according to a nineteenth-century policy statement, "to educate the pupils in the principles and practices of the Catholic faith," now, according to another professor, the school has become "an American Catholic university saturated with American values and culture." According to still another professor, the university's "religious rhetoric" belies the truth: being religious has become "like intramural sports," an activity for those who like it. "Social service programs" exist to help the students "feel good about themselves and good about the school." The quality of student life and education is declining, he said. The dean of academic affairs, on the other hand, maintained that the Catholic identity of the school was greater than in the '50s to '80s. The author's overall impression was that key figures on the campus were working hard to thwart "the inevitability of secularization" and promote "an integration of academic excellence and religious expression" that would exceed the achievements of the past.[197]

The author found a large number of students on the campus, the majority of whom are Catholic, "bored by organized religion, especially organized Christianity," but "seriously invested in spirituality." Many viewed attending Mass as an occasion for socializing; for others, attending Mass is part of a "weekly routine, along with drinking and studying."[198] Some students "mentioned the transformative effect of Jesuits and Jesuit spirituality on their religious lives"; some faculty spoke of "student behavior as completely out of control."[199]

The author reports that a thriving retreat program exists on the Jesuit campus. Approximately eight hundred or 30% of first-year students made

[196] Ibid., 144–46. Though deliberately unidentified, the discussion leaves no doubt the school is Boston College.

[197] Ibid., 148–53.

[198] Ibid., 159.

[199] Ibid., 161–63.

the Ignatian retreat in 1996–1997, a figure the author considered impressive.[200] What may not be so impressive is that these retreats, as described by the author, are expressive of the heavy emphasis at the university now being placed on liberation theology and almost anything except Christ: the retreats that, according to the report, "make constant use of student leaders," focus on "academic work, social pressures, friendships, sexual relationships, and opportunities for community involvement." Other programs said to be run by a female chaplain who left the Church over women's ordination focus "on spiritual development through identification with the poor." Student anger at these programs is aroused "at the injustices of capitalism" and then encouraged to be expressed "in nonviolent ways." Nowhere is the name of Jesus mentioned in this entire discussion, though "more traditional forms of spiritual formation" are said to be made available for the few students who want them. The emphasis is on diversity. As one Jesuit chaplain remarked, "this Jesuit thing is a mantra that everyone can agree with because it is very popular but not pinned down. It can be like 'bullah bullah' at Yale."[201]

But the author admits to having experienced deep division on the campus between the liberal social justice set and the more conservative Church-supporting set. She spoke with several students who expressed serious rejection of the liberalism on the campus expressed in the spiritual and religious life. According to one student, social justice is "an attempt to make up for" the widespread "individual subjectivism" where "whatever feels good for you is OK with me," with no room left for an intellectual discussion of faith. "Students are hungry for Catholic spirituality," the student said, "and they are just given scraps."[202] The irony is that conservative students are experiencing what it means to be countercultural in the world today because of their dedication to the teachings of the institutional Church on a Catholic campus.

In the author's conclusion to her study of East University, she admits to growing in an awareness "of a vast tapestry of Catholic religious life" on the campus. She found "an inclination to sacramentalism" that was "pervasive" in the Eucharist as well as in "finding God anywhere." She found a "deep-seated investment in personal purity," especially in the "widespread disapproval of abortion." She understood the "identification with the poor" as a "means of identification with the suffering of Christ and his love for the poor." She appreciated the conflict between the progressives' view of faith and justice as concern for the poor, and the traditionalists' fear of the politicizing of "a profound mystical reality." She also felt the conflict on the campus between loyalty to the teachings of the Church versus academic

[200] One chaplain tells the author that "about 70–80 percent of students involved in chaplaincy activities were female" (Ibid., 175).

[201] Cherry et al., 168–73.

[202] Ibid., 185–92.

freedom, between "secularization" versus the presence of Catholic life. And yet she is able to conclude by saying she "never found a student who was not involved, in some way, in religious life."[203]

Perhaps the overall conclusion of the three authors regarding the presence of religion in American higher education today may best be summed up by the continuing distinction they heard between spirituality and religion. When they asked if a typical student was religious, the response was, "No, but most of them are very spiritual," where religious was taken to mean connected with institution and being traditional, and spiritual meant "a personal experience of God or ultimate values" or "a quest, a journey, something not yet completed." What this distinction reflects, according to the authors, is that today's youth are "spiritual seekers rather than religious dwellers"—they are seeking to construct a spirituality without regard to traditional religious boundaries.[204] The authors candidly note that as a result of the lesser interest of students in religion, there were more opportunities for religious practices at all four schools than there were student participants: no more than a minority at any of the four schools, and as low as 10% at "West University," participated in such practice.[205]

Many students, according to the authors, take religion courses at all the institutions because such courses help them to find meaning in their lives.[206] Surely anything that helps students in this way has to be a plus. Yet the careful reader cannot help but notice, as we already stated, that the authors find many religious elements in the four schools because the authors include in their concept of religiosity practices such as "volunteer service," "student spirituality," and openness to religious diversity.[207]

The writers are forced to use an umbrella concept of religion that has "different shades of meaning" to see such practices as religious. In fact, the shades are often remarkably different. At West University they find the "evangelical piety of football players," Masses attended by twelve hundred students at the Newman Center, and Bible study groups.[208] At South University, "virtually every major public event on campus was a worship service."[209] At West University and North College, the authors were "struck by the popularity of the evangelical groups" that combine fun and games with "faith-sharing, prayers, Scripture reading, and occasional lectures" to promote "Christian development."[210] All fine and good. But at the Catholic

[203] Ibid., 214–18.
[204] Ibid., 275–77.
[205] Ibid., 282–83.
[206] Ibid., 288.
[207] Ibid., 280, 277.
[208] Ibid., 277.
[209] Ibid., 278.
[210] Ibid., 280.

East University, the emphasis is upon "the integration of academic study, personal formation, and service in the world," all representing a spirituality that focuses on "self-transformation" and the greater social awareness that comes from service-learning and a commitment to the Jesuit ideal of becoming "men and women for others."[211]

The authors may have failed to find a justification for "secularization theories" in their visits to the four campuses, but in the process, they may have exposed the existence of the same thing that Smith found happening among teenagers in *Soul Searching*: the decline of a commitment to anything that has to do with the origins and history of the Christian heritage.

Lack of Commitment among Youth

Clear evidence of the lack of commitment among today's youth is found in many of the above studies, especially in the *NCR*/Gallup study of 2005, which, as we noted, found no commitment to the institutional Church among Catholics 25 years of age or younger in the sample of laypersons it polled. Certainly the survival of commitment to an ecclesial community is what is at risk in the distinction between the "religious" and the "spiritual." Though, as we saw, Smith strongly rejects in *Soul Searching* the use of this distinction by teenagers, he readily admits they are failing to find religious life meaningful to them.

The question is: How could they? Their knowledge of their faith is so dismal. A typical youth's response to Smith's query about what Catholicism is came from an 18-year-old Catholic whom Smith reports replying, "Like, you, you live better, like you, um, you have like a standard for yourself that's higher than like other people. Uh, I don't know."[212] Catholic youth are so uninformed about their faith that it would be difficult for anyone with such paltry knowledge of Catholicism to find meaning in it. Smith concludes that the Catholic Church needs to act quickly to reverse the knowledge drainage.

Davidson notes in his recent study that while the Church continues to affirm the Council of Trent's teaching that for believers the sacraments of the Church are "*necessary for salvation*,"[213] only 38% of "Millennial" Catholics strongly agree that the sacraments are "essential" to their relationship to God. Davidson concludes from the lack of importance of the sacraments for young people that we "should expect that a growing number of young adults will have [a] more individualistic view of their relationship with God and will attach less importance to the institutional church."[214]

---

211 Ibid., 279.

212 Smith et al., *Soul Searching*, 132.

213 *Catechism of the Catholic Church*, par. 1129; hereafter paragraphs noted in the text as *CCC*.

214 Davidson, "Belief in Church," 21.

O'Reilly cites a professor of sociology at Le Moyne College, Syracuse, New York, asking his students to define a "good" Catholic. The professor asked: "Did it mean going to Mass, or confession, or doing this and not that?" The professor added: "And their answer wasn't yes or no. It was more like, 'What a stupid question!' "[215] In fact, only 30% of "Millennial" Catholics said the Church was among the "most important parts of my life" (whereas 59% of pre-Vatican II Catholics did).[216] With the growing consensus about the priority of being a "good person" over religious attitudes, the idea of relating being a good Catholic to the life of the Church becomes meaningless.

Only 23% of Catholics say they are "very strong" in their faith, and of that group, only 12% are young (18–29), 21% middle-aged (30–50), and 36% of the oldest group (over 50). But according to Gallup, it is only in the group of those who are very strong in their faith that the majority agree with the Church's teachings on abortion, extramarital sex, and the prohibition of marriage after divorce (but only on these issues). May we conclude only a minority of Catholics consider themselves very strong in their commitment to the Church? Since the smallest group of those very strong in their faith is the young, may we wonder when Gallup says it is "not surprising" that they "tend to express the strongest opposition to many of the Church's dogmas"?[217]

Youth maintain "a certain level of individual judgment" about Church teachings.[218] They represent a new type of Catholic that "lives the faith on his or her own terms," where a "spiritual autonomy is growing more pronounced among those who count themselves as practicing Catholics," and scholars see little chance this tendency might be reversed.[219] O'Reilly cites one scholar: "My sense is that this is an enduring condition, not just an anomaly" . . . . There's a tension between Catholicism and American culture . . . [and] American culture is winning out."[220] It is the lack of commitment to the Church that explains such an independent attitude.

"Are all religions equally good?" Answers to this question reveal much about how one relates to one's own religious community. Data from a Gallup December 1999 survey showed that 82% of Americans held that other religions are equally as good as theirs, while only 16% felt their reli-

---

215 O'Reilly, "A Faith in Flux."

216 D'Antonio, "Generational Differences," 15.

217 *Gallup Poll 1998*, 148.

218 Mary Johnson et al., "Young Adult Catholics: Conservative? Alienated? Suspicious?," *America* 180 (March 27, 1999): 13.

219 O'Reilly, "A Faith in Flux."

220 Ibid. O'Reilly is citing Chester Gillis, at that time chair of the Theology Department at Georgetown University.

gion was "the best path to God."[221] Data from a 1994 Gallup study show that 74% of young Catholics (13- to 17-year-olds) said all religions are equally good (and 62% of young Protestants agreed).[222] As usual, the Zogby survey of March 2006 is in sharp contrast in that 81% of Catholics in the survey held that the Catholic Church is the one true Church (76% among 18- to 35-year-olds).[223]

For one who holds all religions of equal value, it is indeed possible to be a member of a specific religious group and support its life and teaching as reflective of a dedication to some kind of general religious sentiment, but such thinking is not compatible with a strong identification and commitment to that group. Perhaps this is why post-Vatican II Catholics are about five times as likely to say they are less committed to the Church than they were five years ago.[224] Identification with the Church is simply fading away.

Answers to the question "How important is your religion to you?" are also revelatory of personal commitment. Gallup notes an increasing decline, especially among Catholics, of those who answer "very important": whereas 83% of Catholics and 76% of Protestants said "very important" in 1952, only 53% of Catholics and 64% of Protestants made that claim in 1995.[225] When Gallup asked if they would mind not having a Sunday Mass but only Communion because of the shortage of priests, 70% of Catholics said they would not mind, at least if done only occasionally.[226]

The Obama Effect

As of this writing, the country is still in the throes of the Obama effect that took over the nation during the primaries and presidential election of 2008. Millions of Americans, as well as people around the world, have been caught up into the maelstrom of frenzy over this young, charismatic politician who gained access to the White House after virtually no previous political experience or accomplishment. The election of Obama, a man of African descent on his father's side, is seen by many as an indication of the end of racism in America, as well as the beginning of a new era of détente between the United States and the rest of the world. So exuberant was the frenzy over Obama on Election Day that one woman, when she was shown on television filling up her tank at a gas station, shouted "I am so happy! Now I won't have to pay for gas anymore, and I won't have to pay the mortgage on my house. I am so happy!"

221 Newport, "Americans Remain Very Religious."
222 Gallup, *Religion in America 1996*, 73–74.
223 Zogby, "National survey of Catholic adults."
224 D'Antonio et al., *American Catholic Laity*, 78.
225 Gallup, *American Catholic*, 12; *Religion in America 1996*, 53.
226 *Gallup Poll*, 147; D'Antonio et al., *American Catholic Laity*, 174.

Obama seems to have introduced a new era of liberal or left-wing thinking into American politics and moral opinions.[227] Americans became more oriented toward the Democratic Party and its more left-wing positions in 2008 than to the Republican Party. However, because of the failure of the Obama Administration to fulfill its campaign promises regarding the economy, a major shift in party allegiance seems to be underway. The political scene is presently, indeed, volatile.

Americans have favored the Democratic Party in recent years: from 1984 to 2000, more Americans were identified as Democrats than Republicans on presidential election days. In 2004, the numbers were even, at 37% each. In 2008, Democrats outranked Republicans by 7%—39% to 32%—the biggest margin since 1984. But that's not all: according to Andrew Kohut of the Pew Research Center, "independents broke decisively for Obama, favoring him by a 52%-to-44% margin over John McCain. Obama also won an overwhelming 60% of self-identified moderates. By comparison, John Kerry carried 49% of independents and 54% of moderates four years ago."[228]

The alteration of the American landscape is especially notable among young voters (18- to 29-year olds). The 2008 HERI survey of college freshmen noted an increasing trend toward polarization among the students, with fewer incoming freshmen characterizing themselves as "middle-of-the road," though the percentage still remained the highest: "This category is at an all time low (43.3 percent), returning to roughly the same percentage as in 1970." On the other hand, the survey noted the remarkable increase of students identifying themselves as liberal: "Corresponding increases occurred in the proportion of students who characterized themselves as Liberal (31.0 percent), and Far Left (3.2 percent). This is the largest percentage of students categorizing themselves as liberal since 1973. Approximately one in five students in 2008 characterize themselves as conservative (20.7 percent), a small decrease since the previous year (23.1 percent)."[229]

---

227 "The Democratic Party's advantage in party identification has widened considerably in recent years, but the share of Americans who describe their political views as liberal, conservative, or moderate has remained stable during the same period. Only about one-in-five Americans currently call themselves liberal (21%), while 38% say they are conservative and 36% describe themselves as moderate. This is virtually unchanged from recent years; when George W. Bush was first elected president, 18% of Americans said they were liberal, 36% were conservative and 38% considered themselves moderate. Young people are considerably more likely than older Americans to describe their political views as liberal" (Juliana Horowitz, "Winds of Political Change Haven't Shifted Public's Ideology Balance," November 25, 2008, pewresearch.org).

228 Andrew Kohut, "Post-Election Perspectives," November 13, 2008, pewresearch.org.

229 John H. Pryor, Sylvia Hurtado, et al., *The American Freshman: National Norms Fall 2008* (Los Angeles: HERI, University of California, Los Angeles), 4–5.

The survey noted that with the increase of liberal-oriented students, "overall support for more liberal causes has also risen." Among these, the study listed an increase in the percentage of students "who support the right to legal marital status for same sex couples, indicating that now over two-thirds (66.2 percent) of entering freshmen support such rights."[230]

In the 2009 survey, however, political interest declines, and financial concerns dominate: "Today more incoming first-year students are concerned with their ability to finance their college education . . . . those with 'some' concerns . . . continued to climb to its highest level since 1971. . . . Four and a half percent of students reported that their fathers were unemployed, this is higher than at any time" in the history of the freshman survey.[231]

Regarding political views: the survey notes that those students identifying themselves as liberal in 2009 compared to 2008 "dropped two percentage points to 29.0%, returning to pre-election levels (29.3% in 2007)." Students identifying themselves as conservative rose to 21.8%, a rise of 1.1% over 2008. The study notes, however, that such percentage drops are normal after election years.[232] Perhaps as indicative of the prevalence of a less liberal stance, 64.9% of freshmen now support the right to legal marital status for same sex couples, down 1.3% from 2008.[233]

In five out of the eight presidential elections since 1980, more young people voted for the Democratic Party candidate than the general population did. In 2000, the Democratic share of the vote was almost identical between the young and all voters, at 48% each. But in 2004, the vote of the 18- to 29-year-olds grew to 54% Democratic, while the Democratic share remained at 48% among all voters, a gap of six points. In 2008, however, the Democratic share among youth grew to 66%, thirteen points higher than the Democratic share among all voters (53%). In 2000, the party affiliation among the young between Democrats and Republicans split nearly evenly, but in 2008, a nineteen-point gap separated the Democratic Party affiliation of the young (45%) from the Republican affiliation (26%). Clearly, according to Kohut writing after the November elections 2008, the evidence "suggests that a significant generational shift in political allegiance is occurring" among young voters.[234] In the 2010 midterm election, that generational shift seems still in place:

---

[230] Ibid., 5.

[231] Pryor, HERI, *American Freshman: National Norms Fall 2009*, 6–7. [The comma after "unemployed" is *sic*.]

[232] Ibid., 8.

[233] Pryor, HERI, *American Freshman 2008*, 35; Pryor, HERI, *American Freshman 2009*, 33

[234] Andrew Kohut, "Young Voters in the 2008 Election," November 12, 2008, pew research.org.

according to CNN, 57% of those 18 to 29 years old voted Democratic and 40% voted Republican, a point gap of seventeen percent.[235]

One of the major reasons for these changes seems to be what Kohut calls "the Bush effect": "The Republican brand has been severely damaged by the presidency of George W. Bush. The financial crisis and falling stock market cannot explain away the GOP's troubles here. Iraq, Hurricane Katrina and a long list of criticisms of the Bush administration created a significantly more advantageous party-identification spread for the Democrats than Bill Clinton had in either of his two victories."

The damage created by the perceived weaknesses and/or failures of the Bush presidency were perhaps even more real among the young than they were among older generations; however, the strength of the Democratic Party among the young "was further enhanced by the presence on the ticket of a candidate who was so appealing to younger voters. From the very start Barack Obama swept them off their feet. Obama won voters under the age of 30 by a dramatic two-to-one margin (66% to 31%). By comparison, Kerry won 54% of voters under 30, while Al Gore was not able to carry even a majority of the young vote (48%) just eight years ago."[236]

Kohut points out that there are other factors as well that have a significant role to play when explaining attitudes and behavior among young people today: "Young voters are more diverse racially and ethnically than older voters and more secular in their religious orientation. These characteristics, as well as the climate in which they have come of age politically, incline them not only toward Democratic Party affiliation but also toward greater support of activist government, greater opposition to the war in Iraq, less social conservatism, and a greater willingness to describe themselves as liberal politically." According to Kohut, "just 62% of voters age 18–29 identify as white [today], while 18% are black and 14% Hispanic. Four years ago, this age group was 68% white. In 2000, nearly three-quarters (74%) of young voters were white. . . . Compared with those age 30 and older, fewer young voters say they are affiliated with a religious tradition (16% vs. 12% overall), and fewer report regular attendance at worship services. Among all voters, 40% attend religious services weekly or more often; among those 18–29, just 33% do so."[237]

Among the young, a combination of factors seems to be coalescing—their own greater racial and ethnic diversity, a greater emphasis on diversity education in secondary and higher education, a disillusionment with the Bush administration and Republican Party ineffectiveness—to produce a

[235] CNN Politics, Electioncenter exit polls.

[236] Kohut, "Post-Election Perspectives."

[237] Kohut, "Young Voters in the 2008 Election."

more liberally oriented youth than in the general population: according to Kohut, "nearly a third of young voters (32%) describe themselves as liberal, compared with 22% of all voters."[238]

Young Catholics reflect the same tendency as their peers. Catholics 18 to 34 years old are identifying themselves as more liberal (24%) than Catholics older than 35 years of age (21%), less conservative (28% to 42%), and more moderate (41% to 36%). And while older Catholics are about evenly split in their party affiliation (48% Democrat, 45% Republican), among younger Catholics the gap is a huge 19% (54% Democrat, 35% Republican).

All of these data come from the the Faith and American Politics Survey, *The Young and the Faithful,* released October 8, 2008, by a progressive organization called Faith in Public Life. The survey revealed how great the shift is among young people on political and moral issues today, away from the views of the older generation in general and even more so from older generations within the Catholic Church.[239] The data, however, continue to indicate that those closest to the Church are more faithful to traditional values and traditional Church teaching on moral issues. Salient points follow:

- Voters in general who attend religious services only "once or twice a month" moved from 49% for Kerry in 2004 to 60% for Obama in 2008. But among those who "attend church weekly," only "about four-in-ten" supported Obama. And among those who attended "more than once per week," McCain led Obama 60% to 34%.[240]
- Among Catholics, 51% to 40% supported Obama, but 55% to 40% did so among the 18- to 34-year-olds. Since among Catholics (35 years of age or older), McCain and Obama split virtually evenly (46% to 44%), Obama's support among Catholics as a whole is due to the young.[241]
- Among young people in general 18- to 34-years-old, a "significant edge" supported Obama—59% to 35%. Among the religiously unaffiliated in

---

238 Ibid.

239 The survey was conducted by Public Religion Research August 28 to September 19, 2008, of 2,000 adults 18 and older, and an oversample of 974 respondents ages 18–34. According to Catholic News Service, the views of 1,250 younger Catholics and evangelicals 18–34 years old were included so as to compare their views with those given by the adults. Eileen Casey, "Survey shows young Catholics' political views mirror those of peers," CNS, October 14, 2008, www.catholicnews.com. The survey is available at www.faithinpubliclife.org/tools/polls/faps/The%20young%20and%20the%20Faithful.pdf.

240 Faith in Public Life, *The Young and the Faithful,* The Faith and American Politics Survey, October 2008, 2, 5; faithinpubliclife.org/content/faps/.

241 Ibid., 4.

that group, Obama led McCain by an astounding 75% to 18%.[242] But among "young adults who attend religious services once a week or more, McCain's lead (55% to 38%) is similar to his lead among Americans overall who attend religious services once a week or more." Among young adults who attend religious services "once or twice a month or less," however, Obama led 69% to 25%. So Obama's support mainly lay with less religiously affiliated youth. He was also helped by the fact that these "less-frequent attenders" make up 65% of the young adult population, as opposed to only 56% of the general population.[243]

- Abortion: 60% of younger Catholics say abortion should be legal in all or most cases. In this respect, they are closer to their peers overall (58%) than to older Catholics (51%).[244]
- Same-sex marriage: 44% of younger Catholics say same-sex marriage should be legal in committed relationships. In this respect, they are closer to their peers overall (46%) than to older Catholics (26%, an eighteen-point generation gap).[245] Among younger Catholics, 23% support civil unions, as opposed to 37% among older Catholics, and 26% support no recognition as opposed to 32% among older Catholics.[246]
- Finally, younger Catholics "are the most pro-government constituency of any major religious group and even more pro-government than their peers. Two-thirds (67%) of younger Catholics say they prefer bigger government offering more services rather than a small government offering fewer services."[247] This percentage is twenty-six points higher than among older Catholics (41%) and ten points higher than among their peers (57%).[248]

A Barna Study

A Barna study made of 1,003 adult Americans in May 2008 provides further evidence of how liberal Americans are becoming regarding traditional standards of morality, especially among the young.

According to the Barna Group, for example, 19% of adults "admitted to intentional exposure to pornographic images" in the past week, and "21%

---

[242] Ibid.
[243] Ibid., 6.
[244] Ibid., 15.
[245] Ibid., 16.
[246] Ibid., 15.
[247] bid., 16.
[248] Ibid., 15.

of single adults indicated they had sex with someone" in the past week. Those who "describe themselves as 'most liberal' on sociopolitical issues were twice as likely as those who describe themselves as 'mostly conservative' to participate in activities that conflict with traditional moral perspectives." Barna cites as evidence that "liberals were five times more likely to participate in unmarried sex (20% vs. 4%), more than three times as likely to view pornography (30% vs. 8%), more than twice as likely to lie (21% vs. 8) and to get drunk (17% vs. 7%)." Barna found few differences within the Christian community between Protestant and Catholic attitudes.

But Barna argues that one of the "most stunning outcomes" of the study was shown by comparing "the moral pattern" of the "Mosaic generation"—18- to 24-year-olds—to the "Baby Busters"—25- to 43-year-olds—and the "Baby Boomers"—44- to 62-year-olds. The choices the younger generation now makes, the study says, "made even the Baby Boomers—never regarded as a paragon of traditional morality—look like moral pillars in comparison."

Barna asserts that the Mosaic generation is "more than twice as likely as all other adults to engage in behaviors considered morally inappropriate by traditional standards." The Barna Group cites as evidence the fact that the Mosaics were "nine times more likely than were Boomers to have engaged in sex outside of marriage (38% vs. 4%), six times more likely to have lied (37% vs. 6%), almost three times more likely to have gotten drunk (25% vs. 9%) . . . twice as likely as Boomers to have observed pornography (33% vs. 16%) and to have engaged in acts of retaliation (12% vs. 5%)."

Barna says the results of the study reflect a "significant shift in American life." The Barna Group's conclusion is worth citing at length:

> We are witnessing the development and acceptance of a new moral code in America . . . . Mosaics have had little exposure to traditional moral teaching and limited accountability for such behavior. The moral code began to disintegrate when the generation before them—the Baby Busters—pushed the limits that had been challenged by their parents—the Baby Boomers. The result is that without much fanfare or visible leadership, the U.S. has created a moral system based on convenience, feelings, and selfishness.
>
> The consistent deterioration of the Bible as the source of moral truth has led to a nation where people have become independent judges of right and wrong, basing their choices on feelings and circumstances. It is not likely that America will return to a more traditional moral code until the nation experiences significant pain from its moral choices.[249]

---

[249] CNN exit polls, "Role of Religion in Presidential Election," *America* 199 (November 24, 2008): 7.

Conclusion to Part One

While all of the data examined in chapters 1 and 2 do not point in the same direction, there appears to be enough of a consensus to allow us to draw the following conclusions:

1. There appears to be a growing interest in ending abortion on demand. This movement, especially among the young, seems to have sprung from an increased sensitivity to the value of the life of the unborn, to an appreciation among the young of the fact that they have been allowed to be born, and to a growing awareness of the horror of late-term abortion where the life of a human being is so patently being destroyed. Still, the desire to outlaw all directly willed abortion, in conformity with Church teaching, is lacking, even among Catholics. The anti-abortion movement appears to be heading toward the desire to limit circumstances where abortion would be legal to three situations deemed most pressing—rape, incest, and endangerment to the life of the mother.

2. There is a process of erosion underway in the American Catholic Church regarding standards of Catholic value. In general, the process represents a movement away from the more traditional standards of value toward a laissez-faire approach—from a more conservatively oriented mentality to a more progressive or liberal one. This movement exists especially among the young, and especially since the onslaught of the Obama era, thus showing the transferable effect of politics on people's moral views.

3. There is a growing lack of concern to support the teachings of the Church on any issue, especially among the young. Positions on moral, ecclesial, or dogmatic teachings, even when in agreement with the Church, are not held in response to Church teaching, but reflect the judgments of individual conscience.

4. This process of erosion seems to be part of a larger process of erosion going on in American society in which Catholics gladly join. Standards of morality in general are becoming more relaxed, and Catholics seem to find no reason to counteract this trend. Of major importance for Catholics is the desire to be tolerant of all views even should one not personally be in agreement. Morality thus now resides in personal choice reflecting current moods, and not in objective standards.

5. What is remarkable and distressing is that the temperament of laxity is growing at a more rapid pace among Catholics than among Protestants, so that at times popular Protestant morality is now often closer

to traditional Catholic standards than popular Catholic morality. This can only be reflective of the poverty of the Catholic Church's catechetical program and the lack of commitment to the teaching authority of the Church.

6. There is a growing lack of awareness of the place of moral issues in the life of the Church. A growing number of Catholics, even among those closest to the Church, now assert that views on moral issues are not relevant in determining what it means to be a good Catholic.

7. The process of erosion is slowed among those more closely identified with the life of the Church among Protestants as well as Catholics.[250] Among Catholics, the more people identify with the institutional Church, the more closely they adhere to its teachings. Identification with the Church thus seems to create a force that makes it possible to resist the inroads of a secular society. This is certainly one of the greatest values derived from the studies we have examined above. The Church needs to find ways to increase the covenant relationship between God and his people through Christ and his Church.

   If it is to survive, the Church must increase the numbers of those "highly committed" who are eager to participate in the Church's sacramental life and live by its teachings. Those who are committed must also learn that commitment today entails being countercultural witnesses to the faith. The Church of the future can no longer simply reflect the trends of the culture. The Church will need the loyalty of the few—a core group of faithful—to keep the traditions alive that maintain its role in the service of Christ and his people.

8. The process of erosion is especially prevalent among Catholic youth. Youth have increasingly fallen away from loyalty to and identification with the institutional Church in their understanding of their lives as Catholic Christians. The Church seems terribly in danger of losing its youth, who are increasingly motivated by philosophies of individualism and self-fulfillment. Though we have seen some indication of a reversal of this trend by more conservative, traditionally oriented youth who have grown tired of the laissez-faire agenda and are eager to identify themselves with the institutional Church and return to its fixed standards of truth and morality, their numbers are not yet sufficiently large to indicate whether this is a movement that can revitalize the Church, or only a temporary phenomenon. If the process of

250 Barna Group, "Young Adults and Liberals Struggle with Morality," Barna Update, August 25, 2008, www.barna.org.

erosion is to be stemmed, special effort needs to be made to support the growth of this countercultural movement among the youth. Otherwise, the Catholic Church is destined to become more and more a variant of the liberal mainline churches where dogma, structure, and standards of value are evanescing.

9. Inroads of secularization seem especially evident on many Catholic university campuses that have attenuated or abandoned their identification with the institutional Church, and no longer consider support for its teachings relevant to what they are about as Catholic institutions of learning. The Church needs to reassert loyalty to its purposes among these institutions, or no longer allow them to claim to be Catholic.

   According to the 2009 HERI study of freshmen in America's colleges and universities, the new major orientation of freshmen today is toward "doing volunteer or community service work in college." The study notes that in the first freshman survey in 1990, when students were asked if there was a "very good chance" they would engage in such activity, only 16.9% said yes; in 2009, 30.8% said yes, "an increase of 82.2% in just under 20 years." Another 41.3% indicate there is "some chance" they will perform such activity.[251] In view of the downward trend of Christian identification among youth, could this desire to be of service, in itself commendable, be one of the growing signs of the rise of a secular humanism that will replace Christian humanism as a value among today's youth?

It has been said that America is caught in a cultural war, a struggle between two opposing forces for the domination and control of the American psyche. That culture war, as we shall see, exists also within the Catholic Church. The data we have examined seem to indicate that the forces of erosion within the Church are strong and are winning. One senses we are at a critical moment, where the futures of American society as well as of the Catholic Church are at stake. The Church needs to step back, regroup itself, and revitalize its way of evangelizing.

Our investigation of the sources of the modern conflict begins now.

---

[251] To some extent, this may represent the power of religiosity as well as commitment to one's own church.

[252] Pryor, HERI, *American Freshmen 2009*, 10.

PART TWO

History of Crisis in the Enlightenment

CHAPTER THREE

Enlightenment and Relativism

GEORGE WEIGEL, the noted American theologian, has argued that the secularization process, or the de-Christianization of Europe, is in full force in Western Europe, and it may be only a matter of time before it takes over in the United States.[1]

The European Union, he argues, has committed itself to a "politics without God," a "public space from which the God of the Bible has been excluded,"[2] the latest stage in a process of atheistic humanism that broke out with the onslaught of World War I in August 1914 and inflicted "unprecedented eruptions of human wickedness" through August 1991 with the collapse of the Soviet Union.[3] According to Weigel, the future of Europe now hangs in the balance, depending on whether it will be able to revitalize its origins in Christian humanism.[4]

Cormac Cardinal Murphy-O'Connor, archbishop emeritus of Westminster, England, told the National Conference of Priests in September 2001 (just a few days before 9/11) that Christianity in England had just about vanished. He is quoted by the international news agency Zenit as saying:

> It does seem in our countries in Britain today, especially in England and Wales, that Christianity, as a sort of backdrop to people's lives and moral decisions—and to the government, the social life of the country—has now almost been vanquished. . . . There is indifference to Christian values and to the Church among many young people and, indeed, not only

[1] George Weigel, *The Cube and the Cathedral: Europe, America, and Politics without God* (New York: Basic, 2005), 27–28.

[2] Ibid., 159.

[3] Ibid., 35–36.

[4] Ibid., 171.

> the young. You see quite a demoralized society, one where the only good is what I want, the only rights are my own, and the only life with any meaning or value is the life I want for myself. . . . There are many today who think that to believe in God is to limit one's freedom.

Zenit suggests that "Christian life will be all but dead in 40 years" in Britain. It quotes the former Anglican archbishop of Canterbury, George Carey, as saying: "A tacit atheism prevails. Death is assumed to be the end of life. Our concentration on the here-and-now renders a thought of eternity irrelevant."[5] In January 2003, the same news agency wrote that Murphy-O'Connor told the *London Telegraph* that "Britain has become a pagan nation over the past 50 years, creating a vacuum in which people will believe in anything and everything."[6]

The Spanish bishops' conference published a pastoral instruction, dated March 30, 2006, entitled "Theology and Secularization in Spain, Forty Years after the End of Vatican Council II." The president of the doctrinal commission that produced the document, Bishop Eugenio Romero Pose, said the document points out "both the sickness and the cure" for the present situation of the Church in Spain.

The document states what the sickness is: "The main question that the Church in Spain must face is the secularization inside itself. At the origin of this secularization is the loss of faith and of knowledge of the faith." The document goes on to itemize four areas that summarize the heart of the "crisis": "a rationalist conception of the faith and of revelation; an immanentist humanism applied to Jesus Christ; a merely sociological interpretation of the Church; and secularized subjectivism-relativism in Catholic morality." The document criticizes several contemporary theologians whose "erroneous theories" regarding Christ and the Church "have had serious and grave consequences in the life of the Church," shaking the faith of many by "misleading, ambiguous and harmful theological propositions" that have "precluded the joyful transmission of the Gospel." Finally, the bishops find the cure for the problem in "restoring life to the profession of faith" through a proper "interpretation of Scripture," a recognition of "Jesus Christ as the only savior of all men," "the Church as the Body of Christ," and a proper understanding of "moral life."[7] All of these problems are a direct consequence of the Enlightenment and its aftermath, which we shall be addressing in this chapter.

---

[5] Zenit News Agency, "Christianity Almost Defeated in Britain, Cardinal Says," September 6, 2001, www.zenit.org.

[6] Zenit News Agency, "Britain Is a Pagan Country, Says Cardinal Murphy-O'Connor," January 20, 2003, www.zenit.org. These words are the agency's paraphrase.

[7] Sandro Magister, "The Church in Spain Is Sick, but It's Not Zapatero's Fault," July 28, 2006, www.chiesa.espressonline.it.

Are things as bad in the United States? If not, is Catholicism in America moving in the same direction as Western Europe? The history of the founding of the United States makes our situation unique among the developed nations of the Western world for its fusion of the national spirit with the fervor of the Christian mentality. Yet the data in our first chapters suggest that we must reckon with the likelihood that our nation is on a trajectory leading to a situation similar to that which exists in Europe today. Though we have seen that a significant minority in America still attends church regularly—far more than do so in any countries of Western Europe except probably Ireland[8]—the numbers continue to decline, especially among the young, and the influence of Christian values is sliding precipitously.

The situation of the Church is grave. What is the cause of this situation? Surely there are many. But it is the major thesis of this book that the heart of the problem resides in the gradual destructive effect of a movement known as the Enlightenment, which came into prominence in the Western world in the eighteenth century and is now wreaking havoc in the widespread acceptance of the residues of the movement known as relativism and nihilism, the inevitable ultimate consequences of the Enlightenment mentality.

Benedict XVI has iterated frequently, right up to the day before he was elected pope on April 19, 2005, the central problem of relativism for our time:

> We are moving toward a dictatorship of relativism that does not recognize anything as certain and has as its highest goal one's own ego and one's own desires.[9]

He states definitively:

> So in fact relativism has become the central problem for faith in our time.[10]

Benedict has argued that relativism came into vogue in recent history especially after the collapse of the Marxist philosophy, which had replaced belief, knowledge, and truth with scientific materialism and then left nothing in its wake except either nihilism or relativism: "The failure of the one

---

[8] Catholics attending Mass in Ireland "still number around 40 to 45 per cent each week. In addition, the traditional devotions remain strong: tens of thousands still go to Marian shrines such as Fatima and Lourdes each year, and our own Marian shrine, Knock, remains one of the most visited places in Ireland." David Quinn, "Too Little, Too Late, Again," *The Tablet* 264 (February 27, 2010): 9.

[9] Joseph Cardinal Ratzinger, "Future Pope's Homily for Conclave's Opening," April 18, 2005, *Origins* 34: 720.

[10] Joseph Cardinal Ratzinger, *Truth and Tolerance: Christian Belief and World Religions*, trans. Henry Taylor (San Francisco: Ignatius, 2004 [2003]), 117.

system [Marxism] incorporating a scientifically based solution to human problems could only favor nihilism or at any rate absolute relativism."[11]

This Enlightenment mentality is currently in major combat with the more traditional Christian outlook on life and the latter seems to be losing the battle. Whether the two perspectives can be reconciled is a question we will have to face later in this work, but the heart of the clash between relativism and traditional thinking is over the issue of truth.

What Is Truth?

The focus of the problem resides in one simple word: *truth*. What is it? But there is a second problem allied with the first that is almost equally as important, because, as soon as one asks the first question, the second question logically arises: How does one have *knowledge* of it? For even if there were agreement on what truth is, this would not necessarily provide agreement on how one knew it. In fact, the second question may have been even more troubling throughout the course of history than the first, for without a satisfactory answer to the second question, it really wouldn't matter if truth existed or not, since one could not be sure that one knew it.

The two questions have gone hand in hand throughout the course of history, and really cannot be separated. There is no question that has troubled the history of the human race more than these two, and how they are answered determines not only the meaning and direction of individual personal lives, but also the course of social and political history. By the thirteenth century, the Western world had generally worked out satisfactory answers to these questions, but in the fourteenth century, consensus began to break down. By the eighteenth century, widespread disagreement had set in, leading gradually to the situation today of massive confusion known as postmodernism.

Allied with the questions regarding the existence and knowledge of truth is the equally troubling question of its nature: whether truth is objective or only subjective. If truth is only subjective, then truth is true only for me, the subject; if truth is objective, it has existence in itself, independently of me. This issue has plagued modern thought, and today, much of society holds that there is no objective truth, but only what is true for me. Clearly there are serious philosophical issues involved in the understanding of truth, but the differing perspectives over the centuries do not simply reflect disagreement about abstract questions. Theoretical perspectives are so much influenced by social and political forces that one cannot discuss the question of truth without examining at the same time the persons and movements that directed those forces.

---

[11] Ibid.

There are two possible philosophical conflicts at play here, and three social forces.

Philosophical Conflicts

1. **Reason vs. revelation.** There is the potential conflict between *reason* and *revelation*. How one resolves this possible conflict affects not only one's understanding of what truth is, but also how one knows it. Let us take for granted for the moment that truth exists. Does one know it simply by the powers of reason alone, or is some form of revelation required? And if the latter, where does this revelation come from?

   The issues involved here are extremely complicated. For if one argues that unaided reason knows truth simply by the use of its own intrinsic powers of intuition and logically structured thought, one has apparently a simple foundation for determining truth. But several weaknesses arise. For one, nothing would be true that could not be known by reason. This would necessarily exclude the possibility of God making known truths beyond the power of reason to grasp them. And so, if one argued that God could make known suprarational truth through revelation, a conflict would arise for the strict rationalist. But if an infinite God exists, could not such truths theoretically exist as well?

   Secondly, what would the norm for truth be for reason left to itself? It may be human perception based on scientific experimentation or sensible observation (this is the empirical method). The problem is, our senses so often deceive us. How could one be sure of having truth based on fallible data? Or truth may be based on the clarity of my ideas and their logically structured thought (this is the rationalist method). The problem here is that what is clear and acceptable in my rational processes of thought often conflicts with those of others. Who, then, would decide which is true? Reason, operating by itself alone, finds it especially difficult to conclude with certainty to a truth when another mind, operating by its own intrinsic rational processes, comes to a different and perhaps conflicting conclusion.

   And so a distinct advantage is provided if one holds that reason, in addition to what it can know through its own intrinsic powers, is guided in its understanding of truth by revelation understood as truth provided by God. The certainty of such truth would be axiomatic, because if God has provided it, it must be true (otherwise, God would be either fallible or deceptive and thus not be God). Truth known through revelation is therefore certain and immutable. Stability is thus provided to our process for knowing truth that reason alone could never provide.

A possible systematic weakness here is that the instrument of knowledge in grasping revelation is primarily *faith*: Only the believer can know truths that God reveals. So if one is not a believer, revealed truth becomes inaccessible to that person. A second factor to note here is the role of outside authority: revealed truth is accepted on the authority of God. Though this is not a weakness to reason, it certainly indicates a limitation to its power. Accepting truth on the authority of another is a problem to the Enlightenment mind, for such a system demands a humbling role for reason. Reason's powers become secondary: reason in the case of revelation does not know truth primarily by its own processes of thought, but seeks to *understand* truth given to it by God in a way that is compatible with its nature.

A good example of how faith and reason operate together may be shown in the Christian teaching regarding God. Christianity holds that I can know from reason alone that God exists. There are many good philosophical arguments for the existence of God, the best being the argument from contingency: Everything that exists needs a cause, either itself or another. Since everything that comes into existence is caused by another, ultimately a First Cause is required as the foundation for all reality, and this is God. In this case, though revelation is not strictly speaking required, nevertheless revelation can aid reason, for revelation makes even more certain that there is a God. In Christianity, it is the God who reveals himself in Judeo-Christian history who is ultimately the foundation for my faith in him. But it is valuable and important to have reason's support for what I know from faith.

Other good instances of how faith and reason cooperate give much more of a role to faith, as, for example, in our knowledge of God as a trinity of Persons. If one accepts God as a unity of three divine persons, as Christianity teaches, this truth is surely known only by revelation. The Christian accepts this truth in faith, but then proceeds through rational investigation to make the truth understandable as far as possible to the human mind. The role of reason here is to make sure the revelation is not accepted in a way that would be irrational or incompatible with human reason. In this case, reason is an instrument in the service of revelation, but not the norm of truth. Reason has revelation to guide it and prevent it from accepting deviation from truth. This system that has reason's search for truth supported by faith's acceptance of revelation as the ultimate standard of truth provides a certainty and stability to one's understanding of truth that supersedes all other systems in the search for truth.

2. **Universal vs. particular.** A second potential conflict involves the opposition between the *universal* and the *particular*. Particular knowledge always involves knowledge of the individual or the singular: for example, I am of a friend of Louis, an individual person; or I know that I, an individual human being, exist. Knowledge of universals would mean that I know that Louis and I are both members of the group known as human beings. Or again, I see an individual animal that I address as Fido, but I also recognize that Fido belongs to a group, or a universal, known as dogs. Normally knowledge is understood to involve an awareness of the fact that the singular is an individual within a universal grouping. But the problem here is whether that universal has reality. As we shall see, the history of knowledge is plagued by whether or not there is a foundation to the universal.

This is an especially important question in the realm of morality or ethics, since norms of morality are always applied to universals. It is not simply wrong to murder Louis or me, it is wrong to murder any human being. It may also be wrong to kill Fido, but we do not call such an action "murder." That is because murder applies only to the deliberate killing of an innocent human being. What this implies, then, is knowledge of essences, which are roughly comparable to universals. What I perceive in Louis is that he is essentially a member of the group known as humans, whereas Fido is essentially a member of the group known as dogs. While Fido is a living, sentient animal, Louis is a living, sentient person having intellect and will. While both are intrinsically valuable, the latter is essentially of greater intrinsic value.

We normally think of the evil involved in murder as of a totally different order than the evil involved in killing a dog, even though neither in itself may be desirable. The point here is that, in order to make judgments of morality that have a foundation in reality, there has to be an awareness of the essence of that to which we are referring, and of that essence as having some foundation in reality. Moral judgments are always about universals or essences. But if I don't know or can't know universals, then I am really not able to argue that there is any foundation in reality for moral or ethical statements. Such is the problem that developed in history, then, over whether knowledge is only of existing particulars, or whether knowledge is rooted in the reality of universal essences.

The greatest certainty of having knowledge is provided when there is an integration of what is known through reason and revelation with what is known about particulars and universals; that is, when I know something to be true because what I know by reason is rooted in revelation and philosophically supported by a knowledge of particulars that has a foundation in universals. Without revelation, reason loses a solid basis for truth; without universals, moral statements about the particular have no objective foundation.

Subjective vs. Objective

The problem with the predicament in which we find ourselves today is that a major part of modern society denies the existence of both revelation and universals, or, more to the point, denies that either revelation or universals provide knowledge or have an objective foundation. This problem inevitably raises an allied question about what is *subjective* versus *objective*, the former being that which is true only for me, the latter that which has validity independently of me.

If knowledge is only knowledge of the subjective, all truth is relative to the subject and therefore subjective. If objective truth exists, it inevitably involves a discussion of the existence and knowledge of universal essences that have some foundation in reality as a basis for truth independent of the subject. Our modern world has largely denied the existence of essences, and therefore, the existence of objective truth, and we call the philosophy that does this *relativism.* It is the major scourge afflicting the modern world.

Church vs. Philosophy, Science, and Politics

The problems of reason versus revelation and the universal versus the particular have arisen in the course of history in three different ways during the Christian era:

1. **Between the Church and philosophers.** The Christian Church has traditionally argued for a knowledge rooted in the revelation of God. In the early history of the Church, revelation was the primary source of knowledge. Reason was conjoined with revelation to provide the rational explanation or support of the faith, but was not considered a system of thought independent of revelation as it became in the late Middle Ages. In the time of the Fathers of the Church, revelation was known in the history of the Jewish people as recorded in the Hebrew Scriptures, and brought to fullness in God's Son, Jesus Christ, in the New Testament. This revelation has provided a security and solidity to the theological and moral life of the Church that is unshakable.

   Such knowledge, however, can only have meaning if it is rationally supported by the reality of universals that provide knowledge of essences with a foundation in reality. A typical Christian statement of faith, such as "God has revealed in Jesus Christ that he is the Son of God and savior of the human race," only makes sense if there exists a reality known as the human race. Even to affirm "God exists" implies an ability to know truth independently of myself, a truth that applies not only to me but to the whole human race. Without knowledge of objective truth and an ability to affirm the existence of men and women, all having the same human essence, for whom the revelation of Christ and his saving death are valid, Christianity is without meaning.

The role of reason since the beginnings of Greek philosophy was to search for objective truth and the meaning of life and death. With the coming of Christ and the Christian revelation, Christians understood that search as completed: truth, or "beatifying knowledge,"[12] was now to be found in Christ and his revelation of God and God's will; life became meaningful in that it was destined for salvation in eternal union with God beyond death. Such knowledge was available only to faith, but it was validated by knowledge that came from human reason. Thus faith and reason supported each other, and in their "aim to make all things Christian," Christians joined "the words of Christ with those of men to provide a unified outlook on the world."[13]

According to Ratzinger, a "fusion of Christianity and philosophy" occurred in Christ: "the figure of the philosopher now becomes the image of Christ himself," and Christ becomes "the perfect philosopher": "Philosophy, the search for meaning in the face of death, is now represented as the search for Christ." The philosopher who typified this fusion was Justin Martyr (c. 100–164):[14] "As early as the second century, Justin Martyr had characterized Christianity as the true philosophy, for which he adduced two main reasons. First, the philosopher's essential task is to search for God. Second, the attitude of the true philosopher is to live according to the Logos [Reason] and in its company. Christian existence means life in conformity to the Logos; that is why Christians are the true philosophers and why Christianity is the true philosophy."[15]

According to Justin, there were two ways to explain "how philosophers have found the truth": through their study of the Bible, and

[12] R. V. Harvanek, "Patristic Philosophy," *New Catholic Encyclopedia* (*NCE*), 2nd rev. ed. (Detroit: Gale, 2003 [1967]), 10:959. All subsequent *NCE* references are from this edition.

[13] E. A. Maziarz, "Philosophy," *NCE*, 11:276.

[14] "Justin was the first Christian 'philosopher'—not only because he professed philosophy before his conversion and called himself a philosopher as a Christian, but especially because he made the basic distinction between the logos of revelation and the logos of Greek philosophy or of reason" (Harvanek, *NCE*, 10:958).

[15] Joseph Cardinal Ratzinger, "Faith, Philosophy and Theology," address delivered at the College of St. Thomas in St. Paul, MN, 1984, in Ratzinger, *The Nature and Mission of Theology: Essays to Orient Theology in Today's Debates*, trans. Adrian Walker (San Francisco: Ignatius, 1995 [1993]), 14–15.

independently of the biblical revelation, through their participation in Christ, the "divine LOGOS," the "universal reason, the 'seminal logos' in which all rational beings participate; therefore seeds of truth are found in everyone endowed with reason."[16]

A major problem in the modern world, then, is the growing separation between philosophers and the Church, whereby philosophers argue more and more to the separation of reason from revelation, and to a foundation for truth that is known by the operations of reason alone quite apart from what one may hold in faith. What the history of modern philosophy shows is that philosophy, once it is uprooted from its moorings in revelation, inevitably loses a sure foundation; in other words, it inevitably is reduced to relativism and therefore becomes inconsequential and even nihilist. For a philosophy that has only relative value is in fact no philosophy at all. And that is why, as we shall see, Plato was so concerned to ground truth in the existence of the universal, to keep truth from being relative.

2. **Between the Church and science.** Before the natural and physical sciences became so highly developed in the seventeenth and eighteenth centuries, they did not have an existence independent of the Church. As hard as it is to accept today, it is nevertheless true that the major impetus for the development of the sciences came from the institutional Church and faith in the Christian revelation as the source of truth. It was Christianity that promoted the development of the sciences in the Western world (though credit must be given to Islam as well). Their role was to investigate the world through scientific instruments in order to provide a more technical knowledge of the world that could only be known through mathematics, the hard sciences, and the instruments of technology. That science was cooperating with what was already known by faith was a given.

   But this was to change. Beginning in the fourteenth century and especially in the Ages of Science and Reason in the seventeenth and eighteenth centuries, the union between faith and science became unglued. Louis Dupré finds no principle more conducive to the deism and atheism of the modern age than Descartes' and Newton's notion of a "causality conceived on a mechanistic model" to explain movement in the universe. Such a model relegated God to the order of "a remote Prime Mover responsible for the motion of the universe" or deism. The problem is, once "the need for an external source of mechanical motion

[16] H. Chadwick, "Justin Martyr, St.," *NCE*, 8:94.

ceased to exist," atheism inevitably followed,[17] to the point where it is largely taken for granted today either that faith and science not only have nothing in common, making faith irrelevant to science, or that the two are in fact in conflict with each other (though one is beginning to see signs of some reversal of this alienation).[18]

3. **Between the Church and politics.** For good or for bad (and probably both), the Church had for centuries been aligned with ruling governments. This goes back to the time of the Emperor Constantine in the fourth century. There was much to be gained from this patronage for the Church. For one thing, there was no longer the massive suffering from persecution by the Roman Empire that plagued the life of the early Church. Official acceptance by emperors and kings also aided enormously in bringing prestige to the Church, leading many of the intellectuals and members of the upper classes to convert to Christianity (official approval brings corporate status). Such approval also abetted the spread of the Christian religion throughout the Roman Empire both in the West and in the East. The point is that church and state by and large worked in harmony, so that what was approved by the one was generally approved by the other. Each supported the well-being of the other.

   But there was something undesirable at the same time in this association. Too close an identification of the Church with secular powers risks the Church's losing its identity with the poor and marginal members of society: in France the masses, "pressed by economic

[17] Louis Dupré, *The Enlightenment and the Intellectual Foundations of Modern Culture* (New Haven, CT: Yale, 2004), 243. Dupré's conclusion is confirmed by Michael J. Buckley, who argues in his classic work on atheism that atheism has resulted as a consequence of the Church's arguments for the existence of God not from his revelation in Jesus Christ, but from philosophical design. Atheists argue that "chance rules the lives of human beings, not an orderly providence." The problem is that if the Church roots belief in God primarily in arguments from design and such arguments are rejected, so is a basis for belief in God. Cf. Michael J. Buckley, S.J., *At the Origins of Modern Atheism* (New Haven, CT: Yale, 1987), 48–49.

[18] Two prominent scientists who held numerous appointments in science and religion and stress their compatibility are John Polkinghorne, once professor of mathematical physics, and ordained an Anglican priest in 1982; and Arthur Peacocke (d. 2006), a British theologian and biochemist, who was ordained an Anglican priest in 1971. Francis Collins, a physician and geneticist, formerly director of the National Human Genome Research Institute and now Director of the National Institutes of Health, states that he was an atheist in graduate studies, but came to see DNA as "God's language, and the elegance and complexity of our own bodies and the rest of nature as a reflection of God's plan." Francis Collins, "Why This Scientist Believes in God," CNN.US, April 3, 2007, www.articles.cnn.com/2007-04-03/US/Collins.commentary_1_god-dna-revelation?_s=PM:US.

hardship, felt abandoned by a Church closely linked to a political regime indifferent to their suffering."[19] Church-state alliances increase the likelihood that the Church will take the side of the strong and the wealthy from whom it will seek favors regarding matters of economic well-being and political and social justice. The causes of truth and justice are best aided by the Church when it is unattached to ideological interests.

The fact is, then, that increasingly from the fourth century on, the Church developed a comfortable association with leading rulers of the West and its thinking held hegemony in the West: "In past centuries religion had been the integrating factor of Western culture; in the eighteenth century it was forced to the sidelines. Christianity had once formed the core of Western culture: the Church ruled intellectual life, directed the universities, set the norms of moral conduct. For a long period she had also controlled the political structures."[20]

As a result, the major development for which the Church was not ready was the revolutionary spirit that arose in the modern world against the powerful imperial Church-state structures and establishments. A secular spirit desiring freedom and independence from monarchical rulers became an increasing factor in the spread of nationalism and socioeconomic developments in the middle classes. The problem that this spirit of freedom and independence created for the Church was simply this, that when revolutionary forces struggled to overthrow the overbearing weight of monarchical structures that were felt to be oppressive, these forces generally also felt the need to extricate themselves from the domination of the institutional Church and the Church's hierarchy with which monarchies had generally been allied.

There is nothing intrinsically inimical between the Church and a desire to be free, and in an ideal world no conflict between the two would ever have been necessary. But the historical situation being what it was, freedom became largely identified with revolutionary forces, and oppression with established orders, including the Church. This situation in turn led the hierarchy to view revolutionary, anti-establishment movements not simply as threats to the stability of established governments, often seen as endowed with divine rights to rule and as the sole protectors of peace and order in society, but also as threats to the order and stability of the Church with which those governments were allied, and to the will of God in history. As a result, the right to be free from tyranny was often not recognized by the Church

[19] Dupré, *Enlightenment*, 229.

[20] Ibid., 229–30.

as a legitimate right of the individual, but as a call to social anarchy and to disobedience to the will of God.

The democratic form of government was not seen by the Church in earlier centuries as an acceptable form of government, because it implied not only opening the world to the chaos that comes from excessive individualism, but also accepting an ideology that understood received dogma and Church order, as decreed by God in his revelation for the salvation of the human race, as matters to be overthrown and to be replaced by religious conviction decided on the basis of individual choice.

The Church was caught in a clash between the movement toward personal independence which history was taking, and a tradition espousing the values of external authority, stability, divine right of rulers and hierarchy, and the primacy of God's revelation as the source of truth. Thus history and modernity became an enemy of the Church. This alienation between Church and society, especially felt in France in the eighteenth century where the Church had so long allied itself with political power, made many philosophers, scientists, and revolutionaries see the Church as an institution impeding historical progress that needed to be destroyed, just as much as the Church felt it was necessary to destroy freedom and the chaos that would result if the antiestablishment movement should prevail.

When we look back on history from today's perspective, we can see how unfortunate it was that this alienation developed. There were good reasons for the Church to be fearful of the unleashing of these democratic forces, especially when freedom became identified with license to do and think anything. Politically, that leads to anarchy; philosophically, to relativism. Since Vatican II, there is no political movement more closely supported by the Church than democracy. But it took hundreds of years for the Church to come to the realization that democracy is not necessarily a force of evil destructive of God's plan for the world, but can be with proper direction a political system that is a major instrument in the service of God's purposes for salvation.

We need now to focus more closely on the issues and controversies that occurred throughout history in the struggle between reason and revelation and the particular and the universal, so as to get a better understanding of the roots of the modern crisis in the Church.

Reason and Revelation

Reason got a head start on Christian revelation, since philosophy had its origins back at least to sixth century B.C. Greece. The biblical period is of course caught up in the amazing experience of the revelation of the Incarnation, death, and Resurrection of Jesus Christ understood as the turning point in history and the beginning of the new age. After the end of the New Testament period, when the early Church Fathers began to realize it was necessary to systematize their understanding of the faith, it was inevitable that concepts from the dominant Hellenistic philosophy that surrounded them would be introduced in their understanding of Christianity. Tensions were not unusual at this early stage, however: Was the role of faith to clarify the insights already gained through Greek philosophy, or was philosophy to be used as a tool for understanding the faith? Currents of thought moved in both directions. However, it was not long before the Fathers made philosophy the instrument for understanding the faith. Philosophy was valuable, for one thing, in defending the faith against the pagan philosophers. But philosophy could also be understood as a preparation for the gospel, at least when its views were consistent with the teachings of Christ.[21] As a result, patristic theology became a combination of Judeo-Christian and Hellenistic thought used to clarify and defend the Christian revelation.[22]

Following the initial period of tension and caution regarding philosophy, a second period might be designated where philosophy began to be accepted as a discipline integral to the understanding and defense of the faith. This was especially true in the theology of St. Augustine (354–430), who found the greatest support for understanding Christianity from Platonic philosophy. In Augustine, faith and reason are "distinct but inseparable sources of learning." For Augustine, faith was the primary source of knowledge because it was rooted in the revelation of God in Jesus Christ. But Platonic thought was immensely valuable for providing a systematic structure of thought that made the various elements of the faith rationally intelligible. Augustine seems never to have envisioned philosophy as an autonomous body of knowledge or as having any role other than to explicate the faith.[23] For Augustine, reason and revelation were "parallel paths to the truth," but one believed first and then used reason to understand.[24] It was Augustine, then, who set the tone for the unity of reason and revelation right through to the late medieval period, although a more rational attitude slowly becomes stronger as one moves from a more "pastoral and monastic" use of philosophy during the first ten centuries to a more "scholarly and scientific" attitude with the high Scholasticism of the thirteenth century.[25] It is with the advent of the fourteenth century that this happy integration begins to fall apart.

[21] I. C. Brady, "Medieval Philosophy," *NCE*, 11:290.
[22] F. X. Murphy, "Patristic Theology," *NCE*, 10:964.
[23] R. P. Russell, "Augustinianism," *NCE*, 1:876.
[24] R. J. Teske, "Augustine, St.," *NCE*, 1:862.
[25] L.-B. Geiger, "Christian Philosophy," *NCE*, 3:539.

PARTICULAR AND UNIVERSAL

Plato

Truth—what is it, can we know it, and how do we know it—was the issue that vexed most of all the Greek philosopher Plato (427–347 B.C.). He felt that life was impossible without a foundation in truth—that the human being could not survive without satisfying the need to know truth. But everything in the world is constantly changing. Everything is here for one instant and already different the next. Nothing we see is ever permanent. Truth for Plato could not reside in what is continually changing, for then truth would have no meaning beyond the instant. Truth can only reside in what is permanent and immutable, and then knowing it would provide stability and certainty in life. Thus, for Plato, there had to be not only truth, but also the ability to know the truth, if life was to be meaningful and worth living. So what was the truth for Plato, and how did he know it?

Plato was what philosophers call an ultra or absolute realist. By this we mean that for Plato, truth resided in really existing immutable universals that denoted the essences of things.

When Plato saw Louis and Mary and Henry, he realized that they were all human beings (what Aristotle would later call "rational animals"). But there were many other human beings besides these three. What was common to all of them was that they participated, or shared, in the essence of human being. Plato concluded that this essence was a universal because it applied to all members of the human race. For Plato, the universal essences, or forms, really existed in a realm independent of the experience of changing things. It was the forms that were truly real, whereas sensible things are merely illusion, or if they had any existence, they got it only by participation in the absolute forms. "Only essence [truly] is, with its characteristics of perfection and stability."[26] Knowledge resided in the intuition of the essences of things, a perception of which we are reminded (by a process he called "reminiscence") when we see the mutable, sensible, passing versions.

With Plato, then, there are three orders to consider: the ultimate foundation of truth that resides in the universal and unchanging essences, which truly exist independently of this world; the participated reflection of the universals in the changing sensible versions of them; and the universal concepts in the mind through which we see the ultimate essences of things when we look at the participated versions of them in our world. The universal form really exists, whereas the universal concept has only mental existence, but it has contact with reality and knows truth, which it perceives in its understanding of the universal form as reflected in the sensible participations in the world.

[26] M. Corvez, "Essence," *NCE*, 5:361.

One can see the beauty of this system: it gives stability and security in knowledge of unchanging and immutable truth. I know, for example, the essence of human being, and that that essence will never change. Based on my knowledge of the truth regarding human beings, I am therefore able to develop an ethics or a moral system of values regarding human beings that will also be certain and immutable. I am able to say, for example, that it is wrong to commit murder, based upon an awareness of the intrinsic value of human life that was always true, is true now, and will forever be true. So does that make the moral principle forever true.

Aristotle

Problems already begin to develop with the philosophy of Plato's student, Aristotle (384–322 B.C.). He is called a moderate realist because he denied the existence of immutable essences in a realm independent of the world of existing things, or as one scholar says, he "insisted on the immanence of concrete forms and on the true causality of particular causes on particular effects."[27] Aristotle brought the essences down into the concrete realities of sensible experience. For Aristotle, the human being belongs to the genus "animal," and is specifically different from all other animals by reason of the fact that the human being is rational. The essence of the human being, then, is rational animal. When the human mind looks at Louis and Mary and Henry, then, it abstracts, or draws away, from the individuated rational animal a universal concept of rational animal that it derives from the experience of the individuated essence of human being, which then may be validly applied to all members of that species. Thus I continue to have real knowledge of Louis and Mary and Henry as rational animals through the universal concept I have of them, which I acquired from my experience of them, and from my abstraction of their essence that I perceived as really present in them in that experience.

The difference here, as against Plato, is that the universal as universal exists only in the mind for Aristotle. It exists in reality only as individuated or concrete essence. The universal essence of rational animal as a universal in the mind has a basis of objectivity in the concrete individuated essence or form of rational animal I experience in the world. The basis for truth and knowledge here is only the individuated essence of rational animal, not a universal rational animal existing independently of the singulars.

Though it still seems possible to construct an ethics with Aristotle's system, such an ethics is nevertheless based upon truth or knowledge of reality that has its only objective foundation in the individuated existing essences. Aristotle's system is hampered by the lack of knowledge of an

[27] C. Fabro, "Participation," *NCE*, 10:906.

existing ultimate foundation for a universally valid truth perceived in the essences. To state the matter philosophically, he has lost a metaphysics of universal essences.

Without that ultimate foundation for truth, where does the stability and certainty of immutable truth reside? Only in the perception of the individuated essences I experience in a changing world. I will, therefore, have difficulty justifying the certainty of my perception in the face of conflicting perceptions. So, for example, if I assert that it is intrinsically wrong to commit murder, I must now justify that truth only on the basis of my perception of the intrinsic worth of the human being as I find it present in the individuated essences of human beings. If another disagrees with my evaluation, I have no more ultimate foundation for my conviction to which I can appeal for support. Thus, an Aristotelian system of ethics may be said to be less secure than a Platonic one. It still has a basis of objectivity, but has no existing ultimate immutable principle by which it can philosophically justify its position in the face of controversy. There is no existing immutable essence of human being in which existing human beings participate.

Thomas Aquinas

With St. Augustine comes the theory of divine ideas as the cause of the essences in things. In a sense, this is a restoration of Plato's really existing essences, though they are now placed in the divine mind. It is, then, really the divine essence that is participated in by the existing human essence.

We have a harmonious systematization of all three positions with the philosophy of moderate realism of St. Thomas Aquinas (A.D. 1224–1274). Absolute essences exist in the divine mind in Thomas, and they come by divine causality into existence in creation through participation in the divine essence. Therefore, the three orders are now unified in a more satisfactory philosophical system: The absolute forms of Plato do not exist in some ethereal world, but are identified with the divine mind; the individuated form or essence in the things of the world now exists by participation in the being of the Creator; and the individuated essence is known by the human mind through the universal concept or mental construct that has been abstracted from the perception of the existing essence from which the concept gets its objective validity.

Theological, philosophical, and moral truth obtain solidity in their understanding of truth. Universals get a solid foundation in truth by their being grounded in the existence of Absolute Truth, God; individuated essences get a foundation for truth by their participation in the divine essence that they reflect; and the objective validity of the knowledge that is known through universal concepts in the mind is established by their being grounded in the individuated essence or form present in a single existing being.

By the end of the thirteenth century, the Western world was largely united in accepting that revelation is the ultimate foundation of the knowledge of God, the human being, and the world. Because it is God's revelation, it is certain and immutable; it provides permanent stability. It makes it possible for the human mind to know with a knowledge provided by God himself. No greater solidity for truth can be found.

Revelation by definition provides us with a knowledge that is beyond the capacity of the human mind to know by its own powers. Such knowledge is made known by God through the history of his dealings with the world, especially in Judeo-Christian history, as recorded in the Hebrew Scriptures and in the Incarnation of God's Son, Jesus Christ, as made known in the New Testament.

The role of reason is humbly to accept the knowledge provided by revelation as made known in the dogmas and Tradition of the Church, and to endeavor ever more to probe revelation for greater understanding through rational investigation. When it comes to providing a philosophical apparatus that explains human understanding of reality and the acquisition of truth, Christian scholars concluded to a doctrine of this-worldly participation in the divine essence, and to the ability of the human mind to know through universal concepts the foundation for universal truth in individuated essences existing in extramental reality.

To put it concretely: there is the *universal essence* of the human being in the divine mind; there is the *individuated essence* of the human being existing in the created world; and there is the *universal concept* of the human being in the human mind, and all are interrelated—the second by *participation* in the first, the last by *abstraction* from the second. A foundation is thereby provided for certain knowledge of objective philosophical and moral truths about the nature of the human being.

Thus, I know the essence of the human being as an intrinsically valuable person by reason of its participation by creation in God's own life and understanding of what human existence is; and I know that the universal concept by which I know the intrinsic worth of a human being has an objective foundation in God's own existence and in what it means to be a human being in God's own mind. Thus when I state that it is wrong to commit murder, I know the statement to be true based on an objective understanding of the intrinsic worth of human nature as it participates in God's own essence.

This is the kind of knowledge and certitude regarding truth that was bequeathed to the Western world by the end of the thirteenth century.

How, then, did we get from this secure understanding of truth based on a conjunction of revelation, reason, and universal concepts, to the situation of our postmodern world that rejects revelation as a principle of knowledge, rejects the ability of reason to know objective truth, and rejects the validity of universal concepts? In other words, how did we get from knowing so much to knowing so little?

TRIUMPH OF RELATIVISM AND SUBJECTIVISM

A simple way to explain the forces of opposition in our society today is to see life as a struggle between the idea of truth as objective and truth as subjective, between truth that is real and truth that is only in the mind. Relativism sides with the latter in each pairing, traditional thinking with the former.

The subjectivist mentality is deeply embedded in our culture today. It is rooted in a philosophy based on relativism—the notion that all truth is relative, meaning that truth has no foundation independent of the perspective of the person who holds it. Thus all truth is a product of the subject's viewpoint and has no validity apart from the subject. Objectively, then, all viewpoints are put on an even plane, since one perspective is no more valid than another. This mentality infects the minds of nearly all Americans today, especially the young.

Allan Bloom

Allan Bloom created a sensation in the late '80s when he published *The Closing of the American Mind: How Higher Education Has Failed Democracy and Impoverished the Souls of Today's Students*. Though not especially well written, the book was an instant best seller, and remained on best-selling lists for many weeks, first in hardback and later in paperback. People couldn't get enough of it, though it was often called the most unread best seller in America.

Bloom's thesis was summed up in the ironic introductory chapter, "Our Virtue," and its now-famous first sentence: "There is one thing a professor can be absolutely certain of: almost every student entering the university believes, or says he believes, that truth is relative." Students are unable to defend their position, Bloom argues, nor have they ever tried to do so, because they accept it not on the basis of philosophical insight, but for political reasons. They see it as the condition of possibility for a free society: "Openness—and the relativism that makes it the only plausible stance in the face of various claims to truth and various ways of life and kinds of human beings—is the great insight of our times."[28]

According to Bloom, the students have been indoctrinated to accept this "virtue" of openness by a massive movement in education that began early in the twentieth century. Whereas the Founding Fathers had argued in the

[28] Allan Bloom, *The Closing of the American Mind* (New York: Simon and Schuster, 1987), 26.

Declaration of Independence to the equality of human beings and their right to be free based on the inherent dignity of the human person as endowed by the Creator, students now claim equal rights and dignities as a consequence of the relativity of truth. Should anyone argue that truth is not relative but objective, Bloom continues, that person will be accused of being intolerant and a danger to a free society. For the relativist, "The true believer is the real danger," Bloom concludes. "The study of history and of culture teaches that all the world was mad in the past; men always thought they were right, and that led to wars, persecutions, slavery, xenophobia, racism, and chauvinism."[29] Instead of trying to correct these evils through a search for truth, Bloom argues, students opt for the naïve view that relativism will overcome a basis for conflict, the point being that since with relativism all "truths" end up having equal value, there is no "right" or "truth" to fight over.

With this kind of thinking, the deleterious effect upon educational policies is enormous, says Bloom. In addition to the suspicion it levels against the person of conviction, this "cultural relativism" leads to an "openness of indifference" to the truth, which is in fact not openness, but a closing of the mind to truth.[30] In an effort to be consistent, the student is forced to accept, at least theoretically, being tolerant of falsehood, moral evil, and ironically, even prejudice, because a basis for challenging such views has been lost. But by allowing everyone to champion one's own views as the "truth," a basis for national unity rooted in commonly accepted principles is undermined. For by this philosophy of tolerance, "there is no enemy other than the man who is not open to everything." Thus we have one of many inconsistencies in relativism, for tolerance is extended to every idea and every person—except to the person of moral conviction.[31]

Phillippe Bénéton

In an effort to promote tolerance, convictions regarding truth and morality are reduced to opinion, says Philippe Bénéton, a professor of political science in France. To be tolerant in this view is to cling to the opinion that everything is a matter of opinion, and of equal opinions at that. Each person must take his bearings from his sovereign subjectivity, and no one has the right to put forth a universal standard. To affirm that a particular proposition is true by itself, apart from mere opinion, is considered an attack on tolerance.[32]

---

[29] Ibid.

[30] Ibid., 38, 41.

[31] Ibid., 27.

[32] Philippe Bénéton, "True and False Tolerance," *Crisis* 14 (April 1996): 34. Note Bénéton's observation that with a philosophy of tolerance and truth as subjective comes the loss of the validity of universal concepts of morality.

According to Bénéton, the misconceived idea of freedom as the sovereign authority of individual choice ultimately leads to the destruction of the meaning of choice, since if all ideas are equal, there is no rational foundation "to justify the choice for liberty, equality, or democracy" over tyranny. The fact that persons espousing this kind of tolerance stop short of being tolerant toward what they consider to be intolerant shows the philosophical inadequacy of their system.

But philosophical consistency is not their goal. Like Bloom, Bénéton argues that this misguided notion of tolerance is actually the first stage in a process that is politically motivated. In appearing to reduce all ideas to a relative standard of equality, modernists are subtly moving public thought toward "appropriate ways of being" that favor a "social moralism" where relativism ultimately gives way to generic "moral imperatives" such as "the denunciation of evil and compassion for suffering mankind." When this process arrives at its final stage, these "activists of equality," while not technically renouncing relativism, claim that their moral viewpoint represents the dominant opinion, the views of today's "supposed majority," and therefore should prevail. Thus morality is reduced to statistical play. In this way, traditional Christian perspectives, while not technically accused of being unequal, are viewed as outmoded, limited, and biased perceptions redolent of the past, which should be discarded. These "activists of equality" thus achieve their political goal, which is to win over the minds and hearts of people to the acceptance of their own social mores as the only reasonable ones appropriate for today's Enlightened world.

Who are these "activists of equality," according to Bénéton? They are "philosophers of absolute freedom, radical social scientists, immoderate partisans of rights, radical feminists, [and] militant multiculturalists," and it is especially the young, he argues, who fall victim to their thinking because it pretends to be based on a notion that appeals to today's youth—"autonomy" of thought—even though it is actually based on a policy where "conformity reigns."[33]

Bénéton may be exaggerating in accusing all "activists of equality" of being advocates of extremist positions; nevertheless, his general analysis makes sense. What really concerns both Bénéton and Bloom as political scientists are the intolerant consequences of such relativism, for it is only a short step from the promotion of this relativistic understanding of tolerance to a situation where persons with traditional convictions regarding truth and morality are seen as narrow-minded bigots, relics of a past age, limited in their historical consciousness, unrepresentative of good citizenship, and ultimately worthy of being marginalized if even tolerated. Persons

[33] Ibid., 35–37.

of strong Christian convictions, long heralded as models of good citizenship in our country, become dangerous threats to the well-being of American society, especially if they hold to certain unpopular positions demanded by their faith. This would be especially true for traditionally minded Catholics and their views on the immorality of abortion and same-sex marriage. In a relativist society, a Catholic who supports the traditional teaching of the Church is destined to be viewed as un-American and intolerable.

One might argue that American society is bordering on this situation now: where multiculturalism is understood as implying the equality of cultures, and where it becomes a dominant paradigm as it is today in American higher education, it is difficult to argue to the continuing value of traditional Christian principles upholding the uniqueness of salvation in Christ, the revelatory role of the Scriptures, and the truth content of dogmatic and moral teachings of the Church.

Relativism and the Church

Relativism affects almost every issue that arises in the life of the Church today. For if truth is relative and subjective, there would in fact be no such thing as truth. If all truths were subjective, every idea would represent only one individual's or one group's viewpoint. If truth is subjective, morality and what were formerly thought to be objective life values are subjective. There remains only one unique and supremely "human" value with relativist morality: the right to choose one's own set of values. Once all truth is understood as relative, one is left with no alternative but to argue that "everything is a matter of choice." To choose is to be human; to deny one's right to choose is to be subject to the criminal charge of being inhuman.

The moral conclusion much of society has made today regarding one's right to choose abortion represents the direct implementation of this style of thinking. Pro-choice people have been able to capitalize on this fetish regarding the absolute value of choice (in itself a contradiction, but logical contradiction means nothing when your motives are ideological) in their effort to undercut the pro-life movement. And many well-intentioned Americans are swept up with this kind of thinking, staunchly viewing the right to choose as a primordial American value.

If truth is subjective, so are the contents of faith, and that ends all objectivity regarding the existence of God or Christianity's understanding of God's revelation in Jesus Christ. If truth is relative, so are faith's beliefs, and that destroys the possibility of an unconditional faith commitment to Jesus Christ. If truth is only subjective, there is no possibility of dogma or objective morality, and the Church's claim to authority regarding dogmatic and moral teachings is overruled.

Relativity has these far-reaching repercussions, and more besides. Without a basis in objectivity for social values, there is no enduring foundation for community. Once truth has been made subjective, the only remaining basis for morality is majority opinion based on ideology. But such a morality cannot compel when one's own ideology is best served by the destruction of another's. A society without objective standards of morality is a society doomed to destruction, and if the Church no longer has authority to compel by objective standards, neither will it survive. The Church will be reduced, as Hegy predicts, to a "social movement," or an "appropriate way of being," as Bénéton tells us, that serves populist fancies (read: political correctness). The Church will be tamed to support public conduct acceptable to politically powerful private interest groups. Indeed, mainline Protestant churches may already have done as much.

The fact that the fabric of American society is now unraveling is the inevitable consequence of this subjectivist thinking, for we are replacing principles that provide a foundation for unity with "liberating" nonunifying principles of diversity.[34]

The Problem of Relativism

I submit that the major problem in our society today is the dominance of the philosophy of relativism. Even many Catholics are caught up in the frenzy of relativism, and find themselves standing at a crossroads between accepting their traditional Catholic heritage with convictions based on objective truth, or America's glorification of the right to choose based on the subjectivity of all truth. Our society is moving more and more toward an absolute morality of choice. As we have seen, the Church is often able to stem the speed of this movement, and sometimes even impede its progress altogether, where there are close ties between Catholics and the institutional and sacramental life of the Church. Strengthening these ties is the only hope for the Church's survival.

It is often because they stand at the crossroads between their traditional Catholic values and their allegiance to the absolute value of choice that many Catholics make peace with themselves by affirming what is called a "personal" opposition to abortion that refrains from urging that abortion be made illegal in the land. In this way, such Catholics are able to claim allegiance to their own subjectively held Catholic heritage without violating others' rights to abide by their own subjectively held view of the truth. To ask a Catholic who accepts the subjectivity of truth to support the enactment of an anti-abortion law in the nation is to ask the Catholic to advocate

[34] For further discussion of these ideas, see my "The American Church in Jeopardy." *America* 175 (September 28, 1996): 12–13.

a law that would impose one's own subjective personal views on the right of others to choose to live by their own subjective personal views, as members of a free democratic society. Here the Catholic's logic is impeccable, since no one has a right to impose purely subjective viewpoints on others.

What needs to be done, then, if society is not to self-destruct, is to restore to public consciousness an awareness of the fact that there is an inherent objectivity to morality based on the intrinsic dignity of the human person. Once this standard has been reestablished, there remains the task of educating people to know how to recognize and apply this standard to the choices they make in their daily lives. This will not be easy to do, since even if we accept the objectivity of moral standards, it does not necessarily follow that one's own reading of these standards is any more valid than another's. Once again, the problem of relativism arises: How may I argue that my reading of the presence of objective moral values is valid for all? There is the danger of my being caught up again in my own subjective perspective.

I propose three points to help resolve this issue:

1. First of all, one needs to submit that there are objective truths and that the mind has the ability to know these truths.

   To see that there is a clear basis in American history for accepting this position, one need only call to mind the Declaration of Independence, and the fact that the Founding Fathers accepted the "truths to be self-evident" that human beings are created equal, and that they are inherently endowed by their Creator with the rights to life, liberty, and the pursuit of happiness. One needs to reflect on the fact that history, including the history of America from the time of the drawing up of its founding documents, has accepted, at least until modern times, that human beings have the capacity to perceive the objectivity of these fundamental truths, and have the right and duty to live lives based on principles that follow from these truths. Otherwise legal systems of rights and corporal punishment could never have been imposed. If one argues that truth must now be seen as relative and subjective, one needs to be brought to the clear awareness of the philosophical contradiction involved in asserting the self-evident existence of the fundamental truths by which our country was established, and the denial of the existence of such truths that subjectivism entails.

2. Secondly, we need to restore the necessary linkage of freedom with truth and not simply with choice. Freedom is not found in one's ability to choose, but only in one's ability to live by the truth.

   According to John Paul II, there is a "fundamental dependence of freedom upon truth, a dependence which has found its clearest and most authoritative expression in the words of Christ: 'You will know the truth, and the truth will set you free' (Jn 8:32)." This is because, on the one hand, freedom is a "manifestation of the divine image" in the human being, and, on the other, the human being finds fulfillment and perfection only by seeking God and being united with him. The human being in freedom lives as divine image seeking ever greater divine image. It is for this reason that the human being as a creature of God has the "moral obligation . . . to seek the truth and to adhere to it once it is known."[35]

If what John Paul II is saying is true, what he is asserting on a most fundamental level is that truth and freedom cannot be known and experienced without a relationship to an Absolute Transcendent in whose life one participates in experiences of freedom and visions of truth (shades here of the philosophy of Plato and Thomas Aquinas). Life at its richest moments is experienced as the pursuit of an ever greater participation in the Absolute's life and truth. But there is no philosophically or morally tenable way of understanding who or what that Absolute is other than the Absolute Being, God. This is, indeed, what the Founding Fathers were implicitly saying in their major assertion in the Declaration of Independence: that fundamental human rights are endowments provided by the Creator as inherent natural rights—they are rights endowed by Absolute Truth, God. According to the Founding Fathers, these rights are granted to human beings in no other way.

3. Third, we need to restore the understanding of the faith experience in Jesus Christ as rooted in the objective revelation of God, that Jesus Christ is the objective presence in our world of God's Messiah, the one who really and truly overcame the power of sin and death in his own physical death on the Cross and in his Resurrection to eternal life.

   Christianity has never understood these faith statements as relative or subjective. It is the modern, secular mentality of relativism that has crept into the Christian's consciousness, and deformed these statements by making them purely personal viewpoints. Treating faith convictions as purely subjective undercuts the possibility of a deeply transforming existential experience of Christ, for that which is purely subjective has no existential depth. And so the experience of a deeply transforming relationship to Christ needs to be restored to our understanding of the faith experience, if Christianity is to overcome the modern relativist mentality.

---

[35] John Paul II, *Veritatis Splendor* (Encyclical on the Splendor of Truth), *Origins* 23 (October 14, 1993): 297, 299–334, par. 34.

Overcoming this mentality is the major problem for the Church today. Achieving this goal will demand an effort that consumes all of the Church's energy.

Origins of Relativism

What are the origins of this subjective mentality? How did it become so deeply ingrained in the American consciousness?

We are arguing that today's relativism is the ultimate outcome of the mentality that set into Western thinking in the Age of the Enlightenment. In order to understand this effect of the Enlightenment better, we need to trace its origins back to the fourteenth century where it received its initial impetus from the views of a well-intentioned monk named William of Ockham, who innocently developed a philosophical position that he thought was necessary to save Christianity, but whose effect was nearly to destroy it.

William of Ockham

Weigel rightly finds the "proximate roots" of today's "collapse of a transcendent horizon of moral judgment in European public life" in the "drama of atheistic humanism" of the nineteenth century.[36] But he argues to deeper roots in the religious wars of the sixteenth century, and to ultimate roots in the thought of William of Ockham (c. 1285–1349), whose "work was 'the first atomic explosion of the modern era.' "[37] It was, indeed, Ockham who innocently set in motion the agenda that has led to today's crisis of "cultural and civilizational morale" in Europe, and increasingly, in America.[38]

Ockham was a philosopher-theologian and Franciscan priest famous for what is known as the "modern way" in philosophy, so-called because it represented a departure from philosophical methods used into the Middle Ages. He was called a nominalist and his philosophy was known as nominalism because it placed great emphasis upon names or terms that he understood to be mental signs or concepts that sprang from immediate intuitive knowledge of individual sensible reality. The mind also has universal concepts, he argued, but these had no foundation outside the mind. Ockham is important to us for several reasons, but most of all for his nominalism and antiuniversalism and all of the consequences that follow from these positions, including relativism.

Up until the time of Ockham, it had largely been accepted that universal concepts had an existential foundation—a position we have seen was

---

36 Weigel, *Cube and the Cathedral,* 51–52.

37 Ibid., 82–86. Weigel is citing (p. 83) Servais Pinckaers, O.P., *The Sources of Christian Ethics* (Washington, DC: Catholic University Press, 1995), 242.

38 Ibid., 6, 160.

epitomized in Platonic, Aristotelian, and Thomistic thought. Thus, if I spoke of the essence of the human being as "rational animal," that could properly refer not simply to one human being but to a whole class of beings, all members of the human race who share the common essence or nature of rational animal. In this sense, "rational animal" has in reality not only individual but also universal significance—it properly denotes either a single human being or members of the human race in general.

But for Ockham, this was not the case. He understood universals to correspond to no extramental reality. Whatever exists is always individual and singular for Ockham. Thus if I say "human being," it properly denotes only an individual human being, and not a human nature or essence in which all human beings share.

But, you might say, it certainly looks as though universals exist. For example, it seems reasonable to say that all people fall into a class of beings that share in one common human nature as rational animals. But for Ockham, not so. What these individuals share is not a common essence. What we are noticing is simply that they are all *similar*. Yes, for Ockham, they resemble each other, but this is not to say that they share a common nature. They are just similar to each other.

One might say, what does it really matter—if they are similar to each other, that is enough to allow us to speak of them collectively as human beings, so what is the problem? But that is precisely the problem: similarity alone is unable to provide a foundation for universal moral principles. For how can one apply a moral code that would be valid for all human beings if each individual merely resembles every other? Strictly speaking, if human beings are ultimately utterly individual, each individual forms a class by itself, and each would have principles of morality valid only for itself. A moral code valid for all human beings would have no foundation for establishing its validity.

Ockham employed a philosophical method for which he is famous, based on a principle of economy known as Ockham's "razor." For Ockham, no explanation should be devised for anything when a simpler explanation could be given. Ockham, applying his "razor" to this issue, cut out universal concepts, which he considered unnecessary to provide an adequate explanation of reality. As he put it, "plurality is not to be assumed without necessity." In this sense, he is a reductionist. Thus, for Ockham, if universals existed anywhere, it was only in the mind as a useful tool for understanding individually existing reality. To assert that universals existed outside the mind, as Plato argued, or that universals had a philosophically valid foundation in individually existing reality, as Aristotle and Thomas argued, was for Ockham a contradiction: if something really existed, it was either singular or universal, it could not be both. So for Ockham, "the evidential base of all knowledge is direct experience of individual things and particular events."[39] In this sense, Ockham was an empiricist and a forerunner of modern science.

One might expect, then, that if knowledge requires direct experience for Ockham, it might be difficult for him to prove the existence of God, and that would be correct. Philosophers often argue to the existence of God from the existence of individually existing contingent beings by use of the principle of causality, as Thomas Aquinas had done. Thus, one might argue that God is necessarily the Ultimate Cause of the existence of all beings that can't explain their own existence. But Ockham had difficulty accepting real causality. According to him, while we may accept that a thing has a cause, we are unable to know what that cause is unless we have actually experienced the causality in process. Of course with God we have not. We normally argue to God's efficient causality from reason, based on the nature of contingent being as necessarily requiring the existence of noncontingent being as its ultimate explanation. But for Ockham, we are not able to prove the existence of God, even though it might be reasonable to argue to the existence of God in this way, because we have not had direct experience of him as Ultimate Cause.[40]

In spite of arguing this way, Ockham remained a devout Christian. He was not trying to undermine belief in the existence of God, but only to demonstrate the inadequacy of philosophical proofs of God's existence. Nevertheless, once it became widely known that, for Ockham, reason was unable to provide adequate support for faith, it was only a matter of time before faith and reason would begin to operate on two separate tracks. Skeptical attitudes toward faith not only followed but became acceptable, because faith didn't seem to have reason to support it.

Faith unhinged from reason is what we mean by fideism, a viewpoint that John Paul II adamantly opposed in his last encyclical *Fides et Ratio* (Faith and Reason) because, without rational support, faith loses a basis for objectivity. People begin to wonder if what they hold in faith is really true if it can't be rationally justified. People begin to wonder if they are even being "irrational" in accepting what can only be known in faith. Does faith become simply personal experience? And if so, what meaning do the contents of that experience have for another person who hasn't had the experience? For that other person, the content doesn't exist. Thus a God whose existence is known only in faith becomes a nonexistent God for one who doesn't have faith, because the instrument of knowledge is purely subjective.

---

[39] Ernest A. Moody, "William of Ockham," in Paul Edwards, ed., *Encyclopedia of Philosophy* (New York: Macmillan and Free Press, 1967), 8:307.

[40] Frederick Copleston, S.J., *A History of Philosophy*, vol. 3, *Ockham to Suárez* (Westminster, MD: Newman, 1953), 71, 81.

Faith begins to be undermined without a rational support. And as history shows, if one chooses to have such a faith, it quickly becomes viewed as "my" faith, that is, my personal belief, without any foundation in the real world. And this leads to subjectivism and relativism. Truth becomes a matter of perspective and loses its objectivity or relationship to reality. In fact, there really is no longer anything such as "truth"; it becomes only a name or term (nominalism) loosely applied to things. What is left is really only subjective truth, which is no truth at all. And so truth is replaced by "opinion"—in my opinion, God exists, but only as a "God for me" and not necessarily for you. Without a rational foundation, God becomes indefensible, but also does not need a defense since his existence is only an opinion. I needn't defend his existence any more than I need to defend the fact that my favorite color is blue or that I like cherry pie. Thus all basis for dispute over the existence of God becomes otiose—his existence depends purely on personal whim. God remains secure at that point—he becomes my personal God, and I am free to believe in him if I want to, without fear of being challenged about it by another. God turns into a "security blanket" that keeps me warm and happy. Ockham of course never went this far. He would never have claimed to be a relativist or subjectivist, and never doubted the objectivity of God's existence. But philosophers often fail to see the consequences of their thoughts. Ockham failed to realize that a God without a rational foundation is a God doomed to subjectivity.

Ockham had an ulterior motive for removing a rational foundation to faith. He was deeply concerned about preserving God's freedom. God was not to be compelled in any way by arguments from human reason or by anything related to creation. God's freedom needed to be preserved especially regarding the moral order. And so, for Ockham, there was no natural law. Indeed, there could be no natural law for Ockham because that would lead to universals by which the natural law would be expressed. An action was evil for Ockham not because it was against the natural law, but because it was against God's *will* regarding human action.

Thus Ockham's system was voluntaristic, meaning something was evil for Ockham ultimately because God wanted it to be evil, and not because of laws regarding good and evil that flowed from the existence of essences and their intrinsic values. This would certainly clash with the thinking of realist followers of Aquinas, who would say, for example, that "murder is the deliberate destruction of innocent human life" that has intrinsic value because it participates in the life of God himself. One is not free, therefore, deliberately to destroy human life because of its objective worth, and not simply because God does not will such destruction. Human life is seen in America, moreover, as endowed by God with the rights recognized by the framers of the Declaration of Independence, including the right to life (the basis for the argument used by pro-life people in the fight against abortion). It is intrinsically evil to commit murder, then, because of the objective demands that flow from the intrinsic value of human life on which the moral law is based, and not simply because God wills murder to be forbidden. But for Ockham, murder is wrong ultimately because God wills it to be wrong. In fact, for Ockham God could theoretically have willed it otherwise, and if he did, murder could have been a good thing.

Such a system, based ultimately on God's will and not on a necessity following from the objective nature of essences, may have served Ockham's purposes and preserved God's absolute freedom in relation to his created world, but, as one can readily see, his system leads to chaos in the intellectual, social, and moral orders. Though Ockham may have tried to avoid this weakness by holding that human beings are able to discern by "right reason" what the proper moral code should be, or that acts can be intrinsically and necessarily virtuous (leading to a certain ambiguity in Ockham's thought), this intrinsic character ultimately exists because God chooses to make reality this way, not because reality necessarily is this way. Thus, if human life is intrinsically good, it is because God chooses to make it intrinsically good, not because human life necessarily is that way. God could always choose to make it otherwise. In this way, Ockham seems to have tried to maintain objective intrinsic values even while giving priority to God's will. The trouble is, you can't have it both ways.

Ockham's conception of the moral order as ultimately based on God's free will and not on intrinsic necessity undermined the reality of an objective order of things and the necessity of an objective moral code. Ockham's views inevitably led to the notion that knowledge of God's moral code is known in faith and not by rational knowledge of immutable essences, as had been traditionally done. The reality of immutable essences, such as the nature of the human being, had given solidity to the moral code, based as it was on immutable natural law which reason could discern. Now Ockham was saying that all is ultimately based on God's free choice, which is known by faith in revelation.

Ockham's system left many other problems. With knowledge of individual reality as the only certain knowledge, and with the rejection of universals as conveyors of knowledge of the real world, philosophy could be certain of little knowledge beyond immediate sensible experience. Because the principle of causality had been ruled out as a basis for knowledge beyond trans-sensible experience, it became impossible to know by reason alone if God existed. As a result, the intelligibility of the world, which had been rooted in its relationship to God, became increasingly questioned, and knowledge beyond what the physical sciences provided a fantasy.

Faith had more and more to assume the role of purveyor of truths previously held to be rationally demonstrable. It stands to follow that if one is not a believer, Ockham's vision of "right reason" becomes arbitrary and subjective, since the ultimate certainty that right reason was on the mark came from the norm for truth in the God in whom one believed. For some, right reason now becomes a law unto itself, without the controls of revealed knowledge to guide it. But that creates a problem, since what is right reason to one is not necessarily right reason to another. For others, skepticism regarding a meaning inherent in the real world or the existence of an objective moral code ensues. In other words, an objective order of truth and morality that is ultimately rooted in the God who wills such an order and not in the way things are becomes uprooted and flounders, once one no longer accepts congruence between reason and revelation. And these are exactly the problems that subsequent nonbelieving generations came to experience.[41]

Peter Kreeft has written a clever and humorous dialogue between a relativist and an absolutist that illustrates the problem. When the dialogue gets to the discussion of the consequences of Ockham's thought, the absolutist says it "gave birth to relativism." When asked how, he replies:

> First, through what philosophers today call the "divine command theory." Luther and Calvin and Descartes followed Ockham there; their "divine command theory" got rid of the more complex natural law theory. The divine command theory says that God's command is the only thing that makes an act right, or morally good. The natural law theory says that there is also a natural law, as well as a divine law—a law that comes from the nature of the act itself, and the nature of man, and that this natural law also makes an act good or evil. The natural law is the proximate cause; the divine law is the ultimate cause. Two causes instead of one.[42]

Though slightly oversimplified, the point is clear: there is an intrinsic rationality to the created order that is a reflection of divine law. That intrinsic order is not ultimately based simply on God's willing it to be so but because it *is* so, rooted in the nature of being. By making creation's intrinsic rationality ultimately dependent upon God's will, and not upon his essence of which it is a reflection, the intelligibility of the intrinsic order was ultimately made ambiguous, arbitrary, and not necessary; in fact, reality ceased to have an intrinsic rationality. As Louis Dupré so well puts it, in his masterful study of the Enlightenment:

---

[41] Cf. H. R. Klocker, "Ockhamism," *NCE*, 10:535–37.

[42] Peter Kreeft, *A Refutation of Moral Relativism: Interviews with an Absolutist* (San Francisco: Ignatius Press, 1999), 41.

> As nominalist theologians began to attribute the origins of all things to the inscrutable will of God, they abrogated the link of intelligibility that connected the source of reality with its created effect. As a result, by the beginning of the modern age reality had ceased to be intrinsically intelligible and God no longer provided the rational justification of the world. Henceforth meaning was no longer embedded in the nature of things; it had to be imposed by the human mind.[43]

It was only a matter of time, then, that when secularists eliminated God, the intrinsic laws of nature disappeared as well, since their very existence had been based on divine will. The real world was reduced to putty in their hands, capable of being manipulated for their own personal gain. And what manipulation there was to be.

The Enlightenment

Our discussion of the contents and historical development of the Enlightenment in this chapter and of modernism in the next will necessarily be brief. It does not serve the purposes of this study to provide an in-depth and thorough analysis of the many different and conflicting currents that occurred within these movements—that is for scholars of the Enlightenment and of modernism to do. Our purpose here is served by providing an overview highlighting those elements within these movements that in our judgment prevailed upon modern society and contributed to the situation of crisis in today's Church.

I want to avoid here a possible criticism that this study is being directed only by my own agenda and does not lead to a proper evaluation that would include an investigation as well into what is positive in these two movements. Such a criticism is not warranted. I admit that there are many positive elements to be found, at least in the Enlightenment, that it would be of value to present and discuss at length, but this study's purpose would not be served by such a presentation. I am investigating why crisis exists today in the Catholic Church, and so our purposes are only to expose those elements that helped produce that crisis.

Starting, first, then, with the Enlightenment: the period of the Enlightenment is roughly identified with eighteenth-century philosophical thought in England, France, and Germany, though the character of the movement differs considerably from one country to the next. One may perhaps establish its beginning more precisely with the close of the Thirty Years War in 1648, and its end with the French Revolution in 1789.[44]

---

[43] Dupré, *Enlightenment*, 2–3.

[44] This, following James C. Livingston, *Modern Christian Thought*, vol. 1, *The Enlightenment and the Nineteenth Century*, 2nd ed. (Upper Saddle River, NJ: Prentice Hall, 1997 [1988]), 5; hereafter, *MCT* 1.

The Enlightenment rises out of the development of thought that can be traced back to Ockham and the two dualisms in his thought: between faith and reason, and between universal ideas and concrete sensible experience.[45] A split largely occurs between those who continue to believe in God and the relevance of his existence for an adequate understanding of reality, and those skeptics and nonbelievers who downgrade God's importance or make him irrelevant to an understanding of reality.

Among the former were those called "rationalists" who explained reality primarily as a function of ideas. Descartes was the archetype of this kind of thinking. He developed much of his understanding of reality based on the clarity of innate ideas and the rational consequences of those ideas.

The other, by far the more dominant group and the more important for its influence upon subsequent history, were the empiricists, who explained reality primarily on the basis of what can be known through sense experience. This latter group's influence can be especially noted in the thinking of such philosophers as John Locke (1632–1704), David Hume (1711–1776), and Immanuel Kant (1724–1804), to mention only three. It is mainly reason operating under the influence of the empiricists that places its stamp on the thought that has commonly been identified with the Enlightenment.

In this study, rather than focus on the intricacies of the Enlightenment—the fact is, when one considers all the scientists and philosophers who make up Enlightenment thought, the movement takes on conflicting characteristics—we will focus on the major Enlightenment thinking that has had the greatest impact upon our own age, an impact that has been enormous. Most people's thinking is unconsciously the product of the French Enlightenment. It has become the dominant influence in Western thought since the eighteenth century, and its spirit is foundational to the thought of its nineteenth- and twentieth-century counterpart, modernism.

Reason

The tenor of Enlightenment thinking may be aptly discerned at the beginning of Immanuel Kant's famous essay entitled "Answer to the Question: What Is Enlightenment [German: Aufklärung]?":

> Enlightenment is man's release from his self-incurred tutelage. Tutelage is man's inability to make use of his understanding without direction from another. Self-incurred is this tutelage when its cause lies not in lack of reason but in lack of resolution and courage to use it without direction

[45] For an excellent discussion of this split, cf. E. Hegel, "Enlightenment," *NCE*, 5:254–55.

> from another. *Sapere aude*! [Dare to know!] "Have courage to use your own reason!"—that is the motto of enlightenment.[46]

Perhaps the two most important characteristics of Enlightenment thought are highlighted in Kant's remark: the primacy of the role of reason in forming one's understanding, and independence from submission to any external authority when doing so. This did not necessarily mean that the tenets of traditional Christianity were rejected, although more often than not that was the case, but that its teachings had to be accepted on the basis of the independent approval of reason.

But what was reasonable? For the Enlightened mind, reason's norms were normally stipulated by conclusions derived from empirical scientific investigation, even in areas not usually seen as susceptible to purely empirical study, such as morality and religion. Since the Enlightenment's goal was originally to produce a rational faith, it did not have much tolerance for nonrationally grounded dogma, and so, in many cases, "many of the orthodox Christian doctrines—original sin, predestination, vicarious atonement, the eternity of punishments" and resurrection—were rejected. In some cases, as in the early German Enlightened period, doctrines such as the Trinity and the Incarnation could be accepted as a product of revelation, but even then, it was "reason that must determine the criteria by which a true revelation can be recognized."[47]

The independence of reason was perhaps best summarized by the French atheistic philosopher Baron Paul-Henri d'Holbach (1723–1789):

> The *enlightened man*, is man in his maturity, in his perfection; who is capable of pursuing his own happiness; because he has learned to examine, to think for himself, and not to take that for truth upon the authority of others, which experience has taught him examination will frequently prove erroneous.[48]

---

[46] Immanuel Kant, "What Is Enlightenment?," in Kant, *Critique of Practical Reason: And Other Writings in Moral Philosophy*, trans. and ed. Lewis White Beck (Chicago: University of Chicago Press, 1949), 286. The article originally appeared in the journal *Berlinische Monatsschrift* 4 (1784): 481–94.

[47] Livingston, *MCT*, 1:29.

[48] Cited in Gary Hatfield, "Reason," in Alan Charles Kors, ed., *Encyclopedia of the Enlightenment* (Oxford: Oxford University Press, 2003), 3:407. This four-volume work has to be one of the finest compendiums of present-day scholarship on the Enlightenment.

Buckley argues that d'Holbach presents the most systematic argument for atheism prior to the twentieth century, and that the "emergence of modern atheism lies with Diderot and d'Holbach. This fact seems uncontestable." But the springboard for their argumentation against theism resides in their rejection of the conclusions of two "figures that dominated the European philosophic and scientific world": Newton

It is for these reasons that the Enlightenment is also called "the Age of Reason" (though Dupré argues the epithet belongs more properly to the seventeenth century[49]). Reason becomes the dominant principle of operation for the Enlightened mind: nothing is to be accepted or rejected—including faith if one is a believer—except insofar as it satisfies or fails to satisfy the demands of reason. The dominant feature of the age of the Enlightenment by comparison with the mentality of the Middle Ages is that it moves the fulcrum for the acceptance of truth from the revelation that is known in faith to the insights and empirical observations accepted by unaided reason.

The effect that this radical shift in thought had on the European Christian mentality is not difficult to discern. For the traditional Christian, faith is based on the God who reveals himself. Christians inherit this approach from the Jews. The God of the Old Testament is known to Moses in the burning bush experience as "I AM" (Ex 3:14), and it is only because God reveals himself as "I AM" that Moses and the Jewish people know him this way. Without this revelation, God might still be known by purely rational investigation—as was the case with Aristotle in fifth century B.C., but as Prime Mover. Aristotle would never have dreamed of God as personal, and even less as one who could have any interest in human beings, an imperfection for an all-perfect being. So the knowledge of the Judeo-Christian God as personal being is firmly rooted in God's revealing himself as such.

Under these circumstances the Christian does not rely only or even primarily on the power of reason for an understanding of God. It is true that Christian faith, in an effort never to be irrational, seeks the support of reason in its pursuit of truth, but never accepts the primacy of reason. For the typical Enlightened mind, however, one need not look beyond reason for the power to know, because "human reason was the apt and only instrument for solving problems connected with man and society." Those who continued to believe—and as the movement progressed their numbers gradually dwindled—based their religion "on reason, without reference to unquestionable divine revelation. . . . In the moral sphere the tendency was to separate morality from all metaphysical and theological premises and in this sense to make it autonomous."[50] One cannot exaggerate the Enlightened person's faith in the power of reason to know. Satisfying reason's principles of investigation would be the ultimate goal the Enlightened person would have as the basis for accepting whatever is true.

---

and Descartes, both of whom may be said to have precipitated by their thought the origins of modern atheism. Buckley, *Modern Atheism*, 34, 32.

49 Dupré, *Enlightenment*, 53.

50 Frederick Copleston, S.J., *A History of Philosophy*, vol. 4, *Descartes to Leibniz* (Westminster, MD: Newman, 1961), 34.

Accepting the autonomy of reason normally meant refusing to accept anything as true on the basis of any external authority, institution, or tradition. One is supposed to accept truths because of their inherent rationality, because it is reasonable for the mind to do so, or on the basis of induction from empirical investigation. Thus scientism assumes a position of prominence for the Enlightened. The nonbeliever, championing the autonomy of reason and scientific evidence, would automatically exclude the value of faith, seen as irrational; for the Enlightened believer, faith would rest on rational argumentation rather than on the authority of Scripture, or, even less, of the Church. The major figures of the Enlightenment

> counted the Church and confessional religion not as allies, but as adversaries. . . . Voltaire and the Enlightenment with him insisted that the evidence for the reality of god be obtained independently of any religious community. The natural religion of human beings sensitive to the world around and within them was discovered here, and it could provide criteria by which the truth and falsity of confessional doctrines could be sifted. . . . The existence and meaning of god must be established without appeal to the Church, and, even more critical for the historical European religious sensibility, without appeal to Jesus Christ.[51]

With this kind of thinking, the Catholic Church, with its emphasis upon the binding force of dogma and the teaching authority of the pope, becomes even more repulsive than the Protestant churches (even though papal infallibility was not declared a dogma until 1870).

This Enlightened way of operating has a serious deleterious effect upon one who wishes to be a good Catholic. For when such a person accepts revealed dogma and the moral authority of the Church, the standard for doing so for the Enlightened mind cannot be God's revelation or the fact that the Church has been entrusted by Christ with the power to dispense authoritative teaching to its members, but because of the rationality of the dogma or of the wisdom of Church teaching. In other words, even in the best of circumstances, the truly Enlightened person normally acts on the basis of reason and not of revelation or authority. In this scenario, the Church, as an authoritative teacher and dispenser of God's revelation, becomes an obstacle, rather than an instrument, to faith.

Many twenty-first-century Christians, so imbued with the spirit of the Enlightenment, might not see a problem with satisfying the dictates of reason as the norm for accepting truth—why not make reason the final arbiter of truth?

---

[51] Buckley, *Modern Atheism*, 38.

In the history of the development of Christianity, considerable thought has been devoted to this question: Should I examine the tenets of the Christian faith to see if they are rational before I accept them, or should I accept them and then seek to make them as rationally acceptable as possible? Or simply, Do I accept the Christian faith because it is reasonable, or do I accept the faith as revelation, and then seek to make it reasonable? This is just a variation on the question asked by St. Anselm in the eleventh century: Is Christianity a process of faith seeking understanding, or of understanding seeking faith? The latter would correspond with the Enlightened approach: only if the faith is shown to be reasonable would I accept it. But Anselm concluded the proper approach had to be the former: faith seeking understanding. Anselm realized that understanding, an operation of the human mind, could never by itself arrive at the experience of faith, an activity that is beyond the capacity of reason to produce.

That Anselm's approach is consistent with Jesus' teaching is profoundly manifested in a key passage from the Gospel of John, where Jesus states: "Unless you eat the flesh of the Son of Man and drink his blood, you do not have life within you" (Jn 6:53). In itself this is a shocking statement that could not but scandalize anyone hearing it for the first time, as Jesus recognized (Jn 6:61). Why? Reason is repelled by such a thought—it sounds like cannibalism. How could anyone be expected to accept it? As we see in John's Gospel, Jesus' words were repugnant to many of his rationally oriented disciples—"How can we accept this?" (Jn 6:60) they said. We read the sad effect of Jesus' words: "Many of his disciples returned to their former way of life and no longer accompanied him" (Jn 6:66).

Then Jesus turns to the twelve apostles and says, "Are you going, too?" To which Peter replied, "Lord, to whom shall we go? You have the words of everlasting life" (Jn 6:67–68). In other words, Jesus doesn't say, in an effort to maintain the support of his disciples, wait a minute, I can explain what I meant and make it rationally acceptable to you. He sticks to his words, and is willing to lay the success of his mission on them. Peter, speaking for the twelve, makes the decision of faith. He doesn't understand Jesus' words any better than those who left, but his approach is based on faith and not understanding. In other words, if Jesus said it, it must be so, even if reason is repelled by it.

We see here why the Christian approach must always be one of giving priority to faith over reason. If Jesus' disciples had given reason final authority, all would have turned away. If faith is given priority, however, the experience with Jesus is able to continue, even though reason lags behind.

This same approach is necessary regarding the acceptance of all Christian dogma. The example of the Trinity clarifies this point most of all: if we wait for the requirements of reason to be satisfied before we accept God as three Persons, we will never arrive at faith. In fact, the truly Enlightened person has a difficult time accepting that article of faith because it has never been explained adequately. The Christian who gives priority to faith, however, accepts dogma as the revelation of God, revealed in the Scriptures and made known by the Spirit in the Church's Tradition, and seeks to come to an ever greater understanding of that teaching with the aid of reason.

For the Enlightened mind, autonomous reason is crucial to maintaining one's freedom. To accept something on the authority of another is to be dependent on the other and to be dehumanized by that other. To acquiesce simply on the basis of authority is to be "irrational," and leads to the destruction of the powers of the human mind and of the authentic self. There is no operation more heinous to the Enlightened mentality than to accept something without first having it rationality justified.

Anyone who teaches in a classroom knows how much our students today are imbued with Enlightenment thinking, a situation that was not common in the pre-Vatican II Church. This change represents, in my view, the major feature of the gap between the mentality of the pre-Vatican II and post-Vatican II Church. Parents who date from the earlier era are often unable to provide a rational explanation to their children for the teachings of their faith because they had never felt such a need. They had accepted such teachings simply because the Church taught them. Children of the Enlightened mentality want a rational explanation of the teaching if they are to accept it. Since such an explanation is often not available or not adequate when provided, such students react in disgust at the notion that a teaching should be accepted simply on the basis of authority. The sharp opposition between the two mentalities is manifested in the fact that that which is disgusting to the Enlightened mind is the height of faith to the non-Enlightened mind.

My comments here are not meant to imply that reason has no role to play in accepting what is known in faith. The Catholic Church, much more than the Protestant communities, has always insisted on the importance of reason in accepting the Christian faith. Indeed, what would be the role of theology, whose nature is to seek a rational understanding of the faith, or of catechetical "instruction" to converts, if reason had no role to play? The issue I am addressing is best understood when one examines the Anselmian choice that must be made: a faith that gives priority to reason is anthropocentric—makes the human reason the norm for the acceptance of the Christian faith—whereas a faith that gives priority to faith rooted in revelation is theocentric—the voice of God gets priority. In Christianity, the only acceptable way is Christocentric and theocentric.

Because the Church insisted for so many centuries, and perhaps too strongly, upon the traditional standards of belief in Church life with little concern for providing rational support, many in the age of the Enlightenment attacked the Church, not only for being irrational and enslaving, but also ritualistic and superstitious. The Church's sacramental life for many became reduced to meaningless and even pagan behavior, and accepting it ultimately absurd and demeaning. When seen this way, the Catholic Church becomes an enemy of the Enlightened person, an institution that wants to retard individual self-growth and human progress rather than promote them. It is no wonder that the French Revolution in the late eighteenth century, so steeped in the Enlightenment mentality, did everything it could to destroy the Catholic Church in France for representing all the evils that had to be wiped out if the liberated human being was to make any progress.[52] Do Enlightened Catholics today sympathize with these French Enlightenment views?

Nature and Progress

Another key role in Enlightenment thinking is played by nature.

Nature was a universal principle of well-being in the Enlightened age, the bedrock in which all reality was grounded. It was the companion of reason: "It served with Reason as the standard against which other ideas, activities, and aspirations were evaluated."[53] Nature was reason's replacement for God. For Locke, the contents of God's revelation were no more than the laws of reason.[54] If one believed in God, one could read the laws of nature for knowledge of God, of his presence in the universe, of the order he built into the structure of the universe beneath the world of flux, and of the moral code he intended human beings to obey. "Nature is the book that everyone can read."[55] In these ways, the Enlightenment built upon the thinking of seventeenth-century writers where nature and its laws had already begun to replace revealed Christianity with a natural Christianity:

> In the place of the revealed laws of the Christian God, these writers substituted a set of laws and philosophical principles that they believed had universal validity. These laws and principles were provided by the model of physical Nature that was being constructed by the Mechanical Philosophy and the Scientific Revolution. Divine, revealed law was replaced by Natural Law, rooted in the physical order of the universe. As a result,

---

[52] Livingston, *MCT*, 1:6–7; Hegel, *NCE*, 5:257–58; R. Z. Lauer, "Enlightenment, Philosophy of," *NCE*, 5:259–64.

[53] Peter Hanns Reill and Ellen Judy Wilson, *Encyclopedia of the Enlightenment* (New York: Facts on File, 1996), s.v. "nature," 302–4, at 302. This one-volume work provides an excellent understanding in brief form of present-day scholarship on the Enlightenment.

[54] Dupré, *Enlightenment*, 244.

[55] Buckley, *Modern Atheism*, 41.

> political theory and positive law, like so many other enlightened disciplines, acquired a foundation in the natural, secular order of things.[56]

According to Livingston, the basis of this "equation of the reasonable and the natural . . . can be traced very largely to the new science of Newton."[57] Sir Isaac Newton (1642–1727) was a mathematical physicist who inherited the Cartesian understanding of the universe as a system that operated in accordance with universal mathematical and self-contained mechanical principles:

> The new model of Science advocated abandoning inquiries about the essences (natures) of things. It proposed, instead, to concentrate on describing events that occur in the terrestrial and celestial worlds. . . . In this new world, mathematical law, put in place by God at the time of creation, actually determined the course of events. God was remote from the world for most theorists, stepping in only occasionally to wind up the clockworks. Reason dominated in this world and assured that natural operations would be accessible to the rational minds of human beings.[58]

Newton was able to see universal mathematical and physical laws at work in the order and harmony of the universe, and, since he was a believing man, he saw these laws as an expression of God's active involvement in the universe. For example, he saw a universal law of gravitation at work in the attraction of celestial and terrestrial bodies to one another, and from the phenomenon of motion, he argued to mechanical laws operating in the universe. In other words, he specialized in the scientific analysis of material reality by a process of induction based on observation of its actions that led to universal conclusions.[59]

What is important in Newton for our purposes is that this order and harmony that he saw operating in the universe gave rise to the notion of nature as a principle of goodness in the universe that reason could discover by its own inductive operations upon the real world. He concluded that reason working together with nature could lead to the progressive advancement of life in the universe.

For the Enlightened mind, this order rooted in nature and discovered by reason largely came to replace the need for the God of revelation and nonverifiable faith statements (dogma). Philosophers such as Jean-Jacques Rousseau (1712–1778) saw the developed social, cultural, and political

[56] Reill and Wilson, *Enlightenment*, s.v. "political theory," 330–32, at 330.

[57] Livingston, *MCT*, 1:7.

[58] Reill and Wilson, *Enlightenment*, s.v. "nature," 302.

[59] Fredrick Copleston, S.J., *History of Philosophy*, vol. 5, *Hobbes to Hume* (Westminster, MD: Newman, 1959), 147–56.

worlds around them as degenerations of the pristine beauty and nobility of nature with which the person of reason was in tune, once he was able to perceive it beneath the corruptions of evil society. According to Livingston:

> What is reasonable in human affairs is what is natural, i.e., what is universal beneath the divergences of culture and outward appearance. What was called for, then, was the excision of all the beliefs and practices that had taken hold as a result of humanity's deviation from nature. Society had become artificial, the victim of all kinds of heteronomous influences—the monarch, the church, the conventions of society—which had destroyed freedom and corrupted natural integrity.

The point was to return to "that state in which humans existed before they were corrupted."[60]

It is not difficult to see, especially in France, the role relegated to the Church in this scheme of things: it belongs to those conventions in society that stifle the freedom of the individual and natural wholeness. The clarion call is now back to nature governed by reason, and away with the destructive and dehumanizing structures such as the Church, which inhibits rational humanity's natural prospects.

Those who remained religious believers in this era, such as Kant, saw the beauty of the order of nature as a reflection of God's design for the universe. So far, so good. The problem arises, however, when nature becomes synonymous with the life of the natural man, and reason sees this natural order of being as self-sustaining. Then the God of Christian faith can be seen as superfluous to well-ordered nature to which insightful reason is quite capable of responding.

> Originally, deism had not excluded revelation. . . . English deism drew heavily upon Stoic philosophy and more particularly upon Roman writers who had developed that philosophy into a monotheist, natural theology. . . . Eventually Stoic philosophy became a weapon in the battle for atheism . . . . The development is not too surprising. When nature serves as the only ground on which the idea of God rests, it may easily turn into a substitute for God, or, as in Spinoza's case, become equated with God.[61]

Following this line of thinking, the religiously minded person becomes one who is in harmony with himself and God by being in harmony with nature. Where the various Christian religions could not agree among themselves as to who God was and what he asked of humans to the point where divisions, wars, and persecutions became such a prolonged and intolerable

---

[60] Livingston, *MCT*, 1:8.

[61] Dupré, *Enlightenment*, 243–45.

part of sixteenth- and seventeenth-century life, this notion of pure nature, to which reason was progressively able to be attuned through ever greater scientific analyses of empirical data, became an enticing way to foster religious unity among believers, to overcome the divisions generated by advocates of conflicting revealed religions, to explain the prodigious growth in scientific advances, and to justify getting rid of the stifling influence of institutional Christianity. It was not long before many people concluded that the primary instruments of truth were no longer philosophy and theology, and certainly not faith, but the natural and physical sciences and the progressive understanding of the world created through their instruments of empirical discovery:

> As writers addressed human destiny, models of change and future development came to the fore. Enlightenment thinkers perceived that civilization was making rapid, wholesale changes to the physical environment—building cities, draining marshes, constructing harbors, digging canals, sinking mines, and modernizing agriculture—and they praised the power over Nature conferred by science and industry. Such changes were changing the very people in physique and appearance, ways of thinking, social existence, and expectations. Viewed in this light, *homo rationalis* ("rational man") was not, after all, some immutable essence, but the malleable product of various stimuli and responses. Man was *homo faber* ("man the maker"), but he was also *homo hominis faber*, made to be the maker of his own destiny.[62]

Already in the seventeenth century, Leonard Lessius (1554–1623), a Dutch Jesuit priest, arguing as a philosopher, treats of God as a God of divine providence and the ultimate basis for morality. Jesus and the Scriptures enter into his arguments for God's existence "almost in passing."[63] Lord Edward Herbert of Cherbury (1583–1648), whose influence was not largely to be felt until the eighteenth century, reduced all religions to "common notions" or universally shared principles that God in his goodness had imprinted upon every human mind and which could be known by a kind of "natural instinct." These were principles that it was taken for granted all persons of goodwill would accept: that God existed and was to be worshipped, that the main form of worship was a life of virtue, that one should repent of one's sins, and that everyone would be rewarded or punished in the afterlife according to the kind of life that was led here.

By emphasizing that the essence of religion is contained in a moral order reflective of this "universal natural religion" (a notion that was later to be

---

62 Roy S. Porter, "England," in Kors, *Enlightenment*, 1:412.

63 Buckley, *Modern Atheism*, 42, 44, 54.

shared by the Founding Fathers in America), Cherbury did not specifically reject dogmas held by different religious traditions, although these had to pass the test of rationality to be accepted. Rather, he hoped to bring tolerance into the religious community by making a kind of civic religion, independent of specific dogmatic differences, available to all people.[64] The effect, however, was to downgrade the importance of sectarian religious dogma, and to reduce all religions to a basic common denominator.

Happiness was "the natural goal of life" for the individual and "the ultimate aim of human life on earth" in the political and moral philosophy of the Enlightenment. Since ancient times, "the rational exercise of virtue" was considered necessary for happiness, and that notion, sometimes admixed with good fortune and good health, generally prevailed in the Enlightenment—even if on the one hand some orthodox Christians continued to insist it could be truly found only in the afterlife, and on the other some freethinkers, such as the French encyclopedist Denis Diderot (1713–1784), separated happiness altogether from morality, even to the extent of finding it in practices of immorality.[65]

But by the middle of the century, happiness was not simply the goal of individual life, but came to involve "an ideal of rational activity in political society." Certain legal scholars and jurists of the period held that happiness was a collective social goal as well as an individual pursuit. According to one scholar, " 'Public happiness,' understood as the measurable wellbeing of the aggregate of individuals in a community, is perhaps the Enlightenment's chief contribution to the history of ideas."[66] Such thinking greatly influenced the Founding Fathers when they included in the Declaration of Independence the "pursuit of happiness" as an "unalienable natural right." The Founding Fathers saw the individual's pursuit of happiness as integral to the community's pursuit of that same goal and never to be understood apart from the larger agenda. In this way, the individual's personal life was seen as intrinsically related to the social order and the pursuit of its goals, from which the individual may never be properly extricated without detriment to both.

This emphasis upon the integration of the well-being of the individual into the well-being of the community was the reflection of a heritage passed down from Augustine through the Middle Ages.[67] Prior to the Enlightenment, "most European theory and practice placed greater emphasis on social groups than on individuals. Legal privileges, rights, and obligations were defined according to a person's membership in a specific group. . . . The job

---

64 Livingston, *MCT*, 1:15–16; Copleston, *History*, 5:53–54.

65 Adam Potkay, "Happiness," in Kors, *Enlightenment*, 2:181–83.

66 Ibid., 182.

67 Christopher F. Mooney, S.J., *Religion and the American Dream: The Search for Freedom Under God* (Philadelphia: Westminster, 1977), 133n9.

of law and of the government lay in protecting the rights of these groups."[68] This emphasis upon the corporate role of the community in which the individual finds fulfillment has always been a major principle in Roman Catholic thinking, and is well represented in the political philosophy of the young Karol Wojtyła, later John Paul II.

Individualism

Nevertheless, it would seem that a second major epithet of the Enlightenment (in addition to the Age of Reason) is the Age of Individualism: "The eighteenth century decisively transformed political thought by granting the idea of individual freedom a primary position in its theories."[69] This could also be called the Age of the Self: "Despite the persistence and development of rationalist trends, the Enlightenment could more accurately be described as an age of *self-consciousness*" than as an Age of Reason. Dupré bases this conclusion on the fact that science's advances in knowledge of the cosmos brought a new awareness that human beings were no longer the center of the universe and that the solar system no longer existed for their benefit. This led to two reactions: a focus on the human mind as the source of this knowledge, and a focus on the human self as having an interior life whose meaning could be explored.[70]

Dupré finds one of the first to focus on the life of the self, Anthony Ashley Cooper, Third Earl of Shaftesbury (1671–1713), who, rejecting Descartes's emphasis on self-consciousness as *cogito ergo sum*, emphasized "self-knowledge" as "an awareness of one's feelings." Others, such as Rousseau, "argued that not reason, but the deeper, more diffuse self-awareness attained in feeling forms the core of mind."[71] The success of the novel in France promoted "reflection on the complex interaction of feelings, passions, and emotions in love." Even for Descartes, the passions had "assist[ed] the will in executing what reason commands." Philosophers began to realize that it was the passions that gave impetus to life and moved to action. Though the primacy of reason was rarely questioned, "gradually passions came to be regarded as the stronger and often the only impulse to action."[72] It is with Rousseau that the self is really displaced from the *res cogitans* (the thinking being) of Descartes and the "streams of perceptions" of Hume, and becomes the "subjective core of feeling from which all specific acts of consciousness, ideas, passions, and emotions, emerge."[73]

---

[68] Reill and Wilson, s.v. "individualism," 214.

[69] Dupré, *Enlightenment*, 185.

[70] Ibid., 53–54.

[71] Ibid., 54.

[72] Ibid., 55–56.

[73] Ibid., 65.

Exaggerated Individualism

One must give major credit to Enlightenment thinkers for their strong emphasis on the rights of the individual, especially in the advancing of individual freedom. At the same time, one may justly criticize the Enlightenment for an exaggerated individualism that has come to plague modern society and is dominant in American life today, so often spearheaded by present-day judicial decisions, such as the 2003 gay-rights decision handed down by the Massachusetts Supreme Court, that sacrifice the well-being and good order of the community for putative individual rights wholly inconsistent with the principles our Founding Fathers intended in the writing of our Constitutions, to say nothing of principles of good social order that pervade the history of the human race.

Another factor to be noted contributing to an exaggerated individualism in the Enlightenment is the role Epicurean philosophy played.[74] One finds its influence, for example, in the thinking of the Jesuit-trained Claude-Adrien Helvétius (1715–1771). His publication in 1758 of *De l'esprit* (Of the mind) brought a condemnation from French censors who "lamented that the book contained all the poisons characteristic of eighteenth-century modernity." Helvétius argued that a "pleasure-pain principle" was behind all human motivation, and, as a result, "all human behavior, including moral behavior, is based on this fact and is therefore rooted in self-interest." His political philosophy was based on the equation of individual self-interest with that of society; that is, a "functional political culture required shaping individual per ceptions of self-interest so that they would correspond exactly to the general interest of the society." He rejected the idea that the individual could be asked to suppress or sacrifice self-interest for the good of society, and argued to a philosophy of manipulation to lead the individual to see his own personal pursuit of happiness as identical with the public interest. This process of manipulation was to be achieved through public education.[75]

Legislation would also be enacted by Helvétius based on the principle that the pursuit of pleasure and the avoidance of pain were the goals of all human behavior. The role of law was then to enact legislation that would pursue goals advantageous to society by motivating the individual to pursue them out of self-interest, since it was not to be expected that one would pursue such goals in any other way. A dedicated exponent of the Enlightened principle that social progress is achieved through the progressive perfection of the rational human being, Helvétius belonged to the group who saw the freedom of the individual and state progress as mandating the separation of

---

[74] Reill and Wilson, s.v. "Epicurean philosophy," 134–35; Potkay, "Happiness," in Kors, *Enlightenment*, 2:181.

[75] Reill and Wilson, s.v. "Helvétius, Claude-Adrien," 196.

church and state, as well as the dissolution of clerical privileges that undermine that separation.[76]

Religion Reduced to Morality

A major achievement of the Enlightenment deists was to reduce religion to morality. According to Buckley, when the focus of religion was upon God, "his providence became the fundamental issue." But when under the deists the focus turned to the human person, "moral life became the fundamental issue." This shift in religious focus brought with it a "reassessment of Jesus; he became a teacher of ethics."[77] According to Dupré, religion and ethics became virtually coterminous: "For the deists, God had scarcely any function left but that of sanctioning morality. As Voltaire had written with characteristic assurance: 'I understand by natural religion the principles of morals common to the human race.'" Advocates of deism originally had good intentions: they hoped that by detaching God from revelation, "the religious conflicts that had torn Europe apart would end."[78]

Buckley argues that the seventeenth-century Lessius was a major innovator of the movement of religion toward morality. For Lessius, "the existence of a provident god and the immortality of the soul" are of "sovereign importance and pressing necessity" because "a negative decision on either of these issues would be the ruin of the moral enterprise . . . . To deny the reality of god is to deny that there is any final sanction in moral life . . . . To eliminate the awareness of such a god is to eliminate the police force from human life."[79]

It was Kant who picked up on the reduction of religion to morality that had already begun with Lessius in the seventeenth century and promoted it even more in the eighteenth, in a way that was consistent with his own philosophical system.[80] One must remember that Kant followed Hume in the history of thought, a philosopher who had fundamentally reduced all known reality to that which can be verified by empirical analysis. For Hume, if it was not experienced through sense impression, it was not knowable. This meant that all religion and religious systems Hume cast on the pile of pious sentiment, completely devoid of rationality:

> Belief in God, Hume taught, does not come from man's reasoning but from human desire for happiness, fear of death and future misery, and the thirst on the part of many for revenge. Because we have these emotional

[76] Reill and Wilson, s.v. "Helvétius, Claude-Adrien," 195–96; "atheism," 21–22.
[77] Buckley, *Modern Atheism*, 41.
[78] Dupré, *Enlightenment*, 248.
[79] Buckley, *Modern Atheism*, 44.
[80] For much of this discussion of Kant, I am indebted to Livingston, *MCT*, 1:58–69, and Fredrick Copleston, *History of Philosophy*, vol. 5, *Wolff to Kant* (Westminster, MD: Newman, 1960), 308–48.

> and impulsive characteristics as human beings, we construct a belief in God and then seek to prove that such belief is justified by reason. . . . While, from the point of view of reason, we must be skeptical about God, from the fact of our impulsive and emotional nature we do believe in God and construct a theory about God which is necessary for us.[81]

Kant was not as radically empirical as Hume. Kant believed in God (Hume was agnostic), regretted the threat to religion that Hume's system presented, and sought to provide a philosophical basis for religious thought, even while not abandoning the hegemony of reason and the empirical principles advocated by Hume. Kant agreed with Hume that all knowledge is derived from sense experience and may not transcend sense impressions and still remain knowledge. But if that was the case, how was Kant to save religion and the existence of God from the purely subjective realm of personal feeling to which Hume had relegated them?

For Kant it was possible to be a rational person and still be a person of faith because faith is implied in certain human experiences. For Kant, empiricists made the mistake of seeing knowledge purely as a product of sense experience, without factoring in the fact that the mind does its part in organizing that experience by applying its a priori, or predetermined, categories of thought to that experience. It follows, of course, in view of the delimitation of knowledge to that which is strictly knowable by sense experience, that God cannot be an object of rational knowledge for Kant either. But this did not prevent him from accepting the existence of God, though that acceptance had to be arrived at in some way other than through rational knowledge.

This Kant did by arguing that in addition to the a priori categories of "pure reason" by which we have rational knowledge of sensible experience, we have a priori categories of "practical reason" regarding moral action. One of these categories is "oughtness": we all have a duty, out of reverence for universally valid moral law, to act in accordance with such law. We have, for example, a duty to be honest. All persons of goodwill will be honest for the sake of duty or out of reverence for the moral law. This moral code is rationally autonomous, that is, it proceeds from the rational will itself and is not imposed upon the will from outside (such as from external authority, a process which the Enlightened mind could never accept). It is a product of the will's own legislation based upon reason's awareness of the universal validity of the moral law and of our need to implement it. The universal validity of this law has its basis in the universal value of the human being, who exists as an end in itself and never merely as a means to an end.

---

[81] S. E. Frost, Jr., *Basic Teachings of the Great Philosophers: A Survey of Their Basic Ideas*, new and enlarged ed. (Garden City: Doubleday Dolphin, 1962 [1942]), 119.

There are postulates or presuppositions, according to Kant, required to sustain this moral order: freedom, immortality, and the existence of God. Freedom is a necessary condition of morality, for we can act to obey duty only on the condition of our being free. But why are immortality and the existence of God necessary conditions as well?

Reason, according to Kant, seeks the *summum bonum*, or the supreme or highest good, which includes perfect virtue, or holiness, and happiness. Since the virtuous life, which reason commands the soul to pursue, is never attained to perfection in this life, it must be pursued *ad infinitum* or until one's will is perfectly in accord with moral law. This is possible only with the immortality of the soul, which therefore makes that immortality a necessary postulate of practical reason.

Nor does virtue in this life necessarily produce happiness, which Kant defines as "the state of a rational being in the world with whom in the totality of his existence *everything goes according to his wish and will.*"[82] So if happiness and perfect holiness are included in the highest good of the moral order and they can never be achieved perfectly in this life, then the moral law demands for its rationality that there be a final outcome where all of these goods may be experienced. The One who causes this final confluence of virtue, or holiness, and happiness must, moreover, apportion this happiness according to the just demands of the law and the quality of the virtuous life lived. But to do this, this Being must operate with reason and will. Thus this Being must be an omniscient and omnipotent God, and so God must exist as a necessary postulate for the existence of the moral order.

Kant does not posit to "practical reason" a knowledge of God that he refused to allow to "pure reason" bound by empiricism; nevertheless, he could not "really conceive the possibility of the perfect good being realized except on the supposition that there exists a God. Hence, though the moral law does not directly enjoin faith in God, it lies at the basis of such faith."[83] In other words, these postulates of practical reason are ultimately principles necessary for the reasonableness of our hope in the highest good, but not principles that give us *knowledge* or a certainty of the fulfillment of the hope other than through a practical or moral faith.[84]

Critique of the Reduction of Religion to the Moral Order

According to Dupré, traditional laws of morality that had been in place since early Christian times, with roots even in pre-Christian Greek and Hebrew life, began to be questioned in the eighteenth century, and the sit-

[82] Cited from Kant's *Critique of Practical Reason*, in Copleston, *History*, 6:339.
[83] Copleston, *History*, 6:340.
[84] Ibid., 6:343.

uation created was one of "crisis": "The ensuing moral predicament was unprecedented."[85]

The ethical turmoil was largely caused by the new hegemony of science and scientific method: science did not decree what ought to be, but only what was. In many cases, law thus changed its meaning from what was normative for human conduct to the merely descriptive. Among naturalists, the law of survival operative in the natural world seemed operative also regarding human conduct. Though the age as a whole did not go to this extreme, says Dupré, many did accept the residue of scientism, that "no moral absolutes exist."[86]

Kant wanted to bring an order of necessity into morality, which meant that, like scientific knowledge, morality "had to be rooted in a priori principles."[87]

What we saw in the atheist Helvétius is that religion is replaced with morality, but with Lord Cherbury and even more with Kant, religion is reduced to morality. The practical effects are not all that different.

For Kant, the moral law is what drives religion, or as Livingston puts it, "our moral nature *demands* the reality of the objects of religious belief," which are "logically required" as "implications of the moral law."[88] But for Kant, to be religious is equated with "obeying the moral law, acting for the sake of duty,"[89] and has little to do with prayer or acts of worship: "worshiping God" is "synonymous with obeying the moral law," and anything else for Kant is mere illusion. Since the only way to knowledge of God is through the "moral conscience," the "only genuine theology is moral theology."[90]

Obviously the roles of Christ and the Church are at best minimal for Kant: Christ becomes "the historical exemplification of the archetype of humanity well-pleasing to God," and the institutional Church a distraction from "the faith of pure rational religion." Since the fulfillment of moral duty is all that remains of religion for Kant, the institutional Church is hardly necessary. Indeed, that Church eventually needs to be replaced by "loyalty to the pure religion" which is found "within reason alone."[91]

This Kantian reduction of religion to a morality that by itself leads to eternal happiness caps off the rationalistic thought of the Enlightenment. As inheritors of the Enlightenment mentality, Catholics and Christians widely hold today that religion is equated with morality, and, indeed, for most Americans today, being religious is essentially reduced to being moral.

85 Dupré, *Enlightenment*, 112–13.
86 Ibid.
87 Ibid., 41.
88 Livingston, *MCT*, 1:63.
89 Copleston, *History*, 6:344.
90 Livingston, *MCT*, 1:63–64.
91 Ibid., 68.

That explains why, when Gallup asked teenagers (13–17 years old) in 1994 if "all religions are about equally good," 64% agreed very much or somewhat.[92] It is disheartening to note that among Catholic teenagers, the figure was much higher: 74%.[93] Catholic youth are being very logical in their thinking here, since, if Christianity is nothing more than being moral, it is no better than any other religion, almost all of which advocate good morality. One of the most common arguments against the need to attend religious services today, leveled especially by nonpracticing Catholics, is that to be a good Christian, one need only be a good person, which means leading a good, moral life. Such an understanding does not necessarily include attending public worship. To show how irrelevant attending Mass is to achieving this goal, Catholic students will often add, "Look at all the people who attend Mass, and then come out and fight with other people in the parking lot!" The implication is: I don't do that because I am a good person, so why should I go to Mass?

This line of thinking, I would argue, explains why charitable activity is so popular among young people today: they see good works as synonymous with being a good Christian and all that is required for being saved. This reduction of Christianity to morality leading to salvation appeals to natural Enlightenment instincts and is taken as axiomatic: it is not questioned, it is not thought through, it is not the result of an intellectual investigation—it is simply part of the apparatus of acceptable Christian thinking today.

We have already seen data in the first two chapters that make it clear that people do commonly conclude that Christianity achieves its fullness when one is a good person. We saw it represented in the study made by Hegy, who concluded on the basis of his data that the Catholic and Protestant churches were losing their specific identities because religion is being increasingly equated with "social movements" such as liberation theology and feminism.

That the Catholic Church is moving in this direction is clear also from James Davidson's study. He found that, while pre-Vatican II Catholics tended to emphasize the importance of following the Church's teachings and participating in its sacramental life, these views were not present among most post-Vatican II Catholics. As opposed to the objective approach to being a good Catholic for the pre-Vatican II person, the post-Vatican II approach tended to be more subjective, and the categories of understanding more moralistic, purely personal, and content-free, reflecting the heavy emphasis in education today upon the need to be tolerant of

[92] Although notice again the influence of church attendance: among those who had attended church in the past week, the figure was reduced to 56%.

[93] Gallup, *Spiritual Life*, 88.

diversity and the reduction of religious conviction to personal feelings. As a result, when younger Catholics were asked what a "good Catholic" is today, Davidson says:

> Most stated that they did not want to judge others according to criteria set forth by the Church because "what really counts is what's in your heart," that what is important is "that you're doing the right thing for you," and that "whether a person is a good Catholic or not is between the person and God." Many respondents of this generation indicated that participation in the sacraments, Mass attendance, and contributing to the Church financially are not important when considering the essentials of being a "good Catholic." When asked whether a "good Catholic" needs to attend Mass weekly, one focus-group participant answered, "No . . . why have the middle person when you have a direct line to God . . . ? I'm a good Catholic because I'm a good person." In an individual interview, a 26-year-old woman answered this question by saying, "I think being a 'good Catholic' is not necessarily going to Church every Sunday, but being good to other people and loving people, and being the best person you can be doing God's acts and work." Another interview respondent said: "I think being a 'good Catholic' is like your personal behavior more than following the rules and regulations of the Church. . . . I don't really think God distinguishes on religions and there are lots of different religions, but I think we all have the same God. So I don't really think being a good Catholic is any different than being a good person." [94]

Davidson notes: "Just as with the pre-Vatican II cohort, post-Vatican II participants were relatively uninformed about the Church's social teachings."[95] A telling observation. The data show that Catholics are not motivated by the movement for social action as a response to the teachings of the Church, but by the more nebulous feeling of "being good to other people and loving people," which is usually reduced to being kind to others because it makes everybody "feel" good. While a willingness to support social action is largely present among the Catholic populous today, a real commitment to social action as a consequence of Catholic teaching registers only among a militant minority of post-Vatican II generation Catholics. One reason for this may well be that living a life based on principles of social action consistent with Jesus' teaching requires self-sacrifice and a revision of the basic motivating values that define one's life, and not just "being a good person."

---

[94] Davidson, *Common Ground*, 118–20.

[95] Ibid., 120.

Negative Consequences of the Enlightenment

For all of the good that followed from the Enlightenment, and there is much—the increased awareness of the rights of the individual to be free in the pursuit of personal goals, the power of reason to investigate and ascertain what is knowable independent of external coercion, the separation of the political and religious spheres, the increased role given to the empirical sciences in our understanding of our world, the value of critical thought in biblical scholarship, the need for tolerance of another's views—we have at the same time in the Enlightenment one of the most fundamentally destructive movements in the history of Christian thought, not only because of its exaggerated emphasis on the importance of self-fulfillment at the risk of the well-being of the community, but especially because of the relativism and subjectivism it has bequeathed to us.

That relativism and subjectivism regarding truth, knowledge, and values are products of the Enlightenment should not surprise us. Though I do not think the original Enlightened thinkers deliberately intended to relativize all thought and principles of action, such was the inevitable consequence of Enlightenment attitudes for several reasons.

First, the Enlightenment's desire for tolerance regarding religious differences, in itself a noble pursuit, led to a religion in the public forum reduced to commonly accepted principles of good order—what is often called in America today "civic religion," a religion of principles considered necessary to maintain the well-being of any social order. Certainly America's Founding Fathers operated with such a civic religion in mind. This public religion did, indeed, originally include beliefs considered fundamental to an understanding of human existence, necessary for good moral order, and accepted without question by all rational beings, such as the existence of God and the necessity of good moral living. In this way, religion often served as a principle of unity, as it should.

Perhaps it was not necessary for the maintenance of civic order to have more than a civic religion, and perhaps having such a religion did well in leading to a general acceptance of a religious dimension to human culture. But this public religion inevitably marginalized the uniqueness of sectarian principles and beliefs, and made them in their uniqueness optional and irrelevant to public life. Since it is in the public forum that most people live most of their lives, it was inevitable that sectarian religious beliefs would increasingly be considered divisive of civic harmony if they penetrated the public forum. Except among sectarian religious individuals staunchly committed to the teachings of their faith, religious groups seem gradually to have felt the need to adapt their beliefs to fit the character of civic religion itself, and come increasingly to accept the Kantian reduction of faith to commonly accepted principles of good moral living.

Second, by increasingly removing religion from involvement in public life and reducing civic religion to good moral living, room was ironically provided for atheism in the public forum. Being an atheist, in spite of the influence of the publications of the French atheist *philosophes*, such as the *Encyclopédie* of Diderot, still remained largely unacceptable in the eighteenth century,[96] but it was moving in the direction of respectability in view of the growing irrelevancy of private religious convictions. As religion became increasingly identified with practical civic-mindedness, it made few demands that an atheist could not readily accept. This led to a leveling process even of public religion. But what happens when that public religion makes the universal acceptance of the existence of God optional? Not only do specific religions become unnecessary and irrelevant, but so also does any conviction beyond the need for being virtuous. But history now also shows that even the need to be virtuous may be called into question, for without God, all things become possible.

Third, for all of Kant's attempts to save the respectability of religion by placing it in the moral order of practical reason, his philosophy dealt it a mortal blow. The death blow came with the uprooting of religious conviction from its base in rational knowledge, a process already underway, as we saw, from the time of William of Ockham. When philosophy concludes that good rational thinking is unable to establish with reasonable certitude that God exists, there is no recovery for religious faith: it becomes more and more relegated, as Rousseau said it was, to the order of feelings, and becomes purely private and subjective, "irrational," publicly indefensible, and therefore irrelevant.

Kant's efforts to justify religion as the necessary postulate of duty to universal moral law is, first of all, hardly religion, but secondly, hardly a satisfactory way of saving what he understood religion to be, because the moral order without an intellectual foundation necessarily becomes subjective and personal. All of Kant's efforts to justify morality by the force of its universal value does not, in fact, escape the subjective foundation from which the argument began, for the universal value of the moral law without a rational

96 Even into the nineteenth century, being called an atheist was still unrespectable and made matter for imprisonment in England (Buckley, *Modern Atheism*, 11). According to Buckley, the first use of the term "atheist" in England seems to occur in 1540 with Sir John Cheke, a professor at Cambridge, but a long history of ambiguity over the use of the term is evident from earliest Greek times. Its use occurs "almost exclusively in a polemical context" to accusation against "one's enemies" (ibid., 9). Nevertheless, what began as a "boast" by a few intellectuals in the eighteenth century increasingly became "the mark of an elite" in the nineteenth century, and presently includes "more than twenty percent of the world's population," so that now we live in a "culture" that is characteristically "'the age of atheism'" (ibid., 27–28, citing Gerhard Ebeling).

support inevitably turns into nothing more than a universally valid moral law "for me." Even Livingston argues that with Kant, "we cannot know God as he exists in himself, only as he exists *for me*."[97] To argue that God is a necessary postulate of moral law can go no further in establishing God's existence than the ultimately subjective basis on which Kant's whole moral order is founded. God finally remains ultimately personal, purely subjective, merely optional, and not necessary for public order. In such a context, it becomes difficult to see what worth faith has, for a God who is reduced to a moral prop who has no objective presence is no more than a security blanket. Such a God is not worth the bother. Such a God is surely not the God of the Judeo-Christian faith. It is a God reduced to manageable categories of logic for reasoning by overzealous philosophers.

And yet, a God reduced to a product of reason and a necessary postulate of duty hardly promotes the Enlightenment's desire for tolerance; ironically, it leads to intolerance. For what is decreed as known by reason can easily be reduced to what is demanded by reason, and that, coupled with historicism and in the hands of tyrants, is easily reducible to whatever program is presently in vogue. Dupré argues that "one of the main problems of the Enlightenment stems from the assumption that the mind alone is the source of meaning. This often led to an unwarranted intellectual confidence," reinforced by the successes of scientific operations.[98] The twentieth century plainly witnesses to what happens with this exaggerated emphasis on the power of the mind to control reality: in fact, in enforcing one's view of what is rational, the mind strangely can become irrational and destructive.

Finally, so many of the principles for which the Enlightenment stands—the glorification of the power of reason, the importance of progress in the natural sciences, the unlimited ability of empirical investigation to explain the world and one's role in it—have created an atmosphere that makes religious faith today seem unreal and anachronistic—a superstition, an illusion. When an Enlightened person today is confronted by one who believes in the God who reveals himself in the death and Resurrection of Jesus Christ, the Enlightened person is likely to screw up his face and with an unbelieving gaze say: "You can't be serious!"[99] The clash between the Enlightened mind and a religious faith rooted in a two-thousand-year-old tradition of religious and moral teaching is insurmountable. There is no room for religious faith in the Enlightened inn.

The Enlightenment laid down the gauntlet for Christian faith: either give up your pre-Enlightened convictions and adopt a religion acceptable

---

[97] Livingston, *MCT*, 1:64.

[98] Dupré, *Enlightenment*, 336.

[99] "Nietzsche himself specified [that] God has become incredible" and "finally irrelevant" (Buckley, *Modern Atheism*, 30).

to reason, or maintain your faith and become obsolete and irrelevant. That is the challenge that every true believer faces today. No wonder, then, that many a young person, already facing the difficulty of trying to discover oneself amidst the insecurities and tensions of a harsh post-9/11 world, and eager to learn how to succeed by buying into the socially acceptable and monetary standards of today's world, reduces Christianity to "being good," a harmless and inoffensive way to retain the best of both worlds: being a Christian, and being acceptable to the secular way of life. Having to cater to a religion that requires benign charity is a small price to pay for the freedom to do whatever one wants to climb the ladder of success in this world and still be saved in the next. Given the array of possible options, the religion of Pious Christian Secularism turns out to present an unbeatable bargain, acceptably inoffensive to the Enlightened mind, and religiously acceptable to a Christianity reduced to morality.

Only a minority of Christians today seems to be aware that such thinking is an aberration of the Christian faith, and these are often marginalized as lingerers from a distant past. Time marches on, and the Enlightened world marches with it—to a distant but enticing future goal, too important for the Enlightened person to be sidetracked by the irrelevancies of a Christian faith that, by maintaining its authenticity, might lead one to be irrelevant to the modern world.

CHAPTER FOUR

Liberalism, Modernity, Modernism, and Americanism

WE ARE listing these four movements together—liberalism, modernity, modernism and Americanism—because, though distinct, they have much that allows them to be treated in common.

LIBERALISM

Liberalism was a multifaceted movement that in many ways represented the continuing application of the Enlightenment mentality to the political, social, and religious issues of the nineteenth century. As a secular movement, liberalism may be identified with an emphasis upon the natural over the supernatural, upon the scientific or positivistic approach to reality, upon human rights and the freedom of the individual over against institutional authority.

Insofar as liberalism operates within religious circles as liberal theology, one can see the influence of the Enlightenment in the scientific, rational, and humanistic elements considered common to this theology:

> Throughout the gamut of theological liberalism the same themes occur: a certain confusion of revelation and human reason; the reduction of dogma to the philosophy of religion; and the identification of the development of the deposit of faith with the speculative unfolding of man's self-consciousness. Certain corollaries of these basic principles also appear frequently: a radical distinction between the "Jesus of history" and the "Christ of the creeds"; maximum optimism concerning the status of man in relation to God, with an attenuated doctrine of sin and its effects. And throughout the entire system the constantly recurring note is the exaltation of the faith experience as the ultimate authority in matters of religion.[1]

[1] M. B. Schepers, "Liberalism, Theological," *NCE*, 8:543.

One can see the influence of the Enlightenment upon liberal theology in this succinct summary of the two main perspectives that dominate its thinking:

> The first of these consists in an assimilation of the theological view of the Enlightenment, which reduced the doctrine of faith to religious and moral principles capable of being discovered and understood by unaided human reason. . . . The other . . . set forth the doctrine of immanence in terms that constitute a denial of the distinction between the natural and the supernatural. In the same vein knowledge of God communicated through Jesus Christ is considered to be quite excellent, but no different in kind from any other knowledge of divine reality.[2]

The tendency was to consider Jesus as a remarkable teacher and a profound thinker, but not a person specifically different from any other person.

Liberalism entered into Roman Catholic circles where the movement urged the personal, rational, or subjective nature of faith; historical development of Church dogma and Tradition; freedom of the laity from hierarchical authority; and a highly critical, nonliteral approach to an understanding of the Bible. Liberal theology dominated in Protestant circles in the nineteenth and twentieth centuries, especially due to the influence of the German theologian, Friedrich Schleiermacher (1768–1834), often called the father of liberal theology, who made the heart of religion the personal experience of one's dependence upon God.

MODERNITY

The term "modern" may be used in many different ways.

Buckley states that " 'modern' without qualifications is not a period." At the same time, he notes that "in historical studies it denotes that period which begins after the medieval." He cites the philosopher James Collins as confining "the range of modern European philosophy to the three centuries between 1600 and 1900"; others speak of the termination of the modern period "with the end of colonialism, the emergence of atomic energy, the decline of Europe, the unifications of mass communication and transportation, or a particular turn in world consciousness or philosophic focus" that might be identified with the twentieth century as the beginning of the "post-modern world."[3]

---

[2] Ibid.

[3] Buckley, *Modern Atheism*, 25–26.

Modernity is characterized by one scholar as "the desire for an all-encompassing mastery of reality by rational and/or scientific means."[4] When we consider it as a movement distinct in itself, we are referring to the nineteenth-century development of the Enlightenment that is largely coextensive with liberalism. Modernity as a secular movement also emphasizes many of the attributes typical of the Enlightenment mentality: emphasis upon knowledge as rooted in the empirical, giving a priority to the scientific as the realm of truth; belief in the progress of human development based on the increasing ability of the mind to know and control the world; and the rejection of the metaphysical (and thus the supernatural) as a realm of superstition and illusion indigenous to the early and medieval mentality and surpassed by modern advances.

Modernity as a secular movement may be distinguished from the eighteenth-century Enlightenment by the increased role given to objective scientific investigation in our understanding of the world, and by its advanced technological manipulation of the environment. But there is another and even more important way in which modernity may be distinguished from the Enlightenment.

Stanley Grenz brings out that distinction well, in arguing that modernity is the movement that ultimately emerged from Kant's philosophy.[5] In placing meaning and knowledge in the categories of the mind and their constructive ordering of the phenomena of the sensible order, Kant ultimately made the mind the creator of its own world. In doing so, he presumed universality to the operations of the mind, both in the realm of knowledge as well as of the moral order: morality was based on the universal sense of "oughtness" held by all human beings, and knowledge on the categories of understanding operating uniformly among all human beings.

The problem with Kant's perspective was that the mind became the subject of its own self-creating world, which led to an imminent solipsism. This exaggerated focus on the self as the generative principle of reality led to a direction of thought distinct from that of the Enlightenment that may be seen as the beginning of modernity:

> Kant's elevation of the active mind as the definitive agent both in the process of knowing and in the life of duty encouraged subsequent philosophers to focus their interest on the individual self. The centrality of the autonomous self, in turn, laid the foundation for the modern

---

[4] Gavin Hyman, *The Predicament of Postmodern Theology: Radical Orthodoxy or Nihilist Textualism?* (Louisville: Westminster John Knox, 2001), 11.

[5] And may have been "most fully incarnated in the speculative metasystem of G. W. F. Hegel" (1770–1831) and his quest for complete mastery of knowledge (Hyman, *Predicament*, 11).

> engagement in the Enlightenment project and in fact became the chief identifying characteristic of the emerging modern era. . . . Kant thus provided the foundation for the final emergence of modernism as a cultural phenomenon. And his work marked the inauguration of modernity in its fullness, the era characterized by a focus on intense self-reflection.[6]

As we shall see later, it was that same exaggerated emphasis on the autonomous self and its universalizing presumptions that later led to postmodernism's rejection of modernity for its unjustifiable, unilateral outlook on reality.

Modernism

Although liberalism operated largely within Protestantism, toward the end of the nineteenth century, certain features of the movement sprang up within Catholic circles as well, giving rise to a movement known as modernism.[7]

When exactly does modernism occur? One scholar dates the movement, perhaps too narrowly, to approximately twenty years at the turn of the nineteenth century:

> By "modernists" I shall mean those who were in one way or another implicated in the movement in the Roman Catholic Church that is called by that name—the movement which originated about 1890, was condemned by Pope Pius X in 1907, and was snuffed out to all intents and purposes in 1910.[8]

What Alec Vidler is referring to here is a group of philosophers and theologians in France, England, Italy, and Germany who were generally thought

---

6 Stanley J. Grenz, *A Primer on Postmodernism* (Grand Rapids, MI: Eerdmans, 1996), 78–79.

7 Modernity and modernism are not always as carefully distinguished as we are doing in this chapter alone. Here, we will understand *modernity* as the modern development of the Enlightenment mentality, whereas we understand *modernism* as a distinct branch of the mentality of modernity that developed within Roman Catholicism.

8 Alec R. Vidler, *A Variety of Catholic Modernists* (Cambridge: Cambridge University Press, 1970), 1. According to Vidler, "modernism" as a term was originally applied to the movement that developed in the Roman Catholic Church from about 1890 to 1910. Alec R. Vidler, *The Church in an Age of Revolution: 1789 to the Present Day* (New York: Penguin, 1990 [1961; rev. ed. 1974], 179). One may also speak of modernism in literature: "Literary historians and critics . . . are generally agreed that modernism in literature and the arts can be dated rather precisely from the 1890s to the 1930s" (James C. Livingston and Francis Schüssler Fiorenza, *Modern Christian Thought*, vol. 2, *The Twentieth Century*, 2nd ed. [Upper Saddle River, NJ: Prentice Hall, 2000 (1997)], 494; hereafter, *MCT* 2). Our focus here is on modernism in theology.

of as partisans of the modernist movement, though no one was ever officially designated as a member.

Modernism has its philosophical roots in the Enlightenment, especially in the thought of Kant. Two of the most notable figures related to the movement are Alfred Loisy (1857–1940) in France and George Tyrrell (1861–1909) in England, whose views we shall consider shortly.

Modernism's theological outlook developed from the liberalism and positivism of the nineteenth century, and its sociopolitical formulations may even be seen as developments of the American and French Revolutions (1776, 1789, respectively), all of which ended in several papal condemnations.[9] Modernist thought was already condemned as a "heresy" in its early stages by Pius IX in his *Syllabus of Errors* (1864). The Vatican's Holy Office condemned sixty-five propositions reflecting the views of Loisy and others in its decree *Lamentabili Sane Exitu* (1907), approved in the same year by Pius X. Finally the condemnation of modernism, officially so named, occurred in Pius's encyclical *Pascendi Dominici Gregis* (1907). His "Oath against Modernism" (1910) required that clerics promise to accept the teachings contained in *Lamentabili* and *Pascendi*. The oath effectively put an end to modernism—or so it seemed at the time.

Modernism may be linked with modernity and even secular humanism because they have so much in common. They all emphasize accommodating the mentality of the modern world: accommodation of theological thought for modernism, of all other suprarational thought for modernity. Modernism represented, as it were, an updating of Enlightenment thought focusing directly on biblical and ecclesial issues. In modernism, the emphasis is on the role of reason over revelation, the role of science over metaphysics, the power of subjective feeling over objective reality, the primacy of experience over the inherited traditions of the Church, the primacy of modern critical textual analysis and historical-critical methods over the literal understanding of the Bible, the primacy of individual self-determination over submission to external authority: in every way, the Church was to accommodate its traditional theological perspectives and practices to the methods of the modern world.

As with the Enlightenment, there was truly much of value in the modernist movement because of its emphasis upon the power of reason, the role of the empirical sciences in our understanding of our world, and the need for critical analysis in scriptural studies and theological thought. The problem was that, in modernism's accommodating spirit, priority was always given to

---

[9] David G. Schultenover, S.J., *A View from Rome: On the Eve of the Modernist Crisis* (New York: Fordham University Press, 1993), 24.

the natural and the scientific over the supernatural and the metaphysical, normally to the exclusion of the latter.

At certain times such prioritization was appropriate. But modernism went too far too fast. It removed the dogmatic, the theological, and the spiritual from the control of the Church and from the authority of revelation, and placed them in the hands of reason. It undercut the primacy of the Church's role in an understanding of Christianity, at the same time as it naïvely thought that unencumbered reason could handle matters by itself. Along with removing faith in revelation as the foundation for theological thought, it outlawed traditional Church practices as vestiges of a primitive era. This was more than the Church could take.

It was, I fear, the extremist elements within modernism that led to a backlash by the Church in its rejection not only of the modernist movement, but along with it anything with which it was identified. This included most of the scientific, psychological, social, and political advances being made in the modern world as well. Modernism seemed to typify for the Church the contemporary world's threat to everything the Church stood for. As a result of this sharp and harshly created mutual antipathy, the Church became increasingly reactionary to the modern world, and the modern world increasingly secularized.

Modernism had serious weaknesses. One was its principle of vital immanence which excluded transcendence. Enamored with the theory of evolution, modernism espoused the idea of an immanent divine power inexorably in movement toward a superior future. In this way, many modernists thought they had effectively demythologized transcendence by replacing it with nature. Natural progress was such a seductive idea to many modernists that there seemed no longer to be need for the God who revealed himself from outside the vital immanent process. The result was an understanding of history as self-sufficient. If there was anything left of the divine, it had to be found inside the historical-natural process. The human being, emancipated from the shackles of the past represented by the authority of the Church and its fixation on external revelation, becomes for the first time free to be self-creative, in a world whose own creative spirit is waiting to be liberated and directed by human inventiveness.

The problem with this kind of thinking is that the divine is made subject to human control, and the human becomes a law unto himself. Gone is dependence on the God who challenges the human to be more than what reason and nature can offer. The world is remade to anthropocentric proportions, and the human becomes tied to his own limited powers of perfection. What starts with modernism's understanding of the truly liberated person becomes in the end a person newly enslaved by the limitations of his own creative powers.

Americanism

Americanism was the name given to certain teachings rejected by Leo XIII in his apostolic letter *Testem Benevolentiae* in 1899.[10] The movement, an offshoot of modernism, developed in the United States by the 1870s, though its origins may be traced back to 1789 and to John Carroll, a Jesuit before the 1773 suppression of the order who became the first United States Catholic bishop and who "was an intellectual heir of the Enlightenment" with modernist leanings. He "wanted to adapt certain practices of the church to the American environment,"[11] and thus set the foundations for the Americanist movement.

Americanists, also known as Integrationists, were first of all Americans, imbibing the spirit of America as much as any other red-blooded Americans. They were interested in moving the Church in America in the direction of adaptation and integration into the American culture. This would mean emphasizing typical American values, such as separation of church and state, religious freedom, freedom of thought, cooperation with Protestants, and "democratic decision-making in the Church."[12] It would especially emphasize the independence of the American Church vis-à-vis the Vatican.

The Americanists were strongly opposed by Europeanists or Restorationists, who saw adaptation to American values as detrimental to the life of the Church. This group emphasized hierarchical authority, especially that of the Vatican, and fidelity to the pope and the official teachings of the Church, as the appropriate form of Catholic living and the source of truth and morality.

The opposition between the two positions could not be clearer: whether to orient the Church toward fidelity to the Vatican and the official teachings of the Church, or toward adaptation to the democratic conception of freedom and the values that typify life in American society. The purpose of Americanism was clearly not only to integrate the Church into American society, but also to make the Church more attractive to non-Catholic Christians, and in that sense, the movement had evangelical overtones. Its position is sometimes rightly called accommodationist—it accommodates the life of the Church to the values dominant in America. The Europeanists, then, are called countercultural—their basic tendency is to view Christian values as opposed to the values that typify American society.

The opposition is fundamentally ecclesiological: whether the Church should be viewed as so deeply imbedded in history that it is dominated by

---

10 T. T. McAvoy, "Americanism," *NCE*, 1:354.

11 Jay P. Dolan, *The American Catholic Experience: A History from Colonial Times to the Present* (Notre Dame: University of Notre Dame, 1992 [1985]), 304.

12 D'Antonio et al., *American Catholic Laity*, 7.

historical-mindedness, or whether the Church, while involved in history, represents primarily a reality that transcends history and derives its primary meaning from what it embodies beyond history. To put it simply, is the Church primarily the embodiment of eternal truths rooted in divine revelation, or of developmental truth and a product of historical consciousness?

According to T. T. McAvoy, Leo XIII condemned five specific errors the Church could not accept in Americanism: "the rejection of external spiritual direction as no longer necessary; the extolling of natural over supernatural virtues; the preference of active over passive virtues; the rejection of religious vows as not compatible with Christian liberty; and the adoption of a new method of apologetics and approach to non-Catholics." As so often happens in the face of papal rebuke, those who felt they were being attacked as Americanist denied that the condemned teachings reflected their own positions. Nevertheless, the Americanist movement was dealt a serious blow, and for all practical purposes, went down to a resounding defeat.

Or so it seemed. As D'Antonio brings out so well, while Leo XIII saw to it that Americanism was defeated in 1899, Vatican II in the mid-1960s decidedly reoriented the life of the Church back toward many of the values with which Americanism was identified. So did Americanism actually die at the end of the nineteenth century? But more on that later.

Alfred Loisy

Specific weaknesses may be found in the views of Loisy and Tyrrell, undeclared leaders of the modernist movement.

Born in 1857, Loisy was ordained to the priesthood in 1879.[13] He taught at the Institut Catholique de Paris until 1893 when he fell into disfavor over his views on biblical inerrancy and was dismissed. He continued to exercise his role as a priest, even though he had abandoned the faith and become an atheist, many years before his formal excommunication in 1908. He died outside the Church in 1940.

His initial and well-intentioned attempts were to serve the Church by bringing its thought into harmony with modern developments. He early on opposed biblical inspiration, and challenged the historicity of Genesis. Regarding the New Testament, he was an exponent of the new historical-critical method of exegesis, which argued, among other things, that the early Church had already adapted the teaching of Jesus, which had originally been wholly oriented toward the end-time coming of the Kingdom of God, to respond to its own needs. Thus the attempt to accommodate the Gospels to developing historical perspectives in our own time is nothing new.

---

[13] I am indebted for this explanation of Loisy's life and thought especially to Livingston, *MCT*, 1:365–71, and to L. A. Bushinski, "Loisy, Alfred," *NCE*, 8:765–66.

Loisy's historical-critical analysis of the scriptural texts is a method widely used by biblical exegetes today, a method that the Church does not reject. So why did the Church bridle at Loisy's views? The problem was that Loisy went too far. For him, the gospel Jesus proclaimed was a primitive form surpassed by historical development and the alterations made by the early Church. For Loisy, the heart of the gospel is to be found in its continuing, developed form in the life of the Church rather than in its initial proclamation. Priority for Loisy is to be given to progress, development, and openness to the new: fidelity to the gospel is found in its accommodation to each historical period and the varying conditions in the life of the Church.

As a result, there is for Loisy no such thing as immutable truths or dogmas; rather, dogma is in a continuing process of development as it meets the challenges of new thought patterns and modern religious experience. Dogma for Loisy is, therefore, not the historical realization of immutable truths contained in the initial deposit of revelation made known by Jesus and handed down in the Scriptures and Tradition, as the Church has traditionally understood it; rather, dogma is a developing and historically conditioned understanding of the faith based on the thinking of the Church in each surpassing generation.

Since Loisy reduced Jesus' teaching purely to the proclamation of the Kingdom, he was forced to conclude that Jesus had never established the institutional Church. Loisy did not intend to threaten the life of the Church by this conclusion; on the contrary, he felt that his position increased the importance of the institutional Church, since in every age it embodied the latest stage in the developing life of the gospel.

Finally, Loisy was totally wedded to the spirit of scientific positivism widespread in the nineteenth century, according to which any element of the Bible inaccessible to empirical scientific investigation is rejected as an expression of an age from which the Church needs to be "demythologized." Loisy therefore challenged the validity of Church teachings regarding the Incarnation and bodily Resurrection of Christ.

George Tyrrell

This rejection of the role of the supernatural in our understanding of Christian revelation is also to be found in George Tyrrell's thought. Tyrrell, born in Ireland and raised a Calvinist, was converted to Roman Catholicism in 1879, and entered the Jesuits the following year. Like Loisy, he firmly intended to remain faithful to the Church, but was so thoroughly caught up in the modernist mentality that he was unable to see how complete accommodation to that perspective could be detrimental to the life of the Church.

Tyrrell made a distinction between the spiritual core of religious truth and the symbolic, historically conditioned form in which it is expressed. For Tyrrell, it is the spiritual core contained in Jesus' eschatological proclamation that must be retained, while discarding as historically conditioned the form in which he presented it. And the same two-fold distinction is valid for every age in the history of dogma.

What is distinctive in Tyrrell is his understanding of revelation as an interior religious and personal experience. Borrowing from Friedrich Schleiermacher, Tyrrell roots revelation not in the events of history or in doctrinal knowledge, but in the experience of the divine "presence" in one's spiritual life. Unlike Loisy, Tyrrell does not hold for a development of dogma, nor are the spiritual insights of Jesus superseded. They are always normative of the faith. What is developmental is not really dogma as immutable truth, but theology's ability to understand the dogma as well as the insights of biblical criticism.[14]

As personal experience, revelation is always subject to change. Theology is constantly trying to formalize revelatory experiences into a science, but its efforts are necessarily fallible. By this distinction between revelation as personal experience and the events of history and the formulations of theology and dogma, Tyrrell was able to subject theological formulations and dogmatic definitions to the contingencies of historical development. Similarly, our understanding of the foundational events of Christian history, such as the reality of the Virgin Birth, was made subject to the conclusions of modern biblical criticism. This he thought acceptable, because none of these formulations or events touched the heart of the Christian faith that is found in the universally held religious insights of the spiritual life.[15]

What we see in Tyrrell, then, is another form of immanentism in the exaggerated role he gives to personal experience in his understanding of revelation. Revelation as present in one's interpretation of one's own religious experience discounts any objective revelation of God from outside that experience. Talk about extra-experiential reality, categorized since the time of Kant as "metaphysical" meaning beyond the power of the intellect and reason to know, has now been recategorized as the product of personal moral consciousness.

The problem with this understanding of "revelation" is that it is always a product of historical contingencies, such as progressive developments in our understanding of the divine, and is therefore always subject to change.

---

[14] A principle which Vatican II came to accept. *Dei Verbum* (Dogmatic Constitution on Divine Revelation), par. 8, in Abbot, *Documents of Vatican II.*

[15] Livingston, *MCT,* 1:371–76.

As a result, there can be no such thing as immutable truth. As Copleston says, for the modernist,

> Revelation in a general sense can be considered as the work of God, even if from another point of view it is man's work. But the idea of God revealing absolute truths from outside, as it were, truths which are promulgated by the Church in the form of unchangeable statements of unchanging truths is incompatible with the concept of evolution, when applied to man's cultural and religious life, and with the accompanying relativistic view of religious truth.[16]

Tyrrell never renounced his convictions. He was dismissed from the Jesuit order in 1906. When he publicly criticized Pius X's condemnation of modernism in 1907, he was excommunicated from the Catholic Church. He died in England in 1909.

Conclusions Regarding Modernism

The Catholic Church saw modernism, and indirectly the Enlightenment, as a major attack on its teachings. Five of the main teachings that the Church felt were threatened are presented in Pius X's 1910 "Oath Against Modernism." Here is one author's summary of those Church teachings:

> (1) God can be known and proved to exist by natural reason; (2) the external signs of revelation, especially miracles and prophecies, are signs giving certainty and are adapted to all men and times, including the present; (3) the Church was founded by Christ on earth; (4) there is a deposit of faith and the assertion that dogmas change from one sense to another one different from that held by the Church is heretical; (5) faith is not a blind sense welling up from the depths of the subconscious under the impulse of the heart and of a will trained to morality, but a real assent of the intellect to truth by hearing from an external source.[17]

Item 4 represents the Church's rejection of the notion of an evolutionary development of dogma à la Loisy, and item 5 the rejection not only of Tyrrell's immanentism and personalism, but also of Kant's nonintellectual formulation of the truths of faith.

Enlightenment and Modernist Mentalities Today

Whereas the modernist movement was formally terminated by the "Oath against Modernism" in 1910, modernism and the Enlightenment did not

---

[16] Fredrick Copleston, *A History of Philosophy*, vol. 9, pt. 2, *Maine de Biran to Sartre* (Garden City, NY: Doubleday/Image, 1977 [1974]), 41.

[17] J. J. Heaney, "Modernism, Oath Against," *NCE*, 9:757.

in fact die; indeed, many scholars argue that the teachings of Vatican II in the 1960s vindicated many of the modernist positions by recognizing them as principles acceptable in Catholic teaching today. The truth probably calls for a more nuanced position.[18]

The historian Philip Gleason argues that modernism is alive and well today, and is known as Americanism. Though Americanism had been condemned by the Church in 1899, it was back in vogue by the 1950s with "the great reawakening of democratic fervor and rededication to national ideals set off by World War II, and particularly by the heightened visibility it lent to issues like pluralism, tolerance for diversity, and improved intergroup relations."[19]

A Catholic adaptation of liberalism, Americanism was driven primarily by the desire for social and cultural reform. Since the immigration at the turn of the century, Catholics had been separated from mainstream life in America by a so-called "ghetto" mentality, which fostered Catholic identity and gave strength to the institutional Church, but did little to make Catholicism an integral part of American culture. Many Catholic scholars felt it was time to rise out of that mentality, become socially acceptable, and enter into the currents of modern life. The condemnations of Americanism and modernism at the turn of the century, it was argued, were at best distortions of true Americanist positions, and therefore should not be seen as making it unacceptable to be Americanist today.

The election of John F. Kennedy, a Catholic, to the presidency in 1960 could not have been more symbolic of the beginning of a new age of Americanism—the integration of Catholicism into American secular life. Kennedy, to defend his rightful place as an American citizen who could be

---

[18] R. Scott Appleby, a scholar of modernism, argues rightly that the Church's controversy over modernism goes back to the longstanding disagreement with the Enlightenment and "concerns the proper sphere of rational critical inquiry and the limits of the scientific method." He argues that Vatican II avoided the extreme "either/or" positions that had dominated the discussion, and "invoked the historic 'both/and' of the Catholic tradition (in this case, room within the Church for *both* rational critical inquiry concerning doctrine *and* the ahistorical and supernatural character of divine revelation) in the hope of easing the Scylla-Charybdis tension of the 'either/or' that had dominated Catholic self-understanding since Vatican I (*either* non-critical acceptance of the objective fact and particular expression of divine revelation *or* complete and absolute perfidy). The resulting paradigm for Catholic self-understanding stressed the ongoing human experience of the divine and incorporated the results of modern biblical and historical criticism." R. Scott Appleby, "*Church and Age Unite!*": *The Modernist Impulse in American Catholicism* (Notre Dame: University of Notre Dame, 1992), 240–42.

[19] Philip Gleason, *Contending with Modernity: Catholic Higher Education in the Twentieth Century* (New York: Oxford, 1995), 285. I am indebted to Gleason, 283–314, for much of the following.

president even if Catholic, strongly argued for what we commonly call today the separation of church and state. His point was that in no way would his membership in the Roman Catholic Church interfere with the upholding of his duties in the office of president of the United States.

Pope John XXIII's call to the world's bishops to meet in Rome starting in 1962 for the updating of the life of the Church at a new ecumenical council had the impact of revitalizing hopes for a new theological relevance of the Church to the modern world. In spite of the social and political turmoil that occurred in the world early on in the 1960s, which could have distracted the bishops from the work of renewal at the Council, Vatican II truly opened the doors of the Church to the modern world and to the new theological role the world would supposedly play in promoting the Catholic mission. During and after the Council, new calls for individual freedom and personal responsibility in the Church reflected the same calls in the secular world for freedom and against established authority, especially as represented by the political, corporate, and educational institutions of the time.

It was widely felt that there was serious need for change in the Church, and the mood was ripe for it. One cannot exaggerate the impact of Harvey Cox's *The Secular City*, which appeared in 1965, emphasizing the secular world as the new arena of theological activity for an Enlightened Christianity. Calls were going out to reformulate the understanding of the Church in terms representative of the new "demythologized," secular, and immanentist outlook. The Church was meant for the here and now; life beyond this world became questionable and no longer relevant. The role of the Church was to address the problems of today; it was to the social and political issues now tearing society apart that the Church needed to speak. If the Church was any longer to be relevant, it needed to speak to the modern, "secularized" world; it needed to speak with a theology translated into categories that would be meaningful to the modern world, such as social justice. It needed to become a secular Church.

CHAPTER FIVE

Postmodernism

WHAT WE SEE in postmodernism is the ultimate trajectory of Ockham's nominalism and the Enlightenment movement, which nominalism bred. This section will show how that was possible, and the terrible consequences that followed.

Three points are to be recalled: First, with Ockham, knowledge became oriented toward individual reality. Universal statements were no longer of philosophical value, for there were no universal essences to make such statements meaningful. With this development came the loss of a metaphysical foundation for standards of morality. A consensus regarding a natural law of morality that all rational persons could agree on was held by many as a vestige of Christian morality, but it was only a matter of time before an adequate foundation for such rationality would be called into question.

Secondly, the same rootlessness occurs regarding truth. We have, starting with Ockham and even more prominently with the Enlightenment, the institution of reason as the ultimate norm of truth. But with reason's loss of an objective standard of truth independent of its own rational processes and peculiar human experiences, metaphysical truth is lost, including objective knowledge of the existence of God. As we have seen, God is gradually relegated to the realm of purely personal faith and private religious experience. Whether or not to believe is simply the product of personal conviction, or, as with Kant, a postulate of practical reason's need that moral law be rooted in a Transcendent. But thinking based upon need eventually becomes purely optional, and, with Schleiermacher, loses any objectivity apart from personal feelings.

Thirdly, once the knowledge of the Transcendent became relegated to the realm of unknowable reality and the categories of reason limited to reflection upon the data of empirical experience, the world was left open to the dominance of scientism, and, in the moral and social orders, secularism.

And so we are arguing that a rootless rationalism, subjectivism, and secularism become the ultimate systems for understanding who we are, once universal essences, external revelation, and a rational foundation for metaphysical truth in the Transcendent are revoked. The loss of essences means the loss of a secure foundation for morality and truth; the dominance of pure reason means the loss of knowledge of the God who reveals himself; and the reign of empiricism means the rule of scientism and secularism.

What postmodernism adds to this mix is that the natural and logical consequence of this Enlightened process is relativism and, ultimately, nihilism—life without a foundation for meaning.[1]

In sum, then, we are arguing that the scheme of things that began with Ockham's nominalism inevitably led to the dominance of relativism, and with relativism inevitably came the Enlightenment's reduction of the relationship to the Transcendent as meaningless metaphysical musing, which eventually left only sense experience devoid of any meaning beyond itself. But when all data, both conceptual and sensible, have no meaning beyond the sensible, there is no basis for meaning beyond the eternally mutable, which is life without meaning, or nihilism.

But what do we mean by postmodernism—or postmodernity,[2] the movement that follows the modernist era[3]—and the period in which many argue we find ourselves today?

Postmodernism gets its name from the fact that it basically rejects everything for which modernism stands. That in itself makes it difficult to define the movement, since its ethos is derived from what it is not. It is also such a new movement experience that it is still without a system (if a postmodern system is not an oxymoron) and therefore still undefinable. There are also many different currents operating within postmodernism, each current focusing on different elements it opposes within modernity, depending on which aspects of modernism it highlights in its rejection of that movement. As a result, postmodernism cannot be characterized as a movement with a single identity. Nevertheless, there is enough of a drift to what is going on

---

1 Gavin Hyman's excellent treatment of postmodern theologians Don Cupitt and John Milbank shows how, while they are at opposite ends of the spectrum regarding their reaction to postmodernism, they are in agreement that "modernity is inherently unstable, that it must deconstruct itself according to its own premises, and that it must ultimately culminate in nihilism" (Hyman, *Predicament*, 52).

2 From hereon in, "modernism" is used interchangeably with "modernity," and "postmodernism" with "postmodernity."

3 Or that breaks out within the modernist era as a reaction to modernism. In this case, both movements coexist, though postmodernism is exposing the limitations of modernism, and is gradually overtaking and replacing modernism.

under the name "postmodernism" that there is a bevy of characteristics that are used to describe the movement. Livingston does this well when he summarizes its distinctive trait as a

> heightened sense of radical pluralism, cultural fragmentation, and indeterminacy . . . , what postmodernists refer to variously as "the emptiness of the Absolute," "absence," "the loss of self," "the movement toward silence," "the unrepresentable," and "the crisis of legitimation." The deconstructive propensity of postmodern culture often reveals a "will to unmask," a strange mélange of radical relativism, cool insouciance, and apocalypticism. Yet it is also true that the postmodern plunge into immanence and becoming manifests a positive, celebratory, and quasireligious side, which is apparent in the use of terms such as "the feast of becoming," "gay relativity," "anticipation," "holy silence," and a kind of post-Nietzschean "fictive" constructivism.[4]

Postmodernism represents what happens to a society that has lost its integrity, its drive for objective truth, and its determination to live by that truth. It is what results when the worst of what modern society has to offer is allowed to have an overwhelming impact upon naïve human consciousness, such as has occurred in the mass media's manipulation of human beings and human values in its frenzy to dominate culture and economics; in the power maneuverings of major corporations in their efforts to dominate the market whatever the cost to human dignity; in the sleaze of party politicians doing whatever it takes to win, disdaining any notion of a standard of morality that might cause them pangs of conscience; in the willful debasement of modern educational institutions in their greed for the outlandish profits provided by the sports and broadcasting industries. Social structures in recent times have become so enamored with personal and corporate interests that they have willingly abandoned the limits that standards of value normally imposed on their operations, and have made the unmitigated lust for power, success, and money the norms for their activities. The loss of objective standards creates a vacuum of public morality that leaves one free to capitalize on the situation at hand with virtually no limitation to what one might do to achieve self-centered personal goals.

Postmodernism represents the tragic consequences that result when society is overcome by these new "truths": vast discouragement and disillusionment. When social and personal structures of evil have been allowed to become so strong, they produce extreme negative reactions, and that is what postmodernism is: a retreat from a reality that is no longer operative, a mocking cynicism that sees any purported statement of truth as nothing but an expression

---

[4] Livingston and Fiorenza, *MCT*, 2:494.

of self-interest, power politics, and deceitful manipulation. That one would justify one's position on the basis of universal truth to postmodern ideologues is laughable, except in those few cases where hope remains of a distant utopia where self-interested "truth" no longer abides. For most postmodernists, however, even hope of such a future does little to enhance the present.

Postmodernism, as we said above, is the ultimate Enlightenment trajectory. At the same time, there is a major break between the Enlightenment-modernist mentality, where reason still reigns supreme, and postmodernism, where an embedded context of self-interest rules. The contrast is brought out well in the following quote:

> "Modernity," in contrast to the self-perceptions of the postmodern self, tends to be optimistic. It draws its confidence from the mood of the Enlightenment when scientific method appeared to open up new possibilities for the self as active agent to carve out and control its own destiny. Leaving behind the constraints of authority and medieval hierarchy, the self of modernity becomes, with Descartes, the starting-point for knowledge. With Kant it becomes the locus of autonomy and free decision. This mood of optimism in which the human self seems to be situated at the centre continues from the Enlightenment until perhaps around the end of the 1960s or the early 1970s.[5]

Although there is no commonly accepted date for the beginning of postmodernism, the first use of the term "postmodernism" dates back to literary circles of the 1930s, and the common use of the term dates from the 1960s and developments in the field of architecture.[6] Grenz gives remarkable precision to the advent of the movement: "Postmodernism was born in St. Louis, Missouri, on July 15, 1972, at 3:32 P.M." That was the moment when a housing project "hailed as a landmark of modern architecture" was razed. It had stood, according to Grenz, "as the epitome of modernity itself in its goal of employing technology to create a utopian society for the benefit of all." Grenz sees this event as symbolizing the "death of modernity and birth of postmodernity" because, like the project, "the edifice that housed thought and culture in the modern era is crumbling." Modernity's emphasis on the rational and the scientific is being replaced by "the emotions and intuition" and going "beyond reason to nonrational ways of knowing."[7]

It has also been argued that postmodernism began with the dropping of the atomic bomb on Hiroshima on August 6, 1945, when American air-

---

[5] Anthony C. Thiselton, *Interpreting God and the Postmodern Self: On Meaning, Manipulation, and Promise* (Grand Rapids, MI: Eerdmans, 1995), 121.

[6] Hyman, *Predicament*, 13. Postmodernism very early was identified with developments in architecture.

[7] Grenz, *Primer on Postmodernism*, 11–12.

men killed 70,000 people and left 130,000 to die slowly.[8] That event was a watershed because it belied the Enlightenment notion that reason and nature were cooperatively progressing to a this-worldly state of perfection. After Hiroshima, the idea of enduring progress no longer made sense.

But what really began with that event was a new Age of Senselessness. How could anyone make sense out of such a staggeringly deliberate destruction of human life? Or of the events that led up to it? No longer could the human being be seen as the apex of a meaningful historical process; rather, the human being was being consumed by forces of technology and social disintegration that seemed to make a mockery of any system of intelligibility. This senselessness, this lack of intelligibility, this utter lack of meaning or purpose to *anything*, is perhaps what most typifies the age of postmodernity.

And yet, as we saw in Livingston's remarks, there are those who try to make sense even out of the Age of Senselessness, in a "feast of becoming" or a " 'fictive' constructivism." For many of these, there are at least four major characteristics of postmodernity that prove helpful for our understanding:

1. **Language.** Postmodernity begins with a focus on language and the contextual nature of all that is thought or spoken. Though the modern-postmodern philosopher Ludwig Wittgenstein (1889–1951) was the main source of this insight, the philosopher Jacques Derrida and his deconstructionist thought largely established the parameters of postmodernism today. As explained by Christopher Butler, professor of literature at Oxford University, in a remarkably succinct work on postmodernism:

> The central argument for deconstruction depends on relativism, by which I mean the view that truth itself is always relative to the differing standpoints and predisposing intellectual frameworks of the judging subject. . . . [A]ll language systems are inherently unreliable cultural constructs. . . .
>
> [P]hilosophy and literature in the Western tradition had for too long falsely supposed that the relationship between language and world was, on the contrary, well founded and reliable. (And even, for some religions, guaranteed by God.) This false "logocentric" confidence in language as the mirror of nature is the illusion that the meaning of a word has its origin in the structure of reality itself and hence makes the truth about that structure directly present to the mind. All this amounts to a false "metaphysics of presence." . . .

[8] Desmond Fennell, "A Fragile World: Post-Western Civilization," *Studies* 86 (Autumn 1997): 225. Fennell quotes Norman Cousins, editor of *The Saturday Review*, who wrote on August 18, 1945: "It should not be necessary to prove that on August 6, 1945, a new age is born" (p. 225).

> For the relativist claim is that once we see our conceptual systems in this way, we can also see that the world, its social systems, human identity even, are not *givens*, somehow guaranteed by a language which corresponds to reality, but are *constructed by us* in language, in ways that can never be justified by the claim that this is the way that such things "really are." We live, not inside reality, but inside our representations of it.[9]

2. **Culture.** Language—the words we speak and through which we think—is a product of the *culture* out of which we come. Our very ideas bespeak our culture. The smaller our world becomes, the more we realize that the structures of our thinking are largely a product of the questions and answers, assumptions and arguments, regarding our world as our environment sees it. Therefore language represents culture, and culture speaks through language. Each shapes the other. And each culture is conditioned by the plurality of differing cultural perspectives. That plurality gives no reason to think that any one culture is any "better" than any of the others. To argue otherwise is to make unwarranted conclusions. Such an argument implies the ability to make a judgment independently of the relativity of the cultural perspective out of which one speaks. Such an unconditioned judgment is not possible. We never escape the limitations of our own cultural contexts. If there is any "meaning" to any of the universe's enterprises—and that is not a given—that meaning must ultimately be ascribed to the Great Unknown, in the face of which one best responds with a "holy silence," or if one must, the "game" of language.
3. **Context.** But not only does language, with its conflicting self-interests in various bureaucracies, illustrate the *contextual* nature of all thought, but also scientific studies, especially in physics, now show that time, space, and order—the categories of meaning that Kant supplied for everything we know and understand—are contextual. They do not lead us to an understanding of the real world, but only of *a* world.

   Einstein's theory of relativity and our understanding of the infinite reaches of the universe make it clear that human beings are an insignificant element in that universe, and represent what they perceive only as they see it from their own small vantage point, which is worth little within the billions of galaxies that make up the universe. Our small world is thus limited by the billions and billions of other possible worlds, which makes it laughable, so the postmodernist would say, to

[9] Christopher Butler, *Post-Modernism: A Very Short Introduction* (Oxford: Oxford University Press, 2002), 16–17, 21.

essay giving significance to the minute perspective we have.

4. **Plurality.** Which leads to the fourth important element in the postmodern mentality: Our world (and perhaps the universe) is made up of a *plurality* of cultures. Multiculturalism is the name of the game today, and each speaks and thinks in its own way in terms of its own limited world.

   And so, if one could summarize postmodernism in one sentence, it could be: *All is contextual*, in a plurality of contexts. There is no centeredness from which one can draw any principle of unity or meaning or purpose: "The postmodern ethos is centerlessness. No clear shared focus unites the diverse and divergent elements of postmodern society into a single whole. There are no longer any common standards to which people can appeal in their efforts to measure, judge, or value ideas, opinions, or lifestyle choices." We are left with only "a conglomerate of societies," a "'multiverse' that has replaced the universe of the modern quest."[10]

CRITIQUE

While the postmodernist mentality is very insightful, the problem comes with its overreaching comprehensiveness. For while it is true that language is a product of culture, it is another thing to argue that it is *only* a product of culture, as the postmodernist does. One who holds that truth is rooted in an eternal and absolute reality would understand language not as a game of words, nor simply as a product of cultural relativism, but as a product of the human being's ability to grasp reality as it is. Thus, if I speak of a human being as a creation of God, I understand that statement to be an insight into the nature of reality and some comprehension of truth, and not simply a cultural construct. For the postmodernist, however, there is no known truth. Actually, although postmodernism would not even use the word "reality" if such a word were permitted, it would understand "reality" to be a product of a specific culture that would have no meaning apart from that culture. In other words, all insights simply bespeak the cultures that produce them, and represent a way of understanding from the perspective of that culture.

What we have here is what happens to Enlightenment's reason when its light goes out—nothing but reflections of different cultures representing perspectives of different mentalities, none of which has any foundation in anything beyond its own culture—in other words, scientific, historical, and metaphysical emptiness, based on a relativism pushed to the extreme, leaving nothing but contextualism in its wake.

---

[10] Grenz, *Primer on Postmodernism*, 19–20.

And for the Christian believer, what is the effect of such a perspective? Devastating. For how can Christianity mean anything to one who accepts no truth beyond context? To the postmodernist, Jesus Christ may indeed be absolutely fascinating, and provoke a "holy silence" or a "'fictive' constructivism," but so do oriental watercolors to a Western mind. To the rootless and aimless postmodernist, all that is left to reality is fascination with differing colors. Life is comparable to entering a cafeteria full of exciting choices that provide momentary pleasure. Since providing such pleasure is all that is left, quality within postmodernism is estimated by how much "excitement" the art of life can produce.

Attempts at Reconciliation

Many a postmodern theologian has made attempts, as any theologian should, to speak to the postmodern age, but, so far as I can determine, the efforts are largely unsuccessful. The following is an excellent attempt that bedazzles with its many fascinating ideas, but these cannot cloud the fact that the attempt ultimately fails because, while accommodating to the postmodern mind, it destroys the uniqueness of the person of Jesus Christ and the essence of the Christian faith in the process.

Paul Lakeland

Paul Lakeland, professor of religious studies at Fairfield University, is the first holder of the Aloysius P. Kelley, S.J., Chair in Catholic Studies there. He has devoted a complete work to an understanding of postmodernism, and presents his own efforts to accommodate Christianity to the movement.[11]

Lakeland begins by clearing the table of discussion of definitive dogmatic teachings, thereby preventing them from disrupting the possibility of dialogue. He then focuses on three issues central to the Christian narrative: God, the Church, and Christ. His purpose will be to present the Christian perspective on each of these in ways that are faithful to the Christian vision and yet acceptable to the postmodern mind.

- God: Taking on the postmodernist perspective, Lakeland argues that our new understanding of the size and scope of the universe, plus the possibility of other galaxies of living persons, makes the traditional Christian cosmology and anthropology centered on a divine plan for the human person no longer acceptable. Humans are simply an insignificant part of a larger cosmological perspective.

  The new widened perception of the universe also rules out discussion of sin. Christian dialogue must also be compatible with post-

[11] Paul Lakeland, *Postmodernity: Christian Identity in a Fragmented Age* (Minneapolis: Fortress, 1997).

modernity's understanding of God as silent. Taking his cue from the book of Job where God is present in the whirlwind challenging all human conceptions of God, Lakeland concludes that God is a God whose providence extends to the whole universe, but not directly to any individuals within it. In this way, God does not intrude in history. Rather, as a self-effacing God, God responds to human needs by letting human beings create their own futures through their own individual agencies with futures where there are no guarantees. This, then, is who the Christian God of love is: "the compassionate outpouring of realistic affirmation," the one who in "self-effacement . . . enables free human agency."[12]

- The Church: Lakeland sees the need here to retain some distinctive form of Christian "sociality" that is faithful to the Christian tradition and gives Christians a distinctive role to play in the world; otherwise, why bother being a Christian? He finds this need will be satisfied if he can give a distinctive mission to the community of faith in the postmodern world.

  Lakeland rejects the notion that the Christian vision could be superior to others, since a pluralistic world would find that unacceptable. Yet he recognizes that not to hold this superiority causes problems for Christianity, which normally argues to a unique way of salvation and a gospel valid for all peoples. Lakeland solves the problem by focusing on what he calls "reaching consensus through conversion." He sees the Church as the "community of revelation" having a responsibility toward a world that is the "community of redemption." But the problem is, for this community of redemption, all things are relative. Taking its cue, then, from who the God of love is, the Christian community sees its mission as an expression of "the compassionate outpouring of realistic affirmation." (Does this mean anything more than do whatever you want?)

  Lakeland then reinterprets the traditional understanding of the priestly, prophetic, and royal understanding of the People of God.

  Priesthood is no longer a term of reference to the Eucharist; rather, it refers to the Messiah and to the human shape of God's presence to the world. In the fate of the Messiah on the Cross, moreover, is seen the human shape of the community's discipleship. In its own "compassionate outpouring of realistic affirmation," the community empties itself to the world to awaken it to the "interpenetration of the cosmos and the divine" and to the world's "responsibility" to this cosmos and the divine.

[12] Ibid., 93–101, at 101.

The role of the prophet is to speak the truth to the world. But since the concept of truth as the Christian understands it would be too harsh, this prophetic speaking becomes a matter of "demanding—through acting out—an uncompromising openness to the future revealed through unconstrained discourse." Finally, as a royal people, the community will "exercise leadership through service" in building a future for the world. This means responding to the needs of the world—in the concrete, participating in the world's struggle for liberation.

In sum, the Church's mission is to "be deeply involved in its world, engaged in collaborative efforts toward the amelioration and elimination of problems, and confidently oriented toward a radically open future."[13] (If this isn't liberalism revisited, what is it?)

- Christ: The Christian perspective must again retain its uniqueness, Lakeland says, at the same time expressing a message relevant to the postmodern world. This means that Christ must be the "distinctive element *behind*" the Christian's task—behind, in the sense of not making Christ directly known—speaking from the Christian's "background consciousness," representing the "silent and distant God . . . in a non-coercive way." How does this "background consciousness" do this?

> Thus, in the death of Christ on the cross one sees at once the destructive freedom of the human race in face of the divine, and a representation of exactly the message of the divine for the human, namely, that human selflessness, self-abnegation, and the embrace of failure and death are the way in which the world can be saved from and for itself.[14]

What the Christian makes known by presenting this "message of the divine" is that Christ represents the "only way" of salvation that God extends to human beings, speaking to them through their mode of receptivity. Thus, in following the pattern of Christ's death on the Cross, Christ is "not merely *the way* to salvation [but] is salvation" because the following of Christ as the "divine other" escapes the limitations of anthropocentrism, and yet reveals that God has determined to express in Christ the human way of fitting into "the divine scheme of things."[15]

But this message, Lakeland readily admits, is not distinctive of Christianity. What is distinctive is Christ in whom the "human face of the divine" is made known. But this distinctive element, Lakeland

[13] Ibid., 101–7.
[14] Ibid., 109.
[15] Ibid., 109–110.

> concedes, in no way gives Christianity any superiority over other religions. Moreover, other expressions of the Christian insight might be more acceptable to other religious traditions. What remains valuable for all others in the Christian insight is that it expresses a "salutary challenge to postmodernity's insouciance, that among the great variety of options, *it is important to choose one.*"[16]

Critique of Lakeland's theology. Lakeland's attempt to present a postmodern Christian theology that remains faithful to the Christian experience and yet is meaningful to the postmodern perspective is, in my opinion, woefully inadequate. It fails on both counts. First, while Lakeland's "salutary challenge" is to accept "human selflessness, self-abnegation, and the embrace of failure and death" as a universally valid way to salvation, he ultimately fails to provide a way of understanding that message that escapes what a postmodern would consider the Christian's own limited and relative cultural context. The implication in Lakeland's thought is that the romantic beauty of the notion of the divine presence in the human Christ's self-abnegation somehow escapes cultural relativism and would necessarily appeal to the postmodernist. But there is little reason to see why this would be. Rather, there is every reason to believe that the postmodernist would see Lakeland's Christ as providing another scintillating and perhaps fascinating approach to understanding our world, but nothing beyond that. Lakeland's Christ is designed to keep the postmodernist interested and amused for a few moments at best.

Secondly, Lakeland indeed recognizes that he must retain distinctiveness to Christianity if he is to make the Christian revelation worthwhile. But what is distinctively Christian about a theology that focuses on "human selflessness"? Nothing that I know. Indeed, Lakeland admits that his postmodern theology is only distinctive in presenting Christ as the "human face of the divine." Lakeland correctly argues that it is Christ that remains distinctive in Christianity, but he fails to realize that it is not simply because Christ is the human face of the divine. The uniqueness of the Christian faith only begins there. It is the distinctiveness of the interpersonal relationship with Christ that is at the heart of the Christian faith experience. But unfortunately Lakeland feels he must leave the person of Christ in the background in his humanistic reconstruction of Christ's death on the Cross, apparently lest Christ's distinctiveness be offensive. But does a theology that hides its distinctiveness make sense?

Lakeland further fails to recognize that the faith experience with Christ includes a new and transformed life with Christ within this world that

---

[16] Ibid., 108–13.

endures beyond this world's history. The transhistorical dimension of this life never gets spelled out in Lakeland's postmodern adaptation of Christianity. Moreover, he repeatedly describes Christianity with empty substantives whose explicit Christian meanings must remain unexpressed: Lakeland urges salvation, but for what? Service for what? Responsibility for what? Prophetic truth about what? And "compassionate outpouring of realistic affirmation" of what, and why? Lakeland never says, because he cannot say; to put content into any of these assertions would be to affirm a reality the postmodern mind would be unwilling to accept.

Thirdly, Lakeland plays at deception by hiding Christ in Lakeland's "background consciousness," making Christ the "silent God" represented in "human selflessness." This purely natural, moralistic subterfuge represents a system that is fair neither to Christ nor to the postmodernist.

Conclusion regarding Lakeland's theology. Lakeland's adapted Christian postmodern efforts fail because, in the last analysis, there is no way to provide meaning to the Christian faith experience in the face of postmodernism's utter relativism. As we have seen, postmodernism is the ultimate trajectory of the process that began with William of Ockham and became intensified with the Enlightenment, ending where no truth can be affirmed because there is no longer any truth to be affirmed. Once pure reason is made the ultimate norm of truth, and sensible experience the primary or unique data provided to reason for discerning the truth, objectivity is lost, subjectivity takes over, and reality loses trans-subjective content. The ultimate consequence is total absence of meaning, and a life that reflects that meaninglessness. Lakeland and others make valiant attempts to inject meaning into the trajectory of meaninglessness that postmodernism inherits. But his accommodationist theology, in the last analysis, is acceptable neither by Christian standards nor by those of the postmodernist: it fails, on the one hand, to retain the uniqueness of Christianity, and on the other, brings more meaning into postmodernism than the latter's categories are able to handle.

Stanley J. Grenz

Stanley J. Grenz, a professor of theology and ethics in the evangelical tradition in Canada, does a better job of remaining faithful to the integrity of each discipline—Christianity and postmodernism—in his attempt to reconcile the opposing viewpoints, but in the end, fails as well.

Grenz willingly accepts the postmodern rejection of much of the Enlightenment mentality. He argues further that Christianity cannot ignore the emerging postmodern youth culture, increasingly contemptuous of the rationalistic and dualistic mentality of the modern world. Christianity, as he says, "must think through the ramifications of the phenomenal changes occurring in Western society for our understanding of the Christian faith and our presentation of the gospel to the next generation."[17] But how to make that gospel presentable?

Grenz argues that we must "embody the gospel in a manner that is *post-individualistic, post-rationalistic, post-dualistic*, and *post-noeticentric*," meaning that we must take into consideration and adapt to all that is good about the postmodern perspective: its emphasis upon context in community for the creation of the individual's ideas, upon the existence of the realm of "mystery" beyond the rational, of the soul-body unity of the human person, and of the goal of existence as not simply growth in knowledge, but as wisdom in action involving "the transformation of our character and the renewal of our entire lives as believers."[18] All well and good.

But on the other hand, as a deeply committed Christian, Grenz refuses to compromise on the essentials of the Christian faith, such as its centering in a personal encounter with Jesus Christ, or the sin-grace dimensions of the saving relationship experienced in the journey through life with God in Christ. While he is willing to accept the rejection of the Enlightenment mentality that exaggerated the correspondence of knowledge to the objective, scientific conception of truth, he insists on "standing our ground" in "rejecting the rejection of the metanarrative," in other words, in rejecting the postmodern view that there is no "unified whole that we can call 'reality,'" that there is no "universal, ultimate truth" beyond "a host of conflicting interpretations or an infinity of linguistically created worlds." Nor can we allow Christianity "to be relegated to the status of one more faith among others. . . . It embodies the truth—the truth of and for all humankind."[19]

But if Christianity is to reject so much that postmodernism stands for, how is it able to speak to postmodernists in categories acceptable to them, as Grenz insists we must do? With all the good will in the world, Grenz is ultimately asking the postmodernist to concede more to the Christian's outlook than the Christian is willing (or able) to concede to the postmodernist's. Ultimately, Grenz refuses to accept the fact that there are differences between the Christian faith experience and postmodern contextual categories that are simply irreconcilable.

Basis for Optimism?

There are some who see a basis for optimism in postmodernism, and, lest I seem too pessimistic regarding the impasse the movement creates for Christianity, let me quickly insist that there is a basis for optimism. Perhaps every

[17] Grenz, *Primer on Postmodernism*, 162.
[18] Ibid., 167–74, at 173.
[19] Ibid., 163, 165.

cloud does have a silver lining, and there is such a lining to be found in postmodernism.

For one, the movement, as an attack on modernism, represents a rejection of the basic premise on which modernism stands, namely, that reality is coterminous with the purview of the rationalistic and scientific. Said simply, for modernism, that which is real is that which is sensate or logically structured, as in mathematics; that which is excluded is the reality of the meta-empirical. By rejecting that purview, postmodernism rejects scientism, and refuses to explain the meaning of life in terms of it. Any movement that rejects such a purview has to be good, at least, in some sense.

Secondly, at the same time as it rejects the comprehensiveness of the scientific mentality, postmodernism also insists on reopening our horizons to the meta-rational, the invisible, the realm of "mystery" that surrounds all of life, a realm that adds a dimension of beauty, the surreal, the fascinating and mystical dimension that gives richness and fullness to life. Postmodernism, in other words, attempts to recapture the existence of a world of the incomprehensible that cannot be contained in rational and scientific categories, but which gives zest to life. Thus postmodernism reopens life to a realm from which we had been cut off by the modernist mentality. Postmodernism thereby opens up our vistas to the possibility of readmitting one day the religious realm, the mystical realm, even the existence of the God of Christianity, into our world, the God who cannot be circumscribed by the limitations of the scientific and the sensible, and who one day may give life the meaning and purpose longed for.

Jean-Luc Marion

One can find elements of this kind of optimism in the views of a postmodernist such as Jean-Luc Marion (1946–), Andrew Thomas Greeley and Grace McNichols Greeley Professor of Catholic Studies and Professor of Religions and Theology at the University of Chicago Divinity School, who holds that God exists, yet refuses to allow him to be captured within the categories of being to which modern rational philosophy reduces everything:

> With respect to God, is it self-evident that the first question comes down to asking, before anything else, whether he is? Does Being define the first and the highest of the divine names? When God offers himself to be contemplated and gives himself to be prayed to, is he concerned primarily with Being? When he appears as and in Jesus Christ, who dies and rises from the dead, is he concerned primarily with Being? No doubt, God can and must in the end also be; but does his relationship to Being determine him as radically as the relation to his Being defines all other beings? . . . I am attempting to bring out the absolute freedom of God with regard to all determinations, including, first of all, the basic condition that renders

> all other conditions possible and even necessary—for us, humans—the fact of Being.[20]

The God who exists for Marion is the God of theology, and not philosophy. For Marion, the Christian understanding of God begins with his revelation of who he is, not with our ontological constructs of him. Thus Marion separates himself not only from empirical reductionism, as found in modernism, but also from the reductionism to the categories of being of much of Catholic philosophy, including Thomism with its heavy emphasis upon the rationality of the God of Christianity. For Marion, the Christian God does not primarily reveal himself as the highest in the realm of being, nor even primarily as being above all other being, as the analogy of being understands him, but primarily as gift, as the God of love:

> If, to begin with, "God is love," then God loves before being, He only is as He embodies himself . . . . This radical reversal of the relations between Being and love, between the name revealed by the Old Testament (Exodus, 3:14) and the name revealed, more profoundly though not inconsistently, by the New (First Letter of John, 4:8), presupposes taking a stand that is at once theological and philosophical.[21]

The meaning of this love is revealed above all in Jesus' suffering and death on the Cross, that cannot be comprehended by philosophical categories of being:

> Jesus gambles, upon the Cross, his Lordship. He gains it only in undertaking to lose it. This kenotic loss, going so far as death and, above all, the descent into hell, appears as the highest lordship—that, precisely, of love without reserve, universal and hence all-powerful.[22]

It is this kind of perspective that may open up the postmodern mind to the penetration of a reality that destroys the limitations of human thought to which modern philosophy denigrated itself from the time of Descartes, and to which Catholic philosophy often submitted itself in its attempts to accommodate to the modern mind. In doing so, primacy was given to the God who proved his existence by the Five Ways of Thomas Aquinas, rather than to the God who revealed the uniqueness of his existence in Jesus Christ.

---

[20] Jean-Luc Marion, *God without Being*, trans. Thomas A. Carlson (Chicago: University of Chicago, 1991 [1982]).

[21] Ibid.

[22] Ibid., 193.

Following Marion, Christian scholars in the postmodern age may begin not by accepting as a given modernism's rationalist and empirical reductionism, which it then tries without success to broaden so as to include the reality of the God of Christ, but by refusing to concede the perspective on truth to modernistic categories. Let postmodern Christianity present the meaning of reality that the Christian faith, when true to itself, challenges the world to accept: that all of reality is grounded in a God of love who reveals himself in suffering, and who calls for our union with him in and through the experience of suffering with and at the side of his Son.[23]

Anthony C. Thiselton

A further reflection on the God of love who opens up the possibility of overcoming the limitations of the postmodern perspective is provided by Anthony C. Thiselton, emeritus professor of Christian theology at the University of Nottingham.

Thiselton, borrowing from the hope and promise vistas emphasized in the theologies of Wolfart Pannenberg (1928–) and Jürgen Moltmann (1926–), argues that God calls us to a future of hope and promise of the fulfillment of his love directed toward all humanity. Because it is the selfless love of the divine lived in the interest of others, it has the capacity to overcome the postmodern criticism, leveled against all modern contextual perspectives, of representing nothing more than manipulative power plays motivated by myopic egocentric considerations. The fulfillment of God's promises has yet to come to pass, but "promise beckons 'from ahead' to invite the postmodern self to discover a reconstituted identity." One who accepts the call of this promise enters into a faith "that has world-transforming and self-transforming effects. . . . The self perceives its call and its value as one-who-is-loved within the larger narrative plot of God's loving purposes for the world, for society, and for the self."

If one is suspicious that this God of love represents only "wishful thinking," Thiselton admits that in Christianity "everything rests on divine promise," but just as Jesus entered into the "*larger narrative* which only in its wholeness defined his selfhood," so the "definitive interpretation of true humanness as it was meant to be" may be found in a future already dawning in Christ where the self is defined "by giving and receiving, by loving and being loved unconditionally," where "the human self, like Christ," comes to bear ever closer "affinities" to God and finds "grace."[24]

---

[23] For a brief but excellent treatment of Marion's thought, cf. Livingston and Fiorenza, *MCT*, 2:504–6.

[24] Thiselton, *Interpreting God*, 160, 163.

Anguish of Hopeless Meaninglessness

As promising as the theologies of Marion and Thiselton may be for finding a way that the Christian believer may be able to speak to the postmodernist, one has to accept the fact that this fascinating spirit of optimism and openness to the future of the God of love does not represent the dominant mood in postmodernism today. Rather, the hopeless meaninglessness with which most of today's postmodernists are afflicted is brought out in a recent article by Joseph Feeney, S.J., in which he presents the anguish so many of his students express in his English classes at Saint Joseph's University in Philadelphia. Feeney describes "the essence of postmodernism" this way:

> Postmodernism is a set of attitudes: Human feelings, human art, and the world itself are exhausted; humans are limited and lonely; human existence is random, impermanent, nightmarish, without firm values; humans cope with absurdity by laughter and parody. Postmodernism shows itself in art's content: Humans are objects or comic-strip characters; action takes place on the surface; colors are simple and bright; fact and fiction blur into the bizarre and the fantastic; reality and art grow untrustworthy; self-contradiction is normal . . . . A reader, viewer or listener should never be shocked or surprised; never expect coherence or meaning; be ever willing to help construct the text or art-object; be willing to see a work self-destruct; always be cool and distant, protecting the self through laughter, play and parody.

Feeney finds in his students "a sense of exhaustion, a loss of feeling and meaning, minimal expectations and hopes, and a desire to parody everything." He quotes statements from student papers: "I view most subjects as having no meaning." "No reason can be found in the world. This is a comic state." "Parody is my life. I never take anything seriously." "I have no passion. I have no spirit. I have no religion."

Feeney is "moved by the pain . . . so common among college students," and seeks to offer them "the possibility of hope and meaning and stable values." He asks if "we, as educational heirs of an integrated renaissance worldview, present a coherent view of life." As professors in Catholic education, can we "examine different worldviews and clarify their underlying values and suppositions"? Can we "probe what it means to be human and offer a coherent worldview that includes both meaning and the spiritual"? Can we "offer a living God, redemption in Christ, a community of believers and hope for this world and in eternity"? He concludes: "If we respond well, we might truly be healers of our students."[25]

---

[25] Joseph J. Feeney, S.J., "Can a Worldview Be Healed? Students and Postmodernism," *America* 177 (November 15, 1997): 12–16, passim.

Perhaps Feeney is correct. But it will take a concerted effort on the part of many to overcome all of the ill effects of the Enlightenment mentality. After so many years of inculcation of the irrelevance of religious and moral values, of the subjectivity of all thought, of the absence of truth in any statement affirmed, of the utterly contextual nature of all standards of judgment, of the arbitrariness of all convictions, how does one restore the "integrated renaissance worldview"?

Conclusion

To conclude these chapters on the Enlightenment: it is the dregs of the Enlightenment represented in the postmodern mentality that have come to roost in the minds of many American Catholics today, and this is why all statements of truth are widely held simply to be matters of private conviction. This is why the statements of the hierarchy are understood to be purely personal and have no greater authoritative value than anyone else's. This is why one is now an island unto oneself, and why each individual Catholic is left to make up his or her own mind on moral and dogmatic questions. This is why there is a major breakdown in the unity of the Church, a unity which to the postmodern mentality, unlike the pre-Vatican II mentality, has lost its theological or ecclesial purpose.

The Catholic Church has in its official declarations tried to hold out against the Enlightenment-cum-postmodern mentality, and it continues to do so today. That is why Catholics who heed the official declarations of the institutional Church and Catholics who subscribe to any stage of the Enlightenment-cum-postmodern age, are living in two different worlds. Is there any way to bring these two "churches" together? Are modern or postmodern theologians even interested in trying to do that? Have we come to an intractable division between the two churches? Or are there some principles of union that could restore wholeness to the Body of Christ? To find such principles is the purpose of this study.

But first we examine contemporary expressions of the effects of the Enlightenment mentality on our world. We begin with Catholic higher education and the papal decree *Ex Corde Ecclesiae*.

PART THREE

Enlightenment and Crisis in the Contemporary Church

CHAPTER SIX

Enlightenment and Catholic Education

THE ENLIGHTENMENT has had a major impact upon many areas of modern Catholic life. There is arguably no area where the impact has been more deeply felt than in Catholic higher education. This chapter will indicate major ways in which that impact has been felt, and discuss the serious rift that now exists between representatives of the Enlightenment mentality and those who support ecclesial policies and procedures.

There are several factors that explain the advancement of the Enlightenment or modernist mentality in Catholic education today:

Low Intellectual Productivity

Severe criticism was leveled in the late 1950s against Catholic higher education in the United States, even by the most ardent of Catholics supporters, for the fact that the Church's intellectual productivity in this country was one of the lowest among Catholic communities in the world.[1] Many felt that the American Church's strongly moralistic concerns had had the effect of downplaying the importance of the intellectual life.

Catholic educators were enormously embarrassed by the criticism, which they recognized as valid, and set about to rectify the situation. Perhaps it was inevitable that Catholic leaders would make the decision they did, which was to have a decisive impact upon the course of Catholic education: they

[1] The shot heard 'round the American Catholic educational world exposing this situation was fired mainly by Msgr. John Tracy Ellis, a Church historian at the Catholic University of America in Washington, DC; cf. his "American Catholics and the Intellectual Life," *Thought* 30 (Autumn 1955). His volley was perhaps the single, most decisive catalyst of the revolution that occurred in Catholic education's structures and policies in the 1960s and '70s.

adopted many of the structures, policy procedures, and standards of measurement used by the non-Catholic educational world. This in effect meant becoming integrated into the surrounding secular culture and competing by Enlightenment standards. In this way, Catholic education set upon a path that made it increasingly Americanized and secularized.

Fear of Loss of Government Funding

Since the early 1960s, Catholic higher education felt threatened by what appeared to be a new wave of secularism sweeping the country. Many institutions felt that, when challenged in state legislatures or in courts, government funding for private, religiously founded colleges and universities would be removed for violating separation of church and state.

There were solid reasons for this fear. In 1966 in the *Horace Mann* case in Maryland, state funding for Catholic colleges was declared unconstitutional "on the grounds that they were 'sectarian.'"[2] An even more famous case occurred in 1968 in New York State with the so-called "Bundy money" which the state was unwilling to grant to "denominational" or sectarian schools. Fordham University in New York City feared its church-related situation as a Jesuit university would jeopardize crucial public funding, which initially it did.[3] To avoid what would be a crippling financial loss, many schools sought ways to alienate themselves from their religious identity and to emphasize policies and procedures that put them on a par with secular institutions, notably by establishing separate incorporation, that is, financial independence from founding religious communities, and legal transferal of ownership of schools to lay or predominantly lay boards of trustees. Some Jesuit schools, such as Fordham, started calling themselves schools whose origins were "in the Jesuit tradition" rather than "Jesuit schools."

Response to Vatican II

And then along came Vatican II (1962–1965). Many of the Catholic elite were only too ready to respond to the new openness and accommodation to the world that seemed to be officially validated by the Council, especially in its decree *Gaudium et Spes* (The Role of the Church in the Modern World). Catholic theology, which had been beholden to Thomistic scholastic thought since the beginning of the century, was simply unable to cope

---

[2] Alice Gallin, O.S.U., *Independence and a New Partnership in Catholic Higher Education* (Notre Dame: University of Notre Dame, 1996), 102.

[3] Gallin covers the lengths to which Fordham went to alienate itself from its religious affiliation in order to receive the public funding. The tumultuous period from 1966 to 1969, when Fordham was receiving the Bundy funding, is carefully delineated in Gallin, *Independence*, 85–101.

with this new spirit of freedom from the straightjacket of traditional structures. Thomism was largely encrusted in Aristotelian forms and categories that provided a clarity of thought that served well in the Middle Ages, but that lacked the existential outlook and vitality necessary to speak to the new personalistic "I-Thou" philosophies coming out of Europe and taking over the modern mentality.

Vatican II also strongly supported a new theology of the laity. The dawning of the age of the laity meant that many operations in the life of the Church under the control of the clergy should be turned over more and more to the control of competent laypersons. There was a practical reason as well for this transfer: Would Catholic higher education be able to vie with the best of the secular institutions of learning, if it was controlled by clerics who often had little or no competence regarding academic procedures, and limited resources for meeting the challenges of superior modern educational policies and structures? If the role of the laity was now to be crucial to the Church's understanding of its social and political mission in the world, as Vatican II mandated, that role would have to be crucial for its mission in academia as well.

In Jesuit circles, this came to mean that there should be separate incorporation in the colleges and universities—that institutions of higher education should no longer be owned or operated by the Society of Jesus, but by boards of trustees, who would be both lay and Jesuit. In many Catholic schools, laypeople overnight constituted the majority on these boards, as was already the case in 1967 at Jesuit-run Saint Louis University and Holy Cross's University of Notre Dame.[4] Saint Joseph's University followed in 1972.

Spirit of the 1960s

There were other currents operating in America in the 1960s: a strong movement away from corporate powers' domination of civic life, a movement toward correcting the social injustices of the previous decades, a movement away from authority, and a resurgence of the spirit of modernism where reason held sway and faith became increasingly irrelevant in the public square.

As in the Enlightenment, the overweening power of the institutional Catholic Church now began to be felt as burdensome and regressive. It became, as in the eighteenth century, an obstacle to progress. The widespread sense of frustration in the 1960s with supposedly inadequate traditional institutional and corporate structures generated social and political upheavals never before seen in the United States, fueling a sense of frustration in Catholic circles with the institutional Church and its failure to

[4] David J. O'Brien, "The Land O'Lakes Statement," *Boston College Magazine* 58 (Winter 1998): 42.

respond to the critical issues facing modern America, such as systemic racism, injustice, and poverty.

Vatican II had also given new emphasis to the role of the Enlightenment principle of independence to individual conscience. Vatican II had never mandated that the role of clerical rule and authority should be downgraded, but these began to be interpreted "in the spirit" of the Council as vestiges of the past to be sent on their way out ("in the spirit" meant "if you read between the lines, this is what Vatican II *really* meant to say"). Most Catholic education was run by religious orders who, as arms of the Church, held almost as tight a rein on the operations of their institutions of secondary and higher education as they did on their seminaries and parishes. But now their authoritarian hold was seen as an impediment to the freedom of thought necessary to allow the Catholic intellectual enterprise to compete effectively in the marketplace.

So much of what had been handed down from the past suddenly seemed outdated and stifling. Catholic higher education was looking more and more with envy on many secular institutions that had alienated themselves from control by their Christian founders, and where emphasis on academic freedom, institutional autonomy, and professional excellence had made many of them major institutions of teaching excellence and research in the nation. In 1940 the American Association of University Professors (AAUP) adopted a statement on academic freedom that supported such alienation. It was perhaps inevitable that Catholic schools would want to do the same. Such alienation was a mark of the modern spirit, and if Catholic schools were to compete with secular institutions, it seemed they would have to adopt the same values as these institutions.

LAND O'LAKES

Land O'Lakes is known to most people as a name for butter. But Land O'Lakes is the name of a small town in Wisconsin where a major conference of twenty-six leaders in American Catholic education, headed by Fr. Theodore Hesburgh, C.S.C., then president of the University of Notre Dame, was held July 20–23, 1967, to compose the philosophy of Catholic education that would legitimize new and reorganized structures of administrative and academic life—free from the authority of the institutional Church—that the conveners felt was necessary for the survival of Catholic higher education in the United States. The process of installing those structures was already underway with the newly appointed, dominantly lay boards of trustees at Saint Louis and Notre Dame Universities, already announced in January and March 1967, respectively. Land O'Lakes was convened to legislate that independence for all of modern Catholic educational life.

The opening paragraph of the "Land O'Lakes Statement" is revelatory and monumental in its importance. Not only does it set out the new agenda that would set the course for most of Catholic higher education in America, but it also unconsciously reveals how the Enlightenment, which had struggled so hard to prevail upon Catholic thinking in early twentieth-century modernism, had finally come to prevail in American Catholic intellectual life:

> The Catholic University today must be a university in the full modern sense of the word, with a strong commitment to and concern for academic excellence. To perform its teaching and research functions effectively the Catholic university must have a true autonomy and academic freedom in the face of authority of whatever kind, lay or clerical, external to the academic community itself. To say this is simply to assert that institutional autonomy and academic freedom are essential conditions of life and growth and indeed of survival for Catholic universities as for all universities.[5]

The statement is replete with typical modernist jargon asserting lofty and unproven principles enunciated simply to support the preconceived educational agenda of the conveners. Do all universities "in the full modern sense of the word," especially Catholic ones, have a "strong commitment to and concern for academic excellence"? To "perform its teaching and research functions effectively," why are institutional autonomy and academic freedom essential to the Catholic university? And why are these necessary for the survival of any university, let alone Catholic? Did other major sectarian institutions of higher education, such as Yale and Harvard, separate from their religious congregations to perform their "teaching and research functions effectively," or did they separate to support partisan interests? Arguments supporting these presuppositions were never provided by the conference participants because they had already decided what their conclusions would be prior to the meeting. The statement was simply an ad hoc declaration deemed necessary to substantiate and legitimate what they had determined to be the new *modus agendi* in Catholic higher education.

Let us turn to the statement's true purpose—to announce and implement the new principle that "institutional autonomy" and "academic freedom" are now to be the governing principles in the life of the "modern" Catholic university. The statement calls for autonomy from external "authority of whatever kind, lay or clerical." But there was no external lay

---

[5] Alice Gallin, O.S.U., ed., "Land O'Lakes Statement: The Nature of the Contemporary Catholic University," in *American Catholic Higher Education: Essential Documents, 1967–1990* (Notre Dame: University of Notre Dame, 1992), 7–12, at 7.

authority troubling the composers of the statement. What was being asserted was independence from the authority of the Church.

By "institutional autonomy," the authors meant freedom from the authority of the hierarchy of the Catholic Church, as well as from religious superiors who had traditionally governed the institutions founded by their order, regarding the administrative policies and procedures of the university, including mission statements, hiring, firing, curricular decisions, and internal discipline. The "academic freedom" being referred to, though not defined, was in reference to instructors or teachers, who were to be free from external discipline or censorship in the pursuit of their scholarly research and in the content of their classroom presentations.[6] Implicit was the approbation of new boards of trustees already being formed, which were increasingly to become predominantly lay. Though the persons present at the meeting were technically speaking only for themselves, they spoke as if the new prescriptions drawn up by them would be operative throughout Catholic higher education in the United States in general.[7]

ENLIGHTENMENT INFLUENCE

Significant in the document is the reflection of the Enlightenment mind to which we referred earlier, which was gradually coming to prominence in the thinking of Catholic educators in the United States since the 1950s, and especially since Vatican II. This is indicated in various ways.

Land O'Lakes, without using the word "secular," nevertheless stresses in many ways the identity of the Catholic university with modern secular institutions of higher education: The Catholic university "participates in the total university life of our time"; the Catholic university "has the same

---

6 No doubt the authors of the statement were advancing their notions on the basis of the American Association of University Professors' (AAUP) *1940 Statement of Principles on Academic Freedom and Tenure*, www.aaup.org/AAUP/pubsres/policydocs/contents/1940statement.htm. According to the statement, "institutions of higher education are conducted for the common good." The statement does not define academic freedom, but states that "teachers are entitled to full freedom in research and in the publication of the results," and "to freedom in the classroom in discussing their subject," and that "when they speak or write as citizens, they should be free from institutional censorship or discipline." According to the document, the freedom in research is "fundamental to the advancement of truth," and the freedom in the classroom "fundamental for the protection of the rights of the teacher in teaching and of the student to freedom in learning." It is uncanny how the promotion of the "common good" and the search for "truth" are central also to the Catholic Church's understanding of the purposes of Catholic higher education, though with different results, as we shall shortly see.

7 In fact, the president of the Catholic University of America was not in agreement with the statement, though his representative at the meeting signed it.

functions as all other true universities and, in general, offers the same services to society." What is, indeed, remarkable is the lofty social role educators give to their institutions, making them, as it were, the conscience of society. The educators assert, for example, that, like every university, the Catholic university is "the critical reflective intelligence of its society," and that its service is to "society and all its parts, e.g., the Federal Government, the inner-city, etc." Even more remarkable is that, where the document asserts that a Catholic university does have some distinctiveness, this service does not appear to be primary, but merely "added" to the functions it already carries out with all other universities in its service to society.[8]

The document mentions Catholic education's ties with the Catholic Church, but these are expressed in an attenuated fashion. The document repeatedly calls for maintaining the Catholic character of the university, but not in ways that make the Catholic university markedly different from a non-Catholic university.

What is indicated as special to the Catholic university over against secular institutions is nebulously expressed and difficult to measure: for example, that in the Catholic university, "Catholicism is perceptibly present and effectively operative." How could one ever verify whether either of these conditions was being met? One way in which this Catholic presence should be evident, according to the document, is in the existence of "a group of scholars in all branches of theology" at the university. But many non-Catholic universities have representatives of different theologies on their campuses, and this does not make them Catholic. Again, according to the document, the theological faculty should explore "the depths of Christian [note: not Catholic] tradition and the total religious heritage of the world" so as to come to "the best possible intellectual understanding of religion [note: not Christianity or Catholicism] and revelation, of man in all his varied relationships to God." But many non-Catholic institutions also do this.

The need to elaborate a "Christian anthropology"—again, not Catholic—is highlighted, as well as the need to "serve the ecumenical goals of collaboration and unity." The importance of dialogue between theology and modern cultures is stressed as a way to enrich and be enriched by them. "Interdisciplinary discussions" within the different disciplines within the university are encouraged, and the "theological dimension to most intellectual subjects" is supposed to be made evident. These directives are, indeed, more likely to be made at institutions identified as Christian, but they cannot be said to make the institutions specifically Catholic.

[8] Gallin, *American Catholic Higher Education*, 7, 9.

Jesus Christ is never mentioned in the document, and no mention is made of the study of Catholic dogma or fostering a Catholic faith experience, factors that would truly make the university distinctively Christian and Catholic.

There are some directives urging that room be created for Catholic thought on the campus, but more often it is a religious perspective or the Christian tradition that is urged rather than the specifically Catholic. Missing are any instruments for measuring how well the directives are being heeded, or whether or how they would be enforced if they were not. Without instruments of measurement or enforcement specified, it is difficult to conclude that the directives were meant to be taken seriously.

With a "hubris" that is surprising for its time but typical of the Enlightenment mentality, the document states that the Catholic university is to serve as the "critical reflective intelligence" of the Church. This it will do in "a continual examination of all aspects and all activities of the Church" by "objectively" evaluating them. The Church will thus "have the benefit of continual counsel from Catholic universities." What is noteworthy about this watchdog activity is that, while the Catholic university is understood as offering a service of critical examination of Church life (a service, by the way, which the Church does not seem to have invited), there is no evidence that the Church in any way is to perform a similar service for the university.

What is missing from this statement of the university's life is any dimension of commitment to the Church, either on the part of the administration and faculty or the students: no mention of fidelity to the Church, to its teachings, or to furthering a mission toward the world other than in secular humanist categories. A pastoral dimension appears to be deliberately excluded from the university's life, as if to indicate it has no relevance to the intellectual environment of the campus. Instead, the campus provides an arena where "the consequences of Christian [not Catholic] truth" will be "taken seriously," and where the importance of a "religious [not Catholic] commitment" is "accepted and constantly witnessed to."

When attention is given to the university's obligations toward its undergraduate students, the stress is on the world of "knowledge and ideas" to which the student must be exposed, rather than to Catholic teaching. The role of "the theological disciplines" is to "affect" the "education and life" of the students, but only in ways that are said to be "distinctive." The education must be "truly geared to modern society," with "no boundaries and no barriers" to the intellectual life (there are to be "no outlawed books or subjects"). Students should be able to "carry on a warm personal dialogue with themselves and with faculty." Undergraduate education should lead the student to "a basic understanding of the actual world in which he lives today."

The social dimension of Catholic existence is prominently mentioned, but only in secularly acceptable ways: Students are to enter into "Christian service" through "inner-city social action, personal aid to the educationally disadvantaged, and so forth." There is to be "concern with the particularly pressing problems of our era, e.g., civil rights, international development and peace, poverty, etc."—all this so that the student might "fulfill himself," not deepen a faith experience.

The only area mentioned of the internal life of the Church is in regard to a "full, meaningful liturgical and sacramental life" that is to be made available to the students and in which they will be able to participate. But this is so that they will be able to discern "the meaning of the sacraments for themselves."

Finally, the "total organization" of the university should "emphasize the university's concern for persons as individuals." A democratic spirit is to operate in administration: there should be "appropriate participation by all members of the community of learners in university decisions."[9] Ironically, this gives more of a say to the students in the operations of the life of the university than to the Church, especially since the Church is given none.

Significance of Land O'Lakes

I do not want to suggest that the writers of the document, prominent among whom was Fr. Robert J. Henle, S.J., then academic vice-president of Saint Louis University, lacked a concern for Catholicism. The educators do indicate the need that "a competent presentation of relevant, living, Catholic thought"[10] be provided at the Catholic university. But what is the meaning of "presentation," and how would one oversee its existence, if one were charged with doing so? The statement is so utterly vague as to allow for the presence of much or almost nothing of what is distinctive of Catholic life. The theology department is not even required to teach Catholic theology, but only to "engage directly in exploring the depths of the Christian tradition."[11] Apart from the nodding suggestion of the availability of "liturgical and sacramental life"[12] on the campus, the Catholic Church is not involved in the life of the university. There is no mention of the need to foster a Catholic spirit that would permeate the life of the university in an integral way. The Church is effectively marginal to the university's life. The document is truly an Enlightenment document, as it was intended to be.

---

[9] Ibid., 8–11.
[10] Ibid., 10.
[11] Ibid., 8.
[12] Ibid., 11.

When Philip Gleason, professor of history at the University of Notre Dame, in his masterful work on Catholic higher education in the twentieth century, seeks to understand the changes that took place around the time of Land O'Lakes, he argues that the downgrading of the role of religious communities and the increasing influence of the laity represented a "tilt toward secularization" caused by three factors: first, "Vatican II's call for fuller participation of lay people in the life of the Church"; secondly, the serious need to get the financial input of lay people, as well as to involve their professional competence in the operations of the institutions; and thirdly, the fear that government aid to "sectarian" institutions would be found unconstitutional. The last turned out eventually not to be a problem, but by the time that was discovered, the process of laicization was too advanced to be stopped—if, indeed, anyone wanted to.[13]

For Gleason, Land O'Lakes was significant because it represented "a declaration of independence from the hierarchy and a symbolic turning point." While the Church may have won the battle with modernism in 1910, it lost the war in 1967. Land O'Lakes signified, in Gleason's words, that which John Cogley, a leading Catholic journalist (later turned Anglican), the previous year (1966) had stated as true: that "the church's future path might remain unclear, but her 'cold war with modernity' was definitely over."[14]

Or was it?

Ex Corde Ecclesiae (From the Heart of the Church)

From 1968 to 1990, a series of meetings of leading Catholic educators occurred in various parts of the world with numerous documents published, as the Vatican moved steadily toward composing a papal document emphasizing the new relationship between the Church and Catholic higher education in the light of the teaching of Vatican II. The circuitous and intricate route toward the development of that document is detailed elsewhere.[15] One generally finds, on the one hand, on the part of Catholic educators, an increasing assertion of independence from ecclesial control through the establishment of boards of trustees predominantly under lay control,[16] and resist-

---

[13] Gleason, *Contending with Modernity*, 315–17.

[14] Ibid., 317.

[15] Cf. Gallin, *Essential Documents*, and the complete issue of *Current Issues in Catholic Higher Education* 20 (Fall 1999). For a historical tracing of this development, with some discussion of its significance, see my article, "*Ex Corde Ecclesiae*: A History from Land O'Lakes to Now," *Review for Religious* 59 (September–October 2000): 454–70.

[16] Cf. Gallin, *Independence*. This work contains the study of the gradual movement of Catholic colleges and universities toward independence from the control of the

ance in the last phase of this period to what they feared would be Vatican encroachment upon the freedom accorded them since Land O'Lakes; and on the other hand, on the part of the Vatican and some of the hierarchy, a growing effort to restore a tighter relationship between the universities and the Church than Land O'Lakes had warranted. Noteworthy are the educators' efforts to exclude any enactment of Church legislation that would impinge upon university self-governance and academic independence. The issue of creating a juridical tie between the Church and the university becomes the major bone of contention especially in the last phase of this period.

John Paul II's *Ex Corde Ecclesiae*, the apostolic constitution on Catholic universities, finally appeared in 1990.[17] It did not restrict itself to vague generalizations about Catholic presence at Catholic universities, or simply to the need to establish trusting relationships between the Church and Catholic education, as previous documents had done, but contained the binding juridical elements that American Catholic educators had hoped to forestall.

Perhaps the most significant of these elements was canon 812 of the new Code of Canon Law of 1983. The canon stated that every Catholic theologian teaching in a Catholic university would have to sign a mandate (or mandatum) affirming the consistency of the theologian's teachings with official Catholic Church teachings. American Catholic educators had sought to keep a requirement to follow that canon out of *ECE*. But when the document was finally approved, it mandated that that canon was to be implemented. Catholic educators had lost that battle.

But now they turned to the more significant battle. A document was to be drawn up regarding how the constitution would be applied to the United States. Perhaps that application would allow an exemption to United States institutions from following the canon. At first, Catholic educators were not too concerned. They did, indeed, believe that Catholic theologians in America would be exempted because, they felt, the canon could never be enforced in the United States without violating constitutional separation of church and state. Thus, the apparently damaging ramifications of the canon's incorporation in *ECE* would be stemmed at the outset, and *ECE* would turn out to be only a paper tiger.

Church and religious founding communities through the establishment of lay-dominated boards of trustees and separate incorporation starting in 1967. As noted above, the Jesuit-run Saint Louis University and the Holy Cross's University of Notre Dame were noteworthy in establishing the trend. Whether they had canonical and civil rights to enact this alienation has never been resolved, and continues to be a bone of contention in the discussions of *Ex Corde Ecclesiae*.

[17] John Paul II, *Ex Corde Ecclesiae* (Apostolic Constitution on Catholic Universities), in *Origins* 20 (October 4, 1990): 265, 267–76; hereafter paragraph numbers noted in the text as *ECE*.

But anxieties grew when it came time for drawing up the application document. National attention was drawn to the 1999 international conference on Jesuit higher education at Saint Joseph's University in Philadelphia, where Archbishop Giuseppe Pittau, S.J., secretary of the Vatican Congregation for Catholic Education, was to give a major address. Would he reveal the congregation's hand on the direction the Vatican would take? As it turned out, Pittau was discretely vague, and ended up mainly urging American Catholic educators to strive for excellence.[18]

Last minute appeals were made to the Vatican to keep a juridical element out of the application document. But the Catholic educators' worst fears came to pass. Over the objections of the overwhelming majority of American Catholic higher educators still basking in the light of the freedom granted them by Land O'Lakes, the United States Conference of Catholic Bishops (USCCB) in November 1999 approved an application document that included the juridical implementation of canon 812. The document was sent to Rome where it was approved May 2000, and went into effect May 2001. The document appeared as "*Ex Corde Ecclesiae*: An Application to the United States."[19]

What specifically does the Application assert? It presents and affirms the prescription of canon 812: "Catholics who teach the theological disciplines in a Catholic university are required to have a *mandatum* [mandate] granted by competent ecclesiastical authority" (App 2.4.4e). Whereas *ECE* had included canon 812 in a footnote (50), the Application includes it in the body of the text, perhaps to affirm the canon more strongly.

ECE explains what receiving the mandate signifies: "Catholic theologians . . . are to be faithful to the magisterium [teaching office of the Church] as the authentic interpreter of sacred Scripture and sacred tradition" (2.4.3). The Application clarifies the significance of the *mandatum* more fully: a) it is a "juridical expression of the ecclesial relationship of communion that exists between the church and the Catholic teacher of a theological discipline"; b) it is a recognition that Catholic theologians are "not separate from the church's teaching mission," and that in "responding to their baptismal call, their ecclesial task is to teach, write and research for the benefit of the church and within its communion" (n. 41; cf. 2.4.4e1); c) it "recognizes the professor's commitment and responsibility to teach authentic Catholic doctrine and to refrain from putting forth as Catholic

---

[18] Archbishop Giuseppe Pittau, S.J., "Nature and Mission of the Catholic Colleges and Universities," in Martin R. Tripole, S.J., *Jesuit Education 21: Conference Proceedings on the Future of Jesuit Higher Education, 25–29 June 1999* (Philadelphia: Saint Joseph's University Press, 2000), 365–68.

[19] USCCB, "*Ex Corde Ecclesiae*: An Application to the United States," in *Origins* 30 (June 15, 2000): 68–75; hereafter, App. numbers noted in the text.

teaching anything contrary to the church's magisterium" (2.4.4e3). Normally this commitment to "teach in communion with the church" is to be expressed by the professor's making a "profession of faith and oath of fidelity" (App, n. 42) "in writing" (App 2.4.4e4c).

With full theological clarity, the Application's justification for requiring the *mandatum* "is grounded in the right and responsibility of bishops to safeguard the faithful teaching of Catholic doctrine to the people of God and to assure the authentic presentation of the church's magisterium" (n. 41). The requirement is presented as a prescription without clear disciplinary consequences. Should the theologian not ask for or receive the *mandatum*, the follow-up is left to the university, which "must determine what further action may be taken in accordance with its own mission and statutes" (App, n. 41). Thus much leeway is provided here between the Church's requirement that the theologian receive the *mandatum* for permission to teach theology, and the action, if any, that the university might take, should the theologian not fulfill the requirement. Presumably universities more in sympathy with the Church's teaching would tend to discipline the teacher or even sever its relationship with the professor, while institutions having a looser relationship with the Church would take no action.

It is not immediately obvious why a theology instructor would have problems with signing the *mandatum*, though the most critical element at issue appears to lie in the Application, part 2, article 4.4e3. Yet, professional honesty would seem to require that a good professor not propose as official Church teaching viewpoints that were not. Anyone who did otherwise would be deceiving the students and should not be in the classroom. Strictly speaking, the mandate does not insist that the professor be *personally* committed to authentic Catholic doctrine, but only that the professor accept a commitment to teach it, should such teaching be part of a course curriculum. Why should this present a problem? If a particular doctrinal matter is addressed in a given theology course, why would anyone, even a non-Catholic theology professor, object to stating the official Catholic position? After all, the course is being taught in a Catholic school. The answer to our problem lies at a deeper level—the clash between the Enlightenment mentality and subjection to ecclesial directives, which we will clarify below.

Additional contentious elements are present in the Application over and beyond what had been directed in *ECE*:

1. *ECE* had only "contemplated" that all Catholic universities not directly established by ecclesiastical authority (such as most religious orders' schools) would implement the constitution's general norms or directives, "internalizing them into their governing documents and, as far as possible, [conforming] their existing statutes both to these general

norms and to their applications" (2.1.3). The Application makes the implementation a juridical directive: such universities "are to make the general and particular norms their own, include them in the university's official documentation by reference and in other appropriate ways and, as much as possible, conform their existing statutes to such norms" (2.1.2b). Such a directive could be seen by universities as a violation of their autonomy and, if implemented, a matter for litigation.

2. Going beyond *ECE*, which simply stated that university administrators are to be recruited who "are both willing and able to promote . . . or at least to respect" the "Catholic identity of the university" (2.4.1 and 2.4.2), the Application asserts that the "university president should be a Catholic" (2.4.3a), though it does not juridically mandate it.

3. According to *ECE*, boards of trustees must be informed of their "responsibility for maintaining and strengthening the Catholic identity of the institution" (2.4.1), whereas the Application is more stringent in stating that "to the extent possible, the majority of the board should be Catholics committed to the church" (2.4.2b). However, while the Application is more rigorous here, it nevertheless demands implementation only "to the extent possible," leaving room for exceptions. The critical issue here, however, is what criteria you use to determine if a Catholic is "committed to the church." Obviously, this could be a highly contentious issue.

4. When the university president assumes office, according to the Application, the Catholic should express to the local bishop a "commitment" to the "university's Catholic identity and to the Catholic faith." If the president is a non-Catholic, only a "commitment to the university's Catholic mission and identity" is required (App, n. 36). The requirement for the Catholic applicant clearly crosses the line between normal requirements for job placement skills and private faith experience. And again, how does one measure a commitment to the Catholic faith? Such directives may seem unduly rigorous to many Catholics and a violation of personal freedom and separation of church and state.

5. Whereas *ECE* states that non-Catholic teachers and administrators need only "recognize and respect" the "distinctive Catholic identity of the university" (2.4.4), the Application again demands commitment: "All professors are expected to be aware of and committed to the Catholic mission and identity of their institutions" (2.4.4a). Though the directive does not demand a commitment to Catholicism but only to the Catholic mission and identity of the institution, such a directive could still be considered a violation of individual religious

rights, especially for non-Catholic instructors who might not agree with everything involved in the Church's understanding of its mission. Such a directive could well create procedural problems at times of tenure and promotion.

6. *ECE* declares "the number of non-Catholic teachers should not be allowed to constitute a majority within the institution, which is and must remain Catholic" (2.4.4). The Application states "the university should strive to recruit and appoint Catholics as professors so that, to the extent possible, those committed to the witness of the faith will constitute a majority of the faculty" (2.4.4a).

   In this case, the Application appears, on the one hand, to be slightly more lenient—only "to the extent possible" need Catholics constitute the majority, rather than non-Catholics "not be allowed" to constitute a majority—yet, on the other hand, more demanding, since the majority are not simply to be Catholic, but are to be "committed to the witness of the faith." The directive thus challenges the applicant to have a personal faith experience as well as to share in the Church's mission. Must administration also have adequate accounting procedures, to insure that a majority of the faculty is "committed to the witness of the faith"? Again, judging the value of a person's "commitment" and "witness" could be a contentious issue at crucial times of hiring and firing.

7. Finally, one of the most stringent declarations in *ECE* states that "all Catholic teachers are to be faithful to, and all other teachers are to respect, Catholic doctrine and morals in their research and teaching" (2.4.3), whereas the Application states only that "all professors" are to "exhibit . . . good character" as well as "respect for Catholic doctrine" (2.4.4b). While apparently more lenient, the Application asserts that, if these qualities are found lacking, the university statutes are to specify "the process to be followed to remedy the situation" (ibid.). Though the Application does not clarify what the remedy should be, it makes clear that the university should have an institutional remedial policy in place.

Two Mind-Sets in Opposition

The views represented in *ECE* and the Application, when contrasted with the major objections against them by the liberal Catholic establishment in the United States, provide the most striking example of the clash between the two opposing mind-sets that afflicts the modern era: between the Enlightened thinker and the traditionalist. The former emphasizes the primacy of reason over faith, the independence of reason from external authority, the right of the mind to operate by its own principles of investigation, and the ability of the mind, through its own reasoned processes, to attain "truth" or an understanding of one's world, however these should be defined; the latter recognizes the primacy of faith over reason, the binding power of divine revelation that enters into the historical process from outside history, and the authority of the Church in expressing what that revelation is and safeguarding its authenticity.

According to *ECE*, the goal of a Catholic university is therefore to be of service both to the Church and to society. It is the latter as a university in its "continuous quest for truth through its research, and the preservation and communication of knowledge for the good of society" (30), as well as being an "instrument of cultural progress for individuals as well as for society" (32). But as a *Catholic* university, its mission is "to assure in an institutional manner a Christian presence in the university world confronting the great problems of society and culture" (13). The Catholic university is to develop "a true Christian anthropology founded on the person of Christ" (33). Both of these missions can never be separated from the university's larger mission (shared by all members of the Christian community) to deepen an understanding of the presence of Christ in the world (16).

One of the roles of the university, according to *ECE*, is to "promote dialogue between faith and reason" so that the world might become more fully aware of the "unity of all truth," a mission key to the life of the Church. Since, according to the document, "the things of the earth and the concerns of faith derive from the same God," faith and reason are in a common search "to know the one truth" as well as to arrive at "a more comprehensive understanding of the meaning of human life and of the purpose of God's creation" (17). Accordingly, the university's quest for truth and the promotion of the dignity of the human person can never be separated from the vision of Truth that comes through revelation and is made known by the Church through the magisterium's teaching "in matters of faith and morals" (27).

The difference between the two mind-sets as we have presented them here is strikingly brought to light when one examines the sharp opposition that results from their disparate analyses of an educational principle they both in fact accept: there should be no outside interference in the internal operations of a Catholic university. Both agree, and both argue strongly for that position.

For example, most of the critics of *ECE* assert, as we have seen as early as the Land O'Lakes statement in 1967, that Catholic universities must enjoy "a true autonomy and academic freedom in the face of authority of whatever kind, lay or clerical, external to the academic community itself."[20]

[20] Gallin, *Essential Documents*, 7.

But *ECE* argues for autonomy and freedom for the university as well: the Catholic university "possesses that institutional autonomy necessary to perform its functions effectively and guarantees its members academic freedom."[21] Catholic educators also argue, and have repeatedly argued, that the theologian "must be able to pursue his discipline in the same manner as other research scholars"; theologians must have their scholarship evaluated only by peers "as is the case in other disciplines."[22]

Both, then, agree that there should be no outside interference in the internal operations of a Catholic university. What, then, is the problem? Each understands the meaning of institutional autonomy and academic freedom differently.

The Catholic liberals' interpretation of these terms is the easier to understand. It may be presented in the form of the following argument: Institutional autonomy and academic freedom mean no outside interference in the operations of the institution or in the procedures of its teachers in their writings or classroom presentations. And no outside interference means no involvement in the hiring and administrative policies and academic life of the university by any authority or agencies external to the higher education community.[23] But governance by religious orders as such

---

21 Ibid., 12.

22 "Rome Statement: The Catholic University and the Aggiornamento," 1969, in Gallin, *Essential Documents*, 20.

23 It is interesting to note here that Catholic institutions make no objection to secular accrediting agencies, such as the Middle-Atlantic States Association (MASA), which put pressure on institutions to conform to their educational philosophies, forcing them, for example, to introduce hiring policies and curricula that promote diversity as a requirement for accreditation. The institutions would perhaps respond that there is no inconsistency here, that associations such as MASA are made up of educators from within higher education circles, and so do not constitute authorities "external to the academic community itself." Needless to say, that expression from the Land O'Lakes statement is unclear. But such associations are certainly outside agencies in relation to each institution submitting itself for accreditation. How does this differ from a Catholic institution receiving approval for its programs and policies from external ecclesiastical authorities, especially if these are composed mainly of educators? Of course one might argue that an institution does not have to ask for accreditation, and so, in choosing to do so, necessarily accepts the associations' standards for accreditation. The problem, however, is that not having accreditation can severely damage the well-being of an institution and its standing in the academic world. The institution is therefore almost forced to apply for accreditation and submit to an agency's norms for approval, if it wishes to survive. Similar pressure comes from the American Association of University Professors, which will blacklist any institution that does not submit to its standards. That Catholic institutions do not object to these intrusions illustrates the point we noted earlier, that the Catholic educators at Land O'Lakes were targeting only Catholic Church control in their documents affirming their independence.

or by hierarchical agents of the Church such as the local bishop represents external constraints on the operations of the higher education institution and its teaching community. Therefore such governance is a violation of the institutional autonomy and academic freedom of Catholic institutions and is unacceptable.

The crux of the conflict resides in the fact that, while the Church agrees with the argument's major premise—the definitions of institutional autonomy and academic freedom, and the rejection of external interference in the life of the university and its faculty—the Church does not agree with the minor premise that the Church and religious orders are external to the operations of the Catholic higher education community. The title of the apostolic constitution *Ex Corde Ecclesiae* ("From the Heart of the Church") suggests the Church's position: If the university is Catholic, the Church is not external to the life of the university, because the university exists within the orbit of the life of the Church. And so the Church is internal to the university's autonomy, and does not violate that autonomy by exercising its governance over the university. The neuralgic issue, then, is what is meant by "institutional autonomy."

As *ECE* states, "Every Catholic university . . . has a relationship to the church that is essential to its institutional identity" (27). Catholic universities exist as an integral part of the life of the Church, as everything Catholic does. As such, the Catholic university is like any other Catholic entity, all of which share in various ways in the mission of the Church and are therefore subject to the authority of local bishops and through them to the magisterium of the universal Church. Therefore, as *ECE* states, "even when they do not enter directly into the internal governance of the university, bishops 'should be seen not as external agents but as participants in the life of the Catholic university' " (28) because the university is integral to the total life of the Church.[24]

The university, then, has its specific mission as a university, as we have seen (*ECE* 30), but this mission can never be separated from the larger mission (shared by all members of the Christian community) to promote "a vision of the human person and the world that is enlightened by the Gospel and therefore by a faith in Christ, the Logos, as the center of creation and of human history" (ibid., 16).[25] The explicit mention of the life of the university as "enlightened by the Gospel" and "by a faith in Christ" makes it clear that, as far as the Church is concerned, the life and teachings

---

[24] The constitution is citing a passage from an address John Paul II gave to leaders of Catholic higher education at Xavier University of Louisiana, September 12, 1987.

[25] Notice there is an "enlightenment" granted in the document, but it comes not from reason but from "the Gospel."

of the university must always manifest the direct influence of the Gospel teachings and of a faith experience with Christ. The university therefore is not to be motivated primarily by secular values, but by those consistent with the teachings of the Church and with the faith experience in Christ.

The Application expresses even more richly and deeply the theological foundation for the integration of the Catholic university into the life of the Church. Based on the teaching of Vatican II, the Application argues from an "ecclesiology of communion" that the "church is made up of individual faithful and communities linked with one another [and with the triune God] through many active ecclesial relationships." The "dynamic of communion" unites on a deeper level "the various communities in the church" through which its "mission of salvation" operates. According to the Application, "the Catholic university is a vital institution in the communion of the church and is 'a primary and privileged place for a fruitful dialogue between the Gospel and culture.' "[26] This "richness of communion" brings out the complementary teaching roles of bishops and Catholic universities." Each has its own "distinctive autonomous nature and goal," but in the unity of communion they "are joined as complementary activities," embracing "both the pastoral work of bishops and the academic work of Catholic universities, thus linking the bishops' right and obligation to communicate and safeguard the integrity of church doctrine with the right and obligation of Catholic universities to investigate, analyze, and communicate all truth freely" (App 1.2).

The Catholic university as such has a "twofold relationship"—one as a member of the "international community of knowledge," the other as a community of the Church, whereby it "expresses its Catholic identity through an explicit link with the church." This identity "marks concretely the life, the services and the programs of the university community," and guarantees "in institutional form a Christian presence in the university world." [27]

Maintaining this two-fold relationship entails continuing dialogue between the various individuals and groups who "share responsibility for the character of Catholic higher education." Among these groups are not only faculty, students, and administrators, but also the "sponsoring religious communities of the educational institutions," as well as the "bishop and his collaborators in the local church [who] are integral parties in this dialogue".[28] Thus the Application no less than *Ex Corde Ecclesiae* understands the Catholic university as an integral part of the life of the Church,

[26] The Application is quoting *ECE*, 1.43.

[27] All citations in this paragraph, except the first, are taken from the Application from the Congregation for Catholic Education, "The Church's Presence in the University and in University Culture," 2.2.

[28] Ibid.

and thereby subject to the authority of its hierarchy, just as any other individual or institution in the Church.

WHAT DOES IT MEAN TO BE CATHOLIC?

Why have *Ex Corde Ecclesiae* and its "Application to the United States" caused so much excitement in higher-education circles?

ECE originally received favorable press from Catholic educators because it restored an awareness of the importance of maintaining the Catholic identity of Catholic schools, a principle with which most Catholic educators are in agreement. Whereas in the 1970s and '80s educators were affirming that Catholic schools were "in the Catholic (and Jesuit) tradition" implying a certain aloofness from that tradition, now, in this new era that stresses individuality and uniqueness, stressing Catholic (and Jesuit) identity came into vogue. The problem comes with understanding what precisely being Catholic entails.

Had the teachings disseminated in many of the theology departments of Catholic higher education post-Land O'Lakes remained generally consistent with the authoritative teachings of the Church, probably no conflict between the Vatican and American Catholic educators would ever have arisen. Indeed, *ECE* would probably never have been written. A problem arose in view of the growing dissonance and now long-standing gap between the teachings of the Church and the theological aberrations widespread in Catholic education, to which the Vatican's attention was gradually drawn.

To correct the problem, the Vatican saw the need to establish a juridical understanding of the word "Catholic" for Catholic educators, meaning that schools that wish to identify themselves as Catholic must maintain communion with the Catholic Church as well as fidelity to its authoritative teachings. Progressive educators have a broader understanding of the nature of Catholic identity, allowing for a more attenuated relationship to the Church, with greater freedom of thought and reduced Catholic presence. Thus the opposition between two entirely different mind-sets, between those who understand Catholic identity to include conformity to the teachings of the Church and those who do not. And so it is the juridical aspect of the Application's understanding of "Catholic" that focuses on the center of the controversy.

ECE and the Application's understanding of the issues at play in Catholic higher education comes from a mind-set totally at variance with the Enlightened mentality that is widespread in American Catholic education today. Merely to address an issue such as "truth" is to speak to the Enlightened mind out of an antiquated, metaphysical mold dating from the pre-Kantian period. It is to speak of a concept that the Enlightened mind is no longer able to grasp within the rationalistic and empirical horizons that now limit the modern human being's realm of thought. It is to speak in terms of absolutes where these are no longer rationally negotiable. Truth for the Enlightened person becomes a vestige of a primitive, archaic mind-set replaced by historical-critical investigation, by pragmatic inductions from within the ad hoc horizons of the modern pluralistic and multicultural world, where, if one speaks of "truth" at all, one does so only from within the relative, subjective viewpoint of one's own limited mind-set (already the beginnings of postmodernism).

Just to reflect on *ECE*'s use of this one word, "truth," tells us all we need to know about the wide gap between the two mind-sets, and how far liberal Catholic intellectuals have come from the metaphysically based spiritual outlook of the Church. Ironically, when the AAUP wrote their *Statement of Principles on Academic Freedom and Tenure* in 1940, they also spoke, as *ECE* does, of "the advancement of truth" and promotion of "the common good" as goals for higher education: "Institutions of higher education are conducted for the common good and not to further the interest of either the individual teacher or the institution as a whole. The common good depends upon the free search for truth and its free exposition. . . . Freedom in research is fundamental to the advancement of truth."[29] In *ECE*, the advancement of truth and the promotion of the common good are understood as limiting factors and as norms for guidance on what a university and its instructors may do. Presumably when the AAUP composed their 1940 statement, the same was true for them. The AAUP may have since abandoned those guidelines. More than likely, however, even when the AAUP spoke of truth and the common good in 1940, these were terms already affected by the relativistic and even postmodern mentalities that were overtaking the American educators' mentality. Thus, while *ECE* would understand truth and the common good to have concrete content, in terms of God's purposes for the human being and the well-being of the community in its search for union with the Truth, for the AAUP and its postmodern educators, the terms had probably already begun to become void of all intent.

In view of this tremendous gap in understanding, one can see how far away the Enlightenment has brought many Catholics from union with the institutional Catholic Church, a union that no longer has any value for those who bought into the rationalist scholarship of the so-called historical-critical method as the only basis for theological conclusions.

Thus, since Vatican II, Catholic higher education has taken two roads: (1) toward greater integration into the life of the Church and conformity to the Church's teachings; and (2) toward greater separation from the institutional

---

[29] AAUP, *1940 Statement*, 1.

Church, with Catholic identity determined by individual criteria and self-regulation. Ultimately what is at issue is the role of the institutional Church in determining the meaning of "Catholic" in modern Catholic life.

Catholicism and Secular Humanism

And therein lie the deeper roots of the controversy between the Catholic Church and the thinking of many modernist Catholics regarding Catholic education.

The depth of the division was made clear in the conference on Jesuit higher education held at Saint Joseph's University, June of 1999. The conference brought together over three hundred laypersons and Jesuits from around the world, with more than eighty presentations made by prominent educators.

Though their concerns were decidedly pro-Catholic, and their desires to preserve the Catholic and Jesuit dimensions of higher education, the participants never came to a consensus on what being Catholic and Jesuit meant, or how Catholic and Jesuit values, whatever they might be, could be preserved.

In his address to the conference, Joseph A. O'Hare, S.J., then president of Fordham University, pointed out that

> the future of Jesuit higher education will depend on an unqualified commitment to the Catholic religious and intellectual tradition, expressed in part by an active relationship to the wider Catholic community, a relationship to the Church; in other words, either by statutory bond or by an institutional commitment, to recall the terminology of *Ex Corde Ecclesiae*.[30]

O'Hare went on to argue that the distinctiveness of Jesuit education would be found in its roots in St. Ignatius's *Spiritual Exercises* and in an Ignatian spirituality that finds "its continuing vitality in the service of the Church and the Kingdom of God."[31]

Many others, however, were more eager to separate Jesuit values from a too close association with the Church. The proceedings provided good grounds to conclude that the secularization that occurred in many Protestant schools in the early twentieth century is well underway at Jesuit and other Catholic institutions as well.

A basis for this view may be found, for example, in the distinction especially made by admissions recruiters between Jesuit values and Catholic identity. In open discussions held during the conference, many said they emphasize the former and downplay or ignore the latter as a matter of pol-

---

[30] Joseph A. O'Hare, S.J., "What Are the Odds of Jesuit Higher Education Surviving in America?," in Tripole, *Jesuit Education 21*, 437.

[31] Ibid., 441.

icy. But why? The distinction, they said, enabled them to identify Jesuit schools to potential applicants as institutions promoting humanistic values rather than Catholic identity. The effect was to make being Jesuit distinguishable from being Catholic.

Such a distinction seemed to appall some Jesuits. Nevertheless, that recruiters make such a distinction as part of their effort to appeal to potential students may indicate how ingrained secularization has already become among students as well as among recruiters (and, as we shall see, how much Jesuit education may have catered to such secularization). The point is that a striking new opposition is being created here, where being Catholic is identified with membership in the Catholic Church and acceptance of its official faith and moral teachings, whereas being Jesuit is identified with secular humanism.

That dichotomy may be illustrated further in the hiring of new faculty members increasingly being chosen for their professional competence and support of humanistic values, rather than for an interest in fostering a Catholic culture on the campus.

One extremely pertinent but overlooked presentation at the conference illustrating this point was given by a lay administrator at a prominent Jesuit university, who bluntly admitted without comment or apology that Jesuit institutions will no longer consider support for the Catholic mission a factor in the hiring of new faculty. He argued that Jesuit distinctiveness is now identified with humanistic values, and that, when the Jesuit character is understood in this way, "Jesuit education can and will thrive independently of the fortunes of the institutional Catholic Church." He went on to say that "if you were to tell faculty tomorrow to 'hire for mission' with an emphasis on Catholic rather than, or over and above, Jesuit, I know what will happen. . . . The present faculty simply will not do it."[32] The peremptory nature of these remarks indicates how difficult it would be to reverse this trend toward secular humanism, since the faculty are the primary decision-makers for hiring in their departments.

But our administrator then went on to apply "Catholic" merely to the inculcation of these humanistic values. He argued that "Catholic" might be understood not as O'Hare had understood it, identifying it with the institutional Church, but "in a more inclusive, less juridical sense." In this case, Catholic becomes identified with the humanistic values themselves, as a "way of looking at the world," a "secular mysticism," seeing the world as "profoundly sacramental," "love show[ing] itself in deeds," "a principle of

[32] The speaker was Francis L. Fennell, then associate dean of the College of Arts and Sciences at Loyola University Chicago, responding to O'Hare's talk; "Respondents," in Tripole, *Jesuit Education 21*, 444–47, at 446.

ultimate meaning,"[33] or a call for "compassionate service." When taken in this sense, Jesuit education can still remain Catholic.[34]

What is remarkable here is not the emphasis upon humanistic values in an understanding of what is Catholic—Catholicism has always been associated with humanistic values—but that that identification is distinguished from a relationship to the Church and without any mention of the person of Christ. Whereas up to now, admissions recruiters and administrators had understood "Catholic" to include fidelity to the Catholic Church and acceptance of its teachings, from which they sometimes reluctantly felt the need to alienate themselves, here being Catholic is redefined as simply espousing secular human values. The Enlightenment mentality expressed here finds the institutional Church obsolete and irrelevant, and replaces it with a so-called "Catholic" secular humanism.

Deeper theological roots of secular humanism on our campuses may be found in the increasing acceptance of a principle never accepted by the Catholic Church, that faith is a private matter. This perspective includes relegating faith matters to campus ministry and pastoral counseling, rather than considering a Catholic culture something all university personnel should share in. This dichotomy between faith and reason or faith and society's values may have much to do with the above-mentioned division between humanistic values and Catholic identity, but above all, it represents the increasing encroachment of Enlightenment thinking upon Catholic circles.

In view of the wide disagreement between the Church and liberal Catholic educators over what Catholic education means, one wonders why the liberals continue to insist on retaining the term "Catholic" as a designation for their schools. Why not abandon that cumbersome designation, since the term leads the general public to identifying the institutions with a relationship to the Church that is no longer considered desirable? Why not simply call the schools private institutions of liberal arts education, as many other well-respected institutions do?[35]

To make such a suggestion, however, would bring terror to the minds of many liberals. The fact is, the life-blood of these universities was originally generated by the Catholic Church, and it is hard to believe many of them

---

33 The last four quotes Fennell borrowed from O'Hare's talk.

34 Fennell, in Tripole, *Jesuit Education 21*, 447.

35 Some institutions have already done this: When the Archdiocese of New York recently removed the designation "Catholic" from Marymount Manhattan College, college officials agreed with the action and argued that the college had not been Catholic since 1961 when it became separated from its founding religious order. Marist College in Poughkeepsie has also apparently declared itself no longer Catholic. Catholic World News, "Archdiocese removes college's Catholic designation," April 29, 2005, www.catholicculture.org/news/.

could survive today without maintaining that same life-blood. Since the majority of Catholic university students still come from Catholic high school "feeder" schools, where administrators often send their students to Catholic universities because they are "Catholic," ceasing to use the term could represent a significant loss of revenue, especially where many Catholic institutions have often not attained a level of academic excellence that allows them to compete successfully for top-notch students by secular academic standards. It is difficult not to conclude, therefore, that the liberals want to have it both ways: to hold on to the designation "Catholic" primarily because to lose it would mean an official diminishment of identity for their schools, while dropping the meaning of the term "Catholic" for the university as an integral part of the intellectual and spiritual life of the Catholic Church.

We have in the reaction to *ECE* just one more example of the divisive impact of the Enlightenment mentality on contemporary Catholic culture. It is difficult to see how the two outlooks have any possibility of being reunited "in the heart of the Church."

Formulas for Maintaining Catholic Identity

Peter Steinfels

Against the secularist inroads being made on Catholic higher education have come calls from respected and significant Catholic scholars to do what is necessary to maintain the Catholic identity of our institutions.

One such call has come from Peter Steinfels, former religion writer for the *New York Times*, university professor and now co-director of the Fordham University Center on Religion and Culture. Steinfels is quietly troubled by the secularist trends in Catholic higher education, and in his latest book seems sincere in his calls for reversing those trends. But his suggestions reflect the refrain of many liberals who recognize the problem and want to suggest reform, but without ever saying exactly what must be done, lest they be accused of actually having a position. Thus his recommendations continually lack teeth.

For example, he argues that it might be best to "speak of Catholic identities in the plural" depending on the different histories and constituencies of different schools, rather than to search for a "single way" of fulfilling the prescriptions of *ECE*. Such an approach leaves the door open to almost anything.

Steinfels asks whether Catholic institutions present any distinctively *Catholic* approaches to studies in various areas of academic life, such as in "history, social theory, literature, art, spirituality, ethnic studies, political science, and philosophy." Catholic identity, he argues, must be "centered in the Catholic university's intellectual life," and unless it "pervade[s] the curriculum of the university as a whole," Catholic identity is lacking.[36] Steinfels feels the Catholic identity should leave an imprint upon "the character of the campus community and culture." But he doesn't give a very clear indication of what that imprint would look like.

He asks, for example, "Should honorary degrees or other awards be bestowed on pro-choice or pro-capital-punishment politicians? Should groups advocating access to abortion or calling for an end to marriage laws distinguishing between heterosexual and homosexual couples receive student-government funding?" But he doesn't answer his questions, choosing to leave such answers to unnamed persons who would make "judgment calls." "What counts," he argues, is "the *overall pattern of vibrant engagement* with Catholic concerns and traditions in the intellectual and communal life of the institution."[37] Thus he provides a beautifully composed and exciting standard of judgment regarding Catholic identity that would call all worthy Catholic academicians to arms, if they had any standard by which to measure when that "vibrant engagement" was actually present.

Equally nebulous standards are invoked in other areas: Eschewing the notion that Catholic identity would be "imposed from the top down" by "authorities like the bishops" who are "outside the scholarly community," Steinfels argues that "the religious [not the Catholic] character of colleges and universities" is to "be determined by the faculty." He does not seem to realize that without a mandate from above, there is no way to know in what desert area this might abandon the *Catholic* identity of the institution if the faculty is not inclined to foster it.[38]

Catholic identity is "inescapably linked to hiring practices." Steinfels broaches the question of "hiring for mission" as a way of insuring that the slippery slope to secularism brought on by hiring simply on the basis of qualification without regard for religion be avoided. While Steinfels admits that hiring for mission would inevitably provoke "objections" of imposing orthodoxy, discrimination, and violating privacy, he thinks that such objections can be satisfied by four components: "achieving clarity about mission, distinguishing between hiring for Catholic identity and hiring Catholics, embedding concerns about the religious dimension of mission into the entire hiring process and beyond it, and eschewing mechanical or inflexible rules."

1. To achieve clarity of mission, he "imagines" a brochure faculty applicants would receive that would indicate "institutional commitment to viewing reality in terms of creation, incarnation, and redemption in

[36] Peter Steinfels, *A People Adrift: The Crisis of the Roman Catholic Church in America* (New York: Simon & Schuster, 2003), 148–50.

[37] Ibid., 151.

[38] Ibid., 152.

Jesus." This is the one time Jesus is mentioned anywhere in Steinfel's idea of a Catholic university, and it is the closest he comes to suggesting a Christian faith dimension that all faculty hired might be asked to support. But, alas, if they sign on to this "responsibility" that only the "Catholic community" at the university undertakes, doing so should entail no more than "rigorous scholarship," openness to "diversity," and "conversation and dialogue" with "diverse religious perspectives." In other words, no demands upon the faculty necessarily different from those made at any secular institution.[39]

2. The hiring is not necessarily linked to hiring Catholics; rather the primary issue would be public scholarship, not personal creed, the workings of one's mind and not the state of one's soul. Steinfels allows that "at some subtle point" such intellectual concerns might intersect with "personal creed," but the matter should never be broached. Inasmuch as non-Catholics might exhibit "mission-related priorities" more in keeping with the institution's priorities than those of many Catholics, the important point is that the candidates' "scholarly research and teaching agenda" reflect "the institution's Catholic identity." Even if this should produce a faculty with only 25% of "nominal and active" Catholics, Steinfels feels that is not a problem.[40]
3. Steinfels considers "embedding" concerns about religion "essential" to the hiring process. He readily accepts that such a process is not fulfilled simply by having candidates read a mission statement and then agree to foster the mission, as is presently done at many Catholic institutions; rather, hiring for mission would need to influence the entire process of hiring, including an ongoing education into the mission after hiring "with lectures, film series, panel discussion, seminars." People who are hired even "with minimal potential" may turn out, says Steinfels, "to be major contributors if their knowledge is deepened."[41]
4. Steinfels spurns the idea of "mechanical principles" that apply across the board without nuance. Decisions about hiring in any department should, nevertheless, reflect the degree to which a department is in need of persons comfortable with the university's religious identity.[42]

Though Steinfels is confident that hiring for mission following these four components will work, he admits there must be "constant alertness" to insure

[39] Ibid., 152–55.
[40] Ibid., 155–56.
[41] Ibid., 157–58.
[42] Ibid., 158.

the success of the mission. Nor can the goal be accomplished "without leadership." Presidents must make the mission among their "top concerns." Attaining the goal will not be easy, admits Steinfels, because those in academia willing to be a part of such a mission are decreasing.[43]

Finally, after this long discussion of what is required and is so important for hiring for mission, Steinfels agrees with Monika Hellwig: "Discerning a Catholic identity appropriate today 'is not a matter of something we have lost and must retrieve. It is a matter of discovering how to do something we have never done before.'"[44] But if that is the case, how does one hire for mission when one is not even sure what that mission is?

One hardly knows where to begin in critiquing Steinfels's analysis of today's issues regarding Catholic identity, as well as his prescriptions for restoring that identity. Note, for one, that candidates are called to accept the "religious" identity of the institution, rather than its "Catholic" identity. Secondly, they are not called to identify with the institution's commitment to Jesus Christ or the Church, but only to a willingness to support the identity through interest, scholarship, and teaching. Thirdly, Steinfels's formulas are riddled with conditional and qualifying words, such as "might," "perhaps," and "maybe," lest there be any specific requirements for employing his agenda. Though he admittedly recognizes the importance of leadership, he ultimately places the success of his project in the hands of the faculty, whose desire to implement a mission in any way compatible with the Catholic mission is never questioned. But what if the faculty who have been hired without mission for decades are not interested? Finally, he never clearly identifies the Catholic mission as anything necessarily more than principles compatible with secular humanism—and without a mission beyond that, Catholic education will remain as secularly humanistic after Steinfels's prescriptions are put into effect as they are today.

George Dennis O'Brien

An excellent approach to devising a philosophy of education that validates the existence of a Catholic university comes from George Dennis O'Brien's *The Idea of a Catholic University*.[45]

O'Brien argues that both the university and the Church are in search of truth, but there are different types of truth, such as "scientific, artistic, and religious."[46] O'Brien takes it for granted that the university is in search of scientific or rational truth. But the modern university has also come to

---

[43] Ibid., 159–61.

[44] Ibid., 161. Steinfels is citing Hellwig.

[45] George Dennis O'Brien, *The Idea of a Catholic University* (Chicago: University of Chicago, 2002).

[46] Ibid., 26.

accept artistic truth, a truth attached to the experiences, insights, and vision of individuals that at the same time transcends their individuality and historicity to attain universal dimensions.[47]

The truth of Christianity is like the truth of art, "always to and from the person,"[48] rooted in "a deep *personal* vision,"[49] at the same time addressing a value having meaning for the universal "*human* condition."[50] And yet, with religious truth, the Christian comes to know not simply by scientific investigation, scholarly research, or artistic experience, but by experiences far deeper. O'Brien argues from the ancient Church principle *lex orandi, lex credendi*, "the law of prayer is the law of belief," meaning that the beliefs that the Church accepts as truth follow from its life of prayer.

As O'Brien puts it, "There is no appropriation of the truth of faith, the reality of God, except through the attitude of worship, prayer, or love." God is not discovered as a neutrally observable object, as in science, nor is God known simply as the product of insightful experience, as in the arts. Rather, God is known "in the sacramental act, the central ritual of worship." This ultimately makes an "epistemology of prayer . . . or worship necessary conditions for apprehending belief."[51] To perceive this truth—religious truth—is to enter what O'Brien calls the realm of "the real," where "final, absolute, infallible truth" is revealed. This truth is known only "within some mode of personal participation."[52]

In Christianity, however, faith is based on *privileged* truth: Jesus does not simply reveal truth, he is the Truth. Such an understanding of truth as identified with a person "is fundamentally antithetic to the assumptions of universal reason and scientific truth."[53] Jesus—the "*I* am the Truth"—is "life itself," "the real," and the sacraments, like iconic art, make Jesus really present: the Eucharist is "a symbol that participates in the reality it depicts," at the same time making that reality present to the one who participates in it.[54] For O'Brien, the sacraments represent a third kind of truth: beyond what can be captured by either scientific truth (factual or propositional) or artistic truth (engaging the human and experiential through individual personal depiction) lies the "truth of presence," the truth *inside* "the real," the truth inside "the too-muchness of existence" that lies "beyond the neat orders of 'normal' academic pursuit."[55]

---

[47] Ibid., 46.
[48] Ibid.
[49] Ibid., 40.
[50] Ibid., 43.
[51] Ibid., 169–71.
[52] Ibid., 172.
[53] Ibid., 33.
[54] Ibid., 55, 64.
[55] Ibid., 57, 59, 64.

The Gospels are also iconic: they open to "the reality of God" and make that reality present. What we experience in the Gospels is also "the real" as "a totality, as a whole," as an overwhelming presence. There is no before or after, but only "totalizing existential presence" that lifts one out of an isolated world of sin.[56] In Jesus, one experiences "the fullness of God's word, the Truth that encompasses the mystery of existence," the "word" that stands for "the real" beyond science and art.[57] It is this presence that leads to the hope of salvation, in a life beyond death with the resurrected Jesus.[58]

As a belief experience, this presence is available only to one who is open to it: "Reading a depiction iconically is not something that occurs automatically. . . . The one who would read the Gospel as icon must also be a participant in some way in the Jesus story." Thus, appreciating the Bible demands a sharing in "a worshiping, sacramental, liturgical community as an instrument of its sense of life meaning."[59]

O'Brien addresses the question of how this Christian, Catholic understanding of "iconic presentations" can fit into the life of the university. For O'Brien, the university must address questions regarding "the final meaning of life, ultimate reality, the 'really real' ":[60] "if the university claims to encompass *all* that is legitimate for human consideration within the array of its usual academic subjects," it cannot exclude theology that investigates "consideration for 'a way of life' as it relates to the ultimate, to 'the real.' " The Catholic university "holds that Salvation is a deep human quest." This necessarily means, then, presenting "the Catholic choice" regarding the meaning of life and the way to salvation.[61]

O'Brien devotes a chapter to the contentious issues *ECE* confronts. O'Brien addresses in his book the basic question "Is a 'Catholic university' a contradiction?"[62] Such appears to be the case, he argues, when *ECE* employs the juridical model of the Church, which presents the Church as "an *official* witness, *the* official witness, the *infallible* official witness." It is the Church's power of infallibility that is the heart of the problem, since it implies "definitive *answers*," whereas "open inquiry" normally "marks the academic enterprise."[63] The problem is that, while competence in the methodologies and investigative procedures of a discipline normally provides the green light for what a professor might pursue, in theology, *ECE*

[56] Ibid., 72, 74–75.
[57] Ibid., 77.
[58] Ibid., 79.
[59] Ibid., 82–83, 87.
[60] Ibid., 97.
[61] Ibid., 104–6.
[62] Ibid., 164.
[63] Ibid., 146–47.

provides "an *external* test" seen as compromising academic freedom, namely, that "Catholic theology [must be] taught in a manner faithful to Scripture, Tradition and the Church's Magisterium (*ECE*, 20)," the last represented "in the person of the local bishop."[64]

O'Brien admits that "it does seem reasonable to insist on some sort of authentication of *Catholic* competence,"[65] as well as to require the Christian theologian to accept "at least some of the 'orthodox' beliefs."[66] But, says O'Brien, when *ECE* makes the test for orthodoxy that which is acceptable to the Church's hierarchy, this involves a reduction of the Church to the institutional, juridical model, as presented by Avery Cardinal Dulles in his book *Models of the Church*.[67] But if the Church is the People of God, that model does not seem "appropriate."[68]

O'Brien finds Dulles's fifth model, the *sacramental*, the only acceptable model of the Church applicable in this discussion. The sacramental model overcomes alienation between the university and the Church by preserving "the given reality as detailed in science and art while at the same time opening up a supernatural dimension of human life and perception." For O'Brien, the Catholic university becomes the "conjunction of the sacramental and the scientific," so that "Catholic university – sacrament + science."[69] Such a view would include recognizing "the legitimacy of science and art, of 'ordinary' reality," but by seeking "the real," would challenge the university to probe beyond the realms of science and art to realms to which science and art "are methodologically barred": "Sacramental perception deepens ordinary reality, it does not destroy it. Jesus is a figure of ordinary history not myth; only in that way can our experience of him be deepened into an icon of God."[70]

In spite of his devotion to the sacramental model, O'Brien does not think the institutional model can be abandoned completely, and so he seeks to incorporate the institutional into the sacramental model.[71]

O'Brien suggests that by "centering on a definitive experience," like the Resurrection, "the real" takes on "an 'institutional' cast," with "a 'law' of prayer that creates the 'law' of belief": "one cannot avoid" institutionalizing in the sense of written "creeds," "codes of behavior," and "rituals" because "they hold that there is something definitive in the core experience of 'the real.'"[72] But, says O'Brien, one must not confuse the "*definitive*"

[64] Ibid., 149.
[65] Ibid.
[66] Ibid., 159.
[67] O'Brien cites from the New York: Doubleday, 1978, edition.
[68] O'Brien, 160.
[69] Ibid., 175.
[70] Ibid., 183.
[71] Ibid., 184.
[72] Ibid., 185–86.

with "the notion that one can *define* it." The definitive opening to "the real" that the Resurrection provides is clear in that it is "appropriated in prayer, love, worship," but to move from the "defining experience to a *once-and-for-all definition*" would be to prescind from the experience "in favor of intellectual distancing and appraisal." Such a move would mean that the Church "misunderstands its own inner life as a worshiping community and improperly interferes with the task of the university." In fact, because "the real" is "mystery" that "engages the totality of the believer at the deepest levels of his life participation," "church talk" is inevitably no more than "words and images" that touch upon the mystery and yet miss the mark. But the inability to define the mystery does not vitiate its nature as definitive, but rather enhances it, since that is the nature of "the compelling involvement at the heart of mystery."[73]

How would one construct theology courses within a curriculum where "participation, praxis, and prayer" are "investigative tools" of "the real"? Such is the question O'Brien must finally face.[74] He argues that, in a Catholic university, which operates "around a definitive historical memory" of Jesus, the undergraduate curriculum should include courses in both fundamental and dogmatic theology. But for O'Brien, fundamental theology means exploring "the 'logic' or 'grammar' of 'the real.'" To discover God requires that one be "addressed" by "the real," and so fundamental theology must address "the status of love, commitment, and decision." O'Brien even suggests that the course for freshmen be called "Love, Commitment, and Decision (LCD)." Such a course would "point beyond academic review to life choice, to participation beyond appraisal," and address such fundamental questions as "Is love possible? Is love a reality? . . . What is life without love and decision?" This course would be required of every student at a Catholic university "lest the ultimate existential meaning and base of the university's fundamental enterprise be distorted or go unrecognized."[75]

The second, dogmatic theology course, as O'Brien understands it, would present "traditional Catholic orthodoxy." By this, O'Brien means the "enormous body of liturgy, theology, dogmatic pronouncements, meditations, catechisms, moral instructions, spiritual guidance, and so on that constitutes the language of Catholicism." But doesn't this bring back the juridical model of the Church that O'Brien wants to avoid, especially when the curriculum includes the presentation of "dogmatic pronouncements"?

Not, according to O'Brien, if the proper "grammar" is used. The mistake of the past has been to present these teachings as if one were "drilling

---

[73] Ibid., 187, 190.

[74] Ibid., 199.

[75] Ibid., 201–3.

in the orthodox language . . . without first ensuring the grammar is understood." Done properly, the course will show the depth of the "grammar of God," that orthodoxy "rests on a fundamental grammar of love, commitment, and decision." Such a grammar will illustrate all the value to be found in "participation in life," and will show in dogmatic theology "what attitude and life stance emerges from confrontation with the density of 'the real.' " In ecumenical dialogue, where there might be differences among claimants about "the real," to the extent that each view follows from a genuine "participatory encounter with 'the real,' " there can be no effort to "de-center" the encounter: "The reach to 'the real' of other insights cannot be negated or de-centered." O'Brien suggests "concentric circles where all insights converge on a common center."

To move instruction about love, commitment, and decision out of the abstract, O'Brien suggests students be placed in "life situations that demand love, commitment, and decision," such as social service programs. O'Brien recognizes, however, that even with praxis students may not enter into the reality of love and commitment. He argues, therefore, that praxis must come from "structure from within which beliefs are to be articulated and then judged appropriate." "Good works" cannot simply be added on to the curriculum: "They are necessary epistemological moments in the development of theology."[76]

Critique

O'Brien's study is a profound, systematic presentation of a theory of reality that goes beyond the usual understanding of the work of a university as limited to the scientific and aesthetic realms, to the deeper study of "the really real." There is no doubt it is a valuable and masterful systematic justification for the study of religion within a university curriculum, especially on a Catholic campus. O'Brien points to the participatory nature of contact with "the real" as a necessary epistemology for knowledge of it, and in this respect goes beyond what is normally a part of the university classroom.

And he is right: If the university should study whatever is real, the study of the religious dimension of life should be included in that investigation. Even atheists have to admit the possibility of God's existing, and on that basis alone, should encourage a study of that question. Since most Americans believe in the existence of God, even more reason for a study of the religious encounter with life, especially on a Catholic campus. Most Catholic universities, without being able to formulate their theory at a level so profound as O'Brien's, probably do allow for a study of the religious dimension of life, but without appreciating the epistemological importance

[76] Ibid., 203–6.

of the participatory encounter. By explaining the need for that encounter, O'Brien makes a major contribution.

There is a more pointed question, however, that O'Brien fails to handle well: How much must the authority of the hierarchy be allowed to leave its imprint on what goes on in the Catholic university, especially in its study of dogmatic theology? O'Brien provides a solid basis for the study of theology as such, but is weak when it comes to determining what kind of theology is to be studied there. O'Brien rightly argues that belief comes out of a life of prayer: "We pray, *then* we fashion statements of belief."[77] But is it as simple as that? *Lex orandi, lex credendi* cannot simply mean that participation in the liturgical and sacramental life of the Church reveals all that is necessary for a formulation of beliefs. The Latin formula has to mean that the formulation and understanding of doctrine flow from a life of *faith*.

The early Church surely did not begin with prayer; it began with the experience of the physical Jesus Christ, and in that interpersonal faith experience arose the knowledge of who Christ is and the meaning of his teaching. But who Christ is was ultimately not simply known by a personal encounter with him. A study of the early life of the Church makes it clear that different, conflicting understandings of who he is rose from these encounters. The early Church, therefore, early on realized that it was necessary to have an authoritative body, one of whose functions would be to discern which were accurate perceptions of who Christ is and which were not. O'Brien himself admits that participation in the sacramental life of the Church opens the receiver to a profound personal experience that cannot be fully captured on the formulaic level. Indeed true. But it is equally true that, sooner or later, one has to arrive at some attempt to formulate what one understands to be encountered in the faith experience, lest the experience lack all clarity. It is this kind of formulation that is known as doctrine and dogma. To arrive at this level, however, requires a juridical body that determines what that dogma is.

While O'Brien rightly states that "there is no belief in the religious 'facts' except through the 'perception' of prayer, worship, or love,"[78] there ultimately comes the time when for the sake of understanding Truth one must formulate exactly what those "facts" are, and to do that inevitably entails the work of an adjudicating body. Surely a proper "grammar" is necessary to read the experience properly, as O'Brien argues, but by barring the juridical Church from an influence on the life of the Catholic campus, he fails to provide a bridge from having knowledge of that "grammar" of "love, commitment, and decision"[79] to knowledge of the precise teachings of the Church that follow from that grammar.

[77] Ibid., 169.
[78] Ibid., 170.
[79] Ibid., 204.

Without the controlling authority of the juridical hierarchical Church, the sacramental dimension of the Church risks being reduced to the purely symbolic presence Protestantism espouses. O'Brien's sacramental theology of the Church is an admirable enlargement of the discussion on how Catholicism can be justified on a university campus, but leaves no structures for safeguarding that Catholic practice remain Catholic.

By failing to produce a way of integrating the received dogmatic teachings of the Church into his sacramental model, O'Brien fails to provide an acceptable alternative to the arguments provided in *ECE*. Curiously enough, even after devoting a chapter to the views treated in that encyclical, he never gets around to discussing the arguments provided by that encyclical for making academic freedom and the authority of the Church compatible.

Melanie Morey and John Piderit, S.J.

Perhaps the best work to analyze the current crisis in Catholic higher education and propose an adequate response to it, *Catholic Higher Education: A Culture in Crisis*, is sure to cause contention for its hard-hitting, down-to-earth, honest appraisal of the situation and the strong Catholic-oriented measures it will take to correct it.[80] Authors Melanie Morey and John Piderit, S.J., accept the fact that crisis is not only "looming," but that it threatens the ability of the institutions to survive. Their findings are based on data gathered from interviews from January to May 2002, with 124 senior administrators from 33 Catholic colleges and universities.

Based on these interviews, the authors drew three perspectives the administrators considered central to maintaining a Catholic institution: the presence of (1) a "Catholic intellectual tradition" that shows the connection between faith and reason, (2) an environment or "institutional culture" that will impact the Catholic formation of the students, and (3) a "commitment to the Catholic faith" on the part of administrators and faculty. Regarding each of these areas, Morey and Piderit looked for practices at the institutions that indicated what they called "distinguishability"—characteristics that made Catholic institutions unique—a factor that they consider essential if Catholic institutions are to survive amid the plethora of nonsectarian institutions.[81] They reluctantly concluded they were unable to find "much evidence" in any of these three areas of "specifically Catholic contributions" distinguishing the Catholic institutions from their nonsectarian counterparts.[82]

Lack of distinguishability was evident elsewhere as well. For example, the administrators made it clear they intended their institutions to be "fully

80 Melanie M. Morey and John J. Piderit, S.J., *Catholic Higher Education: A Culture in Crisis* (New York: Oxford University Press, 2006).

81 Ibid., 8–9.

82 Ibid., 9.

Catholic,"[83] and that a "vibrant Catholic culture" was an "asset" for Catholic education. But Morey and Piderit felt this was an expression of hope rather than of concrete programs and policies that would foster such goals. Such hope, the authors argue, needed to move "into the arena of effective action" if a Catholic culture was not to evaporate into the surrounding "secular academic atmosphere."[84]

Morey and Piderit emphasize the importance of a Christocentric and ecclesial dimension that is rarely found in other well-known studies of Catholic higher education: that "Catholics who teach, administer, and serve at Catholic institutions" are "called first and foremost to respond to God's gift of faith in belief and action and to follow Christ in the Church." Such a faith life must be supported by a Catholic culture, our authors argue, which they define as "the group of practices and behaviors, beliefs, and understandings that form the ever-deepening context that nourishes the community of believers and energizes their commitment to Christ through the Church." This culture provides "plausibility for belief in Christ" for nonbelievers, and reinforces the faith of believers as well as their "appreciation of the teachings of the Church."[85] The authors argue that "course corrections" enhancing the Catholic culture "need to be undertaken at Catholic colleges and universities if they hope to sustain a vibrant religious character."[86]

The authors distinguish between "cultural catalysts" and "cultural citizens." The latter "live and process" within the culture and are important to the operational life of the institution. But the writers repeatedly stress the importance of cultural catalysts: These are "role models, knowledge experts, and heroic leaders" who "sustain, enhance, and transmit a vibrant culture." Without them, a culture cannot survive.[87]

One of the major factors is the crisis caused by the fact that leadership roles have been turned over to laypersons not equipped with the "religious formation and education" and "religious commitment and knowledge" formerly provided by the religious orders that founded the institutions. Nor can the laity count on much support from the Church to provide the formation necessary to assume their responsibilities.[88]

Part of the problem also follows from the fact that while the basic questions remain the same—what is "Catholic identity," what constitutes an "authentically Catholic" institution, how to balance religious and secular

---

[83] Ibid., 49.
[84] Ibid., 33.
[85] Ibid.
[86] Ibid., 45.
[87] Ibid., 29.
[88] Ibid., 3.

missions—answers are widely disparate. Yet administrators seem to think that a hopeful sign is found in the fact that, while as late as three years earlier, being Catholic was considered an embarrassment, now emphasizing Catholic identity is considered a value, though perhaps not as much among faculty as among administration and students:[89] "Faculty hostility to the religious mission of Catholic colleges and universities" is a big worry to administrators. Repeated expressions of indignation at the fostering of the Catholic mission are found on many campuses.[90]

Many administrators emphasized pride in their institution's strong "Catholic intellectual tradition" and the "significant contribution" they were making to American higher education.[91] And yet, the problem of distinguishability rose again, in that reality did not support these assertions. For example, "no administrator . . . offered any evidence beyond course grades that students were actually appropriating any significant aspects of the Catholic intellectual tradition that could be called upon after graduation." Administrators expressed great eagerness that the Catholic dimension on their campuses be enhanced, but most of this was expressed only "in the optative mood." They recognized the "centrality of the Catholic intellectual tradition," yet they expressed their need to "proceed slowly and with considerable caution" in implementing "new academic programs with Catholic flavors," since they were "dependent on persuading, not commanding, faculty to introduce them."[92] The authors conclude that, apart from the select group of institutions deeply immersed in Catholic education, most institutions "likely fail to educate their students about the Catholic intellectual tradition at even the minimal levels prescribed by their given institutional model."[93]

Many administrators recognized, on the one hand, "theology as the heart of the Catholic intellectual tradition," yet, on the other hand, admitted that theology requirements are generally minimal and often have "little Catholic content." They felt, moreover, that few theology faculty relate theology to the Catholic tradition. In addition, few of the administrators saw philosophy courses being taught in any way linked to Catholic theology.[94] In addition, "the faculty is often illiterate in terms of Catholic culture and the students are in even worse straits."[95] One administrator's complaint resonated with the general reaction among them: that while Catholic schools

89 Ibid., 4.
90 Ibid., 99.
91 Ibid., 91.
92 Ibid., 114.
93 Ibid., 115.
94 Ibid., 106.
95 Ibid., 99.

expose the students "to ways of thinking that are more caring, compassionate, and civic-minded, to encourage belief in social justice, and in community service," students will not at the end of their four years "be able to articulate any more clearly than they did at the beginning what this has to do with Catholicism." Often the students do not see where there is any value in a Catholic dimension to their education. Such a dimension is seen by many students as "irrelevant" in a market-driven environment where "ethics seems to be totally relative."[96]

Morey and Piderit break down the institutions they visited into "four models." One is amazed at the major assumptions they presume about all Catholic institutions within these models, based on the presidents' statements: that each "is faithful to the Catholic Church," and wants to develop "programs and activities that are in accordance with Catholic teaching with the intent of educating Catholics who support Catholic teaching."[97] (One gets the impression the authors accepted too readily presidential rhetoric.) To be truly Catholic, the authors argue, each institution must be distinguishable from nonsectarian universities across five major sectors within the institution: "academic program, residential living, student activities, religious activities, and personnel."[98]

The first is the model that puts the greatest emphasis upon Catholicity, the *Catholic immersion* model. The goal is "to attract committed Catholic students, to educate them more deeply about the Catholic tradition, and to both encourage and actively support their practice of the faith." At least four courses are taken in Catholic theology and philosophy. The residence system is ruled according to Catholic moral teaching with policies that insure compliance. There is a strong presence of Catholic liturgical activity, and strong support for hiring for the Catholic mission so as to have a faculty that is dedicated to "educating students in the Catholic tradition." Institutions in this model are known for their "clearly distinguishable Catholic culture."[99]

The second is the *Catholic persuasion* model. Here the goal is to instill a "certain religious maturity" in knowledge and practice of the Catholic faith. Academics have a "clearly identifiable Catholic component." The majority of the students are Catholic, and "all students are expected to take a course related to Catholic teachings" and another theology course that treats "of some facets of the Catholic tradition." Programs and practices, such as those within the residence system, are to be consistent with Catholic policies. The features of this model are much the same as in the first model, except there

---

96 Ibid., 6.

97 Ibid., 62.

98 Ibid., 61.

99 Ibid., 62–63.

is less emphasis on academic and institutional requirements and more on desire or expectation. Residence halls are expected to be faithful to Catholic moral principles, and violations are expected to be dealt with in a "firm manner." Faculty and staff are "actively recruited" who are supposedly "well trained in the Catholic faith," and who "promote and nurture academic, social, and religious components of the Catholic culture."[100]

Though this model would seem to be intended as the location for most Catholic institutions today, such a conclusion would seem far too optimistic. Many schools, even though the majority of the students are Catholic, do not see education in the Catholic faith and the promotion of Catholic practice of any significant importance in their mission. Rather, such a mission is largely understood, even by the theology department, as the work of campus ministry.

The goal of the third model—*Catholic diaspora*—is "to orient students to the Catholic Church without requiring much knowledge or practice." The majority of the students are non-Catholic. Students are encouraged to take a course in Catholic teachings, and do not necessarily learn much about Catholicism. As in the first two models, students may not "promote activities that are contrary to official Catholic teaching," nor may groups operate on campus that take "positions at variance with official Catholic teaching." The majority of the faculty is not Catholic, so that at least a small group of committed Catholic faculty and administrators are present to support the Catholic agenda. Residential living rules conform to Catholic teaching.[101]

The goal of the fourth model—*Catholic cohort*—is "to graduate talented students" to operate in influential sectors of society, to "promote the practice and general knowledge of religion," and even "to promote Catholic viewpoints." A substantial number (though less than a majority) of students will be Catholic, and the focus with these students is to "deepen their knowledge of and commitment to the Catholic faith." Students are not required to take any courses regarding Catholic teaching, but are encouraged to take courses regarding the importance of religion in history and society. Student groups are expected to abide by Catholic teaching. Residential living consonant with Catholic principles is encouraged, but not enforced. No policies favor hiring Catholic administrators or faculty, though they are "valued." The focus at such schools is to provide resources that encourage the Catholic perspective and heritage, but never to enforce it.

Recall that each model, according to Morey and Piderit, must maintain a certain degree of distinguishability to survive. The first model achieves

[100] Ibid., 63–64.
[101] Ibid., 64–65.

that by its strong emphasis upon the Catholic component in its culture. The second model achieves it by a narrower focus on a committed group of Catholic faculty and students. Importance to distinguishability is also placed in the fact that students learn much about the "content of the Catholic faith." According to Morey and Piderit, if that is lacking, which by the presidents' own admissions seems often to be the case, the "distinguishable criterion can hardly be fulfilled."[102]

The third model requires "promoting and protecting the Catholic mission and identity" through "a relatively small group of Catholic faculty and administrators." Because of the weakness of the Catholic dimension of the academic program, some other ways must be found, such as through campus ministry or religious practices or other Catholic activities, to give Catholic distinctiveness to the institution.

Finally, in the fourth model, distinguishability will be maintained by the existence of "special institutes and programs that promote the Catholic identity of the institution," such as a Catholic studies program and students who are identifiable as having interest in such programs. A "small cohort of well-trained and committed Catholic students and faculty" is also important.[103]

In all four models, Catholic leadership and governance is assumed: "Each of the models assumes the president is an informed, committed, and practicing Catholic."[104] All also "emphasize the importance of social justice."[105] Only those, however, that link social justice programs to aspects of the Catholic heritage make the programs distinguishable from those at nonsectarian institutions.[106] In this respect, the authors felt that the Catholic institutions that will survive must assert more than the importance of justice as they emphasize the values of their Catholic tradition.[107]

Administrators insisted their institutions "educated students within pervasive and transformative Catholic cultures." Yet the authors again concluded that "the reality on campus" suggests a "religiously tepid student culture."[108] Administrators admitted encountering "real obstacles to creating pervasively Catholic cultures" in their residence halls,[109] and recognized they are in a serious struggle with modern American youth culture "for the minds and hearts of its students":[110] one administrator expressed the think-

[102] Ibid., 74.
[103] Ibid., 74–79, 89.
[104] Ibid., 65–67.
[105] Ibid., 56.
[106] Ibid., 57–59.
[107] Ibid., 6–7.
[108] Ibid., 155, 158.
[109] Ibid., 160.
[110] Ibid., 166.

ing of many, that "our society is becoming so secularized that the real danger is our Catholic institutions will become secular."[111] Sexual activity appears to be especially uninfluenced by Catholic morality—says one administrator, "the sexual activity of students is actually shocking"—and, with little support from parents, most felt there was little to be done about it.[112]

Most administrators were dismayed at the low attendance at Mass, though not at immersion institutions where the "vast majority of the community . . . celebrates the Eucharist on a daily basis."[113] Curiously, when discussing religious activities on campus, administrators frequently heralded "social justice and service programs" as "the religious activity with the greatest potential to change students."[114] They saw that the "motivations of Catholic students" in such activity "had a religious orientation" that would not be found at nonsectarian institutions. But our authors disagreed. They argued that there may be a "mixed bag of reasons" for student involvement in volunteer service at any institution, even Catholic.[115] They argued that, unless service programs were clearly linked "to the mystery of salvation through Christ" and to some aspect of the Catholic tradition, such programs were undistinguishable, and thus failed to serve the goal of the institution "to strengthen the Catholic culture and enhance the possibility of student religious transformation."[116]

The authors note the negative impact of the decades of the '60s and '70s when Catholic identity became muted at Catholic institutions due to the fear of loss of public funding to sectarian institutions: "Catholic colleges made a decision to mute their religious self-identification beginning in the late 1960s in order to survive" (compare to our discussion earlier in this chapter of the Land O'Lakes movement begun in 1967). The authors argue there were unintended consequences of such a decision: the "deemphasis of religious self-identity . . . was interpreted by many as religious cultural erosion," which led in time to "actual cultural drift" that "contributed mightily to the leeching away of religious culture."

The fact that the senior administrators, while talking about the Catholic identity of their institutions, avoided "the use of richly evocative Catholic language, thereby abandoning one of the tradition's richest symbol sets," shows that, as a result of the decision to downgrade Catholic identity in those decades, they are "still religiously timid." They were able "comfortably" to refer "to God's presence among us or in all things," Morey and

111 Ibid., 162.
112 Ibid., 163.
113 Ibid., 185, 192–93.
114 Ibid., 198, 201.
115 Ibid., 199.
116 Ibid., 202.

Piderit noted, but they rarely spoke "about the 'gospel,'" and "almost all completely avoided the words 'Christ,' 'Jesus Christ,' 'Lord,' sacrament, sanctity, virtue, holiness, or sin. No one spoke of the Holy Spirit, the Trinity, or the Blessed Virgin." At the same time, the administrators "were at pains to distance themselves from the evangelical colleges and universities that use religious language quite openly." The irony is that these colleges and universities retain their Christian identity and are succeeding in promoting that identity, while the muted policies the other institutions employ are not working. Interviews with the university presidents resulted in a "culturally bland" religious vocabulary, marked by the use of a "common language" that "worked against cultural distinguishability." The administrators, say the authors, were "locked into a language pattern" of "verbal timidity," and "even in the face of a weakening institutional Catholic culture they clearly want to strengthen" seemed "more committed to the religious sensibilities of non-Catholics than they are to reclaiming symbolic religious language that is clearly 'Catholic.'"[117]

The book ends with four chapters of comments and recommendations. Some of these follow:

Responsible Leadership

The authors lay much of the blame or credit for the Catholic culture of the campus at the feet of presidents and boards of trustees: "Cultural enhancement and change in any organization require strong leadership at the highest level. Almost to a person, the group of 124 administrators we interviewed talked about the importance of deepening Catholic culture. Making progress on this front, however, will depend in large measure on the performance of Catholic college and university presidents." One of the duties of the president is to shape "the religious culture" of the institution.[118] Doing this, however, also requires direction from the board of trustees: "Trustees are guardians of Catholic universities, and no other group has ultimate responsibility in the area of Catholic character, mission, and identity." Trustees are to maintain the "vibrancy of Catholic culture," and "make changes when they judge the Catholic culture at their institution is in need of a correction."[119]

Formation of a Catholic Culture

"Catholic knowledge and commitment to the faith" are necessary among faculty and administrators. Faculty and administrators must become knowledgeable about "the Catholic intellectual tradition," so that they can

[117] Ibid., 219–21.
[118] Ibid., 275–76.
[119] Ibid., 305–6.

increase students' acquaintance with that tradition, "including both Catholic social teaching and the Catholic moral tradition." Institutions also need to know how effective their educational programs are, such as "how much religious knowledge students retain and how committed they are to the practice of their faith" and to the influence of that commitment upon "their professional lives," their "friendships and marriages," and "their service to society and to the Church."[120]

Maintaining Distinguishability Essential

Our authors conclude that, whereas senior administrators were quite sanguine about "sustaining institutional Catholic culture" on their campuses, their optimism was "unfounded." Our authors boldly state the principle that must be faced: "The situation that senior administrators actually described created serious doubt in our minds about whether the religious legacy of Catholic colleges and universities will survive, let alone thrive, if present policy approaches persist."[121]

The authors found distinguishable dimensions of Catholic cultural presence hard to find, and often were able to note them only after deliberate efforts were made to point them out. Apart from campus ministry, few elements were "clearly Catholic and touched the hearts and minds of most of the undergraduates." The major exception in all of this were the immersion institutions, which were distinguishable by almost all accounts.[122]

The authors recognize how much administrators are conflicted. While wanting to distinguish their institutions by the Catholic dimension, they are caught in the maelstrom of modern American society that tears down public displays of religious commitment: "Religion in the United States is controlled, constrained, and tamed in ways that assure that it does not threaten the dominant secular culture of the land." As a result, Catholic institutions try to offer "basically the same education as their nonsectarian counterparts," and Catholic elements are made addenda that "count for nothing in terms of institutional legitimacy and consequently appear more decorative than useful." The "religious culture" they present ends up as being "fairly bland."[123]

To break out of this maelstrom, a "contrary strategy is required" if Catholic institutions' "religious cultures are to survive and flourish."[124] The authors suggest a number of ways to fulfill this prescription, some of which are:

---

[120] Ibid., 308–10.
[121] Ibid., 347.
[122] Ibid., 347–48.
[123] Ibid., 348–49.
[124] Ibid., 350.

- Take "bold and dramatic initiatives for strengthening Catholic culture on campuses."[125] The point is: rather than hiding or diminishing the Catholic identity, emphasize it all the more.
- Give the faculty "the requisite knowledge and skill to weave religious themes and topics into their course work."[126]
- Create a "critical mass of faculty and/or administrators . . . that would step in to take the place of vowed religious and provide knowledgeable, committed, and visible religious leadership."[127]
- Accept and implement a program that recognizes that "educating students in the basics of Catholic faith and practice is part of the mission of a Catholic institution."[128]
- Focus on hiring for "Catholic competence," asking candidates "what they could actually contribute to the Catholic character, culture, and mission of the institution."[129]
- "Forthrightly explain . . . to candidates" the need for "the existence of the CIC [committed, informed, and Catholic] cluster and its function." The fact that a candidate is a "practicing Catholic" should make the candidate "attractive."[130]
- Recognize that the immersion schools often produce "the most effective graduates in terms of their service to the Church and their distinctively Catholic contribution to society." But because such institutions "lack broad appeal," the authors encourage such schools to find ways of broadening their programs, so that, over time, their value to Church and society might be "magnified."[131]
- Initiate greater involvement of faculty, administrators, and pastoral staff in residence halls where "they could help create living environments where students are mentored in the Catholic tradition."[132]
- Find ways for schools to be "at least partially countercultural with respect to consumerism." The authors suggest a voluntary program of "simple living."[133]

---

125 Ibid.
126 Ibid., 352.
127 Ibid., 353.
128 Ibid., 354.
129 Ibid., 356.
130 Ibid., 357.
131 Ibid., 359.
132 Ibid., 362.
133 Ibid., 364–65.

Conclusion

Morey and Piderit are unduly positive in their assumption that all Catholic schools are "faithful to the Catholic Church," and want to develop programs and policies that "are in accordance with Catholic teaching with the intent of educating Catholics" who support the Catholic Church and practice their faith. This assumption is curious in view of the fact that the authors conclude from their study that the Catholic culture is lacking on Catholic campuses, and that without serious efforts to restore that culture, the institutions will lose their distinguishability and cease to exist. The authors duly note that much of the problem is due to the fact that Catholic cultural catalysts are missing from the campuses, and there is not yet the serious effort being made to correct the problem. Their study also exposed how inflated were the administrators' judgments of the Catholic quality of their campuses. When the authors sought evidence to support the glossy presidential rhetoric, there was often little to be found.

Secondly, more satisfactorily than O'Brien, Morey and Piderit emphasize the importance of the existence of a Catholic culture on the campuses in Catholic higher education. The authors insist that without the Catholic dimension as the distinguishing element on the Catholic campus, Catholic higher education will not survive. So important is that element to the Catholic campus that the authors urge presidents and boards to go out of their way to make the presence of the Catholic tradition the centerpiece of their programs of study.

Thirdly, it is not simply a Catholic intellectual formation that the authors urge in order to overcome the widespread illiteracy on Catholic campuses. They urge that colleges and universities make efforts to promote Catholic participation in the life of the Church, especially participation in liturgical activities and other programs that promote Catholic life.

Fourthly, they urge Catholicity not only among the students, but among the faculty, staff, and administrators as well. Their call for "cultural catalysts" who make the Catholic dimension of the campus alive and real is on the mark, since, as the authors frequently remark, religious congregations are no longer able to serve that role.

Fifthly, the authors emphasize that major social activist programs must be integrated into the Catholic dimension of the institutions, as an outgrowth of the spirituality of the Church. So many of the presidents emphasized their social justice programs as emblematic of their institutions, and yet the authors rarely found any evidence these programs were any different from those practiced at nonsectarian institutions. Once again, an integration of the intellectual, spiritual, moral, and social dimensions of life must be shown as outgrowths of the Catholic teaching of the Church, to make Catholic education distinguishable.

Finally, the authors are not hesitant to make clear that Catholic education finds its roots in its fidelity to Jesus Christ and his Church, and that that dimension must be broadly understood by the faculty and staff, and supported by enough of the institution to bring about the Catholic culture that will foster future fidelity to the Church.

Major lessons can be learned from this important study of Catholic higher education, the main one being that Catholic education will not survive by blending into the fabric of education as exercised on nonsectarian campuses, but rather by emblazoning its distinctiveness. Instead of hiding their Catholicism, Catholic educators must recruit faculty, staff, and students who champion the causes of Christ and his Church, and are willing to speak to that identity in their Christian lives.

James T. Burtchaell, C.S.C., formerly of the University of Notre Dame, in his massive study of the decline of Christian education in Christian-founded institutions of higher education, points out how non-Catholic Christian institutions that once heralded their role in the service of their churches gradually downgraded their Christian identity. The same process, he shows, is underway in the life of many Catholic campuses. He cites a figure from Georgetown who delights in the idea that Georgetown might become " 'just' another distinguished center of research." This would, supposedly, indicate the " 'coming of age' of Catholicism in this country." A president of Fordham at a recent commencement address celebrated the fact that that institution had achieved "assimilation into American culture" and freedom from "ecclesiastical control."[134] If Morey and Piderit's study indicates anything, it is that fostering the assimilation of Catholic education, rather than emphasizing its distinguishability, is the wrong way to go, and that such a philosophy is leading to the demise of Catholic higher education. Morey and Piderit's predication of the future is already underway.

THE OBAMA EFFECT

One of the most divisive events in modern Catholic life in the United States occurred on May 17, 2009, when at the invitation of the University of Notre Dame, President Barack Obama gave a commencement address and received an honorary doctorate in law from the university. The event reverberated like nothing else has in recent memory in the world of Catholic higher education. Said one Catholic commentator:

134 James Tunstead Burtchaell, C.S.C., *The Dying of the Light: The Disengagement of Colleges and Universities from Their Christian Churches* (Grand Rapids, MI: Eerdmans, 1998), 633.

> Obama's relationship with the Catholic Church remains clouded and tense following the controversy over the University of Notre Dame's decision . . . . American Catholics are deeply divided in their responses to this aggressively pro-choice president. . . . [His] remarks at Notre Dame evoked typically divided reactions ranging from disgust to adulation.[135]

George Weigel of the Washington Ethics and Public Policy Center wrote: "Never in our history has a president of the United States, in the exercise of his public office, intervened in such [religious] disputes in order to secure a political advantage" until Obama did in his Notre Dame commencement address. According to Weigel, Obama sought to "secure a political advantage" he gained among Catholics in the November 2009 elections by deciding to "insert himself into the ongoing Catholic debate over the boundaries of Catholic identity" and defining "what it means to be real Catholics in 21st-century America." Declaring himself "the Primate of American Catholicism," Obama, like the "good postmodern liberal" that he is, settled "the decades-long intra-Catholic culture war in favor of one faction—the faction that had supported his candidacy and that had spent the first months of his administration defending his policies"—to restore the "seamless garment" approach of the late Cardinal Joseph Bernardin, seeking to find "common ground" in support of "that progressive 'consensus' [that] is so self-evidently true."[136]

Those who objected to the Obama event had a hook on which to hang their complaints. The United States Conference of Catholic Bishops at their semiannual spring assembly in 2004 had issued a directive: "The Catholic community and Catholic institutions should *not honor* those who act in defiance of our fundamental moral principles. They should not be given awards, honors or platforms which would suggest support for their actions."[137] Notre Dame's invitation to Obama was a direct challenge to that directive. The issue was sparked not so much by Obama's giving an address at a Catholic institution (though to many even that was problematic), but by the fact that the university was honoring him with a doctorate of law. Was not doing so in defiance of the bishops' decree? The Catholic population was divided.

There have been few figures in the modern presidency who have caused more polarization in American society than Obama.[138] By and large, Catholic traditionalists, who were already outraged by the fact that the

---

135 Russell Shaw, "Obama Addresses Abortion at Notre Dame Commencement," accessed May 31, 2009, www.osv.com.

136 George Weigel, "Obama and the 'Real' Catholics," May 18, 2009, www.nationalreview.com.

137 USCCB, "Catholics in Political Life" (emphasis in original).

138 But there has been one. According to Gallup, the Democratic-Republican gap in Obama's presidential approval rating was 63 points in a survey conducted March

majority of Catholics in the United States had voted for the election of Obama to the presidency in the previous year, were now further outraged by the fact that what is widely considered the flagship Catholic university in the country publicly applauded and honored a man who as the most prominent figure in the United States promotes policies diametrically opposed to the most basic teaching of the Catholic Church on the central moral issue of our time: abortion.[139]

The announcement of Notre Dame's intentions in this regard brought a unity in opposition among American bishops rarely seen: 83 American bishops publicly voiced their dissent, including then president of the United States Catholic Conference, Francis Cardinal George of Chicago, Obama's home town.[140] At least 1,400 alumni and other benefactors pledged to withhold nearly $14 million dollars in future donations until the current university president is replaced by "someone who will be more loyal to the teaching of the Catholic Church."[141] According to the Cardinal Newman Society's web page, over 367,000 persons signed a petition opposing the commence-

---

30–April 5, 2009, with the Democratic approval rating at 90%, the Republican at 27%. The highest gap so far in Obama's presidency occurred in mid-March at 65% (91% vs. 26%). The highest gap ever recorded by Gallup occurred in the fall of 2004, with a record 83-point party gap for George W. Bush. From Harry Truman to Jimmy Carter, the typical partisan gap in approval rating was 35 points (Jeffrey M. Jones, "Obama Approval Rating Stable, Polarized," April 7, 2009, www.gallup.com).

139 Obama has an agenda decidedly pro-abortion. On the thirty-sixth anniversary of *Roe v. Wade*, he affirmed his commitment to that ruling: the next day (January 23, 2009), he nullified the pro-life "Mexico-City Policy," thus making agencies that perform abortions eligible for foreign aid; in March he released $50 million to the United Nations Population Fund that aids China in carrying out its program of coerced abortions; again in March, he "opened the door to federal funding of research that requires the killing of human embryos"; he has committed himself to rescinding "a conscience-protection regulation" issued by the Bush administration for doctors and hospitals refusing to perform abortions; and he has chosen many pro-choice persons for cabinet and other administrative posts, including many pro-choice Catholics (National Right to Life, "The Presidential Record on Life: President Barack Obama 2009–Present," accessed June 2009, www.nrlc.org). Obama has pledged to make the choice to have an abortion a fundamental human right of every woman in America by signing the Freedom of Choice Act.

140 LifeSiteNews.com, "List of Bishops Opposing," May 6, 2009, www.lifesitenews.com.

141 LifeSiteNews.com, "Notre Dame Alumni Confirm $13.9 Million in Withheld Donations," May 15, 2009, www.lifesitenews.com. On October 25, 2010, CatholicCulture.org reported that "Contributions to the University of Notre Dame fell by over $120 million during the fiscal year in which President Barack Obama was awarded an honorary degree." The news service noted that the "decline in donations largely coincided with the late-2000s recession, which officially began in December 2007 and ended in June 2009." CatholicCulture.org, "Gifts to Notre Dame plunged $120M during Year of Obama's Appearance," October 25, 2010, www.catholicculture.org/news/headlines/index.cfm?storyid=8036.

ment address and honor to Obama.[142] Ten priests from the Congregation of the Holy Cross, the order that founded the university, asked the university president and the board of trustees to reconsider their invitation to Obama, saying the university could risk losing its "true soul," and that "failure to do so will damage the integrity of the institution."[143]

According to a Pew Forum poll, American Catholics in general were split on the vote, with the usual division based on whether one attended Mass regularly: "Among white Catholics who attend church at least once a week, a plurality (45%) say it was wrong for Notre Dame to invite Obama, while the majority of less-observant Catholics (56%) take the opposite view, saying Notre Dame was right to invite him."[144] A Quinnipiac University Polling Institute survey of 2,041 registered voters came to a similar conclusion: "U.S. voters say 56–31 percent, including 60–34 percent among Catholic voters, that Notre Dame University should not rescind its invitation" to Obama, and even among weekly-Mass-attending Catholics, 49 to 43 percent agreed.[145] A Rasmussen Reports survey, on the other hand, reported overwhelming opposition to the event: by a 60% to 25% margin, American Catholics opposed awarding the degree to the President, and even among all Americans, 52% opposed the honor, with 25% supporting it. Even pro-choice Americans were "evenly split as to whether Notre Dame should snub the Catholic bishops."[146]

This gave rise to an opposite reaction from prominent American Catholics, most of whom were progressive. Among these were San Francisco's Archbishop Emeritus John Quinn, the only Catholic prelate who was recorded as publicly voicing disagreement with the protest,[147] and twenty leading Catholic theologians from Catholics in Alliance for the Common Good who, according to *NCR*, "sharply *criticized those who are attacking the University*," and who wrote in their published statement that Obama is "a Christian with a deep respect for the role of faith in public life."[148] Then

142 Cardinal Newman Society, "U.S. Bishops Praise Bishop D'Arcy in Wake of Notre Dame Scandal," June 22, 2009, www.cardinalnewmansociety.org.

143 Associated Press, "10 Holy Cross Priests Object to Obama Notre Dame Invite," April 8, 2009, www.foxnews.com.

144 Catholic World News, "Catholics Split on Notre Dame Invitation to Obama, Poll Shows," May 1, 2009, www.catholicculture.org/news/.

145 Quinnipiac University, "Notre Dame Should Not Disinvite Obama," release detail, May 14, 2009, www.quinnipiac.edu.

146 LifeSiteNews.com, "Catholics Overwhelmingly Oppose Notre Dame Honor to Obama: Ramussen [*sic*] Poll," May 7, 2009, www.lifesitenews.com.

147 Kathleen Gilbert, "San Francisco Abp. Emeritus Issues Letter of Support to Obama amid ND Scandal," May 15, 2009, www.lifesitenews.com.

148 Jerry Filteau, "Theologians back Notre Dame honoring Obama," *NCR Today*, May 14, 2009, ncronline.org (emphasis in original).

president of the Association of Jesuit Colleges and Universities, Fr. Charles Currie, S.J., is also cited in NCR as saying that he, as well as the presidents of the twenty-eight Jesuit institutions in the United States, had privately expressed support for the University and its president, and that they had been "talking to individual bishops to see if we can't lower the volume and lessen the heat of the discussion."[149]

Many of those who support Obama and the Notre Dame invitation argue that he is really pro-life, in spite of his many public statements supporting pro-abortion agendas, because of his politics of promoting social and economic agendas that would reintroduce equality of wealth, and universal health-care benefits that would make it possible for women to find an outlet from the dire situations of poverty that often give them little choice but to abort a child. Thus, Obama's policies, they argue, will eventually lead to the promotion of life more successfully than have previous agendas promoted by so-called pro-life Republican presidents.

For some of the opponents of the Obama invitation, the granting of an honorary doctorate to the President represented the ultimate outcome of all that had been started by the Land-O-Lakes conference of 1967 and, oddly enough, by the man who initiated and became the guiding force behind that conference, then president of Notre Dame, Fr. Theodore Hesburgh. The clearest expression of this view comes from an editorial in the *Catholic World Report*:

> The scandal at Notre Dame originated not in 2009 but in 1967, when its then-president Theodore Hesburgh . . . signed a de facto declaration of independence from Catholicism . . . . That declaration gave birth to the modern American Catholic university, which would henceforth be modern and American but not very Catholic. . . . That a majority of Catholics, many of whom graduated from colleges and universities like Notre Dame, voted for Obama is one of the legacies of the Land O'Lakes manifesto.[150]

Russell Shaw, a columnist for the conservative *Our Sunday Visitor*, saw the Obama invitation as the "latest chapter in an old story by the name of 'Americanism.'" The movement, which we discussed in chapter 4 (see pp. 199–200), was condemned by Leo XIII in 1899 as a "'reprehensible' error," according to Shaw, because it aimed to "adjust Catholic belief and behavior . . . to suit contemporary secular standards in unacceptable ways."

---

149 Tom Roberts, "Jesuit educators back Obama Notre Dame invitation," *NCR*, accessed April 13, 2009, ncronline.org.

150 George Neumayr, "*Ex Corde Ecclesiae* and the Notre Dame Affair," editorial, *Catholic World Report*, May 2009, 1.

According to Shaw, "Notre Dame's invitation to President Obama . . . is part of this Americanist pattern."[151]

A popular conservative columnist observed that inviting someone who regarded judgment about the rights of the unborn "above my pay grade"—as Obama stated in August 2008—to speak and be honored at a Catholic university further contributes "to the moral ambiguity tearing at our nation's fabric."[152]

Robert W. Finn, bishop of the Kansas City-St. Joseph diocese, addressed pro-lifers in April 2009 with the declaration "We are at war!" and said the Church Militant was ultimately in "a spiritual battle for the eternal salvation of souls." He brought up the controversy over Notre Dame's invitation, calling it "scandalous, discouraging and confusing to many Catholics." He predicted the president of the university "will probably lose his job."[153]

The top Catholic prelate to rail against the invitation was then Archbishop Raymond Burke, prefect of the Vatican's highest court, the Apostolic Signature, and former archbishop of St. Louis. At an address he delivered on May 8, 2009, at the National Catholic Prayer Breakfast in Washington, DC, Burke sharply rebuked Notre Dame:

> The profound granting of an honorary doctorate at Notre Dame University to our President who is as aggressively advancing an anti-life and anti-family agenda is a source of the gravest scandal. In a culture which embraces an agenda of death, Catholics and Catholic institutions are necessarily countercultural. If we as individuals or our Catholic institutions are not willing to accept the burdens and the suffering necessarily involved in calling our culture to reform, then we are not worthy of the name Catholic.[154]

Charles J. Chaput, O.F.M. Cap., then archbishop of Denver, wrote on the archdiocesan web page of the "intellectual vanity" of the university and the quarter century of Notre Dame's "softening Catholic witness in Catholic higher education," which has "given the next generation of Catholic leadership all the excuses they need to baptize their personal conveniences and ignore what it really demands to be 'Catholic' in the public

---

151 Russell Shaw, "Error of Americanism," *Our Sunday Visitor*, May 3, 2009, 18.

152 Star Parker, "Moral relativism and Obama at Notre Dame," May 17, 2009, townhall.com.

153 Robert W. Finn, "Warriors for the Victory of Life," keynote address at the 2009 Gospel of Life Convention in Overland Park, KS, in "Kansas City Bishop to prolifers: 'We are at war!,'" *NCR*, April 28, 2009, ncronline.org.

154 "The Teachings of the Catholic Church: Archbishop Burke's Keynote Address from Friday's National Catholic Prayer," May 8, 2009, 19, www.lifesitenews.com/news/archive/ldn/1990/50/9050819.

155 "Archbishop Chaput on Notre Dame and the Issues That Remain," May 18, 2009, www.archden.org/index.cfm/ID/2081.

square."[155]

Among the supporters of Notre Dame's invitation was Douglas W. Kmiec, the professor of constitutional law at Pepperdine University and onetime ambassador to Malta, who argued that without the university's invitation,

> which opened the oval office door to the Catholic perspective and this President's implicit understanding and embrace of *Gaudium et Spes* "to show respect and love to those who think or act differently . . . in social, political and even religious matters," the ubi caritas prayer that "all divisions cease" would have gone unarticulated.[156]

Kmiec saw Obama as a "fifth rider" to the "legendary four horsemen of Notre Dame," who, instead of inspiring "fear" as those players did, "conquers with a message of hope and a call for common ground—and he did so masterfully on graduation Sunday, 2009."[157]

Fr. John W. O'Malley, S.J., university professor at Georgetown University, also heard the spirit of Vatican II in Obama's address:

> We have a Vatican II president. Barack Obama . . . [in his commencement address at Notre Dame] embodied and professed in his public persona the spirit of the council. . . . He called for civility, for the end of name-calling, and for a willingness to work together to deal with our common problems, including abortion, rather than a stand-off determination to impose one's principles without reckoning what the cost to the common good might be. . . . Is it not ironic that not a bishop but the President of the United States should today be the most effective spokesperson for that spirit?[158]

Fr. Thomas J. Reese, S.J., senior fellow at the Woodstock Center at Georgetown University, agrees that "the bishops have lost what John O'Malley, S.J., refers to as the spirit of Vatican II," and urges the American bishops "to return" to that spirit.[159] Reese has repeatedly berated the bishops for their failing in leadership: they have "stopped listening and teaching

---

156 Douglas Kmiec, "Obama at Notre Dame: Incomplete Eloquence," *NCR*, May 18, 2009, ncronline.org/news/politics/obama-notre-dame-incomplete-eloquence. Kmiec is quoting from Fr. John Jenkins' 2009 commencement address at the University of Notre Dame. Further reference to this passage is found below.

157 Ibid.

158 John W. O'Malley, S.J., "Barack Obama and Vatican II," *America*, May 25, 2009, www.americamagazine.org.

159 Thomas J. Reese, S.J., "The Bishops' Dispirited Agenda," Georgetown/On Faith: This Catholic's View, June 16, 2009, www.washingtonpost.com/blogs/georgetown-on-faith/.

and started ordering and condemning," as they did at Notre Dame for inviting Obama. Reese has his own theory as to what is happening to the bishops: they are being duped by a "conservative conspiracy" fomented by the Republicans:

> The bishops are being egged on by Republican activists whose presidential candidate lost the election. There is clearly a conservative conspiracy to do whatever is possible (including lying about *ambassadorial candidates*) to create conflict between the Catholic Church and the Obama administration. They want the Catholic Church to be the Republican Party at prayer. Some bishops are falling for this.[160]

Fr. Richard P. McBrien, Crowley-O'Brien Professor of Theology at the University of Notre Dame, has complained strongly for a number of years about the "leadership crisis" in the American hierarchy, and took this occasion to address further "the crisis of pastoral leadership" and the "ill wind" blowing in the "negative reaction" of the bishops to the controversy.[161]

Reese also took this occasion to scold other Catholic college and university presidents, most of whom were "AWOL during the entire controversy." Calling them "the dogs that did not bark," Reese asked, "Why did they not speak out?" He offered five theories as possible explanations, none of which he espoused, and concluded:

> The presidents owe Notre Dame and Jenkins an explanation; they owe Catholic higher education better leadership; their job is to defend academic freedom and autonomy. They stood silent while another educational institution was unfairly and viciously attacked. The next time when one of their institutions is under attack, they should not be surprised when no one comes to their defense.[162]

McBrien supported Reese's position.[163]

Perhaps one of the strongest supporters of the invitation to Obama came from the president of Notre Dame, Fr. John I. Jenkins, C.S.C., who argued in his speech welcoming Obama to the commencement ceremonies that the invitation was given to him in an effort to further "dialogue."

---

160 Thomas J. Reese, S.J., "Memo to Bishops: Most Catholics Aren't Listening," Georgetown/On Faith: This Catholic's View, May 5, 2009, www.washingtonpost.com/blogs/georgetown-on-faith/.

161 Richard McBrien, "More on the Leadership Crisis," *NCR*, June 1, 2009, ncronline.org.

162 Thomas J. Reese, S.J., "Notre Dame—Opinion: With one of their own under fire, university presidents stood silent," *NCR*, accessed June 26, 2009, ncronline.org.

163 Richard McBrien, "The silence of the presidents," *NCR*, June 8, 2009, ncronline.org.

Ignoring the directive of the U.S. bishops not to honor those who support principles contrary to fundamental Catholic moral values, Jenkins appealed to Vatican II's *Gaudium et Spes*:

> As the Fathers of the Second Vatican Council wrote in their pastoral constitution Gaudium et Spes: "Respect and love ought to be extended also to those who think or act differently than we do in social, political and even religious matters. In fact, the more deeply we come to understand their ways of thinking through such courtesy and love, the more easily will we be able to enter into dialogue with them."[164]

Perhaps recognizing that there could be no dialogue with Obama at the commencement ceremonies, Jenkins pointed out that "dialogue is never instantaneous; it doesn't begin and end in an afternoon," but is "an ongoing process made possible by many acts of courtesy and gestures of respect." Jenkins pointed out that Obama, knowing "we oppose his policies on abortion and embryonic stem cell research," accepted the invitation anyway, thus demonstrating he is "not someone who stops talking to those who differ with him," and that is "a principle we share."

Jenkins went on to enumerate the various "qualities and accomplishments the American people admired in [Obama] when they elected him." These included Obama's mastery of "the most rigorous academic challenges," his turning his back on wealth "to serve the poor," and his leaving the election campaign "to go to the bedside of his dying grandmother who helped raise him." Other points: Obama's "great respect for the role of faith and religious institutions in public life"; his powerful transcendence of race; his "ambitious goals" to extend "health care coverage to millions who don't have it, improving education especially for those who most need it, promoting renewable energy for the sake of our economy, our security, and our climate"; his goal "of a world without nuclear weapons"; his "pledge to accelerate America's fight against poverty"; and finally, his embrace of "the burdens of leadership and the hopes of his country."[165]

Obama devoted considerable time in his address to the conflict over "the issue of abortion." An incident he recounted that had recently occurred to him was telling: He told how he had once been criticized for an entry on his web page that said he would fight "right-wing ideologues who want to take away a woman's right to choose." An e-mail was sent to him scolding him for his partisan remark and saying he should use "fair-minded words." Obama accepted the criticism and removed the harsh-sounding

---

164 "Text of speech by Notre Dame President Rev. John I. Jenkins," May 17, 2009, www.southbendtribune.com.

165 Ibid.

words. He explained that by extending the "presumption of good faith to others, we open up our hearts and minds to those who may not think precisely like we do" and "discover at least the possibility of common ground." He added, however, "I didn't change my underlying position."

"Common ground" for Obama seems to include promoting issues that surround procuring an abortion, such as reducing the "number of women seeking abortions," reducing "unintended pregnancies," making "adoption more available," providing "care and support for women who do carry their children to term," honoring the "conscience of those who disagree with abortion" (without clarifying how one would honor them), drafting "a sensible conscience clause" (without defining what is meant by "sensible"), grounding health-care policies "not only in sound science, but also in clear ethics, as well as respect for the equality of women" (without explaining which science is "sound," or what could possibly be meant by ethics that are "clear"). All of these proposals received loud applause, in spite of the resounding generalities.

After all this talk about the search for "common ground" over the issue of abortion, Obama added, almost imperceptibly, that while each side is to "make its case to the public with passion and conviction" and "without reducing those with differing views to caricature," "at some level, the views of the two camps are irreconcilable." He failed to indicate that public policy has to side eventually with either one or the other of the two "irreconcilable" positions, and that the policy to be accepted would be his. So much for dialogue.

Finally: Will there be any consequences for Notre Dame and its president over the Obama event? Two follow-ups will amply answer that question:

First, the bishops did not introduce any public discussion of the issue at their assembly of June 17–19, 2009, in San Antonio. Instead, they discussed it behind closed doors, and, apparently unable to come to any consensus on how to react to the incident, simply published one of the blandest statements that could possibly be written of support for Bishop D'Arcy, who had publicly rebuked Jenkins and the university for the Obama invitation:

> The bishops of the United States express our appreciation and support for our brother bishop, the Most Reverend John D'Arcy. We affirm his pastoral concern for Notre Dame University, his solicitude for its Catholic identity, and his loving care for all those the Lord has given him to sanctify, to teach and to shepherd.[166]

Secondly, the board of directors of the Association of Catholic Colleges

166 USCCB, "U.S. Bishops Express Support for Bishop D'arcy [*sic*] and His Pastoral Concern for the University of Notre Dame," June 22, 2009, www.usccb.org.

and Universities (ACCU) met June 11–12 at the University of San Diego. Was there any rebuke of Notre Dame? Just the opposite. We are told, according to their summer newsletter, that there was "lengthy discussion" over "campus speaker policies" that "continued a dialogue" begun in 2006, and they concluded that the document "Catholics in Political Life," which presented the standard against which many bishops had found Notre Dame's actions wanting, "warranted further clarification regarding its application to Catholic higher education." The board also called for a new document to be composed that would set up "principles which guide Catholic higher education's mission, programs, and processes." These would be "national in scope," but also reflect "considerable differences among institutions."[167] In other words, from now on, Catholic institutions will have great flexibility in adapting the principles of Catholic education to their local situation, so that nothing like the Notre Dame controversy will ever arise again. This is just another way of saying there will be no national standards in the future—that Catholic education will be whatever individual Catholic educators want it to be.

Will there, then, be any rebuke of the University of Notre Dame's board of trustees or its president for the Obama event? Apparently not. Neither the U.S. bishops nor ACCU seems to want to touch the issue. Each has abdicated its role in directing the course of Catholic education. And Jenkins has recently had his tenure as Notre Dame's president renewed.

As a result, there likely will be serious negative consequences for Catholic higher education. The structures have been radically changed. The principle of relativism will become even more deeply embedded in the Catholic consciousness as the Catholic intelligentsia are given free rein to "do their own thing" without any fear of outside interference in their operations, and they will increasingly set the tone for Catholic thought, with the perspective of the U.S. bishops more and more marginalized.

Indeed, Land O'Lakes will have finally achieved its purpose—to alienate Catholic higher education from any and all ties of fealty to the Catholic Church and its teachings. As a result of Obama's insinuation of his own left-wing perspective into the operations of Catholic higher education, such education, if it endures at all, is likely to differ only in name and prestige from the secular institutions that surround it, and which it has been struggling to emulate for more than forty years.

---

[167] ACCU's newsletter, *Update* 35 (Summer 2009), 5.

CHAPTER SEVEN

A Church of Social Justice or of Love?

WE HAVE ALREADY noted that among Enlightenment thinkers who accepted a religious dimension to life, religion was normally reduced to an acceptance of the existence of God and the need to live a virtuous life in order to attain eternal salvation. For many of the Enlightened, especially in France, such reductionism provided the warrant for attacking the accretions of Catholicism; for others, it was a way of overcoming the religious conflicts that had troubled so much of recent history. The Enlightenment mind, moreover, as we have noted, placed reason at the top of instruments of knowledge. Reason by itself alone, it was argued, was able to attain a proper knowledge of God, making faith, revelation, and church doctrines regarding a supernatural order either at best irrelevant, or at worst superstitious and illusory. It was perhaps Kant who capped off this whole naturalistic development with his noble but erroneous attempt to save belief in God by arguing that, while God could not be known by reason, he could nevertheless be believed in as a postulate of the moral order—as a necessary requirement to justify a life of doing good and avoiding evil. After Kant, the Enlightenment is virtually entrenched in the notion that religion and even religious worship are expressed in virtuous living.

This reduction of religion to morality has become the bane of the Christian religion, and it has a history. I have said that the movement of thought beginning with Ockham's razor in the fourteenth century and growing through the eighteenth-century Enlightenment led finally to the notion that all truth and morality are relative, and that this principle has become the greatest evil of modern society. Enlightenment thought, we have argued, has ultimately led to postmodernism and nihilism, where truth and morality no longer mean anything outside of one's own context of life. I would argue that this equation of the Christian faith experience with good moral living is the second major evil afflicting the modern world, and the Church of Social Justice is a consequence of it. And this reduction logically follows from the relativizing of all truth. For if all truth is relative and therefore subjective, it has no relevance to the public forum, where only values that have a common denominator are permissible. Thus whether one accepts that there is a triune God or an Incarnation, or whether one holds that Jesus Christ has been superseded by Mohammed, becomes at best a matter of private conviction. What remains as religion's contribution to the public forum is merely the moral dimension of religious conviction—the need for virtuous living. Being moral also becomes the norm for good citizenship, whether one is religious or not, as well as the standard for judging criminal action. Since religious truths have become private "conjectures," and morality the only dimension of religion that has public relevance, it is only logical that those who still claim to be "religious" would be increasingly influenced by society to reduce their understanding of what it means to be religious merely to being morally good persons.

This reductionism is beneficial in two ways: First, it makes it easy to be "religious." A religion reduced to morality demands no convictions, no commitment, makes no demands that good citizenship would not already have made. Being a good Christian is equated with being a good citizen. One has the best of both worlds.

The second benefit follows: such a religion becomes nonconflictual. It provides no reason for controversy, disagreement, argumentation, disruption of life, war, oppression—whatever. Since it stands for nothing other than being good, a principle that nearly all rational persons accept and seek to abide by though it is largely devoid of content, it provides no basis for confrontation. One can be "religious" and still have friends. A religion reduced to morality is no longer countercultural or "obnoxious"—it doesn't conflict with reason's assessment of what is desirable in human life. Being a believer no longer presents any challenge to the secular world.

In an effort to avoid conflicts that could arise from religious conviction, the Supreme Court has seen the need to separate religious expression from lower public education: this obviates the conflicts that would supposedly arise if certain religious traditions were given a platform where they could "indoctrinate" youth. A curious mentality operates here: to obviate the possibility of conflict and undue influence from religious thought, rid the classroom altogether of the First Amendment right to religious expression. The reasoning seems to be that the best way to preserve a constitutional freedom is to remove the possibility of exercising it.

We have argued that these two principles—the relativizing of truth and its corollary, the reduction of religion to morality—have led to the secularization of Christianity, to a growing value-free social order, and to the increasing meaninglessness of the idea of objective value. Even as crimes are being committed by young people at a staggeringly high rate,[1] the older generation, increasingly indoctrinated with the relativizing and secularizing of all values by the intellectually Enlightened, has lost the ability to do anything about it, since trying to correct this trend would imply imposing long-held principles of traditional morality on a society in which they can no longer be justified.

The older generation has yet to grasp the full effects of this new thinking upon the postmodern younger generation, many of whom are quick to conclude that if all values are only subjective, why must anyone be bothered with them, especially if it is more fun not to be? Why not shoot and kill another who teases you too much, rather than put up with "harassment"? Why not annihilate parents if they insist on discipline? Is killing an annoying person any different from killing an annoying fly? The older generation, still harboring the vestiges of traditional objective morality, would cringe at the thought of comparing a human life to a fly, but would a young postmodernist who has a gun at his disposal share that feeling of horror? Inevitably the older generation exclaims, "How could anyone do such a thing!" when another of our Columbine-style shootings occurs; perhaps a more realistic question is, how come it doesn't happen more often?

Peter Singer and the Equation of Human and Animal Morality

One might rightly be appalled at the noxious equation just made between killing a human being and killing a fly. But the fact is we are losing a basis for arguing that human life has any more value than that of a fly—or at least of a gorilla. The Australian-born utilitarian atheist Peter Singer, Ira W. Decamp Professor of Bioethics at the University Center for Human Values at Princeton University, recently wrote that he wants to put "human and nonhuman animals, *as such*, on the same moral footing," and that the view that gives a priority to human rights over those of animals "owes more to our own selfish interests" and "ancient religious teachings that reflect these interests than to reason or impartial moral reflection." Singer has now become renowned for launching the Great Ape Project International, which "seeks to extend the

[1] "In 2008, law enforcement agencies in the United States made an estimated 2.11 million arrests of persons younger than age 18." While juvenile arrests in 2008 were 3% fewer than in 2007, the figures are still alarming. Charles Puzzanchera, "Juvenile Arrests 2008," *Juvenile Justice Bulletin*, Office of Juvenile Justice and Delinquency Prevention, December 2009, www.ojp.usdoj.gov/ojjdp.

'moral community of equals' to include human beings, chimps, gorillas and orangutans because of their 'morally important characteristics.' "[2]

Singer inveighs against what he calls "speciesism," which he defines as "the idea that it is justifiable to give preference to beings simply on the grounds that they are members of the species *Homo sapiens*," a "prejudice that survives because it is convenient for the dominant group," namely, "humans." Such "speciesism," for example, would give priority to "infants and those with severe intellectual disabilities" over animals who have a level of self-awareness and some interest in living. Since in Singer's view animals, like humans, have "interests," "if we ignore or discount their [animals'] interests, simply on the grounds that they are not members of our species," we are no different from "the most blatant racists or sexists who think that those who belong to their race or sex have superior moral status."[3]

It's not hard to see that Singer is not a theist, much less a Christian. He speaks of the "Judeo-Christian tradition" as having "an unjustifiable bias in favor of human beings" over "nonhuman animals." Since human beings have no intrinsic worth, he argues, killing them should be justified on the basis of whether or not characteristics indicative of personhood are present, such as whether or not they have "a capacity to feel life" and are "capable of anticipating a future." Operating by this principle, argues Singer, newborn babies would not have an intrinsic right to life: "Killing a newborn baby—whether able-bodied or not—I think, is never equivalent to killing a being who wants to go on living."[4] Singer feels that many animals, such as gorillas, have a "capacity to feel life" or a certain "sense of existing over time" whereas newborn babies do not, and so such animals might sometimes be given a right to life over the "rights" of newborn babies. Indeed, Singer goes

---

[2] From a letter Singer posted on the online magazine *Slate*, June 2001, www.slate.com, as quoted in Celeste McGovern, "Human Rights for Apes?," *National Catholic Register*, July 8, 2001, 1, 10, at 10. An attempt to get a chimpanzee legally declared a person failed in Austria in May 2008, but an appeal was made to the European Court of Human Rights in Strasbourg, France, where the case is pending (Thaddeus M. Baklinski, "Quest to Have Chimps Declared Persons Rejected by Austrian Supreme Court," May 23, 2008, www.lifesitenews.com). Singer's cause is expected to succeed in Spain where the environment committee of the Spanish Parliament in June 2008 voted to "bind Spain to the principles of the Great Ape Project" and "grant limited rights to our closest biological relatives, the great apes" (Donald G. McNeil, Jr., "When Human Rights Extend to Nonhumans," *New York Times*, July 13, 2008, www.nytimes.com).

[3] Peter Singer, "Animal Liberation at 30," *New York Review of Books* 50 (May 15, 2003): 23.

[4] When once asked if he would "kill a disabled baby," Singer responded: "Yes, if that was in the best interests of the baby and of the family as a whole" (John-Henry Westen, "Princeton Professor Singer: And I Repeat, I Would Kill Disabled Infants," September 12, 2006, www.lifesitenews.com).

so far as to say that it is only because a human being has this "sense of existing over time" characteristic of personhood that "it's normally worse to kill a human being than to kill a chicken." Note here his use of the word "normally," which means on a regular basis, but not necessarily.[5]

Fortunately Singer's views on the moral equivalence of humans and animals have not yet become widely accepted, though they reflect a movement gaining momentum among certain animal rights' groups. Singer has been at work fostering utilitarian and positivistic principles regarding human and animal rights for some forty years, and is only now approaching his peak. Society still holds on to moral principles based on intrinsic values because most people continue to accept existing laws that were formulated when intrinsic values were still the basis for moral law. But for how long and on what basis, in view of the fact that Singer and others like him continue to work at the undermining of any foundation for traditional moral values?

In fact, principles of traditional morality are increasingly being jettisoned. There is a growing coarsening of moral sensitivity. We were all at one time horrified by the idea of legalized abortion, but now 1.3 million abortions are carried out each year in America and most people accept it as part of life. We were all at one time horrified by the notion of mercy-killing or euthanasia, but now it has been legalized in Oregon, Washington, Montana, and parts of Europe, and people seem to take it in stride.

Nor does anyone seem troubled by the fact that certain organizations are now urging that pedophiliac activity be made legal in some cases. As in the case of legalized abortion, traditional morality based on intrinsic values is here gradually being replaced by morality based on choice. Rep. Gerry Studds in 1983 was formally censured by the U.S. Congress for having a sexual affair with a seventeen-year-old male congressional page. Studds never apologized, argued the investigation was an invasion of his privacy, and brought the page to the House floor to boast of their consenting relationship. He was welcomed with applause, retained his House seat, and retired in 1996. At his death in 2006, he was heralded as a "role model" by certain political leaders.[6]

Recently members of the European Parliament issued a report that included a chapter on the rights of children in which the organization lamented the fact that countries still have penal codes where "discriminatory dispositions are still enforced on the age of consent of the minor for

---

[5] "Bob Abernethy Interview with Princeton University Professor Peter Singer," *Religion & Ethics Newsweekly*, September 12, 1999, 1, 2, 5, www.pbs.org.

[6] Eric Fettmann, "The Page-Stalker that Dems Lionized," *New York Post*, October 17, 2006, www.nypost.com.

homosexual relations."[7] Judith Levine, a journalist, argues that sex between adults and teenagers is not always wrong: "For some teens," she argues, "a romance with an older person can feel more like salvation than victimization."[8] The American Psychological Association has published a study "that claimed to find little or no harm—and sometimes benefit—in consensual pedophilia between men and boys."[9] And the North American Man-Boy Love Association has a web page supporting adult-child sexual relationships as long as they are a matter of choice.

We continue to be horrified by certain outrageous killing actions, but not by all. Only recently, thousands of people were being systematically slaughtered in southern Sudan by the northern ruling Muslim government, but most of the world seemed unconcerned. Several hundred babies, many of them viable in the second and third trimesters of birth, were once killed by partial-birth abortion each year in the United States, but there was no national outrage.

A bill designed to outlaw such action was repeatedly vetoed by President Clinton over many years, and could never be overruled by the Congress because a two-thirds majority could never be mustered. This was due in part to the many Catholic senators who voted in opposition to the ban, but there was little Catholic outcry. A law outlawing such action was finally passed with the support of President George W. Bush, a Methodist, but has now been enjoined by the courts as a possible violation of *Roe v. Wade*, and there is no national outrage.

We continue to be horrified at a Timothy McVeigh, who could wantonly destroy innocent human life by blowing up the Alfred P. Murrah Federal Building in Oklahoma City on the weekday morning of April 19, 1995, or an Osama bin Laden, who could destroy the lives of thousands of innocent people on a bright summer Tuesday morning on September 11, 2001. But is the day to come when we will have to be tolerant even of these two people and their supporters because they are only exercising their right to choose, as pro-abortionists do? Some argue that governments should stop infringing on the rights of people "in their bedrooms." But what gives governments the right to infringe on people's rights when they are not in their bedrooms? What objective standard of morality can one point to, to argue otherwise?

---

[7] Zenit News Agency, "European Parliament Recommends Recognition of Homosexual Couples," March 17, 2000, www.zenit.org.

[8] From Levine's *Harmful to Minors: The Perils of Protecting Children from Sex*, as quoted by Robert F. Worth in "Renegade View on Child Sex Causes a Storm," *New York Times*, April 13, 2002, 1, www.nytimes.com.

[9] Brian Donnelly, "Pedophilia: Abnormality or Alternate Lifestyle?," *Our Sunday Visitor*, August 15, 1999, 19.

Indeed, the basis for maintaining objective standards of morality in the United States has virtually disappeared. One of the most ominous signs of this, though it went largely unnoticed, appeared in the Supreme Court decision *Planned Parenthood of Southeastern Pennsylvania v. Casey* (June 29, 1992). In continuing to maintain the right of a woman to terminate her pregnancy, which the Supreme Court narrowly reaffirmed by a 5–4 decision (Justice Kennedy, a Catholic, being the deciding opinion), the Court went beyond simply reaffirming that supposed right, and philosophized about its understanding of the liberty that the Bill of Rights grants to every person. The Court affirmed: "At the heart of liberty is the right to define one's own concept of existence, of meaning, of the universe and of the mystery of human life. Beliefs about these matters could not define the attributes of personhood were they formed under compulsion of the state."[10] In other words, everyone has the right to decide for oneself what has value and what does not regarding the totality of human existence, and everyone is then free to live according to the values each creates for oneself. Could it possibly have dawned on the misguided minds of the five justices who concurred in this opinion that no society could maintain the unity necessary to survive on the basis of the anarchy that such a morality would entail, were it lived out to its fullest?

Social Justice and Secularization

One of the most common forms of reductive Christianity today is the social justice movement. This movement, especially as it is used in Catholic circles where it is often separated from the deeper dimensions of the Christian faith, is another example of the theme we noted above, the reduction of religion to morality.

Supporting social justice causes is the culturally acceptable and politically correct way of being religious in American society today because it comes without all the "baggage" associated with being overtly religious. Standing for social justice doesn't separate you from others, nor does it demand adherence to principles that can be socially unacceptable, alienating, and even countercultural. As a result, advocating social justice is a way of pleasing both religionists and nonreligionists. Nonreligionists are happy because it removes the suprarational—the transcendent, or faith dimension—from public discourse. But religionists are happy for the same reason, because the transcendent dimension is embarrassing to superrational religionists. Put simply, by reducing faith to social activism, one can be a believer without having to believe. A religious person simply becomes a "good person" with feeling.

---

[10] "Supreme Court Rules on Pennsylvania Abortion Control Act," *Origins* 22 (July 9, 1992): 117.

Social justice programs sans overt religion increasingly are becoming the politically correct way for college students to show they care about others, which is the prime motivating principle at the heart of this new "religion." Such programs are often based on the notion that being a good Christian means more than just being a "good person": it involves assisting the less fortunate, at least at times, in their moments of need. Recall the data in the Morey and Piderit study of Catholic higher education in our previous chapter (see pp. 261–72) where college and university administrators argued that the practice of their Catholic students in social justice causes was a "religious activity" that had "the greatest potential to change students." Yet there was little evidence of the social justice programs as expressions of Catholic social teaching.[11]

According to *America*, "a growing number of college students are taking part in service projects," such as "building homes, tutoring students, registering voters, visiting the sick and elderly and volunteering in homeless shelters and soup kitchens" during spring break, rather than going off, as many students continue to do, to beach parties on sunny shores.[12] At one university, the applicants for a spring-break "Appalachian Experience" with the poor rose in one year from 230 to 370 students, so that an emergency meeting had to be called to create new sites to accommodate the volume. This led the director of the program to conclude "students are willing to dedicate their lives in any way to giving themselves and their time to those in need."[13]

Perhaps, but not all scholars agree on the loftiness of student motives. A study released by the federal agency Corporation for National and Community Service (CNCS) in 2006 recorded an astounding rise in college students (between 16 and 24 years old) volunteering: "The number of college students volunteering grew by 600,000 from 2.7 million in 2002 to 3.3 million in 2005. . . . In 2005, approximately 30.2 percent of college students volunteered, exceeding the volunteer rate for the general adult population of 28.8 percent."[14] While the study notes the "positive outcomes for

---

11 Morey and Piderit, *Catholic Higher Education*, 201.

12 "College Students Once Again Spend Break Helping Others," *America* 184 (April 2, 2001): 4. To be sure, many Catholic youth resist social-service projects, finding efforts to aid the poor and oppressed unappealing, since such persons are thought to be personally responsible for their plight for failing to live the work ethic that naturally leads to success. Our youth are still by and large enamored with the desire to get ahead, to become rich, and to succeed by climbing the corporate ladder. For such youth, the social justice movement is not attractive unless it supplies personal dividend.

13 Kate MacNair, "Massive Amount of Apps Mean More Sites for Appalachian Experience," *The Hawk* (student paper at Saint Joseph's University), October 12, 2006, 5.

14 CNCS, *College Students Helping America* (Washington, DC: CNCS, October 2006), 2, www.nationalservice.gov.

communities and students" from such volunteering, it also reports that "some researchers have started questioning the nature of volunteering among young people," arguing that "many youth volunteer out of self-interest and to 'pad their resume.'"[15] Another study notes: "Paradoxically, while more students are volunteering than ever before, they are not espousing the civic values that community service is intended to encourage. For some students, involvement in community service could be motivated less by caring than by other factors, such as personal interest, group norms, or the social benefits they derive from participation."[16]

Little is made of the fact that students often seem to be dedicated to the poor at far-off places, for which free round-trip air flights are provided by wealthy benefactors or are financed from auctions of goods donated by well-intentioned benefactors.

And so, since the dreaded 1960s when all institutions had their raison d'être questioned and all values that were not rationally justified were rejected, Catholicism felt that if it was to survive, it needed to translate the faith into categories the new generation would accept. And so it force-fed the young the idea that you could indeed translate the faith into rationalistic and social categories and devote some time to social justice causes as a way of being a good Catholic. Other matters of faith that demanded some degree of overt religiosity beyond the purely rational and social, such as participating in the sacramental life of the Church, could be ranked secondary, or even better, ignored.

Many in the Church have seized upon this new wave as a way of saving Catholicism from extinction, without noticing the disastrous effects the secular morality of social justice has had upon mainline Protestant denominations. A revealing study as to why mainline Protestant churches had diminished so greatly in the twentieth century led three sociologists to conclude that for young people, religion "had become low on their list of personal priorities," resulting largely from the fact that the tenets of their religion had gradually been reduced to a "common moral code" respecting "such virtues as honesty, helping others, and generally 'leading a good life.'" The principle reason for having churches had increasingly been reduced to "support basic morality" so that people would turn out to be

---

15 Ibid., 16; the citation is from Lewis A. Friedland and Shauna Morimoto, *CIRCLE: Working Paper 40: The Changing Lifeworld of Young People: Risk, Resume-Padding, and Civic Engagement* (Center for Information and Research on Civic Learning and Engagement, University of Madison-Wisconsin), September 2005, 3, www.civicyouth.org.

16 Helen M. Marks and Susan Robb Jones, "Community Service in Transition: Shifts and Continuities in Participation from High School to College," *Journal of Higher Education* 75 (May/June 2004): 308.

"good." The problem for the modern generation was that, with their so-busy lives and so many commitments of time and energy to other projects, there was "no real point in getting involved" in a religious culture that asked so little of them and promised so little. So bad has the situation gotten, according to the three scholars, that there appears to be nothing the churches can do today to reverse their disintegration, since the churches have lost the "spiritual conviction required to generate the enthusiasm and energy needed to sustain a vigorous communal life."[17]

Many Catholics seem unaware of these reasons for the disintegration of modern Protestantism. Even less are they aware of the conclusions Hegy drew from his study, as we also noted in our second chapter (see p. 97–98), that all divisions among Christian religions are destined to become obsolete as they become increasingly reduced to "social movements."

And so the evil that I have argued follows from the reduction of religion to morality, namely, the disintegration of organized religion, has now begun to have its effect upon the Catholic Church, and the social gospel advocates are either oblivious of the effects of their movement or simply unconcerned about it.

It is important to note that the argument is not that the social justice movement has no place in the Christian faith experience. How could one argue such? Benedict XVI, as we shall see shortly, has made it clear that the creation of a just society is of deep concern to the Church. The problem, however, is that virtuous action for a Christian should always be a direct consequence of a personal relationship with Jesus Christ, lived through a vital sacramental life in his Church, and never a replacement for that life. It is indeed not possible today to believe in Jesus Christ as the Messiah who came not to be served but to serve and to give his life for the many (Mk 10:45) without being committed to the establishment of equality and justice for all and to the realization of the well-being of all members of society. The problem is not with the importance of the social justice agenda, but with such an emphasis upon its importance that it leads to the reduction of the Christian faith to the service of that agenda.

There are many scholars today who argue that the Jesus of history was primarily a social revolutionary who wanted to destroy all political and social oppression, all divisions in society between the rich and the poor, between the establishment of his day and the marginalized, but these scholars are reinterpreting Jesus and his teaching to suit their own preconceived political and social agendas. I say preconceived because liberation theology began in the late 1960s and early '70s as a grass-roots movement that sought

---

[17] Benton Johnson, Dean R. Hoge, and Donald A. Luidens, "Mainline Churches: The Real Reason for Decline," *First Things* 31 (March 1993): 15–18.

a theological justification to bolster its sociopolitical agenda, and garner forces within the powerful Catholic Church that would provide the impetus to overcome the political and social injustice and oppression of the poor and marginalized in Latin America.[18] It is to the study of the ill effects of that reductive movement on the life of the Church that we now turn.

Liberation Theology and the Latin American Bishops

The Church in Latin America has traditionally aligned itself with the interests of government authority, military leaders, and corporate powerhouses.[19] The turning point in the life of the Church came with the meeting of the Second General Conference of Latin American Bishops at Bogotá and Medellín, Columbia, August 24–September 6, 1968. For the first time in modern times, service of the poor and oppressed becomes a preeminent leitmotif in the life of the Church. The Church identifies itself with the marginalized in its efforts to liberate all strata of society from oppressive structures that inhibit the greater participation of humanity in the life of the Kingdom of God.

The bishops at the conference take seriously Christ's commandment to "evangelize the poor," by which they mean to distribute resources and personnel in a way that "effectively gives preference to the poorest and most needy sectors and to those segregated for any cause whatsoever." The bishops intend to "come closer to the poor . . . making ourselves accessible to them" and fostering "solidarity" with them.[20]

The bishops' concern, however, is not simply with the poor. They speak to the liberation of all peoples who "hunger and thirst for justice," in an effort to elevate the dignity of all human beings and all human activity.[21] The bishops call the Church to "lend its support to the downtrodden *of every*

---

[18] In fact, liberation theology's origins can be traced to European theologians, such as Jürgen Moltmann and Johann Baptist Metz, whose theologies of hope and liberation, sprung in the aftermath of the Nazi holocaust, spoke to various parts of the world that needed a basis of hope for rising out of economically impoverished and politically oppressive situations.

[19] Our discussion of liberation theology will be limited to its earliest developments in Latin America, since that is where the movement began, and where fundamental principles directing the movement were established. Liberation theology later spread to other Third World areas, such as Africa and the Far East, and to minority groups in North America formulating black and feminist theologies in their struggles to overcome oppression.

[20] Second General Conference of Latin American Bishops, "Document on the Poverty of the Church," in Alfred T. Hennelly, S.J., ed. and trans., *Liberation Theology: A Documentary History* (Maryknoll, NY: Orbis, 1990), p. 116, nos. 9–10.

[21] Ibid., "Document on Justice," pp. 98–99, nos. 3–5.

social class so that they might come to know their rights and how to make use of them."[22] The bishops intend to work "for a new order of justice that incorporates *all persons* in the decision-making of their own communities."[23] They express compassion for those who yearn for justice "*in every sector* of the respective national communities," including peasants, workers, women, and those eager to advance their lives through studies in higher education.[24]

The expression "preferential option for the poor" with which liberation theology is identified today first appears in Church documents of the Third General Conference of Latin American Bishops that met at Puebla de los Angeles, Mexico, January 27–February 13, 1979.[25] We quote the paragraph in full:

> With renewed hope in the vivifying power of the Spirit, we are going to take up once again the position of the Second General Conference of the Latin American episcopate in Medellín, which adopted a clear and prophetic option expressing preference for, and solidarity with, the poor. We do this despite the distortions and interpretations of some, who vitiate the spirit of Medellín, and despite the disregard and even hostility of others. We affirm the need for conversion on the part of the whole church to a preferential option for the poor, an option aimed at their integral liberation.[26]

Even here, however, the bishops continue to speak of the ecclesial base communities that operate in the Latin American Church as embodying not simply the Church's preferential option for the poor, but more broadly "the church's preferential love for the common people."[27]

---

[22] Ibid., p. 104, no. 20 (emphasis added).

[23] Ibid., "Message to the Peoples of Latin America," p. 93 (emphasis added).

[24] Ibid., "Document on Justice," p. 98, no. 1 (emphasis added).

[25] Gustavo Gutiérrez tells us the expression first "emerged from within Christian communities, between the time of the conferences of Medellín and Puebla (1979)"; Gustavo Gutiérrez, "The Task and Content of Liberation Theology," trans. Judith Condor, in Christopher Rowland, ed., *The Cambridge Companion to Liberation Theology* (Cambridge, UK: Cambridge University Press, 1999), 27. Peter Hebblethwaite tells us that the phrase "option for the poor" was "first used in a letter from Pedro Arrupe to the Jesuits of Latin America in May 1968"; Peter Hebblethwaite with C. Rowland (1994–1999), "Liberation Theology and the Roman Catholic Church," in Rowland, *Liberation Theology*, 179.

[26] Third General Conference of the Latin American Bishops, "Public Final Document: 'A Preferential Option for the Poor,'" no. 1.1, in Hennelly, *Liberation Theology*, 254.

[27] Third General Conference of the Latin American Bishops, "Base-Level Ecclesial Communities (CEBs), The Parish, and the Local Church," no. 2.2, in Hennelly, *Liberation Theology*, 251.

Bishops' Understanding of the Poor

The burning issue throughout this discussion concerns the core principle behind the cause of liberation theology: the preferential option for the poor. Who, according to liberation theology, are the poor?

The initial clarification regarding the meaning of that term is supplied by the Second Conference of Bishops held at Medellín in 1968. The bishops distinguish three ways to understand poverty:

1. "As a lack of the goods of this world necessary to live worthily as human beings." The bishops denounce this poverty as "contrary to the will of the Lord" and generally the result of "human injustice and sin."
2. As "spiritual poverty." It is "the attitude of opening up to God, the ready disposition of one who hopes for everything from the Lord." One who practices this poverty "values the goods of this world," but "does not become attached to them" and "recognizes the higher value of the riches of the kingdom." The bishops cite the Magnificat (Lk 1:46–55) for the understanding of poverty in this sense. Even though the word "poor" or "poverty" is not used by Mary in that canticle, the song of praise expresses, according to the bishops, "the theme of the poor of Yahweh."
3. "As a commitment, through which one assumes voluntarily and lovingly the conditions of the needy of this world in order to bear witness to the evil it represents and to spiritual liberty in the face of material goods, follow[ing] the example of Christ who took to Himself all the consequences of our sinful condition and who 'being rich became poor' in order to redeem us."

According to the bishops, the Church is called to denounce the first form of poverty, preach and live the second, and is "bound" to the third. Indeed, "all members of the church are called to live in evangelical poverty"—the third form of poverty—"but not all in the same way," depending on their "vocations," their "diverse styles of life," and their "various modes of acting."[28]

In their subsequent discussion about the consequences of this teaching, the bishops present a position regarding their own exercise of poverty that is not entirely unambiguous. Curiously, after making the distinction regarding the three ways of understanding poverty, they express their need

[28] Second General Conference of Latin American Bishops, "Document on the Poverty of the Church: Doctrinal Motivation," 115.

to "evangelize the poor" as Jesus did, and their "duty of solidarity with the poor," without saying in which sense they are using that word.

However, one may presume from the content of their discussion to which group they are referring. For they explain that their "duty of solidarity with the poor" means to "make ours their problems and their struggles, that we know how to speak with them," to criticize all forms of injustice and oppression to which the poor are subjected, and to "dialogue with the groups responsible for that situation in order to make them understand their obligations."

The bishops indicate, furthermore, that their "resources and apostolic personnel" will be distributed so as to give "preference to the poorest and most needy sectors and to those segregated for any cause whatsoever." Finally, the bishops plan to "come closer to the poor in sincerity and fellowship, making ourselves accessible to them." The poor in all of these statements appear to be only the poor in the first sense, a group for whom the bishops have been largely remote and uncommunicative. But what about the needs of the spiritually poor? Do they not also experience injustice and oppression? Are they not also in need of fellowship? In other words, once the three-fold distinction has been made, the spiritually poor seem to be forgotten.

Secondly, the bishops have stated that all the members of the Church are called to live the second and the third forms of poverty. But in accepting that the third form has various styles and modes depending on one's vocation, no clear lines are given as to how that form of poverty is concretely to be lived, perhaps because none can be given. But some indication of parameters regarding spiritual and evangelical poverty seems necessary.

Finally, regarding their own lives, the bishops say their "houses and style of life [are] to be modest, our clothing simple, our works and institutions functional, without show or ostentation." Are they speaking only for themselves as Latin American bishops or for all bishops of the Church? They seem to be mandating principles appropriate for all bishops. But if so, this is a tall order for princes of the Church and members of the modern hierarchy, one to which few seem to have responded.

Nevertheless, the categories of poverty presented by the bishops at Medellín are a welcome clarification of three ways in which the meaning of poverty may be validly understood. The tripartite classification should prove helpful in our understanding of poverty throughout our discussion of liberation theology as well as the scriptural uses of the term. We shall see, however, a major weakness in liberation theology: it tends to follow the same route the bishops take in distinguishing various ways in which poverty may be understood, and then limit the focus of its attention to the first.

Gustavo Gutiérrez

If anyone may claim to be the most significant figure behind the origins of liberation theology, it is Gustavo Gutiérrez (1928–),[29] the Peruvian now also Dominican priest who launched the movement in 1968 with his magnum opus *A Theology of Liberation*.[30] The major features of that study were first limned in a paper Gutiérrez presented in July of that year, and published in 1969 as "Toward a Theology of Liberation."[31] That title gave the name to the movement.

Gutiérrez emphasized in that paper that theology is, as traditionally understood, reflection upon the Christian faith. But if that faith involves commitment to God, it also involves commitment to human beings. This, he argues, gives a progressive dimension to theology, as it adapts itself to the historical situation of human beings in every time and place.

The concrete situation at the stage of human life in the world today, according to Gutiérrez, demands efforts toward liberation: "If faith is a commitment to God and human beings, it is not possible to live in today's world without a commitment to the process of liberation" and the "call to action" that process demands.[32] But according to Gutiérrez, this human process of liberation, when understood from the perspective of faith, includes social, economic, and political dimensions calling for emancipation of human beings from oppressive structures within history, as well as a spiritual process of emancipation from sin and the forces of evil. For Gutiérrez, liberation from oppressive forces within history is not accidental to, but an integral part of, the movement of the human family toward eternal salvation in the life of the Kingdom of God. Taking his cue from the words of Paul VI in *Populorum Progressio* (Encyclical on the Development of Peoples, March 26, 1967), Gutiérrez stresses God's saving role in the historical struggle for liberation:

> I emphasize that the work of building the earth is not a preceding stage, not a stepping stone, but already the work of salvation. The creation of a just and fraternal society is the salvation of human beings, if by salvation we mean the passage from the less human to the more human. Salvation, therefore, is not purely "religious."[33]

---

29 Our treatment of Gutiérrez's liberation theology will focus on the basic principles of his thought. It is the use of these principles that has had a major impact on the Church and, in my estimation, contributed heavily to the present crisis of faith in the Church.

30 Gustavo Gutiérrez, *A Theology of Liberation: History, Politics, and Salvation*, rev. ed., trans. and eds. Sr. Caridad Inda and John Eagleson (Maryknoll, NY: Orbis, 1988 [1971]).

31 Gustavo Gutiérrez, "Toward a Theology of Liberation," 62–76.

32 Ibid., 64.

33 Ibid., 71. See Paul VI, *Populorum Progressio*, par. 20: "This is what will permit the fullness of authentic development, a development which is for each and all the

Gutiérrez justifies his integration of the historical in the salvific by the biblical story of creation, which is already "the first salvific act": "Creation is included in the process of salvation, which is God's self-communication." Israelite history in its totality is then for Gutiérrez "nothing else but the prolongation of the creative act. Thus the Psalms speak of Yahweh as simultaneously creator and savior (see Psalm 136)." In the New Testament, Christ's redemptive activity is also God's work of salvation "in the context of creation."

From this it follows that work—understood by Marx "as a humanizing element" tending toward "the transformation of nature to construct a society that is more just and worthy of human beings"—is also "a work of salvation." Similarly, the scriptural promises of the coming of the Messiah "bind tightly together" salvation with historical progress: "the kingdom of God" with "better living conditions for human beings," a "kingdom of peace" with "the establishment of justice, the defense of the *rights of the poor*," and "the punishment of oppressors." For Gutiérrez, the Messiah and the Kingdom of God come with "the suppression of oppression" and "when injustice is overcome."[34]

History for Gutiérrez is "the progressive revelation of the human face of God." Central to this theology is his exegesis of the Last Judgment scene in Matthew 25:31–46, interpreted to indicate that "an action on behalf of a human being is an action on behalf of God. If you gave food and drink, you gave it to me; if you denied it, you denied it to me." Thus the "encounter with God takes place in the encounter with our neighbor. . . . To believe in Christ, therefore, is to believe at the same time in history."

Faith becomes "the motivating force of all human behavior," and "eschatology" the "motor of the historical process," taking Christians always beyond a contentment with the present to a search for ever greater horizons of liber-

---

transition from less human conditions to those which are more human" (Boston: Daughters of St. Paul, n.d.). There is no document more instrumental in the formation of liberation theology than this encyclical of Paul VI. It stressed the crying need for overcoming structures of injustice, and the integration of human historical development in spiritual growth: "To wage war on misery and to struggle against injustice is to promote, along with improved conditions, the human and spiritual progress of all men, and therefore the common good of humanity" (76). Among those conditions that for Paul VI are "more human" are "increased esteem for the dignity of others, the turning toward the spirit of poverty, cooperation for the common good, the will and desire for peace, . . . faith, a gift of God accepted by the good will of man, and unity in the charity of Christ, Who calls us all to share as sons in the life of the living God, the Father of all men" (21). When investigating the causes of 9/11, we need to reflect upon what is lacking in our own efforts to promote what is always the "more human."

[34] Gutiérrez, "Toward a Theology of Liberation," 71–73.

ation. For Gutiérrez, contemporary history has made faith "radicalized": "One cannot be a Christian in these times without a commitment to liberation." But faith is also "relativized," for the "process of human liberation is never ending." The contemporary issue for Christianity is whether it will understand the Kingdom of God "in its integral reality," as a Kingdom measured by the processes of historical emancipation of the human person and social and political structures, or whether it will remain tied to the Marxist image of Christianity, as a system that uses other-worldly reality to try to compensate for the injustices of poverty and oppression within history.[35]

In addition to the above conjunction of the salvific and the temporal in the horizon of eschatology, Gutiérrez's theology is guided by two other fundamental principles: First, theology begins with praxis (from the Greek, meaning "an acting" or "doing" or "action"; one sees in the word the English "practice"). This position directly undercuts the traditional perspective that theology begins with a systematic reflection upon the faith's understanding of Christian revelation (following St. Anselm's principle, "faith seeking understanding"). In other words, instead of theology starting "from above," from God's word to humanity, and then systematically explicating the meaning of that revelation for our lives and the world in which we live, liberation theology starts "from below," from the concrete issues of conflict in the world in which we live, which it then analyzes as a Christian believer, finally ending in a grasp of the meaning and theological relevance of God's revelation for our world.

The fact is, however, that the concrete world in which we live could be examined from many different perspectives. And so, secondly, we must ask: From what perspective, from what angle of investigation does liberation theology look at our world? Which world is the real world of praxis for liberation theologians?

The answer to that question constitutes the paramount distinguishing element in liberation theology: it starts from the situation of the poor, and looks at the world from their viewpoint. "If one day someone posed the question, 'What is the most important perspective in the theology of liberation?' " Gutiérrez writes, "I would reply that it is the preferential option for the poor." So crucial is this preferential option to Gutiérrez that, if the theology of liberation movement should one day cease to exist, as he expects it will, it would make no difference to him as long as the option for the poor remained. Why? Not because the poor are necessarily good (he says they aren't), nor because we should have compassion for them (although we should), nor because it is reasonable to do so, but because God in fact prefers them: "God is good and prefers the forgotten, the

[35] Ibid., 74–76.

oppressed, the poor, the forsaken."[36] Gutiérrez knows this from Genesis, where God preferred Abel, "the younger brother, the last," to Cain.[37] But he knows it most of all from the New Testament and his exegesis of Matthew 25:31–46, which we shall examine later.

But who are the poor, according to Gutiérrez?

In an essay published in 1999, Gutiérrez distinguishes three concepts of poverty, which he says were first developed "around July 1967," and which closely resemble those later presented by the bishops at Medellín:

1. Real poverty (frequently called material poverty). This is defined as the lack of those goods required to satisfy the most basic needs of human beings.
2. Spiritual poverty. This is not primarily the putting aside of worldly goods; it is rather an attitude of openness and acceptance toward the will of God. The Gospel also calls this spiritual childhood, of which the renunciation of worldly goods is a consequence.
3. Poverty as a commitment to be assumed by all Christians. This expresses itself in solidarity with the poor and in protest against poverty. Jesus assumes the sins of humanity in this way, both out of love for the sinner and in rejection of sin.[38]

In his earliest seminal work on the theology of liberation, Gutiérrez recognized these same three conceptions of poverty, but integrated them in an important way. Poverty "designates in the first place *material poverty*," he says, but there is a second line of thinking in the Bible known as *spiritual poverty*, which is "synonymous with faith, with abandonment and trust in the Lord, . . . to be totally at the disposition of the Lord." But Gutiérrez says he accepts neither of these as an adequate understanding of the biblical conception of poverty, since the former is too oriented toward canonizing socioeconomic hardship, the latter too removed from such hardship. He therefore understands the third concept of poverty as a synthesis of the two, "as a commitment of solidarity" with those who "suffer misery and injustice . . . to protest against it and to struggle to abolish it." This solidarity "must manifest itself in specific action, a style of life, a break with one's social class" so as to help the poor "to become aware of their exploitation and seek liberation from it." Christian poverty, then, is "an expression of love, is solidarity *with the poor* and is a protest *against poverty*."[39]

[36] Gustavo Gutiérrez, "Option for the Poor: Review and Challenges," *Promotio Justitiae* 57 (September 1994): 17.

[37] Ibid., 16.

[38] Gutiérrez, "Task and Content," 25–26.

[39] Gutiérrez, *Theology of Liberation*, 163, 169, 172.

Returning to the 1999 essay, we find Gutiérrez formulating three types of liberation related to these three types of poverty. The first type of liberation sees the poor primarily as the economically poor and politically marginalized, focusing on understanding their plight and calling for "political and social liberation, which points towards the elimination of the immediate causes of poverty and injustice, especially with regard to socio-economic structures." But two other types of liberation probe more deeply: the second, human liberation, means that, while we are aware that changing social structures is important, we need to go deeper. It means liberating human beings of all those things—not just those in the social sphere—that limit our capacity to develop ourselves freely and in dignity. Here we are speaking of what Vatican II called a "new humanism."[40] The third type, crucially, is liberation from selfishness and sin. In the analysis of faith, this is the last root of injustice that has to be eliminated. Overcoming this leads to re-establishing friendship with God and with other people.[41] It is clear that only the grace of God, the redeeming work of Christ, can overcome sin.

For Gutiérrez, these "three dimensions of liberation" are "linked" in a "broad process whose meaning is ultimately to be found in the salvation of Christ."[42]

Gutiérrez explains each of the terms in the expression "preferential option for the poor" based on the conjunction of these three notions of poverty and liberation:

1. The *poor* are those who are "victims of material poverty."[43] Who they are is best described by the situations to which they are subject: they are liable to premature "physical death" and repressive situations of "cultural death"; they are "non-persons, the *in-significant*, those who do not count in society," those "without social or economic weight," those "robbed by unjust law," "despised," and "culturally marginalized."[44]
2. Gutiérrez understands *option* to explain the Church's and the individual Christian's "spirituality" of commitment: "*option* relates to the idea of commitment that—as we have suggested—means solidarity with the poor and rejection of poverty as something contrary to the will of God."[45] James Nickoloff explains the option as "a free decision to side

[40] Cf. *Gaudium et Spes*, par. 55, in Abbott, *Documents of Vatican II*; hereafter paragraph numbers noted in the text as *GS*.

[41] Cf. *Lumen Gentium* (Dogmatic Constitution on the Church, November 21, 1964), par. 1, in Abbott, *Documents of Vatican II*; hereafter paragraph numbers noted in the text as *LG*.

[42] Gutiérrez, "Task and Content," 26–27.

[43] Ibid., 27.

[44] Gutiérrez, "Option for the Poor," 15.

[45] Gutiérrez, "Task and Content," 27.

with the oppressed and powerless in their fight for justice and to stand against all persons and structures that oppose their liberation." It is a "decision to make a commitment" that "transforms the world into a place of justice."[46]

3. *Preferential* "is inspired by the notion of spiritual childhood or the capacity to accept the will of God in our lives."[47] It means "what comes first." It "implies the universality of God's love, which excludes no one." According to Gutiérrez, it is "only within the framework of this universality that we can understand the preference."[48] Preferential means "having priority," not that "only the poor count."[49]

Note in Gutiérrez's understanding of this preferential option for the poor that while poverty is understood to have three different meanings, it is only those who suffer from "real poverty," meaning "material poverty," who are the object of the preferential option. This is again based on Gutiérrez's understanding of the type of poor whose needs are satisfied according to his exegesis of Matthew 25:31–46. For reasons we shall see, the poor in this text are for Gutiérrez the *really*, or *materially* poor, and not the spiritually poor.

Christopher Rowland summarizes perhaps best of all and quite succinctly the main points of liberation theology when he says that it focuses on "the presence of God in the persons of the poor, the emphasis on action rather than belief, the hope for the reign of God on earth, and a reliance on an action-reflection model." The "thread" running through all the theology is "a commitment based on contemplation of God in the suffering Christ whose presence is hidden in the poor."[50]

What Happened to the "Poor in Spirit"?

Gutiérrez accepts, as we have seen, the category of the "poor in spirit," and recognizes there are such people, yet he never seems to take them seriously because of the importance he gives to the teaching of the Beatitudes and his narrow exegesis of its meaning. He argues that, in spite of the recent "stubborn resistance" of those who support "spiritualistic interpretations" of the Beatitudes, Jesus in that passage clearly affirms the preferential

> love of God for the poor for being just that—poor—and not necessarily, or even primarily, for being more believing, kinder, or better, morally

[46] Nickoloff, *Gustavo Gutiérrez*, 13.
[47] Gutiérrez, "Task and Content," 27.
[48] Gutiérrez, "Option for the Poor," 15.
[49] James B. Nickoloff, "Introduction," *Gustavo Gutiérrez: Essential Writings*, ed. James B. Nickoloff (Maryknoll, NY: Orbis, 1996), 13.
[50] Rowland, "Introduction," in his *Liberation Theology*, 12.

> speaking, than others. God loves them simply because they are poor, because they are hungry, because they are persecuted. Only on this basis is it possible to appreciate subsequent efforts to enrich or define precisely the evangelical meaning of the poor person.[51]

For Gutiérrez, if we "spiritualize" the gospel by maintaining that the poor addressed in this passage "refers first and primarily to the 'spiritually' poor rather than to the 'materially' poor, then we 'humanize' God" by making God "love, by preference, those who are good because they deserve it—just as we do ourselves." On the other hand, if we allow the Gospel to present the love of God for the poor "precisely as poor people (materially speaking if you want to use that language)," then we accept the "mystery of God's revelation and the gift of his kingdom of love and justice," and a God who "will not be reduced to our mode of thinking, and who judges us on the basis of our concrete, historical actions toward the poor (Matt. 25)." We also allow God to "block the path of a false love which forgets sisters and brothers while claiming to direct itself spiritually toward God." If God's love is primarily to the materially poor, then "to know and to love God, one must know the concrete life situation of the poor today, and radically transform a society that produces them."[52]

Critique of Gutiérrez

Gutiérrez's argumentation betrays many weaknesses.

First of all, to argue that God's love is directed toward those who are "good" or who are "poor in spirit" does not imply under any circumstances that these receive his love because they "deserve it." This is simply bad theology. No one deserves God's love, and certainly not those who attain poverty of spirit only with the help of God's grace. But if, following Gutiérrez's argument, God's love is to be preserved from being humanized, how is that achieved if, as Gutiérrez argues, God judges us "on the basis of our concrete, historical actions toward the poor"?

Secondly, Gutiérrez misunderstands the meaning of "poor in spirit" when he sees it to be compatible with "false love which forgets sisters and brothers." A love that is truly "poor in spirit" could never be a "false love."

Thirdly, Gutiérrez's inadequate exegesis is a result of the faulty methodology of liberation theology, arguing from praxis to revelation rather than from revelation to praxis. His exegesis of Matthew 25 should be directed by the fact that the Gospel writer wrote "blessed be the poor in spirit," rather than by imposing on the text the ideology of his liberation theology that makes God who he wants God to be.

---

51 From Gutiérrez's *The Power of the Poor in History* (1979), in *Gutiérrez: Essential Writings*, 104–5.

52 Ibid., 105.

Gutiérrez is not alone in his downgrading of the theological importance of poverty of spirit. His views appear to be endemic to liberation theology. For example, Leonardo Boff and his brother, Clodovis, also spurn the notion of the "poor in spirit." Giving theological value to the "poor in spirit," say the Boffs, is done by those who want to be included in the beatitude but "cannot really be counted among the poor." But then why did Matthew in his Gospel say "poor in spirit" and not "poor," as in Luke? Perhaps because Matthew, the former tax collector, is one of those who also wanted to be included but felt left out by the more narrow "poor."

The Boffs' conception of poverty appears to be even more radical than Gutiérrez's in its rejection of capitalism and popular culture. The poor are the *socioeconomically poor*, narrowly defined as "all those who lack or are deprived of the necessary means of subsistence—food, clothing, shelter, basic health care, elementary education, and work." Their situation, according to the brothers, is "in most cases" the product of the unjust, exploitative, and oppressive capitalistic system "that constitutes injustice on a societal and even international scale."

Those considered poor would, however, also include all those "*discriminated* against by reason of their race . . . their culture, . . . or their sex." As an example of such poverty, the brothers describe a woman "oppressed and impoverished on six counts: as a woman, as a prostitute, as a single parent, as black, as poor, and because of her tribal origin." For such a woman, they argue, the Christian faith means "trying every possible avenue of escape from such a set of social iniquities."[53] But doesn't the Christian faith offer so much more, and isn't it unfair to reduce all who receive God's preferential love only to those suffering social and economic injustices?

LIBERATION THEOLOGY ON THE WANE

Gutiérrez makes liberation theology indispensable to the Christian dispensation. The Boff brothers seem at least theoretically more open-minded: They admit that liberation theology "is not the only possible and legitimate reading of the Bible," and that its views even "may not be the most *important* themes in the Bible." It's simply that, "for us in the Third World today, however, it is the obvious one, the 'hermeneutics' for our times," "the most *relevant* (to the poor in their situation of oppression)."[54] That primacy of relevance is, indeed, questioned by many, but one may at least respect the Boff brothers for their honesty.

---

[53] Leonardo Boff and Clodovis Boff, *Introducing Liberation Theology*, trans. Paul Burns (Maryknoll, NY: Orbis, 1987 [1986]), 46–47.

[54] Ibid., 32–33.

Nevertheless, most advocates of liberation theology seem mesmerized by the importance of its perspective for contemporary theological discourse. One scholar not too long ago asserted "it is the most significant and influential theological movement in the Catholic Church since the Second Vatican Council," representing a "completely new epoch in church history," so significant that "three distinct eras" may now be addressed in the life of the Church: "the first centuries," "the Constantinian era," and the era with which liberation theology is identified, "social construction."[55]

Though the movement is on the wane today in Latin America, it still continues to have its admirers among certain theologians in the United States, especially among those guilt-ridden over past failures to be concerned for the less fortunate; among those who identify with groups formerly marginalized, such as feminists (who have insisted on inserting their cause into the movement even though one struggles to see how many feminists today could seriously rank themselves alongside the peasants of Latin America); and among those who have written their dissertations on the movement and know little else. For many, however, championing the goals of liberation theology is just another way to reduce Christianity to a socially and politically correct system of morality, and that may be the major reason for its popularity in American Catholic circles. The movement is especially designed to make Christianity palatable to people who have lost the faith and still want some principles they can hang onto, or people who fear that Christianity would otherwise become irrelevant. Thus it is the mentality of crisis in the Church since the '60s that continues to feed liberation theology in much of the northern hemisphere as its value and influence wane south of the border.

What remains to be critically investigated, however, is liberation theology's claim to a foundation in the New Testament, especially in the Beatitudes. But as we investigate the Beatitudes, we shall see there a much richer and deeper theological perspective than liberation theology is able to provide.

"The Poor" or "Poor in Spirit" in the Beatitudes

There are two New Testament texts that liberation theologians use to justify their position that Jesus was primarily concerned about the materially poor and politically marginalized. The first of these is Luke 6:20 from Jesus' Sermon on the Plain: "And raising his eyes toward his disciples he said: 'Blessed are you who are poor, for the kingdom of God is yours.' " Reference is rarely made to Matthew's version of the same beatitude, since, if properly exegeted, it broadens the range of Jesus' teaching and does not

[55] Hennelly, general introduction to *Liberation Theology*, xv–xvi.

support liberation theology's agenda: "Blessed are the poor in spirit, for theirs is the kingdom of heaven" (Mt 5:3). The question arises as to who exactly are these "poor" or "poor in spirit"?

It is patently the teaching of the Matthean version, but probably also intended in the Lucan, that those who are considered blessed by Jesus are more than simply economically and materially poor people; otherwise, why refer to them as "poor in spirit"? Liberation theologians are also too literal for Jesus, who often used words whose first meaning applied to the material world, but whose reference extended to the spiritual ("My mother and my brothers are those who hear the word of God and act on it" [Lk 8:21]; "Jesus said to them, 'Come after me; I will make you fishers of men' " [Mk 1:17]). Liberation theology's approach represents far too literal an understanding of the opposition between "the poor" and "the rich" in the Gospels, and fails to bring out the nuances that an adequate reading of such statements would require. For, as one writer rightly points out, "the poor man may be far from being poor in spirit," and "the rich man may occasionally exhibit just that attribute in his dealings with God and with his neighbours."[56]

Furthermore, in both Matthew and Luke, Jesus is addressing his "disciples" (Lk 6:20; Mt 5:1–2). Some of these may have been both blessed by Jesus and economically poor, but surely not all: Peter as a fisherman was part of a thriving and "intensive" fishing industry that existed on the shores of the Sea of Galilee, and would not have been considered poor by contemporary Palestinian standards;[57] and surely tax-collectors such as Matthew raked in considerable profit from their collections for the Roman rulers. In fact, more recent scholarship is concluding that Jesus himself, as a woodworker or a carpenter's son, would not have been economically poor, which makes his so-called "preferential option for the poor," if understood in the sense of material poverty, curious to say the least. As one writer says:

> Indeed, Jesus Himself was not poor in the normally accepted sense. The story of the birth of Jesus in an outhouse in Bethlehem is in terms of this discussion quite beyond the point. Symbolic though it may be, the circumstances were created by the exigencies of travel rather than by lack of money. He did not belong to the proletariat; He inherited a business from His father. He was self-employed. He became a "mendicant" only in the sense that He sacrificed the securities of home and employment for the life of a wandering evangelist dependent upon the resources of others.[58]

[56] Stuart Blanch, *Way of Blessedness* (New York: Ballantine, 1985), 81.

[57] Madeleine S. and J. Lane Miller, eds., *Harper's Encyclopedia of Bible Life*, third rev. ed. (San Francisco: Harper & Row, 1982), 383.

[58] Blanch, *Way of Blessedness*, 81; see Lk 8:3.

John P. Meier, in his celebrated study of Jesus and his times, notes that many people in Nazarean society would have fallen "into a vague middle group" that would have included "business people and craftsmen in cities, towns, and villages, as well as freehold farmers with fair-sized plots of land." On this scale, Meier concludes that Jesus "would have ranked somewhere at the lower end of the vague middle, perhaps equivalent—if we may use a hazy analogy—to a blue-collar worker in lower-middle-class America," and certainly above the situation of "day laborers" and "hired servants."[59]

Jesus, moreover, had a domicile, at least for a while (Mk 2:1, 15). He seems to have frequently dined with tax-collectors (he was accused of being a "glutton" and a "drunkard" while dining with them [Lk 7:34; Mk 2:15]), and even stayed with the tax-collector Zaccheus who was wealthy (Lk 19:2–5). If Jesus' preferential option was for the poor in the sense of the socioeconomically deprived, why was he consorting with types such as these? One suspects a larger, more comprehensive understanding is necessary if one is to grasp correctly who these blessed persons were who were "poor" as well as "poor in spirit."

While Luke may have been referring to the disciples of Jesus insofar as they were as a group economically poor[60]—which I think is unlikely in view of the means that at least some of them had available to them—their situation of being blessed, even in the eyes of Luke, would not have been caused by the poverty of their existence (why would poverty in itself make anyone blessed?), but by the relationship of dependence on God that stamped their whole existence and was the focus of Jesus' concern in the light of his proclamation of the coming of the Kingdom. It is likely, then, that Matthew, by speaking of the "poor in spirit," deliberately intended not only to clarify by broadening the scope of what Jesus really meant when he spoke of the "poor," but also to heighten the disciples' awareness of their transcendent relationship to God that would have constituted the reason for their blessed state either as economically "poor" or "poor in spirit." Quite likely, Luke also intended the transcendent relationship to God as the basis for the blessedness of his "poor" even as Matthew did for his "poor in spirit."

A better exegesis, then, would understand these terms to denote the disciples as a group who were "poor" in the sight of God, which is the only

[59] John P. Meier, *A Marginal Jew: Rethinking the Historical Jesus*, vol. 1, *The Roots of the Problem and the Person* (New York: Doubleday, 1991), 282.

[60] Raymond Brown understands it this way in Luke: "These beatitudes address those who are actually poor, hungry, mournful, and hated 'now.' " But Matthew has "spiritualized" the meaning to address those in his community "who are not physically poor and hungry," to let them know "that there was an outreach of Jesus for them as well, if they have attitudes attuned to the kingdom." Raymond E. Brown, S.S., *An Introduction to the New Testament* (New York: Doubleday, 1997), 239, 178–79.

referent for which Jesus had any interest. Such "poverty" is surely not meant to exclude material poverty, but not meant to be limited by it either.

In Jesus' speech, to be "poor" is more closely identified with being humble, in the sense of recognizing one's lowliness before God, and being detached from the things of the world in the sense of being utterly dependent upon God for all that one has. To be sure, the Matthean text brings out this meaning with greater clarity ("poor in spirit"). But Jesus must be understood as speaking always, not in reference to the things of the world, but in reference to the Kingdom of God, which he has come to bring into the world and whose heavenly realm he is equipping people to attain: "The Beatitude is more concerned with our relationship with God than it is with our place in society."[61]

In that case, "poor" or "poor in spirit" would be terms for those who recognize their dependence on God and live the whole of their lives in the light of that dependence. Gutiérrez's concern to avoid humanizing God's love by making it directed toward those who deserve it has no place here. A person who is "poor in spirit" has a transcendent dimension incorporated into life, or better, has allowed that dimension to be the life source of all human action, a gift one would never consider to be deserved. Such a person, of course, would surely not be living an extravagant life, nor be unconcerned about the welfare of those less fortunate, as Gutiérrez fears, since such attitudes would contradict the nature of the "poverty" intrinsic to the transcendent orientation. The state of poverty of the disciple of Jesus would follow from recognition of the utterly baseless foundation within oneself for pride or arrogance or vanity, in view of the fact that all of one's "riches" are received from God in the light of a life of dependence on him. It is, in fact, in this sense that Jesus is actually in favor of being "rich": "Thus it will be for the man who grows rich for himself instead of being rich in the sight of God" (Lk 12:21). If Jesus has a preferential option for the poor, it is because only in being "poor" in the sight of God is one capable of being "rich."

Jesus' Understanding of the "Child"

Further clarification about Jesus' call to humility and dependence on God as the foundation for life in the Kingdom can be found in his teaching regarding the child in Luke 9:46–48. Indeed, if one insisted upon Jesus' preferential option for the poor and understood his use of "the poor" to designate the materially disadvantaged, one would have difficulty making Jesus consistent with himself when he speaks about the child as the greatest in the Kingdom of God. If the child is the greatest in the Kingdom, how does that give priority to the materially poor?

---

[61] Blanch, *Way of Blessedness*, 84.

As the question about greatness arose, Jesus placed a child in front of his disciples and boldly identified himself with the child: "Whoever receives this child in my name receives me." He then continued to assert that "whoever receives me receives the one who sent me" (Lk 9:48). In other words, the child becomes identified with the Father through the child's identification with Jesus. Jesus concludes in the same verse by drawing from his words the maxim: "The one who is least among all of you is the one who is the greatest," and finally, explains why that status is given to the child: "Whoever makes himself lowly, becoming like this child, is of greatest importance in that heavenly reign" (Mt 18:4).

Whether the child is materially rich or poor seems not to be the issue; the point is that the child's lowliness, humility, and situation of utter dependence for all that the child has make the child the symbol of the type of person for whom the Kingdom of God is intended. In this case, Jesus is being perfectly consistent with his teaching regarding the poor when understood in the spiritual sense: the need for humility in one's understanding of one's own worth, and of leading a life of detachment from the world consistent with the awareness of one's utter dependence on God for all that one has.

The annotated edition of the New American Bible (NAB) has this footnote at Matthew 5:3:

> *The poor in spirit*: in the Old Testament, the poor (*ʿanāwîm*) are those who are without material possessions and whose confidence is in God (see Is 61, 1; Zep 2, 3; in the NAB the word is translated *lowly* and *humble*, respectively, in those texts). Matthew added *in spirit* in order either to indicate that only the devout poor were meant or to extend the beatitude to all, of whatever social rank, who recognized their complete dependence on God. The same phrase *poor in spirit* is found in the Qumran literature (1QM 14, 7).[62]

The annotation accepts two possible interpretations of the "poor": either those who are materially poor, or those of any social status. The point, however, is that even while the materially poor *may* have been intended (and I think not, for the reasons given above), it is not meant to suggest all of the poor, but only those who formally qualify for the beatitude by "their complete dependence on God." This sets the reference on the poor in the context of Jesus' disciples, and not simply on the poor as a class by itself.

The reference is to the *ʿanawîm*, the remnant of Jews in the Old Testament who were to be among the saved. While the annotation asserts that the *ʿanawîm* are both lacking in material possessions and living a life of

[62] Commentary from the New American Bible, St. Joseph Medium Size Edition (New York: Catholic Book Publishing, 1992 [1970]), New Testament, p. 16; hereafter pages noted in the text as NT.

dependence on God, other noted exegetes are not so sure. Some, such as Meier, argue that the use of that word originally had a more literal reference to the materially poor, and had already taken on an extended meaning in the Old Testament in the Psalms and the writings of the prophets. In a chapter devoted to a fundamental disagreement with certain liberation theologians for their misunderstanding of "the poor," Meier states:

> *'anawîm*, "the poor ones," along with similar Hebrew adjectives, had become a description of those who had seen through the illusory security of this world and had learned to trust in God alone for their salvation. At times no particular socioeconomic connotation is attached to *'anawîm* . . . . The poverty-vocabulary is coming to mean humility, meekness, almost Matthew's "poor in spirit." Indeed, according to some scholars, Matthew's very phrase has now been found in the documents of Qumran (ironically, in the War Scroll!). As the quintessentially pious group, the Essenes called themselves "the poor of God." They provide the prime example of the theology of poverty applied to a whole Jewish sect at the time of Jesus.

In fact, Meier and others argue, quite correctly in my view, that the term "the poor" may have come to be a designation "applied to the Jerusalem church" as a whole,[63] and a state appropriate for any disciple of Christ who would inherit the Kingdom of God.

LAST JUDGMENT SCENE

The other text commonly used to argue that Jesus had a preferential option for the socioeconomically poor is Matthew 25:31–46, the Last Judgment scene. This presents Jesus' final discourse to his disciples before entering into his Passion, and is unique to Matthew. The scene is the final judgment at the end of history, and "all the nations" (Mt 25:32) of the world are assembled before him. Jesus, as king and judge, designates who will enter the Kingdom of God and who will not. The norm for distinguishing those who are saved from among the people assembled is whether or not one has responded to the needs of "these least brothers of mine" (Mt 25:40) or to the needs of "these least ones" (v. 45). To examine this issue carefully, two questions need to be answered: which people are designated by "all the nations," and who are Jesus' "least brothers" or "least ones"?

Scholars are sharply divided into two major groups. The more traditional exegesis holds that "all the nations" refers to all the people of the

[63] John P. Meier, "Jesus among the Theologians: II: Sobrino and Segundo," in his *The Mission of Christ and His Church: Studies in Christology and Ecclesiology*, Good News Studies 30 (Wilmington, DE: Glazier, 1990), 64–65.

world. Exegetes holding this position include the distinguished biblical scholar William F. Albright[64] and liberation theologians.[65] "All the nations" are all peoples being judged by how they respond to the needs of "these least brothers of mine," understood as the world's materially poor and socially oppressed.[66] But is this the best exegesis of these terms?

It is true that some of the needs of the "least brothers" enumerated in the Matthean text fall into the category of those who are materially poor: Some of the "brothers" are said to have been hungry, thirsty, and naked (Mt 25:35–36). But others are said to have been ill or in prison (Mt 25:36), a situation not necessarily proper only to those who are materially poor or socially oppressed. But the designation of another group as "strangers" (Mt 25:35) indicates even more clearly the weakness of this position, since hospitality is offered to the stranger as one who is alone and alien to the environment and not because of a situation of material poverty or social oppression. But there are more serious weaknesses to this exegesis.

First, it is curious that this Last Judgment scene, which according to this exegesis is of major importance because it presents teaching regarding the one thing necessary for salvation—responding to the needs of the materially poor and socially marginalized—is found only in Matthew. Since such a teaching would obviously be central to Jesus' proclamation, it is difficult to understand how it could be overlooked by the other Gospel writers.

Second, the teaching proposed by this exegesis is found nowhere else even in Matthew. Thus it is a unique teaching in a unique Matthean passage, leaving one to wonder how anyone would have known about it had the passage been omitted. Some of those who support this exegesis admit to its uniqueness, yet continue to assert that, in spite of that oddity, that's the way it is. I would assert that its uniqueness is an argument against this interpretation. A better exegesis would be one that shows the passage at least to reaffirm a teaching central to the Matthean corpus.

---

64 Albright translates Matthew 25:32 as "all the peoples," meaning all the nations of the world. W. F. Albright and C. S. Mann, eds., *Matthew*, The Anchor Bible 26 (Garden City, NY: Doubleday, 1971), 310.

65 "According to the Gospels, the poor are the primary addressees of Jesus' message. They constitute the eschatological criterion of the salvation or condemnation of the human race and every one of its members (Matt. 25:31–46)." Leonardo Boff, O.F.M., *Faith on the Edge: Religion and Marginalized Existence*, trans. Robert R. Barr (New York: Harper & Row, 1989 [1978 and 1980]), 60–61.

66 According to Gutiérrez, *all the nations* "includes . . . 'all persons: pagans, Jews, and Christians,'" and *my least brethren* "designates 'all the needy, whoever they may be, and not only Christians.'" *Theology of Liberation*, 112, citing Heribert Mühlen, *Esprit dans l'Église*, and Pierre Bonnard, *L'Évangile selon Saint Matthieu*. For Boff, the poverty has material, social, and religious dimensions (*Faith on the Edge*, 60).

Third, if "these least brothers of mine" or "these least ones" refer to the materially poor and socially and politically oppressed, as this first group of exegetes argues, "all the nations" who respond to their needs would have to refer to everyone else. This would mean that the whole human race apart from these needy ones is designated for salvation or condemnation on the basis of how it responds to their needs. And this would mean, as Gutiérrez argues, that Jesus' disciples would be judged on the same basis as pagans.

But this poses a serious problem: Are Jesus' disciples to be considered no different on their route to salvation than all the nonbelievers on the face of the earth? If so, why does Jesus stress so often the importance of faith for salvation (Mt 7:30; 8:13, 26; 9:22, 28; 10:32; 13:58; 14:31; 15:28; 17:20; 28:19–20)? By this interpretation, only service of the poor, not faith, seems to be important. Could Jesus really have been saying that? Such a notion sets up a major conflict within Jesus' teaching, and a serious challenge to the importance of the interpersonal relationship with Jesus that is at the heart of the Christian faith experience.

Sometimes supporters of this exegesis respond that faith is presumed among "all the nations," so that Jesus is stressing that faith must be put into action as a necessary dimension of discipleship.[67] But this is surely eisegesis (unscholarly and unfounded interpretation) at its worst, since "all the nations" clearly leaves no room for a breakdown based on faith.[68] And even if it did, what about the destiny of nonbelievers who served others? Are they not being considered at all as having the possibility of salvation? But if they would somehow have that possibility, we are remanded back to the question of the role of faith regarding salvation. And if they would not be saved, they seem to be condemned for not having seen Jesus in "these least ones" (Mt 25:45–46), an advanced teaching that surely many of them would never have had an opportunity to learn. Are they to be condemned for their ignorance? While some fundamentalist groups do indeed argue this way, Catholic teaching does not.

Others argue that those among the respondents who are Christian would have the faith, nonbelievers would not, but both could be saved because of their response to the needs of the poor. But again, how could

---

[67] According to Benedict Viviano, the passage "presents a practical religion of deeds of loving kindness, love of neighbor." Jesus is addressing it "to Christian disciples, and discipleship is understood in a very bold way as identical with care of the needy. This is not a denial of faith; it is of the essence of faith." Benedict T. Viviano, O.P., "The Gospel according to Matthew," in Raymond E. Brown, S.S. et al., *The New Jerome Biblical Commentary* (*NJBC*) (Englewood Cliffs, NJ: Prentice Hall, 1990 [1968]), 42:145.

[68] The NAB argues that "the phrase *all the nations* includes the Jews also, for at the judgment 'the Son of Man . . . will repay everyone according to his conduct' (16:27)" (NT 26, note for Mt 25:32).

responsible exegesis find this in the text rather than as a theological distinction being imposed upon the text to save this interpretation?

Finally, one might argue that, by responding to the poor and oppressed with whom Jesus identifies himself, those who attain salvation do so because, even though they do not know of Jesus' presence in the poor, they were in fact responding to Jesus in his "least brothers," and thereby their response in some minimal way equates the response of faith (a kind of anonymous Christianity).

While such an interpretation has the advantage of maintaining an element of faith (if one may call it that) as an instrument of salvation, it creates another problem: Since all those who are saved, as well as those condemned from among "all the nations," are unanimous in their failure to recognize Jesus' identification with his "least brothers," how is it that Jesus' disciples, if they are included as members of "the nations," would be unaware of this fundamental teaching of Jesus? And if the answer is, Jesus' disciples would not be included in the group of "all the nations" but only nonbelievers, then where are Jesus' disciples represented? One would have to argue that they have been omitted entirely from the scene because the discourse is not addressing their situation.

Since the Greek word translated as "nations" is ἔθνη, which can also mean "the Gentiles," such an exegesis is possible. The text would represent Jesus, then, teaching his disciples regarding the possibility of salvation for nonbelievers who had received no introduction to him (they would not have been put into a position where they would have had to decide about believing in him or not), nor would they have been exposed to his teaching regarding his identification with the poor. Jesus' point would be that these nonbelievers, even while never having attained faith, could nevertheless be saved simply on the basis of how they responded to the needs of the poor in general.

While this exegesis, unlike all the previous, may be cogently argued, some questions remain: What about Jewish nonbelievers? Since they are not included among the Gentiles, is the possibility of salvation for them simply being ignored? Secondly, since this is the final judgment, it is curious that Jesus' disciples would be entirely omitted from the discussion, especially since they would be the primary hearers and readers of the Gospel. Would they not also be required to respond to the needs of the poor? Perhaps not, in which case this would be an anomalous dimension of Jesus' teaching, implying faith without works is acceptable. Or is their response simply taken for granted, without any need for discussion? But how could such an important dimension of Jesus' teaching not be made explicit for his disciples? Finally, and perhaps most importantly, the text still remains a unique passage within the Gospels, and even within

Matthew itself, meaning that it doesn't fit into the general scheme of the teaching of any of the Gospels. This may be the most serious weakness, since there is a better exegesis that fits comfortably within Jesus' teaching as presented elsewhere in the Gospels.

The number of difficulties with this exegesis is too great to be ignored. Surely there must be a better interpretation of the Last Judgment scene. And there is.

A growing number of the better exegetes argue that "these least brothers of mine" are Jesus' disciples, or more specifically, Jesus' disciples on mission. According to Bruce Metzger and Roland Murphy, the "*little ones*" [italics in original] are "disciples of Jesus."[69] Coming as it does at the end of Jesus' public ministry and before he goes off to his Passion, the passage presents Jesus' final mission statement, sending his disciples to "all the nations" of the world to hear and accept his message. In this case, a better translation for ἔθνη would probably be "the Gentiles," which would include all those who have not yet heard of Jesus and his teachings. As Metzger and Murphy write: "*The nations* [are] probably those who do not know the God of Israel."[70]

This provides an adequate explanation for why "all the nations" are unaware of this fundamental teaching of Jesus that salvation comes through a response to him in his "least brothers": In responding to Jesus' disciples on mission, these nonbelievers would be unaware that they were responding to Jesus as he lives in his disciples, and thereby performing an action equivalent to the response of faith, the only actionable faith available to them.[71] Those who did not respond would be equally unaware that they were failing to respond to Jesus, but their actions would have the same effect because they would be rejecting Jesus and his teachings as embodied in his disciples. Their failure to respond merits condemnation since all salvation comes through Jesus alone (Acts 4:12).

---

[69] Bruce M. Metzger and Roland E. Murphy, gen. eds., The New Oxford Annotated Bible (New York: Oxford University Press, 1991), NT 27, note for Mt 18:6.

[70] Metzger and Murphy, New Oxford Bible, NT 39, note for Mt 25:32. I agree with Metzger and Murphy. However, the NAB states: "the phrase *all the nations* includes the Jews also, for at the judgment 'the Son of Man . . . will repay everyone according to his conduct' (16, 27)" (Jean Marie Hiesberger, gen. ed., The Catholic Bible, Personal Study Edition [New York: Oxford University Press, 1991], NT 56, note for Mt 25:32; ellipsis in original).

[71] Gutiérrez admits that this interpretation solves the problem created by the first exegesis regarding the Christians' "failure to recognize Christ implied in the question, 'When did we see you hungry,' etc." However, in spite of this solution, he belittles the issue by considering it a "minor" problem, cuts through all of the scholarship devoted to a study of the question, and continues to justify the first exegesis by simply begging the question: the second exegesis "go[es] against the obvious sense of the text and the context" (*Theology of Liberation*, 112). But the sense of the text and the context is exactly what is at issue!

Our interpretation is supported by the NAB annotation at Matthew 25:31–46:

> The criterion of judgment will be the deeds of mercy that have been done for the *least* of Jesus' *brothers* (40). A difficult and important question is the identification of these *least brothers*. Are they all people who have suffered hunger, thirst, etc. (35–36) or a particular group of such sufferers? Scholars are divided in their response and arguments can be made for either side. But leaving aside the problem of what the traditional material that Matthew edited may have meant, it seems that a stronger case can be made for the view that in the evangelist's sense the sufferers are Christians, probably Christian missionaries, whose sufferings were brought upon them by their preaching of the gospel. The criterion of judgment for *all the nations* is their treatment of those who have borne to the world the message of Jesus, and this means ultimately their acceptance or rejection of Jesus himself.[72]

Many plausible arguments can be brought forth to support this view. Jesus repeatedly identifies himself with his disciples in the Gospel of Matthew. In the long discourse of Matthew 10, Matthew specifically mentions that Jesus is addressing the Twelve (10:1; 11:1), and at the end of the discourse and before sending them on mission, Jesus identifies himself with his disciples as "these little ones" (10:42) and says:

> Whoever receives you receives me, and whoever receives me receives the one who sent me. Whoever receives a prophet because he is a prophet will receive a prophet's reward, and whoever receives a righteous man because he is righteous will receive a righteous man's reward. And whoever gives only a cup of cold water to one of these little ones to drink because he is a disciple—amen, I say to you, he will surely not lose his reward. (10:40–42)

The passage has significant parallels in the Final Judgment scene. First, there is the near identity of the term of designation: here, Jesus is identified with his disciples who are "these little ones"; there, he is identified with "these least ones." Secondly, here, those who give a cup of cold water to one of his disciples will be rewarded; there, anyone who responds to the least ones who are thirsty receives the reward of membership in his Father's kingdom. Could these two groups be different? The parallels would seem to indicate they are the same.

Also, the interpretation of the Last Judgment scene as involving Jesus' disciples on mission is supported by a parallel scene in Luke 10:1–16,

---

[72] Hiesberger, The Catholic Bible, NT 56, note to Mt 25:31–46.

where Jesus concludes his charge to the seventy-two who will precede him on mission with, "Whoever listens to you listens to me. Whoever rejects you rejects me. And whoever rejects me rejects the one who sent me" (v. 16). This is similar to the mission of identity in John's Gospel, where Jesus identifies himself with his disciples on mission and tells them, "Whoever receives the one I send receives me, and whoever receives me receives the one who sent me" (Jn 13:20). In other words, while the Last Judgment scene is unique to Matthew, its teaching is not: Jesus repeatedly asserts that the response of nonbelievers to Jesus' disciples on mission has eternal saving significance because of Jesus' identification of himself and his teaching with his disciples.

Additional supporting data for the disciples-in-mission exegesis of Matthew 25:31–46 can be offered:

Jesus calls his disciples here his "brothers." In a teaching situation before the crowds in Matthew 12:48–50, Jesus asks, "Who is my mother? Who are my brothers?" and answers, "Whoever does the will of my heavenly Father is my brother, and sister and mother." Thus the designation of his disciples in the Last Judgment scene as "these least brothers of mine" (Mt 25:42) would be a conjunction of two ways by which Jesus refers to his disciples—as "these little ones" and "my brothers."

We see in Matthew 18:1–5 a remarkable conjunction of Jesus' understanding of "the child" and "his disciples":

> At that time the disciples approached Jesus and said, "Who is the greatest in the kingdom of heaven?" He called a child over, placed it in their midst, and said, "Amen, I say to you, unless you turn and become like children, you will not enter the kingdom of heaven. Whoever humbles himself like this child, is the greatest in the kingdom of heaven. And whoever receives one child such as this in my name receives me."

It is both the "children" and "the disciples" who become "like children" who are "the greatest in the kingdom of heaven." Moreover, in verse 5, Jesus affirms that "whoever receives one child such as this in my name receives me," paralleling the reception given to the thirsty "little ones" because they are Jesus' disciples (in Matthew 10:42), and those "least ones" who are "thirsty" and are given to drink (in Matthew 25:42). In verse 6, "these little ones" are designated as those "who believe in me." Obviously "the children" and "these little ones" are not simply designations for children; they are terms designating Jesus' disciples as well. We see the disciples being compared to children again in Mark 9:37, and the disciples are called "childlike" in Luke 10:21. In John, Jesus explicitly addresses his disciples as "children" (Jn 21:5).

There is every reason to believe, therefore, that "these little ones" of the Last Judgment scene would also refer to Jesus' disciples. To speak of his disciples in diminutive terms was clearly an indication of their endearment to Jesus. Jesus is also highlighting the children's and his disciples' common dispositions of humility or lowliness or dependence, all qualities of fundamental importance for entrance into the Kingdom of God.

Further, a prominent role is also given in Matthew, as well as in John, to the disciples as they carry Jesus' mission to the world. As we have already noted in Matthew 10, Jesus is concerned that the Twelve proclaim the coming of the Kingdom of heaven. Similar calls of the Twelve to mission are found in Mark (3:13–19; 6:6–13) and Luke (9:1–6), along with the mission of the seventy-two in Luke 10:1–16. Mission seems to be especially important in Matthew in view of the fact that he ends his Gospel with the risen Jesus commissioning his eleven disciples to go out and make disciples "of all nations" (28:19), with the same Greek word used for "nations" as in Matthew 25:32. Clearly the "nations" referred to in Matthew 28:19 are all nonbelievers, supporting that same understanding of ἔθνη in Matthew 25:32.

The disciples-in-mission explanation of the Last Judgment scene has other benefits. It harmonizes all the parts of the scene without the strains induced by the explanation of "these least ones" as simply the poor. A consistently plausible explanation may now be given for why those who respond as well as those who do not respond did not know that Jesus was present in "these least brothers of mine": all are ἔθνη and therefore, unlike the disciples, would have no familiarity with Jesus' teaching. The disciples as "these least brothers of mine" are put in the position of knowing Jesus' teaching, which would certainly have been the case in view of its prominence in the Gospels, whereas to include the disciples in the group of "nations" who do not know Jesus' teaching makes no sense.

The disciples-in-mission exegesis also explains well why faith is not at issue in the judgment regarding the salvation of the nations. The disciples on mission know the importance of faith, but the people to whom the mission is being carried do not. And so the passage clarifies that, while the nations are nonbelievers—being Gentiles and perhaps also Jews who have not yet heard about Jesus and his teaching—they are nevertheless capable of being saved because of their response to Jesus' disciples and his teaching.

The point is, then, that rather than seeing the Last Judgment scene as a unique occasion in the Gospels presenting Jesus' concern for the poor and oppressed of the world, the passage is better understood as a powerful statement of the important role that Jesus' disciples play as his ambassadors (consistent with Paul's theology in 2 Corinthians 5:20) who make him continually present to the world, making it possible for the whole human race throughout history to enter into a saving relationship with Jesus through their mission activity. No greater statement could be made of the need for Jesus' disciples to carry on this saving mission to all the peoples of the world. No greater statement could be made of the importance of the witness value of their lives, of the need for their continuing fidelity to Jesus and his teachings so that the whole human race may be saved through them.

This mission activity, to be sure, should continue to be directed toward non-Christians as called for in the above passage. Today's mission, however, needs also to be directed just as forcefully toward the re-evangelization of many Christians who have lost their commitment to Christ, as well as toward Christians who have departed from the faith for lack of an understanding of who Christ is, or who have never experienced the value of a faith relationship with him.

Conclusions regarding the Beatitudes and the Last Judgment Scene

For all these reasons,[73] it seems better to understand "these least brothers of mine" and "these least ones" in the Last Judgment scene, and "the poor" and "the poor in spirit" in the Beatitudes, as references to Jesus' disciples who are totally oriented in their lives toward God, who live lives of utter dependence on God for meaning and purpose and satisfaction in their lives; and in the Last Judgment scene, the reference would be to Jesus' disciples more precisely as they carry out his mission to the world. In this latter case, some situation of material poverty for Jesus' disciples is, of course, implied by the fact that his disciples are in need, but it is not their situation of need as the "poor" that determines who these people are, but their mission to the world as disciples of Jesus. In the case of the "poor" of the Beatitudes, it is again not their material poverty which informs the members of the group, though that condition may be implied, but their relationship of utter detachment from the values of the world and their complete identification with the values appropriate to life in God's Kingdom.

Therefore, if it is proper to speak of Jesus' "preferential option for the poor," as is commonly done today,[74] this is because Jesus called his disciples

---

[73] Further discussion of the proper exegesis of the Beatitudes and the Last Judgment scene may be found in my book *Faith Beyond Justice: Widening the Perspective* (St. Louis: Institute of Jesuit Sources, 1994), 101–16.

[74] John Paul II frequently spoke of the preferential option for the poor, and so many refer to his usage as support for liberation theology's position. But one must note what the Pope meant by the poor: In a Christmas message in 1984, in which he affirmed his "solidarity with all the poor of the modern world," he included fourteen separate groups among the poor, going all the way from those who are starving in Africa, to "families that are suffering from the moral upheaval introduced into them

"poor" in their spirit of poverty before God. In this way, the preferential option is intended to include anyone—rich or poor, weak or strong, Jew or Greek, oppressed or nonoppressed (if there is such a person)—all those who respond to Jesus' proclamation of the Kingdom, and who accept God and a relationship of dependence upon him as the heart of their self-identity and as that which gives meaning to their lives.[75] These are the ones who are brother and sister and mother to Jesus, where all individuating distinctions break down because all become united as one with Jesus in doing the will of his heavenly Father (Mt 12:50).

This means, therefore, that Jesus was not focusing on the role of social justice for the economically poor as the norm for entrance into God's Kingdom in these two passages. But this is not to deny that social justice has a role in the lives of Jesus' disciples today. Whether the call to social justice as we understand it today can be found in the Scriptures is hotly debated;[76] nevertheless, few would deny the importance of the social justice mission in our contemporary world. The issue is not so much whether the Church should be involved in the promotion of social justice, but the degree to which and the way in which the Church should be involved in an activity that in itself has widely secular overtones (cf. below, our discussion of Benedict XVI's encyclical). The real question, then, is whether so much emphasis is being placed upon promoting social justice that it undercuts the primary mission of the Church to lead humanity to an active participation in a life of faith in God in Jesus Christ, and to a life of dedication to the service of God through identification with Jesus and his redemptive mission.

---

by the cynical society of consumerism," to those whose conscience is attacked by "psychological violence" ("The Beatitude of the Poor: Christmas Message of John Paul II," *Origins* 14 [January 10, 1985]: 498). The object of Jesus' preferential option here seems to correspond more closely to those who in whatever way suffer. The Pope is hardly restricting himself to the socioeconomic understanding of the poor.

[75] Cardinal Ratzinger writes: "At the beginning of his public life Jesus says: I have come to evangelize the poor (Luke 4:18). This means, 'I have come to respond to the fundamental question of your existence. I am here to show you the path of life, the path to happiness. I am, in fact, that path.'" For Ratzinger, the "deepest poverty" is "not material poverty but spiritual poverty: the inability to be joyful, the conviction that life is absurd and contradictory. In different forms this poverty is widespread today, both in the materially rich and in the impoverished nations." As quoted in Robert Moynihan, ed., *Let God's Light Shine Forth: The Spiritual Vision of Pope Benedict XVI* (New York: Doubleday, 2005), 83–84.

[76] Cf. the excellent discussion of this issue by Joseph A. Fitzmyer, S.J., professor emeritus of biblical studies at the Catholic University of America, "What Do the Scriptures Say About Justice?," in Tripole, *Jesuit Education 21*, 98–123. In his paper at the conference (pp. 99–112), Fitzmyer argued that social justice as such is not to be found in the Scriptures. While other scholars at the conference agreed, some found enough of a foundation in the Bible to warrant special emphasis upon the social justice movement today.

Review of Recent Ecclesial Teachings on the Role of Social Justice

Vatican II

Though the roots of the social justice movement in the Catholic Church go back to 1891 and Pope Leo XIII's encyclical *Rerum Novarum* (Encyclical on the Condition of Labor, May 15, 1891), which affirmed social justice principles regarding the equality of all human beings, and championed the rights of workers in the industrialized world over against worker exploitation by wealthy corporate owners, there is no doubt that the impetus that gave rise to the social justice movement in the modern Church is Vatican II—especially the teaching of one of the most magnificent documents the Church has ever composed, *Gaudium et Spes*.

This document in many ways reversed the hostile mentality toward the world created by the Church's decisions against modernism in the nineteenth century, and justified more concretely than had ever been done before the need for the Church to look outside itself to the issues and problems facing the world, and to make those issues and problems the Church's own: "The joys and the hopes, the griefs and the anxieties of the men of this age, especially those who are poor or in any way afflicted, these too are the joys and hopes, the griefs and anxieties of the followers of Christ" (*GS* 1). Though *Gaudium et Spes* was approved only at the end of the Council, discussions toward its composition set the tone for Vatican II—a conciliatory tone toward the modern world, an eagerness to treat the world as a partner in furthering the mission of our time to establish peace, equality, and prosperity for all.

Gaudium et Spes had a sense of the universal community of humankind, of which the Catholic community was a part, as the arena of the Church's concerns. The document challenged Christians as no other document had done before to bring the Kingdom of God into the world by transforming that world into the new creation of the Kingdom. Ecclesial concerns were no longer primarily to be focused only on intra-Church issues and problems; Christians had now staked their rightful claim and responsibility, as members of the human community, to work for the betterment of life within that community.

But this they would do by incorporating in the world practices consistent with the teachings of that other community in which they dwelt, the community of Christ's disciples who live by the gospel of Christ in their daily lives. A process of inculturation would entail restructuring that world according to Christ's teachings, namely, promoting the dignity of the human person in every area of life and promoting the common good, including efforts for racial and social equality, justice in the workplace and in the political community, global peace, and economic and spiritual well-being, wherever in the world these were lacking. The Church would enlist its efforts alongside those of all people of goodwill to develop the human potential to achieve the fullness of life for every member of the human family.

The shock effect of this kind of document on the Catholic community of the '60s and '70s was monumental—no one who has not lived through it could appreciate the effect this new spirit generated. Whereas the dominant perspective in Church teaching up to Vatican II, reflecting the ill effects of the Church's clash with the Enlightenment and modernism, viewed the world as a negative reality—something from which good Catholics separated themselves to avoid contamination from sin and anti-Catholic bias—now, suddenly, the world was a legitimate arena for wholesome Catholic living.

A careful reading of Vatican II, of course, makes it clear that the bishops at the Council had not simply become rosy optimists regarding life in the world. They continued to recognize that the spirit of the world could be detrimental to the life of the soul. But a careful reading was not being done by many in the immediate post-Vatican II Church. Most Catholics felt that the Council bishops had deliberately downplayed the problem of evil because of the need to present an appreciation of the world as a place outside the Church where one could rub elbows with non-Catholics and still grow in the experience of God's love. This nonecclesial yet Christian perspective regarding the world was so new and refreshing to Catholic thinking that it assumed a dominant role in the Catholic mentality. The social justice movement then took off at the speed of lightning, as the nonconfrontational way for a Catholic to be involved in the world in a secular way consistent with being Christian.

Perhaps in hindsight, after more than forty years to reflect, a more balanced view of the Church's teaching at Vatican II is possible. While *Gaudium et Spes* and *Apostolicam Actuositatem*[77] provided the foundation that was needed for the modern social justice movement within the Church, these teachings never intended for that movement to have a primacy in Church life, even less to have a self-understanding independent of the greater life of the Church, in spite of what many Catholic theologians understood at the time. In fact, the documents make it clear that the Church's primary purpose in all of its nonevangelical activity is to provide an arena of preparation for the reception of the gospel and for entrance into the saving life of the Church.

We read in *Lumen Gentium*, Vatican II's major doctrinal statement on the nature and role of the Church in God's plan of salvation:

[77] Paul VI, *Apostolicam Actuositatem* (Decree on the Apostolate of the Laity, November 18, 1965), in Abbott, *Vatican II*; hereafter paragraphs noted in the text as *AA*.

> Nor does divine Providence deny the help necessary for salvation to those who, without blame on their part, have not yet arrived at an explicit knowledge of God, but who strive to live a good life, thanks to His grace. Whatever goodness or truth is found among them is looked upon by the Church as a preparation for the gospel. She regards such qualities as given by Him who enlightens all men so that they may finally have life. (*LG* 16)

Along the same lines, Church efforts to promote justice are not seen as ends in themselves, but as measures preparing the world for the implanting of the seed of "the Word of God":

> Moreover, let the laity also by their combined efforts remedy any institutions and conditions of the world which are customarily an inducement to sin, so that all such things may be conformed to the norms of justice and may favor the practice of virtue rather than hinder it. By so doing, laymen will imbue culture and human activity with moral values. They will better prepare the field of the world for the seed of the Word of God. (*LG* 36)

In *Gaudium et Spes*, Vatican II did, indeed, support natural moral goals consonant with its saving purposes. It saw as one of the major goals of the Church to make "the family of man and its history more human" (how wonderful indeed that, whereas being human is so commonly understood as a justification for shortcomings, here it takes on a noble status as a goal to be achieved!). The Church was also told to hold "in high esteem" all that other "Christian Churches or ecclesial communities" had done toward achieving that same noble status. But, as noble as that goal was, it was not enough. The Council bishops immediately added: "At the same time, she [the Church] is firmly convinced that she can be abundantly and variously helped by the world in the matter of preparing the ground for the gospel" (*GS* 40).

It is the saving purpose that ultimately motivates all that the Church does in the world. In the eyes of the Church, all the scientific, technological, and social advances made in the world are of value not only because of what they do to promote the well-being of the human community, but also because they "provide some preparation for the acceptance of the message of the gospel—a preparation which can be animated with divine love by Him who came to save the world" (*GS* 57). The Church never forgets that she "com[es] forth from the eternal Father's love" and is "founded in time by Christ the Redeemer, and made one in the Holy Spirit," for "a saving and an eschatological purpose, which can be fully attained only in the future world" (*GS* 40).

Thus it is clear that in Vatican II, the purpose of all Church efforts in the world in the promotion of natural moral values is not simply the ennobling of human life, even though that is indeed a lofty goal, nor even to make the world a better place to live, as valuable a goal as that is in itself, but to integrate these goals into the Church's ultimate mission of preparing the way for the proclamation and acceptance of the gospel of Jesus Christ.

Synod of Bishops of 1971

The groundswell promoting social justice within the Catholic Church is heavily indebted to the Synod of Bishops of 1971 for giving impetus to the movement. Perhaps no statement has been cited more often than the following produced by that synod, as a justification for emphasizing the importance of the social justice movement:

> Action on behalf of justice and participation in the transformation of the world fully appear to us as a constitutive dimension of the preaching of the Gospel, or, in other words, of the Church's mission for the redemption of the human race and its liberation from every oppressive situation.[78]

The precise meaning of "constitutive dimension," the most critical words in the statement, is in dispute. The words are widely understood to affirm that the mission to proclaim and implement the gospel cannot be adequately undertaken without action fostering the establishment of just relations, or to put it simply, that promoting social justice is an element intrinsic to the gospel teaching, and therefore the two are inseparable. But the words almost certainly were not intended to convey that kind of philosophical clarity, which bishops would rarely do in what was intended as a pastoral document, but to emphasize the importance of social action in the mission of the Church when understood in its totality.[79] Liberation theologians usually seize upon the stricter interpretation of these words in an effort to bolster the basis for their social justice agenda, and force Christians to admit that they are not living according to the teachings of Christ unless they are promoting social justice. That can hardly be what the bishops wanted to say.[80]

What the bishops intended to say was that action on behalf of justice is an integral part of the total redemptive mission of the Church. They

---

[78] "Justice in the World: Synod of Bishops Second General Assembly," November 30, 1971, note 6, in Joseph Gremillion, *The Gospel of Peace and Justice: Catholic Social Teaching since Pope John* (Maryknoll: Orbis, 1976), 514.

[79] Perhaps John Paul II put it best when he referred to "works on behalf of justice" as an "indispensable part of its [the Church's] evangelizing mission" ("Pope John Paul II: Opening Address at the Puebla Conference," in John Eagleson and Philip Scharper, eds., *Puebla and Beyond: Documentation and Commentary*, trans. John Drury [Maryknoll: Orbis, 1979], 66). No pope has ever used "constitutive dimension" to express the relationship between action for justice and the gospel.

[80] Further clarification of the meaning the bishops wished to convey in their use of this expression may be found in Tripole, *Faith Beyond Justice*, 45–52.

wished to avoid the extremes of seeing efforts to promote social justice as comprising either the totality of the mission of the Church, or an optional activity that Christians may legitimately ignore in their understanding of the gospel. For the bishops, the work of liberating people from all forms of oppression spiritual as well as temporal is a "must" in today's understanding of the gospel. Though most liberationists are careful not to argue in theory that action for social justice comprises the total mission of the Church, they do in fact often champion the cause to such an extent that they effectively reduce the gospel message to that pursuit, or understand it as the work of supreme importance in the life of the Church. Such reductionism constitutes one of the major weaknesses of liberation theology, which the statement from the synod of bishops would definitely not support.

Popes subsequent to the promulgation of the bishops' statement, and none more so than John Paul II, have been wary of the liberation theology movement because of its tendencies toward this political and social reductionism and liaisons with anti-Catholic ideologies. They have consistently emphasized the importance of efforts to promote social justice, but they have just as emphatically insisted that the primacy of the Christian mission must be given to the redemptive saving action of Jesus Christ in liberating human beings from enslavement to sin and death, and that the fullness of freedom is only to be found in a relationship of love with Christ, now and forever in the Kingdom of God. Liberation from poverty and oppression, the Church insists, must always be integrated into that larger context, and is never adequately Christian without that integration.

Evangelii Nuntiandi

We see integration into that larger context clearly and emphatically presented in Paul VI's extraordinary apostolic exhortation on the Church's mission of evangelization and the role of social justice within that mission, *Evangelii Nuntiandi*. There the Pope affirms, with a clear awareness of the need to bring proper balance to the teaching of liberation theology, that Christ brings liberation "from everything that oppresses man," but this means "above all liberation from sin and the Evil One, in the joy of knowing God and being known by him, of seeing him, and of being given over to him."[81] For Paul, this process of liberation is a key aspect of the Church's mission, but its "essential mission" is more broadly understood as the need to evangelize, that is, "to preach and teach, to be the channel of the gift of grace," to proclaim "Christ to those who do not know him, . . . to reconcile sinners with God," and to confer "Baptism and the other Sacraments"

[81] *Evangelii Nuntiandi* (On Evangelization in the Modern World, December 8, 1975) (Washington, DC: USCC, 1976), par. 9; hereafter, paragraph numbers noted in the text.

(14, 17). Evangelization means bringing "the Good News into all the strata of humanity, and through its influence transforming humanity from within and making it new" (18).

To achieve this transformation, the Good News of the gospel needs to be what we would call today "inculturated" at the deepest levels of society and of the human psyche, by "affecting" and "upsetting . . . mankind's criteria of judgment, determining values, points of interest, lines of thought, sources of inspiration and models of life": cultures have to be "regenerated by an encounter with the Gospel" (19, 20). Evangelization will also contain as the "summit of its dynamism—a clear proclamation that, in Jesus Christ, the Son of God made man, who died and rose from the dead, salvation is offered to all men, as a gift of God's grace and mercy" (27).

The Pope pointedly notes that this salvation exceeds all that the world has to offer: It is "not an immanent salvation . . . restricted to the framework of temporal existence . . . but a salvation which exceeds all these limits" (27). It is a proclamation of liberation that is "incomplete" if the Church does not proclaim that "salvation [is] in Jesus Christ" (34).

The Pope stresses nevertheless the importance of evangelization's impact upon the temporal order. He speaks of "profound links" (and deliberately not of a "constitutive dimension") between "human advancement, development and liberation" and evangelization (31). He insists on the need to "build up structures which are more human, more just, more respectful of the rights of the person and less oppressive and less enslaving," yet nevertheless argues that "all temporal liberation, all political liberation," even if it is justified by scriptural foundations in the Old and New Testaments, even if it is rooted in acceptable "theological data and conclusions," even if it conforms to the needs of contemporary theological perspectives, carries within itself "the germ of its own negation" unless its motives are informed by "justice in charity" and its "final goal" is "salvation and happiness in God" (35).

The Church "links human liberation and salvation in Jesus Christ" (35), but "reaffirms the primacy of her spiritual vocation and refuses to replace the proclamation of the Kingdom by the proclamation of forms of human liberation" (34). The Church knows that, in order for God's Kingdom to come, it is "not enough to establish liberation and to create well-being and development" (35):

> Evangelical liberation . . . cannot be contained in the simple and restricted dimension of economics, politics, social or cultural life; it must envisage the whole man, in all his aspects, right up to and including his openness to the absolute, even the divine Absolute; it is therefore attached to a certain concept of man, to a view of man which it can never sacrifice to the needs of any strategy, practice or short-term efficiency. (33)

The Pope recognizes the legitimate role of "pre-evangelization"—the use of philosophy and the arts and sciences—as a way of proceeding for those who are not yet ready for an explicit introduction to the gospel of Christ. Nevertheless, even this stage is a form of evangelization—"initial and still incomplete" (51), and a "preparation for the Gospel" (53; citing *LG* 16).

The Pope argues that the Church needs to confront a "phenomenon which is becoming almost its [the contemporary world's] most striking characteristic: secularism," by which he means a movement that sees the world as "self-explanatory, without any need for recourse to God, who thus becomes superfluous and an encumbrance." Hand-in-hand with secularism goes a "man-centered atheism," a "consumer society" mentality, an "inhuman" humanism that seeks to make "the pursuit of pleasure" and "a desire for power and domination" the supreme values (55). In the face of these issues, the Church needs to find "the proper means and language for presenting . . . God's revelation and faith in Jesus Christ" (56). Here Paul VI clearly sets the foundation and tone for the repeated attacks on secularism and consumerism that run through the teachings of John Paul II.

Evangelii Nuntiandi represents one of the more emphatic statements of the Church in opposing the reduction of Christianity to a worldly morality and to secular values, a scourge that has increasingly plagued the Church since the beginning of the Enlightenment. Paul VI clearly saw that, while liberation theology highlights values of crucial importance to the modern Church—namely, the need for action on behalf of the economically poor and politically oppressed—the movement's goals, if they are to remain Christian, must always be set within the deeper and more theologically meaningful understanding of liberation as redemption from sin with a view to union with God in Jesus Christ.

John Paul II

Less than six months after becoming pope, John Paul II delivered the opening address at the Puebla Conference in January 1979. There was great anxiety over how he would address the Latin American bishops, in view of the general recognition of the fact that he was less than kindly disposed to liberation theology. Liberation theologians were relieved when the Pope did not totally reject their movement; nevertheless, his criticisms were serious enough to undercut its strength. Whether he represented the movement adequately in his remarks could be debated, but there was no denying the fact that he had serious misgivings about some of its basic tenets. This address encapsulates the fundamental shortcomings John Paul noted in liberation theology.

The Pope was concerned that the Christian message was being separated from the totality of the truth that includes "the truth about Jesus Christ":

> So we must profess Christ before history and the world. . . . "There is no authentic evangelization so long as one does not announce the name, the teaching, the life, the promises, the kingdom, the mystery of Jesus of Nazareth, the Son of God."[82]

It is the truth about Jesus Christ that "is at the core of evangelization and constitutes its essential content": a truth whose knowledge will strengthen the faithful's "adherence to the church" and their lives as active Christians in the world.[83]

Liberation is, indeed, a genuine goal of the Christian mission, according to the Pope, but it must be understood as "authentic liberation," which includes a sociopolitical dimension, but which must never be reduced to that dimension. John Paul II criticizes the Puebla Conference for separating the Church from the Kingdom of God and giving the Kingdom a "rather secularist sense" by arguing that "we do not arrive at the kingdom through faith and membership in the church but rather merely by structural change and socio-political involvement." The Pope attacks one of the major impressions given by liberation theology by citing the words of John Paul I: "It is a mistake to state that political, economic, and social liberation coincide with salvation in Jesus Christ; that the *regnum Dei* is identified with the *regnum hominis*." Citing *Lumen Gentium*, paragraph 5, John Paul II argues that the bishops forget that it is the Church's mission "to establish among all peoples the kingdom of Christ and of God," and that it is the Church that is "the initial budding forth of that kingdom" on earth.[84]

John Paul II inveighs against " 'rereadings' of the gospel that are the product of theoretical speculations rather than of authentic meditation on the word of God." False rereading of the Scriptures leads to Jesus being depicted "as a political activist, . . . a political figure, a revolutionary, . . . even as someone involved in the class struggle," all of which "does not tally with the church's catechesis." The Pope attacks the "claim that the cause of [Jesus'] death was the result of a political conflict" rather than his "willing self-surrender or even his awareness of his redemptive mission." Though Jesus surely serves "the least of [our] brothers and sisters, the poor, the needy, the marginalized," his mission includes "all those whose lives reflect the suffering countenance of the Lord," and "goes much deeper" to a "complete and integral salvation through a love that brings transformation, peace, pardon, and

---

82 "Pope John Paul II, Selections from 'Opening Address at the Puebla Conference' (January 28, 1979)," 1.2–3, in Hennelly, *Liberation Theology*, 226; the Pope is citing *Evangelii Nuntiandi*, par. 22.

83 John Paul II, "Opening Address," no. 1.2, p. 226.

84 John Paul II, "Opening Address," 230, citing John Paul I from his "Catechetical Lesson on the Theological Virtue of Hope," September 20, 1978. Emphasis in the original.

reconciliation." As a result, any evangelization in Latin America that ceases to affirm "the great gift of God that is salvation" obtained through union with Christ in "the power of his mystery . . . diverges from the church's faith" and "cannot be the valid content of evangelization."[85]

Peter Hebblethwaite perceptively points out that John Paul fundamentally disagrees with the primacy liberation theology gives to praxis. According to Hebblethwaite, one of the main theses of liberation theologians is that the truth God speaks to us "cannot be discovered *outside* the political and social world in which they are embroiled." This makes the starting point of theology the concrete situation of poverty and oppression rather than the revelation of God as proclaimed by Christ, and risks reducing Christianity to an ideology (Marxism). For John Paul II, the primary sources of theology are the traditional ones—Scripture and Tradition—and the "primary mission of pastors is to 'be teachers of the truth, not a human and rational truth, but the truth that comes from God.' "[86]

Congregation for the Doctrine of the Faith

In the face of the increasing popularity of liberation theology in Catholic circles, the Vatican's Sacred Congregation for the Doctrine of the Faith, headed at that time by Cardinal Ratzinger, did a major study of the movement and issued two instructions, the first in the summer of 1984, the second the spring of 1986. The first emphasized many of the theological inadequacies of liberation theology, while the second looked to ways in which the movement could be validly understood as an expression of an important dimension of Catholic teaching.

The first instruction lauded the fact that liberation has become an "almost irresistible aspiration" of people today.[87] The document recognized that this desire is rooted in a "perception of the dignity of the human person" (1.2) as well as of the vocation of the children of God, as called for by the gospel, to "a peaceful and just fraternal life in which everyone will find respect and the conditions for spiritual as well as material development" (1.3). The instruction argues that "the consciousness of the oppressed" has been awakened, and "mankind will no longer passively submit to crushing poverty with its effects of death, disease and decline" (1.4). It recognizes that "the shocking inequality between the rich and the poor," whether between nations or social classes, is a "scandal" that is "no

---

85 John Paul II, "Opening Address," 227–28.

86 Hebblethwaite, "Liberation Theology and the Church," 183; last citation is Hebblethwaite quoting from the introduction of John Paul II's "Opening Address," 225.

87 Congregation for the Doctrine of the Faith (CDF), "Instruction on Certain Aspects of the 'Theology of Liberation,'" *Origins* 14 (September 13, 1984): pp. 193, 195–204, sect. 1, no. 1; hereafter, sections and numbers noted in the text.

longer tolerated" (1.6), and sets out to examine the "meaning of this deep yearning of people for justice" (1.4), as well as the theological movement that this yearning has spawned.

The instruction accepts the expression "theology of liberation" as a "thoroughly valid term" to designate "theological reflection centered on the biblical theme of liberation and freedom" (3.4). It affirms the movement's concern for "the poor and the victims of oppression, which in turn begets a commitment to justice." But it inveighs against the reductionism to which the movement often succumbs in its understanding of the "Christian meaning of poverty and the type of commitment to justice" called for (3.3).

The Congregation traces the meaning of liberation to the Old Testament event of the Exodus, where freedom includes liberation "from foreign domination and from slavery." But the "specific significance" of the Exodus comes from the purpose that motivates the event, namely, God's establishment of a covenant relationship with his people. Since it is God alone who brings liberation through a relationship with him, "the liberation of the exodus cannot be reduced to a liberation which is principally or exclusively political in nature" (4.3). The Old Testament is primarily a call to "an essential religious experience" with God from whom alone one "can expect salvation and healing" (4.5).

The Congregation insists that the theology of liberation, if it is to be correctly understood, must express the biblical "experience of Christian liberty" that finds its "first point of reference" in "Christ, our liberator, [who] has freed us from sin and from slavery to the law and to the flesh." Thus, the "most radical form of slavery is slavery to sin," and freedom "in the full Christian sense" is freedom "in a new life of love," in the "new life of grace," and in the "life of the Spirit" (4.2). This liberation should indeed have effects in the social and political orders, but the sin in question is not simply "social sin," nor is it to be found "principally or uniquely in bad social, political or economic 'structures' " (4.12, 4.14–15). In a major disagreement with liberation theology, the Congregation insists that these are the "consequences more than the causes" of evil. The root of evil must be referred back to "free and responsible persons who have to be converted by the grace of Jesus Christ in order to live and act as new creatures in the love of neighbor" and in the "search for justice" (4.5).

The second instruction continues these same themes, but puts greater stress upon "the main elements of the Christian doctrine on freedom and liberation."[88] The document reaffirms the Old Testament origins of the Christian understanding of liberation, but stresses that the spirituality of

[88] CDF, "Instruction on Christian Freedom and Liberation," *Origins* 15 (April 17, 1986): 713, 715–28, par. 2; hereafter, paragraph numbers noted in the text.

the Old Testament only achieves its "full significance in Christ" (49). The "heart of the Christian experience of freedom is in justification by the grace received through faith and the church's sacraments," which free us from sin and place us "in communion with God" (52). It is through Christ's Cross and Resurrection that he brings about "our redemption, which is liberation in the strongest sense of the word since it has freed us from the most radical evil, namely sin and the power of death" (3).

The experience of freedom, according to the instruction, is radically linked to the experience of truth. The instruction recognizes that it is the truth that " 'will make you free' (Jn 8:32)" and that this truth "comes from God" and "has its center in Jesus Christ, the savior of the world." It is the "truth of the Gospel" of redemption which "is at the heart of the mystery of faith" and the "measure of all liberating action" (3). It follows that a person "becomes free to the extent that he comes to a knowledge of the truth and to the extent that this truth . . . guides his will" (26). Freedom in the true sense of the word is found only in a "knowledge of the truth" and in a relationship of "dependence on God" whereby one enters into a "friendship with God" and shares in his life (26, 28–29).

The Church is concerned about "an integral liberation" (63) in the sense of an "integral salvation of the world" (62). While by this is meant the liberation of the individual "from everything that hinders" the development of the person "in all his dimensions," this liberation speaks first of all to the person "as a member of the city of God and [only] then as a member of the earthly city" (63). In view of the priority of the spiritual, the salvific dimension of liberation "cannot be reduced to the socio-ethical dimension" which is rather a "consequence" of the salvific (71): "The first thing to be done is to appeal to the spiritual and moral capacities of the individual and to the permanent need for *inner conversion*, if one is to achieve the economic and social changes that will truly be at the service of man" (75, emphasis added).

To give priority to the "conversion of heart" in no way denies the need for transformation of oppressive and unjust structures, but rather recognizes that transformation of structures alone will not guarantee a just society. It is "sin which is at the root of unjust situations," and "moral integrity is a necessary condition for the health of society. It is therefore necessary to work simultaneously for the conversion of hearts and for the improvement of structures" (75). The "distinction between the supernatural order of salvation and the temporal order of human life must be seen in the context of God's singular plan to recapitulate all things in Christ."

The purpose of the Church is "to spread the kingdom of Christ so that all men may be saved and that through them the world may be effectively ordered to Christ" (80). This will require the creation of a "civilization of love," that is, the integration of the commandment of love of God and neighbor with the "radical cultural transformation" of the entire social order (81–82).

In the light of this teaching, the instruction calls for "inculturation" not in the sense of "an outward adaptation" to the world, but as "an intimate transformation of authentic cultural values by their integration into Christianity and the planting of Christianity in the different human cultures." The Church's evangelization of culture is "necessary" to give cultures "fresh life by their encounter with the Gospel." The instruction considers it a "tragedy" if the gospel is separated from this transformative process (96).

We have carefully considered here the teaching contained in these two instructions because they stress so emphatically the point of this chapter: that the pursuit of justice is indeed a work of the Church, but only when that work is integrated into the larger mission of the Church of which it is an expression, namely, the proclamation of the gospel, the liberation of all peoples from the destructive power of sin and death in both their spiritual and temporal dimensions, and the orientation of humanity toward a personal friendship with the Lord in Christ, and in the community of universal salvation which is Christ's Body, the Church.

Congregation's Understanding of the Poor

Before we leave the second instruction, it will be helpful to note an important contribution it makes to our discussion above about the Christian meaning of "the poor."

In the Old Testament, according to the instruction, "the prophets vigorously condemn injustice done to the poor." Yahweh is considered "the supreme refuge of the little ones and the oppressed," and any injustice done "to the little ones and the poor is a grave sin." Further, "whatever the forms of poverty, injustice and affliction they endure, the 'just' and the 'poor of Yahweh' offer up their supplications to him in the Psalms": they all are reduced to "servitude" because of "their sins." Finally, "on the threshold of the New Testament, the 'poor of Yahweh' make up the first fruits of a 'people humble and lowly' who live in hope of the liberation of Israel" (46–48).

We may note from the Congregation's discussion here the similarity of the relationships Yahweh has with "the poor," "the little ones," "the oppressed," "the just," and those in "servitude" before the Lord because of "their sins": these expressions are used by the Congregation as parallel or interchangeable terms denoting the same group of people whose common identity is epitomized not as people suffering from economic deprivation, but as the "poor of Yahweh" who stand humbly and lowly before the Lord, living in hope of liberation.

We find in the texts of the Congregation, in its discussion of the poor in the New Testament, that it is liberation that is repeatedly being offered them in a context larger than simply one of economic deprivation. Liberation is proclaimed to "the poor" for whom wealth is not offered, but who have the "good news proclaimed to them" (Mt 11:5). Christ who had been "rich" has made himself "poor" so that he can be recognized "in the poor, in those who suffer or are persecuted" (50). The "liberating mission of the Church" (61) is manifested in a "love of preference for the poor." Christ is the "Messiah of the poor": it was "among the latter, the humble, the 'poor of Yahweh,' who were thirsting for the justice of the kingdom, that he found hearts ready to receive him."

The Congregation clearly indicates that the poverty "that Jesus declared blessed" is "made up of detachment, trust in God, sobriety and a readiness to share" (66). Jesus comes to many different groups who experience "material deprivation, unjust oppression, physical and psychological illnesses, and finally death" (68). The Church carries on the witness of Christ to these groups, whatever their situation "of poverty, scorn, rejection or powerlessness" (68).

To indicate that the meaning of poverty in the biblical sense reaches beyond those who lack the goods of the world, the Congregation states that Jesus "wished to be near to those who, though rich in the goods of this world, were excluded from the community as 'publicans and sinners,' for he had come to call them to conversion" (66). The Church therefore expresses her solidarity with those who "do not count in a society by which they are rejected spiritually and sometimes even physically" (68). The Church is also and especially on the side of "children" who "will never be brought forth from the womb to the light of day, as also for the elderly, alone and abandoned" (68).

The instruction argues that the preferential option for the poor, which liberation theology emphasizes and which has become an acceptable principle in the teaching of the Church, cannot be expressed "by means of reductive sociological and ideological categories which would make this preference a partisan choice and a source of conflict" (68). Such categories would take the preferential option to be a "sign of particularism or sectarianism," whereas in fact the option is intended to manifest "the universality of the church's being and mission," the fact that "this option *excludes no one*" (68; emphasis added).

The point of the preferential option, according to the instruction, is to emphasize that God's love is directed toward the human person as such, and stresses the dignity of the person rooted in the essence of the person as such and not in what the person has (68). The document expresses the "supreme commandment of love of God and neighbor in justice" that flows from the teaching of Christ. It recognizes the foundation for this teaching in the fact that every human being is "created in God's image," and that it is from this image that "flow natural rights and duties," including the right to be free (72–73).

Deus Caritas Est

Pope Benedict XVI's encyclical *Deus Caritas Est*[89] is of immense value for the purposes of this chapter, especially in part 2 of the encyclical, where the Pope emphasizes the social apostolate as an essential element of the nature of the Church, and yet not the direct mission of the Church but only of the laity.

Benedict argues first of all that "love of neighbor, grounded in the love of God," is a "responsibility" for every member of the Church community. That responsibility includes never allowing "a poverty that denies anyone what is needed for a dignified life" (*DCE* 20). But the apostles, who had been entrusted "primarily" with "prayer" and the "ministry of the word," designated others for concrete diaconal work in the service of the community. These persons, "full of Spirit and of wisdom," initiated a "social" and "spiritual" work that gradually became one of the three essential elements in the life of the Church: proclamation of the Word, administration of the Sacraments, and a ministry of "concrete charitable activity" responding to the temporal needs of the community (*DCE* 21–22). The latter is not to be belittled. It has come to be clearly seen as a part of the Church's "nature," an "indispensable expression of her very being" (*DCE* 25a), though it has been "an essential part of her mission from the very beginning" (*DCE* 32).

Nevertheless, "the just ordering of society and the State is a central responsibility of politics." The Church is "the social expression of the Christian faith," and while independent of the state, helps to "form consciences in political life." It seeks "the promotion of justice," and to "stimulate greater insight" into "the demands of the common good."

The Church's role is not, however, to "make this teaching prevail in political life." The Church has only an "indirect duty" toward "the formation of just structures," in that "she is called to contribute to the purification of reason" and the "reawakening" of arguments, on the basis of natural law, to promote its social teaching. But since "building a just social and civil order" is "a political task," it "cannot be the Church's immediate responsibility": "The Church cannot and must not take upon herself the political battle to bring about the most just society possible. She cannot and must not replace the State. . . . A just society must be the achievement of politics, not of the Church." In these efforts, church and state are "distinct, yet always interrelated" (*DCE* 28a, 29).

---

[89] *Deus Caritas Est* ("God Is Love," Encyclical on Christian Love, December 25, 2005), (Washington, DC: USCC, 2006), hereafter paragraph numbers noted in text as *DCE*.

While the Church's duty toward the formation of a just society is indirect, it remains a "direct duty" of "the lay faithful." Since charity must animate their entire lives and they are "citizens of the State," they are to exercise their mission of "social charity," including personal involvement in the area of "public life" with all other citizens, in an effort to "configure social life correctly" (*DCE* 29).

The Church, however, through its "charitable organizations," such as Catholic Charities, does have a "direct responsibility" to practice charity. Acting as "an organized activity of believers," the Church operates in correspondence to her very nature where her action is not primarily one of justice but of "love," where there will always be need (*DCE* 29, 31a).

The Pope is eager to counteract "the growing secularism of many Christians engaged in charitable work" (*DCE* 37), so that "the Church's charitable activity maintains all of its splendor and does not become just another form of social assistance" (*DCE* 31). Christian charity, while it remains a "simple response to immediate needs," must also be understood as a consequence of an "encounter with God in Christ," and of "a faith which becomes active through love" (*DCE* 31a). Since "God is love" (1 Jn 4:8; cf. *DCE* 31), "practical activity will always be insufficient, unless it visibly expresses a love for man, a love nourished by an encounter with Christ" (*DCE* 34).

Michael Novak's Critique of Liberation Theology

Numerous theologians have had major problems with liberation theology. Most notable among these is Michael Novak, formerly a political liberal and now a conservative and the George Frederick Jewett Scholar in religion, philosophy and public policy at the American Enterprise Institute in Washington, DC.

Novak's criticism of liberation theology dates from immediately after John Paul II's 1979 criticism of the movement at Puebla, and in that critique he makes much use of the Pope's own words.[90] Novak understands the earliest formulations of liberation theology as "formal attempts to translate Christianity into Marxist categories."[91] This is the perennial and probably the most serious criticism leveled against liberation theologians, as they attempted to adapt Christianity to the dominant political movement of the age, an effort seen as desirable by the left-wing Christian establishment in spite of the fact that millions of Christians in Eastern Europe and Russia had been and continued to be enslaved and slaughtered by Marxist-Russian ideological systems.

---

[90] Michael Novak, "Liberation Theology and the Pope," in Hennelly, *Liberation Theology*, 272–81; originally published in the June 1979 issue of *Commentary*.

[91] Ibid., 273.

Novak's most serious criticism of liberation theology occurs in his 1986 work *Will It Liberate? Questions about Liberation Theology*.[92] Two of his criticisms presented there concern its inadequate evaluations of political and capitalistic systems: (1) its erroneous evaluation of the worth of two opposing political systems—capitalism, and a socialism combined with revolutionary action; and (2) its exaggeration of the theological significance attached to these two systems.

First, Novak sees in liberation theology a "flawed vision of political economy,"[93] a misguided attempt to attribute the underdevelopment of Latin America to its economic dependency on foreign capitalistic systems, especially the United States, which supposedly dominate and exploit its rich supply of raw materials.[94] Two problems with this theory of dependency is that North America has become a far larger exporter of raw materials than all of Latin America and this has not worked to its economic dependence, and Far Eastern countries with far fewer resources and at one time far greater poverty than Latin America have managed to build booming free economies today.[95] While the goal of raising up the poor from economic destitution is a worthy one on which all would agree, one may legitimately question whether capitalistic exploitation is the problem, or whether Latin America's own "pre-capitalist, disproportionately state-directed," aristocratic, and militaristic societies are what need to be liberated by "a theology of enterprise, of commerce, of economic dynamism—in short, of capitalism."[96]

Second, regarding theological method, Novak's most serious criticism is one widely directed against liberation theology: its identification (or quasi-identification) of the Christian dispensation of salvation with political structures. According to Novak, Latin American liberation theology is "a *Christian* re-interpretation of Marxism and socialism" that often associates capitalism with death and socialism with life.[97] Liberation theology's "single greatest flaw lies in combining two quite different methods of analysis in an effort to overcome 'dualism' . . . [between] religion and politics, church and state, theological principles and partisan practice. Liberation theology says that truth

92 Michael Novak, *Will it Liberate? Questions about Liberation Theology* (New York: Paulist, 1986).

93 Ibid., 30.

94 Ibid., 13; Novak cites Gutiérrez: "There can be authentic development for Latin America only if there is liberation from the domination exercised by . . . the United States of America" (*Theology of Liberation*, 54).

95 Novak, *Will It Liberate?*, 25.

96 Ibid., 22.

97 Ibid., 6. Valpy Fitzgerald explains the reasoning behind this: Life in this context as well as work and land "are both economic *and* spiritual realities." Life is "tangible human life expressed by work, land, house, food, health, education, family, participation, culture, environment, and even *fiesta*. . . . Death is immoral: unemployment,

lies in revolutionary praxis." As a result, economic socialism combined with revolutionary action becomes identified with the Christian message of salvation. Such an equation Catholicism can never accept because the latter stands for the "transcendence of religion beyond politics, the primacy of the spiritual, [which] can be surrendered by no Christianity worthy of the name."[98]

SOCIAL JUSTICE AND LOVE

Perhaps the most serious matter of concern caused by an undue emphasis upon the promotion of social justice is the fact that such an emphasis undermines the primacy that should be given to the role of love in the Christian faith experience.[99]

The basic meaning of justice is to give to each what is due. Justice is to be exercised toward other persons individually as well as toward the community as a whole. But justice is also due to God. We only know what true justice toward another is if we make it an integral part of a just relationship with God. As Bernard Häring tells us, "Justice among men will become a genuinely Christian virtue only if it is an extension of that grateful justice that is owed to God."[100] True justice does not exist outside of a just relationship to God.[101]

We know from revelation that "God is love" (1 Jn 4:8), and that he has freely bestowed the abundance of his blessings on each human person whom he has created in his image. Justice demands, therefore, that the human being respond to God's love by recognizing one's dependence upon God for all that one has, and praising and thanking God for his generosity. But to do this is to love God. Justice is exercised toward God in the fullest sense of the word only if it is integral to a love relationship with God where the justice exercised toward God and love for him become as one. But the

---

hunger, and illiteracy are economic problems but also forms of death and thus a perverse ethical reality." The fact that all should have life leads to a "logic of life" based on the economic and spiritual needs of the poor, as opposed to the "logic of the majority" where "rationality is based on maximising corporate profits and private wealth. . . . In sum, . . . adequate provision of basic needs for all is the crucial criterion for distinguishing between authentic and false spirituality—or rather between a spirituality of life and a spirituality of death." Thus, "economy (i.e. life) and theology" are "inseparable in theory and practice." Valpy Fitzgerald, "The Economics of Liberation Theology," in Rowland, *Liberation Theology*, 222–24.

98 Novak, *Will It Liberate?*, 26.

99 The hermeneutical role of love in the life of the Church and in the service of God's Kingdom will be discussed in our final chapter. Here our discussion is limited to the relationship of love to social justice in the life of the Church.

100 B. Häring, C.S.S.R., "Justice," *NCE*, 8:65.

101 Similarly, regarding the experience of fidelity: John C. Haughey, S.J., *Should Anyone Say Forever? On Making, Keeping, and Breaking Commitments* (Garden City, NY: Doubleday, 1975), 157–58.

fullness of what we need to return to God is best expressed not as justice, but as our love for him, in view of his inherent goodness as well as his abundant mercy toward us. Justice demands that our response be complete, and when it is, it is a response of love. It is the return of our love that completes the cycle that is initiated by God's love for us.

Clearly the promotion of an awareness and of an experience of God's love for the human race, and the union with God that results from the return of God's love, should be primary in the Church's apostolic mission. As John says, "God is love, and he who abides in love abides in God and God in him" (1 Jn 4:16). Since the ultimate goal of life is to be reunited with God, it follows that our return of God's love to him brings us into an intimate union with him now, a union which leads into the fullness of union with him in the life beyond death. It is for this union that we were born and that his plan of history was conceived.[102] Surely such a response is an exercise of justice toward God since it returns to him what is his due, but the fullness of the relationship is known and experienced as a relationship of love. The supreme example of human justice toward God is expressed in Jesus' loving response to God's request that he become Victim for our sins.

It stands to follow, therefore, that the Christian mission understood in its completeness can be no less than to proclaim that God is love, and to make life lived in the experience of that love and response to it the fiber of all human activity. This will surely include the exercise of social justice where that justice is missing. But whereas it would be a misstatement to say that the ultimate goal of the Church's role regarding human beings is to bring them to an experience of just relations with God and with one another, it would not be remiss to say that the fullness of what is intended by justice is only attained in the experience of love of God and one another. Love completes justice and brings it to its fullness.

Häring makes this point clear in his analysis of the roles of justice and love in the human community. If one looks first to "external relations," he says, and sees them as objective, and regards personal relations as merely subjective, justice takes priority in society and becomes the maintaining of "mere external order." If, however, the person and personal relations in the "intimate community of the family" where the order of love resides are "seen as primary," justice is not understood as merely the ordering of external relations, but as the necessary "mediator . . . preserving the capacity of the person for love." Theology corroborates this integration of the role of justice in the

[102] "By her relationship with Christ, the Church is a kind of sacrament or sign of intimate union with God, and of the unity of all mankind. . . . The conditions of this age lend special urgency to the Church's task of bringing all men to full union with Christ . . . . The eternal Father created the whole world. His plan was to dignify men with a participation in His own divine life" (*LG* 1–2).

service of love in God's dealings with humans: "God is love, and every revelation of His justice, all His justifying action, speaks primarily of His love."[103]

Every exercise of justice is at least minimally an expression of love, in the sense that justice intends what is due to another and thereby intends the well-being of another. But an expression of love is not necessarily an exercise of justice, in the sense of what is due to another. Such is the case, for example, when the expression of love exceeds the requirements of justice. This is present above all in God's love for human beings, which is not due them, but is rather an expression of God's bountiful goodness toward them. So, while justice demands right relationships between human beings, love supersedes right relationships by intending a well-being that goes beyond what is due. Once again, we see the fullness of right human relationships expressed in love and not in justice.

Finally, neither love nor justice can live if the other is lacking. There is no true love if it omits a justice that is due[104]—a love without such justice is patronizing—nor will a justice that is not at least tending toward love endure. Justice without love becomes lifeless, mechanical, begrudging, and ultimately oppressively legalistic. Thus, if the Church works to achieve just relationships among human beings, but does not integrate that effort into the larger perspective of promoting human relationships motivated by love, the justice project will not succeed.[105]

According to Novak, social justice is a concept originally coined by an Italian priest in 1840.[106] According to Häring, what social justice adds to the legal rights and duties contained in the more traditional concepts of commutative justice (the rights of persons toward each other), distributive justice (the rights of the person from the community), and general or legal justice (the duty of the community to work for the common good) is a concern for "the natural rights of the community, its members, and the member communities of the family of nations in their relations to one

103 Häring, "Justice," 65.

104 This is what is so distressing about Gutiérrez's suggestion that one could be "poor in spirit" and unconcerned about the social and material needs of others.

105 John Paul II in his 1980 encyclical *Dives in Misericordia* ("Rich in Mercy," Encyclical on the Mercy of God, November 30, 1980) repeatedly affirms the priority of love over justice in God's activity toward the people of Israel in the Old Testament, and in Christ's redemptive activity in the New. Regarding events in the modern world, the Pope states: "The experience of the past and of our own time demonstrates that justice alone is not enough, that it can even lead to the negation and destruction of itself, if that deeper power, which is love, is not allowed to shape human life in its various dimensions" (Washington, DC: USCC, 1981), par. 12. See also *Gaudium et Spes*, where peace is called "an enterprise of justice" (citing Is 32:7), but "likewise the fruit of love, which goes beyond what justice can provide" (par. 78).

106 Michael Novak, "Defining Social Justice," *First Things* 108 (December 2000): 11.

another."[107] J. Y. Calvez, however, argues that Pius XI incorporated social justice into the Church's teaching, and understood it to have "exactly the same meaning as general and legal justice." Calvez quotes from the papal encyclical *Divini Redemptoris*[108] for the clearest Church teaching on the meaning of social justice:

> It is of the very essence of social justice to demand from each individual all that is necessary for the common good. But just as in the living organism it is impossible to provide for the good of the whole unless each single part and each individual member is given what it needs for the exercise of its proper functions, so it is impossible to care for the social organism and the good of society as a unit unless each single part and each individual member . . . is supplied with all that is necessary for the exercise of his social functions.[109]

Though originally intended to refer to the rights of industrial workers, social justice grew in scope with the increasing understanding of the nature of the human person as by definition social, and of God's goods as intended for the well-being not only of the individual but of the total human community. Social justice, then, intends as its goal the realization of the potentialities of the individual person as well as the well-being of the whole human community.

In their discussion of the meaning and role of social justice, scholars note that it refers to the well-ordering of acts or relations between individuals and does not speak to the interior lives of individuals as such. Indeed, Calvez gives as his own definition of social justice the "virtue that ordains all human *acts* toward the common good."[110] Therefore, whereas the virtue of love addresses the quality of the inner life of the person who loves, justice speaks to how that spirit of love is mediated when put into action.

All the more reason, then, why it is important to distinguish the role of social justice from that of love, and to emphasize the priority of the latter over the former. It seems clear that in the Christian dispensation, primacy must be given to the role of love over social justice. But the maintaining of that primacy is often what is at stake in some circles in the contemporary Church, especially in liberation theology when it emphasizes the need to promote social justice.

No doubt liberation theologians in Latin America were well-intentioned as they sought to provide a theological foundation for garnering the support

[107] Häring, "Justice," 67.

[108] *Divini Redemptoris* (Encyclical on Atheistic Communism, March 19, 1937).

[109] J. Y. Calvez and T. Massaro, "Social Justice," *NCE*, 13:243 (ellipsis in original). Calvez is citing from *Acta Apostolicae Sedis* 29 (1937): 92.

[110] Calvez, "Social Justice," 24, emphasis added.

of the Church hierarchy and the wider Christian community, in an effort to dig the majority of Latin Americans out from under the reign of poverty and oppression that had so long afflicted them. But whether it was ever advisable to stress the importance of social justice to such an extent as to risk secularizing the gospel with social justice exegesis, especially of Jesus' teachings, and thereby demoting the primacy of love and a faith relationship with God, is another matter. The effect was to rework the deeper theological and spiritual dimensions of the Scriptural teachings toward the fulfillment of a political agenda. As valuable as that agenda may be, it is not worth distorting the Scriptural teaching to justify it, when a more nuanced understanding of the Scriptures preserves their spiritual dimension and provides a proper foundation for social justice as well.

It is clear that the Vatican has not been pleased with the liberation theology movement for its politicization of Christianity. Yet even from a political standpoint, one might question how successful the movement has been in rectifying the social order in Latin American countries: little in its efforts to overcome poverty seems to have been accomplished by its teachings, when much more might have been achieved, without political confrontations, acrimonious relationships, and sacrifice of human life, by promoting a theology that placed the emphasis upon the implementation of the more comprehensive Christian principles of love, equality of all humans in the sight of God, and service of others as a response to God's love.

There is also an increasing presence of Protestant evangelical churches in Latin America, where Catholicism once reigned supreme.[111] Indeed, there is an increasing protestantizing of Latin American Catholics in the United States.[112] Perhaps there is good reason for this: while the evangelical movement is not unconcerned about the social conditions of third-world peoples, it has never let that concern replace the primacy of the proclamation of salvation in a faith relationship with Jesus Christ. The clarity of that message seems to appeal to a deeper level of human need. Perhaps the evangelical movement is telling the Catholic Church that it

---

[111] "By any standard, the realignment of Christianity in Latin America during the twentieth century was breathtaking. Conversion of Catholics to Protestantism actually surpassed, in numerical terms, the results of the Protestant Reformation in Europe in the 16th century. Evangelicals soared from 50,000 to 64 million, and nearly 40 percent of the world's Pentecostals now live in Latin America"; John L. Allen, Jr., "Evangelical Strength in Latin America Is Homegrown," *NCR*, August 25, 2006, ncronline.org.

[112] "Fabiola Briones . . . Mexican-American Catholic . . . is one of thousands of Latino immigrants who [has] left behind the ritual and perceived formality of the Roman Catholic Church for the personal experiences and boisterous services of Pentecostalism"; Sonya Geis, "Latino Catholics Increasingly Drawn to Pentecostalism," *Washington Post*, April 30, 2006.

needs to restore to a position of primacy the evangelizing of the good news of redemption in Christ. This is not to say that liberation theology has no place in Christ's teaching; indeed it does. But Jesus' primary message was not sociopolitical or economic. It was a message of salvation through faith and justification leading to union with Christ in the Kingdom of his Father. Everything else was a value only in the light of that goal.

Justice and Justification

Social justice is sometimes confused with the biblical understanding of justice as God's justice in the world or in the Kingdom of God. There is a considerable difference between social justice and the justice of God.

In the Old Testament, the justice of God occurs within his covenant relationship with his people Israel, and connotes all the saving elements contained in that relationship. The term "justice" is often used in parallelism with God's saving activity (Is 45:21) because it expresses God's fidelity to his people when in his mercy he delivers them from foreign oppressors or enslavement brought on by their sinful ways. If there is one word that stands at the core of what is intended in the justice God extends to his people, it is *salvation* from whatever seeks to destroy them. This saving covenant relationship provides the foundation for the enduring life of the Israelites. It gives them stability and hope in the midst of conflict. They can always count on God's saving relationship with his people.

Justice was also appropriate to the response the Israelites made to God's saving justice. It expressed their fidelity to the covenant to which they had committed themselves at Mt. Sinai. This they did by fulfilling within the Israelite community all the terms of the covenant as expressed in the Ten Commandments and the ensuing developments of the law. Living in just relationships with fellow Israelites is one of the ways in which the just person fulfills the terms of his commitment to covenant fidelity toward God. Especially in Isaiah and Jeremiah, one looks forward to the coming of the Messiah who "would live in justice with God and procure justice for others by judging them according to the covenant."[113]

In the New Testament, especially in Paul's Letter to the Romans, justice continues to be shown in God's saving deliverance of his people as an expression of his covenant fidelity. The major difference is that the promise of salvation in the Old Testament has now been fulfilled by the eternal covenant ratified with God by Christ in his redemptive life, death, and Resurrection. The human being, in spite of being a sinner, becomes purified of sin and is made justified or righteous, that is, shares in the life of God himself. The

---

[113] D. M. Crossan, "Justice of Men: In the Bible," *NCE*, 8:73; and D. M. Crossan and T. G. Weinandy, "Justice of God: In the Bible," *NCE*, 8:70–71.

objective state of righteousness established by God through Christ is made available to every human being by accepting God's saving gift in faith. Indeed, Jesus was "handed over [to death] for our transgressions and was raised for our justification. Therefore, since we have been justified by faith, we have peace with God through our Lord Jesus Christ, through whom we have gained access by faith to this grace in which we stand" (Rom 4:25–5:1).

One of the most significant passages explaining justification through faith in Christ is found in Romans 3:21–26, and the NAB annotation regarding Romans 3:21–31 summarizes well Paul's theology of justification: "These verses provide a clear statement of Paul's 'gospel,' i.e., the principle of justification by faith in Christ. . . . Divine mercy declares the guilty innocent and makes them so. God does this . . . through forgiveness of their sins, in virtue of the redemption wrought in Christ Jesus for all who believe. God has manifested his righteousness in the coming of Jesus Christ, whose saving activity inaugurates a new era in human history" (NT 235).

Thus we see that in the New Testament, God's saving fidelity to his covenant, which was primarily experienced in the Old Testament as freedom from material want and sociopolitical evils, has been largely spiritualized in Paul to mean liberation from sin and participation in God's own life in faith.

Derivative Meanings of God's Justice

God's justice has its first derivative meaning in the New Testament when it refers to the work of justice among human beings. This is expressed primarily by members of God's community in their attempts to transform human relationships of whatever kind into more adequate experiences of the life appropriate to membership in God's Kingdom. God's justice then becomes a transformative saving power working within history, exercised through the activity of God's justified people.

Especially valuable in this context is Romans 12:1–13:14, where the NAB states that Paul "explains how Christians can function, in the light of the gift of justification through faith, in their relation to one another and the state. . . . Christians are liberated for the exercise of good judgment as they are confronted with the many and varied decisions required in the course of daily life." To assist them in this, they are provided with many charisms, such as the gifts of "prophecy, teaching, and exhortation" (NT 246).

The works of justice in this sense may be equated with efforts at evangelization or the proclamation of Christ and his gospel to all peoples of all times, in fulfillment of Jesus' command to his disciples (Mt 28:18–20), calling them to be reconciled to God through a sharing in Christ's death and Resurrection so that they might share in the new life of grace. This process of evangelization corresponds to what is now sometimes called inculturation, which, when properly understood, has two facets: (1) the formulation of who Christ is and what the teaching of his gospel is in a way that makes use of the symbols that a culture uses in expressing its thinking, feelings, values, and actions; and, conversely, (2) the adaptation and even enlargement and restructuring of the community's symbols so that they are made capable of representing adequately who Christ is and the Good News he proclaimed. It is only when inculturation has achieved an adequation between Christ, his gospel, and the mind-set of a given culture that evangelization is made possible.

We come finally to the second derivative meaning of justice as the work of social justice, which, unlike "prophecy, teaching, and exhortation," is a concrete application to one specific area within the wider process of justification carried on by all Christians in their daily lives in their various interactions with others.[114] According to S. C. Mott, the biblical understanding of God's justice is incomplete unless the social dimension is included. Mott argues that God's saving relationship to his people in the Old Testament includes social justice, and in the New, Jesus' proclamation includes a challenge to correct the various social situations of inequality when they exist.[115]

If that is the case, the implementing of just relationships among God's people was a significant element in the teaching of the Old Testament as well as of the New, in that the covenant relationship with God was inadequately realized without it. Nevertheless, it must be recognized that this effort to form just human relationships is a specification, and only one specification, of the wider work of justice in the sense of evangelization, carried on by the whole Christian community in its efforts to bring the power of God's saving activity into every dimension of human life. And, as important as that wider work of justice is, it should never overshadow the primacy to be given to God's direct justifying action in history, that is, the salvation of the human race wrought by God's Son, Jesus Christ, through his life, death, and Resurrection. Losing sight of that primacy is what the Christian community is in danger of doing when it does not clearly make its social justice efforts a consequence of faith in Jesus and the saving paschal mystery.

Indeed, it may be questioned even on a pragmatic level whether promoting social justice is the best way of achieving the goals so desperately sought by many social activists, if, as Häring and Calvez seem to indicate above, the object of social justice is "acts" in "concrete social relations" that "mediate" more equitable conditions within the human community. The

---

[114] Other such concrete applications might be promoting goodwill among neighbors, teaching professional skills, creating self-help programs, or fostering community development.

[115] S. C. Mott, "The Use of the New Testament for Social Ethics," *Journal of Religious Ethics* 15 (Fall 1987): 225–60.

problem is that such acts do not in themselves achieve the necessary transformation of the inner life of human beings—their thoughts and feelings, the values that motivate them, the goals for which they live, the principles that give meaning and direction to their lives—or, in other words, as we saw, social justice acts do not by themselves create love.

Reaching this level of transformation, which is necessary if we are to have a just society, requires something more than acts of social justice. Such acts will never achieve their purpose if they are not integrated into a more fundamental outlook on life that produces them. Without a more holistic system of values in which they are grounded, such acts are inevitably reduced at best to subset values, appended to life to satisfy the demands of "political correctness," or actions that assuage guilt feelings for past insensitivities, or, at worst, necessary responses to legalistic injunctions.

What is really lacking in modern society is not so much a culture that adequately implements social justice principles as one that lives by the life of God's Spirit. It is the Spirit that introduces into the world the values destined to be inherited in the life of God's Kingdom. Our present culture is so overwhelmed by the secular mentality and the values connatural to it, where achievement is based on success attained through self-aggrandizement and measured by the amount of money and power acquired, by whatever methods are necessary to do so. Such an ethic is limited only by its ability to succeed. Such a standard is in opposition to the standard of success proclaimed by Jesus in the Beatitudes, where the norm is to be "poor in spirit" by loving God and living a life of dependence on him, exercising love and mercy toward others, and living for the ever-increasing realization of God's Kingdom in history. Christianity often fails to make clear that these two standards of success frequently stand in opposition to each other, producing clashing mind-sets in daily living, and are ultimately incompatible as primary motivating standards. Focusing primarily on efforts to enact social justice will not in itself produce the life of virtuous justice consonant with the "poverty of spirit" required for membership in God's Kingdom.

Inculturation of Evangelization

The promotion of the inculturation of evangelization seems by far the better way for Christians to go, where the values of the world are confronted head-on by the values of the gospel and the former's primacy overthrown. Christianity really has no other choice if it is not to sell out to modernity. But to enter into the challenge of this confrontation is to enter into the ongoing historical process of transformation that the gospel creates, moving from the culture of relativism and secularism that the Enlightenment has bequeathed to the Western world to the culture of the Beatitudes that leads to the life of the Kingdom.

But in addition to surpassing social activism by a call to a deeper level of spiritual activity, the challenge to enact a transformation of culture consonant with the Christian vision supersedes efforts to implement social justice in another way, in that the challenge is directed not only toward those who would hear the call and put it into effect, but also toward those who initiate it. Merely to proclaim the call to social justice and see that it is enacted nicely avoids the self-examination that recognizes the need to transform our inner lives, where materialism, pragmatism, comfort, self-esteem, and other secular values often remain at their highest priorities even when the social justice agenda is in action.

Our Catholic education, for all the good that it does, is quite capable of reducing what it means to be Catholic to being motivated to implement social action programs. We are then able to relegate efforts for justice to the Office of Campus Ministry, to "service-learning" courses in the theology department, or to a few days of vacation ministries to far-off places to offer token gestures of help to people in serious economic need. All of this fills our need to feel we really care about others, even while we continue to foster a culture of acquisitiveness, seeking all that is possible through the implementation of secular humanistic standards.

Fostering such a social justice agenda alone falls well short of what is really needed from our students, which is a response to the call to discipleship of Christ that involves the total transformation of the inner life of students that makes it possible for them to accept and live in response to that call. Responding to such social justice programs can lead to the impression that Christ's call is being answered, when in fact such efforts provide only a veneer that leaves untouched the heart of core curricular and major departmental programs that train in the art of succeeding in life by following the standards of the world. Social action thus becomes one agenda to be ranged alongside others promoted in education, such as development in professional skills, or the art of mastering a capitalistic system that has as its goal the acquisition of unlimited quantities of money, fame, and power. Few are troubled by the fact that fostering such an extremist spirit of capitalism, decried so often by John Paul II in his frequently unread encyclicals, is incompatible with life in the true service of justice.

The social justice movement normally has the weakness of being comfortably integrated into a larger framework of self-identity, even when it is most effective. The promotion of justice is put on par with other advocacy movements or charitable causes that are not life-altering, and so fundamental mind-sets are largely unaffected by them. We contribute a suitable amount of time to programs of service to others, but when the time is up, we return to the secular aims and pursuits that characterize the fundamental orientation of our lives. The deeper mind-sets of our students are not likely to be altered much by participation in special advocacy programs, because a set of worldly values has been so deeply ingrained in them that such programs do not jar their commitment to such values. Against such a backdrop, advocacy causes are reduced to "feel-good" distractions that fulfill the contribution to humanity that political correctness and a secularized Christianity deem necessary for those who would want to be considered model citizens or good Christians, but they do not call for a thorough renunciation of living by the standards of the world that Christ proposed in his Sermon on the Mount.

That many students who consider themselves good Catholics and Christians have happily bought into the world of unlimited success by capitalistic standards, we know from the heroes they hold up, most of whom epitomize this system at its worst (Donald Trump, Kobe Bryant, Madonna, to name a few). We assuage our consciences that recognize the disparity between what the Catholic faith stands for and the standards of the world by teaching our students to esteem social justice relationships in theory, and occasionally in practice, and hoping that something greater might eventually follow. Generally it doesn't. To recognize this disparity and seek to overcome it apparently represents a challenge too demanding of us—a transformation of our own self-image and of our own identification with "the American way of life." But it is the need for that transformation that the events of recent memory show.

Life since 9/11

In the light of the major life-threatening events of recent years, such as 9/11, the destruction of hundreds of innocent lives every year in late-term abortions, and the gravity of the priest sex-abuse scandal, perhaps the most serious question to be asked of advocates of social justice is whether their agenda represents the most effective way of meeting the crucial challenges of our time.

The roots of the horrendous actions of the Middle East terrorists on 9/11 may be found on many different levels—economic, social, cultural, and religious. Surely an Enlightened awareness of the failure of the United States to promote equitable forms of justice among its own people and certain other nations may be a factor to be reckoned with in drawing up a response to the issues that prompted that day. But whether one is Palestinian or Israeli, European or American, Democrat or Republican, man or woman, the issues to be addressed today cannot be formulated in terms of whether or not to promote social justice, since surely no one in the world today is in favor of being unjust. Such a formula is completely inadequate for today's needs.

The most pressing question today is how to discern the fundamental values that will motivate all human beings to want to promote the well-being of all, and to find the practical means that will lead to the satisfaction of all human yearnings for truth, justice, and love.[116] This is a major challenge to all human societies that will not be easily satisfied. Faith does not endow Christians with the ability to discern what such means might be, nor does shallow Enlightenment thinking provide any guidance. Adequate answers continue to elude the best of political scientists, whatever their faith. But faith does provide a motive for seeking the best of methods and choosing honestly the most prudent and equitable moral action.

The issues on the table since the attacks of 9/11 are fundamental. The very survival of humanity is at stake. It would be naïve for Christians to think they have made a contribution to the problems created by 9/11 merely by seeking to promote social justice. The stakes are far too high, the dimensions of the problem too great, for talk on that level to be adequate. The world has a right to expect more from people of faith.

America's scandalous practice of partial-birth abortions, permitted for so long a time, subjected a child to brutal dissection and destruction at any stage of its life short of actual birth. This shows that the attack on the right to life created by legalizing abortion was not really based on a genuine and sincere lack of clarity over when a human being actually came into existence, but upon a concerted effort to allow free and unlimited sex to be entered into without any ensuing responsibilities. As a result, choice without responsibility is now becoming the dominant morality spreading across all moral issues in our society. No culture that gives greater value to mere whim than to the intrinsic value of life can expect to survive in any civilized way for any length of time. And so, again, the very survival of humanity is at stake.

The sex scandal among the clergy, which we will discuss in chapter 9 (see pp. 441–71), that became so widespread that it drew national attention beginning in January 2002, is another form of attack on the intrinsic value of life, and calls for a major rethinking among all Christians of what it means to be a disciple of Christ. If those who have been singled out by the Church to be model "artisans of a new humanity" (*GS* 30) have instead become instruments of dehumanization, more is demanded to correct the situation than a call for social justice.

To respond to the demands of our day, Christians are being called to a thorough reformation of their lives—abandoning self-interest and recentering their mind-sets on the Christ who renounced himself on the Cross for the salvation of the world. Christians must become persons who are themselves transformed and at work revamping the human psyche so that it is

[116] We read in *Gaudium et Spes*: "This social order requires constant improvement. It must be founded on truth, built on justice, and animated by love" (par. 26). An intercession in the Liturgy of the Hours for the Morning Prayer of Friday of the Fourth Week reads: "O God of mercy, guide us toward spiritual growth; fill our minds with thoughts of truth, justice and love."

motivated no longer primarily by secular and material values. The goal is a transformation of culture so that the person of Christ and the pattern of his life will willingly be accepted as the ideal of what it means to be human.

What other efforts could Christians be expected to make? The mission for Catholics today is to go all the way or not go at all. What we need is not simply a social justice agenda, however valuable that might be, but a new vision of humanity where God's Spirit, rather than being optional or marginal to life, is recognized as the power driving generous and beneficial human action toward global well-being. Our goal cannot merely be social justice, but must ultimately be the justice of God's Kingdom that destroys demonic forces in the world, restores community between the human race and God, and ennobles human dignity by seeing human life as a sharing in God's own life. Our goal cannot simply be to be just, but must be to spread the fire that Jesus came to earth to ignite (Lk 12:49), brightening people's minds with a radically new vision, and warming their hearts with a selfless desire to make the world whole by whatever means that takes.

Christ's call to true Christian living is not simply carried on by those who respond to the needs of the economically poor, but by the "poor in Spirit" who recognize that primacy must be given to love of God and others, and that greatness in life is achieved in self-donating love rather than in self-aggrandizement. Without the acceptance of this Spirit as the foundation of Christian living, efforts at social justice lose a Christian base, are made marginal to our true identities, and range among the many acceptable and optional ways of being respectable in a secular world of comfortable mediocrity. As such, these efforts will never produce true Christians nor significantly alter our world in ways so desperately needed for our times.

Conclusion

On balance, much good and much not-so-good has come from liberation theology.

It has done much to redress the undue emphasis upon the other-worldly dimension of Christianity. As one supporter of the movement argues: "There is the disturbing fact that even if liberation theologians have made some mistakes, they have put their finger on something fundamental to the theological task: speaking of God in a world that is inhumane."[117] For too long Christians had ignored the plight of the poor and the downtrodden. Insufficient attention for too long had been given to the inequality and injustice widespread among the masses of humanity. God's concern for the well-being of the marginalized of society is present from the very beginning of his relationship with his covenant people. Unjust *laissez-faire* capitalistic ideology too

[117] Rowland, "Introduction," *Liberation Theology*, 12.

long associated with Christianity has led many Christians to ignore the unjust social relationships within society to which the Christian faith must address itself. Liberation theology has made a major impact upon our understanding that the Christian faith can never be properly lived undisturbed by the existence of unjust relationships. American Christianity has a serious problem in that it allows the wealthy to consider themselves worthy Christians as they insulate their lives by unbelievable luxury, leaving millions in our nation and throughout the world suffering excessive indigence.

But liberation theology has taken Christianity from one extreme to the other. By unduly equating the Christian faith with service of the economically poor and politically oppressed, it has served to undercut the meaning and importance of the specifically spiritual, theological, and liturgical dimensions of the faith, depriving Christians and the Church of growing in an understanding of the fact that Christ came to bring all humanity to a personal faith relationship with the Father through a union with Christ in the sacramental life of the Church.

But proof of the inadequacy of liberation theology for our times is in the pragmatic:

1. Had liberation theology led to evidence of greater equality in society, one might be more lenient in criticism. But the facts tell us otherwise. Even with the introduction of free-trade policies including the eradication of economic barriers in Latin America,

   > the number of absolute poor, the truly destitute, was estimated by the World Bank at 1.3 billion in 1993, and is probably still growing. One fifth of the world lives in countries, mainly in Africa and Latin America, where living standards actually fell during the 1980s. Several indicators of aggregate poverty—1.5 billion lack access to safe water and 2 billion lack safe sanitation; more than 1 billion are illiterate, including half of the rural women—are no less chilling than a quarter-century ago.[118]

   Moreover, in the 1970s and '80s, democratic structures incorporating equality of human rights were finally introduced in many Latin American countries, so that the problems created by unjust political policies could no longer be blamed upon foreign domination and unrepresentative government. And yet the political situation seems not to have improved. A recent report, entitled "Latin America: All Coherence Gone," reads in part:

---

[118] Commission on Global Governance, *Our Global Neighbourhood* (Oxford: Oxford University Press, 1995), 139; cited by Fitzgerald in Rowland, *Liberation Theology*, 232.

> Democracy in Latin America has crumbled; institutions supporting democracy have very little credibility. The conclusions of the Truth Commission lie forgotten in Peru; 70,000 have died in the decades between 1980–2000, most of them Quecha-speaking indigenous people. In Ecuador, with the withdrawal of indigenous support, the government has tilted increasingly to the right. Bolivia fears that popular participation in the referendum called by Carlos Mesa will be low. The peace process in Colombia seems to be threatened by a new insistence on "national security" that aims at protecting investments rather than people. Argentina has found no alternative political development to Peronism, a political system based on clientelism and patronage. Paraguay allows crimes to flourish with impunity; Mexico is disillusioned with the changes introduced by President Fox; the Dominican Republic, troubled by financial fraud, has elected a neoliberal government to power; and Brazil's Lula is afraid of confronting the IMF [International Monetary Fund]. Chile alone seems to benefit from an able President, but increasing prosperity has led to increased secularization. In the face of such collapse, it was humbly acknowledged at the meeting that collaborating to strengthen democratic and transparent political institutions is imperative.[119]

Of the eighteen Latin American countries having democratic regimes considered in a recent groundbreaking report, "Democracy in Latin America: Towards a Citizens' Democracy," produced by the United Nations Development Program, only three were democracies in the '70s.[120] Yet the study reports that "in 2002 43.4 per cent of Latin Americans live under the line of poverty," and that "Latin America continues to be the region in the world with the highest levels of inequality." The study shows that social parity and civil rights continue to be violated by "powerful business interests" and "state agents acting independently of elected officials." Nearly half the citizens (44.9%) are already so disillusioned with democracy they would prefer "an authoritarian government" if it would resolve their economic problems.[121]

An excellent and thorough report supporting the findings of the United Nations Development Program on the inadequacy of the Latin

---

[119] Report of Fr. Jorge Julio Mejia, S.J., Assistancy Coordinator of the Social Apostolate for Latin America, at the annual meeting of Jesuit Coordinators of the Social Apostolate, held July 6–10, 2004, in Peru, in *SJS—Jesuits and Partners together for Justice*, "Headline articles: Latin America: All Coherence Gone,"www.sjweb.info/sjs/headlines/news Show.cfm?PubTextID=2731.

[120] United Nations Development Program, "Report on Democracy in Latin America: Overview," released April 21, 2004, 1, www.undp.org.

[121] United Nations Development Program, "The Report on the Development of Democracy in Latin America, Brief to the Secretary General of the United Nations, February 2004," April 21, 2004, III, 5–6, www.undp.org.

American experience of democracy is detailed in a ten-part *National Catholic Reporter* series, "Latin America: Search for a Future." According to the introduction, there is widespread corruption, and "whatever statistics you cite, they all reflect increasing inequality. In land ownership, in access to credit, in income distribution, it's the region of the world with the most pronounced inequality. The gap is wide and getting wider."[122] Thus, there is little or no evidence that liberation theology has made any contribution toward making social equality any more present in Latin America today than was underway through progressive political and diplomatic programs already in operation.

2. Had liberation theology led to a renewed vitality in the faith and sacramental life of the Church, once again one might be more lenient in criticism. Surely so, since a movement that fostered growth in the Church's interior life could never be an aberration. But there is no evidence that life in the Church has improved in the last forty years through the insights or actions of liberation theology. On the contrary: life in the Church has increasingly been reduced to social activism, and fewer and fewer young people seem to find a home in the Church. Indeed, this is one of the reasons why this book is being written, to challenge movements such as liberation theology whose ideologies foment the gradual conversion of the Christian life into various forms of social activism.

For all the good that liberation theology may have accomplished, it is difficult not to think that greater progress in the social mission of the Church could have been achieved in much easier and less traumatic ways, through greater fidelity to the total perspective of Vatican II, and the constant teachings of the popes in their encyclicals thereafter.

The social justice agenda, as it is promoted by many Christians today, often represents a distraction away from the lofty challenges of the Christian faith experience and toward a Christianity of accommodation to quick-fix movements that sell human nature short. The agenda takes as a given that society is intractably secular, and that Christians have bought into that secularity and cannot be changed. As a result, a spiritual transformation consonant with the Christian mind-set of the Beatitudes is considered impossible. Only reform on a secondary level of social action is considered feasible, where Christians can be motivated by a popular Enlightenment mentality that "all you need is love" (John Lennon).

But if the crass secular values that pervade our culture have provided any indication of where our society is headed, reform of the

[122] Barbara Fraser and Paul Jeffrey, "Latin America: Search for a Future, Part 1: Introduction; Power or Credibility?," *NCR*, May 14, 2004, ncronline.org, 1–2.

social order by a social justice movement that is derivative of the values of that very culture will achieve at best only minimal results. We have already witnessed how minimal those results are. By all objective accounts, the social justice agenda can only be rated a failure in its service of the Church and in enhancing the spiritual life of its "poor."

CHAPTER EIGHT

Does the Bill of Rights Call for Separation of Church and State?

THERE IS ONE THING on which almost all Americans agree: that church and state should be separated, and that the First Amendment to the U.S. Constitution mandates it. While the former may be true, the latter is certainly not.

When asked what separation of church and state means, Americans generally say that church and state should constitute separate realms of life and activity, and neither should exert any influence upon the other. This uninformed and unexamined understanding of the First Amendment allows left-wing extremists to capitalize on it, and to gain popular support for removing the exercise of religion from public fora.

Many supporters of this unnuanced idea of separation of church and state come from innocent Catholics who have little understanding of the ideas that motivated the Founding Fathers, or of what the consequences of total separation would be. The fact is that it would give Enlightenment extremists full discretionary power to remove God or religious convictions from any influence upon public policy. The question is, is there anything wrong with that? Does it really make any difference whether God has any role in the operations of society?

The removal of God, however, is only one part of what secularists are trying to accomplish today. Perhaps even more significant is the reason why they are trying to remove God from society: in doing so, they would remove the Absolute as the basis for all objective standards of morality from the public forum. The currents of Western society are in general moving in secularist directions, and the issues that have confronted America since the fall of 2003 made that trend especially clear.

Recent Political Currents

Perhaps no one event brought out the general erosion of traditional standards of morality more clearly than the 4–3 decision of the Massachusetts Supreme Judicial Court on November 18, 2003, legislating that gays and lesbians have a legal right to marry in Massachusetts under that state's constitution, and giving the state legislature six months to rewrite state marriage laws to accommodate state same-sex couples. The state judiciary decreed, against the wishes of the majority of the people of Massachusetts, that restricting marriage to monogamous relationships between a man and a woman was not constitutionally approved. In recent years, judiciaries have grown accustomed to legislating against the will of the people with little reaction from most Americans, who largely accept the will of judiciaries as if they were infused with divine truth and power, but this time, perhaps because the decision represented such a fundamental undermining of the fabric of family and social life, the decision shocked many Americans into taking action.

The November 2004 national elections followed, and provided a critical juncture: Senator John F. Kerry, the Democratic contender for President of the United States, was supported by many left-wing factions representing the erosion of traditional values. Though a Catholic, he advocated (though with the usual sadness) abortion on demand, had voted against federal legislation banning partial-birth abortion, and was supportive of civil unions of same-sex couples. Though he advocated rejecting same-sex marriages, many doubted his sincerity. He had appeared on stage with left-wing Hollywood celebrities whose views he cited as representative of the values of the nation, even though they had openly mocked traditional values. Kerry and his coterie seemed to stand for all that would happen to traditional values if he were elected President.

The critical nature of the situation was apparent—especially to right-wing evangelical Christians, but also to all those who realized how adrift the nation was becoming. The left-wing sought to unite the 18- to 29-year-old voters, especially those who had never voted before, and Hispanic and African-American voters, who traditionally vote Democratic. Never before did so many people become so galvanized about coming out to vote for the candidate who represented their deeply felt values. The current of the pre-election period seemed in the end to be moving in Kerry's direction.

Then a semi-amazing phenomenon occurred: George W. Bush, the conservative Texan whom the liberals disdained and who stood for traditional values, was reelected President for another four years, in spite of the turbulent Iraqi situation at the time and the general economic unease, both of which should have ruined his chances. The exit polls, however, showed that a whopping 22% of the electorate asserted that "moral values" was the primary factor motivating their choice for President, and 80% of these had voted for Bush.[1] Bush won the election by over three million votes, and garnered the majority in practically all of the states, the major exceptions being the coastal states in the upper Northeast and the far West. Later analysis of the referendum indicated two things: that it was the largely elitist and wealthy nonchurchgoing members of the population who had supported Kerry, and that these were considered to be directing society toward embracing secularist values against the will of the general populace.

The Democratic Party, recognizing that their success resided mainly with secularist voters but that this was not enough to win, tried in 2006 to appeal more strongly to religiously inclined voters, and that effort may have paid off. The 2006 congressional contests, which Democrats generally won in close races, added new wrinkles to the political map.

According to the Pew Research Center, Americans who worship weekly or more continued to support the Republican Party, but not by as comfortable a margin: 59% to 40% in 2004, 55% to 43% in 2006. Among white Catholics (considered an important swing vote) who attend church weekly or more, a majority of 58% to 41% favored Republicans in 2004, but a less comfortable majority still existed in 2006: 52% to 47%.

Among those who are less religiously affiliated, the Democratic vote increased in 2006: among all Americans who worship a few times a month or a few times in a year, 45% were Republican to 54% Democratic in 2004, but 39% Republican to 59% Democratic in 2006. Among Catholics who attend church less than weekly: 50% Republican to 49% Democratic in 2004, but a Democratic majority in 2006 (53% to 46%). Among all Catholics, while the majority went to the Republicans in 2004 (50% to 49%), the majority went to the Democrats in 2006 (55% to 44%.) But Americans across the board who never go to church even more strongly supported the Democrats in 2006: 60% in 2004, but 67% in 2006. Thus, while the Democratic Party increased its numbers among churchgoing Americans, it still did not get a majority among them, although it did increase its numbers significantly among what might be called secularist or secularist-leaning Americans.[2]

Did those who stand for traditional values swing to the Democrats? Some probably did. The fact is that while the Republican Party had such strong support in 2004 from this group, many of these seem to have become disillusioned with that party in 2006. Among white evangelical Protestants, the majority of whom surely stand for traditional values, some shifting may have occurred: whereas there was a 49% spread between the

[1] According to the Edison-Mitofsky exit poll as of November 10, 2004, www.cnn.com.

[2] Pew Research Center, "Election '06: Big Changes in Some Key Groups," November 16, 2006, pewresearch.org.

Republican and the Democratic vote in 2004, there was only a 42% spread in 2006, when 70% voted Republican and 28% voted Democratic.[3]

Nevertheless, the Washington Post reported that it was not over social issues that evangelicals swung to the Democrats, but for "corruption and big spending" among Republicans.[4] Also, according to exit polls, when voters were asked which issues were "extremely important" to their vote, the largest percentage—42%—said "corruption and ethics."[5] But according to James Dobson, founder of Focus on the Family, "many of the values voters of '04 stayed at home" in 2006.[6]

In 2008, the division between the religiously observant and the secularists seemed to intensify. The Democratic Party with its left-wing agenda found strong support among less-observant religious groups, but not among observant groups. Though the Party made a strong attempt to court religious voters, traditionalists remained faithful in general to the Republican Party, though usually less so than in 2006—41% of observant white Catholics (who attended services at least once a week) voted for Obama, while 39% had voted for Kerry; observant white evangelical Protestants voted 20% for Obama, while 17% had voted for Kerry; but 38% of observant white Protestants voted for Obama compared to 42% for Kerry. Less-observant white Catholics, however, significantly increased their support for Obama over Kerry (52% to 47%), and less-observant white evangelical Protestants did the same (36% for Obama, 28% for Kerry), while less-observant white Mainline Protestants remained the same at 47%.[7]

In 2010, a mid-term election year, a strong surge toward the Republican Party occurred among all demographics, and, among those who attended religious services at least weekly, "nearly six-in-ten . . . voted for the Republican House candidate in their district (58%), compared with 44% Republican support among those who attend religious services less often."[8] Among Catholics overall, "Fifty-four percent . . . cast the ballot for Republican congressional candidates in the midterms, which was an increase of 12 points compared to 2008." While one might wish that their religious

[3] Cited in NewsMax.com, "Democrats Narrow Gap in Religious Vote," November 19, 2006.

[4] Ibid.

[5] CNN.com, "Corruption Named as Key Issue by Voters in Exit Polls," November 7, 2006.

[6] Cited in NewsMax.com, "Democrats Narrow Gap."

[7] Pew Forum on Religion & Public Life, "Religion in the 2008 Presidential Election," August 11, 2010, www.pewresearch.org/pubs/1697/exit-poll-election-support-among-religious-groups.

[8] Pew Forum on Religion & Public Life, "Religion in the 2010 Elections," November 3, 2010, pewresearch.org/pubs/1791/2010-midterm-elections-exit-poll-religion-vote.

convictions played a part in this surge, it is largely understood that the major cause of the majority swing to Republicans among Catholics was no different than it was for the American population in general: dissatisfaction with the economy and unease with the current political situation.[9]

What conclusions may we draw? Perhaps that most of those who stand for traditional values continue to do so, and that some who may have wavered in the 2008 election, out of disillusionment with the Republican Party, have turned back. The problem with the Republican Party, however, is that many Americans have become so disillusioned with its failure to remain faithful to its core principles that voters could swing back again in desperation toward the Democratic Party. The problem for the Democratic Party, however, is that secularists continue to be staunchly Democrat, so that traditionalist voters will continue to have difficulties moving toward that party. More moderate Democratic leaders, such as Jim Wallis, editor of *Sojourners* magazine, have tried to make the Democratic Party an "umbrella" party catering to all political viewpoints. So far, his efforts seem to have produced meager results, since it is difficult to get such groups as pro-abortionists and pro-lifers to identify with the same political party.[10]

Thus our treatment of the constitutionality of separation of church and state feeds into our more general discussion of the deeper problem: our society's replacement of the transcendent dimension to life, and the perennial values rooted in that perspective, with the secularist mentality and its relativistic understanding of moral values.

The Secularist Agenda

We have argued from the beginning of this book that since the Enlightenment, there has been a growing movement among situational ethicists to

---

[9] Jade Mardirosian, "Religious voters motivated more by issues than doctrine," *The Lariate Online*, November 19, 2010, www.baylor/edu/lariat/news.php?action=story&story=84457. Mardirosian cites Dr. Patrick Flavin, a political science professor of Baylor University: "Catholics are kind of like the rest of voters and are fed up with the Democrats more than the Republicans."

[10] Wallis has made a valiant attempt to form this "umbrella" party with his book *God's Politics: Why the Right Gets It Wrong and the Left Doesn't Get It* (San Francisco: Harper, 2005). He seems to think that by emphasizing what Jesus would want in social issues and sliding over the deep divisions in America over sexual and moral issues, all well-intentioned voters will come together in the Democratic Party. Suffice it to say that when Wallis tried to address his agenda at a session of the American Academy of Religion annual meeting in Washington, DC, in 2006, his attempts to foster the umbrella party broke down. It became clear that gay rightists, for one, were not interested in the social unity that might be established when soft social issues were given priority, if it meant sacrificing the priority that should be given to promoting gay issues.

remove God and objective standards of morality from the operations of society. Such ethicists feel that only a predominantly secularist society will accept a nontraditional, left-wing political and social ideology as the dominant motivating force of the day. We have already discussed these issues at great length.

Our purpose now is to determine whether the Constitution supports the secularist agenda. In doing so, we examine the teaching of the First Amendment to the Bill of Rights of the United States Constitution regarding the relationship of religion to society and of church to state, to determine what role, if any, that amendment gives to religion in American society.

In support of their position, secularists argue that the Constitution mandates separation of church and state. Their purpose is to validate their secularist views from the teaching of the document that founded American life at its very beginning. Such a foundation would protect their position from any further challenge, for if in fact the Constitution mandated this separation, one would have little recourse but to accept the secularists' position as the law of the land. The fact is, however, that the Constitution does not support the secularist position, and so their erroneous interpretation of the Constitution needs to be exposed, if there is any hope of derailing their ideology from gaining popular support.

There are two things to which Americans, and especially Catholics, give a sacral aura: the Constitution, and the Supreme Court in its interpretation of the Constitution. At one time the pope commanded unquestioning allegiance among American Catholics, but he has now been replaced by the Supreme Court, and it is easy to see why: without the Supreme Court to provide the last word on the meaning of the Constitution, the foundations of American life would be undermined, and our world would be thrown into chaos. The fact that the Supreme Court is already undermining American life by its extremist antireligious and amoral interpretations of what the Constitution mandates has so far failed to come to the consciousness of most.[11]

Should Religion Be Separated from Society?

The question we are addressing may be presented this way: Does the Constitution call for the separation of church and state, and does this entail the removal of God and objective morality from the operations of society?[12]

---

[11] This sacral nature of the Supreme Court has in most recent times begun to erode, though mostly among fundamentalist Christians, who are particularly attuned to the damaging social effects resulting from the many antireligious decisions of the Court in the last sixty years.

[12] Some of what follows is a revision of and elaboration upon what first appeared in my article, "Religion and the First Amendment: How the Supreme Court Has Misinterpreted the Constitution," *Christianity in Crisis* 5 (June 1987): 12–20.

The question is a curious one, since I don't know of any other type of separation popularly supported in our society. Our culture does not normally insist that different areas of life be legislated as mutually exclusive; for example, we don't say, "This is a conference about business matters so we mustn't let *politics* enter our discussion," or "let's consider the value of this painting, but we must exclude any *philosophical* perspective the painter might have had." To be sure, different areas of life operate by different sets of principles—a painting is not normally considered well-done because it is logically consistent, nor a political viewpoint normally thought to be worthwhile because it is beautiful—but there are no laws legislating the separation of these domains from any contact with or influence upon each other. So why should religion be legally separated from the operations of society?

Moreover, even if one tried to isolate business or art or physics from the operations of society, it would not be possible to do so, for our lives are not made up of totally discrete areas: we cannot really discuss politics, for example, without bringing our liberal or conservative mind-sets, our emotional and rational inclinations, our understanding of history, scientific progress, and the meaning of life to the table. Indeed, Supreme Court Chief Justice Warren Burger once asserted: "No significant segment of our society and no institution within it can exist in a vacuum or in total or absolute isolation from all the other parts, much less from government."[13] The fact is, since our whole being is engaged in every activity of our lives, every facet of our lives penetrates every other. Even to suggest that our views regarding science or art or psychology or philosophy should be necessarily isolated from each other would be naïve—it cannot be done. Why this mania, then, about isolating a religious perspective? For what is impossible regarding other areas of life is equally impossible regarding religion: religion cannot be isolated from the other operations of our lives so as not to have an effect upon them.

Since it is therefore unrealistic and impossible to isolate religion totally from the operations of society, perhaps we should ask whether it would be desirable to extricate the influence of religion from society as much as possible? Should we really try to do the best we can—to go as far as we can—to remove religion from society? My answer is no, for without religion, public life inevitably loses the transcendent dimension that brings meaning, purpose, order, and direction to our lives in society.

Without a transcendent dimension, social structures lose an objective raison d'être. They lose the foundation that makes it possible for them to

---

[13] *Lynch v. Donnelly*, 465 U.S. 668 (1984). Chief Justice Burger delivered the opinion of the Court, sec. II A, at web page *FindLaw* for Legal Professionals, www.findlaw.com/casecode/index.html. Unless otherwise noted, all cases are from *FindLaw*.

endure when challenged. They become instruments for individual personal manipulation, and victims of social forces.

Without a transcendent dimension that grounds life in the social order, people would also be unable to see the relevance of faith to their daily lives. Faith would become a superstructure detached from and optional to determining the meaning of life in the public forum. As a result, people would begin to explain reality without a relationship to God. The meaning and purpose of the social order would be determined by personal gain. Immediate historical and personal perspectives severed from any meaning beyond themselves, that is, historicism, would prevail.

Structures of society will initially take on a nontheistic, but eventually, a-theistic,[14] configuration. For, divorced from its proper relationship to a Transcendent Being, the public order does not become "neutral" regarding the existence of God, as many argue in this case, in an effort to imply that objectivity is obtained when a reference to God is removed; rather, the public form necessarily takes on a configuration that claims to have meaning without taking into consideration its divinely created origins. That is in fact not "objectivity" but a-theism. It is also a falsehood, a statement of reality that is not in conformity with the truth. It therefore leads to an atheistic distortion of reality. The result may not be atheism by explicit intention, but it will be at least atheism in practice—an attempt to deal with life in a social order where the God who created all reality is treated as irrelevant to it.

Church and State: Separate Realities?

To argue for the validity of a religious dimension to life in the social order, however, is not necessarily to argue for the involvement of the Church as an ecclesiastical institution in the affairs of the state as a governing institution. Religion and the Church are not the same. One might be in favor of maintaining a religious dimension to life without necessarily affirming a role for the institutional Church as such in state operations. The institutions of the Church and the state have distinct interests, goals, and ways of proceedings, and these should remain separate. When we argue to the existence of a religious dimension to life, we are referring not necessarily to the Church but to a transcendent dimension—a relationship to God—that is intrinsic to our understanding of the world and the operations of society. And it is this we would be arguing must be maintained, if the social order and the structures of society are to survive and maintain their proper configurations.

Widespread among Americans today is the notion that the First Amendment to the Constitution legislates not only a separation of church and state, but also the separation of faith from the operations of the political

[14] "A-theistic" meaning to be actively against or opposed to the existence of God.

and social order. Many would be surprised to learn that the words "separation of Church and State," words now commonly known by more people than the words of the First Amendment itself, are nowhere to be found in the Bill of Rights or the Constitution. Many, moreover, are unaware that it is strongly argued by reputable scholars of constitutional law that the Constitution does not mandate such a separation, even though a majority on the Court in recent years has continued to support that separation. What antiseparationist scholars are asserting is that the recent Court's understanding of church-state separation does not remain faithful to what the Framers of the First Amendment intended in the writing of that amendment, and that an examination of the discussions held at the time of the First Amendment ratification reveal no desire to make such a separation. As one noted scholar writes:

> Debates on the adoption of the First Amendment [by the Framers] reveal no request for a "separation of church and state." The phrase simply was not used in these debates, and the idea was not advocated. . . . In light of the failure of dissenters [to the amendment] to seek a separation of church and state and the failure of the framers to mention separation, the historical claims that the amendment adopted this principle are, at best, improbable. . . . American dissenters demanded a religious liberty very different from separation of church and state, for they did not want separation. Their distaste for separation . . . explains why separatism is without historical authority.[15]

What is also seriously being discussed today is whether the modern Supreme Court has not only distorted the original understanding of the Framers on this issue, but has also so deviated from their intentions as to be legislating in direct opposition to them, even to the point of violating fundamental human rights granted by the Constitution. To arrive at conclusions regarding this very important issue, therefore, we need to be clear about what the First Amendment does in fact say, and the mentality of the men who wrote it.

The Mind-set of the Founders

Michael Novak recently devoted a whole chapter of a book to show "the depth and power of the Hebraic view of reality shared by this nation's founding generation."[16] People of the colonial period were commonly rooted, he says, in the biblical perspective of history and the origins of the universe, and frequently peppered their thought and publications with citations from the

[15] Philip Hamburger, "Against Separation," *Public Interest* 155 (Spring 2004): 179–80.

[16] Michael Novak, *On Two Wings: Humble Faith and Common Sense at the American Founding* (San Francisco: Encounter, 2002), 5–24, at 13.

Old Testament. One of the least religiously inclined of all the Founders was probably Thomas Jefferson, yet while he was President, he attended and supported the largest church service in the United States that took place every Sunday in the Capitol Building.[17]

As a rule, however, the Founders tended not to be deeply religious in the sense of being committed to devotional worship. As one might say today, they were spiritually oriented people, rather than religious. Though believers, they were men of the Enlightenment. Faith and reason worked together for them, but faith tended to confirm what was already known from reason. Some who were deists or rationalists held that reason by itself alone provided a sufficient foundation for religious beliefs. Though many were members of specific religious groups—hardly any Catholic—they tended to leave aside sectarian convictions when they moved into the public forum, and concentrated instead on values they considered common to all religious groups. Thus, (1) that there is a God who created the universe, (2) that human beings are created to live according to a universal code of moral conduct, and (3) that if human beings live by that code their final destiny is salvation—these were Enlightenment religious viewpoints accepted by all.

Common agreement was important to the Founders. They had come from Europe where, from the sixteenth to the eighteenth centuries, deep religious conflicts prevailed. Many in their families had been objects of persecution, and had come to the New World to escape this. Europe had finally resolved its religious conflicts by establishing national or territorial Christian churches for free expression of differing religious convictions. This seemed to be an equitable way to resolve disputes where there was no hope of compromise. Once these geographical divisions were accepted, there was for the most part peaceful coexistence. Atheism was still widely considered a social evil in Europe, in spite of the existence of French iconoclasts like Voltaire and Diderot, and was barely tolerated anywhere, for atheists rejected the commonly accepted conviction that all reality was grounded in a transcendent relationship to God, and that the well-being of society depended upon fostering that relationship. Americans felt the same:

> Hostility to atheism was nearly universal in America, on the ground that where there is no omniscient Judge, political power knows no moral check. . . . Were atheism widely promulgated, most believed, everyday morals would slide into decadence, and reason would lose its steel. . . . Atheism, the founders thought, undermines republican institutions . . . . It erases the Creator Who (the Declaration states as a truth) endowed all individuals with inalienable rights, beyond the power of the state to take away.[18]

---

[17] Ibid., 31.

[18] Ibid., 28–30.

The seventeenth- and eighteenth-century settlers in America brought with them the background of the European solution of specific churches for specific territories or states. They were initially no more tolerant of each other's religious views than were their forebears: the "true" religion was always one's own. But gradually they came to realize, far more fundamentally than those left behind in Europe, that they lived too closely to profit from war, that they were dependent on each other for survival, and that some tolerance of religious views was necessary for the well-being of all.

Tolerance was gradually exercised regarding each other's staked-out territory. Our modern concept of toleration where, regardless of where one lives, each is free to choose whichever religious commitment one wishes to make, or to make no commitment at all, was eventually accepted by American settlers for pragmatic reasons: because no one religion had hegemony throughout the land, and because toleration was the best way to escape the endless religious wars of the past and live in peace. By the end of the eighteenth century, the colonists had largely settled their religious differences peacefully, by a sort of "separate, not equal but, for pragmatic purposes, tolerant" relationship.

There was also a sentiment brought over by the Puritans that America had a "covenant with God" and that Americans were "God's chosen people." An American way of life developed into a civic religion in which the basics of all religions were amalgamated, leading to a kind of national destiny:

> An interesting aspect of the great diversity of religions in Colonial America was that they all developed a common image of the American nation. This brought about the extraordinary American development of a generalized religion integrating a society even while the nation had many religions. Within American society, the collective religion became America's civil religion, incorporating secular as well as religious values and emphasizing a national purpose. In its simplest form this identification of a generalized Protestant religion with America's national purpose cast America's "mission" as one of bringing the American way of life, democracy, and free enterprise to all parts of the globe.[19]

It is against this background that we look now to the two principal documents of the American founding, the Declaration of Independence and the Constitution of the United States with its Bill of Rights.

DECLARATION OF INDEPENDENCE

The second sentence in the Declaration is crucial to our investigation: "We hold these Truths to be self-evident, that all Men are created equal, that

---

[19] Barry A. Kosmin and Seymour P. Lachman, *One Nation Under God: Religion in Contemporary American Society* (New York: Harmony, 1993), 20, 22.

they are endowed by their Creator with certain unalienable Rights, that among these are Life, Liberty, and the Pursuit of Happiness."

The Framers assumed there was no need to prove the "Truths" in question, for the truths were obvious and accepted by all, because their basic validity was found in the transcendent dimension to life that was accepted by all: that people are "endowed by their Creator with certain unalienable Rights." The fact that the Framers could affirm these truths in an astonishingly simple yet profound statement of conviction, indicates that the writers possessed a common background that supported the clarity of their vision. One scholar explains what was included in that background:

> It was, of course, the existence of God, who by his act of creation orients every human creature toward the goals of life. This common dependence of all human beings upon a Creator is what constitutes their equality, and endows them with rights freely to pursue their personal destinies in society. If such rights do indeed belong to men and women precisely as human, then it follows that they are unalienable and hence exempt from all arbitrary government action. Any arbitrary interference with them would clearly be an affront to the dignity of the human person. However, all this is self-evident only if one first believes in a God from whom we receive in creation our corporate destiny in society. In other words, the self-evidence of which the authors speak was founded upon a prior and transcendent faith experience.[20]

Thus, for the Founding Fathers, the basis for the equality of human beings is found in their common origin in the Creator. What is clear from this key sentence is not only that the Founders discovered the basis for this conviction in humanity's common creation by a Transcendent Being, but also that, without a foundation in the Transcendent, the assertion had no basis. Human beings have a right to life which achieves its greatness in the free pursuit of happiness. But the Founders understood the new nation to be built not only upon the pursuit of happiness for one's own good but for the good of others as well. But that pursuit was intelligible to them only in view of a common "destiny under God" where the will of the people would be "the surest clue to the will of God," a God who they felt would ultimately "guide the pursuit itself" toward his own divine purposes.[21]

---

[20] Christopher J. Mooney, S.J., *Religion and the American Dream: The Search for Freedom Under God* (Philadelphia: Westminster, 1977), 43–44.

[21] Ibid., 50–51.

FIRST AMENDMENT

The First Amendment asserts regarding religion: "Congress shall make no law respecting an establishment of religion, or prohibiting the free exercise thereof."

There are two important clauses here: the Establishment Clause, which holds that Congress shall not establish religion by law in this country; and the Free Exercise Clause, stating that Congress shall do nothing to obstruct people's freedom to believe and worship according to their convictions. Both clauses are deceptively simple, for their precise meaning is not easy to determine. Supreme Court efforts over the last sixty years to analyze and rule authoritatively on their precise meaning and relationship to each other have led to much distortion and confusion regarding the relationship of church to state and religion to the public forum prescribed for this country by the amendment. Since the Founders are not here today to provide clarification, we must find other means to decipher the clauses' meaning. To do that, it seems we may legitimately draw upon the Founders' other writings where they discuss these same issues, as well as on their understanding of the world in which they lived, as aids in the resolution of these ambiguities. But first let us examine the Religion Clauses for their possible meanings.

Establishment Clause

Two questions are apt regarding the Establishment Clause ("Congress shall make no law respecting an establishment of religion"):

First, what does the clause forbid? There are two possibilities: Does it forbid the government to establish or foster *religion* in general as opposed to *nonreligion* throughout the land, or does it forbid establishing a *national* religion, that is, giving a place of priority or privilege to one religion, as opposed to being favorably disposed toward and supportive of *all religions*? Which is the intended meaning is crucial: in the former case, the clause would be insisting on *neutrality* toward religion—neither favoring religion nor opposing it; in the latter case, the clause would be opposed to establishing and supporting one religion as a *national* or established state religion of privileged rank and power, but not forbid the government to be *supportive of all religions* in general and on an equal basis. The consequences would be quite different, depending on which interpretation is valid: in the former case, the government would be forbidden to take a position or play a role regarding the presence or absence of religion in society, but in the latter case, religion and its values could be promoted by government as long as it was done on an equal basis toward all religions. Thus, whether or not the government must be neutral toward the presence of religion in society is the crucial element to be understood in the intention of this clause.

Secondly, what is the scope of the clause? Does it refer simply to the obligations pertaining to the *federal* government, or does it apply to *state* governments as well? On the face of it, since we are talking about an amendment to the federal Constitution, the statement seems to refer to legislative action by the Congress of the United States, and not to legislative policies of state congressional houses.

In regard to the first question, the Supreme Court has in recent years asserted that the clause forbids *both* favoring religion over nonreligion, and the establishment of one specific religion over others. In other words, government must not only not establish one religion as a *national* religion, but must also be *neutral* toward the presence or absence of religion in society. In regard to the second question, the Supreme Court applies the above prohibition today (in view of the Fourteenth Amendment) to the *states* as well as the *federal* government.

Since the Supreme Court has so decreed, most Americans accept these interpretations as definitive, as if the Court spoke with infallible power. Yet the Supreme Court possesses no infallibility. The very possibility that the Court has erroneously interpreted the clause must be recognized in view of the fact that the Court's many opinions on religious questions have often been decided by narrow 5–4 margins. Should the views of one judge carry that much judicial weight? In addition, there is considerable disagreement among scholars of constitutional law over the Court's decisions on religious issues.

Following Edward Harrington, United States Senior District Judge for the district of Massachusetts, we understand the Establishment Clause to be asserting *only* that Congress shall make no law establishing a *national* religion:

> The Establishment clause says that government shall not establish a religion, nor enforce its observance by law, nor compel any citizen to worship in a manner contrary to his conscience.[22]

The clause does not forbid the government to be *supportive of all religions* in general. As Mooney states, "The Founders wanted to formulate a principle that would guarantee the participation of all churches in the common social unity of the republic, while at the same time not compromising those distinctive modes of worship and belief proper to each."[23]

Thirdly, we understand the clause to be addressing *only* the prohibition of a national religion by the *federal* government, not the issue of a *state* reli-

---

[22] Edward F. Harrington, "The Metaphorical Wall," *America* 192 (January 17–24, 2005): 12.

[23] Mooney, *Religion and the American Dream*, 97.

gion within any of the federated states (though the Fourteenth Amendment may have extended this prohibition later to the states as well).[24]

In sum, the clause intends that Congress shall make no law establishing one religion over others as the national religion, as exists, for example, in Great Britain. It does not address the matter of supporting religion over nonreligion. Therefore the clause does not require the government to be *neutral* toward religion, but rather allows government to be supportive of the well-being of religion in society, so long as government does so in an even-handed way.

In fact, the clause could not be mandating government neutrality because the religious foundation of human values was commonly accepted at the time as necessary to the well-being of society, so much so that to be neutral about fostering that foundation would not only mean being neutral about maintaining the presence of such values, but also about the undermining of the well-being of society. Some of the Framers of the Constitution would in fact have been inconsistent had they intended to be neutral toward religion, since they had made it clear in signing the Declaration of Independence that religion was considered by them an integral dimension of human life. It was in that document that they had accepted as "self-evident" that the fundamental rights of human existence—equality, life, liberty, the pursuit of happiness—were a product of the human relationship with the Transcendent. For them to have affirmed that foundation in 1776, and then claim to be neutral toward such a foundation in 1791, would have been incongruous and put them at cross-purposes with their role as Founding Fathers. Affirming the transcendent foundation of human rights and maintaining support for that foundation was the only way not only to establish the rights of human existence but also to preserve those rights for the well-being of society on a permanent basis.

Historical Background

Most of the original settlers believed that their own religion was the true religion, and each group felt it had its God-given right to establish its own religion in its own territory. The historical situation at the time of the writing of the Establishment Clause of the First Amendment clarifies that it was intended to prevent the encroachment of the *national* government upon the free exercise of religion, and not to address states' authority regarding religious matters in their own territories. What makes this interpretation lucidly

---

[24] It should be noted that the First Amendment, strictly speaking, addresses only the actions of Congress. It has been argued that the amendment leaves the President and the federal judiciary free to be involved in the area of religious establishment, but this is probably a minority view; see Robert L. Cord, *Separation of Church and State: Historical Fact and Current Fiction* (New York: Lambeth, 1982), 37.

clear is that a number of states at the time of the writing of the amendment had already established state religions and continued to maintain them after the ratification of the amendment in 1791. Nine of the original thirteen colonies had established religions in place in 1775, five still had them in 1787, and three still had them as late as 1818. Massachusetts had an established religion as late as 1833.[25] How could this have been allowed if the amendment had made state religions illegal by insisting on religious neutrality throughout the land? What the data indicate, therefore, is not only that state-established religions were not forbidden by the First Amendment, but a fortiori that it was permissible to be favorably disposed toward religion over nonreligion throughout the land.[26]

Secondly, other historical data also support the view that only the establishment of a *national* religion was being rejected by the First Amendment, not federal support for religion in general.

For example, in 1785, six years before the First Amendment was adopted, Thomas Jefferson

> reminded his state of Virginia that the states of Pennsylvania and New York had long had an official policy of no establishment. "The experiment was new and doubtful when they made it," he said. "It has answered beyond conception. They flourish infinitely. *Religion is well supported*; of various kinds, indeed, but all good enough; all sufficient to preserve peace and order."[27]

Jefferson's statement shows he did not understand a no-establishment clause on the state level to exclude the possibility of a state supporting religion in general, and that he was in fact delighted that such support was happening for the maintenance of peace and order.

We also have an insight into the intentions of James Madison, the primary author of the First Amendment, when he proposed the original wording of the amendment in 1789 as follows: "The civil rights of none shall be abridged on account of religious belief or worship, nor shall any national religion be established, nor shall the full and equal rights of conscience be in any manner, or any pretext infringed."[28] Some feared at the time that including the word "national" might imply that the government was a

---

[25] Ibid., 4.

[26] Many constitutional scholars argue that the Fourteenth Amendment, ratified in 1868, extended the First Amendment rights to the individual states as well (cf. below, see p. 371, n. 38). If so, it follows that the amendment now forbids on the state level exactly what it forbids on the national level and nothing more.

[27] Mooney, *Religion and the American Dream*, 97, citing Saul K. Padover, ed., *The Complete Jefferson* (Duell, Sloan & Pearce, 1943), 676 (emphasis added).

[28] As cited by Philip Hamburger, *Separation of Church and State*, 105.

national as opposed to a federated government (built on states' rights). Madison insisted he had intended his words only to forbid the establishment of a national religion, and not to imply that the American government was national rather than federated. Others feared that without the term "national," the passage might be misunderstood to have a negative impact on religion in general, or be seen as a support to those who expressed no religious convictions.[29] Madison felt these interpretations would not be made, and so the word "national" was dropped—an unfortunate decision in view of subsequent history. This and similar discussion of the contents of the First Amendment substantiate the position that only the rejection of a national religion was the intention behind the writing of the Establishment Clause.

A sorry footnote here: Madison failed to recognize that by limiting the First Amendment to a directive not to establish a national religion, he did not include a provision safeguarding principles he took for granted, namely, the need to foster a civic understanding that fundamental civic laws are based upon a recognition of the existence of God, and that human beings have an obligation to worship the Creator—principles without the acceptance of which the "foundation of religious liberty crumbles."[30] It is the failure to set in legislation this religious foundation and the natural law principles that follow from it, which the Founders took for granted, that has allowed today's Supreme Court to reject this foundation, and to replace it with the purely relativistic perspectives of religious and moral values that prevail in the Court today.

Thirdly, various amendments guaranteeing religious liberty were proposed to state constitutional ratifying conventions. Virginia and New York both insisted on an amendment to their constitutions guaranteeing "no particular religious sect or society ought to be favored or established, by law, in preference to others."[31] North Carolina and Rhode Island insisted upon the same. Such directives further clarify that the concern the states had was not to be neutral toward the presence of religion in society, but rather not to prevent the flourishing of religion in society by giving one religion preference over others.

Americans at that time took for granted that to be religiously oriented was the duty of every citizen, and that government should support that duty. Though atheism had begun to be accepted as a viable alternative, it was not yet generally accepted as such. In any case, atheism was not a position the writers of the First Amendment supported. However, while they sought to

---

[29] Novak, *On Two Wings*, 56.

[30] Ibid., 60.

[31] Article 20 of Virginia's "Bill of Rights" adopted June 27, 1788; Cord, 7.

favor religion, they did not wish to deprive anyone of the freedom to abstain from religious belief and practice. In other words, they sought ways to favor the expression of religion for the well-being of the nation and its citizens, but without coercing religious belief. Persuasion was left to the efforts of religious sects, while general support was to be a public phenomenon.

It is the constitutional scholar Robert L. Cord who expresses so well the correct interpretation of the meaning of the First Amendment:

> I conclude that, regarding religion, the First Amendment was intended to accomplish three purposes. First, it was intended to prevent the establishment of a national church or religion, or the giving of any religious sect or denomination a preferred status. Second, it was designed to safeguard the right of freedom of conscience in religious beliefs against invasion solely by the national Government. Third, it was so constructed in order to allow the States, unimpeded, to deal with religious establishments and aid to religious institutions as they saw fit. There appears to be no historical evidence that the First Amendment was intended to preclude Federal governmental aid to religion when it was provided on a nondiscriminatory basis. Nor does there appear to be any historical evidence that the First Amendment was intended to provide an *absolute separation or independence* of religion and the national state.[32]

Separation of Church and State

We are asserting, therefore, that based upon the rationale behind the formulation of the Establishment Clause and the context of ideas operating at the time in which it was written, the clause forbade the establishment of a national religion and nothing more, and that this is the only "separation of church and state" intended by the writers of the First Amendment. As Hamburger points out so well, neither religious dissenters nor state-supported established churches in eighteenth-century America wanted to separate religion from society, since "it was widely accepted that civil government depended upon religion and upon the morality it inculcated."[33]

According to Hamburger, with few possible exceptions, "it is difficult to find . . . many individuals in America prior to 1800 who clearly advocated the separation of church and state."[34] What troubled religious dissenters from state religions was not the influence of government upon religion, which they readily accepted, but the privileged position state governments had given established churches, and the inhibitions such privilege created for the free exercise of religion by nonestablishment religionists. Ministers of the established churches, for their part, had their own fears about reli-

---

32 Cord, *Separation of Church and State*, 15.

33 Hamburger, *Separation*, 66.

34 Ibid., 64.

gious dissenters—that their desire for independence from the established churches would lead to the alienation of church and state: "Some prominent establishment ministers worried that the religious liberty sought by dissenters would have the effect of separating religion and thus morality from civil government."[35]

According to Hamburger, it was religious dissenters campaigning against the established churches "whose claims seem to have affected the wording of the constitutional guarantees against establishments." But these dissenters were only interested in making "demands for a religious liberty that limited civil government, especially civil legislation, rather than for a religious liberty conceived as a separation of church and state."[36] Even while asking for the removal of the privileged position given to the established churches, dissenters continued to feel the need for government protection for the free exercise of religion: "Therefore, when, in opposition to establishments, various dissenters asserted that government should not make laws taking cognizance of religion, some of these dissenters . . . hastened to add in qualification that government should, of course, be able to provide protection for the free exercise of religion."[37]

The point is, then, that virtually no one at the time of the writing of the First Amendment was interested in the separation of church and state, but only in establishing religious liberty, as contained in the Free Exercise Clause, and curtailing the role of government regarding religion except insofar as government was necessary for the free exercise of religious belief and worship. The purpose of the Establishment Clause, then, was certainly not to separate religion and state, as its meaning is widely misunderstood today, but to buttress the position taken in the Free Exercise Clause—to "protect individuals in the free exercise of their religion."[38] The free exercise of religion clause "bans the state from restraining a citizen's unfettered choice to believe the tenets of his faith and to worship in accordance with his conscience."[39]

---

35 Ibid., 19.

36 Ibid., 107.

37 Ibid., 102.

38 Ibid., 101. This meant that the federal government would not establish a national religion subsidized by the State, as is the case with the Anglican Church in England, whose power and privileged position could infringe upon the equal rights of all religions. But since the federal government had no authority over the states regarding state establishment of religion, the First Amendment left intact the situation in many states where established religions were in place, as, for example, the Congregationalists in Connecticut. Whereas the equality of all religions was thus mandated by the First Amendment on the national scene, situations of unequal rights among religions could still exist on state levels, and did so into the nineteenth century.

39 Harrington, "Metaphorical Wall," 12.

Everson v. Board of Education

Unfortunately the Supreme Court since 1947 has found much more in the Establishment Clause than the Framers of the First Amendment had ever intended.

In *Everson v. Board of Education* (1947), the Supreme Court in a 5–4 decision charted a new course in our understanding of church-state relations. The Court's interpretation of the Establishment Clause went far beyond anything that had ever before been seen in that clause. Justice Black, writing for the majority, now called for "a wall of separation between Church and State" (citing the words of Thomas Jefferson)[40] that would be "high and impregnable." [41]

According to Black, the state was now to be "neutral" toward religion: the First Amendment "requires the state to be a neutral in its relations with groups of religious believers and non-believers; it does not require the state to be their adversary. State power is no more to be used so as to handicap religions, than it is to favor them."[42] But that was only the beginning. According to Hamburger, the wall metaphor would be used to demand even more than neutrality: "Rather than simply forbid civil laws respecting an establishment of religion, it has more ambitiously tended to prohibit contact between religious and civil institutions."[43] The new thinking led to a policy of rigid exclusion of national as well as state governments from aid to or involvement in religious activities or the life of religious institutions.

Justice Rutledge, in spite of his dissenting position, was to be even more influential than Black, in that Rutledge "laid out the broad arguments concerning the Founders that the later Court would come to accept as virtually self-evident."[44] Rutledge, using the wall imagery, and arguing from what he claimed to be the views of Jefferson and Madison, asserted that the Religion Clauses together were intended "to create a complete and permanent

---

[40] Contrary to popular thought, the wall imagery is not original to Jefferson. Its origins can be traced back at least to the Anabaptist Menno Simons in a 1548 letter, and, later, to the Anglican theologian Richard Hooker (1554–1600), the colonial advocate of religious liberty Roger Williams (1603–1683), and the Scotsman James Burgh (1714–1775), whose political writings Jefferson read, and from whom Jefferson probably borrowed the phrase. Daniel L. Dreisbach, *Thomas Jefferson and the Wall of Separation between Church and State* (New York: New York University Press, 2002), 71–82.

[41] *Everson v. Board of Education of the Township of Ewing et al.* 330 U.S. 1 (1947), in *FindLaw*, 1–38, at 6–7. Mr. Justice Black delivered the opinion of the Court.

[42] Ibid.

[43] Hamburger, *Separation*, 3.

[44] James Hitchcock, *The Supreme Court and Religion in American Life*, vol. 2, *From "Higher Law" to "Sectarian Scruples"* (Princeton, NJ: Princeton University Press, 2004), 7.

separation of the spheres of religious activity and civil authority by comprehensively forbidding every form of public aid or support for religion."[45] The wall imagery had remained dormant since its use by Jefferson in 1802 (except for one Supreme Court reference in 1879), but after *Everson*, the wall with its "high and impregnable" barrier became so popular in constitutional discourse that it supplanted the words of the First Amendment:

> Jefferson's architectural metaphor, in the course of time, has achieved virtual canonical status and become more familiar to the American people than the actual text of the First Amendment. . . . The *Everson* ruling marked the metaphor's entrance into public consciousness; shortly thereafter, its use proliferated in legal, political, and popular discourse. . . . Remarkably, the Jeffersonian metaphor has eclipsed and supplanted constitutional text in the minds of many jurists, scholars, and the American public.[46]

In the same way that religion, "with respect to its free exercise, was to be understood in the broadest possible sense, so it was to be understood with respect to establishment as well."[47] As a result, instead of the Establishment Clause finding its meaning, as was intended by the Founders, from its ability to protect the free exercise of religion, the Establishment Clause has taken on a life of its own and undercut free religious expression: The "federal and state constitutional provisions designed to protect religious liberty have, ironically, come to be understood in terms of an idea that substantially reduces this freedom."[48]

Problems Created by the Everson *Decision*

There are serious problems with the *Everson* decision.

First, the "wall of separation" metaphor is not found in the Constitution or the First Amendment, which, insofar as it speaks to religion, addresses only two things: *nonestablishment* and *free exercise of religion*. This hardly justifies legislation supporting a wall of separation between religion and state, and statements by Supreme Court justices arguing that the amendment contains such a separation are erroneous—separation is simply not there.

Secondly, while President Jefferson did indeed make use of the wall metaphor, he did so in the context of a letter to the Danbury Baptists in 1802, eleven years after the ratification of the First Amendment in 1791, and about thirteen years after the congressional debate and approval of the final text—a debate in which Jefferson did not participate, since he was out

45 Justice Rutledge, in *Everson*, in *FindLaw*, 12.
46 Dreisbach, *Jefferson*, 4–5, 3.
47 Hitchcock, *Supreme Court* 2:6.
48 Hamburger, *Separation*, 14.

of the country at the time as an American minister to France.[49] Therefore, his thinking could have had no direct influence on the debate.

Thirdly, Jefferson certainly did not intend his phrase to have reference to state governments, whose religious authority was not under scrutiny. Moreover, authority regarding religious affairs, including the relationship of religion to education, which is such a hot-button issue today, was in the hands of the states at that time, and so neither the First Amendment nor Jefferson's comment could have had any bearing upon the role of religion in state educational policies: "Jefferson's 'wall' was a metaphoric construction of the First Amendment, which governed relations between religion and the *national* government. His 'wall,' therefore, did not and *could not* specifically address relations between religion and *state* authorities."[50]

Therefore, if Jefferson's words had any bearing on our understanding of the First Amendment, they could only have referred to a wall of separation "in regard to possible federal action such as a law establishing a national religion or prohibiting the free exercise of worship [since] Congress had no other power in religious matters to curb."[51]

In addition, if we assume that Jefferson had intended a rigid wall of separation, we are unable to explain how, as President from 1801 to 1809, he authorized the allocation of public monies to support religious activity—in one case, in the early 1800s, for the Society of the United Brethren in Pennsylvania for the purpose of promoting Christianity; in another case in 1803, for the building of a church and for a Catholic priest to carry out his priestly duties.[52] Would not such allocations be in violation of the wall of separation, if that is in fact what he intended?

In fact, Jefferson used the "wall of separation" imagery as a metaphor not to explain that the federal government should not have any relationships with religion, but only to erect "two distinct walls of separation: one between the federal government and religious institutions, thereby prevent-

---

[49] Dreisbach, *Jefferson*, 98–99. "Thus, his [Jefferson's] influence on the actual text of the First Amendment was at most indirect" (Ibid., 99).

[50] Dreisbach, *Jefferson*, 65.

[51] Cord, *Separation of Church and State*, 115. James Hitchcock indicates that the Court's "espousal of the separationist position" in the *Everson* case "is usually explained on the grounds" that the case "marked the first time the Court recognized the Fourteenth Amendment as applying the Establishment Clause to the states, thus requiring the justices to face entirely new questions." James Hitchcock, *The Supreme Court and Religion in American Life*, vol. 1, *The Odyssey of the Religion Clauses* (Princeton, NJ: Princeton University Press, 2004), 159. But it necessarily follows that the application of the First Amendment to the states could contain no more than was contained in the First Amendment itself, which leads back to the initial question as to what was intended by the First Amendment.

[52] Cord, *Separation of Church and State*, 38–46.

ing the establishment of a national church, and the other between the federal and the state governments on matters pertaining to religion, thereby preventing the federal regime from interfering with religious establishments and practices endorsed by state governments."[53]

Thus, Daniel L. Dreisbach sees Jefferson's wall imagery more focused on preventing the *federal* government from interfering with the people's right to practice their religions as they saw fit, rather than on the issue of freedom of religion itself.[54] The image was not intended to prohibit civil government from benevolence toward religion or even to prohibit the church from influencing the conduct of civil government.

Harrington sees Jefferson's and the Bill of Right's purposes to include both a concern for religious freedom and a concern to shield religions from infringement from the federal government. He argues, moreover, in agreement with Dreisbach, that there was never any concern to shield the federal government from the influence of religions upon its operations:

> the metaphor "wall of separation" was used by Jefferson as a shorthand formula to endorse religious liberty against the power and control of the state [the federal government]. The term served solely as an aid to religious belief. . . . The Bill of Rights thus was designed not to shield the state [the federal government] and its policies and practices from the exercise of those individual rights by its citizens, but rather to protect the exercise of those individual rights from infringement by the state. The Bill of Rights was erected as a bulwark, a "wall," as it were, against the state. . . . The "wall of separation" permits maximum freedom to religious ideas and expression and deprives the state [the federal government] of any power to curtail that freedom.[55]

It is interesting to note that this parallels the guarantee provided the press by the First Amendment: civic government may not restrict the freedom of the press, but no restriction is placed upon the role of the press

[53] Dreisbach, *Jefferson*, 68.

[54] This is probably because Dreisbach sees Jefferson's purposes focused on preventing governmental interference with religion solely on the federal level: "Jefferson's 'wall,' like the first Amendment, affirmed the policy of federalism. This policy emphasized that all governmental authority over religious matters was allocated to the states." Dreisbach argues that the First Amendment and Jefferson were concerned more about restricting the authority of the federal government than about asserting a "universal principle of religious liberty": the amendment "offered little in the way of a substantive right or universal principle of religious liberty." Nevertheless, Jefferson may have been in favor of a corresponding juridical wall of separation on the state level "between ecclesiastical and state authorities" (Dreisbach, *Jefferson*, 68–69).

[55] Harrington, "Metaphorical Wall," 11–12.

regarding civic government. "Any construction of Jefferson's 'wall' that imposes restraints on entities other than civil government exceeds the limitations imposed by the First Amendment."[56]

The fact is that when the Supreme Court in 1947 misinterpreted Jefferson's words to restrict the freedom of religion as well as any support the state might provide religion, both positions were exactly contrary to the meaning Jefferson had intended. The Court in *Everson*, in an amazing act of judicial activism that has begun a long history of such activism, composed principles from out of nowhere: that the "wall of separation" meant, according to Justice Black:

> At least this: [1] Neither a state nor the Federal Government can set up a church. [2] Neither can pass laws which aid one religion, aid all religions, or prefer one religion over another. . . . [3] No tax in any amount, large or small, can be levied to support any religious activities or institutions, whatever they may be called, or whatever form they may adopt, to teach or practice religion. [4] Neither a state nor the Federal Government can, openly or secretly, participate in the affairs of any religious organizations or groups and vice versa.[57]

Little of the above represents a valid interpretation of the First Amendment, nor does most of it even represent principles that functioned in government policies in the life of early America. The first statement is accurate, as we have shown, but only to the extent that it states that the First Amendment prohibited the establishment of a (national) church. The second statement is accurate, except for the clause "aid all religions." Herein lay the Court's major deviation from the meaning of the First Amendment. As Cord points out, "There is no historical evidence to suggest, however, that the Establishment Clause in any way constitutionally precludes *non-discriminatory* governmental aid to religion. In fact, the converse is confirmed historically."[58]

The third and fourth sentences suffer from the same weakness, namely, that they rule out nondiscriminatory aid to religion in general. The sentences create a provision not found in the First Amendment nor intended by the Framers. In support of his position, Cord rightly argues:

> Did not the prayers of Congressional Chaplains in the First Congress, which formed the Establishment Clause, constitute "religious activities"? Were their salaries not paid from tax revenues? Are not these same

---

[56] Dreisbach, *Jefferson*, 195–96n51.

[57] Justice Black delivering the opinion of the Court in *Everson*, in *FindLaw*. I have added the enumeration for purposes of the following discussion.

[58] Cord, *Separation of Church and State*, 112.

> activities, performed in the U.S. Congress by clergymen today, irreconcilable with the Court's interpretation? How can the clear and direct financial aid to missionaries and the U.S. treaties to build Churches [in the late eighteenth and nineteenth centuries] be reconciled with the *Everson* definition?[59]

So far removed is *Everson* from the wording and true intent of the First Amendment that it is difficult not to conclude that an antireligious and perhaps anti-Christian bias motivated the majority of the justices in this new strictly separationist interpretation of the amendment.[60] In any case, what happened in the *Everson* decision unfortunately set off a wave of antireligious interpretations of that amendment that set the tone for a continuing and far-reaching removal of the religious dimension from the public operations of American society: *Everson*'s "wall" metaphor "has become the central icon of a strict separationist dogma that champions a secular polity in which religious influences are systematically stripped from public life."[61]

Antireligionist Consequences of Everson

The Court continued to base its decisions thereafter on the erroneous interpretations made in *Everson*. For example, in 1948 the majority ruled that public school property could not be used for religious instruction, since such a practice constituted state "aid" to religion. Thus began the costly, arduous, and time-consuming process of "bussing" students from public schools to church lands for religious instruction, then back to public schools, a system that has never been proven to be worth the effort.

In 1962, a case was brought against the State of New York for authorizing the following nondenominational prayer at the beginning of the school day: "Almighty God, we acknowledge our dependence upon Thee, and beg Thy blessings upon us, our teachers, and our country." In the first in a series of decisions to eliminate religious activity that had traditionally been a part of the public forum, the Court held that the Establishment Clause prohibited the state from authorizing any prayer in public schools, even if the prayer was nondenominational.

---

59 Ibid., 113.

60 To be fair, however, we note that Hitchcock indicates that an expansion of the Court's understanding of the Free Exercise Clause occurred during World War II and thereafter—for example, in the incongruous expansion in the 1960s of the right of religious liberty to include nonbelieving conscientious objectors—and that this expansion of religious liberty seemed to the Court "necessarily to require" an expansion of the Establishment Clause as well, in an effort to maintain "stringent separation between government and religion" (Hitchcock, *Supreme Court* 1:160).

61 Dreisbach, *Jefferson*, 117.

The following year, Madalyn Murray (later Madalyn Murray O'Hair), the founder of American Atheists, became famous as one of the litigants involved in further cases to ban organized prayer in public schools. In June of that year, by an 8–1 majority, the Court declared unconstitutional the recitation of the Lord's Prayer or the reading of a passage from the Bible at the opening of school, even if participation was voluntary. Justice Clark, in his majority opinion, firmly committed the Court to the principle of neutrality toward religion, which such exercises were said to violate.

In 1980, the Court held that a Kentucky law requiring the posting of the Ten Commandments on the walls of classrooms did not have a secular purpose and therefore was unconstitutional. Thus the Court overruled the state's right to support religious teaching, even when, presumably, the people chose it.

In 1985, the Court issued several rulings antagonistic to religion: it overruled a Connecticut law giving employees a right to a day free from work on their chosen Sabbath; it declared unconstitutional "shared time" programs supplementing courses offered by the state and community education programs, both providing classes to nonpublic school students at public expense in classrooms located in and leased from the nonpublic schools; it declared unconstitutional New York City's use of federal funds received under the Elementary and Secondary Education Act of 1965 (a program that had been in place for twenty years without problems) to pay salaries of public school employees who taught educationally deprived children from low-income families in parochial schools (later overturned, so that what was unconstitutional in 1985 became constitutional in 1997); and it held a 1981 Alabama law authorizing a one-minute period of silence in public schools "for meditation or voluntary prayer" unconstitutional because the law was said to be motivated for the purpose of advancing religion.

In 1989, the Court majority ruled that a Christmas nativity scene displayed inside a government building was in violation of the Establishment Clause.

In 1992, the Court ruled that clergy could not lead prayer at high school graduation ceremonies, and in 2000 threw out a Texas ruling that allowed high school students to have a school prayer read at athletic events.

On the other hand, there have been rulings that have tended to favor or support religion, although the Court justified them on the basis that they did not: for example, the 1981 ruling that when a state university allows its facilities to be used by student organizations, religious student groups must be allowed "equal access"; the 1983 ruling that a Minnesota law permitting parents to claim state tax deductions for children's school expenses, including tuition, textbooks, and transportation expenses, even if they attend nonpublic schools, is constitutional; and a 1983 ruling by a 6–3 decision permitting the beginning of state legislative sessions with prayer given by a publicly funded chaplain. The ruling in this last case was based not on the fact that a religious activity was being carried on, but that the practice was seen as consistent with the long-standing tradition of doing the same thing in the Supreme Court and the Congress. So in this case, tradition overrules the Constitution?

In 1984, a 5–4 ruling allowed the use of taxpayers' money for the display of a nativity scene at Christmas, as long as it was on private land. A crèche had been erected at a city shopping center that included other displays, and so the majority on the Court was able to argue that the display had "legitimate secular purposes." Further examples include the 1989 ruling that upheld the right of states to celebrate Christmas with a joint menorah-Christmas tree display; the 1990 ruling that required high schools to give religious groups the same access to school facilities given to other groups for extracurricular activities (basically reaffirmed in 2001); the 2000 ruling that federal monies could be used to purchase educational equipment for parochial schools; and the 2002 ruling, by a 5–4 decision, upholding for the first time a voucher program in Ohio allowing tax dollars to parents to send their children to religious schools.

Though it is often difficult to decipher how all of these rulings do not favor religion (which a proper reading of the First Amendment should allow), the Supreme Court justified each of them *only* because it was able to interpret them as not favoring religion, thus (at least in its own eyes) standing by its continuing norm of neutrality toward religion.

Lemon *Test*

In many of the above decisions, the norm for determining exactly where to erect the wall separating church and state and maintaining neutrality toward religion was definitively set in place by the Court in the *Lemon v. Kurtzman* decision of 1971. Chief Justice Warren Burger wrote the opinion of the majority in that case, ruling that direct government aid to religious schools was unconstitutional.

In his opinion, Burger constructed a three-part formula (the first two parts of which had already been set in place in a 1968 decision) for testing most laws regarding a state's relationship to religion: "First, the statute must have a secular legislative purpose; second, its principal or primary effect must be one that neither advances nor inhibits religion . . . ; finally, the statute must not foster 'an excessive government entanglement with religion.' "[62]

---

[62] *Lemon v. Kurtzman* 403 U.S. 602 (1971), in *FindLaw*, 1–36, at 6. The citation is from *Walz v. Tax Commission of New York* 397 U.S. 664 (1970), in *FindLaw*. Chief Justice Burger delivered the opinion of the Court, sec. II.

Justice William Brennan later added a fourth criterion (which he argued was contained in *Lemon* but which the Court added "albeit without express recognition of the fact"):[63] that the given statute not create "a serious potential for divisive conflict over the issue of aid to religion."[64] Thus for Brennan, the serious possibility that a statute might contain a "divisive political potential"[65] is enough to constitute a violation of the Constitution and prohibit state aid. But what makes a given potential "serious" rather than "not serious"? Creating such broad latitude for rejecting state aid on the basis of such imprecise law obviously leaves judicial decisions open to the whim and fancy of any judge who might find a statute not to his or her liking. That the supreme law of the land could be reduced to this kind of vague and unstructured formulation is utterly mind-boggling, and opens to question the sincerity of any court that would devise it.

As is fairly obvious, the consequences of adjudicating on the basis of such a complicated and totally unfocused formula could be devastating, and the Court has created serious problems for itself over the years in its efforts to produce consistent adjudications. In more recent decisions, it has begun, in a curious irony, to back away from the standard of the "high and impregnable wall of separation" it had set up for itself in 1947, and to adjudicate on the basis of Lemon's criterion of avoiding "excessive entanglement." But formulating decisions consistent with the imagery created by these two conflicting metaphors is not easy to do. In 1984, Justice Burger gave a majority decision where he continued to insist upon a "wall of separation" between church and state, but it was not to be "absolute" and not without "accommodation":

> Nor does the Constitution require complete separation of church and state; it affirmatively mandates accommodation, not merely tolerance, of all religions, and forbids hostility toward any.[66]

By this decision, the Court is now supposedly permitting state statutes that accommodate religion without "excessive entanglement." The Court deliberately does not want to make the separation absolute or remove all involvement, because it deems such separation not only undesirable, but impossible to enact. But then the critical question becomes how to determine this "fine line" of separation between acceptable accommodation and "excessive entanglement."

---

63 *Meek v. Pittinger* 421 U.S. 349 (1975), in *FindLaw*, Justice Brennan, concurring in part and dissenting in part.

64 Ibid.

65 Ibid., 15.

66 *Lynch*, in *FindLaw*. Chief Justice Burger delivered the opinion of the Court, sec. II A.

The Court has had an extremely difficult time trying to apply its three- (or four-) part *Lemon* formula. Chief Justice Rehnquist pointed out the extremely circuitous and conflicting if not self-contradictory route the Court had to take in trying to measure up to its established criteria. When Rehnquist enumerated in 1985 a list of some decisions the Court had made, it proved laughable:

> For example, a State may lend to parochial school children geography textbooks that contain maps of the United States, but the State may not lend maps of the United States for use in geography class. A State may lend textbooks on American colonial history, but it may not lend a film on George Washington, or a film projector to show it in history class. A State may lend classroom workbooks, but may not lend workbooks in which the parochial school children write, thus rendering them nonreusable. A State may pay for bus transportation to religious schools but may not pay for bus transportation from the parochial school to the public zoo or natural history museum for a field trip. A State may pay for diagnostic services conducted in the parochial school but therapeutic services must be given in a different building; speech and hearing "services" conducted by the State inside the sectarian school are forbidden, but the State may conduct speech and hearing diagnostic testing inside the sectarian school. Exceptional parochial school students may receive counseling, but it must take place outside of the parochial school, such as in a trailer parked down the street. A State may give cash to a parochial school to pay for the administration of state-written tests and state-ordered reporting services, but it may not provide funds for teacher-prepared tests on secular subjects. Religious instruction may not be given in public school, but the public school may release students during the day for religion classes elsewhere, and may enforce attendance at those classes with its truancy laws.[67]

Such decisions, according to Rehnquist, have caused the Court to end with "hopelessly divided pluralities"; its "historically faulty doctrine" has "proved all but useless as a guide to sound constitutional adjudication," and "should be frankly and explicitly abandoned."[68] Hamburger concurs: "The aptly-named *Lemon* test . . . has already been squeezed dry, and the Court should now expressly and completely discard it."[69]

Free Exercise Clause Violated

Former Chief Justice Burger once concluded that the Court's decisions could no longer be interpreted as neutral, but rather manifested "hostility toward

---

[67] *Wallace v. Jaffree* 472 U.S. 38 (1985), in *FindLaw*, Justice Rehnquist dissenting in the 6–3 decision.

[68] Ibid.

[69] Hamburger, *Separation*, 190.

religion."[70] His point introduces a new dimension to the Court's problem, for even if it were granted that the First Amendment called for "neutrality" toward religion (which I have argued it does not), is such a stance possible for the state? I think not. It is possible to enact laws favoring religion or antagonistic to religion, but not neutral toward religion, for any legislation that does not recognize the need to have a religious dimension in an adequate understanding of the operations of society inevitably signals that that dimension is not required for that understanding. Such a position is hardly a neutral one.

The Court has, for example, permitted states to grant tax exemptions to parents who send their children to parochial schools. This may seem in the Court's eyes to be "neutral" toward religion, but there is no getting around the fact that such legislation benefits Catholic families by providing them financial assistance, which enables the continuing existence of parochial schools and furthers the standing of the Catholic culture. Again, students who receive by the Court's ruling free bus transportation to parochial schools are thereby supported in their efforts to receive a Catholic education. A nativity scene is a Christian religious presentation on public display, whether it is justified as a part of the secular holiday spirit or not. Legislatures may seek to justify continuing to display them by contrived arguments purporting the contrary, but the fact is that such scenes are recognized by all who see them as religious symbols depicting the birth of the one whom Christians call their Savior.

On the other hand, legislation which prevents public school students from hearing prayer in school does not represent a neutral stance toward religion, but deprives them of the right to the free exercise of their religious beliefs in a public setting. Moreover, legislation that forbids the presentation of religious symbols in the classroom inevitably gives priority to a secular, nonreligious, or irreligious perspective regarding life in the public forum, and thus is biased in favor of an irreligious attitude toward issues of public relevance. Such legislation necessarily imprints upon the minds of young people that when adjudicating issues of public policy, faith plays no role. Such a stance inevitably creates an understanding of faith as something partisan, subjective, and irrelevant to life in the world, a position totally unacceptable to Christianity as well as to most other religions.

---

[70] *Wallace*, in *FindLaw*, Chief Justice Burger dissenting. The context: *Wallace* held that "a 1981 Alabama Statute authorizing a 1-minute period of silence in all public schools 'for meditation or voluntary prayer' . . . is a law respecting the establishment of religion and thus violates the First Amendment" (opening paragraph). The fuller statement of Burger's reaction was: "To suggest that a moment-of-silence statute that includes the word 'prayer' unconstitutionally endorses religion, while one that simply provides for a moment of silence does not, manifests not neutrality but hostility toward religion."

Thus the faith life of the entire community, Christian or otherwise, is threatened by what is being called a "neutral" stance toward religion, but which is in fact bias against religion. As Hamburger asserts, "Although suggestive of nondiscrimination, these ideas [of neutrality] perpetuate separation's discrimination against churches or distinct religions by depriving them and their adherents of ordinary rights and relations to government that do not constitute an establishment."[71] Such legislation is not only hostile to religion, as Chief Justice Burger concluded, but, ironically, violates the Free Exercise Clause, the very principle that the legislation supposedly tries to uphold. The only ones who delight in such "neutrality" are Enlightened secularists, who know that what the Court is providing them is a public square in which their perspective has won the day.

Establishment vs. Free Exercise

One might suppose that at times, a conflict might ensue between legislation that would tend to support the Establishment Clause and legislation that would support the Free Exercise Clause. In such cases, laws that guaranteed the preservation of the one might have to be cut back so that the greater good provided by the other might be maintained. If so, to which clause should there be given priority? Which clause supports the greater good? In other words, does the Establishment Clause exist so as to preserve the free exercise of religion, or does the Free Exercise Clause exist only so long as it does not risk the establishment of a specific religion?

The answer is clear from examining the purposes of the Founding Fathers: They wanted to support the free exercise of religion, which had been forbidden in the countries from which they had come. Thus, the Establishment Clause was composed to prevent the state from erecting one church as the state church, giving that church a dominant position in society, and reducing other religions and those who practiced them to a lesser position or even preventing them from exercising their religious rights altogether. The Establishment Clause expressed a principle legislated only because of its value as an instrument serving the free exercise of religion. Or as Mooney puts it: "Separation *ordinarily* promotes religious freedom, and is defensible only so long as it does so."[72]

An example of how the two clauses comfortably interrelate may be seen from the long-standing practice of the chaplaincy program that exists in our armed services. According to Mooney, "Strict church-state separation would mean the elimination of this program, thereby seriously limiting the free exercise of religion by making it impossible to provide opportunities

---

[71] Hamburger, *Separation*, 190.

[72] Mooney, *Religion and the American Dream*,105.

for worship and instruction." Such a policy, according to Mooney, "has never been followed or even advocated." Mooney concludes:

> As in the case of the armed services, the state may do a great deal which appears superficially to aid religion. "It may do these things, not because impartial aid to religion or encouragement of religion is an appropriate object of government, but because insistence upon strict separation would limit religious freedom and would thus violate neutrality." Government neutrality aims therefore at maximizing religious freedom and requires only that degree of separation which is compatible with maximum freedom.[73]

Our Supreme Court has, however, unfortunately chosen in recent years to make its main object of concern the enforcement of the Establishment Clause rather than the preservation of the rights granted by the Free Exercise Clause. An example of this in practice: the Court has decreed that public expression of prayer or Bible reading in public schools is not permitted because such activity would be coercive upon "impressionable young minds."[74] But as a result of this decision, children are not free to exercise their religious rights in a public forum.

The complexity and intriguing nature of this opinion begins to appear when one examines this curious matter of coercion. While coercion of various sorts is part of everyday life and is necessarily and inevitably injected into the classroom by its nature as an enclosed, forced environment for educational purposes, the Supreme Court seems fixated on the presence of coercion when it comes to matters religious. But students are forced to go to school until age sixteen; they are forced to accept an education in what are considered essential tools for knowledge—communication, trade, math, and science; they must accept basic disciplinary structures and procedures, or if not, disciplinary consequences, even to the point of being dismissed; they are sometimes even forced to be involved in extracurricular activities, seen as a desirable part of the process of growth of a healthy, well-rounded person. But the Court forbids them to have formal prayer presented or merely suggested to them, even for voluntary consideration, lest coercion be implied. Two questions are in order: Why is religious education not a part of the development of a well-rounded person—and who makes

---

[73] Ibid., 105–6. Mooney's citation is from Wilber G. Katz of the University of Chicago Law School, in his essay "The Case for Religious Liberty," in John Cogley, ed., *Religion in America* (Meridian, 1958), 100. What Mooney calls "neutrality" I would argue is not really "neutrality" since the government aims at "maximizing religious freedom."

[74] *Grand Rapids School District v. Ball* 473 U.S. 373 (1985), a 7–2 decision, in *FindLaw.* Justice Brennan delivered the opinion of the Court, sec. II A.

that decision—and why this extreme fear of using coercion regarding religious matters, with little or no concern over the fact that coercion is exercised regarding other matters?

Though the answer the Court gives invokes the demands of the First Amendment, such demands are hard to substantiate. Where is there any indication in the First Amendment of a concern for "impressionable young minds"? Practically all agree that the Framers of the First Amendment could not even have had public school education of young people in mind when they wrote that amendment, since education at that time was handled at the state level, and was largely religiously sponsored. One would have to argue at best that the Court's opinion is a valid interpretation or extension of the intentions of the Framers, updating their purposes to today's needs. Whether the Court has a right to legislate on the basis of such interpretation is in itself open to question and contested, as many scholars argue that by doing this the Court usurps the role of the legislature and thereby commits unacceptable "judicial activism."

Some purists argue that the Supreme Court has no right to exceed the literal meaning of the amendment as understood and intended by those who wrote it. The basis for such a position resides in a philosophy that understands law to have no built-in evolutionary principle. This position has its merits. It frees the populous from arbitrary manipulation of the law by activist judges with their own political agendas, or by minority groups who are unable to get faddist agendas implemented by ordinary legislative means. But this position may also have its weaknesses. It would seem to mean that many laws would become useless in a short time, and that legislators would be unduly and unnecessarily burdened to update previously enacted laws. The teachings of Christ might not even be allowed to survive to this day by such rulings, since when Jesus proclaimed his message, he probably did not have in mind situations that would arise two thousand years later.

The problem, as we see it, is not so much that the Supreme Court should not be allowed to interpret the Constitution in the light of the needs and situations that arise today, but that it should not be allowed to do so by creating law that is not a legitimate interpretation of the Constitution; in other words, not be allowed to create law that so deviates from the meaning of the Constitution as to violate, contradict, or thwart the original intention. But that is exactly what many scholars argue the Court is doing today when it so extends the range of the Establishment Clause that it violates the free exercise of religion.

Due Exercise of Free Exercise Clause

The Free Exercise Clause prohibits the Congress from interfering with the free exercise of religion. The Framers recognized the right of the individual to be free from outside coercion in choosing religious beliefs and in expressing religious convictions. They held that preserving such a right was necessary, if there was truly to be a society founded on life, liberty, and the pursuit of happiness.

But they also recognized that maintaining the free exercise of religion was essential to the flourishing of life in the public forum; they knew, as Mooney points out, that "the well-being of society depended upon a body of shared religious beliefs—the nature of man, his place in the cosmos, his destiny, and his conduct toward his fellowmen." These statesmen believed the churches were important to the well-being of society and that they "should flourish in America because . . . all churches held and taught in common the 'essentials of every religion,' and that these essentials were not only relevant but vital for the health of the nation." Thus, the Founders "wanted to formulate a principle that would guarantee the participation of all churches in the common social unity of the republic" for the sake of preserving the well-being of the republic, while at the same time not infringing on those religious tenets distinctive to each.[75]

Conclusion

It is this free exercise of religion that the Supreme Court has violated by its exaggerated concern for legislating government neutrality through the enforcement of the Establishment Clause. Neutrality implies impartiality, noninvolvement, or disinterest in sides or outcomes. But the Free Exercise Clause was not written to establish impartiality toward religion, but precisely the opposite: it was intended to favor the exercise of religion, though not one rather than another—religion in general, as an ingredient important to the well-being of the individual and of the entire fabric of society.

The Framers would have understood such neutrality as in fact undermining the best interests of society and would have opposed it. They wanted public space to be open and broad enough for all religions to flourish. The point was that the state was not to sanction or adhere to any specific religion in such a way that its actions would be detrimental to the well-being of others, and lead to the instability and social and political unrest previously known in Europe. But the role of the state was, indeed, to sanction the religious dimension of life because that was the sole ultimate guarantee of the well-being of society. Thus the state was to be benevolent toward religions and those who practiced them.

---

[75] Mooney, *Religion and the American Dream*, 97–98, 101; Mooney is citing from Sidney E. Mead, *The Lively Experiment: The Shaping of Christianity in America* (Harper & Row, 1963), 66.

The Supreme Court, by removing the public elementary and secondary school classrooms from the realm of the free exercise of religion, has in fact created a public delimitation of the free exercise of religion, and thereby unconstitutionally sought to remove the free exercise of religion from the public domain. Not only, then, is this a deprivation of the rights granted to Americans by the First Amendment, but it also sends signals contrary to the intentions of the amendment by implying that religion is a purely private matter and has no public relevance.

In that sense, the Supreme Court has created a public arena that is antithetical to religious thinking and ultimately a-theistic in its temperament. A world that relegates religion to the private sphere does not in fact remain neutral toward religion, but inevitably gives preferential treatment to nonreligious viewpoints. As religion is removed more and more from life in the public order, nonreligiously oriented thinking increasingly assumes dominance in the explanation of public policy and the resolution of public issues. The divorce of religion from society inevitably makes the world unreceptive to religious discussion and ultimately antagonistic to religious expression.

The mood of modern America amply illustrates the veracity of this perception. Rarely is God allowed to enter into popular discussion of current issues. Secularists are on a rampage to remove every consideration of a religious perspective from modern discourse. Hollywood is especially in the forefront of this movement, and secularists seemed to be succeeding with unquestioned authority—until the unbelievable success of Mel Gibson's movie "The Passion of the Christ," released by design on Ash Wednesday 2004.

What that movie so eloquently evoked was the views of the vast numbers of the silent religious majority living in the United States, who suddenly had a spokesperson for their convictions. They ran to see the movie in rampaging forces! Everyone in the country was shocked. In fact, the movie's success with almost every religious group in the country was remarkable. To see evangelical Protestants going to a movie depicting a Catholic representation of the Christ seemed never to be possible. Though many Jews were not sympathetic to the depiction of Christ's death in the movie, even accusing Gibson of anti-Semitism, others admitted that the movie largely represented the events as presented in the Gospels, especially John's. The point was: don't blame Gibson, blame John!

The division over the movie was a premonition of what was to come in the November 2004 presidential elections: those who regularly attended church or synagogue tended to support the movie, while those only loosely connected to religion or those who were atheists tended to reject it, just as the religiously inclined tended to vote for George Bush, while those less inclined voted for John Kerry. In fact, Kerry was the first Catholic presidential nominee not to capture the vote of Catholics who regularly attended Mass.

While the proreligionists may have suffered a setback in the 2008 elections, as, for example, the pro-life movement seemed to be overwhelmed by the large election of pro-choice candidates, the results of the 2010 election show once again that the pro-life movement is alive and well, and that traditional values may be resurging. Whether these events indicate a temporary or long-lasting backlash against the secularist tendencies of Western society that are so militantly marching to destroy the Christian way of life of Western Europe and North America remains to be seen.

As matters stand now, however, many Christians have unwittingly become victims of the secularist trends of the postmodern world, so that the secularist agenda is now comfortably situated in our lives. The decisions of the Supreme Court in recent times have had an extraordinary role to play in augmenting this secularist movement. Through its decisions, the Court has undoubtedly been a paramount force for establishing the Enlightened mentality, because it has increasingly legitimated the secular mentality and provided us with the lingua franca of our daily lives. That is why the role of the Supreme Court in America in mapping this secularist trend is so significant. The Court's Enlightened decisions, especially those that have moved faith and religious values to the margins of society, have in effect made Americans members of an Enlightened world. The fact that the secularist mentality has taken hold of so many of us Christians is evidenced by the fact that we largely seek the values and goals of the secular world just as much as non-Christians do. Some of the results of the 2008 election showed how much in line many American Catholics are with popular trends in society. Many Catholics, especially our politicians, have learned to apply the freedom of conscience principle of Vatican II to their lives, in such a way that they consider themselves good practicing Catholics while publicly supporting anti-Catholic teachings. This evidences how well secular values have entered into our lives. Catholics often seem no more eager to redress injustices and erect a culture counter to the secular world than the most secular in society. Many Christians seem to have bought into the values of the secular world, so that we are not so much concerned to fulfill the ideals of Christ's teachings as to win success in the eyes of the world.

To return to our point of departure: as the Declaration of Independence makes so clear, fundamental human values are rooted in the human being's relationship to the Transcendent, and without that relationship, there is no ultimate basis for establishing or justifying human values. The loss of the transcendent dimension of life, therefore, is not simply destructive of the life of the Church because it increasingly secularizes the world in which Christians live, and thereby imposes a secularizing force upon them; it also destroys the basis for maintaining fundamental human values in general, and thereby leads to a breakdown of the order and harmony of life in society. Today's crime statistics bear this out. As Americans and as Catholics, and in spite of the success of the Supreme Court up to now in secularizing our lives, we must seek to return the Transcendent to its rightful place as an integral part of life in the public square, or we are destined to see a movement toward secularization even more destructive than that we have already known.

CHAPTER NINE

Church in Crisis

"It seems certain to me that very hard times await the Church. Her own crisis has as yet hardly begun."*

IS THERE CRISIS in the Church today? Hardly anyone would deny it. In fact, crisis has become part of the vocabulary of almost anyone who studies the Church today.

The idea of crisis has become no less intense with the advent of Pope Benedict XVI. Controversy will probably rage for some years over whether his installation has aggravated or lessened the crisis. In fact, one may suggest, with slight fear of exaggeration, that the Church has a crisis of major proportions, and that only by the grace of God will it be overcome. But it is not exactly clear what in fact the nature of the crisis is. It depends on whom you talk to. If anything, the new Pope has probably muddied the waters on this question. Though, as we shall see, while he has made it abundantly known that he sees the Church in crisis, his understanding of the crisis differs from the usual, and his solution may be exceedingly different as well.

While the perception that the Church is in crisis is a truism today, it was not always so.

Before Vatican II (1962–1965), the last ecumenical council of the Church, no one ever said the Church was in crisis. There was crisis addressed at the Council, but not in the Church. In *Gaudium et Spes*, the bishops stated that the "human race is passing through a new stage of its history" where it is undergoing "a true social and cultural transformation," which the bishops called a "crisis of growth" (*GS* 4–5). The modern world is experiencing "new forms of social and psychological slavery" as well as "imbalances" that lead to "mutual distrust, enmities, conflicts, and hardships" (*GS* 4, 8). According to the bishops, this crisis of growth inevitably

* Benedict XVI, in Moynihan, *Let God's Light Shine*, 144.

"has repercussions on man's religious life as well": because of it, there is "spiritual agitation," "many people are shaken" in their convictions, and "growing numbers of people are abandoning religion in practice" (*GS* 5, 7). Finally, in the same document, though in the context of a discussion on war and peace, the bishops speak of "the whole human family" having "reached an hour of supreme crisis in its advance toward maturity" (*GS* 77).

One reason the bishops chose not to speak of crisis specifically in the Church is due to the fact that "Church" has a double meaning: it is both a divine and a human reality. To speak of the Church in crisis risks implying that the Church as a divine reality is in crisis, which would be completely out of the question. (The same problem occurs when discussing sin: the Church never says that the Church sins, but only that members of the Church sin. Pope Paul VI edited the documents of Vatican II carefully before they became official, to make sure that that distinction was maintained.)

While the bishops never said the Church was in crisis, they certainly said that the Church shared in the world's problems: "The joys and the hopes, the griefs and the anxieties of the men of this age, especially those who are poor or in any way afflicted, these too are the joys and hopes, the griefs and anxieties of the followers of Christ" (*GS* 1). They spoke of serious problems in the Church. Vatican II, for example, speaks of "extremely serious errors" that "are gaining currency" and are beginning to "undermine the foundations of religion."[1] One of these errors is atheism, which Vatican II considered one of "the most serious problems of this age" (*GS* 19); another is the split between faith and reason, considered one of "the most serious errors of our age" (*GS* 43). But that was not *crisis.*

It was not long after Vatican II, however, before writers started speaking directly of crisis in the Church, though at first rarely. The earliest use of the term that I can find (though the author does not appear to be coining an expression) is by a non-Christian named Raymond Williams, writing from London in 1967 for *The Nation.* His essay, "Letter from London: The Catholic Crisis," already gives us some understanding of what the crisis is. Writing after the renowned English theologian, Charles Davis, left the Church to become an Anglican, Williams speaks of the "continuing crisis within the Catholic Church in Britain," referring to the tension "between a cautious and conservative Church hierarchy, dragging its feet over implementing recent Vatican Council reforms, and an articulate and progressive section of the laity, concerned with freedom of speech and of conscience, and in general with a kind of modernization." Perhaps revealing his political tendencies, Williams sees this "crisis in the Catholic Church" as part of a "deeper crisis," the "long crisis of belief in advanced capitalist societies"

[1] Paul VI, *Apostolicam Actuositatem,* November 18, 1965.

between a conservative and corrupt capitalism and a New Left "Socialist humanism" in their concerns for the poor. His use of "crisis" here is reflective of the social and political struggle of the '60s, where the institutional Church is seen as part of the larger problem of the lack of a "connection of Christian action and organization with radical politics," and the need for the Church to become the "bearer of Christianity's primary message and mission of social revolution."[2]

Shortly after, in November of the same year, an article along the same lines written by the historian David J. O'Brien appeared in a Chicago monthly called *New City*. While O'Brien does not speak specifically of crisis in the Church but only of the "Catholic crisis," this is again seen as part of a larger social crisis, in a way that parallels Williams's view.

O'Brien sees the Church confronting the larger "American crisis," and torn in the tension over whether the Church should become assimilated into an American culture that appeared to be "a vicious society, which necessarily excluded the poor from power and inadvertently but necessarily devoured men's souls," or remain aloof. The problem is that different factions within the Church chose either assimilation or aloofness, and the result was visible "as the crisis of the 1960s deepened, when nuns and priests joined picket lines to receive insults and rocks thrown by Catholic laymen."[3] O'Brien understands the "divisions" and "paradoxes" and "contradictions"[4] occurring at that time in American Catholicism as happening in the midst of "a cultural crisis" where the "matrix of meaning itself has broken down."[5]

The first Catholic priest and theologian I can find who spoke of crisis in the Church was the celebrated French Jesuit traditionalist named Henri de Lubac.

In an address given at Saint Louis University in St. Louis, Missouri, on May 29, 1969, de Lubac, in a way reflective of the views of the two previous authors, expressed that the "church in crisis" is part of a larger "crisis of civilization." For de Lubac, this crisis is "more acute and more accelerated than those of other periods of history," and is entering into a "new phase" that is fast becoming associated with "the word 'destruction.' "[6] A "violent crisis" has ensued, he says, especially among the young, generated by a "crisis of

[2] Raymond Williams, "Letter from London: The Catholic Crisis," *The Nation* 205 (July 17, 1967): 51–52.

[3] David J. O'Brien, "American Catholics in an Age of Crisis," *New City* (November 1967), revised and reprinted in David J. O'Brien, *The Renewal of American Catholicism* (New York: Oxford University Press, 1972), 9.

[4] O'Brien, *Renewal*, 9.

[5] O'Brien, *Renewal*, 36–37. O'Brien takes the two quotes from Herbert W. Richardson, *Toward an American Theology* (New York: 1967), ix.

[6] The address was published under the title "The Church in Crisis," in *Theology Digest* 17 (Winter 1969): 312–25; here, reference to p. 312.

intelligence . . . reduced to computer-thinking" that "becomes a principle of oppression for man." A "violent revolt" ensues that, on the one hand, exalts an irrational meaningless life in a meaningless world, and on the other, "criticizes the alienating results of rationalized society." A "universal confrontation" occurs between the forces of "nihilism" and "the structures of established society" and its "intellectual patrimony."

This confrontation is also taking place "at the very heart of Catholicism," de Lubac argues, operating "with great force both within and against the church," because the "same spirit of confrontation" has turned so many believers, "fascinated by this modern world . . . against the community to which they belong." Authority in the Church is seen as "hostile" and "tyrannical"; declarations of the magisterium are seen as "abusive, bitterly debated, and at times rejected entirely" by "sons of the church" who, "urged on by an unknown and unknowing crowd, become the accusers of their mother and their brothers." In such a mentality, Christian faith is reduced to an "out-dated . . . fact of culture." Divine revelation becomes a "series of thoughts and interpretations which are entirely human," and "the unity of revealed truth" is lost. What is happening, according to de Lubac, is a faith dissolving itself and becoming "unable to engender anything whatever," and a "community" that is "incapable of radiating or of attracting others."

What is needed to renew and revitalize the Church, according to de Lubac, is "an energetic revival of faith" that will "liberate the Christian conscience from a morbid negativism which is eroding it," "from an inferiority complex which is paralyzing it," and "from a web of ambiguity which is smothering it."[7] Above all, according to de Lubac, the unity of the Church is "wounded" when the "center of unity [the successor of Peter] becomes the target of the most impassioned attacks . . . on any point whatever." For de Lubac, the need to maintain Catholic unity is "prior to and subsequent to all legitimate discussion . . . of the best means of governing the church at a given time and in given circumstances."[8] This is exactly the conclusion at which we arrive in part 4 (see pp. 475–544) of this work.

"The crisis for the church is one of major importance." So argued the renowned Jesuit theologian Avery Dulles in his lecture at Saint Louis University on October 8, 1969.[9] He even argues that John XXIII "unquestionably contributed to the present crisis" when he reoriented the Church in a "radically new direction" toward "dialog" and "involvement in . . . the modern world."

Crisis here for Dulles mainly results from the outdated modes of operation of a traditionalist magisterium, and a modern world that is unwilling

---

7 Ibid., 314–18.

8 Ibid., 324–25.

9 Avery Dulles, S.J., "The Contemporary Magisterium," *Theology Digest* 17 (Winter 1969): 299.

to accept them. The conflict is "between the current style of operation of the Catholic magisterium and the decision-making processes that have come into general usage in modern secular society."[10] The magisterium continues to promote a concept of doctrine, as developed especially in the nineteenth century, that is abstract, metaphysical, absolutist propositions of "revealed truth," whereas modern society's approach to truth is self-critical, relativist, particular, and individual, "concrete and contextual."[11] The crisis became openly manifest when the post–*Humanae Vitae* magisterium could no longer assume "the implicit and unquestioning confidence of all Catholic priests and faithful."[12]

Dulles asserts that the Church must continue to "function as a living community of faith and witness," and cannot do so without being able to "say within certain limits what views and attitudes are required, or permitted, or excluded, by Christian revelation."[13] Nevertheless, for Dulles, the major need for the Church is to develop a magisterium that understands Tradition as primarily open to the future (à la Jürgen Moltmann).[14] The magisterium must be "reshaped to meet the demands of our time." "Modernization" would take on a positive meaning here, as representing "the new ecclesiological possibilities which our age affords." Based on *Lumen Gentium*'s thinking that "the teaching office of pope and bishops" is set "within the total context of the people of God as a dynamic communion in the life of grace," and where infallibility resides in "the entire church," the "faithful as a whole" should be allowed to "participate in the magisterium."[15]

The above views seem to reflect a less conservative period in Dulles's thinking, when he also emphasized the thirteenth-century role of the "scholarly magisterium" that recovered the views of Clement of Alexandria and Origen that "teachers stand, in their own way, in the apostolic succession and therefore need not look exclusively to the hierarchical magisterium for purely apostolic doctrine."[16] The later Dulles found the traditional role of the magisterium much more congenial.

The idea of the Church in crisis was soon to come into increasingly standard parlance through the writings of many renowned historians, scholars of the Scripture and theologians. In 1973, the priest theologian Richard P.

10 Ibid., 302–3.
11 Ibid.
12 Ibid., 299.
13 Ibid., 299–300.
14 Ibid., 310. The magisterium's "primary task will be less to preserve what is already explicit in the teaching of the past . . . than to make men sensitive to the breathing of the Spirit in the world today and to open their minds to the future to which God is beckoning his people" (p. 310).
15 Ibid., 304–5.
16 Ibid., 300–301.

McBrien published *The Remaking of the Church*, a work we will shortly discuss at greater length. Here already he speaks of "the current ecclesiastical crisis" or of the "present crisis within the Catholic Church," which he sees as created by the opposition between those who would implement the reform movements in the Church generated by Vatican II and the resistance to that reform by the hierarchy. He describes the 1973 state of the Church as "an organization marked by excessive conflict, polarization, and a debilitating drainage of human resources." Raymond Brown, S.S., published *Biblical Reflections on Crises Facing the Church* in 1975, and Avery Dulles, S.J., speaks of a "crisis of identity" in the Church in his book *The Resilient Church* in 1977.[17]

To my recollection, the notion of a Church in crisis did not really gain prominence until Andrew Greeley's series of articles entitled "The Crisis in American Catholicism" published in 1976 (and later in his book, *Crisis in the Church*).[18] Greeley, a priest sociologist, had very quickly made a name for himself by his strong and biting attacks on the American bishops in the early '70s, stating, for example, that after the synod of bishops in 1970 the "credibility of ecclesiastical authority" was "battered," that the Church looked "ridiculous," and that some bishops were "quite devoid of any sense of personal integrity" and would "reward competent work with a knife in the back."[19] By 1972 he saw the striking change in the Catholic mind-set toward accepting abortion as "one more sign of the crisis in the culture and structure of American Catholicism."[20]

In the 1976 series Greeley made a number of statements and revelations that were quite shocking at the time, such as "the Roman Catholic Church in the United States has been shaken by a major crisis since the end of the Second Vatican Council" and was in such "disarray," "being torn apart by internal forces it cannot control," that its very survival was in doubt.[21] Nearly two years later he added that we were in "one of the worst disasters in the history of Christendom."[22] His conclusions were based on the number of men who had left the priesthood, the seminaries that had closed, the

---

[17] Richard P. McBrien, *The Remaking of the Church: An Agenda for Reform* (New York: Harper & Row, 1973), 17, 14, 71; Raymond E. Brown, S.S., *Biblical Reflections on Crises Facing the Church* (New York: Paulist, 1975); Avery Dulles, S.J., *The Resilient Church* (Garden City, NY: Doubleday, 1977), 12.

[18] I read the series in the Rochester, NY, diocesan paper *Courier-Journal* (*CJ*), April 7, 14, 21, 28, and May 5, 1976; Andrew M. Greeley, *Crisis in the Church* (Chicago: Thomas More, 1979).

[19] Andrew M. Greeley, "After the Synod," *America* 125 (November 20, 1971): 424–26.

[20] William C. McCready and Andrew M. Greeley, "The End of American Catholicism?," *America* 127 (October 28, 1972): 338.

[21] Greeley, *CJ*, April 7, 1976, 10.

[22] Greeley, *CJ*, January 18, 1978, 8.

decline in Catholic school enrollment and Mass attendance, and the number leaving the Church.

Perhaps the greatest and most controversial revelation in the series were Greeley's figures on the high percentage of Catholic laypersons—83%—who in 1974, within only six years after its publication, rejected the Church's teaching on birth control as set forth by Paul VI in his encyclical *Humanae Vitae*, and the high percentage of American Catholic women—68%—who were "practicing some form of unapproved birth control."[23] It was in this study that Greeley also noted the substantial decline in the acceptance of the authority of the hierarchy, and drew the shocking conclusion that almost all the decline was attributable to the rejection of the encyclical's teaching on the pill: "The pill, in other words, introduced a crisis in the Catholic sexual ethic," as a result of which Catholics "have substantially reduced their devotion and loyalty to the Church." Thus the encyclical was "a disaster in its effect for American Catholicism."[24] Greeley continued publishing dire remarks about the consequences of the rejection of the encyclical, such as his 1979 statement that "American Catholicism was in a crisis of decline of the sort that had not been seen since the French Revolution or perhaps even the Reformation."[25]

The year 1985 seems a critical one for awareness of crisis in the Church. More and more lower-level Catholic leaders, theologians, and publishers were now willing to speak of crisis in the Church. Robert Johnson, president of the National Federation of Priests' Council, stated in the mid-'80s that "priesthood is in crisis. The vocation of the ordained priest is not what it used to be. The data tells us that. Our own experience tells us that also." The crisis is described as "a crisis in numbers," a drop in vocations that was especially troubling in view of the fact that the number of those whom the priests were ordained to serve was multiplying greatly.[26]

Edward C. Herr, while not using the word "crisis" in a report on "The State of the Church" in 1985, all but affirmed one. He stated that, whereas in a similar report in 1983 there were "hopes that a relatively stable and tranquil period" was about to arrive in the Church, he must now report those hopes were "naïve," that "the tensions and turmoil have increased and show no signs of ebbing."[27]

But even in 1985, when more and more people began to speak of the Church in crisis, the hierarchy never did. For example, Bishop James Malone

---

23 Greeley, *CJ*, April 14, 1976, 21.

24 Ibid.

25 Greeley, *CJ*, April 25, 1979, 17.

26 Edward C. Herr, "The Catholic Priesthood," *Overview* 19 (published August 1985), 1, citing a report in *NFPC News Notes* of March 1984.

27 Edward C. Herr, "The State of the Church," *Overview*, May 1985, 1.

of Youngstown, Ohio, when he was president of the National Conference of Catholic Bishops, submitted a report to the Vatican in the summer of 1985 on the state of the Church in the United States, in preparation for the extraordinary synod of bishops that met in Rome November 25–December 8 of that year, on the twentieth anniversary of the end of Vatican II. In his report, the bishop stated that the Church in the United States was "basically sound." Malone makes mention of "confusion," "abuses," "false ideas," and "difficulties" in various areas of Church life, but not of crisis.[28] The hierarchy were using the word "crisis" regarding the drift of American culture, but still not about the Church. But they were being criticized for "looking at the Church in the United States through 'rose-colored glasses.'"[29]

Then an amazing thing occurred that year. Someone whom no one ever expected to use the term "crisis" in a way that applied it to the Church did so, and with some frequency: Joseph Cardinal Ratzinger, then prefect of the Vatican's Congregation for the Doctrine of the Faith, one of the most respected and powerful figures in the Church, and now Pope Benedict XVI. An Italian reporter conducted an extensive interview with the cardinal and published it as a book.[30] The interview showed the cardinal deeply distressed by what had happened to the Church since the end of Vatican II, with language that clearly expressed it. Where so many had expected a period of great hope for the Church after Vatican II, he argues, the opposite occurred: the time after the Council has led to "dissension," "self-destruction," "boredom and discouragement," "a progressive process of decadence . . . whose catastrophic consequences are already incontestable."[31]

Ratzinger saw crises of various types just about everywhere in the "post-Vatican II" Church, although he rejected the use of that term: "There is no 'pre-' or 'post-' conciliar Church: there is but one, unique Church." States Ratzinger, "My diagnosis is that we are dealing with an authentic crisis and that it must be treated and cured."[32]

What is the nature of the crisis? It is a crisis of "*faith in the triune God* in his Persons," a "crisis of 'original sin,'" "the crisis of the understanding of the Church, on ecclesiology" [that is, the Church being understood as a "human construction"], "the crisis of the Church in the Western world," "a

---

[28] James Malone, "Vatican II and the Postconciliar Era in the U.S. Church," *Origins* 15 (September 26, 1985): 227, 230–31.

[29] *National Catholic Register*, September 29, 1985, 8, expressing the view of the Catholic ethician Germain Grisez.

[30] Joseph Cardinal Ratzinger with Vittorio Messori, *The Ratzinger Report: An Exclusive Interview on the State of the Church*, trans. Salvator Attanasio and Graham Harrison (San Francisco: Ignatius, 1985).

[31] Ibid., 29–30.

[32] Ibid., 35.

crisis of faith and of the Church," a crisis of the "*men of the Church*," religious orders "seem to be shaken by an identity crisis," a "*crisis of trust in the dogma* proposed by the Magisterium," the *crisis of confidence in Scripture* as it is read by the Church," and a "*crisis*—likewise grave—*of the morality* proposed by the Magisterium"—against all of which there is the need to "rediscover the courage of nonconformism in the face of the trends of the affluent world."[33] Put simply, the crises seem to be of faith—of fidelity to the Church in the teaching authority of the hierarchy, in acceptance of the Scriptures and of the traditional moral teaching of the Church. Each of these crises is caused by a radical departure from the acceptance of the Church's traditional teachings, values, or truths.

The consequences of the crises are many: "Catechesis is . . . exposed to dismemberment and to constantly changing experiments"; the "traditional faith of the Church no longer seems justified by critical exegesis but appears only as an obstacle to the authentic 'modern' understanding of Christianity"; Christology is beginning "to lose the dimension of the divine" based on a purely human conception of Jesus and "a project of salvation that is merely historical, human"; there is "an attempt to transform man, to manipulate him as one does every other 'thing': he is nothing but a product planned according to one's pleasure."[34]

No one had ever itemized so many crises in the Church. And the fact that it was now being done openly by the second most important figure in the Vatican meant that one could now admit that the Catholic Church was officially at a critical juncture in its life. From then on, the fact that the Church is in crisis has been almost universally held.

But it might be wise today to reflect on one important statement Ratzinger mentioned regarding crisis: the fact that it "must be treated and cured." What exactly does that mean? So far as I can see in *The Ratzinger Report*, it means that the "healing process" is found in "a reading of sacred Scripture in and with the Church" and a "return" to the teachings of Vatican II, understood not "as merely a point of departure from which one gets further away by running forward"—as those who speak of the "spirit" of Vatican II would do—but as "a reality that must be fully accepted" and "as a base on which to build solidly."[35] We must "*return to the authentic texts of the original Vatican II*," and "defend the true tradition of the Church today," which means "to defend the Council": "We must remain faithful to the *today* of the Church, not the *yesterday* or *tomorrow*. And this today of the Church is the documents of Vatican II, without *reservations* that amputate

---

[33] Ibid., 77, 80, 45, 43, 44, 55, 55, 71, 74, 83, 114.

[34] Ibid., 72, 74, 77, 84.

[35] Ibid., 118, 34.

them and without *arbitrariness* that distorts them."[36] So far, Pope Benedict has remained strikingly faithful to these principles.

Since the spring of 2002, whenever the word "crisis" is used, it almost always refers to the major sex-abuse scandal that came to light in the Church that year. But that scandal is only the tip of the iceberg. The roots of the crisis go much deeper. Indeed, this book aims to show that the roots of crisis go back to the consequences of the gradual disjunction of faith from reason, which as we have seen began as early as the fourteenth century. Here we want to focus on the pre-Enlightenment effects of the Protestant Reformation in the sixteenth century, and look to the ambiguities that followed in the theology of the Church after Vatican II that contributed to the intensifying of the faith-reason disjunction.

Scholasticism Pro-and-Con

The Protestant Reformation constituted the most significant rupture to the integrity of the life of the Catholic Church since the break with the Eastern Orthodox Church in 1054. Perhaps no one thing characterizes what the Protestant Reformation stands for more than the rejection of the nature, role, and authority of the institutional Church, and in this way the pre-Enlightenment mentality of the Protestant Reformation was already evident. But Protestantism had more problems with the Church than authority.

We may recall, from our discussion in chapter 3, that up until the thirteenth century in the Christian world, philosophy as a rational field of thought distinct from theology did not exist:

> As a rough generalization, therefore, one may say that the philosophic ideas of the early Christian writers were Platonic or neo-Platonic in character (with an admixture of Stoicism) and that the Platonic tradition continued for long to dominate Christian thought from the philosophic viewpoint. In saying this, however, one must remember that the Christian writers did not make any clear distinction between theology and philosophy: they aimed rather at presenting the Christian wisdom or "philosophy" in a very wide sense, which was primarily theological, though it contained philosophical elements in the strict sense.[37]

What did exist, however, was theology as the rational investigation of revelation, and included in that theologizing, or perhaps allied with it, were the operations of reason seen as supportive of both theology and revelation.

---

[36] Ibid., 31.

[37] Frederick Copleston, S.J., *A History of Philosophy*, vol. 3, pt. 1, *Mediaeval Philosophy: Augustine to Bonaventure* (Garden City, NY: Doubleday Image, 1962 [1950]), 29.

In this way, there was a dimension of rational investigation of the faith that was certainly philosophical. Again, Copleston explains:

> Starting with the endeavour to understand the data of revelation, so far as this is possible to human reason, early mediaevals . . . applied rational dialectic to the mysteries of faith in an attempt to understand them. In this way they laid the foundations of Scholastic theology, since the application of reason to theological data, in the sense of the data of revelation, is and remains theology: it does not become philosophy. . . . So far they were certainly acting as theologians, but such men, who did not make, it is true, any very clear delimitation of the spheres of philosophy and theology, certainly pursued philosophical themes and developed philosophical arguments.[38]

In this sense, there was a synthesis of reason and the Christian faith. Thus it was generally held that the mind knew through revelation who God was, but that one could also know through reason that there is a God. Faith, however, arrived at a greater knowledge of God, such as the Trinity, that did not conflict with what was known by reason, but transcended that knowledge to a deeper and more complete understanding of who God is. Thus Christian writers were people of faith: they were theologians, secondarily; they were philosophers, incidentally. But the important point for our discussion here is that, on the whole, faith and reason worked together: they were compatible; they were mutually acceptable.

With the discovery in the late twelfth and early thirteenth centuries of the Aristotelian philosophy, which presented an integral understanding of reality independently of revelation, philosophy came of age. The harmony that had perennially existed between faith and reason suffered a serious blow, because the Aristotelian system seemed to explain all reality from the powers of reason alone. It was Thomas Aquinas, however, who showed that this was not so. It was his great achievement in the thirteenth century to synthesize Aristotelian philosophy with the more complete truths of the Christian revelation, and Scholasticism as a movement represented that synthesis of reason and faith. As we have already noted, it was the fourteenth-century movement started by William of Ockham—nominalism—that tore apart that happy synthesis, and it is this nominalistic spirit that is represented in Martin Luther's thought. In Luther's rejection of the Church, he rejected everything with which the Church was identified, including Scholasticism.

Scholasticism as a system of philosophy and theology was already under attack by Christian humanists in the fifteenth century for its recondite terminology, its abstruse language, its heavy emphasis upon abstraction, its

---

[38] Ibid., 18.

seemingly useless subdivision of thought, its convoluted form of argumentation, its remoteness from concrete reality.[39] Originally designed in theology as a rigorous method of disputation over biblical questions, Scholasticism had gradually begun to wean itself from contact with the Bible. Scholasticism became caricaturized by its rigorously logical argumentation over subtle abstract philosophical questions and highly refined terminology, resulting in a "rigid formalism" where the emphasis was upon "the mechanics" of knowledge "rather than on an intellectual grasp of reality."[40] The thirteenth-century discovery of Aristotle's compendium of philosophical knowledge encompassing the cosmos had a major impact on theology. Scholasticism "came face to face with a world-system, a *Weltanschauung*, which relied completely on reason and appeared almost entirely at variance with the Christian faith." Scholastics "were faced with doctrines such as the Prime Mover, eternal motion, denial of creation and providence, uncertainty on the immortality and spirituality of the soul, and a morality based on reason alone," which challenged the value of the Christian revelation.[41]

It was Thomas Aquinas's great achievement to bring Aristotelian philosophy into harmony with Christian theology: "For Thomas Aquinas, the basic problem was to discover how as a Christian scholar he could order anew the whole structure of Christian wisdom in such a way that pagan philosophy would be made tributary to the Christian faith." Aquinas achieved his goal, integrating both philosophical truths, such as proof for the existence of God, and theological truths, such as knowledge of God as a Trinity, into his system. Yet in doing so, some argued that Aquinas's philosophy overshadowed his theology. At times, Aquinas seemed to make Christianity a Christian philosophy by bringing "Aristotelian naturalism and metaphysics into the heart of theology."[42] By emphasizing how much reason could explain what had previously been known through faith and revelation, Aquinas risked making revelation an adjunct to reason, useful in tangential ways to buttress reason's range.

That Aquinas gave a priority to reason's arguments for the existence of God over the knowledge that comes from a faith experience of God through Jesus Christ may be seriously argued. Michael Buckley has done so.[43] Buckley argues that the priority given to modern philosophy's arguments from

---

39 Frederick Copleston, S.J., *A History of Philosophy*, vol. 3, pt. 2, *Late Mediaeval and Renaissance Philosophy: The Revival of Platonism to Suárez* (Garden City, NY: Doubleday Image, 1963 [1953]), 22–26.

40 W. H. Crilly, "Scholastic Philosophy," *NCE*, 12:749.

41 I. C. Brady, "Scholasticism," *NCE*, 12:759.

42 Ibid., 761.

43 Buckley, *Modern Atheism*, 55, 342–43.

reason undercut the compelling arguments for the existence of God that come through the Christian's faith experience. Then, when science mounted a successful campaign against the compelling nature of reason's arguments, acceptance of the existence of God fell by the wayside.

The process that set in motion the demise of reason's arguments for the existence of God and the rise of modern atheism began, according to Buckley, when Descartes and Newton made the existence of God the explanation for the universe. For Descartes, the existence of God was necessary to explain the existence of the world and movement. But this made God as Efficient Cause an appendage to the universe. For Newton, God existed as the efficient cause of Universal Mechanics, the one who gave nature its unity, order, and beauty.[44] In both cases, Christian faith willingly "abandoned the justification intrinsic to its own nature and experience, and insisted that its vindication would be found in philosophy, become natural philosophy, become mechanics."[45] The problem is that, once philosophers, such as Diderot and d'Holbach, were able to make the universe self-explanatory, either by explaining the universe as creative matter "eternally productive of all change and all design" (Diderot),[46] or as "dynamic matter" that can account for its own existence, its own movement, and be "the basic category for everything that is" (d'Holbach), there was no longer a need for a God extrinsic to the universe.[47] The troubling fact for Buckley is that theologians, hoping for a common ground of discussion with scientists, had acquiesced in this philosophical proof for the existence of God as a deus ex machina, rather than in the God who reveals himself in an interpersonal faith relationship with God in Jesus Christ. According to Buckley,

> For the Christian, Jesus belongs to the intelligibility and to the truth of god. What god is, and even that god is, has its primordial evidence in the person and in the event that is Jesus Christ. This person and this event make claims about god. These claims take precedence if one is to establish the truth of any conclusion that such a god exists. . . . the personal lies at the heart of this confession. Nothing can substitute for it and still sustain the affirmations of the great monotheistic religions.

Once theologians abandoned this personal encounter with God as the basis for their religious convictions and turned over justification for faith in Christ to the rationalizations of philosophers and scientists, it was only a matter a time before God would become a "*deus otiosus*,"[48] removed from the

[44] Ibid., 347.
[45] Ibid., 359.
[46] Ibid., 250.
[47] Ibid., 319.
[48] Ibid., 359.

modern mentality as the explanation for reality, and replaced by atheism: "The origin of atheism in the intellectual culture of the West lies thus with the self-alienation of religion itself."[49]

This philosophizing of Christianity, largely supported by Catholic theologians in the sixteenth century, provided further cause for Martin Luther to become alienated from the Catholic Church. Luther, who stood in the forefront of the Reformation, explicitly fostered the separation of faith and reason—except that Luther, unlike many of the secularists of the era, took the side of faith against reason, which was a reflection of his conversion experience based on his study of Paul's Letter to the Romans and his close attachment to the thinking of Augustine. The summation of Luther's thinking may succinctly be identified with the point made by Paul in Romans 1:17: The just man lives by faith in Christ. Once that idea sunk into Luther's mind, he rejected the value of everything human preliminary to justification by faith, namely, human works in accordance with law and thought produced by human reason.

For Luther, reason was part of the baggage of the natural person "characterized as 'total depravity' " where "no aspect of life or activity is exempt from the corruptions of self."[50] Luther did not deny the possibility of knowing God through reason, but spurned its usefulness. Thoroughly Augustinian, he had an increasingly "dark view of human potential" coupled with "the primacy of the revealed will of God in Scripture." Whatever reason produced represented the mentality of the person who had not been redeemed, who had not been brought to the vision of the truth that comes from faith, and who, lacking a faith relationship with Jesus Christ, would not be saved. Thus Luther's attitude toward Scholasticism: "He loathed the ethics of Aristotle, which were among his earliest teaching assignments, and he developed a lifelong hatred of this philosopher who was so important in scholastic learning." Again, his Augustinian bent made him emphasize the primacy of grace for salvation, and made him equally unsympathetic to humanistic values. He devoted his whole life to rebelling against a nominalism that had taken root in some circles of Scholastic philosophy and theology where God found a certain value in the role of the human in its efforts toward salvation.[51]

Luther gradually got caught up in a controversy with Pope Leo X (1513–1521) and his Thomist representative Cardinal Cajetan over indulgences and the role of human works in attaining salvation, and became

[49] Ibid., 361, 363.

[50] John Dillenberger and Claude Welch, *Protestant Christianity: Interpreted through Its Development* (New York: Scribner's Sons, 1954), 28–29.

[51] Diarmaid MacCulloch, *The Reformation* (New York: Viking Penguin, 2003), 114–15, 107–8.

"convinced that Thomists like the cardinal had formed a powerful conspiracy with pagan Aristotle against the truth."[52] Then he turned against the clergy, especially the hierarchy, as a separatist, deviant group representing a destructive force in the life of the Church.[53]

On January 3, 1521, Luther was formally excommunicated from the Catholic Church. His problems with the Catholic Church had focused on three areas: First, he objected to the authority of the Church over the Scriptures. Second, he insisted that all Church teachings had to have their foundation in the Scriptures, and not simply in Tradition, or they were unacceptable. Thus Luther objected to the existence of seven sacraments when he found no basis in Scripture for four or five of them (eventually, only baptism and the Eucharist passed muster with Luther). But while accepting the Eucharist, he railed against the Church's understanding of the Mass as sacrifice (since this infringed upon the uniqueness of Christ's sacrifice on the Cross), and the explanation of the consecration with the use of the Aristotelian term "transubstantiation," which he considered another serious intrusion of reason to explain an event explainable only by faith.[54] Third and finally, he insisted that salvation was only through faith in Jesus Christ, and not in works.

To allow any role for human effort in the process of salvation was to Luther an infringement upon the unique role of Christ's death on the Cross as the instrument of redemption. Thus when the Church allowed the sale of indulgences for the remission of sin, Luther was enraged: only the merits of Christ's redemptive action could overcome the power of sin and death. For Luther, "remission of sin [is] through the merits of Christ, whose sacrifice the Father accepts on our behalf."[55] The role of the individual is passive: to be open in, by, and through faith to Christ as Redeemer, and to trust in Christ as the one who saves. In regard to each of the three areas listed above, one can see that with Luther it is the role of the Church that is at issue: its authority is not supreme, but only that of the Scriptures; the instrument to salvation is not the Church, but only the person of Christ.

Though Luther became disenchanted with nominalism after 1515, he remained influenced by Ockham and the nominalist movement in its "emphasis on the limits of human reason."[56] Scholasticism emphasized the unity of reality known in universals, and that reason had the power to know God by its own rational operations, though revelation was necessary for the fullest knowledge of God and the gift of redemption in Christ. But

---

[52] Ibid., 123.

[53] Ibid.

[54] Ibid., 126.

[55] M. B. Schepers, ed., "Lutheranism," *NCE* 8:894.

[56] P. Soergel and W. S. Barron, Jr., "Reformation, Protestant (on the Continent)," *NCE* 12:12.

with Ockham, reason no longer has the power to know with certainty God's existence, and even more importantly, has no role to play in the understanding of God's revelation. Luther's understanding of the inadequacies of reason in respect to knowledge of Christ and faith leading to salvation turned him strongly against Scholasticism and its exaggerated attempt to explain much of the Christian message without faith.

Though Luther was not a humanist—the very term would have appalled him—he was nevertheless influenced by the humanist movement thriving in the sixteenth century under Erasmus, which advocated reform of the Church, a return to the Bible, and "criticized clerical corruption, scholastic theology, and popular superstition."[57] Humanism rejected the arid and stylistic abstractions of Scholastic thought, which Luther would have found appealing, but emphasized the nobility of the human being, and looked to the Greek and Roman classics for an understanding of the human, which Luther would have rejected. And the general worldly excesses of the Church, especially in its hierarchy, with their drive for money, political power, and moral laxity, did little to enhance the standing of the Church in the mind of the young Luther.

COUNTER-REFORMATION

In 1973, the noted theologian Richard P. McBrien, at that time professor of theology at Boston College and now at the University of Notre Dame, published his thesis that the Church from the sixteenth century to Vatican II had been operating with a Counter-Reformation mentality.[58] By that term he was referring to the Catholic Church's movement of reaction against the Protestant Reformation which began with the Council of Trent (1545–1563) and which had, in his view, stamped the life of the Church ever since.

The thesis has merit. The Council of Trent represented the Catholic Church's awareness of and response to the decided inroads made by the Reformation on the hegemony of the Church over Christendom since the earliest days of Christianity. Suddenly that control was being seriously eroded. It is remarkable how quickly after Luther's posting of his ninety-five theses of disputes with Catholic teaching on the door of the Castle Church in Wittenberg, Germany, in 1517 that Western Christianity turned against the Catholic Church and accepted Protestantism.[59] Vast territories in Western Europe within a period of about two decades went over to Protestantism. Why?

---

57 Ibid., 12:15.

58 In McBrien, *Remaking*. McBrien is consistently representative of the liberal or progressive wing of Catholicism.

59 Dillenberger and Welch, *Protestant Christianity*, 17.

The movement represented the confluence of many different rebellious mentalities, including the growing nationalistic spirit, the increasing fallout with Rome over its control of the political and religious life of Western Europe, Europeans' increasing irritation over the gross economic demands made on the populous to sustain the political and military activities of the pope, and the disillusionment with the papacy over corruption in the Church and the widespread failure of the Church to respond to the cultural and social needs of its people.

When the Catholic Church woke up to the seriousness of the threat created by Luther and the Protestant reformers, it convened a council to affirm what it considered to be the true doctrines of Christianity, against an atmosphere of widespread confusion, and to initiate a countermove that would reform and revitalize the Church and restore allegiance to the true faith. The Council of Trent represents the foundational organization of that attempt, and the movement that characterizes that spirit of reform and the counteroffensive taken by the Catholic Church against Protestantism is commonly known as the Counter-Reformation.

The effect of the Counter-Reformation mentality was to make the Catholic Church largely a reactionary Church—reacting against whatever the Protestant churches were saying. It is rarely a good idea to identify what you stand for by formulating it in opposition to what you don't stand for, but that is basically what the Catholic Church did: the Church emphasized whatever the Protestant churches didn't. And so, whereas the Reformers downgraded the role of reason in matters of faith, the Catholic Church emphasized the rational dimension of the faith, so much so that faith often seemed to be reduced to a product of reason.

Again, whereas the Reformers downgraded the role of the Church, the importance of its traditions, the authority of its hierarchy, and its dogma, and upgraded the authority of the Scriptures—the motto of Protestantism became *sola Scriptura*, "only the Scriptures," meaning that if it's not in the Scriptures, it's not part of the faith—the Catholic Church tended to look upon the Scriptures and the early history of the Church as only the beginnings of Christianity, which paled in comparison to the more developed form of Christianity found in the history of the Church's traditions under the direction of the hierarchy. Thus the accent was placed on the power of the hierarchy and their teaching authority, over against which the Scriptures became of secondary importance. As time went on, Catholics became increasingly ignorant of the Scriptures, whereas Protestants became more and more grounded in its teachings.

Again, Luther reduced the number of the sacraments to two because he couldn't find a basis for seven in the Scriptures. Even then, for Luther, primacy was always given to the Word—the Scriptures—over the sacraments, since faith comes, as Paul tells us, from hearing and believing the Word. And so Luther made the sacraments instruments promotive of the faith rather than instruments of grace in themselves.

Luther discarded the sacrifice of the Mass since he felt such a notion detracted from the unique sacrifice of Christ on the Cross. In response, Catholicism emphasized the importance of the Mass as a re-presentation of the sacrifice of Christ on the Cross and as the central event of Catholic living. Such an emphasis on the Real Presence of Christ in the Eucharist (which Luther also maintained) led to a diminution in Catholic understanding of the importance of the Word—so much so that Catholics came to feel that the only important part of the Mass was the consecration to confect the Eucharist.[60]

One of the most important effects of Luther's reform was his restoration of the importance of faith as an interpersonal experience—in the Old Testament with God through the covenant, in the New Testament with the Father through communion with the Son in the power of the Holy Spirit. Nothing could be more central to the Christian faith than the importance of this interpersonal dimension. But by emphasizing a direct relationship of the believer with God in personal faith and not in the sacraments, Luther undercut the importance of union with Christ in his Body, the community of the Church. This meant, for example, that repentance for sin was directly communicated from God and not through the sacrament of penance, and that interpretation of the Scriptures was ultimately a matter between the individual and God.

In response, the Church emphasized the importance of communicating with God through the Church, as Christ had designed the role of the Church. But unfortunately, this led to a heavy emphasis upon membership in the Church and obedience to its rules and regulations rather than upon the spiritual encounter with Christ through his Church. There is perhaps no greater loss to the life of the Catholic Church than this failure to emphasize the personal encounter with Christ as central to the faith experience. This is undoubtedly the source of many of the Church's present ills.

McBrien, speaking from a decidedly progressive perspective, characterized the mentality that prevailed in this four-hundred-year Counter-Reformation period as one that "betrayed an exceedingly hierarchical and institutionalized understanding of the Church," as "principally a visible society, hierarchically structured." If so, this would have been to counter

---

60 A Catholic priest, later laicized, once told me he didn't understand why the Mass was not simply reduced to a two-minute consecration followed by reception of the Eucharist.

the Protestant version of the Church seen largely "as an invisible, spiritualized community without the requisite appurtenances of law and order."[61]

McBrien enumerated in his book various characteristics of the pre-Vatican II Counter-Reformation Church, many of which ring true for older Catholics: bishops running their dioceses without diocesan or parish councils; priests and religious carrying out the mission of the Church as those who are "called to a higher form of Christian life"; the laity without a direct mission, but participating in the mission of the clergy at the latter's discretion; women considered "by the will of God, subordinate to men"; the laity as a whole "not really expected to strive for perfect holiness"; the clergy having little interest in political, social, or economic issues, which are not considered to have anything essential to do with the work of the Church since the mission of the Church is "the communication of salvation"; active participation in the worship life of Protestant churches strictly forbidden since they had broken away from the true Church of Christ; criticism of the Church forbidden, since it is generally held that "the Church was already the Kingdom of God on earth" and "to criticize the Kingdom" is "to criticize God himself"; the liturgy of the Mass "an incomprehensible experience" for most Catholics since it is celebrated in Latin (but this is of little import since the sacramental rites have their effect without the need for comprehension or involvement); "apostolic succession," meaning that only Catholic bishops can validly trace their lineage back to the apostles, and the pope, as Peter's successor, chooses them, not the people; finally, the assumption that since the Church is the "ordinary means of salvation," "outside the Church . . . there is no salvation." This structure, accepted by all Catholics, gave the Church remarkable unity and uniformity: "Catholics acted the way they acted, and thought the way they thought, because this was clearly the way they were supposed to act and to think, by the will of Christ himself—or so they were convinced."[62]

Eruption Caused by Vatican II

And then along came Vatican II, and the transformation and disruption in the life of the Church occurred overnight. A new theology of the Church burst upon the Catholic community without any attempt to prepare either the clergy, or especially the laity, for the difference. A shock effect occurred around the world. Overnight people were expected to accept a theology and practices that in many ways contrasted and sometimes even contradicted what had been going on for centuries in the life of the Church. What had always been accepted as intrinsic to the life of the Church as designed by

[61] McBrien, *Remaking*, 28.
[62] Ibid., 30–35, 23.

God was suddenly shown to be changeable. It is difficult today, so many years after the event, to imagine the shock effect that occurred, but it was enormous. It is safe to say that to this day, the Church has not recovered from the aftershocks. Here, I believe, lies the root of much of the crisis in today's Church, which we will address shortly.

Let us briefly itemize some of the ways in which the new Vatican II theology contrasts sharply with that of the Counter-Reformation Church:

Centrality of Jesus Christ and the Scriptures

In drawing up the theology of the Church, instead of focusing primarily on the Church's visible structure, its organization and its dogmatic teachings, Vatican II's focus is on Jesus Christ and an understanding of the Scriptures, while the Church is understood as deriving all of its meaning, understanding, and mission from its relationship to Christ and his purposes.[63]

The primary decree of Vatican II, *Lumen Gentium*, is on the Church. And yet the opening words of the document are "Christ is the light of all nations," and all the understanding of the Church is developed in view of "her relationship with Christ" (*LG* 1).

The purpose of the Church is integrated into the Council's understanding of God's saving plan for the human race and the mission of salvation wrought through entrance into his Son's redemptive life, which inaugurated God's Kingdom on earth and made possible union with God through membership in the Kingdom. The Holy Spirit, the third Person of the Trinity, is the Spirit of life in the Church, whose work is to bring humanity into the Kingdom through incorporation into the life of the Church (*LG* 2–5). The Church is understood by its relationship to the members of the Trinity indicated through various symbolic images, such as "the Flock of Christ, the Vineyard of God, the Temple of the Holy Spirit, and the Spouse of [Christ] the Immaculate Lamb" (*LG* 6, note 12, written by Avery Dulles, S.J., editor). Above all, the Church is the "Mystical Body of Christ" (*LG* 8).

---

[63] Even pre-Vatican II studies of the Church had recognized inadequate approaches of the Counter-Reformation mentality: "The negation of the visible character of the Church of Christ and of its hierarchical constitution [by the reformers] has led to such stress being laid upon the visible, tangible aspects of the Church that those who are not Catholics have come to think of it in terms of its external organization and of its recent dogmatic definitions, and not a few Catholics, concentrating their attention upon the argumentative, apologetical, and controversial side of the doctrine concerning the Church, have been in danger of overlooking theoretically—though practically it is impossible for them to do so—the supernatural, the mysterious, the vital, the overwhelmingly important character of the Church as the divinely established and only means of grace in the world, as the Mystical Body of Christ." George D. Smith, D.D., *The Teaching of the Catholic Church: A Summary of Catholic Doctrine*, 2 vols. (New York: MacMillan, 1952), 2:659.

Church Is a Mystery

Instead of the Church being understood principally as a visible hierarchical monarchical structure, the Church "is first and foremost a mystery," meaning that "God is somehow present within it." The Church is "the public, historical sign of God's invisible, redemptive presence to the world and to mankind. . . . God is therein present to the world: the Church is 'a kind of sacrament.' " Instead of emphasizing the Church as an "institution . . . to deliver salvation," the Church exists as " 'a sign of intimate union with God, and of the unity of all mankind,' " and " 'also an instrument for the achievement of such union and unity.' "[64]

One need only reflect on the difference in the quality of the ideas and the terminology used here to recognize the change in the spirit of Vatican II: a change from the Counter-Reformation tone—somewhat unnuanced, canonical, and pragmatic, though clear and easy to understand ("the Church delivers salvation")—to a richer, more inviting terminology, leading to a much deeper perception of the fullness of the life into which one enters in the Church. The Church as sacrament signifies, as well as leads to, union and unity with God in Christ.

Church Is "New People of God"

Whereas in the preconciliar Church, the tendency was to identify the Church with the hierarchy, in whose ministry the laity participated by their service, Vatican II understood the Church primarily as the "new People of God" (*LG* 9).

To emphasize the priority of the consideration of the Church as the People of God over the consideration of the Church as a hierarchical structure, the Council fathers moved the chapter in *Lumen Gentium* treating the latter consideration to chapter 3, giving precedence to the chapter on the Church as the People of God as chapter 2. No single action could have done more to emphasize that "the Church is the whole People of God—laity, religious, and clergy alike—and that the hierarchical structure of the Church exists to serve the whole People of God."[65] This may have been the single most important action to indicate the new emphasis in the Council on the Church as the entire community of the People of God, all of whose members participate fully in the life of the Church.

According to Dulles, in the commentary on the document, the title of "People of God" "met a profound desire of the Council to put greater emphasis on the human and communal side of the Church, rather than on

[64] McBrien, *Remaking*, 43–44. McBrien is citing from Vatican II's *LG* 1.

[65] Richard P. McBrien, *The Church: The Evolution of Catholicism* (New York: HarperOne, 2008), 167.

the institutional and hierarchical aspects which have sometimes been overstressed in the past for polemical reasons" (*LG*, note 27).

The understanding of the Church as the People of God also allowed the Council to give greater consideration to the Church as a pilgrim people "going forward in this present world . . . in search of a future and abiding city" (*LG* 9). By introducing the understanding of the Church as the new People of God, the Council fathers took over the historical dimension of the community the Church inherited from the covenant community of the Old Testament. Thus, history entered into the fathers' understanding of the inner life of the Church, which means that the Church on her historical pilgrimage is no longer best described as a perfect society; rather, the Church attains "her full perfection only in the glory of heaven" (*LG* 48). In the meantime, the Church, "embracing sinners in her bosom, is at the same time holy and always in need of being purified, and incessantly pursues the path of penance and renewal" (*LG* 8).

By introducing a historical dimension, the Church becomes "a pilgrim people still laboring in imperfection." In addition,

> responsibility for the mission of the Church is no longer to be conceived as the exclusive prerogative of the hierarchy; it is a responsibility, rather, whose dimensions are universal, applying equally to laity, religious, and clergy, all of whom are joined together in a multiplicity of pluriform ministries in the service of the one mission.[66]

Church Is God's Presence in Community

Whereas pre-Vatican II theology had emphasized in its consideration of the Church its structure and authority, Vatican II emphasized the Church as a community in and through which God is present to the world.

Along with the understanding of the Church as the new People of God, another point that further epitomized the transformation that occurred in Vatican II's understanding of the life of the Church is undoubtedly its consideration of the Church as "a community called forth by God to embody the presence, and carry on the work, of Christ and his Spirit."[67] This was not to deny the importance of the Church as hierarchy, but to emphasize the importance of viewing the Church as a community. The hierarchy exists as a group *within* the community and derives its role from its service to the community:

> The external side of the mystery [of the Church] is the community itself, not its hierarchy or its doctrines. This holy people—laity, religious, and clergy alike—share in the prophetic, priestly, and kingly min-

[66] McBrien, *Remaking*, 44–45.

[67] McBrien, *Remaking*, 44.

> istries of Christ. There is a common bond uniting the priesthood of the ordained and the priesthood of the nonordained: "Each of them in its own special way is a participation in the one priesthood of Christ. . . . For their part, the faithful join in the offering of the Eucharist by virtue of their royal priesthood."[68]

An enormous revamping of the understanding of the Church has been mandated. What we have here is the introduction of a theology of the Church that was to have an indelible and far-reaching effect on the way Catholics looked at their Church. For with this new importance placed on understanding the members of the Church as a community having a common mission to spread Christ and his teachings to all nations, at least four important theological principles follow:

1. There is an *equality of the membership*. A new awareness of its importance invades the life of the Church: "The chosen People of God is one: 'one Lord, one faith, one baptism' (Eph. 4:5). As members, they share a common dignity from their rebirth in Christ. They have the same filial grace and the same vocation to perfection. They possess in common one salvation, one hope, and one undivided charity. Hence, there is in Christ and in the Church no inequality on the basis of race or nationality, social condition or sex, because . . . 'you are all "one" in Christ Jesus' (Gal. 3:28)" (*LG* 32).

   All members are of equal dignity. The hierarchical dimension denotes not a priority of membership but a duty, among all those who are called to service, to serve "in the sacred ministry . . . by teaching, by sanctifying, and by ruling with the authority of Christ," and in that particular way to promote the building up of the Body of Christ and the spread of the gospel teaching (*LG* 32). Least of all does being a member of the clergy imply that one is a "better" Christian.

2. With equality of membership and participation in the common mission comes *collegiality*.

   Vatican I in 1870 addressed the hierarchical structure of the Church and papal infallibility. Vatican II primarily addresses collegiality. The term does not mean belonging to a college as an educational institution, but rather membership in a community where the horizontal dimension is addressed. Collegiality emphasizes colleagueship, partnership, corporate responsibility, and shared power for the successful undertaking of a project—here, shared in carrying out the mission of Christ to introduce the whole world to a personal experience of Christ and to the acceptance of his teaching.

[68] Ibid., 47. McBrien is quoting *LG* 10.

Vatican II addresses colleagueship between the pope and the bishops and among the bishops themselves throughout the world: the "collegial nature" of the relationship is said to be present from the beginning of the Church in the "college of apostles" in union with its head, Peter, and expressed in "bonds of unity, charity, and peace"; in "conciliar assemblies which made common judgments"; in "ecumenical councils"; and in the college's sharing, with its head, "the Roman Pontiff, . . . supreme and full power over the universal Church" (*LG* 22). Almost immediately after Vatican II, collegial practices sprang up: synods of bishops were called by the popes to discuss major ecclesial issues, and national and territorial episcopal conferences were established.

3. But if understanding the Church as community implies colleagueship, it also implies some element of democracy. Vatican II does not understand the Church in any proper sense to be a democracy; that is why I speak of "some element of democracy." By this I mean only that there is some element of sharing in decision-making regarding practices and procedures in the life of the Church. If a collegial spirit has become part of the life of the Church, this provokes shared responsibility. Such a spirit has led to the formation of diocesan and parish councils, priests' senates, and religious conferences.

4. Finally, if the entire community shares in Christ's mission, this dimension needs to be concretized in a *theology* that emphasizes the importance *of the laity*, and this development remains one of Vatican II's greatest achievements. An entire document—*Apostolicam Actuositatem*—along with a section of *Lumen Gentium*, is devoted to the delineation of this innovative theology in the life of the Church.

In this theology, Vatican II makes a point of insisting that all followers of Christ, and not simply the clergy, are called to *holiness*. This in itself was a leveling principle, but also a challenge to the laity, since it indicated that the laity could no longer passively accept a secondary role in the life of the Church.

Furthermore, as we have already seen, all Christians share in Christ's redemptive mission. But the Council spells this out in a way that had never been done before. The laity do not simply share in the mission of the clergy as pre-Vatican II theology felt, but receive their mission directly "from their union with Christ their Head." They are no longer "assigned to the apostolate" by the hierarchy, but "by the Lord himself" (*AA* 3; *LG* 33).

The laity's mission is distinctive to themselves, and is so essential to the life of the Church that its importance cannot be exaggerated: a mission to spread the Kingdom of Christ and his saving redemptive activity in the temporal order in the various areas of daily life where the clergy as ordained ministers do not normally operate: "The laity are called in a special way to make the Church present and operative in those places and circumstances where only through them can she become the salt of the earth" (*LG* 33). Vatican II repeatedly emphasizes the nature and importance of this mission of the laity to the temporal order:

> The laity, by their very vocation, seek the kingdom of God by engaging in temporal affairs and by ordering them according to the plan of God. They live in the world, that is, in each and in all of the secular professions and occupations. They live in the ordinary circumstances of family and social life, from which the very web of their existence is woven.
>
> They are called there by God so that by exercising their proper function and being led by the spirit of the gospel they can work for the sanctification of the world from within, in the manner of leaven. In this way they can make Christ known to others, especially by the testimony of a life resplendent in faith, hope, and charity. The layman is closely involved in temporal affairs of every sort. It is therefore his special task to illumine and organize these affairs in such a way that they may always start out, develop, and persist according to Christ's mind, to the praise of the Creator and the Redeemer. (*LG* 31)

The laity have a task that is uniquely theirs: to transform the world from within so that it more adequately reflects an arena of Christian values:

> The laity must take on the renewal of the temporal order as their own special obligation. Led by the light of the gospel and the mind of the Church, and motivated by Christian love, let them act directly and definitively in the temporal sphere. . . . The temporal order must be renewed in such a way that, without the slightest detriment to its own proper laws, it can be brought into conformity with the higher principles of the Christian life. (*AA* 7)

Vatican II itemizes specific areas of the temporal order where the laity achieve their apostolic effectiveness in a way available only to them: these include "the family, culture, economic affairs, the arts and professions, political institutions, international relations, and other matters of this kind, as well as their development and progress" (*AA* 7). By "properly fulfilling their secular duties in the ordinary conditions of life, they do not disassociate union with Christ from that life. Rather, by performing their work according to God's will, they can grow in that union" (*AA* 4). In all of these ways, the laity are able to "offer spiritual sacrifices through everything they do," and "witness to Christ throughout the world" (*AA* 3). What more glorious apostolate can there be?

Humanizing the World Is Intrinsic to Church Life

Whereas the pre-Vatican II Church had essentially viewed social, political, and economic problems as peripheral to the life of the Church, Vatican II made concern for these issues *intrinsic* to its life.

The Church's mission is no longer simply to proclaim the Word and administer the sacraments, even though those activities still remain central. The Church now recognizes that it must work so that "this world might be fashioned anew according to God's design and reach its fulfillment" (*GS* 2). This means that the Church does not simply leave worldly concerns to secular organizations, but that it too must "contribute greatly toward making the family of man and its history more human" (*GS* 40).

It was *Gaudium et Spes* that created the second greatest transformation in the life of the Church (after the theology of the laity) by introducing efforts to make the secular world "more human" directly into the Church's mission. Vatican II is now famous for admitting that the Church had become too separated from life in the world, that a great divide had been generated between faith and action in Christian life. The stereotypical accusation that Christians practice their Christianity inside the Church on Sunday and leave their Christian values behind on Monday, made so often by nonbelievers as well as by many believers, was recognized as valid.

But Vatican II did not simply mention this division between faith and life in the world; rather, it used some of its strongest language to declare that "this split between the faith which many profess and their daily lives deserves to be counted among the more serious errors of our age." Included in this condemned "split" is the "false opposition" created "between professional and social activities on the one part, and religious life on the other," or between "acts of worship" and "certain moral obligations" on the one hand, and "earthly affairs . . . divorced from the religious life" on the other. According to Vatican II, Jesus threatened those who catered to such a split "with grave punishments" (probably a reference to Jesus' condemnation of hypocrisy), and Vatican II itself leveled one of its harshest condemnations against those who fail to put into action Christian teaching: "The Christian who neglects his temporal duties neglects his duties toward his neighbor and even God, and jeopardizes his eternal salvation" (*GS* 43, with references to Mt 23:3–23 and Mk 7:10–13).

Worldly Enterprises Witness to God's Glory

Two additional points need be noted:

- (1) *What goals are to be sought when the Christian spirit is activated in the world?*: All earthly activities are to be promoted in order to further "the work of justice under the inspiration of charity" (*GS* 72). Such activities, including "humane, domestic, professional, social, and technical enterprises," are to be brought into "one vital synthesis with religious values," so that under God's "supreme direction all things are harmonized unto God's glory" (*GS* 43).

- (2) *Who is specifically commissioned to put this spirit into practice?*: A further explication of the theology of the laity is addressed: "Outstanding among the works" of the laity's apostolate is "Christian social action" (*AA* 7). It is the laity to whom "secular duties and activities belong properly although not exclusively." Working with all people who share their goals, it is the laity who are to see to it "that the divine law is inscribed in the life of the earthly city." The laity are "not only bound to penetrate the world with a Christian spirit," but "called to be witnesses to Christ in all things in the midst of human society" (*GS* 43).

With this innovative theology emphasizing the Christian's duty to penetrate the secular order with the spirit of Christ and his teachings, *Gaudium et Spes* provided the springboard for liberation theology and the orientation toward political activism, pacifism, and economic justice toward the poor that has motivated a major part of the life of the Church since 1965.

Ecumenical Communion with Non-Catholic Communities

Whereas the Counter-Reformation Church had emphasized the uniqueness of the Catholic Church as the true Church of Christ over against non-Catholic Christian communities, Vatican II speaks of the latter as "Churches or ecclesial communities," and says their members "have a right to be honored by the title of Christian, and are properly regarded as brothers in the Lord by the sons of the Catholic Church."[69]

Such openness to the non-Christian communities constitutes the third great transformation occurring in the life of the Church in Vatican II. *Unitatis Redintegratio* is truly remarkable for the various ways in which it expresses this openness. Before Vatican II, Protestants were considered heretics and generally viewed with suspicion. Catholics were expected to shun all contact with Protestant communities in their life of worship. The average Catholic would rarely if ever enter a Protestant house of worship, and then only with trepidation.

But *Unitatis Redintegratio* goes out of its way to open the Catholic Church's arms to non-Catholics in every way possible: it accepts non-Catholic Christians with "affection" as "brothers in the Lord." It accepts that, though separated from the Catholic Church, they are nevertheless Christians

[69] *LG* 15; Paul VI, *Unitatis Redintegratio* (Decree on Ecumenism, November 21, 1964), par. 3; hereafter paragraphs noted in the text as *UR*.

born in Christian communities, properly baptized in Christ, and "brought into a certain, though imperfect, communion with the Catholic Church," and that many of the elements that give life to the one true Church of Christ exist in these non-Catholic communities, such as "the written word of God; the life of grace; faith, hope, and charity, along with other interior gifts of the Holy Spirit." Perhaps no change was more shocking than the indication that the life of grace lived by those born into these communities can provide them "access to the community of salvation" (*UR* 3). What, Protestants can be saved?! This inevitably led to the question: If so, what was the point of waging this four-hundred-year battle with them?

The Church Shares the Blame for the Lack of Christian Unity

Finally, the Council indicates that the Catholic Church accepts at least partial "blame" for the divisions that destroyed the unity of the Church throughout history, and urges that all Catholics join in ecumenical efforts to restore unity among the Christian communities (*UR* 3–4).[70] Perhaps one has to have lived in the pre-Vatican II period to recognize the enormous transformation in the Church's mentality that is indicated by the Church accepting "blame" for the Reformation. Such remorse hit the Catholic community like a boulder, and, to be sure, without any advance preparation.

Renewal of the Liturgy

A major change that occurred with Vatican II and in the years immediately afterward concerned the liturgy, especially the Mass. The prayers of the

---

[70] This point is undoubtedly what eventually led to John Paul II's apologies (close to 100) to various groups for offenses committed by the Catholic community throughout its history. For example, on May 4, 2001, the Pope addressed the Greek Orthodox authorities and the Holy Synod in Athens, and asked "forgiveness" for sins "by action or omission" committed by "sons and daughters of the Catholic Church . . . against their Orthodox brothers and sisters" ("Pilgrimage to Greece: Pope John Paul II Address to Holy Synod," par. 2, May 4, 2001, www.ewtn.com/library/PAPALDOC/J2XADDR.HTM). In his homily at Vatican City on the "Day of Pardon," March 12, 2000, the Pope asked for "forgiveness for the past and present sins of [the Church's] sons and daughters . . . for the divisions which have occurred among Christians, for the violence some have used in the service of the truth and for the distrustful and hostile attitudes sometimes taken towards the followers of other religions" ("Homily of the Holy Father," "Day of Pardon," March 12, 2000, par. 3–4, www.vatican.va/holy_father/john_paul_ii/homilies/documents/hf_jp-ii_hom_20000312pardon_e...). In the Prayer of the Faithful the Pope led after his homily, he asked for God's "forgiveness" for "the behaviour of those who in the course of history have caused these children of yours to suffer." The Pope was referring to previously noted sins committed by Christians against the people of Israel throughout the course of history ("The Celebration of the Great Jubilee: Holy Father's Prayer for Forgiveness," sec. IV, March 12, 2000, www.ewtn.com/library/PAPALDOC/JJP2UNPR.HTM).

Mass had always been recited in Latin: the Tridentine Mass—the Mass to which Catholics had been accustomed every Sunday—had been in place since 1570. But some changes in the liturgy began gradually to occur over a period of a few years, such as the transition from a wholly Latin Mass to an English one. But other changes occurred almost overnight.

No change in the Church had more impact, more immediate shock value, than just this one transformation in the liturgy from what had been totally unacceptable one week to what became the norm the next. One Sunday, people entered the Church with the priest praying the Mass at the altar facing the wall; the following Sunday they entered to see an altar set toward the middle of the church with the priest celebrating Mass facing the people, and the tabernacle containing the Eucharist—always the central focus for private prayer—removed to a side altar or to a separate chapel of repose:

> The tabernacle was moved from the main altar to a side altar or special chapel. The "feel" of Catholic churches changed dramatically. Catholic church architecture was traditionally designed to draw the eye to the tabernacle, the focus of attention. Now the focus shifted to the altar of sacrifice, to the "action" of the Eucharistic banquet rather than the "static" presence of the reserved sacrament.
>
> By any measure, the council had introduced a vast revolution in the practice and sensibility surrounding the Eucharist.[71]

The shock to the older generation, who knew an unchanging liturgy their whole lives and who presumed by divine decree that change would never occur, was unimaginable. Though all revisions had been intended to make the Mass more understandable and meaningful, the effect was just the opposite, since all had been done without any warning or advance explanation. For many Catholics, the Mass had largely been a meaningless ritual attended out of obligation, to fulfill requirements for salvation. Those who sought some fruit from the experience usually found it by entering into their own private spirituality, such as praying silently to God or saying the rosary. Comfort was found in the repeated presentation of the same Latin rituals, expressive of the Church's continuing battle against the Protestants. Now, suddenly, those barriers of division were breaking down. If anything had distinguished a Catholic church from the Protestant, it was the Real Presence of Christ in the Eucharist in the tabernacle. Now that presence was being downgraded or even removed from sight. Was the Church finally after four hundred years conceding victory to the Protestants? Many thought so, and found it unacceptable. So great was the shock

---

[71] Howard P. Bleichner, S.S., *View from the Altar: Reflections on the Rapidly Changing Catholic Priesthood* (New York: Crossroad, 2004), 25.

that it caused a minor rebellion in some parishes. In the church I attended at that time, the Blessed Sacrament was returned to the main altar the following Sunday, much later to be removed again.[72]

Right to Freedom of Conscience

A remarkable new teaching on the nature and value of *religious freedom* was introduced into the Church. Over the long run, confusion over the meaning of this transformation may have had the most to do with the fomenting of crisis in the Church.

McBrien speaks of the "error has no rights" mentality that was dominant in the pre-Vatican II Church. In that era, it was commonly understood that, since the Catholic Church was the one, true Church of Christ, every other religious community, living in error, had no right to exist. If the Church, therefore, ever arrived at a position of political power where it could ban other religious groups, it would be bound to do so.[73]

In its Declaration on Religious Freedom, *Dignitatis Humanae*, the Council established three major principles that put an end to this mentality: First of all, that "the human person has a right to religious freedom," meaning that all persons "are to be immune from coercion" so that "in matters religious no one is to be forced to act in a manner contrary to his own beliefs" or to be "restrained from acting in accordance with his own beliefs." This right is rooted "in the very dignity of the human person" as a being "endowed with reason and free will" and therefore having "personal responsibility . . . to seek the truth, especially religious truth" and to be "bound to adhere to the truth, once it is known."[74]

Secondly, the human person has freedom of conscience in seeking, accepting, and living by the truth: "In all his activity a man is bound to follow his conscience, faithfully, in order that he may come to God, for whom he was created." As a result, "he is not to be forced to act in a manner contrary to his conscience. Nor, on the other hand, is he to be restrained from acting in accordance with his conscience, especially in matters religious" (*DH* 3).

Such teaching strongly counteracted the rigorous rejection of the value of a free conscience proclaimed by Gregory XVI in 1832 in his encyclical *Mirari Nos Arbitramur*, where he spoke of "the absurd and wrong view, or rather insanity, according to which freedom of conscience must be asserted

---

[72] I can still remember one faithful Catholic woman's horror at finding the bells no longer being rung at the consecration. She took this as a sign of concession to Protestants.

[73] McBrien, *Remaking*, 11–12, 32.

[74] Paul VI, *Dignitatis Humanae* (Declaration on Religious Freedom, December 7, 1965), par. 2; hereafter paragraphs noted in the text as *DH*.

and vindicated for everybody."[75] One should see this somewhat rigorist teaching of Gregory against the background of the modernist teachings of the French Enlightenment, which he understood as leading the unguided conscience to a rejection of the Christian revelation, to accepting the rationalist anti-Catholic modernist teachings, and to departing from the true faith, the acceptance of which is necessary for salvation.

Unfortunately, *Dignitatis Humanae*'s teaching on freedom of conscience became abused by many who understood it to mean license to do whatever one wanted, as long as one was convinced of the veracity of one's position. Such thinking has contributed to the rise of relativism as well as widespread independence in attitudes toward the Church, as the statistical data we studied earlier verifies. Such thinking also ignores passages noting that "the Church is, by the will of Christ, the teacher of the truth . . . that Truth which is Christ Himself"; that "the Christian faithful ought carefully to attend to the sacred and certain doctrine of the Church"; and that the "disciple is bound by a grave obligation toward Christ his Master ever more adequately to understand the truth received from Him, faithfully to proclaim it, and vigorously to defend it" (*DH* 14).

Finally, *Dignitatis Humanae* reaffirms the teaching of the Church regarding the nature of faith: since the "act of faith is of its very nature a free act, . . . man's response to God in faith must be free." As a result, "no one is to be forced to embrace the Christian faith against his own will," nor can he "give his adherence to God revealing Himself unless the Father draw him to offer to God the reasonable and free submission of faith." This freedom is confirmed by Jesus' ways: "He bore witness to the truth, but He refused to impose the truth by force." His disciples followed his way, seeking to convert others to Christ "not, however, by the use of coercion or by devices unworthy of the gospel, but by the power, above all, of the Word of God" (*DH* 10–11).

The Church Is Not Identical to the Kingdom

The pre-Vatican II Church typically held that "the Church was already the Kingdom of God on earth. To criticize the Church is to criticize the Kingdom, which is to criticize God himself."[76]

This identification of the Church with the Kingdom is commonly known as "triumphalism," and had two consequences: First, salvation was identified with membership in the Church. The Church had long accepted the principle *extra ecclesiam, nulla salus* (outside the Church, no salvation),

---

[75] Gregory XVI, "Encyclical Letter *Mirari Nos Arbitramur* (1832)," in J. Neuner, S.J., and J. Dupuis, S.J., eds., *The Christian Faith in the Doctrinal Documents of the Catholic Church*, 6th rev. and enlarged ed. (New York: Alba House, 1996 [1973]), 384–85, at 385.

[76] McBrien, *Remaking*, 32.

though when the well-known American priest Leonard Feeney, S.J., drew the apparently logical conclusion from this dictum that one could not be saved without actually being a member of the Catholic Church, he was roundly corrected.[77]

Secondly, criticism of the pope or Church policy was unthinkable. Since the pope and the hierarchy spoke with the authority that had been given them by Christ (Mt 16:18–19), to criticize the Church was to criticize Christ and his plan of salvation in the Church.

Vatican II saw remarkable change in this area:

First, the Council no longer made the Church and the Kingdom coterminous. Though one statement might seem to imply identification—"The Church, or, in other words, the kingdom of Christ now present in mystery" (*LG* 3)—elsewhere the Council makes clear that the Church is not identified with the Kingdom—the Church is "on earth the initial budding forth [*germen et initium*] of that kingdom" and "strains toward the consummation of the kingdom" (*LG* 5).

Vatican II did, however, continue to teach *extra ecclesiam, nulla salus*—"the Church is necessary for salvation"—to the consternation of liberals, and reaffirmed that teaching by leaving no doubt as to its meaning: "Whosoever, therefore, knowing that the Catholic Church was made necessary by God through Jesus Christ, would refuse to enter her or to remain in her could not be saved" (*LG* 14). But the Council nuanced the teaching to allow exceptions to the necessity by invoking the longstanding, though formerly quietly held, principle that invincible ignorance removes culpability.[78] Thus Vatican II formally declares that non-Catholic Christians, Jews, and Muslims, as well as unbelievers, "can attain to everlasting salvation" when they "through no fault of their own do not know the gospel of Christ or His Church" and "strive by their deeds to do His will as it is known to them" (*LG* 15–16).

Second, the distinction between the Church and the Kingdom opened the door to validating criticism of the Church. If the Church was not yet

[77] The possibility of salvation for non-Catholics was affirmed in an August 8, 1949 letter of the Holy Office of Archbishop (later Cardinal) Cushing of Boston; cf. "Letter of the Holy Office to the Archbishop of Boston (1949)," in Neuner and Dupuis, *Christian Faith*, 305–7; cf. also note 58 to *LG* 16.

[78] "In view of the stress laid upon the necessity of membership of the Church for salvation it is understandable that the possibility of salvation for those outside the Church is mentioned only hesitantly" (Ludwig Ott, *Fundamentals of Catholic Dogma*, trans. Patrick Lynch [St. Louis: Herder, 1964 (1952)], 313). Invincible ignorance is the same as innocent ignorance, namely, lacking awareness of something and not being personally responsible for not knowing it, as, for example, in a case where I might kill a human being without being guilty of murder, since I did not realize it was a human being and was not responsible for not knowing it. More on invincible ignorance later.

the fullness of the Kingdom but strains toward completion of the Kingdom, if the Church embraces sinners with Christian failings (*LG* 8; *GS* 43), if the Church by its failure to witness properly to the faith induces atheism (*GS* 19), if the Church shares "blame" for the break with Protestantism (*UR* 3), then the Church is in some sense still an imperfect realization of the Kingdom and in need of revision and reformation. Theologians with pent-up desires to criticize the Church now found a theological foundation for the airing of their views, and many needed little time to make their criticisms known, sometimes in painfully explicit terms.[79]

So What Happened?

The changes implemented by Vatican II were indeed remarkable. In a matter of a few years, centuries dedicated to mounting a reversal of the Reformation had ended; the Church had entered a time of *aggiornamento*—bringing the Church up-to-date with the times—turning the page on an old era, opening the window to a new era, new ideas, and a new vision of the Church ready to commune, after centuries of fighting it, with the ideals of the modern world. But something happened along the way, and we need to investigate what that is, because it has led to the experience of crisis in the Church long before today's crisis of sexual abuse.

The causes of crisis came from both inside and outside the Church.

Causes of Crisis from Within the Church

Vatican II created circumstances that made crisis *inevitable*, though with better care and understanding its gravity could have been avoided.

Vatican II constituted a seismic reorientation of the theology and life of the Church, from a Counter-Reformation mentality to *openness* to virtually everything—to the spirit of the modern world and its problems, to other Christians, non-Christians, the laity, technology—you name it! All in a matter of a few years! Its effects upon Catholics were similar to those experienced by "born-again" Christians: shock and total transformation.

The transformation was put into effect too quickly—within a matter of three years—but its effect at the parish level, as we saw above, was sometimes felt in a matter of days. What was formerly frowned upon the Church suddenly promoted: personal freedom, shared power, options regarding development of Church life. The changes involved "a profound

[79] Andrew Greeley in 1972 said, for example, "I believe the present leadership of the church to be morally, intellectually and religiously bankrupt," and spoke of the "collapse of confidence [and] credibility" in the Church; quoted in "Religion: To Save a Bankrupt," *Time*, February 21, 1972. Other adjectives used by many to describe the Church are better left unrepeated.

reexamination of the meaning of faith itself" by "disrupt[ing] an old system without substituting a new one."[80]

To introduce radical changes in the life of the Church in a matter of weeks, without recognizing and preparing for the effect they would have, represented a gross unawareness of the role of the psychological in human actions and of the inability of the Catholic mind to adapt to such consequential changes. As one Catholic intellectual at the time stated: "We were woefully remiss in understanding of social and psychological factors."[81]

The traumatic effect of the changes also pointed out the failure of the hierarchy to understand their relationship to the rank-and-file members. They assumed that the clergy and the laity would simply accept what they were told and obey, as they had always done. By and large the clergy did fall in line as directed, although there were glaring exceptions, but the laity did not. The hierarchy never adequately measured the mettle of their flock, and in failing to do so, a minor rebellion ensued.

The shift involved a massive number of people—about 52 million Catholics in the United States, over a billion in the world. There is no way a population of that size could absorb such a fundamental shift in its thinking without cataclysmic repercussions. And that is exactly what happened. And so, it must first be recognized that there was no way crisis could have been avoided.

Crisis as a Lack of Effective Leadership

While crisis was inevitable, it could have been greatly diminished. There were measures that could have been taken to reduce its dimensions.

One of the most common criticisms modern scholars make is that the present crisis in the Church is due to a large extent to the failure of the hierarchy to exercise effective leadership. We will examine examples of this criticism shortly, made by Donald Cozzens, David Gibson, Paul Lakeland, Peter Steinfels, and others.

We have already seen how Greeley mercilessly attacked the hierarchy in the early '70s for this weakness. Another example of this criticism has been made recently by David Carlin, one of the most pessimistic of contemporary Catholic writers. In his chapter entitled "The Church Faces a Crisis of Leadership," Carlin rightly asserts that "the Church is in a crisis situation, as it has been since the time of Vatican II."[82] He speaks of the "*appallingly poor*

---

80 Steinfels, *A People Adrift*, 203.

81 Daniel Callahan, *Commonweal*, March 3, 1967, 624, as cited by James Hitchcock, *The Decline and Fall of Radical Catholicism* (Garden City, NY: Doubleday/Image, 1972 [1971]), 28.

82 David Carlin, *The Decline and Fall of the Catholic Church in America* (Manchester, NH: Sophia Institute, 2003), 297–315, at 315.

level of episcopal leadership in the past generation"[83] in the Catholic Church, and compares the leadership's failure to react to the threat coming from "an extremely hostile secularist culture" as well as from the "liberal Christians who have embraced the values of anti-Christian secularism" to the failure of Western leaders to recognize the threat of Adolf Hitler until September 1, 1939, when Hitler invaded Poland and forced the West finally "to abandon all illusions."[84] Carlin concludes by holding out little hope that the Church will cease trying to be "modernized" even while modernizing a religion based on a God-Man incarnational religion is impossible: "The Church in America must cease to compromise," he argues, "or cease to exist."[85]

It is informative to contrast two notable Catholic figures—Richard McBrien and James Hitchcock—in their assessment of the crisis of leadership. McBrien reflects the liberal approach to the post-Vatican II crisis. Hitchcock is a noted conservative Church historian at Saint Louis University. Both argue that extremist right- and left-wing groups caused the crisis, and so both groups are to blame. Yet McBrien long ago placed ultimate responsibility for the crisis squarely on the hierarchy when he spoke of "two of the root causes" of the crisis: "Failure of church leadership to provide the general membership with adequate reasons for change and second, the failure of church leadership to demythologize its own self-image."[86]

McBrien's second "root cause" is perhaps more open to question, but represents his dedication to the idea of the Church becoming a "genuine participatory democracy."[87] Democratizing the Church would surely establish the "demythologizing" of the hierarchy's self-image that he seeks, but probably create even greater problems. The grandiose resolution of Church problems that he argues could be realized by making the Church a democracy represents a romantic dream more acceptable to the rosy ideas of a liberal in the immediate post-Vatican II Church than it is today.

Hitchcock agrees with McBrien that responsibility for the post-Vatican II polarization falls at least on some of the hierarchy, although not on their failure to explain the new theology but on their refusal to accept it. At the same time, he blamed the radical leftists as well:

> Responsibility for the failure of *aggiornamento* must be about evenly apportioned between rigid reactionaries, especially in the hierarchy, who never believed in reform and did little to implement it, and radical innovators with little commitment to historic Catholicism who nonetheless

---

[83] Ibid., 309–10.
[84] Ibid., 297–98.
[85] Ibid., 384–85.
[86] McBrien, *Remaking*, 14.
[87] Ibid., 15.

> had a disproportionate influence in the reform movement. Naturally, these two extremes have constantly fed on each other, each serving as a bogey which gives the other a certain credibility.[88]

Hitchcock, however, places the blame primarily on the progressives. He suspects "that what motivates the radicals is less their concern for the Church and the majority of its members than their continuing process of self-discovery." For Hitchcock, the progressives initially called for reform in the Church to improve the life of the Church, but this was really only "a way of avoiding the ultimate question of their own faith." Gradually they began "to repudiate almost everything which was part of historic Roman Catholicism," which led to "an unbalanced and disoriented kind of radicalism tending to degenerate into fanaticism and bitterness."

According to Hitchcock, a "weakness of fundamental belief" was "at the root of many liberals' dissatisfaction." What progressives were really trying to do was "overcome a gnawing crisis of faith, which they either did not recognize, lacking adequate self-knowledge, or did not want to recognize." The "chief dishonesty of the reformers was their studious concealment, even from themselves, of the problem of belief." Having finally obtained all they had sought for and more in the new theology of Vatican II, they were still unhappy and wanted more. Ultimately, this inability ever to be satisfied made "the problem of faith finally come to the surface, and many progressives found little fundamental belief on which they could rest."[89] This led many to abandon the Church.

Steinfels, in his latest book on the Church, makes the point that, even without the recent sex-abuse scandal, the Church "would still face a crisis," not only because of the lack of leadership among the American bishops, but also because they represent "some egregious examples of negligent, incompetent, duplicitous, and even corrupt Catholic leaders."[90]

Some of these points are well taken, for while crisis was inevitable, it could have been measurably reduced if the hierarchy had had a closer bond with the membership and explained the reasons for the changes. The new theology Vatican II had drawn up needed explanation, and to this day remains largely unexplained, and so continues to be a cause for crisis. And so, even when many Catholics did finally accept the changes, they often did so, as McBrien explains, because they were told to do so, without understanding the reasons for the changes. What we have here is schizophrenia: a Counter-

---

[88] Hitchcock, *Radical Catholicism*, 29.

[89] Ibid., 27–30.

[90] Steinfels, *A People Adrift*, 67. Steinfels repeatedly faults the American hierarchy for their lack of leadership (pp. 308–9), their "mediocrity" (p. 313), especially for their subservience to Rome (p. 315) and their unwillingness to stand up to Rome (p. 347), as well as ineffective priestly leadership (pp. 338–40).

Reformation mentality held by most Catholics obediently accepting practices implemented by a post–Vatican II theology that is no longer grounded in that mentality. McBrien described this problem as a "theory-and-practice gap"—living by principles justified by an outdated Counter-Reformation theology while implementing practices warranted only by the new Vatican II theology. He argued such a gap inevitably leads to *polarization*, a "tug-of-war between these two extremist forces," where traditionalists seek to "restore Catholic life to its preconciliar vigor," while many progressives go to the opposite extreme by trying to "adopt a much freer attitude toward ecclesiastical protocol and disciplinary decrees."[91] While it is impossible to know today how effective delineating the reasons for the changes might have been, there can be no doubt that the hierarchy's failure to do this was a major mistake.

Dual Orientation of the Teaching of Vatican II and Its Aftereffects

One of the greatest reasons for crisis in the Church is the new dual orientation in the theology of Vatican II, which gave rise to confusion regarding how the Church should proceed.

The new progressive elements were pleasing to reform-minded theologians, who took this theology and ran with it. In doing so, they downgraded the role of the traditional teachings still supported by Vatican II with which they had disagreed and which they had hoped Vatican II would dismiss. The old theology should be ignored, they argued, and the new developed. More traditionally oriented theologians, however, took the opposite approach. They grudgingly accepted the innovative measures in Vatican II, but preferred to focus on the traditional teachings that had been reaffirmed.

As a result of this radical reductionism in the teachings of Vatican II, a new political element with ideological divisions developed between the progressives and the traditionalists, or the leftists and the rightists, whom I identify as the "liberals" and "conservatives," pulling the Church's theology and practices in opposite directions.[92] Four examples of this type of conflict follow:

---

[91] Ibid., 57.

[92] Traditionalists often argue with some justification that the terms "liberal" and "conservative" are unacceptable and should not be used when discussing the theology of the Church, since the terms are appropriate to the discussion of different though politically legitimate ideologies in government policies. Thus, in Congress, the Democratic Party tends to be more liberal, and the Republican Party more conservative, but both represent legitimate perspectives on which direction American public policy should take. Traditionalists see in the Church only one appropriate theology, one that is in accord with revelation, Tradition, and the official teaching of the Church, so that when that theology is represented, it is not liberal or conservative but orthodox or "Catholic." The problem for them is that the more progressive wing often bends that theology or even rejects it. While I agree with the

1. Traditionalists emphasize the continuing support for a hierarchical Church in Vatican II teaching and give priority to that perspective, while the progressives insist priority should be given to the newly espoused collegiality. In fact, Vatican II is both hierarchical and collegial, but in combining the two, it failed to find a satisfactory way to align the seemingly contradictory theologies. Perhaps this was inevitable, for how do you reconcile vertical and horizontal ecclesiologies in the same Church? Protestant theology has abandoned the vertical dimension, but Vatican II, while incorporating the horizontal, recognized the need to reaffirm the tradition of hierarchical authority. Thus Vatican II ranked the new alongside the old, and inadvertently provided the breeding ground for dissension.

2. Traditionalists emphasize that the Catholic Church in Vatican II remains the one true Church of Christ; progressives argue that, since Vatican II accepted that there were elements of sanctification and truth that go to make up the true Church of Christ that reside outside the boundaries of the Roman Catholic Church (*UR* 3), the Roman Catholic Church may no longer make the unqualified claim that the true Church of Christ exists only within its borders. Again, both positions accurately represent the teaching of Vatican II, but the disagreement over its significance indicates the need for a more adequate integration of that teaching.

3. Traditionalists emphasize the priority of preaching the Word and administering the sacraments as central elements in the life of the Church; pro-

---

traditionalists in this regard, I find there are no better terms to use to discuss this division. Catholics also generally understand what these terms signify, and so I continue to use them while recognizing their weaknesses.

Some legitimacy for using these terms may be found in a recent study by the Pew Forum which divided religious groups into three subgroups: traditionalists, centrists, and modernists. The study defined traditionalists as "those with the most orthodox theological beliefs within their respective traditions" who "tend to take conservative stands on a host of cultural and public policy issues." Modernists, whom I am calling progressives or liberals, were "the least orthodox in belief and least involved with religious institutions" who "tend to be liberal on most policy issues." Centrists were "somewhere in between, both in terms of level of religious engagement and political orientation." The Pew Forum, "Religion & Public Life: A Faith-Based Partisan Divide" (Washington, DC: Pew Forum on Religion & Public Life, 2005), 1–15, at 3.

Sometimes the term "moderates" is also used instead of centrists, representing those who try to steer a course not ideologically driven by right- or left-wing extremes. These are those who accept the teachings of Vatican II with magisterial developments. These will often be ranked with the traditionalists by liberals and with the liberals by traditionalists. Obviously none of these terms is completely satisfactory but when properly understood they advance the discussion.

gressives insist that the social gospel is equally if not more important if the Church is to make inroads in the life of the modern world. Vatican II could be interpreted as sympathetic to both perspectives.

4. A major bone of contention before Vatican II was whether membership in the Catholic Church was any longer necessary for salvation. Traditionalists argued that it was, while progressives rejected the position. The fact is that Vatican II affirmed both teachings in an intricate, finely tuned theology that insisted on the necessity of membership in the Catholic Church for salvation, but allowed salvation outside the Church for those innocently unaware of that necessity. The teaching was not new, but Vatican II brought it to a level of completeness and consciousness not formerly present. The problem is that in the teaching, salvation outside the Catholic Church depends upon faulty perception of the truth, an unacceptable theology for progressives. And so they choose to abandon the finer points of this theological position and make claims that ignore the full teaching of Vatican II.

These were what one might call major ambivalences in the theology of Vatican II. I do not wish to imply that Vatican II was defective in its teaching, but only that there is a lack of harmonization of contrasting theologies that lent itself to politicization in the life of the Church, which was only to grow and become a dominant force for crisis in subsequent years.

Loss of an Aura of the Transcendent

It is sad to say, but it is true: the introduction of the theology of Vatican II in itself had an unforeseen negative impact on the psyche of the Catholic faithful, which ambivalences exacerbated, and this impact was to have enduring consequences, since it changed the fundamental understanding of the nature of the Church in the eyes of the people.

The pre-Vatican II inability of the people to understand the Latin liturgy had not been all bad; it had supported an aura of mystery in the life of the Church. In addition, since Catholics had little sense of history, doctrinal teachings were not understood as having developed in the course of history but as having been decreed from time immemorial by God, and so a sacral aura was attached to them. There was a sacral aura also to the Real Presence of Christ in the Eucharist: the ritual of transubstantiation dated back to the Last Supper.

What the changes decreed by Vatican II did was to destroy the sacral aura attached to the hierarchy and to Church life and practices. Changing the Mass into the vernacular brought the liturgy down to the human level. Putting the words in English, which was supposed to make it possible for the people finally to participate in a meaningful way in the liturgy, instead reduced the liturgy to words that not only did not inspire, but also destroyed the Mass's sense of mystery.

Even more troubling was what happened at the Council. Steinfels argues that "behind-the-scenes maneuvering" and "subtle shifts in church policy" drove a "dynamic" of "polarization" in American Catholicism during and after Vatican II, with Pope Paul VI left "to moderate the pace of change and maintain unity by placating contending factions" from the right and the left, all of this occurring against the background of "the highly political, questioning, confrontational mood of the 1960s and early 1970s."[93] But the fact that the Council bishops could deliberate over Church teachings and policies indicated that these were subject to change, and were therefore not established by divine decree after all. The sacral aura had vanished.

Theological conflicts created by post-Vatican II disputes over the implementation of the decrees were heavily destructive of the divine aura that had surrounded the Church. But perhaps most destructive of all was the moving of the Eucharist out of the central position in the apse of the Church. This was a truly horrendous act of monumental import: not only did it imply that the Real Presence in the Eucharist was no longer central to the life of worship, but also, as we have seen, it lent credence to the notion that after four hundred years the Church had capitulated to the Protestants' rejection of that teaching.

There was perhaps no greater force for destruction of the sacral aura that engulfed the life of the Church than the three-year period of deliberation over the morality of artificial methods of birth control. This time became something of a grace period for many Catholic women who were frequently advised by their confessors to follow dictates of conscience until the final judgment was made. The indecision lent credence to the idea that God had not decreed clarity on this issue. Pope Paul finally decided to reject the recommendation of the majority of the committee, and declared that the use of artificial methods of birth control was immoral. When this decree was made known with the publication of the Encyclical Letter on the Regulation of Birth, *Humanae Vitae*, in July of 1968, it appeared to be a decision not sent down from heaven by divine mandate, but arbitrarily imposed by human judgment that could just as easily have come down on the opposite side if the Pope had chosen to do so.

The situation was compounded by the fact that the teaching was controversial. No greater force for the politicization of the life of the Church occurred than the rejection of the encyclical's teachings by many respected theologians of a liberal persuasion, and therefore much of the blame for this development must be placed at their feet. Suddenly, Church teaching

---

93 Steinfels, *A People Adrift*, 20.

became the center of political debate: conservative theologians supported the teaching of the Church, liberals rejected it. This bifurcation was even more promoted by the fact that many of the liberal theologians not only disagreed with the encyclical's teachings, but counseled penitents in the confessional that they could act in good conscience in rejecting the teaching as well. It is impossible to exaggerate the negative impact this rejection had, for many Catholics concluded that if theologians could reject the ban, why couldn't they? But if this teaching could be rejected, why couldn't any?

From now on, Church teachings began to be treated like bills before the federal legislature where, if you were Republican, you supported conservative measures; if you were Democrat, you supported liberal measures. So if you were a conservative Catholic, you favored the strict reassertion of the Church's ban on birth control and other doctrinal teachings and disciplines; if you were a liberal Catholic, you rejected them.

The choice of what kind of Catholic you were now going to be was up to you and your conscience, for which the views of the hierarchy were nothing more than recommendations by men of fallible judgment. This new legislative power of personal conscience was supposedly granted by the theology of Vatican II. Thus, along with the politicization of Church teaching went the rejection of the infallible power of the pope and the hierarchy.

Thus the history surrounding the changes made at Vatican II and the publication of *Humanae Vitae* had the effect of making the teaching authority of the Church purely advisory. Abiding by one's conscience from now on was the norm for personal beliefs and practices. This movement away from the sense of the supernatural toward the natural, from the eternal to the temporal, led Catholics increasingly to accept the norms of the secular world as guiding principles of morality and truth, and increasingly led to the question of whether there was anything intrinsically different between religious belief (faith) and rational practice (reason).

Thus a new age of rationalism in the life of the Church began after Vatican II as a result of its effects and the effects of *Humanae Vitae*. But, clearly, much of the responsibility for the deterioration of the life of the Church resided not simply with the failure of leadership on the part of the hierarchy with the implementation of Vatican II; it rested much more with Church theologians who injected their own personal inadequacies, partisan politics, and emotional sympathies into the fray. Had they continued to remain faithful to the pope and united with the hierarchy as they had always been, and accepted Church teaching as obedience servants of the Church, it is quite likely that they could have provided their own leadership to the hierarchy and the laity through this difficult time. Who knows, perhaps the crisis of polarization that began at this time and continues to wreak disintegration in the life of the Church would never have happened.

Church as a Sign of Contradiction

Vatican II's new theology of openness to the world overshadowed its continuing proclamation of the gospel as a sign of contradiction to the world.

Traditional pre-Vatican II thinking had so often focused on the world as an arena of evil against which the Church needed to stand strong. The problems of the Reformation and of modernism contributed much to this mentality. Thus, when *Gaudium et Spes* stressed the need for Catholics to cooperate with all well-intentioned peoples to create a world more fully human (*GS* 40), it unleashed a long-held, pent-up desire to share in worldly values that was difficult to hold in check.

The problem is that sharing in the values of the world is not exactly the same as making the world more human, and this distinction was perhaps not adequately enunciated by Vatican II. Suddenly the secular was no longer evil but good—not to be shunned but accepted. It was not a force that could drag Christians down from their service of God and his Kingdom, but rather the place where God is at work to erect his Kingdom. Since, as we have seen, the Kingdom was no longer identified simply with the Church, the world was now becoming the Kingdom in process, so that to enter into the life of the world could be considered a good thing done to promote the coming of the Kingdom. This was truly no doubt an exhilarating concept. The Church was becoming one of the many forces in the world for the building up of God's Kingdom.

There was much truth in this perspective, but when pressed to an exaggerated degree, it ceased to maintain the Council's focus on the Church as the "initial budding forth of the Kingdom," a statement not made about any force at work in the world other than the Church. Stressing so strongly the role the Church was to play in the world as the arena for Christian activity inevitably led to a spirit of accommodation with the values of the world as an undesirable byproduct of Vatican II.

What effect did this accommodation have on the life of the Church? Many Catholics began to seek to achieve by worldly standards with an even more aggressive spirit than others had. Today, for example, Catholics rank as one of the largest single groups excelling at the height of the corporate ladder. This in itself is not necessarily bad, provided that it represents efforts to fulfill Vatican II's mandate to transform the world into a reflection of the spirit of Christ (*AA* 4; *LG* 31). Unfortunately, that part of the theology of the laity is often left behind.

As a result, the secularism that the modern world espouses has become woven into much of the fabric of Catholic life. Catholic action's new outward thrust took on such a dominant role in many Catholic lives that it seems almost impossible today to stem it. If there is any one reason for crisis in the Church today, perhaps it is this one: Catholics have become engineers of the forces of secularism!

Theology of the Laity before Its Time

This failure of the Church to resist accommodation with the world must be seen as one aspect of the larger failure of the new theology of the laity.

As we have already seen, Vatican II championed a theology of the laity that represented a major force for integrating lay activity into the active life of the Church. The laity were no longer to be second-class citizens; they were now rightfully endowed directly by Christ with a spirituality that made them sharers in his mission as prophet, priest, and king. In view of the approaching downturn in vocations to the priesthood and religious life, many began to see the Church of the future as a Church dependent on the laity for the vitality of its mission, and this prognosis still seems to be true.

Nevertheless, the laity have largely failed to assume their proper role in the post-Vatican II Church. A major failure in Vatican II's theology of the laity is that, while it endowed lay people with powers and privileges of active leadership long overdue in the life of the Church, it failed to recognize that most of the laity were not properly educated into what active leadership would entail.

The Church once again lacked the analysis of the situation that any sociologist or psychologist would easily have made, namely, that, after centuries of being second class citizens whose membership in the Church had been reduced to obedience to hierarchical directives, most of the laity were without any understanding of the theology of the Church beyond basic catechism, and often not even that. This is not to place any blame on the laity for this situation; if anyone is to blame, it is the hierarchy who had given the laity a mostly passive role. One must admit, however, that the laity were largely acquiescent. In any case, the laity were almost totally unequipped to know what a theology of the laity could mean, and not formed enough to realize there might be benefits in learning about their new status as sharers in responsibility for the life of the Church.

As a result, it was impossible for most of the laity to enter responsibly into the new mission of the Church designed for them. If there was any residue of the new theology that made it to their shores, it was known only by the simple principle that what had formerly been forbidden—entrance into the life of the world—was now approved. And so, in accepting this new open-door policy granted them by the Church without a concomitant spirituality to guide them, the laity in general turned to the world's norms for value as a guide for their own spirituality, namely, American democratic conceptions where reason, conscience, and the suasion of the majority dominate.

This dominance of the rational as the norm for Christian living and the guide to Christian value once again represents a major failure on the part of the Church: that it granted a new freedom to the laity—rightly theirs and long overdue—without preparing them for responsible integration of that freedom into the faith life of the Church. This failure to understand all the richness of the theology of the laity remains to this day one of the major weaknesses in the Church, and serves only to promote the increasing division of faith from reason. As a result, the liberals' call for democratization in the Church continues to make greater and greater inroads, because it seems so eminently rational as the paradigm of Christian value just as it is of American value. As the American democratic system increasingly becomes the laity's norm for Christian living, the Church is more and more pressured to accept greater democratization as the standard for its own Christian living.

Causes of Crisis from Outside the Church

Rupture with Traditional Values

The period from the late 1960s on, as is widely known, was one of upheaval in American society. There was a rupture with tradition caused by the questioning of long-held values and structures.

Traditional values seemed to be inadequate in the face of new situations, such as new discoveries in technology that created new moral issues for which received answers no longer seemed adequate. Traditional institutions, such as the corporate structures of the business world, were considered unjust in the treatment of certain members of society, making inflated profits while large segments of society, such as minority groups, were living in poverty. This became the breeding ground for Marxism, which in spite of the tyranny which many Eastern European countries experienced under Marxist domination, seemed to many to provide better economic hopes than unrestrained capitalism. America's unending and ineffective waging of the Vietnam War also called into question the morality of government institutions. Even the Founding Fathers were seriously questioned if not condemned for their unjust and prejudiced interpretation of the fundamental principles and values by which the nation should live.

This rupture with all things traditional was inevitably to lead to rupture with the institutional Church. Suddenly its traditional values and structures appeared no more adequate in resolving the troubling issues of the modern world than were those of secular institutions, for, in truth, the values and principles that motivated Church policies were often no loftier than those of secular society. The Church was condemned for being complicit in the same evil policies that motivated the rest of society.

The fact is that for so long a time, the configuration of Catholic life had been steeped in secular values beneath a piety that was unrecognizably superficial. Catholics in America had for so long a time so eagerly sought acceptance by the secular world that they assumed the values of that world as their own, which made the Church totally unequipped to address the Catholic reformers who challenged the values of that world. If secular institutions were guilty of unjust procedures toward the world, so too, it seemed, was the Church. And if the old was out of date and hopelessly contaminated by the failed values of the world, so too was this true for the Church.

And so there developed a certain confluence of the secular spirit of rejection of the old and openness to the unstructured new in American society with a post-Vatican II spirit of rejection of the traditional institutional structures of the Church and openness to a spirit of unstructured reform. For many, the only way the Church could escape a parallel rejection of its past by the new society was to consent to the values of the new, to reconfigure its self-understanding according to the values aborning in the secular world.

Social Justice and New-World Values

Thus there was born liberation theology in some segments of the Church in America, for if there was any way for the Church to be accepted by the new society, it was not to support the sacramental life of the Church, which smacked of the failed past, but to join the ranks of the reformers and stand for social justice, the only cause that made the new-world values appear acceptably Christian.

But Catholic activists had already been strongly influenced by the civil rights movement and got involved in social justice issues in America. The crusade that Martin Luther King, Jr. waged for fairness and equal treatment for minority groups attracted many Catholics, especially priests, to join in support of his efforts. The civil rights movement promoted the idea that all people had equal rights *as human beings*, and that all fair-minded people should support these rights. The Vatican and the American hierarchy failed at first to take a position on these issues, and though they tried to recover later from their initial hesitancy, the Catholic branch of the movement quickly concluded that it could wage its social justice battles without the support of the Church.

In this way, the institutional Church became irrelevant to resolving political and moral questions of the day. It could offer little or nothing more than what human wisdom and right judgment could offer on its own. And so Catholics quickly concluded they could go it alone in resolving personal moral issues as well. Once again, the mentality of the world invaded the life of the Catholic community, supplanting the traditional moral authority of the hierarchy.

American Society Increasingly Individualistic

As the human being grew in stature in education, technological achievement, and social engineering, there grew an increasing awareness of one's ability to solve one's own problems rather than to call upon God for safety and direction (in other words, a resurgence of the optimism attached to the powers of the human spirit in nineteenth- and early twentieth-century Europe). As the post–World War II human being became increasingly self-reliant and self-made, God seemed less necessary than he had been during the turn-of-the-century immigrant years and the periods of the wars. Therefore, there was less need for his Church as well. As the neo-Enlightenment movement toward reason and self-reliance grew, external authority became an imposition, a violation of one's selfhood, of one's identity, and a crutch for the weak that was no longer needed for the strong.

Secular Idea of Democracy Enters Church Life

There was a too easy association of the *spirit of freedom and democracy* in America granted by the Bill of Rights with the *spirituality of freedom* experienced in the Church. Liberals in the Church seem especially to have been too quick in making this correlation. As the American spirit moved rapidly toward overcoming old boundaries to freedom of thought and action regarding personal conduct, especially regarding rights to abortion and sexual freedoms, American Catholics often felt those same freedoms ought to be available to them, and so they introduced a call for the destruction of old boundaries inhibiting democratic decision-making and personal morality in their lives in the Church.

The problem is that while America is a democracy, the Church is not and never has been. The new theology of Vatican II was collegial and communitarian, but not democratic. The genuine spirituality of freedom appropriate to life in the Church is conditioned, as all Christian spirituality is, by the revealed will of God, and freedom is always to be found within a life in conformity with the Truth contained in that revelation as expressed in magisterial teaching.

The way of life in American society and life in the Church have much in common, since both were founded upon values promoted by Jesus Christ. But since many in the Church wanted it and still want it to be as democratic and open to the unrestricted as life in American society has increasingly become, polarization inevitably follows. Thus the American Church shares in the same internal contradiction increasingly rampant in American society—between doing whatever seems acceptable to human reason stretched to the limits of one's imagination, and living by the standards of the Judeo-Christian revelation on which both American society and the Church were founded, and which led both to their own greatness.

Life after Vatican II

In the immediate aftermath of Vatican II—from 1965 onward—the progressives appeared to have won the "battle" over which direction the Church would take. The new theology of Vatican II was such a shock to the traditionalists, including Paul VI, that their centuries-old position of dominance in the life of the Church seemed ended. Vatican II seemed to have dealt them a powerful blow, whose effects were fatal.

Progressives, on the other hand, clearly felt that with Vatican II they had won the battle—not as if to say that the war was over, but that the Council had generally sided with them, and that only the kinks had to be worked out. More precisely, the progressives mounted, largely unchallenged, their cause to change the Church according to the newly minted principles encoded in Vatican II, while downgrading the role of the vestiges of traditional teachings. A new Church was aborning with a new theology of openness to innovation in inner Church life and congeniality toward the world, with rejection of all of the Church's narrow, hard-line teachings of the past.

One might also characterize the new direction of the Church in this way: Whereas the life of the pre-Vatican II Church had emphasized the theology of the Cross, post-Vatican II theology emphasized the theology of the Resurrection, and its spirit was infectious. No longer was the overcoming of sin and penance and the renunciation of secular values to typify the life of the Church, because Christ had redeemed us! Redemption was not a thing of the future, it had already begun. It was time to emphasize liberation, freedom, and openness to all that was good in God's creation! The world and its values were no longer considered evils to be shunned, but goods to be enjoyed! Those who lived through that period felt a cool refreshing breeze of jubilation and exhilaration from having been liberated from the burdens of past penitential spirituality, and traditionalists who felt otherwise were largely ignored.

This period of domination by the progressives endured from 1965 to 1978, and had it not succumbed to its major weakness, it might have continued to prevail. But it had a major flaw: it had no principle of limitation. The new theology of Vatican II, as formulated in the sixteen published documents to come out of the Council, was considered by the progressives as only the start of an ongoing and unending period of development of new theological ideas and practices. Instead of Vatican II setting up a new theology for the ages, progressives saw the Council's decrees as *only a beginning*!

Vatican II, it was felt, had been cramped by the leftover preconciliar Counter-Reformation theology that was in its death throes at the Council. Those who were able to read clearly the "spirit" of Vatican II, and perceive the "signs of the times" reflected in that spirit, could supposedly intuit that

Vatican II had intended that the outdated, moribund hierarchical theology whose vestiges still remained was to be gradually discarded and replaced with the new collegial, democratic communitarian theology that was only able to be represented in its initial stages at the Council. In other words, the progressives felt Vatican II had given them the mandate to take the innovative elements of the new theology and run with them.

Unfortunately for the progressives, there was nothing in the teaching of Vatican II to which one could point as the basis for this nebulous, open-ended "spirit" supposedly found there. And so progressives like McBrien were forced to argue that in Vatican II there were "many changes implicitly endorsed by the council," or that further change "can be justified as a legitimate extension of the council's teaching" by seeing such change as "the product of the supremely unpredictable Spirit."[94]

Not to be deterred by such flimsy argumentation, progressives ran with this "spirit" with great abandon, and that is where the post-Vatican II crisis began. They felt that the principle of collegiality, the new theology of the laity, and the freedom of conscience enunciated at Vatican II gave them the bases they needed for experimentation, innovation, local ingenuity, creativity, and personal expression, none of which required a mandate from the Church.

As a result, gross aberrations followed, such as "using beer and pretzels (or Coke and potato chips)"[95] for the Eucharist, and Masses without priests. As for the doctrines of the Church, none went unexamined: Hitchcock, commenting on the situation at the time, stated with accuracy that "there is now scarcely a single traditional doctrine of the Church which is not seriously questioned by some prominent theologians, not excluding the 'existence' of God."[96] No teaching of the Church, from the doctrine of the Trinity to the Real Presence of Christ in the Eucharist, went unquestioned. All teachings, disciplines, and practices were placed in doubt. Almost anything was deemed admissible in the new era of experimentation that Vatican II had supposedly engendered. Paul VI, as well as much of the rest of the hierarchy, was appalled at what was happening, but few had presence enough to react decisively. The Church was adrift, and the Pope, a good but introverted man, seemed overwhelmed by the tide, and incapable of coping with the degree of dislocation and confusion that was overtaking the Church.

A new humanistic psychology played a major role in dislocating seminary training in this period. A most enlightening treatment of the disintegration of moral barriers and taboos that allowed easement into a culture that cham-

---

94 McBrien, *Remaking*, 22, 65–66.

95 Steinfels, *A People Adrift*, 175.

96 Hitchcock, *Radical Catholicism*, 18.

pioned self-fulfillment and unrestraint is presented by the Sulpician Howard P. Bleichner, who has been intimately involved in priestly formation since Vatican II. Bleichner rightly argues that a "new form of spirituality" had a major impact on seminary training after Vatican II that did much to promote a new spirituality of liberation, based on the humanistic psychology of Carl Rogers and Abraham Maslow. Based on "the model of self-actualizing human growth," individuals were advised "to get in touch with their own deepest feelings," which they were "to open up to others" in group encounters. Nor was the human spirit weighted any longer with evil inclinations or sinful actions. Rather, "when the self-actualization model is used, it often empties sinful actions of their objective content. Self-actualizers are set on an expanding continuum of personal growth, and 'sins' are regarded as setbacks on the road to ever greater progress. There is only one large sin in this model: the failure to grow."[97] Once sin is redefined as an inhibition or personality block, the height of spirituality is identified with "the fully actualized person," who becomes "the best candidate for growth in Christian virtue."[98]

Along with this spirituality of self-actualization goes the Enlightenment principle of self-rule. According to Bleichner, instead of being bound by conformity to outside agents, with the new spirituality of self-fulfillment "the fully actualized person acts from internal motivation. Such persons are a rule unto themselves. For them rules are not necessary and are counterproductive. The only rule is to get in touch with one's feelings and share them with others."[99]

In my mind, this identification of natural, youthful psychological urges for self-fulfillment dovetailed with the new emphasis on the theology of the Resurrection, and unleashed a new recipe for excellence in Christian virtue that had few restraints.

Arrival of John Paul II

Such was the situation in the Church until that fateful day in October of 1978 when Cardinal Karol Wojtyła of Kraków was elected Pope. The new Pope, John Paul II, was a Pole—with all the determination and dedication that so often goes with being a Pole, at least since the Nazi era—and had Catholics known what that choice meant, they would not have been surprised by the effect his election was to have on the life of the Church.

John Paul was a man who had been able to survive the crushing persecution of Poland under the hegemony of the Nazis, as well as the era of Communist domination under the ruthless Marxist Stalin. He was born

[97] Bleichner, *View from the Altar*, 33–34.
[98] Ibid., 33.
[99] Ibid., 34–35.

into a strongly Roman Catholic family. He was deeply committed to Catholicism. He entered the priesthood in secret training in Kraków, and barely managed to survive imprisonment and death for his beliefs. In short, he was not a man accustomed to accommodating weakness or abuse. The power of his love for and dedication to Christ, and his eagerness to stand up for the dignity and freedom of the human person, was to dominate all of his thinking, and made him a major player in the efforts leading to the overthrow of Communism and the liberation of Eastern Europe in 1989.

Once he became in 1978 the leader of the Christian world, John Paul, unlike Paul VI, not only did not remain silent about the abuses in Church life, but set out to eradicate them. He was a man totally committed to the Church and the following of its teachings, and ready to implement with vigor and force, if necessary, the theology of Vatican II in its traditional teachings as well as in its innovations. So totally was he committed to Vatican II that one might succinctly summarize his theological position by deeming him the Vatican II Pope: if it's in Vatican II, it's in John Paul II's teaching; if not, then it's not.

John Paul was troubled by the post-Vatican II abuses. One of the major new principles that needed to be implemented in his reign was the exercise of greater collegiality, one of Vatican II's major innovations, and this he was ready to do. But if the yin and the yang is true of Eastern life, it is also true in Western theology: because John Paul saw such an extreme leftist drift in the post-Vatican II Church, lest the life of the Church get out of hand, he retrenched by reinforcing the more traditional policies of the Church.

It has often been remarked that many pre-Vatican II liberal theologians became conservatives in the post-Vatican II Church. This was not unlike John Paul's successor, Benedict XVI, who as a theologian at the Council strongly supported *aggiornamento*, but then, as he saw some of the exaggerated calls for renewal being made by some of the reformers, began retrenching to more traditional lines. This apparently occurred especially when he was confronted with the student uprising of 1968 in Germany at the University of Tübingen where he was a professor. He was shocked by the riots and the student invasion of his classroom, and saw these as a threat to order and the freedom of the spirit that arises within order, and so drew back in his thinking.

In the increasing readiness of Catholic theologians to publish widely affronts to centuries-old dogmatic teachings, such as the existence of the Trinity, the divinity of Christ, or his unique role as Savior of the world, Cardinal Ratzinger, as Prefect for the Congregation for the Doctrine of the Faith, became the defender of the faith and frequently banned reformers' publications, all with the support of John Paul. In other words, seeing the abuses to which reform had led in society and in the life in the Church, the Pope and the hierarchy became reactive, and restored a less collegial and a more centralized approach to Church life.

As John Paul II's final years were approaching, and continuing after his death, liberals frequently criticized him as well as his successor for abandoning the collegial directives given by Vatican II. But in doing so, liberals chose to ignore the post-Vatican II excesses in the Church that they had fostered. A good argument can be made that if the liberals had not gone to extremes in their questioning of Church dogmas and teachings, in their refusal to comply with Church discipline, and in their efforts to assert local independence, John Paul II's recentralization of authority in the Vatican might never have been needed, and a more gracious period of collegial development might have occurred. And so, if the cause of the current polarization may be laid anywhere, it seems it must be laid at the feet of the innovators because of their excesses.

The process of recentralization set in motion with John Paul II has so far not been reversed by Benedict XVI. Liberals meanwhile have not abandoned their demands for further reform. As a result, it is commonly accepted today that the polarization that set in in the immediate aftermath of Vatican II has intensified to an extreme that has torn apart the life of the Church—so much so that one might easily conclude that there are two churches in the Catholic Church today, one for those who remain in union with the Pope and accept the official teachings of the Church, and one for those who do not.

It remains to be seen if Benedict XVI will be able to overcome this polarization, but it is not likely. He has frequently argued to the need for the Church of the future to become a "creative minority" or a "small committed Church," and so it is more likely that he will try to purify the Church of heterodox elements. He also feels the future of the Church lies with the youth, among whom he finds a strong and significant committed element that wishes to return the Church to a flock faithful to the Church and loyal to its teachings. There is no doubt Benedict sees his mission to be the restoration of a unity to the Church based on a flock of loyal and committed Christians. In doing this, he is also committed to the mission of spreading the gospel of Christ and the primacy of the Catholic Church among Christian communities. It will certainly be one of the major challenges of Benedict's reign to achieve his goals in the limited time available to him.

Sex-Abuse Crisis

Against all of this background, we are now able to approach today's sex-abuse crisis.

All that has been said above illustrates quite amply that there was crisis in the Catholic Church long before what is today commonly called the "sex-abuse crisis." But the concept of crisis in the Church has only recently garnered popular attention, due to the "sex-abuse" scandal that erupted in the Church in January 2002. Since then, a slew of books has appeared, most offering various solutions to the newly discovered crisis, and dramatizing the critical nature of the Church's situation, which has suddenly become apparent. But the cure-all in most of these publications seems to be greater involvement of the laity in the decision-making operations of the Church.

Not unusual in this respect is the work of the Catholic journalist David Gibson. Gibson states: "Catholicism is at a crossroads." He appears only now to have become aware of a situation that has been true for some forty years, for if the American Church is at a crossroads, it arrived at that point long before the present scandal. The fact that he makes such a statement now only indicates how little American Catholics are aware of the long-term roots of the present malaise and what the nature of the problem really is.

Gibson continues: "The church must find a unity of purpose and a common direction to move forward on her pilgrim way. There is no going backward, as a small but vocal minority would like to do."[100] What exactly does "going backward" mean, and who are the "vocal minority"? "Going backward" characterizes for Gibson what the conservatives want: not change but a reaffirmation of "Catholic orthodoxy," a return to the standards of traditional "moral behavior" and the overcoming of "America's decadent culture," and citing George Weigel, "a Catholicism that has reclaimed the wisdom of the past . . . [and] risks the high adventure of fidelity."[101] What Gibson caricatures as Weigel's "going backward" is actually Weigel's call for a return to "the wisdom of the past" in order to "create the possibility of a genuinely new future."[102] It is difficult to see how anyone could be opposed to such thinking, but Gibson seems to consider it antiquated.

What Gibson touts is "reform,"[103] apparently unaware that Weigel also calls for "reform."[104] For Gibson, reform essentially means "reforms of governance," which means a democratizing of the Church that "would focus on the laity and would help to restore their trust—the critical factor in resolving the crisis—by involving them more closely in the administration of the church."[105] Gibson catalogues the usual list of data supposedly indicating that need: shortage of priests, laity clamoring for greater voice in Church

100 David Gibson, *The Coming Catholic Church: How the Faithful Are Shaping a New American Catholicism* (New York: HarperSanFrancisco, 2003), 342.

101 Ibid., 128–30. Gibson's citation of Weigel is from the latter's *The Courage to Be Catholic: Crisis, Reform, and the Future of the Church* (New York: Basic, 2002), 7.

102 Weigel, *Courage*, 4.

103 Gibson, *The Coming Catholic Church*, 343.

104 Reform is the leitmotif in Weigel's *Courage*: "How [today's Catholic crisis] might become a great moment of reform is the business of this book" (p. 8).

105 Gibson, *The Coming Catholic Church*, 343.

operations, the need for popular input in the selection of bishops, and greater accountability of the hierarchy. Little of this is new, but it makes for good press. All of it fails to see the crux of the problem at a far deeper level, which Gibson hints at when he speaks of the need for "unity of purpose and a common direction." These are in fact exactly what are needed, but they will not come from the kind of reform that Gibson calls for.

Among the works seeing greater involvement of the laity as the panacea for Church crisis, most notable is the work by the widely respected theologian Paul Lakeland, The *Liberation of the Laity*—a title implying of course that the laity are now in some situation of subservience. Lakeland, a former Jesuit priest, goes so far as to claim that the "mission of the church" is now to be "primarily conducted by laypeople, acting in the Spirit and on their own initiative," with the clergy shifting into "an indispensable but ancillary role."[106] The point seems to be that if the clergy have botched up the operations of the Church, turning those operations over to the laity, most of whom have little training in Catholic theology and the intricacies of Church life, and little time and energy to become so involved since they are often gainfully employed full-time and need to raise good Catholic families, will somehow solve the problem. This is the same kind of apotheosis of democracy we saw in McBrien's thinking. Such simplistic solutions can only come from people who either live in a vacuum or who have little understanding of the foibles of human nature, wherever that nature may be found.

Even though the public became aware only in the twenty-first century, thanks to aggressive investigations by *The Boston Globe*, recent studies have shown that the height of the abuse occurred in the 1970s after rising gradually in the late 1950s and '60s, and diminished considerably in the 1980s and '90s.[107] Can any explanation be given as to why the '70s were the most abusive? Perhaps a better way to phrase the question is: Why did the heart of the sex-abuse crisis occur so shortly after Vatican II?

An investigation of the mood of that period goes far in answering the question: as we saw, almost all structure, all rigor in thought and practice, and most of the traditional principles that motivated Catholic spirituality fell by the wayside in the wake of the Council. The spirit of innovation descended upon the life of the Church to such an extent that it shook the

106 Paul Lakeland, *The Liberation of the Laity: In Search of an Accountable Church* (New York: Continuum, 2002), 255.

107 Bleichner, *View from the Altar*, 43–44, reporting on a study by Laurie Goodstein in the *New York Times*, "Decades of Damage; Trail of Pain in Church Crisis Leads to Nearly Every Diocese," of January 12, 2003, 1, 20–21, and the study made by the John Jay College of Criminal Justice, *The Nature and Scope of the Problem of Sexual Abuse of Minors by Catholic Priests and Deacons in the United States* (Washington, DC: USCCB, 2004).

Church to its very foundations. All that had formerly been taken for granted, as a foundation for Church discipline and formative of religious principles, was suddenly open to question.

One cannot exaggerate the traumatic effect Vatican II's *aggiornamento* had on those most devoted to service of the Church. As the reasons for undergoing the long years of formation necessary to be a priest or religious began to be questioned in the wake of the new spotlight on the theology of the laity, seminary life came undone. Bleichner argues that the "most difficult years were 1967 to 1980" when the seminary and seminarians "lost their bearings."[108] Not only did the rigorous years of study and penitential discipline now seem irrelevant, but the spirituality that had condoned such discipline, based on the sinfulness of the human condition and the need to school the soul against the wiles of the world, suddenly appeared medieval. Because Christ had been raised from the dead and his disciples redeemed, a spirituality that witnessed to that Resurrection and redemption was the order of the day. Such a spirituality was not yet in place; it had to be composed, and all the degrees in spirituality seminary professors had from the outdated mentality of a former age provided little guidance on how to do it. It was the spirit of the Enlightenment now coming into its own inside the modern Church that was to provide the principles of guidance.

Attempts to compose the new spirituality for the modern Church led to excesses beyond belief. At or near the beginning of this movement must be placed the rejection by leading Catholic scholars, especially Catholic clergy, of the teaching on contraception in *Humanae Vitae*,[109] as well as the groundswell in the questioning of all principles of traditional sexual morality:

> For a generation after the council, the Catholic Church spoke with two voices on moral issues. There was the voice of Rome and the bishops, traditional positions articulated in older categories. Then there were the voices of Catholic moral theologians, often in tenured positions at universities, who espoused more liberal positions not only on birth control but on a variety of related topics. Newer categories, they argued, allowed for greater flexibility on masturbation, homosexuality, premarital sex, and other sexual issues.[110]

It did not take young seminarians long to understand the significance of such views: If those most noted among educators and teachers of future priests and religious openly rejected the traditional teachings of the Church

---

108 Bleichner, *View from the Altar*, 41.

109 "In the United States, a public protest criticizing the encyclical was signed by over six hundred Catholic scholars" (Steinfels, *A People Adrift*, 255).

110 Bleichner, *View from the Altar*, 31–32.

as outdated, and opened the doors to subjective standards of morality based on one's need for self-fulfillment, how could the clergy of the future be expected to do otherwise? But the moral confusion this period of transition generated was palpable:

> To the contrary, newer developments had the cumulative effect of making younger priests unsure about their own thinking. What is a sin? What is a serious sin? What is a mortal sin? What was crystal clear a generation before now became murky. The fallout of this confusion spread in all directions.[111]

The mood of the time was quickly grasped by all: it was an era of transition, which meant that everything was open to question, and every new procedure justified as experimentation. Perennial moral truths and doctrinal teachings, as well as preeminent disciplinary practices long taken for granted as reflective of an objective order of truth rooted in the mind and wisdom of God (Plato), were now considered situational and subject to change: "The church's faltering stand on birth control fit hand-in-glove with a new set of permissive attitudes on sexuality sweeping the country."[112] It was assumed by many itching for novelty that among those disciplines open to question was the requirement of celibacy for the clergy. It was only a matter of time before this rule would be made optional, many felt, and since a married clergy would introduce the best of both possible vocations—the priesthood and the married life—why not start to live a life already directed by the coming amalgamation?

Human Sexuality and Its Consequences

Concrete evidence of how widespread the rejection of the teaching of the Church was becoming even among Catholics, and how it was being replaced by the Enlightenment mentality of reason and science, were new approaches to morality that came to light in the publication of a study commissioned in 1972 by the Catholic Theological Society of America (CTSA). The board of directors voted to neither approve nor reject the final report, but to "receive" it when presented at the annual meeting in 1976. But there was no doubt that a sizable number of the membership present at that meeting, which I attended, was strongly in approval. The board authorized the publication of the report "as a service to the membership of the Society and a wider public of interested persons," and felt the report would "contribute to the further reflection and discussion that is called for on a topic of such moral and

[111] Ibid., 32.
[112] Ibid.

pastoral significance."[113] There is no document that I know of that epitomizes more concretely and more succinctly the revolutionary direction that some theologians and other liberal scholars in the Church were taking at that time. The late Richard John Neuhaus in 2002 stated: "The seeds of everything that has come to light in recent months are to be found there."[114]

The report took the fundamental position that traditional standards of morality rooted in traditional Catholic doctrine were outdated. They were to be replaced by a situational ethics consonant with modern scholarship regarding the interpretation of the Bible, but the last word was to be given to the latest scientific and empirical data supporting human processes of psychological development and the needs of the individual as the norm for moral truth. We need only cite a few salient conclusions drawn from the report to give some idea of the new spirituality that was developing:

Regarding the Role of the Scriptures in Formulating Moral Positions:

> Every statement in the New Testament regarding human sexuality is historically occasioned and conditioned. . . . We cannot validly abstract statements regarding sexuality out of their biblical context and use them as proof texts to validate any twentieth-century theology of human sexuality. . . . Critical biblical scholarship finds it impossible on the basis of the empirical data to approve or reject categorically any particular sexual act outside of its contextual circumstances and intentions. . . . Anyone who maintains that the Bible absolutely forbids certain forms of sexual behavior, regardless of circumstances, must likewise bear the burden of proof.[115]

The Role of Scientific Data:

The text makes liberal use of the Kinsey reports[116] and Masters and Johnson,[117] as well as other studies to emphasize that empirical data show wide-

---

113 Anthony Kosnik, William Carroll, Agnes Cunningham, Ronald Modras, James Schulte, *Human Sexuality: New Directions in American Catholic Thought*, a study commissioned by the Catholic Theological Society of America (New York: Paulist, 1977), ix.

114 Richard John Neuhaus, "The Public Square: A Continuing Survey of Religion and Public Life: Scandal Time (Continued)," *First Things* 124 (June/July 2002): 78.

115 Kosnik et al., *Human Sexuality*, 30–31.

116 The text cites A. C. Kinsey et al., *Sexual Behavior in the Human Male* (Philadelphia, 1948), and A. C. Kinsey et al., *Sexual Behavior in the Human Female* (Philadelphia, 1953). Kinsey's conclusions even when published and more recently have been called into question by scholars for their lack of objectivity and acceptable scientific methodology. One writer concludes that Kinsey's erratic personal life or "activities . . . almost certainly did affect the objectivity and detachment of his work as a scientist; his celebrated findings, I now believe, may well have been skewed." James H. Jones, "Annals of Sexology: Dr. Yes," *The New Yorker*, August 25, 1997, 98–110, 112–13, at 101.

117 The earliest cited is W. H. Masters and V. E. Johnson, *Human Sexual Response* (Boston, 1966).

spread changes in sexual mores in the country—this meant as an argument for the need to compose new principles of morality that reflect the new attitudes. The text gives an aura of serious scholarship by scanning the history of the Christian Tradition, the latest trends in empirical sciences, "the dynamic view of person emerging from the documents of Vatican II," and what it calls "pastoral guidelines," drawn from the writings of modern theologians sympathetic to the authors' conclusions,[118] but it is clear that only the conclusions drawn from the latest theories in psychology and behaviorism, and the views of supporting theologians, will hold weight for composing the new guidelines. Magisterial teachings are reviewed but hold no weight, since "profound changes in sexual attitudes and behavior patterns in America and elsewhere have led to serious questions regarding the adequacy of traditional Catholic formulations and pastoral responses to sexual matters."[119]

- *Masturbation*: To masturbate seems never to be sinful, at least not gravely. Such action is explained as either a reflection of important changes in adolescents, or a response to repression by "tyrannical parents," or relief from tensions, or maladjustment indicative of psychological disorder. A particularly significant conclusion relevant for today is worth noting here:

  > [For] celibates, married men away from home on business or in military service or prison, or spouses who for health or other reasons must abstain from intercourse for long periods of time . . . . The use of masturbation to obtain reasonable relief from excessive sexual tension or to preserve fidelity would seem to be a matter of prudent choice of values.[120]

- *Homosexuality*: The homosexual's orientation is accepted as "for all practical purposes natural and irreversible." Homosexual behavior is to be evaluated, even as heterosexual activity is evaluated, by whether or not it is "indicative of" a "wholesome human sexuality." Pastoral counseling should help the homosexual to make his or her own moral judgment based on whether or not the "relationships and actions . . . are self-liberating, other-enriching, honest, faithful, life-serving, and joyous." The homosexual is "bound to avoid depersonalization, selfishness, dishonesty, promiscuity, harm to society, and demoralization," but little else. Individuals should make their own "moral assessment" in view of the "broader context of their total life, all their actions and relationships, in particular their relationship to God and the state of

118 Kosnik et al., 99.
119 Ibid., xi.
120 Ibid., 226–27.

their spiritual life of prayer and participation in the sacramental life of the Church."[121]

The same broad and nonjudgmental psychologically and emotionally laden criteria seem to be applied to the use of sex in all walks of life. Of particular note for our discussion is the use of the above criteria for "those who choose to live a life of celibacy or virginity" even within the Church. They are called "to acknowledge the possibility of a unique, intense, personal encounter that at some moment in their lives invites to an intimate, exclusive, lasting relationship."[122]

- *Sex outside of marriage*: The report indicates that "sexual behavior patterns are changing," and concludes that the "traditional moral code regarding premarital sex is inadequate," and calls for a fidelity to the vague, amorphous standards of morality the report repeatedly calls forth: that the relationship be "self-liberating, other-enriching, honest, faithful, life-serving, and joyous."[123]
- *Adultery, "co-marital" (threesome) sexual relations, and "mate swapping" (a foursome, or two couples)*: The report finds it difficult to see how the guiding "principle of creative growth toward integration" could be applied to all persons involved in order to justify such relationships. Nevertheless, it concludes that "empirical data does not as yet warrant any solid conclusions on the effects of such behavior," and therefore recommends that caution be exercised until such evidence is available.[124]
- *Sexual variants*: Finally, under the heading "Sexual Variants," the report briefly treats such issues as bestiality and transvestism. Regarding the former, no moral judgment is made, only recognition that the practice "renders impossible the realization of the personal meaning of human sexuality"; regarding the latter, no moral judgment is made "because of the psychological factors causing the deviation."[125]

There is no doubt that *Human Sexuality*, written by two diocesan priests (now laicized), a religious, and two laymen, all supposedly esteemed scholars of the Church, not only represented the thinking of many theologians in the first decades after Vatican II, but also cleared the way to legitimize sexual activity of many kinds for many Catholics if not others. Neuhaus affirmed how influential the work was:

[121] Ibid., 214–15.
[122] Ibid., 184–85.
[123] Ibid., 167–68.
[124] Ibid., 148–49.
[125] Ibid., 229–31.

> The book has been widely used in seminaries. Seminarians and priests of the time who had a woman or a male lover on the side could, and did, cite *Human Sexuality* to reasonably claim that a very large part, if not the majority, of the academic theological establishment countenanced their behavior. The CTSA report left no doubt that it represented the avant garde, that the Church's teaching would eventually catch up with "the latest research," and that, while waiting for the Church to catch up, priests should exercise discretion in deviating from the present and woefully benighted official teaching. Thus did academic and theological dissent promiscuously issue permission slips for an era of wink-wink, nudge-nudge, the consequences of which are now on scandalous public display.[126]

Weigel points out that the work had great impact in the sense that it reinforced a new politically correct way of dissent from traditional teaching, already underway with the widespread rejection of *Humanae Vitae* among the intellectually elite, especially among up-and-coming theologians who were anxious to be accepted into the liberal academic theology community:

> Dissent was, once again, affirmed as an appropriate response to authoritative teaching. Theologians who defended the Church's sexual ethic were put on notice that their dissent from dissent would be regarded as a betrayal of the theologians' guild. Younger scholars were told, in so many words, that a robust defense of the Church's sexual ethic would not help advance their careers . . . . Distance from that teaching, not an ability to present it in an intellectually satisfactory and pastorally compelling way, was the new criterion of professional acceptability in the CTSA.[127]

The report does not consider sexual deviation with children and adolescents. Were the report written today, one wonders what position the authors might have taken on this issue, in view of the fact that there was no way to limit the application of their new norms of morality based on their empirically based and psychologically driven principles. There seems to be no reason, if the morality of every other form of sexual activity traditionally understood as deviant and gravely sinful was now up for grabs, why any and all forms of sexual activity, even though not explicitly considered, should be excluded from the list of practices worthy of consideration.

The point, then, is that a post-Vatican II climate where the value and the legitimacy of traditional structures were called into question provided a base for situational ethics to plant its seeds and to justify sexual experimentation in novel relationships of every sort. A new spirituality that rejected the credentials and the truths held by the old guard and opened doors to

---

126 Neuhaus, "Public Square: Continuing Survey," 79.
127 Weigel, *Courage*, 75.

the new was already underway with a new Enlightened generation. What was so surprising was how unprepared the older generation was for this development. Not only were they unable to stem the revolutionary tide, they were unable even to justify to themselves why they had been spokespersons for such "antiquated" thinking.

What we must realize today is that this climate of openness to experimentation and novelty not only made it possible to consider broadening one's options in the use of traditionally legitimate forms of morality, such as dropping the Church's rule of celibacy and allowing priests to get married and be priests at the same time, but also to allow experimentation in ways of life formerly considered deviant. Once traditional principles of truth and morality are laid aside and replaced by ambiguous principles based on patterns of psychological growth and human development, as *Human Sexuality* did in such an apparently scholarly and principled way, there is no limit to what the imagination might find conceivable. According to Bleichner,

> The pattern of sexual abuse by priests in the 1970s needs to be placed in a much wider context of sexual experimentation by priests across the board in those same years. The great majority of cases did not sink to the level of abuse. But the experimentation did provide a fertile seedbed for the latter. There were simply very few good reasons to prevent priests so inclined from experimenting with sex. . . . The new climate after Vatican II was now more favorable to giving those instincts free play.[128]

Had it not always been taken for granted that sexual intercourse was only to be practiced among the married, since openness to procreation was intrinsic to the sex act? Not anymore. With the rejection of *Humanae Vitae* by the elites of society, and the indecisiveness of the hierarchy in the face of that rejection, the long-standing moral principle restricting sexual intercourse to the wedded could be bracketed without fear of recrimination. But then, was there any reason why all traditional sexual morality based on the principles of natural law might also be brought into doubt? Was there really any principle of traditional sexual morality that could withstand the onslaught of situational ethics?

> When moral theologians tried to add shading to traditional Catholic positions on sexuality, the result was not greater nuance. Rather, older positions were swept away like sand castles in a riptide and replaced by nothing at all. Catholics began to act like everyone else not only in regard to birth control but also in regard to premarital sex and other sexual

[128] Bleichner, *View from the Altar*, 46.

> behavior. Once again, the church had come, if not to accept, then at least to tolerate such developments.[129]

And in a curious way, many Catholics, such as the authors of *Human Sexuality*, claimed Vatican II as a basis for justifying this new morality, because not only had it given its stamp of approval to the value of achieving the fully human, but also had made fidelity to personal conscience the subjective norm of truth.

In this way, Vatican II inadvertently created a climate of uncertainty in the Church that provided a breeding ground for moral lassitude—not only among Catholics in general, who no longer found a bastion of truth in the Catholic Church to withstand the growing breakdown of traditional morality in secular society, but also among the clergy, although the disintegration of traditional sexual morality among them and the occurrences of sexual abuse only came to light decades later. This post-Vatican II climate explains the aberrations, but does not justify them. Perhaps it is asking too much to pinpoint who is to blame for the aberrations, though virtually everyone blames the bishops. Though they should have known better, the fact is that there were few among them who had the self-assuredness to challenge what was happening—"many of the bishops did not and do not have the intellectual self-confidence to challenge the academic theological establishment"[130]—and even if they did, there were few who would have listened.

This neo-Enlightenment mentality that discards the old for the acceptance of the new has not changed so very much today. Recent history shows that many of the activities justified in *Human Sexuality* continued for some time, and forms of them continue to be justified today. Those who defend traditional natural law principles of morality are in the few, and are marginalized by many of the Enlightened sophisticates in the Church. This is simply another aspect of the cleavage we have continued to note in the Church—between those who inform reason with the teachings of the Church, and those who inform faith with the conclusions of reason, independently of what the Church teaches.

Why the Cover-Up?

Once *The Boston Globe* opened the doors of investigation into the sex-abuse scandal, it was not long before the horrendous dimensions of the problem became known: "There is no disputing the appalling behavior of priest-perpetrators, the toll of pain wrought on victims and their families,

[129] Ibid., 32.

[130] Neuhaus, "Public Square: Continuing Survey," 79.

and the enormous gravity of the scandal."[131] The abuse had been going on for many decades; it was known to the hierarchy that the abuses were there, and yet little was done to correct the problem. In fairness, it must be said that many of those clergymen who were perpetrators of the abuse were sent by their bishops to treatment centers that were thought to correct the sexual aberrations, and that bishops reassigned them only after they had been assured that the abusers had been rehabilitated. But this was not always the case, especially after cases of recidivism. But ordinaries were singularly imprudent in reassigning past abusers to traditional roles of pastoral ministry, often in situations of close contact with young people, and sometimes without any notification to the directors of those ministries.

Suddenly, when the extent of the abuse became known and the cover-up brought to light, the question inevitably arose: How could those who knew of perpetrators' records of abuse not only hide such records, but continue to assign them to ministries where there was danger of further abuse? Did this not constitute complicity in such abuse? And why was more not done to heal the wounds of victims of abuse? At the present time, these questions continue to be asked.

In attempting to provide some perspective on these questions, it is appropriate to consider certain other data.

Are Catholic Priests the Only Abusers?

Are Catholic priests the only abusers, or is there abuse in other religious groups or even among the general population?

Sexual abuse is apparently present among the clergy of other religious organizations. Heads of other religious denominations have admitted that aberrant sexual practices are found in their communities as much if not more than in the Catholic Church. Yet while the sex abuse present in the Roman Catholic Church has been studied and widely reported by the secular media, without whose aggressive and unflinching efforts no scandal would probably ever have occurred, the media have given little attention to the presence of sex abuse in other religious denominations, nor have these bothered to make any serious study of the matter, and so their problem has gone largely unnoticed.[132]

---

[131] Steinfels, *A People Adrift*, 42.

[132] There have been no serious studies of sex abuse among Protestant clergy, but various surmises have been made. According to a SNAP (Survivors Network of those Abused by Priests) press statement: "Yet, even though their own Southern Baptist scholars report that clergy sex abuse is as prevalent among Protestants as among Catholics, Southern Baptists have 'no national policies' and abuse is 'routinely covered up.' (Trull & Carter, Ministerial Ethics at p. 162, 2004)" (June 14, 2006, www.Snapnetwork.org). According to Richard N. Ostling, "Michael Smith, the Lutheran corpo

What is perhaps even more distressing is the fact that meager attention has been given to the much more serious problem of educator sexual misconduct with adolescents and minors in American public primary and secondary education schools. There has been moral outrage over the sexual abuse of 10,667 young people from 1950 through 2002 by 4,392 Catholic clergy,[133] but the nation seems curiously unconcerned about the possible damage done to more than 3 million public-school students throughout the nation who experienced unwanted "contact educator sexual misconduct" "sometime between kindergarten and 12th grade," according to a 2004 report published by the U.S. Department of Education.[134]

---

rate attorney, . . . suspects Protestants and Catholics differ little in the percentage of abusive clergy or the temptation toward denial. He's convinced media reports only scratch the surface of the Protestant problem" ("Protestant Sex-Abuse Data Murky," *Oakland Tribune*, February 23, 2004, findarticles.com). Mark Clayton writes, "Despite headlines focusing on the priest pedophile problem in the Roman Catholic Church, most American churches being hit with child sexual-abuse allegations are Protestant, and most of the alleged abusers are not clergy or staff, but church volunteers. . . . Since 1993, on average about 1 percent of the surveyed churches reported abuse allegations annually. That means on average, about 3,500 allegations annually, or nearly 70 per[cent] among the predominantly Protestant group, Cobble [James Cobble, executive director of Christian Ministry Resources] says. . . . Volunteers are more likely than clergy or paid staff to be abusers. Perhaps more startling, children at churches are accused of sexual abuse as often as are clergy and staff. In 1999, for example, 42 percent of alleged child abusers were volunteers, about 25 percent were paid staff members (including clergy) and 25 percent were other children" ("Sex Abuse Spans Spectrum of Churches," *Christian Science Monitor*, April 5, 2002, www.csmonitor.com). Clearly, the roots of the problem are deep.

133 John Jay College of Criminal Justice, *Nature and Scope of Sexual Abuse*, 69, 26.

134 Charol Shakeshaft, "Educator Sexual Misconduct: A Synthesis of Existing Literature," Office of the Under Secretary, U.S. Department of Education, Washington, DC, DOC #2004–09, June 2004, esp. 16–18.

Among other data, the report draws from a study by Harris International done in the fall of 2000 for the American Association of University Women (AAUW). *Hostile Hallways: The AAUW Survey on Sexual Harassment in America's Schools* (Washington, DC: AAUW, 2001). The study is based upon a representative national sample of 2,065 eighth- to eleventh-grade students. Shakeshaft's secondary reanalysis of the AAUW data, focusing "only on educator sexual misconduct" (p. 4), indicates that "9.6 percent of all students in grades 8 to 11 report contact and/or noncontact educator sexual misconduct that was *unwanted*" (p. 17), and that "8.7 percent report only noncontact sexual misconduct" while "6.7 percent experienced only contact misconduct" (the numbers total more than 9.6% because some had experienced both). Shakeshaft states she then applied this data "to the population of all K–12 students. Based on the assumption that the AAUW surveys accurately represent the experiences of all K–12 students, more than 4.5 million students are subject to sexual misconduct by an employee of a school sometime between kindergarten and 12th grade" (pp. 17–18). This should mean that the 6.7% who have experienced contact sexual misconduct amounts to more than 3 million students.

The report is unfortunately not always based upon adequate scientifically compiled data, and does not clearly distinguish between sexual misconduct and sexual abuse, a failure that has been used to justify making little note of its contents.[135] While the report shows remarkable similarities to what occurred among the Catholic clergy, there is a major difference: the extent of contact misconduct/abuse in public schools is far greater than it is in the Catholic Church, including not only a much greater number of perpetrators, but also a much greater number targeted! And yet little has been done to correct the problem in the public schools or to bring it to public attention. In fact, the report shows that much of the time, leaders in public education did everything they could to cover up the problem just as was done in the Church.[136]

Finally, in 2007, a first-rate report on the problem of sex abuse in the nation's public schools appeared. The Associated Press (AP) ran a three-part series October 21–23 on sex abuse among public-school educators. Its seven-month investigation of disciplinary records in all fifty states and the District of Columbia found

> 2,570 educators whose teaching credentials were revoked, denied, surrendered or sanctioned from 2001 through 2005 following allegations of sexual misconduct.
>
> Young people were the victims in at least 1,801 of the cases, and more than 80 percent [1,467] of those were students.

---

135 Janice Shaw Crouse, "Sexual Misconduct in Schools," July 26, 2004, www.townhall.com.

136 The report notes that "only 5 to 6 percent of child sexual abuse cases [perpetrated by any adult] become known to social services or the police" (Shakeshaft, "Educator Sexual Misconduct," 16). Most of the educator sexual offenders are teachers (p. 24). Examples of similarities with the clergy sex-abuse scandal given by Shakeshaft include a 1994 report of 225 cases of educator sexual abuse in New York, "all of the accused had admitted to sexual abuse of a student but none of the abusers was reported to authorities and only 1 percent lost their license to teach." While all admitted physical sexual abuse, 25% suffered little consequence, and about 39% left the district mostly with "positive recommendations or even retirement packages intact" (p. 44). A 2001 report in New York City indicated that 60% of employees accused of sex abuse "were transferred to desk jobs at offices inside schools," and "40 percent of these teachers were repeat offenders." Agreements are sometimes made to "avoid legal battles with the alleged abuser." "Many school districts make confidential agreements with abusers" (p. 44). "The school or district rarely prescribes a therapeutic and healing intervention for targets of educator sexual misconduct or for others in the school" (p. 45). Finally, Shakeshaft reports that little is being done to correct educator sexual misconduct (p. 47).

The AP reported that there were "criminal convictions in at least 1,390, or 53 percent, of the cases," that "nearly nine out of 10 of the educators punished for sexual misconduct were male," and that "at least 446 of the cases that the AP found involved educators who had multiple victims." The perpetrators the AP found were "everyday educators—teachers, school psychologists, principals and superintendents among them. They're often popular and recognized for excellence." The AP reported "efforts to stop individual offenders but, overall, a deeply entrenched resistance toward recognizing and fighting abuse." According to the AP, "most of the abuse never gets reported. Those cases reported often end with no action."[137]

It is clear from the above figures that the problem of sexual misconduct of youth in America's public schools is far worse than that among Roman Catholic priests. Yet the AP report has received little media recognition. William Donohue reports that "only five newspapers carried the entire three-day series," none of them major American newspapers. His question is: "Where was the *Boston Globe*, which broke the Catholic scandal, and all the other big media outlets?" He rightly concludes: "Just goes to show that it was never the molested who counted, just the identity of the molester."[138]

In 2008, a two-part series on the problem of sex abuse in Oregon's public schools was published February 17–18 in *The Oregonian*. According to the paper, "129 Oregon educators [have been] disciplined for molesting or having sexual relations with more than 215 public school children over the past 10 years." The paper reports lax procedures reminiscent of the Catholic clergy cases:

> In at least a dozen cases in five years, teachers later convicted of sexual misconduct with a student were left unchecked by local school officials, who failed to investigate early complaints, do adequate reference checks or were lax about stopping problem behavior, The Oregonian found. In some instances, principals or teachers did not believe student reports. In others, administrators reprimanded teachers for sexual misconduct but allowed them to keep teaching.[139]

The headline of the second part of the series tells the rest of the story: "Schools cut secret deals with abusive teachers: They call it 'passing the

---

137 Martha Irvine and Robert Tanner, "Sexual Misconduct Plagues U.S. Schools," StatesmanJournal.com (Salem, OR), October 21, 2007, 1–7, at 1–2, www.statesmanjournal.com.

138 Catholic League for Religious and Civil Rights, "Media Ignore Sexual Abuse in the Schools," *Catalyst Online*, December 2007, www.catholicleague.org/printer.php?p=Catalyst&id=2351.

139 Amy Hsuan, Melissa Navas, and Bill Graves, "Schools Let Sex Abuse Cases Slide," *The Oregonian*, February 17, 2008, 1–3, www.oregonlive.com.

trash,' and it's a common policy that lets child abusers resign and move to another district."[140]

The point is not to highlight these cases, nor to downgrade the significance of the evil perpetrated by Catholic clergy. But questions must be asked: Why have the educators covered up their problem, why is the misconduct drawing so little outrage, and why is the existence of the cover-up of so little concern to the media who are able to raise it to the level of a scandal? What is the difference between this problem of sexual misconduct/abuse and that which has been exposed in the Catholic Church? Why is the nation appalled at the latter problem, but so unconcerned about the former? Parents are horrified, and rightly so, at the damage that has been done to their children by their priests. But hasn't the damage done by public educators been as great if not greater? Where is the parental outrage?

Granted, there is a difference between the religious aura many Catholics attach to their clergy and the respect given to educators in general, yet in both cases young people are being entrusted to persons who have considerable influence in the formation of youth. Surely the destructive effects on young people are similar: Shakeshaft reports that most of the students targeted by the educators "suffer emotional, education, and developmental or health effects."[141] Abuse done to a young person leaves a scar no matter who the perpetrator is, and correction of such a serious problem will only follow if there is an exposé similar to that carried on by the media against the Catholic Church.

Whatever the results an investigation of this question might produce, it is obvious where the focus of attention must be placed to bring the situation to public attention: on the media. Unfortunately, our society is such that in almost every case, media attention, rather than the intrinsic horror of the situation, creates scandal. The wanton sex abuse of many unprotected individuals in American prisons is widely known, yet it draws little attention from the media and so Americans are unconcerned about it, but an incident of much smaller proportions that occurred in the Abu Ghraib prison in Iraq drew media outrage and became a national scandal. Isn't the intrinsic worth of human life at stake in both situations—that is, if there is such a thing as intrinsic worth—and not just grist for promoting political agendas? *The Boston Globe* and *The New York Times,* as well as the major television news networks, were unrelentingly dedicated to the pursuit of the truth regarding the Catholic clergy sex-abuse. But where are they regarding the abuse in public education? There appears to be no sense of urgency to expose this problem and correct it.

140 Amy Hsuan, Melissa Navas, and Bill Graves, "Schools Cut Secret Deals with Abusive Teachers," *The Oregonian*, February 18, 2008, 1, www.oregonlive.com.

141 Shakeshaft, "Educator Sexual Misconduct," 42.

We can only speculate about the difference. Anti-Catholic bias inevitably comes to mind, a bias for which the media in America are widely noted. But another major characteristic of the media must be noted: their indiscriminate efforts to dethrone paragons of morality or persons of great prominence. Thus it is more enticing to the media to publish a sexual exposé on the Catholic Church, an organization that stands for high moral standards, than on the failings of a religious sect, or on a member of a political organization that espouses the upholding of traditional moral values, than on an organization that does not. Thus, since the Catholic Church is one of the few remaining institutions in this country to call humanity to live by high moral values—a call that especially infuriates those who live by no other standard than personal expediency—the media salivate at the chance to create a scandal that would imply hypocrisy and bring the Church down.[142]

But surely there are responsible leaders in the American community who are attracted by principle rather than crass media standards. Where are the social, media, and political leaders who care for the welfare of America's youth, and who are willing to expose the abuse of the lives of young and innocent people wherever that may occur, so that the problems may be corrected? Isn't the magnitude of public school educators' crimes so great that someone of stature would come forward to demand correction?

But if we are truly concerned about the well-being of our youth, why not carry the outrage further: What about the exploitation of high school and college athletes by educational institutions often in exchange for an unearned degree, or the commercialization of innocent children on television, or the exposure of youth to the most insidious and degrading forms of music, or the abandonment of their lives to prostitution and drugs on the streets of our major cities—all disguised under the rights of the First Amendment, yet actually motivated by crass profit-making greed? Will no one stand up to defend the well-being of our youth? Until our society, instead of being driven to outrage wherever the media leads us, shows it cares about its youth wherever the quality of their lives is being undermined, the sincerity of our outrage may be seriously called into question.

The fact is that there is a serious moral sickness growing throughout American society that needs to be addressed and no one is prepared to do

[142] A similar accusation of hypocrisy was brought against Rev. Ted Haggard, president of the National Association of Evangelicals and senior pastor of the New Life megachurch in Colorado Springs, CO. He was forced to resign from the first position and was removed from the second after a self-described former gay prostitute accused Haggard of having a sexual affair with him for three years and of using drugs. The media delighted in the supposed hypocrisy of Haggard in that he had "advocated passage of an amendment to the United States Constitution to ban same-sex marriage." John Holusha and Neela Banerjee, "Evangelical Leader Says He Bought Drugs," *New York Times*, November 3, 2006, www.nytimes.com.

so. Americans remain helpless beneath the weight of this sickness because they have been led to believe that the First Amendment gives a priority to the supposed rights of those who would destroy the moral fiber of the nation, rather than to those who would enforce compliance with standards of decency and morality that maintain the nation's health and welfare. More and more, citizens march when their youth are gunned down on their streets, shouting, "Something must be done!" yet benignly accept court decisions that allow big-business corporations to destroy the fabric of our culture.

AGAIN, WHY THE COVER-UP?

The study of sexual misconduct in American public education indicates a cover-up by education leaders, and other religious groups have admitted cover-up in their organizations. Thus attempts to disguise abuse of the young are not unique to the Catholic hierarchy. One is inclined to conclude that attempts to gloss over public crime in all these situations reflect characteristics endemic to human nature.

Several possible reasons come to mind to explain such cover-ups: It is in the nature of administrators to want to save the public image of their organizations, as well as not to tarnish their own self-image with the publicity associated with scandal. They will not want to be exposed to public embarrassment over their failure to maintain decorum in their ranks. Administrators may have compassion for associates and not want to jeopardize their careers and reputations. All of these represent natural attitudes characteristic of human nature that may distort one's vision and lead to an unbalanced perception of where justice resides. No doubt there is also an underlying hope that the problem, once resolved privately, will not reoccur.

But more than these explanations seem warranted in the case of the Catholic Church.

Jason Berry and Gerald Renner

In a blistering attack with all the sordid details of the rampant sexual failings of the clergy, leftist Catholic journalist Jason Berry gives one of the most vicious explanations for the crisis in the Church. Berry does his best to make seminarians, priests, and bishops look about as depraved as imaginable. No degrading terminology available in the English language is left unused in his warped portrayal of how low clergy life has sunk: "Bishops and cardinals, lacking children of their own, had coddled child molesters in a weird parody of incest . . . blind to the psychodynamics behind the church's state of sin."[143]

---

[143] Jason Berry and Gerald Renner, *Vows of Silence: The Abuse of Power in the Papacy of John Paul II* (New York: Free, 2004), 279.

The point of Berry's diatribe ultimately blames John Paul II for much of the abuse: "An ethos of lying to the public about sexual crimes" resulted "from a history of sexual secrecy demanded by the papacy . . . to protect the church from scandal."[144] Berry presents a picture of the Church as a society where a corrupt hierarchy guard their divinely bestowed positions of power and authority by instilling fear and dedication to secrecy in the lower clergy. But Berry also presents John Paul as a twisted man largely abstracted from reality. Concerned about conformity to doctrinal truth and worldwide evangelism, John Paul, "a virgin monarch," was unable to perceive the "sexual underworld inside the castle," where he perceived "scattered sins, not the hungry worms of structural decay."[145] And further, John Paul's "myopia on the church's corruption suggests the kind of hubris we associate with kings in Shakespearean drama, coupled with a tragic naïveté about sexual intimacy."[146] The fact that Berry's book *Vows of Silence*, presented as a careful investigative exposé of "the staggering trail of evasions and deceit" and "the abuse of power" of "a hierarchy so obsessed with secrecy as to spawn disinformation" from John Paul II down,[147] is endorsed on the back cover by some of the most leftist critics of the Church lets one know that this is a book with an axe to grind, which makes it difficult to put one's credence in any of the data supposedly unearthed for the book.

The distinguished Catholic lawyer Robert Bennett, one of the balanced members of the sex-abuse panel set up by the Church to investigate the problem at great length, admitted that the panel could find no clear reason why the cover-up had occurred, but that there appeared to be a "fear of bringing scandal to the Church."[148] That explanation has frequently been given and concurs with Berry's, yet it is not ultimately satisfying, and Bennett recognized the inadequacy of his remarks even as he made them. Yet I have not heard or read of anyone who probed into the deeper question as to why the hierarchy would be afraid of scandal.

Donald Cozzens

One somewhat disappointing study began with the question, "What are we afraid of?" as the opening words of the monograph.[149] This comes from the priest scholar Donald Cozzens, much of whose life was devoted to seminary

[144] Ibid., 99.
[145] Ibid., 279.
[146] Ibid., 301.
[147] Ibid., from front jacket.
[148] Chris Matthews, "Hardball," MSNBC, April 18, 2005, www.msnbc.msn.com.
[149] Donald Cozzens, *Sacred Silence: Denial and the Crisis in the Church* (Collegeville, MN: Liturgical, 2002), 5.

training. I say disappointing because his is another in a long line of those who find no other recourse than to blame the hierarchy.

Cozzens's work is full of righteous indignation laden with emotion and guilt pangs over the present situation of crisis. He may at times be prone to exaggeration: he reports that "there are approximately 100,000 victims of clergy misconduct in the U.S. alone,"[150] when the figure from the national study done by the John Jay College of Criminal Justice is about a tenth of that (see pp. 453).

Cozzens's book is summed up in the opening lines of the work, pointing out that the hierarchy have shrouded themselves in "silence, denial, and minimization," which he explains as "part and parcel of the human condition," instead of having "a passion for the truth," being "honest," and facing "with candor and courage the issues and challenges that weigh heavy on our church."[151] I tend to rear back with caution when I hear that we need to be "honest." That word is usually a euphemism for asking other people to change their views so that they agree with mine.

But why are the clergy afraid? Cozzens at times speaks as if he were a psychiatrist analyzing the "fear, anxiety, and tension" of bishops suffering from "existential guilt," or the hierarchy's "bad faith" in not wanting to confront "painful realities" for fear of the "unpleasant consequences" that would follow.[152] Cozzens mentions that bishops fear that the laity might be "confused or scandalized" by an open investigation of the issues facing the Church, and that facing crucial issues "*might harm the reputation of the church, of the priesthood*,"[153] but again, he never explains what the scandal would be or why such harm to the reputation of the Church or the priesthood would be so frightening. Cozzens also seems to suggest the hierarchy are simply too lazy to want to submit to the possibility of "significant change" that would disturb their peace and comfort.[154]

Other answers Cozzens provides: the threatening of the hierarchy's traditional long-standing "lines of power"; the hierarchy's fear of Catholic "anger" at the clergy's "duplicitous arrogance," especially with the fact that the bishops have placed "the reputation of the priesthood ahead of the safety of children and teenagers"; "anger" at the Church's failure to come to terms with the modern age; or "anger" with the Church's "denial, legalism, controlling power, secrecy." Cozzens's solution is "serious soul-work": the Church needs to "move from denial to reality, from despair to possibility," yes, to "grieve" over the old order that is passing away, but then to open up

---

[150] Ibid., 97.
[151] Ibid., 7, 11, 34.
[152] Ibid., 21, 27–28.
[153] Ibid., 19, 27.
[154] Ibid., 18–20.

to "the horizon of promise and deliverance."[155] All of this within the first few pages of the book, with nary a word of sympathy for the hierarchy.

Perhaps the greatest contribution of Cozzens's work is his call for the Church to confront postmodernism, a concern that has pervaded our entire study. Cozzens rightly sees the Church as "faced with challenges to its mission and message that may well be unprecedented." Cozzens sees the postmodern mentality as so threatening to the Christian mind-set that it will "shake the very foundations of long-held worldviews and belief systems," and perhaps constitute "*the* major challenge" to "vocations to the priesthood and religious life." As a result, the " 'Catholic' reality and its sustaining myths" are at risk of being undercut by a new form of thinking that finds no room for a "saving message" or "saving truth."[156]

Apart from his timely call for the Church to confront the crisis of postmodernism, a confrontation that Cozzens correctly sees as long overdue, Cozzens's work is awash with a preconceived agenda that one cannot fail to notice. Words calling for "honest, humble dialogue" and openness to a "horizon of promise and deliverance" camouflage a liberal agenda, which Cozzens supplies by the end of the book with a call for optional celibacy for priests, restoration of departed priests, ordination of women to the diaconate, review of priestly ordination for women, lay preaching, dropping of the mandatum for Catholic theologians since fidelity to Church teaching may be "assumed"(has he visited the theology departments in any of our schools?), experimentation with new forms of religious life, "openness" to the "lived experiences" of the "straight and gay," new reflection on *Humanae Vitae*, wide Catholic input in the appointment of bishops.[157] All these changes supposedly lead to a new life in the Church that would overcome the present crisis—as if changes like these would do anything but make matters worse.

But could another explanation for the cover-up be that the hierarchy feared the loss of the laity's financial support for the Church? Such a loss seemed to occur sporadically after the scandal, though there was never any clear indication that the hierarchy were distressed by it. But would the hierarchy be so motivated by personal interest that they would sacrifice the well-being of young people for monetary purposes? Such a harsh judgment seems unwarranted. But even if that were the reason in one or two cases, it seems difficult to accept that explanation for a moral problem that is endemic to the American hierarchy and found in other countries as well.

Steinfels puts together a concatenation of reasons from which we are free to choose. He argues that the hierarchy were "acting out of ignorance, naïve

[155] Ibid., 5–7.
[156] Ibid., 86–88.
[157] Ibid., 168–71.

piety, misplaced trust, indifference to children, clerical clubbiness, fear of scandal, subservience to lawyers, concern for church assets, diocesan prerogatives, sheer administrative incapacity, or downright complicity."[158] He faults them for "*a failure of comprehension and empathy*" (the bishops were "psychologically naïve"), "*a failure of decisiveness*," "*a failure of focus*," "*a failure of persistence and follow-through*," "*a failure of openness*," and finally, "*a failure of explanation*," for they did not offer "any satisfactory explanation of why this [scandal] happened in the first place."[159] But neither does Steinfels.

Neuhaus put the blame squarely on the bishops: "Let it be stated unambiguously: the leaders of the Catholic Church, meaning mainly the bishops, are responsible for the crisis and for the consequent frenzy. . . . The bishops . . . are primarily responsible for the shame and humiliation of the Long Lent of 2002."[160] And why did they do it? "If one asks why they did not do their job, the answers are no doubt various, ranging from indolence, naïveté, willful ignorance, doctrinal dissent, and cowardice to active complicity in evil and the fear of blackmail."[161] Or again: "They stopped being bishops and became business managers and practitioners of group dynamics . . . to keep all factions on board and to avoid 'divisiveness.'"[162]

George Weigel

Weigel blames the bishops as well,[163] and adds a series of possible reasons for their failures. He finds they were undergoing "a crisis of identity" whose deepest roots are theological: "They have not believed, with sufficient life-transforming power, the truth of what the Catholic Church teaches they are," namely, successors of the apostles who make present to the Church today "the living headship of Christ the Good Shepherd," men endowed by Christ with the authority to teach, sanctify, and govern in his name the People of God. Rather, desiring to be seen as liberals on social issues, with "misguided compassion" and "misplaced faith in the expertise of therapists"; lacking security in their headship and the "nerve" to confront the inauthentic theologian-teachers in the Church; with fear "of adding 'homophobe'" to the "put-downs of the Catholic Church" and fear "of confronting malfeasant clergy, fear of publicity, fear of financial retribution from donors, fear of looking out-of-step with other bishops, fear of inadvertently doing something that would frustrate one's ambitions," and possibly "fear of black-

158 Steinfels, *A People Adrift*, 42.

159 Ibid., 309–12.

160 Neuhaus, "Public Square: Continuing Survey," 75, 83.

161 Ibid., 80.

162 Richard John Neuhaus, "Public Square: Scandal Time III," *First Things* 125 (August/September 2002): 90.

163 Weigel, *Courage*, 29–32.

mail," they succumbed to "governance-by-bureaucrats" as well as becoming victims of "psychobabble," willing to entrust to bureaucrats and therapists the decision-making authority Christ had bestowed upon them.[164]

There is wisdom in all of these analyses. But I think I am able to offer three deeper explanations of the actions of the hierarchy that will allow for some expression of sympathy for their failures.

Consequence of Sin

Postmodern society has abandoned the concept of sin, and replaced it with human weaknesses. In the case of the clergy sex abuse, therefore, many attribute the cover-up to the human failings of the hierarchy. But that, while it may be true, is too simple an explanation. A deeper and better explanation involves the Catholic Church's understanding of sin.

Sin, while it surely represents human failing, is more properly understood as "an offense against God" that includes "an offense against reason, truth, and right conscience." It is "disobedience, a revolt against God," a setting of oneself "against God's love for us," a turning of one's heart away from God. It is "self-exaltation"—putting oneself on a par with God—as opposed to humble submission to the will of God. It is a "failure in genuine love for God and neighbor." It "wounds the nature of man and injures human solidarity" (*CCC* 1849–50).

The practical effect of a sinful action is that it creates a situation of alienation from God. Sin may be exercised either directly against God, as in the case of blasphemy, or indirectly against God through a violation of God's will for the well-being of members of his human family, as in the case of murder. While sin is normally found in action, one can be living in sin independently of specific actions of aversion to God when one lives a way of life that refuses to recognize one's dependence on God as the source of life and of all that one has.

While sin has traditionally been considered an individual action inducing alienation from God, modern theology has come to recognize that sin may also be more than the sum of its parts. There is collective sin, a situation caused by a collective act of failure to do the will of God. Such sin may be present not simply in an individual action, but in an action toward a community: for example, if a corporation were to adopt an unjust policy toward a community that milks the members of that community of the means of livelihood entitled to them as employees of the corporation.

The Catholic Church recognizes that all are sinners and in need of repentance, which involves the admission of one's sin to God with a firm purpose of amendment of one's life. If the sin is mortal, confession of the

---

[164] Weigel, *Courage*, 93, 96, 100–4, 109, 113–15.

sin must be made to God through the Church, that is, through a priest; if the sin is venial, admission of guilt and remorse may be made either through a priest or privately to God in prayer. If one is truly sorry for having committed the sin, the sin is forgiven, and, if the sin is confessed to a priest, some penance is given to remit some of the temporal punishment for sin. All of this is common knowledge in traditional Catholicism.

All of this is by way of explaining the background for the first explanation for the hierarchy's cover-up: that the sex-abuse actions were understood and treated by the hierarchy as personal sins and not as civic crimes. As sins, they are confessed to priests and forgiven when the individual expresses remorse for the sin and the firm purpose to commit the sin no more. Once sin is forgiven, the soul of the individual is wiped clean. There is always psychological damage done to the sinner by the committing of any sin, and to the human victim where a victim is involved, and often reparation must be made. But I am not normally burdened with the consequences of a sin in such a way that it would permanently impair my relationships with others. In other words, if I commit murder, I am not prevented ever from interacting with other persons lest I be tempted to commit murder again.

The reader should already be aware of the application I am making: Sex abuse was understood by the clergy as a serious sin in violation of God's law and committed against one or more members of his human family. But once the sin was remitted, one was free to return to a normal life within the community. It seems that there was sufficient awareness on the part of the hierarchy that such abuse was a symptom of psychological and social disorder in the abuser, and as a result, they generally recognized the need for corrective treatment. But the understanding was that, after a period of clinical treatment, the disorder could be corrected and the individual restored to a healthy relationship with others.

Under these circumstances, the cover-up was not so much a cover-up as an application of the hierarchy's compassion for the sinner, with an inadequate understanding of the consequences of the psychological disorder that was still present within the life of the abuser. The hierarchy may be credited with an eagerness to correct the problem without destroying the priest's reputation or ability to carry on a responsible life of service to the community. Thus, in most cases, once the period of treatment was ended, most priests were reassigned to general ministry within the community.

It is unfair, then, to read back into the understanding of those times what we have only recently come to realize, namely, the broader and deeper implications of what is involved in sex abuse, the deeper detrimental effects such abuse has on the life of the victims, the often irremediable nature of the perpetrator's disorder, and the fact that crimes were being committed that often should have been reported to civil authorities.

If this explanation applies to this situation, as I think it does, it allows us to see the hierarchy's actions in a more compassionate light. We tend to become so absorbed in the heinous nature of sex abuse of minors that we lose sight of the possibility that there may be deeper dimensions to the issue that mollify our judgment of those involved, and provide a rational explanation for how some well-intentioned people could have failed to respond adequately to the serious nature of what was happening.

Consequence of the Culture of Confusion

I offer a second explanation for the actions of the hierarchy: the cover-up reflects an attitude brought on by the culture of confusion that has pervaded the life of the Church since Vatican II, especially in the immediate post-Vatican II era, as we have just seen. The fact is that the hierarchy in America were so completely disoriented by the turmoil created by the cultural upheaval of the late '60s that they became insecure in their judgments on moral and doctrinal issues. I do believe that one must give this explanation serious consideration. Weigel admits as well the breakdown in theological training in the seminaries as a product of this confusion: "Part of the reason why reflects the period of confusion in U.S. Catholic religious education in the two decades immediately following the Second Vatican Council."[165]

An examination of the history of events in the life of the Church since 1965 shows that whenever priest theologians in America have called into question moral or doctrinal teachings of the Church, official rebukes or condemnations have almost always come from the Vatican, not from the American hierarchy. Moreover, when such rebukes are issued by the Vatican, they have been implemented by the hierarchy reluctantly and only under pressure.

A case in point: of special interest since Vatican II has been the Catholic identity of American Catholic institutions of higher education, a matter that we have already discussed at length. Increasingly since Vatican II, there has hardly been a principle of Catholic teaching that has not gone unchallenged by some Catholic systematic or moral theologian in Catholic colleges and universities, yet the American hierarchy do not react. The Vatican repeatedly puts pressure on the American hierarchy to rectify situations, yet nothing is done. Even when the pressure becomes acute, most of the members of the hierarchy still try to deflect action. Even after the Vatican issued the 1990 encyclical *Ex Corde Ecclesiae* insisting that action be taken to bring theology departments and university policies into conformity with Church teaching, the hierarchy still failed to act. Only after subsequent

[165] Weigel, *Courage*, 166; cf. Ibid., 178: "The decades of confusion in seminaries . . . ran from the mid-1960s to the later 1980s (and, in some instances, beyond)."

pressure from the Vatican insisting that the directives of the encyclical be locally mandated did the hierarchy reluctantly comply.

Still, the compliance was at a minimum at most institutions. Further Vatican pressure would still be necessary for any significant change to come about. But before that could happen, the sex-abuse scandal broke out and all attention was diverted. The effort to implement the mandates of *Ex Corde Ecclesiae* fizzled: Vatican pressure on higher education was deflected, and the American hierarchy, weakened by the scandal, failed to act. As a result, Catholic schools underwent virtually no reformation. Now that the pressure from the sex-abuse scandal has diminished, Vatican pressure to implement *Ex Corde Ecclesiae* has not returned, and, unless the new Pope takes a stand, Catholic education's abuse of the moral and doctrinal teachings of the Church will remain as unhampered today as it ever was.

The culture of confusion must be seen as a major reason for the American hierarchy's failure to act. The hierarchy are simply too unaccustomed to act in the face of local moral or doctrinal challenges, and too weak as a group to confront the hegemony of the liberal intellectuals over all but a small group of conservative Catholic colleges and universities who were already in compliance with the Vatican. If there is trepidation in the left-wing American Catholic institutions once again today, it is not because of the hierarchy but because of their newfound fear that Pope Benedict will not be so casual in his implementation of *Ex Corde Ecclesiae* as his predecessor was. After all, the encyclical had its origins with Benedict when he was prefect of the Sacred Congregation for the Doctrine of the Faith. But so far, little has happened.

Consequence of Extra Ecclesiam, Nulla Salus

There is another reason, in my view, that provides a third explanation for the cover-up that has, so far as I know, gone completely unnoticed. It is a problem indigenous to the life of the Church and a consequence of the Catholic teaching *extra ecclesiam, nulla salus*—outside the Church, no salvation.

The Church's longstanding commitment to this principle haunted the liberals at the time of Vatican II, and they hoped the Council would abandon it. But the principle had been so integral to the Church's life, at least since its first formulation by Origen in the third century, that Vatican II could not and did not drop it.[166] Instead, the teaching was reaffirmed (*LG* 14) but for-

---

[166] The necessity of membership in the Church for salvation is found in the papal bull *Unam Sanctam* (1302) of Boniface VIII: "Outside this [Catholic] Church there is no salvation and no remission of sins" (John F. Clarkson, S.J., et al., eds. and trans., *The Church Teaches: Documents of the Church in English Translation* [St. Louis, MO: Herder, 1962 (1955)], par. 153; hereafter paragraphs noted in the text as *CT*). The Decree for the Jacobites in the Council of Florence (1438–1445) formally teaches that the "holy Roman Church believes, professes, and preaches that 'no one

mally qualified (*LG* 16), as had been quietly done for many years, by arguing that while the principle remained valid, it did not apply to those who were inculpably unaware of its teaching and therefore did not formally reject the Church.[167]

In Catholic teaching, lack of knowledge of a teaching, unless one is culpably negligent in not attaining the knowledge, does not merit the consequences that follow from having rejected the teaching (contrary to the position held by Luther and still by some fundamentalist evangelical circles), and so does not disqualify a person from the operations of grace and some limited membership in the Church. Thus, according to the Catholic Church, while being a member of the Church is necessary for salvation, it is still possible for one not formally a member to be saved.[168] My point here, however, is to note that, in spite of the mitigating factor, the teaching regarding the necessity of formal membership in the Catholic Church has held sway over the life of the Church for centuries, and still holds sway. One does not take lightly Church teaching on the necessity of membership in the Church for salvation.

Vatican II went on to affirm another equally important point regarding the Church and salvation: that the Catholic Church has the fullness of the means made available by Christ for attaining salvation, such as the seven sacraments and unity with the Vicar of Christ. As a result, other Christian communities, to the extent that they lack one or more of these means, "suffer from defects" (*UR* 3). While, then, it is possible to be saved even though one is not formally a member of the Catholic Church, being outside signifies that not all of the means designed by Christ for salvation are available. A member of the hierarchy, therefore, being by office concerned about the salvation of people, would be concerned not only about keeping Catholics in the Church, but also about making membership in the Church attractive.

remaining outside the Catholic Church, not just pagans,' but also Jews or heretics or schismatics, can become partakers of eternal life" (the decree is citing from the sixth century African theologian Fulgentius of Ruspe, *De fide ad Petrum*, c. 38, par. 79; Clarkson, *CT*, no. 165, p. 78).

167 The concept of "invincible ignorance" applies here, meaning that one is not personally responsible for one's situation of not knowing a truth. The concept has its origins at least as early as the teachings of Thomas Aquinas, and is formally presented in Pius IX's encyclical *Quanto Conficiamur Moerore* (1863): "Those who suffer from invincible ignorance with regard to our holy religion, if they carefully keep the precepts of the natural law which have been written by God in the hearts of all persons, if they are prepared to obey God, and if they lead a virtuous and dutiful life, can, by the power of divine light and grace, attain eternal life" (Clarkson, *CT*, no. 814, pp. 287–88). Such persons are understood to be in some kind of relationship to the Catholic Church (*LG* 13), which is all that is absolutely required.

168 Cf. M. Eminyan/eds., "Salvation, Necessity of the Church for," *NCE* 12:624–26; and F. D. Nealy, "Ignorance," *NCE*, 7:314–15.

There is, moreover, another group for whom the Church, especially the hierarchy, must have special concern: those who are Catholic, and who, for some reason, decide to leave the Church. At least many of these would not fall into either of the groups just discussed: those fully Catholic who can be saved by a faithful life within the Church,[169] or those who, inculpably unaware of the necessity of the Church for salvation, have never formally become a member of the Catholic Church and can still be saved by living a life of grace. Lapsed Catholics constitute a third group distinct from the other two because they may include those who have recognized and accepted the necessity of membership in the Church for salvation, but who are so turned off to being Catholic for some reason, such as scandal or disillusionment with the Church, that they leave the Church in spite of that knowledge. They thus become Catholics who know of the necessity of the Church for salvation and yet choose not to be members.

Can these people be saved? That is a big question. The Council of Florence cites from Fulgentius of Ruspe: "And no one can be saved, no matter how much alms he has given, even if he sheds his blood for the name of Christ, unless he remains in the bosom and the unity of the Catholic Church."[170] Such an edict cannot be taken lightly, and so has guided the Church throughout the centuries. In spite of Fulgentius's words, one must still leave open the door to the possibility of salvation (God is free to do whatever he chooses); nevertheless, in view of this longstanding Church teaching, and insofar as the Church's role is to provide all of the means available to attain salvation, no member of the hierarchy would ever want to be responsible for leading a member of the Church astray.

As a result, an overriding concern that guides the hierarchy must be to do whatever they can, consistent with God's revelation in Christ, to promote the possibility of salvation for all people. Their actions must therefore always be guided by the need to promote the well-being of the lives of members of the Catholic Church, at the same time as they create a climate that is inviting to non-Catholics to become members of the Church, and do nothing that would unnecessarily induce Catholics to leave the Church, lest their ultimate salvation be placed in jeopardy. In other words, nothing should be done that would risk undermining the possibility for salvation for everyone.

One additional factor must also always be a matter of concern: the fact that many Catholics have a truncated understanding of what it means to be Catholic. For many, it seems, there is no reason to be Catholic other

---

169 Simple membership in the Church is not enough for salvation; one must "possess the Spirit of Christ" and "persevere in charity" (*LG* 14).

170 Clarkson, *CT*, no. 165, p. 78; citation from Fulgentius of Ruspe, *De fide ad Petrum*, c. 39, par. 80.

than to be saved. Dealing with such Catholics has its problems; one suspects that for many of them, if there were any other way of being saved, they might not remain in the Church.

How widespread this attitude exists of membership in the Church for salvation rather than out of love for Christ can be rather quickly discovered by teaching theology in a Catholic university. A recurring problem in my classes arose when, in dealing with the teachings of Vatican II, I made it known that non-Catholics could be saved. Invariably consternation appeared on the faces of some students because the question that immediately arose in their minds was, why, then, bother being a Catholic? Why bother going to Mass on Sunday? In fact, why bother doing anything that is required of a Catholic?

When I responded that one was Catholic not only to be saved but also to enter into an interpersonal relationship with Jesus Christ, who calls us to a life of union with him in and through his Body, the Church, and that this union was at the heart of the Christian faith experience of which salvation was a consequence, few gave evidence that they had ever heard of such talk or had any comprehension of what I was saying, and few found the explanation satisfying. Such persons are usually not aware of the value of human relationships, and even less of the value of a personal relationship with Christ.

Many, I fear, have endured long years of membership in the Catholic Church for no other reason than to fulfill the requirement for salvation. Indeed, occasionally a student would explain to me that the reason why church attendance today is so much less frequent than in the days prior to Vatican II, especially among the young, is because in those days it was widely held that attendance was necessary for salvation, but now, Catholics know better—one can be saved simply by living a good life!

It is obvious that the lack of understanding of the basic elements of the Christian faith life runs deep, indicating how much the Church has failed to get across the essentials of the gospel. Steinfels argues that without "an energetic response by Catholic leadership, a soft slide into a kind of nominal Catholicism is quite foreseeable."[171] Where has he been? The soft slide began many years ago and is now a landslide! No wonder so many Catholics turn to the rationalism of the Enlightenment for guidance to Christian living—they know of little else to guide them.

But the point here is: since the Church continues to teach, as it has for centuries, the necessity of membership in the Church for salvation, and the teaching is widely held by Catholics, as it should be, it must be at the forefront of the concerns of the hierarchy and the clergy, who are responsible for promoting this teaching in an effort to insure the salvation of all Catholics. It follows, then, that promoting the salvation of all was and is

---

171 Steinfels, *A People Adrift*, 9.

of overriding concern for the hierarchy in dealing with cases of sexual abuse. To have allowed this problem of abuse to be exposed to public purview would have meant risking scandalizing Catholics as well as others, causing many to leave the Church and jeopardize their salvation, as well as preventing others outside the Church from becoming Catholics. Allowing any of this to happen was not something the hierarchy could accept.

That is why I am personally convinced that, had the media not made an issue of the abuse, the hierarchy would never have brought it to light. This same fear for the salvation of the flock may also explain why other abuses in the Church, such as the widespread disregard for Church teaching, are quietly tolerated: the hierarchy are afraid to make an issue of such matters, for fear of the consequences to the membership.

These are, then, three reasons that, in my view, explain the inactivity of the hierarchy, and their willingness to tolerate abuse within the Church rather than to confront problems openly and risk alienation. The fact that internal problems, when left untouched, seriously undermine the life of the Church surely does not go unnoticed by the hierarchy, nor would they be unhappy if some way could be found to overcome the problems without confrontation, but the effects on them of the culture of confusion, plus their unwillingness to face the wrath of strong liberal opponents, as well as their fear of scandal, seem to render them immobile.

It will be for Pope Benedict to alter this situation, and one hopes he will do so. Regarding the sex-abuse scandal, Benedict's open expression of regret at pedophilia among priests in the United States on his 2008 visit, as well as his meetings with some of the abused, did much to assuage the concerns of victims in the United States. Similar efforts seem to have been successful at the World Youth Synod in Sydney, Australia, the same year.

Those who know Benedict say that he puts a priority on preserving the unity of the Church with the commitment of its members to that unity, that he is unwilling to dilute Church teaching or weaken Church discipline simply to maintain membership in the Church, and that he is open to a future where the Church may well be reduced to a small community of the committed.[172]

---

172 Ratzinger reaffirmed in an interview in 1996 what he had originally predicted in 1970, that "the Church would become small, that one day she would become a Church comprising a minority of society . . . [and] organize herself on a more modest scale." He goes on to state about the Church of tomorrow: "Christianity will be doomed to suffocation if we don't learn something of interiorization, in which faith sinks personally into the depth of one's own life and in that depth sustains and illuminates. . . . It's very important that we recall simplicity and interiority." Joseph Cardinal Ratzinger, *Salt of the Earth: Christianity and the Catholic Church at the End of the Millennium*, interview with Peter Seewald, trans. Adrian Walker (San Francisco: Ignatius, 1997 [1996]), 255–56, 267. Seewald also quotes Ratzinger as having said

Benedict does not appear to be representative of a culture of confusion, nor one who will cower in the face of strong opposition. That being so, he is liable to act when the well-being of the Church demands it. This is what endears him most to supporters of the Church, who are willing to risk reducing the Church to a "creative committed minority," if that is what is necessary to maintain the purity of Church doctrine and the clarity of the gospel message. At the same time, Benedict's willingness to act is what frightens most liberals, who, for some inexplicable reason, insist on reforming the Church to reflect their own rational agenda, rather than leaving the Church to form their own.

Steinfels, in his work on the fundamental issues that drive crisis in the Church, begins with the proclamation that "today the Roman Catholic Church in the United States is on the verge of either an irreversible decline or a thoroughgoing transformation."[173] Steinfels focuses on the reduction in the number of priests and religious and parishes and offerings as a sign of "a pattern of decline" and a "signal" of "the onset of crisis."[174] Perhaps so, but if the Church has been in decline since shortly after Vatican II, it may be due not so much to the reduction in numbers as to the fact that many theologians started right away chipping away at the life of the Church, interpreting Vatican II's teachings to mean whatever they wanted, and introducing a new breed into Catholicism known as "cafeteria Catholics." Reductions do not mean decline if in fact the result is purification, as Pope Benedict understands it when he speaks of the Church as a small community of committed and vibrant Christians.

Benedict, one hopes, will seek to restore the Church to theological and communal integrity, and while that will no doubt involve decline in numbers, it will also involve transformation. A loss in Church membership involves decline only if it is a loss of those who were faithful to the Church and its teachings. Such a loss would be dreadful. But a loss of those who had already departed from fidelity to Christ's Church even while remaining in the Church is a loss of that which had already become a negative. It may be time to put priority on restoring unity to the life of the Church. Allowing Church unity to disintegrate over a period of some forty years is, I fear, what has created much of the interior turmoil with which the Church is beset today. Perhaps the new "sign of the times" is the purifying course Pope Benedict takes.

---

many years ago the Church will "become small," a "little community of believers." Joseph Cardinal Ratzinger, *God and the World: Believing and Living in Our Time*, a conversation with Peter Seewald, trans. Henry Taylor (San Francisco: Ignatius, 2002 [2000]), 441.

173 Steinfels, *A People Adrift*, 1.

174 Ibid., 31.

PART FOUR

Solution to the Contemporary Crisis

CHAPTER TEN

Faith and Reason

OUR SOLUTION to the contemporary crisis in the Catholic Church will take us down two different but converging roads. The first road we discuss in this chapter: restoring unity between faith and reason, with priority given to faith and with reason as its rational support. Such an effort will be necessary if we are to overcome the ill effects brought about by an increasing alienation between the two since the beginning of the modern era, and the rejection of the importance of faith for an adequate understanding of truth.

BENEDICT XVI

Benedict has long emphasized the need to maintain the unity of faith and reason for the preservation of the truth of the Christian revelation and of its relevance to our understanding of reality.

In his *Introduction to Christianity* originally published in 1968, Ratzinger argued that the total dichotomy of philosophy and religion in the ancient world made the decline of the pagan religions inevitable, since they were reduced to myths or state codes of behavior devoid of reality and truth. A similar decline would have occurred to the Christian religion if it had accepted a "similar amputation of reason." But Tertullian identified Christ with truth, thus putting Christianity "resolutely on the side of truth" and its conjunction with reason. The Christian faith, in opting "*against* the gods of the various religions" and "*for* the God of the philosophers," allied Christianity with "the truth of Being itself," and preserved its contact with reality.

But the Christian faith had an effect upon philosophy. It brought the unchangeable and sterile God of the philosophers down into the world of human beings, and made this God "*agape*, the power of creative love." By the conjunction of faith and reason, one comes to know God as he truly is, the "real truth and ground of all Being" who is at the same time the "God of love." In this way, the God of revelation corrects the God of philosophy, who is no longer simply pure thought or self-contemplation, but a God of relationship. Truth and love are seen to be "identical," but the God of faith makes the true and absolute God of philosophy a God of "involvement, creative power, which creates and bears and loves other things."[1]

In his conversations with the journalist Peter Seewald at Monte Cassino in 2000, Ratzinger again points out how faith and reason serve each other in the explication of truth. "Faith speaks to our reason, our understanding," says Ratzinger, "because it expresses truth." Reason, on the other hand, "was created for the sake of truth." Faith searches for reason in an effort "to be understood," and seeks "a meaningful whole that embodies something reasonable." Faith in its fullness, however, is not "entirely comprehensible." It "cannot be rationally demonstrated" as a "mathematical formula" because it reaches into "the eternal nature of God, into the mystery of love."[2]

One of the more stirring statements about the need for unity between faith and reason came from Benedict XVI's academic lecture on his visit of September 12, 2006, to the University of Regensburg in Germany. While the lecture caused enormous interest because of the Pope's misunderstood statements regarding the Islamic religion, its main purpose was to argue for outlawing the use of violence and to emphasize the importance of a union of faith and reason in religious dialogue today.

In that talk, Benedict argues that "not to act in accordance with reason is contrary to God's nature." He finds the union of the Greek use of reason as λογος and the biblical idea of faith in the beginning of John's prologue: "In the beginning was the λογος. . . . God acts, σὺν λογω with *logos*. . . . In the beginning was the *logos*, and the *logos* is God, says the Evangelist" (Jn 1:1). But even before John, a process leading to an enlightened understanding of a "profound encounter of faith and reason" was going on in the Hebrew Scriptures, "especially evident in the later wisdom literature."[3]

The Pope finds the development of voluntarism in the late Middle Ages a step backward. It led to a sundering of the "synthesis between the Greek spirit and the Christian spirit," a voluntarism that, in an effort to preserve

---

[1] Joseph Ratzinger, *Introduction to Christianity*, trans. J. R. Foster (New York: Herder, 1971 [1968]), 94–103.

[2] Ratzinger, *God and the World*, 47–49.

[3] Benedict XVI, "Lecture of the Holy Father: Faith, Reason and the University: Memories and Reflections," Aula Magna of the University of Regensburg, September 12, 2006, 2. Text is taken from Vatican website, www.vatican.va.

God's freedom in relation to creation, disconnected his will from reason and claimed that God "could have done the opposite of everything he has actually done." Such a movement so exalted God's "transcendence and otherness" that it left human reason and "our sense of the true and good" as "no longer an authentic mirror of God." In opposition to this, the faith of the Church has always insisted that there is an analogy between God and human reason, even though the "unlikeness remains infinitely greater than likeness": while the God of love of the Christian revelation transcends knowledge, he has nevertheless "revealed himself as *logos* and, as *logos*, has acted and continues to act lovingly on our behalf."[4]

The Pope finds the convergence of faith and reason important to the foundation of modern Europe. And yet the modern age is attempting to "dehellenize" Christianity. This movement takes on three stages.

It began with the Reformation's rejection of scholastic theology, arguing that Scholasticism made faith "totally conditioned by philosophy" or "one element of an overarching philosophical system." The Reformers felt that "faith had to be liberated" from metaphysics so as to become more truly the biblical Word. Kant, with his reduction of faith to practical reason, brought the separation of faith from reason to fulfillment.

The second stage occurs in the nineteenth and twentieth centuries with "liberal theology," where religion is reduced to the realm of the purely personal, and replaced by the scientific and the empirical. Discarding traditional theology and hellenization, liberal theology reduced Jesus to a man with a "simple message" that represented the "culmination of the religious development of humanity." Religion became the morality of practical reason.

In a modern synthesis of Cartesianism and empiricism, reality is reduced to the mathematical, the object of experimentation, the empirically verifiable. Historical-critical exegesis takes over, and theology becomes "essentially historical and therefore strictly scientific." Modern reason is liberated from "seemingly philosophical and theological elements, such as faith in Christ's divinity and the triune God," and replaced by a practical reason that makes theology admissible in a university context. But in a world where only the certainty provided by what can be verified scientifically is acceptable, God becomes an "unscientific or pre-scientific question." And because religion now is a purely personal matter, Christianity becomes "a mere fragment of its former self," and "ethics and religion lose their power to create a community."

The third stage of the process—the current one of "cultural pluralism"—argues that the hellenization of Christianity should be discarded, and cultures should be allowed to return to "the simple message of the New

[4] Ibid., 3.

Testament" to "inculturate it anew in their own particular milieux." But such thought, argues Benedict, fails to recognize that even in the New Testament, Greek thought was present, and that "the fundamental decisions made about the relationship between faith and the use of human reason" are now "part of the faith itself; they are developments consonant with the nature of faith itself."

Benedict concludes by applauding the Enlightenment for its obedience to the truth and for the "progress in humanity" that it has fostered. What must be overcome is its "self-imposed limitation of reason to the empirically falsifiable." Reason and faith must "come together in a new way" in the university—to be involved in dialogue with the sciences not "as a historical discipline and one of the human sciences, but precisely as theology, as inquiry into the rationality of faith."[5]

In his talk, then, Ratzinger rejects the voluntarism that separated faith from reason in order to keep God free to act in any way he chose. By doing so, theology and religion, rather than making use of reason to promote faith, were bereft of reason and exposed to the coercion of violence. Ratzinger also rejects the humanitarian practical morality of the modern age as the sole niche for theology. He calls for a unification of faith and reason that allows theology to dialogue with the sciences in the university as an inquiry into the rationality of the faith. Such unification preserves theology and religion's proper contact with reality, and transforms the God of the philosophers into the richer understanding of God as the "God of love."

Fides et Ratio

The masterful work of John Paul II in his thirteenth encyclical, *Fides et Ratio* ("Faith and Reason"), provides the main focus of this chapter, since the encyclical expounds so well the nature of the modern crisis between faith and reason, and because of their dependence on each other, the importance of restoring unity between them.

John Paul's encyclical reveals how much he is troubled by the modern opposition between faith and reason. And rightly so. We have seen in the preceding chapters the harmful effects produced by the Enlightenment mentality, in the gradual demise of the guidance provided by faith in the lives of many Christians, in the weakening influence of faith in the public forum, and in the erratic path reason takes as it loses its ability to arrive at truth once it has become separated from the guidance of revelation.

What Christianity has failed to get across, even to its own people, is not only how destructive the dichotomy between faith and reason is for a proper understanding of Christianity, but also how inimical the conse-

[5] Ibid, 3–4.

quences of that dichotomy are for arriving at a true understanding of reality. Such a dichotomy would never have been acceptable to Christ nor the Jewish culture in which he lived.

Greek, Hebrew, and Early Christian Thought

John Paul rightly argues that the history of thought has taken it as axiomatic that the human mind has a capacity for knowledge of the Transcendent. Ancient Greek thought, especially Platonic and Aristotelian, had already developed philosophies that were open to knowledge of an Absolute.

But this meant that such philosophies were apt for Christian revelation. As one scholar of John Paul's thought has noted:

> The fact that philosophy is able to attain metaphysical and ethical truth apart from any faith or apart from a Christian faith supports the position that human reason can grasp some metaphysical and ethical truths that are a part of Christian revelation, and thus it supports the position that a union between faith and reason is not only desirable but possible.[6]

A careful reading of the Scriptures reveals a common conviction in both the Old and New Testaments of "a profound and indissoluble unity between the knowledge of reason and the knowledge of faith."

In the Hebrew world, Yahweh was the God who held supreme power over the universe, which he created and which depended upon him for its survival. As the God of history, Yahweh was also present to every aspect of life. Nothing ever happened in the world without his being in some way related to it. Sin, as it tried to separate the human order from its divine dependence, had a major role in disrupting the harmony of Yahweh's relationship with the world. But the Hebrew mentality at its best rejected sin and that separation, recognizing that human life cannot be lived apart from its dependence upon God, and that history moves forward only insofar as it lives in the light of that dependence.

For the Hebrews, reality was normally "assessed with all the resources of reason, but without faith ever being foreign to the process. Faith intervenes not to abolish reason's autonomy," but to bring the human being to an awareness that in the events of history, "it is the God of Israel who acts." Thus faith "sharpens the inner eye, opening the mind" to the "workings of providence." According to Proverbs, " 'the human mind plans the way, but the Lord directs the steps' (16:9)." Reason shows human beings the "path to its end," but is guided to that end "within the horizon of faith." Scriptural

6 Michael Sweeney, "The Medievalism of *Fides et ratio*," in David Ruel Foster and Joseph W. Koterski, S.J., *The Two Wings of Catholic Thought: Essays on Fides et ratio* (Washington, DC: Catholic University of America, 2003), 169–70.

history thus illustrates that "reason and faith cannot be separated without diminishing the capacity of men and women to know themselves, the world and God in an appropriate way."[7]

The Scriptures also recognized that human beings had a "natural knowledge of God" (*FR* 36). The Book of Wisdom had strongly affirmed that position (*FR* 19), and Paul declared the same when he said, "Through all that is created, the 'eyes of the mind' can come to know God" (cf. Rom 1:20). Paul made clear that because of human reason's capacity to surpass the limitations of sensory perception, the human being can reflect on the data of the senses and arrive at "the cause which lies at the origin of all perceptible reality." Paul thus affirmed in philosophical terms "the human capacity for metaphysical inquiry" (*FR* 22).

That capacity was "diminished" by the sin of disobedience when our first parents thought "they could ignore the knowledge which comes from God," the "source and origin of truth." From then on, the human being's "path to full truth would be strewn with obstacles": "Human reasoning became distorted and inclined to falsehood." However, the coming of Christ "redeemed reason from its weakness" (*FR* 22).

History of Unity between Faith and Reason

John Paul emphasizes that throughout the early history of Christianity, the union of faith and reason in the pursuit of truth was maintained.

For the Fathers of the Church, the role of reason was "to provide a rational foundation for their belief in the divinity" (*FR* 36). Though their primary interest was to bring their hearers to a "personal encounter" with Christ, "a conversion of heart," and a "request for baptism" (*FR* 38), the Fathers gradually recognized the value of philosophy in offering a "new way of proclaiming and understanding the God of Jesus Christ" (*FR* 36). Such early Fathers as Justin, Clement of Alexandria, and Origen saw philosophy as "instruction" and the "love of wisdom" that helped to shape their arguments for the faith and "paved the way for the Gospel" (*FR* 38).

As Christian theology developed as "reflection undertaken by the believer" to "express the true doctrine about God," "Christian thought made use of philosophy" even while distinguishing itself from philosophy where the latter might lead it astray. Such adaptation with correction is apparent in the use of Platonic thought, which was adopted by Christian theologians in their treatment of questions profoundly relevant to Christianity, such as "the immortality of the soul, the divinization of man and the origin of evil" (*FR* 39). Use of Plato was especially prevalent in the thought of Augustine, who produced "the first great synthesis of philosophy and

[7] John Paul II, *Fides et Ratio* (Encyclical on Faith and Reason), in *Origins* 28 (October 22, 1998): par. 16; hereafter paragraphs noted in the text as *FR*.

theology" based on the "unity of knowledge" between reason and revelation presented in the Scriptures (*FR* 40).

What was especially valuable in these early Christian thinkers was their ability to perceive how reason could be "purified" from deviant or constricting limitations, and "find its way" to be open "to the transcendent": reason could recognize its ability to "rise to the higher planes of thought, providing a solid foundation for the perception of being, of the transcendent and of the absolute." The "originality" in what the Fathers accomplished was their ability to recognize that reason was "open to the absolute," a drive that they "infused" with "the richness drawn from revelation." Thus they were able to bring together a union of "creature and Creator." Drawing upon the elements of reason that were "consonant with revelation," they brought reason into an acknowledgement of "the supreme good and ultimate truth in the person of the Word made flesh" (*FR* 41).

With Scholastic theology, "the role of philosophically trained reason becomes even more conspicuous." Reason's role is to "find meaning, to discover explanations" that will lead to a proper understanding of the faith. Says John Paul:

> The fundamental harmony between the knowledge of faith and the knowledge of philosophy is once again confirmed. Faith asks that its object be understood with the help of reason; and at the summit of its searching, reason acknowledges that it cannot do without what faith presents. (*FR* 42)

The thought of Thomas Aquinas confirms this harmony, to which he gave "pride of place." Thomas's insight was expressed in a special way: "Both the light of reason and the light of faith come from God, he argued; hence there can be no contradiction between them" (*FR* 43). Thomas's gift was to reconcile two wisdoms: "philosophical wisdom" based on the capacity of the intellect to "explore reality," and "theological wisdom" based on revelation, which "explores the contents of faith" and enters into "the very mystery of God" (*FR* 44). This was also for Thomas "a reconciliation between the secularity of the world and the radicality of the Gospel." Reason was able to maintain its perception of the "world and its values," but faith opened reason to the "inexorable demands of the supernatural order." "Illumined by faith," reason is set free from its limitations to the understanding of nature, and enabled to "rise to the knowledge of the triune God" (*FR* 43).

Separation of Reason from Faith

Then faith and reason entered a period of separation.

The legitimate autonomy that Albert the Great and Thomas recognized as proper to the operations of philosophy and the sciences gradually gave rise in the late medieval period to a separation of the two from faith: "exaggerated rationalism" produced "a philosophy which was separate from and absolutely independent of the contents of faith." This separation led some to distrust reason, others to agnosticism or skepticism and a denial of the rationality of faith. In effect, the unity that had been present for centuries was "destroyed by systems which espoused the cause of rational knowledge sundered from faith and meant to take the place of faith" (*FR* 45).

A gradual alienation from the Christian revelation developed into the nineteenth century, and largely characterized what is known today as "modern philosophy." Such modern systems are known as idealism, which pretended to transfer faith principles to "structures which could be grasped by reason"; "atheistic humanism," which regarded faith as "damaging" to "full rationality"; and positivism, which "rejected every appeal to a metaphysical or moral vision." These philosophies gave rise to totalitarian or scientific-technocratic systems that undermine the person as the center of all human concerns (*FR* 46). Such modern philosophies, by ruling out "truth offered by divine revelation," claim a "self-sufficiency" that is "patently invalid" and self-damaging in denying "access to a deeper knowledge of truth" (*FR* 75).

The encyclical rejects still other currents of thought: eclecticism, which, drawing from different philosophies, operates without concern for "internal coherence" (*FR* 86); historicism, which, by accepting only the truth of the moment and rejecting all previous positions as "outmoded and meaningless," denies any "enduring validity of truth" (*FR* 87); scientism, which accepts only the validity of the operations of the positive sciences, considering all "metaphysical statements to be meaningless" (*FR* 88); pragmatism, which, rejecting "judgments based on ethical principles," makes democracy by majority vote the norm for moral decision-making (*FR* 89); and postmodernism, which rejects the "meaningfulness of being" and denies any foundation for "objective truth."

Such systems undermine the "ground of human dignity" because they erase the possibility of seeing in human beings "the marks of their likeness to God." Such systems replace the ground of objective truth either with the "destructive will to power or to a solitude without hope" (*FR* 90–91). Ultimately a crisis of reason results, leading to a "nihilism"—a "philosophy of nothingness"—asserting the impossibility of arriving at truth, and reducing life to "sensations and experiences" that make everything "fleeting and provisional," with no "definitive commitment" to anyone or anything any longer possible (*FR* 46). By the end of the twentieth century, "one of the greatest threats" to the world is "the temptation to despair" (*FR* 91).

Commentary: Inasmuch as these secularist ideologies removed God and the life of faith from the rational realm, they inevitably led to God's eradication from the public order. Satanists for their part readily perceive that if their efforts to destroy traditional mores are to prevail, they need also to remove Christ from the world by demonizing Christianity. Though secularists cannot be put in the same camp as such extremists, especially since secularists are sometimes well-intentioned believers, their efforts result in the same effect of increasingly marginalizing God's role in our own personal faith lives and his relevance to decisions made in the public forum. The fatal flaw here is that, because God is so intimately involved in the operations of nature, to remove him from history is to distort history, skew our understanding of the role of human operations, and make it increasingly impossible to maintain a stable world order and a humane quality to life.

Secularists typically wish to replace the traditional objective standards of value maintained by the Christian faith with historicism and contextualism or situationalism. Pro-choice secularists of our day are determined to replace so-called antiquated Christian principles with the individual's subjective values based on personal convenience (postmodernism) or the popular *Zeitgeist.* Such a society is inevitably doomed to social division and moral disintegration, as our own troubled culture shows.

For the success of the Christian mission and to overcome crisis in the Church, the trend toward the marginalization of religion and the dominance of social secularism must be thwarted by a return to our Christian heritage where, as John Paul shows so well, faith and reason worked in tandem instead of being separated, and where faith provided reason with ultimate norms for truth that reason could not securely perceive by itself.

Reason Needs God's Revelation to Survive

John Paul's encyclical is a remarkable reaffirmation of the traditional Catholic teaching of the unity of faith and reason, and of the need that each has for the other. The radical separation of the two, according to the Pope, has led to the impoverishment of each. "Deprived of what revelation offers, reason has taken sidetracks . . . losing sight of its final goal," the attainment of truth; human beings have become limited to the immanentism of purely rational analysis. On the other hand, "deprived of reason, faith has stressed feeling and experience," running the risk of no longer having universal value. Faith becomes purely speculative, private, emotional, and irrelevant to our understanding of the world. For these reasons, it is urgent, says John Paul, "that faith and philosophy recover [their] profound unity" (FR 48).

Commentary: John Paul confirms what a study of history shows: when reason is disconnected from faith, reason loses its moorings. The heart of the problem is that, without faith rooted in the revelation of the one true God, reason is unable to explain why any one rational analysis of reality would have any more grounds to justify its conclusions than any other rational analysis. To put it simply, one rational argument becomes as good as another.

For example, rational arguments supporting the existence of God are not necessarily any more compelling than arguments against God's existence. The fact that rational people take different sides on this issue confirms that fact. Sooner or later, no matter what position one takes regarding the issue of God's existence, some intelligent rationalist will provide what many consider equally compelling reasons why opposite conclusions should not be drawn. One has no defense against such conclusions, however irrational they may seem, since reason by itself cannot provide unassailable powers of persuasion—it has no independent standard by which to judge rationality. Reason is unable to stand its ground against opposing argumentation without a transcendent principle of truth to which it can be referenced to validate its conclusions.

If there is truly a God, a rational investigation of the nature of reality that provides a philosophical substructure supporting his existence is necessarily of value because it supports truth. But if there is no God who is Absolute Being, there is no principle to justify the validity of one conclusion about reality over another. Historical positivism is indeed all that is left to us, and the postmodernist view that one is never able to escape the relativist limitations of one's own cultural constructs provides the last word on human thought and belief.

But if there is a God who, moreover, has definitively revealed himself in Jesus Christ—and that is the position to which the Christian faith is firmly committed—the encyclical's reaffirmation of the unity of truth, which opens human reason to the perception of the Transcendent and to the acceptance of the revelation provided by God in the paschal mystery of Christ's life, death, and Resurrection, is the answer that resolves the human being's quest for truth and ultimate meaning to life. And all philosophies of reason that fail to lead to that perception are inevitably skewed and inadequate.

Drive toward the Knowledge of Truth

The primary purpose of *Fides et Ratio* is to reexamine and affirm the nature of truth—what it is, how it is known, and how crucial it is for the salvation of humankind that a philosophy that supports the possibility of knowing truth be restored to a cynical and disillusioned age.

John Paul defines the human being as "the one who seeks the truth" (*FR* 28). But if this is so, it is only by coming to know the truth that the human being comes to an understanding of his own personal existence, as well as an adequate understanding of reality. Such an understanding includes the religious dimension to life, in and through which the human being finds Ultimate Reality, the source of all truth. This knowledge of the whole truth restores a harmony to life that it is otherwise impossible to achieve—a harmony that only comes about with the restoration of unity between the human being's rational ability to know and his ability to accept the divine complement to that knowledge made "certain" by the revelation of Jesus Christ (*FR* 34).[8]

John Paul argues that it is necessary to overcome the barriers to knowledge brought on by the modern age. As one scholar notes, "Since the dawn of modernity, in fact, there has been an ever more vigorous tendency to deny, in various ways, the possibility of expressing the Face of Being through a conjunction of the One and the many."[9] What is necessary, according to John Paul, is to recover a philosophy that accepts the intelligibility of the human being's natural drive toward Being as a capacity to receive knowledge of that Being.

A major insight of John Paul is his equation of the human being endowed by nature with the drive toward knowledge of ultimate truth with the human being's capacity to understand that truth. David Schindler, in commenting on John Paul's position here, explains that knowledge of such ultimate truth is not properly understood as added on to reason's proper abilities, but is in fact already in some sense "contained" in reason's natural drive for truth, inasmuch as reason's drive is "always open—at least implicitly—to the supernatural" (*FR* 75). Schindler calls this a presence by "anticipation" of the formal object of theology—the God who reveals himself—already "inside" the formal object of philosophy: " 'Anticipation': that is, positively open to, but without any claim whatsoever on, the supernatural truth, which remains essentially gratuitous."[10]

The drive toward knowledge of being is fulfilled by God's revelation of himself, which is accepted by reason and known in the experience of faith. For this unity of reason and revelation to be possible, a philosophy of metaphysics has to be restored that prepares the way for nature to go beyond the limits of what can be known by reason and empirical data, to equip the human mind with rational categories to discern, understand, and accept

---

8 This point is also ably made by Norris Clarke, S.J., in his "John Paul II: The Complementarity of Faith and Philosophy in the Search for Truth," *Communio: International Catholic Review* 26 (Fall 1999): 558. The entire issue is devoted to essays on *FR*.

9 Angelo Scola, "The Integrity of Human Experience: Cultural Dimensions and Implications of the Encyclical *Fides et ratio*," in Laurence Paul Hemming and Susan Frank Parsons, *Restoring Faith in Reason: A New Translation of the Encyclical Letter "Faith and Reason" of Pope John Paul II together with a Commentary and Discussion* (Notre Dame, IN: University of Notre Dame, 2002), 262.

10 David L. Schindler, "God and the End of Intelligence: Knowledge as Relationship," *Communio* 26 (Fall 1999): 510–40, at 518–19, esp. note 13. Schindler goes on to say that this implicit knowledge of God, which he finds in Aquinas's thought, means "that reason's intrinsic openness to faith includes a distinctly metaphysical dimension" that "tends to the end for which it exists," namely, God (p. 520).

"something absolute, ultimate and foundational in its search for truth" (*FR* 83).

Reason and Revelation Attain a Truth of Universal Significance

John Paul II focuses more precisely on the knowledge of universally valid truth as the goal of both reason and revelation.

John Paul sees truth as one (*FR* 79). As a result, the two avenues to truth, reason and revelation, though distinct, should never be seen as divergent, for both come from the one Truth, God. There is "the natural knowability of the existence of God" through reason (*FR* 53). Fundamental theology also shows that, "in the light of the knowledge conferred by faith, there emerge certain truths which reason, from its own independent inquiry, already perceives. Revelation endows these truths with their fullest meaning" by directing them toward the revealed mysteries "in which they find their ultimate purpose" (*FR* 67).

Philosophy is thereby empowered to show that reason provides "a truly propaedeutic path to faith" (*FR* 67), a path that illumines the way to "the fullness of light" to what is already known at least in part by reason. Thus philosophy and theology are brought to "a point of encounter and engagement" in their "reciprocal relationship" to revelation (*FR* 79).

Philosophy is necessary to theology and revelation because it provides not only "the structure of knowledge" but also the "forms and functions of language." This is confirmed in the history of the Church where "concepts and terms," as well as "thought forms" from various "philosophical systems," were used in the formulation of traditions and dogmas (*FR* 65). By rooting its understanding in the reality of "objective truth" (*FR* 66, 76), which is of its very nature universal (*FR* 27), philosophy provides a foundation through the use of its concepts and arguments for the intelligibility of theology's universal claims to truth (*FR* 77) as well as for "the universality of faith's content" (*FR* 69).

A capacity for the universal is necessary to Christianity if it is to be free from the limited scope of a particular culture. From its earliest days, Christianity recognized in Christ's mandate to spread the gospel everywhere that "the truth which he had revealed" had universal meaning (*FR* 70). The Church recognized that with the extension of the salvific significance of the paschal mystery to the Gentiles (Eph 2:13–14), God's redemptive activity in Christ "became a universal offer," breaking down the barriers of division among cultures: "From their different locations and traditions all are called in Christ to share in the unity of the family of God's children" (*FR* 70). Thus the encounter with the Christian faith shows "the human being's characteristic openness to the universal and the transcendent." Both human beings and their cultures are open to mystery and have an "impulse" toward "fulfillment," indicating that both have "an intrinsic capacity to receive divine revelation" (*FR* 71).

Through philosophy, the mind of the believer is able to grasp the "logical and conceptual structure" of the propositions of divine truth as well as their "salvific meaning" for the human race. Philosophy provides the language "to discuss theological issues" such as "God, the personal relations within the Trinity, God's creative activity in the world, the relationship between God and man," and "Christ's identity as true God and true man." A similar role is granted philosophy regarding moral issues, such as "*the moral law, conscience, freedom, personal responsibility, and guilt*," all of which are "in part defined by philosophical ethics." In every case, faith builds on "a natural, consistent and true knowledge of created realities—the world and man himself—which are also the object of divine revelation." Church dogma always "presupposes and implies" a philosophy of the human being and of the world, and ultimately of Being itself "which has objective truth as its foundation" (*FR* 66). Moral theology requires an ethics of "sound philosophical vision of human nature and society," to apply its teachings "to the particular circumstances of individual and communal life" (*FR* 68).

More recently, a "*Christian philosophy*" has been developed, "a philosophical speculation conceived in dynamic union with faith." Such a philosophy denotes a way of thinking which, while not necessarily the only acceptable way of philosophizing, provides a pursuit of the truth that "would not have happened without the direct or indirect contribution of Christian faith" (*FR* 76). Such a philosophy is able to handle questions not easily resolved without the cooperation of revelation, such as "the problem of evil and suffering, the personal nature of God and the question of the meaning of life." Other issues that are not necessarily beyond the capacity of reason but are not easily grasped by it, Christian philosophy, with the help of revelation, perceives with greater clarity, such as "the notion of a free and personal God who is the Creator of the world," "the reality of sin," the fact that history is eventful in the understanding of truth, "the possibility of man's supernatural vocation," and "original sin" (*FR* 76).

What is clear in this union of philosophy with theology and revelation is that meaning to life is only properly provided by Christian revelation "in directing the human being to Jesus Christ, the incarnate Word of God, who is the perfect realization of human existence." In so doing, "all forms of relativism, materialism and pantheism" are summarily rejected. The fundamental conviction inherited from the "philosophy" of the Scriptures is that all reality finds its "fulfillment" in Jesus Christ: only in him "does the meaning of life reach its defining moment." Thus the Incarnation is the "central point of reference for an understanding of the enigma of human existence, the created world and God himself." It is in this mystery that the autonomy of both the human and the divine is preserved and their unique relationship "in mutuality without confusion" is revealed (*FR* 80).

Need for a Philosophy of Metaphysics

John Paul now concentrates on the importance of a philosophical structure for understanding Christian revelation. He finds a philosophy of metaphysics best suited to this purpose.

Our contemporary world, the Pope argues, is exploding from so much information and so many differing interpretations of life that "the 'crisis of meaning'" has developed. Many now argue that to assert the existence of meaning itself is no longer tenable. The effect of such assertions is to cause widespread skepticism, indifference, and ultimately nihilism.

At issue is whether there is any meaning in a search for truth. To respond to this question, philosophy needs to "recover its sapiential dimension as a search for the ultimate and overarching meaning of life." Such a search is especially necessary today because, in the midst of the highly technocratic and utilitarian agenda of our times, a philosophy that provides "a renewed and sharpened sense of ultimate values" is called for. Without that dimension, technology risks becoming "inhuman" and a "destroyer of the human race." God's revelation is crucial in clarifying the real and "final destiny" of the human race, but it needs the support of philosophy "in the search for the natural foundation of this meaning, which corresponds to the religious impulse innate in every person." Unless philosophy pursues its sapiential dimension, it deviates from its proper orientation and becomes "false" (*FR* 81).

And so philosophy must recover its proper task: to "verify the human capacity to know the truth" and undertake the search for reality in "its total and definitive truth." To achieve this goal, relativistic outlooks are inadequate: they are incapable of meeting the outlook of revelation as contained in the Scriptures, which assumes that the human being is capable of grasping truth. That Christian theology might maintain a contact with reality, it needs a philosophy that can meet its perspective by accepting the possibility of arriving at knowledge of what is "objectively true" (*FR* 82).

To meet this challenge, philosophy must have a "genuinely metaphysical range, capable, that is, of transcending empirical data in order to attain something absolute, ultimate and foundational in its search for truth" (*FR* 83), the "God [who] alone is the Absolute" (*FR* 80) and "supreme good" (*FR* 83). Philosophy must accept the fact "that reality and truth do transcend the factual and the empirical," and that the human being has the "capacity to know this transcendent and metaphysical dimension in a way that is true and certain, albeit imperfect and analogical." That such a dimension exists and is knowable is implicit in the fact that human beings have "a call to the absolute and transcendent," to "the metaphysical dimension of reality" as it is found "in truth, in beauty, in moral values, in other persons, in being itself, in God." This call forces the philosopher to move beyond the phenomenal, beyond "experience alone," to a metaphysical dimension to reality that gives "a coherent account of the universal and transcendent value of revealed truth" (*FR* 83).

John Paul insists that the Christian faith espouses no one philosophical system; nevertheless, he argues strongly that the philosophy of realism formulated by Thomas Aquinas is most suitable for an expression of reality that is consonant with what the Christian knows through revelation.

Faith Validates Reason's Capacity for Truth

Norris Clarke points out how John Paul, instead of following tradition and arguing that reason can be shown to be supportive of and even lead to the Christian faith, "reverses the process and begins with faith, showing how it is a support and nourishment for reason and philosophy." This is because faith, rooted as it is in "the word of God himself, is much more stable and reliable, transcending human change, than natural reason, relying on its own resources alone." Clarke asserts that the Pope's argument from the position of priority of the faith is original, in that it is based on the fact that Jesus commanded his disciples to proclaim his Good News to all peoples. Unless one would argue that Jesus' command is absurd, it "necessarily presupposes that truth, the same truth, is *universally accessible* to all human beings," and that there is a common language by which everyone can understand and accept that truth.[11] Thus Jesus' command to proclaim the Good News to all peoples argues from the universal nature of the message of revelation to the necessity of reason's having the capacity to accept that revelation:

> Faith clearly presupposes that human language is capable of expressing divine and transcendent reality in a universal way—analogically, it is true, but no less meaningfully for that. Were this not so, the word of God, which is always a divine word in human language, would not be capable of saying anything about God . . . [and] there would be no revelation of God, but only the expression of human notions about God. (*FR* 84)

The fact that there are some truths known in revelation that are also naturally knowable, such as the existence of God, means that revelation at least at times presupposes that the human being has the capacity for knowledge of naturally knowable truths. In these cases, faith supports reason and gives a greater security to reason's knowledge of God's message of salvation. Aquinas's affirmation that reason and philosophy could grasp revealed truths

[11] Norris Clarke, *Communio*: 561–62.

insofar as they are knowable by reason means that "revelation gives to reason a conclusion that it is naturally capable of achieving on its own." Thus, "the revelation of truths accessible to philosophy means that . . . faith [can] be united with reason in theology."[12]

Where revelation makes truths known that are beyond the capacity of knowledge by reason, such as the existence of the triune God, faith, reason, and theology work together in expounding knowledge of these truths (*FR* 66–67):

> Through belief in that which is beyond reason, reason is given an object that it could receive only supernaturally, and from this starting point one can demonstrate truths that follow from it necessarily. Moreover, it is possible to give explanations for those revealed truths, which, although they do not attain the necessity of demonstration, are reasonable—explanations *ex convenientia*, as Aquinas calls them.[13]

There are, of course, philosophies that do not accept the existence of the metaphysical world at all. Here the role of the magisterium is crucial, and John Paul does not mince his words: the Church "can and must authoritatively exercise a critical discernment of opinions and philosophies which contradict Christian doctrine." Thus he gives an extraordinary role to the Church, not easily accepted by liberal theologians, in correcting erroneously oriented philosophies that threaten teachings that directly engage the Church "concerning God, the human being, human freedom and ethical behavior" (*FR* 50).

Though some might argue such a role for the Church infringes upon the autonomy of philosophy, this corrective role is necessary to the Church, says John Paul, because the Church has the obligation to safeguard the faith of those who might be misled, as well as to preserve revelation from teachings which might threaten its acceptance. His words here clarify the position he took in *Ex Corde Ecclesiae*, where he argued for the role of the magisterium in regulating the teaching of Catholic doctrine in Catholic higher education against an unrestricted view of academic freedom, lest the teachings of the truths be threatened:

> It is the magisterium's duty to respond clearly and strongly when controversial philosophical opinions threaten right understanding of what has been revealed, and when false and partial theories which sow the seed of serious error, confusing the pure and simple faith of the people of God, begin to spread more widely. (*FR* 49)

---

[12] Sweeney, "Medievalism," 168.
[13] Ibid., 167.

Christ the Fullness of Truth

Christ is not just truth; he is the fullness of truth.

One of the striking elements in John Paul's encyclical *Fides et Ratio* is that he not only affirms the validity of the Christian revelation of truth, but also its necessity to philosophy if reason is to remain on a right course, and here he strikes at the heart of the views of modern-day theologians who give priority to reason's arguments over the teachings of the faith. Equally striking is his daring political incorrectness when he asserts that the Christian revelation is or leads to the fullness of truth, and the only valid ultimate explanation of the truth, because of the unique revelation that comes with Jesus Christ. But the Pope is only confirming the teaching of *Gaudium et Spes*:

> The truth is that only in the mystery of the incarnate Word does the mystery of man take on light. For Adam, the first man, was a type of him who was to come, Christ the Lord. Christ, the new Adam, in the very revelation of the mystery of the Father and of his love, fully reveals man to himself and brings to light his most high calling. (*GS* 22; cf. *FR* 60)

Such an affirmation is problematic for many Christians today, immersed as we are in a society that prides itself on its tolerance of differing and even contradictory viewpoints. John Paul points out that it was long ago concluded that the principle of noncontradiction is part of the "spiritual heritage of humanity" (*FR* 4), meaning that contradictory affirmations cannot both be true. The Pope held that tolerance is, indeed, praiseworthy and to be esteemed, and to the end of his life fostered tolerance toward Jews and Muslims as well as nonbelievers. But he also held that tolerance loses it meaning when it is not carried out against a backdrop of conviction that truth is "objective" (*FR* 66, 69, 82), "universally valid" (*FR* 95), "absolute or ultimate" (*FR* 80, 92, 95, 97), "full" (*FR* 67, 92, 99), and "unique" (*FR* 80, 92), all of which he ascribed to the truths embodied in Jesus Christ and the Christian revelation.

John Paul never backed away from this position. It is that conviction which he repeatedly reaffirms in *Fides et Ratio*, as the following additional citations make clear:

> By virtue of the splendor emanating from subsistent being itself, revealed truth offers the fullness of life and will therefore illumine the path of philosophical inquiry. In short, Christian revelation becomes the true point of encounter and engagement between philosophical and theological thinking in their reciprocal relationship. . . .
>
> It is to be hoped therefore that theologians and philosophers will let themselves be guided by the authority of truth alone so that there will emerge a philosophy consonant with the word of God. (*FR* 79)

> A philosophy in which there shines even a glimmer of the truth of Christ, the one definitive answer to humanity's problems, will provide a potent underpinning for the true and planetary ethics which the world now needs. (*FR* 104)

> Christian metaphysical tradition . . . allows a full and comprehensive openness to reality as a whole, surpassing every limit in order to reach the One who brings all things to fulfillment. (*FR* 97)

> The fundamental conviction of the "philosophy" found in the Bible is that the world and human life do have a meaning and look toward their fulfillment, which comes in Jesus Christ. The mystery of the incarnation will always remain the central point of reference for an understanding of the enigma of human existence, the created world and God himself. . . . [In this mystery] the meaning of life reach[es] its defining moment. (*FR* 80)

> The word of God reveals the final destiny of men and women. (*FR* 81)

> God alone is the Absolute. From the Bible there emerges also a vision of man as *imago Dei* [image of God]. (*FR* 80)

> The Christian metaphysical tradition . . . is based upon . . . openness to reality as a whole, surpassing every limit in order to reach the One who brings all things to fulfillment. (*FR* 97)

> Speculative dogmatic theology . . . has objective truth as its foundation. (*FR* 66)

> Faith, enlightened and guided by the Spirit, recognizes in the message of salvation the "fullness of grace and truth" (cf. Jn. 1:14) which God has willed to reveal in history and definitively through his Son, Jesus Christ . . . , who is the mediator and at the same time the fullness of all revelation. (*FR* 9, 10, citing *Dei Verbum*)

> In Jesus Christ, who is the truth, faith recognizes the ultimate appeal to humanity . . . . This truth which God reveals to us in Jesus Christ . . . . This unity of truth, natural and revealed, is embodied in a living and personal way in Christ, as the apostle reminds us, "Truth is in Jesus" (cf. Eph. 4:21; Col. 1:15–20) . . . . What is revealed in him is "the full truth" (cf. Jn. 1:14–16) of everything which was created in him and through him and which therefore in him finds its fulfillment (cf. Col. 1:17). (*FR* 33–35)

> In the end, the word of God poses the problem of the meaning of life and proffers its response in directing the human being to Jesus Christ, the incarnate Word of God, who is the perfect realization of human existence. (*FR* 80)

What we have in these statements is John Paul's constant reaffirmation of where the definitive truth regarding ultimate reality is to be found: in the

One God who reveals himself uniquely in the person of Jesus Christ, the one Savior of the human race (Acts 4:12).

This is therefore indeed the truth that all Catholics must affirm. But for John Paul, this is truth not valid simply for Christian believers, as a typical postmodern Catholic might say. Rather, John Paul identifies the Christian perspective, in view of the revelation contained in it from the one true God, with the fullest understanding of being and the nature of reality valid for all humankind. As one scholar notes, for John Paul, "The highest truth is revealed truth and pre-eminently that revealed in Christ."[14] This makes John Paul "the 'Post-modern Pope' "—not in the sense where postmodernism is understood as the system that leads to relativism and ultimately nihilism, but where it "indicates an evangelical opportunity," even for the nonbeliever, to go beyond the "abyss of meaninglessness" to "reconsider metaphysics—and even God" in whom it is "not unreasonable to believe."[15]

The unity John Paul espouses between philosophy and theology he finds analogously represented in the hypostatic union of the divine and the human in Jesus Christ. Each is contained and completed in the other without loss of its uniqueness: "In the mystery of the incarnate Word, human nature and divine nature are safeguarded in all their autonomy, and at the same time the unique bond which sets them together in mutuality without confusion of any kind is revealed" (*FR* 80). As one scholar notes: "It is precisely the hypostatic *unity* of divine and human in Jesus Christ that alone affords the *right sort of distinctness* between the divine and the human—even as the distinctness of each, within their unity, remains 'perfect.' " This unity in "perfect" distinctness, we have noted, gives priority to the divine over the human, since the person of Christ is divine. In the same way, faith and reason are united in our understanding of God in Jesus Christ. Though there is the priority of faith over reason, each one retains its "rightful scope for action" within "this mutual if asymmetrical penetration."[16]

There is no denying, therefore, that in the mind of John Paul, "both disciplines, philosophy and theology, make their best contribution to wisdom when they are integrated in the mind of the Christian believer."[17] Implicitly, therefore, the Pope is arguing that the task contained in the life of every Catholic theologian is to make the call of Christ attractive to men and women of all generations, so that their drive for the fullness of truth may be fulfilled.

---

[14] Janet Martin Soskice, "*Fides et ratio*: The Post-Modern Pope," in Hemming and Parsons, *Restoring Faith*, 292.

[15] Ibid., 294–95.

[16] Schindler, "End of Intelligence," 516–17.

[17] James McEvoy, "Commentary," in Hemming and Parsons, *Restoring Faith*, 198.

Reef of the Cross

What almost tears apart the unity between reason's philosophy of metaphysics and faith's knowledge of the triune God is the Cross, which John Paul himself admits can be the "reef upon which the link between faith and philosophy can break up" (*FR* 23).

It is especially Paul, asserts John Paul, who highlights "the opposition between 'the wisdom of this world' and the wisdom of God revealed in Jesus Christ." The opposition becomes clear on the face of the "crucified Son of God." The "historic event" of the crucifixion exposes the inability of "merely human argumentation" to provide "an adequate explanation of the meaning of existence."

> Man cannot grasp how death could be the source of life and love; yet to reveal the mystery of his saving plan God has chosen precisely that which reason considers "foolishness" and a "scandal." . . . Reason cannot eliminate the mystery of love which the Cross represents, while the Cross can give to reason the ultimate answer which it seeks. . . . The wisdom of the Cross, therefore, breaks free of all cultural limitations which seek to contain it and insists upon an openness to the universality of the truth which it bears. (*FR* 23)

Philosophy must recognize "the 'foolishness' of the cross" as the "authentic critique" of those who "delude themselves that they possess the truth" when in fact they hopelessly "run it aground" with faulty reasoning. The "preaching of Christ crucified and risen" is the "reef" that exposes the opposition between faith and the reason that is left to its own powers, at the same time as it is the "reef beyond which" the union of faith and reason leads to the "boundless ocean of truth." In the crucified and risen Christ, we find "the border between reason and faith" exposed, but also the way by which the two "meet" (*FR* 23).

The Pope does not develop at length how that "border between reason and faith" can also become "the space where the two may meet," but the answer lies in the grasping of death as "the source of life and love" containing the "mystery" of God's "saving plan." The Pope argues that reason "cannot eliminate the mystery of love which the Cross represents," but only accept from the Cross the "ultimate answer" which reason seeks: the "gratuitous nature of the love revealed in the cross of Christ" (*FR* 23).

At the Cross, reason is forced to recognize the limitations of its "self-transcendent orientation toward the truth." It is here, at the point of discontinuity between reason's operations and faith's revelation, that reason is called to accept the challenge where, "with the assistance of faith," it may rise to the recognition of "the 'foolishness' of the Cross" as the "failure" of reason's "every attempt to reduce the Father's saving plan to purely human logic" (*FR* 23).

It is at the point of the Cross that the ultimate dimensions of Trinitarian ontology are present, where, in the death and Resurrection of Jesus, in an ultimate gesture of love in sacrificial self-giving in which Jesus surrenders himself wholly to the Father and wholly for us, that the "original experience of faith" is presented:

> Jesus has given himself up for us, that his surrender, however, is the surrender of God and that in this surrender, the life and the world, the meaning of being, and in fact absolutely all things are transformed, because everything is given in his origin and everything is taken up in the rhythm of *his* self-giving."[18]

It is ultimately the scandal of the Cross that demands a leap into the truth that only faith can provide—to accept the wisdom of God, the Father's love in the sacrificial death of his Son, as the fullest manifestation in the created world of the paradoxical form of God's infinite love.

Tasks for Contemporary Theology

The Pope closes his encyclical by lining up at least seven tasks incumbent upon contemporary theology:

1. He calls for theologians to inculturate the gospel: they must respond "to the demands of different cultures in order then to mediate the content of faith to those cultures in a coherent and conceptually clear way." In this they will be able "to serve evangelization more effectively" (*FR* 92).
2. Arguing against relativism, John Paul asserts that theology and philosophy are both challenged to present God's truth and his plan of salvation in Jesus Christ as "a universally valid truth." Their "joint effort" is to make known "the truth, which is Christ," which "imposes itself as an all-embracing authority." Their task is to "overcome divisions and to journey together toward full truth, walking those paths known only to the Spirit of the risen Lord" (*FR* 92).
3. Theology's "chief purpose" is "to provide an understanding of revelation and the content of faith." In effect, this purpose is realized in "contemplation of the mystery of the triune God." The method is to

[18] Citations from the German theologian Klaus Hemmerle's *Thesen zu einer trinitarischen Ontologie*, as quoted by Bernhard Körner in his "Thinking Beyond the Reef: The Cross, Faith, and Reason in the *Trinitarian Ontology* of Klaus Hemmerle," *Communio* 26 (Fall 1999): 671.

focus on the Incarnation and the paschal mystery in which the grand scheme of God's plan for human salvation are made known. In exegeting the Scriptures, the Pope calls for greater investigation of "the relationship between meaning and truth": human language embodies and communicates "the language of God, who communicates his own truth" through Scriptures. The task is therefore to convey "the deep and authentic truth" about God, "which God himself communicates through the sacred text." Scripture is not to be interpreted as contextual, as historical positivists would do, but as "events" that convey meaning regarding the history of salvation (*FR* 93–94).

4. A problem arises as to how to reconcile "the absoluteness and the universality of truth with the unavoidable historical and cultural conditioning of the formulas which express that truth." According to John Paul, the resolution lies in showing that truth is not limited by language: human beings can "express truths which surpass the phenomenon of language." Truth is not "confined to time and culture." It is known in history but "reaches beyond history" (*FR* 95).

5. Related to this issue is "the problem of the enduring validity of the conceptual language used in conciliar definitions." John Paul points to the fact that certain cross-cultural concepts "retain their universal epistemological value and thus retain the truth of the propositions in which they are expressed." Were it not so, philosophy and science would not be able to communicate with each other nor would their concepts be understood across the span of differing cultures. He urges philosophy to be concerned about deepening "the understanding of the relationship between conceptual language and truth" (*FR* 96).

6. John Paul stresses the importance of developing a "philosophy of being" which "would enable dogmatic theology to perform its functions appropriately," and not allow a "dogmatic pragmatism" where "the truths of faith" are reduced simply to "rules of conduct,"[19] or an ecclesiology reduced to "the model of civil society." Philosophy needs to integrate the wealth of theological truths contained within the "Christian metaphysical tradition" into "a dynamic philosophy which views reality in its ontological, causal and communicative structures." Based on the "act of being itself," such a philosophy needs to allow "a full and comprehensive openness to reality as a whole," able to surpass every limit "in order to reach the One who brings all things to fulfillment."

   Theology is able to confirm the validity of this perspective, in that it draws from revelation "a new source of knowledge," and conveys

[19] As the Enlightenment has often done.

this knowledge through the "intimate relationship which exists between faith and metaphysical reasoning." Moral theology needs to operate with "a philosophical ethics" that includes "a metaphysics of the good" linked to "Christian holiness and to the practice of the human and supernatural virtues," equipping it to engage more effectively various issues of our day, "such as peace, social justice, the family, the defense of life and the natural environment" (*FR* 97–98).

The Pope affirms that the Christian faith provides "a unified and organic vision of knowledge" that calls for a philosophy that responds to this vision: "It is the Gospel which imposes this sapiential task directly upon her pastors." The Pope urges thinkers to return to systems of philosophy that are "in organic continuity" with the Christian Tradition, the Fathers of the Church, and Scholastic thought. His appeal goes out to theologians to devise systems compatible with "the living tradition of the church," and to "recover" the "profound theological tradition of earlier times" that transcends "the boundaries of space and time" (*FR* 85).

7. Confirming again his position in *Ex Corde Ecclesiae*, the Pope states that theology in the Church must "first of all" be at the service of "the proclamation of the faith and of catechesis." Such a task includes "a call to conversion" to the "truth of Christ" especially in the paschal mystery: "For only in Christ is it possible to know the fullness of the truth which saves." Catechesis is integral to this process, since it represents the intimate bond linking teaching with living, "the mystery of the living God" and human life (*FR* 99).

The Pope concludes his encyclical by reaffirming the need for theology and philosophy to recover their true relationship with each other. Each is in need of and a value to the other: philosophy, in the "development of culture" and its influence upon "personal and social behavior," as well as providing "an understanding of the faith"; theology, as the "science of faith" that challenges reason "to remain open to the radical newness found in God's revelation."

By promoting the unity of the two, the Church "promotes both the defense of human dignity and the proclamation of the Gospel message." The Church leads people "to discover both their capacity to know the truth" and "the ultimate and definitive meaning of life." With the help of Christian philosophy and theology, people will understand that "their humanity is all the more affirmed the more they entrust themselves to the Gospel and open themselves to Christ."

In the work of the "new evangelization," philosophers must continue to find ways to explore "the true, the good and the beautiful to which the word of God gives access," and find ways to convey these truths even to nonbelievers "who do not yet grasp the full truth which divine revelation declares" (*FR* 100–4).

Conclusion

Every time John Paul produced a new encyclical, it always seemed like the greatest. When *Fides et Ratio* appeared, it was no exception, because of the power of its arguments reaffirming a unity between faith and reason, its grounding in the history of a philosophical metaphysics working in unity with theology, and the Pope's innovative prioritizing of faith over reason in establishing the rationality of a Christian philosophy.[20] The Pope shows how seriously the unity has been undermined by modern antimetaphysical philosophies, and speaks to the need to return to a philosophy that provides a rational foundation for accepting the Christian revelation.

In fostering this unity, the destructive influence of the extreme rationalism that has invaded much of Catholic thinking will be overcome. Such rationalism loses sight of its goal and the necessity of being guided not ultimately by reason, but by the truths expounded in the proclamation of the Scriptures, in Church Tradition, and in its dogmas. Extreme rationalism makes its goal not fidelity to Christ and his Church, but to the Enlightenment principles of fidelity to oneself and to the absolute authority of the individual mind unfettered by extrinsic forces.

But recent history has clarified, for anyone who still needed clarification, that the Enlightened approach leads to deviation from the truth, to the ideologies of human destruction, and to the breakdown of the life of the Church with every conceivable type of crisis, both theologically and morally, and ultimately, to the despair of nihilism.

If unity is to be restored to the life of the Church, a principle that provides that unity must be reaffirmed. The encyclical *Fides et Ratio* has strongly affirmed that principle: the prioritizing of faith and its reintegration with reason. If we truly accept that truth comes to us through the revelation of God in Christ and his Body the Church, its Scriptures and its teachings, then the last word has to be given to those faith sources over fidelity to oneself and the rational constructs of the finite mind.

---

[20] Avery Dulles shows other areas of innovation as well; cf. Avery Cardinal Dulles, S.J., "Faith and Reason: From Vatican I to John Paul II," in Foster and Koterski, *Two Wings*, 193–208.

CHAPTER ELEVEN

Restoration of Unity in Christ in His Church

THE SECOND ROUTE to be followed toward overcoming the situation of crisis in the contemporary Church is to restore unity to the Church in Christ. This will not be easy to do.

There is nothing more essential to the life and well-being of Christ's Church than its internal unity. No theological principle for revitalizing the life of the Church is more touted among leading members of the Church today than the principle of unity in Christ. Such unity is the backbone of the Church's theology of the Word, the doctrine on the sacraments, and even the role of Catholic education as espoused in *Ex Corde Ecclesiae* and its "Application to the United States." It is to the reasons why unity is crucial to the life of the Church and to its mission as it was established by Christ that we speak in our final chapter.

UNITY IN VATICAN II

The only way a true unity may be returned to the Church is to do it in keeping with the teaching of Vatican II. There we see that the ultimate theological foundation for unity in the Church is found in its relationship to the Trinity and to God's plan for the world: "According to this plan, the whole human race is to form one people of God, coalesce into the one body of Christ, and be built up into one temple of the Holy Spirit."[1]

No greater role exists for the Church in the Trinity's plan of salvation than to foster this unity. Ultimate salvation is achieved for the world through the redemptive activity of Jesus Christ in obedience to the will of the Father and

[1] Paul VI, *Ad Gentes* (Decree on Missionary Activity, December 7, 1965), par. 7, in Abbott, *Vatican II*; hereafter paragraphs noted in the text as *AG*.

in the power of the Holy Spirit. There is no greater determination of the Father's will for humanity than "to dignify men with a participation in His own divine life" (*LG* 2): to bring all of humankind, and indeed all of creation, into a life of intimate union with himself, even now in this world but forever in eternity, through a unity of all reality with the Body of Christ:

> And so the plan of the Creator, who formed man to His own image and likeness, will be realized at last when all who share one human nature, regenerated in Christ through the Holy Spirit and beholding together the glory of God, will be able to say "Our Father." (*AG* 7)

According to Vatican II, "all peoples comprise a single community" and have God as their "single origin" and "final goal." It is this single community that must be brought to realization.

In God's plan of redemption for humankind, the Father willed the excruciating suffering and death of his Son precisely because humankind could thereby return to its union with the Father—a union, however, that exceeded the original union Adam and Eve had, because it was to be a union through incorporation into the life of the Father through an incorporation into the life of his Son. All people are called to this unity with Christ (*LG* 3), and in God's plan of salvation, the Church has been given the "task of fostering unity and love among men, and even among nations":[2]

> By her relationship with Christ, the Church is a kind of sacrament or sign of intimate union with God, and of the unity of all mankind. She is also an instrument for the achievement of such union and unity. (*LG* 1)

That process begins in the life of the individual with the sacrament of baptism, which "constitutes a sacramental bond of unity linking all who have been reborn by means of it." But baptism is only the beginning, for it is "wholly directed toward the acquiring of fullness of life in Christ." Thus baptism is "oriented toward a complete profession of faith, a complete incorporation into the system of salvation such as Christ Himself willed it to be, and finally, toward a complete participation in Eucharistic communion," where the "fullness of life in Christ" is acquired (*UR* 22).

Ultimately, all the just will be "gathered together with the Father in the universal Church" of the Kingdom of heaven (*LG* 2). Through the power of the "Spirit of life" received in faith and baptism, those who were "dead from sin" are "revive[d] in Christ even [in] their mortal bodies" (*LG* 4). As a result, the Church while it exists in time and space is "a people" already

---

[2] Paul VI, *Nostra Aetate* (Declaration on the Relationship of the Church to Non-Christian Religions, October 28, 1965), par. 1.

"made one with the unity of the Father, the Son, and the Holy Spirit" (*LG* 4, citing St. Cyprian, *De orat. Com.*, 23).

What makes today's divisions among the various Christian communities so distressing is that they have deprived us of an experience of being united as a people in the unity of the Trinity. The Church was indeed "established by Christ" as "one and unique," and so it is theologically. And yet it becomes the job of the Church to realize that ontological unity in fidelity to Christ. The Church has repeatedly failed in this effort. Wherever there is "discord" in the Church, it "openly contradicts the will of Christ [and] provides a stumbling block to the world" and "inflicts damage" on Christ's mission "of proclaiming the good news to every creature" (*UR* 1). By their separation from one another, Christians by their own free choice willingly dispose themselves to tear asunder the symbol of unity that Christ intended for his Church, and through which his mission of salvation for humankind is to be obtained. Fortunately, many are eager through the power of the Spirit "for the restoration of unity among all Christians":

> Almost everyone, though in different ways, longs that there may be one visible Church of God, a Church truly universal and sent forth to the whole world that the world may be converted to the gospel and so be saved, to the glory of God. (*UR* 1)

Indeed, "concern for restoring unity pertains to the whole Church, faithful and clergy alike. It extends to everyone," and "every renewal of the Church essentially consists in an increase of fidelity to her own calling" (*UR* 5). What it behooves us as Christians to do is to admit our "sins against unity," and realize that "the more purely [we] strive to live according to the gospel, the more [we] are fostering and even practicing Christian unity" (*UR* 7), and the more we are responding to the fervent prayer of Christ to the Father "that all may be one" (Jn 17:21; *UR* 8).

Pope Is a Major Obstacle to Ecclesial Unity

Though new barriers to unity have recently arisen among Christians, such as the ordination of women among Anglicans, the acceptance of same-sex marriage among certain Protestant groups and even Episcopal ordination of a practicing homosexual, the role of the Pope continues to be the major stumbling block to unity among Christians today. That is ironic, since Vatican II understands the Pope, as he has been understood for centuries in the Catholic community along with the bishops, as the principle of unity established by Christ for the organizational life of the Church.

According to Vatican II, an individual bishop exercises "the office of teaching, sanctifying, and governing . . . that portion of God's people" of the universal Church entrusted to his care in an individual diocese.[3] The individual bishop "represents his own church," and is "the visible principle and foundation of unity in his particular church" (*LG* 23). The college of bishops, moreover, as the "successor to the college of the apostles in teaching authority and pastoral rule," is the "subject of supreme and full power over the universal Church . . . together with its head, the Roman Pontiff, and never without its head" (*LG* 22).

The Pope, however, by himself alone, has "a primacy of ordinary power over all the churches" (*CD* 1). As "Vicar of Christ and pastor of the whole Church," the Pope "has full, supreme, and universal power over the Church," and "can always exercise this power freely" (*LG* 22). As "the successor of Peter," the Roman Pontiff "is the perpetual and visible source and foundation of the unity of the bishops and of the multitude of the faithful" (*LG* 23). This makes the Pope the ultimate principle of unity in the Church, a unity that he achieves by being the ultimate foundation of teaching authority and pastoral care in the Church.

It stands to reason that the role that Christ endowed to the Pope is crucial to the maintenance of Church unity. Lacking that unity in the Pope, it is not difficult to understand why the non-Catholic community has become so theologically divided and corporately splintered ever since it refused to accept him. It also stands to reason that as the members of the Catholic Church themselves refuse to hold to the primacy and ultimate authority of the Pope in matters of faith and morals and discipline, the Catholic Church is bound to be subject to a continuing disintegration among its own members.

This is the unhappy situation in which the Catholic Church finds itself today. It is regarding the need for a restoration of unity among the members within the Catholic Church, as well as among all Christian groups, that our discussion in this chapter is addressed.

Extraordinary Synod of 1985

Two remarkable documents expounding the principle of unity and its relationship to the Church came out of the Extraordinary Synod of Bishops of 1985, which met November 24–December 8 of that year in Rome to commemorate the twentieth anniversary of the end of Vatican II, to assess the impact of the Council on the life of the Church, to correct any aberrant interpretations of the Council's documents, and to urge a deeper knowledge and understanding of the Council's teachings so that they might be implemented more effectively.

---

[3] Paul VI, *Christus Dominus* (Decree on the Bishops' Pastoral Office in the Church, October 28, 1965), par. 11; hereafter paragraphs noted in the text as *CD*.

In its introductory "Message to the People of God," the synod centers its focus, stressed even more in its major document, on Christ present in the mystery of the Church: "The church is, in Christ, the 'mystery' of the love of God present in the history of mankind." It is as this mystery that the Church is already "communion with the living God, Father, Son and Holy Spirit." But the communion is not yet complete. The Church's goal is to "go forward without ceasing in our work, in faith and hope, for Christian unity." The message points out that "through the church which is his body," Christ calls all humankind "to live fully in communion with God," and that it is through his Church that God "offers an anticipation and a promise of the communion to which he calls all mankind."[4]

The second report fleshes out these same themes substantially. Entitled "The Church, in the Word of God, Celebrates the Mystery of Christ for the Salvation of the World," the report stresses the mystery of God and the mystery of Christ as present in the mystery of the Church, and confirms *Lumen Gentium*'s understanding of the Church as the instrument through which communion with God and of human beings with one another is realized: "The church is sacrament, that is, sign and instrument of communion with God and also of communion and reconciliation of men with one another."[5]

The highpoint of the synodal document is the stress on the Church as communion: the "ecclesiology of communion" is accepted as "the central and fundamental idea of the council's documents" (II.C.1). The synod stresses even more than Vatican II that that ecclesiology of communion "is a matter of communion with God through Jesus Christ in the sacraments," especially baptism, which is the "foundation of communion," and the Eucharist, which "signifies and produces" that "intimate communion of all the faithful in the body of Christ which is the church."

According to the synod, it is in the Eucharistic communion that "a correct relationship between unity and pluriformity in the church" is realized (II.C.1). The unity of the Church is created and promoted by its establishment by the one God, the one mediator, Jesus Christ, the one Spirit, the one faith, and the one baptism and Eucharist. To this list, however, the synod adds the "hierarchical unity" established by Christ with its center "in the service of Peter," and stresses its prophetic role: "Ecclesial communion with Peter and his successors is not an obstacle but the anticipation and prophetic sign of a fuller unity." It is this sacramental and hierarchical unity together that make the Church a "Messianic people."

[4] Second Extraordinary Synod of Bishops, "A Message to the People of God," *Origins* 15 (December 19, 1985): 443.

[5] Second Extraordinary Synod of Bishops, "The Final Report," *Origins* 15 (December 19, 1985): 446, II, A, par. 2; hereafter, sections and paragraphs noted in the text.

It is pluriformity, and not pluralism, that the synod considers desirable and integral to the life of this unique Church, a pluriformity that is realized in the "varied spiritual gifts and charisms" of the Church and in the "various places" in which the Eucharist is celebrated. Such pluriformity produces "true richness" and "fullness" of life in the Church. Pluralism, on the other hand, is a negative because it is made up of "fundamentally opposed positions" and "leads to dissolution, destruction and the loss of identity" (II.C.2).

The synod recognizes the importance of the theology of collegiality for true ecclesial communion. It emphasizes, as Vatican II did, that collegiality speaks to the "activity of the whole college, together with its head, over the entire church." The synod reaffirms that "the college exists with its 'head' and never without him," and that the Roman Pontiff exercises by himself alone "supreme and full power in the whole church." All other ecclesial actions, such as synods of bishops and episcopal conferences, are a "sign and instrument of the collegial spirit," exercised through "the whole college of bishops together with the pope" (II.C.4) and in a "service of unity" toward the universal Church (II.C.5).

In the ecumenical service held during the synod, John Paul II expressed his will that the "synod may be a point of revival of the will for unity" among all Christian groups. He pointed out that the Church is already "the incorporation of all humanity into Jesus Christ as the one Lord," and that therefore "divisions among Christians are contrary to the plan of God." He stressed the importance of unity among all Christians for the success of Christ's mission: all Christians, as "bearers of [Christ's] mission must themselves be reconciled" and "show forth his unifying love in action." The need for a "restoration of unity" calls for "a restoration of the inner dimension of the Christian life . . . which makes intolerable any separation among those who share that commitment." The Pope ended by calling for a "change of heart, interior conversion, renewal of the church" as "essential to the ecumenical movement and its growth."[6]

Unity and the Eucharist

That the Eucharist plays a central role in the formation of the unity of the Church cannot be denied. According to the *Catechism of the Catholic Church,* this is because the Eucharist constructs unity: in receiving the Eucharist, Christians "are united more closely to Christ," and through that union, "to all the faithful in one body—the Church." Though this union had already been achieved by baptism, sharing in the Eucharist "renews, strengthens, and deepens this incorporation into the Church" (*CCC* 1396).

---

[6] Second Extraordinary Synod of Bishops, "An Ecumenical Service: The Pope's Address," *Origins* 15 (December 19, 1985): 453–54.

Further exposition on the role of the Eucharist in creating the unity of the Church is stressed in John Paul II's fourteenth and last encyclical *Ecclesia de Eucharistia* ("Church of the Eucharist"): "The eucharist" is called "the sacrament of the church's unity,"[7] which "the eucharist brings about through the Lord's sacrifice and by communion in his body and blood" (*EE* 44). Incorporation into Christ is "renewed and consolidated by sharing in the eucharistic sacrifice," but a "full sharing" takes place in the reception of "sacramental communion" (*EE* 22).

The role of the Eucharist as sacrament of unity is especially underlined in Paul's First Letter to the Corinthians. There he "refers to this unifying power of participation" in the Eucharist: "The bread which we break, is it not a communion in the body of Christ? Because there is one bread, we who are many are one body, for we all partake of the one bread" (1 Cor 10:16–17; *EE* 23). According to John Paul II,

> the argument is compelling: Our union with Christ, which is a gift and grace for each of us, makes it possible for us, in him, to share in the unity of his body which is the church. The eucharist reinforces the incorporation into Christ which took place in baptism through the gift of the Spirit. (cf. 1 Cor 12:13, 27; *EE* 23)

The Pope reaffirms Vatican II and the 1985 Extraordinary Synod of Bishops in their teaching on the ecclesiology of communion fostered by the Church between the triune God and the community of the faithful. He goes on to affirm the Eucharist as "the culmination of all the sacraments in perfecting our communion with God the Father by identification with his only begotten Son through the working of the Holy Spirit." As such, the Eucharist is not "the starting point for communion; it presupposes that communion already exists" and seeks to bring it "to perfection" (*EE* 34–35).

The encyclical distinguishes two dimensions of communion in the sacrament: the "invisible," whereby the faithful are united to the Father in Christ through the Holy Spirit, and the "visible" among the faithful themselves. The latter dimension "entails communion in the teaching of the apostles, in the sacraments and in the church's hierarchical order." It is by combining these two dimensions that the sacrament carries out its role as "the sacrament of salvation." To do this, it must be based on a communion that already informs it as well as one that it serves to intensify (*EE* 35).

According to the encyclical, the invisible communion involves true communion with the Trinity through the life of grace, whereby we share in the divine nature. But this communion is also realized by "the practice of

[7] John Paul II, *Ecclesia de Eucharistia* (Encyclical on the Eucharist), in *Origins* 32 (May 1, 2003): 753, 755–68, par. 42; hereafter paragraphs noted in the text as *EE*.

the virtues of faith, hope and love." Faith by itself is not sufficient; it must be completed by love so that the fullness of the divine grace and participation in the life of the Church is made present (*EE* 36).

Regarding the visible communion, the Eucharist, as "the supreme sacramental manifestation of communion in the church, demands to be celebrated in a context where the outward bonds of communion are also intact." These bonds include union with the one, holy, catholic, and apostolic Church, and participation in the entire life of the people of God. It is essential that this unity include union with the community's own bishop and with the Roman Pontiff, since it would be "a great contradiction" if the Eucharist were celebrated without union with that foundation of unity. Communion with the Roman Pontiff, therefore, "is intrinsically required for the celebration of the eucharistic sacrifice" (*EE* 38–39).

Theological Foundation of Unity

In his encyclical expressing his commitment to ecumenism, John Paul II proposes a basis for bringing unity into the Christian community: that "every factor of division can be transcended and overcome in the total gift of self for the sake of the Gospel." Overcoming such division is necessary, according to the Pontiff, if the gospel's apostolic mission is to be achieved: if "believers in Christ . . . wish truly and effectively to oppose the world's tendency to reduce to powerlessness the mystery of redemption, they must profess together the same truth about the cross" and "do everything possible, with God's help, to break down the walls of division and distrust, to overcome obstacles and prejudices which thwart the proclamation of the Gospel of salvation in the cross of Jesus, the one redeemer of man, of every individual."[8]

This is indeed the point we emphasize in this chapter on unity: that the apostolic mission of the gospel demands the unity of all Christians—not only across the Christian communities, but also within the Catholic community itself—so that no cause, no matter how great, may be allowed to promote a factionalism that undermines the primary mission of Christ to bring all humanity into a union with God in the Body of Christ, his Church.

John Paul recognizes that the obstacles to unity include serious doctrinal divisions that need to be resolved, as well as "the burden of long-standing misgivings." Achieving unity among Christians will demand "conversion of hearts," "prayer," a "purification of past memories," disciples "inspired by love," motivated by "the power of the truth," with "a sincere desire for mutual forgiveness and reconciliation," "the grace of the Holy Spirit," a "vision enlivened by divine mercy and capable of freeing people's minds,"

---

[8] John Paul II, *Ut Unum Sint* (Encyclical on Commitment to Ecumenism), in *Origins* 25 (June 8, 1995): par. 1–2; hereafter paragraphs noted in the text as *UUS*.

and a "renewed willingness . . . to proclaiming the Gospel to the men and women of every people and nation" (*UUS* 2).

John Paul sees the cause of unity as "a specific duty of the bishop of Rome as the successor of the apostle Peter," and therefore directs this encyclical to his own mission "to recalling the need for full communion among Christ's disciples" (*UUS* 4). But the desire for unity must also be the goal of every Christian, for it "goes hand in hand" with "fidelity to the Gospel" and the continuing process of becoming "more radically converted to the Gospel" (*UUS* 15).

This effort to achieve unity is based "upon God's plan . . . to gather all Christians into unity," indeed all humanity into unity, which the Catholic Church sees as its essential role as a sacrament of unity (*UUS* 5–6). Unity is "at the very heart of Christ's mission" and "belongs to the very essence" of Church life because of unity's role intrinsic to the realization of God's love for human beings: "God wills the church because he wills unity, and unity is an expression of the whole depth of his agape." Belief in Christ involves unity through membership in his Church, through which one enters into the life of grace that makes God's plan for all eternity fulfilled: "Such is the meaning of Christ's prayer: '*Ut unum sint*'" (*UUS* 9).

John Paul does not fail to recognize the role the Catholic Church has already played to create unity among Christians, as well as the role more recently played by what are now called "other churches and ecclesial communities" (*UUS* 87): "Christians have been converted to a fraternal charity which embraces all Christ's disciples" (*UUS* 42). A "Solidarity" has been created "in the Service of Humanity" in "projects aimed at changing the world by inculcating respect for the rights and needs of everyone, especially the poor, the lowly and the defenseless" (*UUS* 43); progress has been made on joint studies and translations of the Bible (*UUS* 44) and the renewal of worship (*UUS* 45); there is the "witness of holiness" and "fidelity to the one Lord" that "other Christians bear to God and to Christ," even to the "shedding of their blood" (*UUS* 47–48); theological dialogue (*UUS* 49) has been promoted that shows possibilities for unity in "many disputed questions such as baptism, the eucharist, the ordained ministry, the sacramentality and authority of the church, and apostolic succession" (*UUS* 69); there has been a strengthening of bonds with the churches of the East (*UUS* 50), including the removal of mutual excommunications (*UUS* 52) and the profession of a "common faith in the mystery of the church and the bond between faith and sacraments" (*UUS* 59);[9] and many programs and activities, as well as

[9] From a joint declaration by John Paul II and the Ecumenical Patriarch Dimitrios I, December 7, 1987, *Acta Apostolicae Sedis* 80 (1988): 253 (cited in note 97 of *UUS*).

ecumenical meetings, have been carried on in local churches (*UUS* 71–73). All of these have provided "fertile ground" for dialogue and practical cooperation (*UUS* 74).

Nevertheless, the matter that "constitutes a difficulty for most other Christians" is the authority of the bishop of Rome in the Christian community. John Paul reiterates the position of the Catholic Church: it is "the Catholic Church's conviction that in the ministry of the bishop of Rome she has preserved, in fidelity to the apostolic tradition and the faith of the fathers, the visible sign and guarantor of unity" (*UUS* 88). This "service of unity . . . is entrusted within the college of bishops to one among those" who is to lead them "toward peaceful pastures." The mission of the bishop of Rome is to "keep watch" so that "the true voice of Christ" may be heard in all the churches. The Church is kept one, holy, catholic, and apostolic, "because all the pastors are in communion with Peter and therefore united in Christ" (*UUS* 94).

The "primacy" of the bishop of Rome exists for the service of the "unity of all Christian communities." This "primacy" operates on various levels, including "vigilance over the handing down of the word, the celebration of the liturgy and the sacraments, the church's mission, discipline and the Christian life." When necessary, the bishop of Rome recalls the "requirements for the common good of the church"; he "has the duty to admonish, to caution and to declare" views that are "irreconcilable with the unity of faith"; he "speaks in the name of all the pastors." But he can also "declare ex cathedra that a certain doctrine belongs to the deposit of faith." In all these ways of "bearing witness to the truth, he serves unity." John Paul insists that he is open to dialogue in the "new situation" of the contemporary Church, to seek "the forms in which this ministry may accomplish a service of love," but this can lead "in no way" to his "renouncing what is essential to his mission" as presented here (*UUS* 94).

That mission entails, as part of "God's plan" and as affirmed in the solemn declarations of the Church and in its praxis, the communion of all the churches with the bishop of Rome. This is "an essential requisite of full and visible communion": "This function of Peter must continue in the church so that under her sole head, who is Jesus Christ, she may be visibly present in the world as the communion of all his disciples" (*UUS* 97).

Vatican I on Unity and the Primacy of the Roman Pontiff

The classic statement on the role of the Roman Pontiff in preserving unity in the Church—"The First Dogmatic Constitution on the Church of Christ"—was made in 1870 by Vatican Council I (*CT* 201–20).

The Council defined as a matter of doctrine to be believed by "all the faithful" (*CT* 201) both the primacy and the infallibility of the Pope, and saw each of these as essential for the preservation of unity of the Church.

Jesus himself conferred the primacy upon Peter. This was done when Jesus said to Peter:

> Thou art Peter, and upon this rock [petrus] I will build my Church, and the gates of hell shall not prevail against it. And I will give thee the keys of the kingdom of heaven; and whatever thou shalt bind on earth shall be bound in heaven, and whatever thou shalt loose on earth shall be loosed in heaven. (Mt 16:17–19; *CT* 202)

According to Vatican I, by these words Jesus conferred on Peter a "primacy of jurisdiction over the whole Church of God." The Council understands Christ not to have conferred this primacy upon Peter indirectly through the Church or as "an agent of the Church," but "immediately and directly," making him "the visible head of the whole Church"; that it was moreover a primacy of jurisdiction and not simply of honor (*CT* 202–3); and that what Christ conferred on Peter he intended to endure "for the perpetual safety and everlasting good of the Church . . . until the end of the world." Thus, "whoever succeeds Peter in this Chair [namely, the Roman Pontiff] holds Peter's primacy over the whole Church according to the plan of Christ himself" (*CT* 204–5).

What precisely is the good derived for the Church by papal primacy? The constitution answers that Jesus' purpose was "to render the saving work of redemption lasting" by establishing the Church so that "in it, as in the house of the living God, all the faithful might be held together by the bond of one faith and one love." Therefore, according to this constitution and thus according to the thinking of the Catholic Church, Christ's plan for human beings to attain salvation is achieved by their being united in one faith and one love in a unity as members of God's house (*CT* 201). The saving significance of the role of unity in Christ's Church could not be more strongly emphasized.

Jesus prayed for a unity among his disciples that would reflect his own unity with the Father (Jn 17:20ff). Just as Jesus was commissioned by the Father to bring salvation to the world, so did he commission his apostles for the same mission, to be "shepherds and teachers . . . in his Church until the consummation of the world." Peter was made head of the apostles as a visible principle to effect this same salvation in unity,

> that the episcopate might be one and undivided, and that the whole multitude of believers might be preserved in unity of faith and communion

> by means of a well-organized priesthood. He made Peter a perpetual principle of this twofold unity and a visible foundation, that on his strength an everlasting temple might be erected and on the firmness of his faith a Church might arise whose pinnacle was to reach into heaven. (*CT* 201)

What precisely was the nature of this primacy? What power and effect did the primacy have?

Building on the teaching of the Second Council of Lyons (1274) and the Council of Florence (1438–1445), the constitution defined that the Roman Pontiff had "the full and supreme power of jurisdiction over the whole Church, not only in matters that pertain to faith and morals, but also in matters that pertain to the discipline and government of the Church throughout the world," that he had "the complete fullness of this supreme power," and that the power was "ordinary and immediate . . . over each and every church[,] . . . shepherd and faithful member" (*CT* 206, 211). The power of primacy, therefore, pertains to four elements: faith, morals, discipline, and government. The Pope has ultimate, complete, and unquestioned authority over all of them. Once again, why this primacy? By "this bond of unity with the Roman Pontiff . . . the Church of Christ is one flock under one supreme shepherd" designed to preserve the faith that leads to salvation (*CT* 207).

Vatican I and Papal Infallibility

Within the nature of the primacy of the Roman Pontiff lays, according to Vatican I, "the supreme power of teaching."

The constitution sees the presence of this power confirmed in a history of declarations in the Church: the Fourth Council of Constantinople (869–870), which saw "the first condition of salvation . . . to keep the norm of the true faith," and Christ granting the power to do that through Peter to "the Apostolic See," which has "always" maintained the "Catholic religion" as "unsullied" and "holy" (*CT* 213); the Second Council of Lyons, which saw the role of Peter's successor "to defend the truth of faith" and to make final "judgment" regarding "any questions concerning the faith" (*CT* 214); and the Council of Florence, which defined the Roman Pontiff as "the true vicar of Christ," "the head of the whole Church," and "the father and teacher of all Christians," with the full power granted to him by Christ of "feeding, ruling, and governing the whole Church" (*CT* 215).

Vatican I moreover attached this function to the Pope in order "to propagate Christ's doctrine of salvation among all the people of the world," and to see to it that the doctrine "be preserved genuine and pure." The history of the papacy and ecumenical councils has also shown that the Roman pontiffs have "defined as to be held such matters as they had found consonant with the Holy Scripture and with the apostolic tradition." The purpose of this power, as granted by the Holy Spirit, was to "religiously guard and faithfully explain the revelation or deposit of faith that was handed down through the apostles." If the Apostolic See is to fulfill this purpose, it must always remain "untainted by any error" (*CT* 216).

The Council once again affirms all that is necessary for the preservation of salvation for all:

> This charism of truth and of never-failing faith was conferred upon St. Peter and his successors in this Chair, in order that they might perform their supreme office for the salvation of all; that by them the whole flock of Christ might be kept away from the poison of error and be nourished by the food of heavenly doctrine; that the occasion of schism might be removed, the whole Church preserved as one, and, secure on its foundation, stand firm against the gates of hell. (*CT* 217)

Finally, in order to maintain "the tradition received from the beginning of the Christian faith" for the "glory of God," the "exaltation of the Catholic religion," and "the salvation of Christian peoples," the Council defines "divinely revealed dogma":

> The Roman Pontiff, when he speaks ex cathedra, that is, when, acting in the office of shepherd and teacher of all Christians, he defines, by virtue of his supreme apostolic authority, doctrine concerning faith or morals to be held by the universal Church, possesses through the divine assistance promised to him in the person of St. Peter, the infallibility with which the divine Redeemer willed his Church to be endowed in defining doctrine concerning faith or morals; and that such definitions of the Roman Pontiff are therefore irreformable because of their nature, but not because of the agreement of the Church. (*CT* 219)

Role of Fidelity in Establishing Unity in the Church

It follows from all that has been said that the principles that preserve the unity of the life of the Church are fidelity to Christ as well as to the Church through regular participation in its instruments of life, especially the reception of the sacraments and the proclamation of the Word. But the teaching of the Church has also made it amply clear that the preservation of the unity of the Church has a centerpiece in the Roman Pontiff. He is the principle by which fidelity to the teaching of Christ is preserved. As primate, he symbolizes unity in the Church as the principle of authority and unity of discipline. It is in unity with the pope that the Church maintains its unity in all of its doctrinal teachings. It is by identification with the pope as the symbol of unity that we come closest to realizing what Christ intended for his Church. It is in fidelity to the pope and all that he stands for, then, that union with Christ and his Father is maintained in the total life of the Christian community as well as for the individual person.

It is this fidelity to the pope that is being undermined today. In doing this, the priority of unity achieved through union with the pope is being sacrificed for the sake of promoting factional agendas, both by groups within the Catholic Church and among various other Christian groups. Each group finds a reason for breaking with unity in the Spirit to support different causes, even when such support does not support "pluriformity," but pluralism.

Among the leading factions of division in the Church today are the women's ordination movement, proponents of a married clergy, pro-choice groups, and gay-rights activists. Most of these are identified as liberal groups mainly because they deviate from the teaching of the Church and stand in opposition to the pope. They are able to coalesce as a group of radicals largely because of their disunity with the pope.

Quite independently of whether there is merit to any of these agendas, the point of concern here is that they all give priority to the cause of their agenda over the value of preserving unity in mind and heart and voice in the Church. They fail to give priority to the theological, ecumenical, and missionary value of unity over the value found in promoting their independent agendas, however valuable any of them might be. They fail to grasp how inconceivable it is that Christ would give support to any agenda that would sacrifice the unity of his Church for a divisive factional value. This is not to argue that the pope would be right in his views regarding every agenda. It is to argue that there is no better way of promoting whatever cause one might seek to advance than by doing it within the Church without sacrificing fidelity to the Church and the hierarchy.

Evidence for the value of factionalism is lacking. Witness the breakdown of unity between the West and the East in the eleventh century, as well as the breakdown within the West in the sixteenth century: Has anything promoting the life of the Church been gained from these divisions that could not have been better attained with much less trauma if the breakdowns had been avoided? How could anyone have thought that greater fidelity to Christ would be achieved by instigating division within his Body? That was the weakness of Luther's position, however righteous his cause may have been. This is the weakness of many of the factions' leaders in today's Church, however righteous may be their causes.

Fidelity Is the Answer to the Sex-Abuse Scandal

As to the creation of today's crisis in the Church, it is by all accounts the instigation of these divisions that has provided the history, the context, and the open door that allowed the various crises to develop. As we have tried to argue, the breakdown in the dogmatic, disciplinary, and moral life of the Church that immediately followed Vatican II, especially in the 1970s, provided the ambiance for the development of a laissez-faire intellectual and moral attitude in the life of the Church, which contributed mightily to the sexual abuse of adolescents that has prompted much of today's crisis.

I see no alternative to correcting the intellectual and moral dysfunction within the Catholic Church today than to restore fidelity to the Church and its teachings. The ideas promoted in the publication *Human Sexuality* and the continuation of its brand of loose thinking has given license to experimentation, and justification of a way of life that is profoundly out of step with the Church and its traditions. To continue to follow that track while remaining within the bosom of the Church is to go down a path that can only lead to further destruction of Church unity and the success of the mission, as designed by Christ, to be achieved through that unity: union with him in his Body, which leads to union with his Father and participation in the life of the Trinity.

That the only answer to today's crisis is fidelity was brought out repeatedly by Neuhaus, both in his writings and in his television appearances. He made this point repeatedly in April 2005 during the final days of the life of John Paul II and the installation of Ratzinger as Pope Benedict XVI. But even before that, he had made his point clearly in his "Public Square" column of his monthly journal *First Things*, where he repeatedly emphasized the importance of fidelity by listing it among the *three* things required for a restoration of a virtuous life to the Church:

> At the epicenter of the continuing crisis is the simple, however difficult, virtue of fidelity. What is this crisis about? The answer is that this crisis is about three things: fidelity, fidelity, and fidelity. The fidelity of bishops and priests to the teaching of the Church and to their solemn vows; the fidelity of bishops in exercising oversight in ensuring obedience to that teaching and to those vows; and the fidelity of the lay faithful in holding bishops and priests accountable.
>
> I have been told that the proposition is "controversial," but I suggest it is almost embarrassingly self-evident: if bishops and priests had been faithful to the teaching of the Church and their sacred vows, there would be no scandal. . . . No, I am sorry, it is as simple as that. We are reaping the whirlwind of widespread infidelity. . . .
>
> . . . The problem is fidelity, or, more precisely, infidelity. Every priest . . . took a solemn oath to live, by the grace of God, in uncompromised

> chastity and celibacy. The sadness is that some of them, homosexual and heterosexual, did not really mean it. Because at seminaries they were taught, explicitly or by example, that they were not expected to really mean it. Because bishops turned a blind eye to what seminarians were being taught; or, even worse, bishops by their own example indicated that sacred vows do not really mean what they really say, and what the Church says they mean. . . .
>
> . . . Bishops have the job of seeing to it . . . that their priests teach and live in fidelity to the truth about faith and morals expounded by the Catholic Church.[10]
>
> In a word, fidelity. Or we might go so far as to rehabilitate another word banished by the therapeutic: holiness. . . .[11]
>
> . . . Bishops . . . [have] a historic opportunity for . . . calling others to rediscover, the vocation to fidelity. . . .[12]
>
> . . . I have said it so often on television, radio, and in print that I begin to sound like a broken record, to myself if not to others: this crisis is about three things—fidelity, fidelity, and fidelity.

And Neuhaus laid it entirely on the bishops to correct the problem when he said that the annual meeting of bishops at Dallas in 2002 "would be a debacle if the bishops did not address in a straightforward manner the three causes of the crisis—infidelity, infidelity, and infidelity."[13]

WEIGEL AND FIDELITY

This same issue of fidelity is paramount in one of the best discussions of why the crisis of 2002 occurred and how to resolve it.

George Weigel, in his *Courage to Be Catholic*, leaves no doubt that he considers the Church in crisis: "The combination of clergy sexual abuse and failed leadership by bishops clearly and unmistakably demonstrates that the Catholic Church in the United States is in crisis." He also leaves no doubt about the extent of harm done: the abuse has "scarred young souls," "condemned once-trusting men to miserable lives," "ravaged families," led to "broken vows" that "hurt the entire community," caused "serious damage to the Church's reputation and its ability to be a credible moral teacher," and "casts a long, dark shadow" over the Church's efforts "to preach the Gospel of Jesus Christ."[14]

Weigel agrees that "at its root," the crisis "is a crisis of fidelity—a crisis of faith." The "fundamental reality of clerical sexual abuse is infidelity," and

---

10 Neuhaus, "Public Square: Continuing Survey," 77.

11 Ibid., 82.

12 Ibid., 83.

13 Neuhaus, Public Square: Scandal Time III," 90–91.

14 Weigel, *Courage*, 21–22.

the way to correct the crisis, according to Weigel, is a life of "discipleship," of "deeper fidelity . . . by everyone."[15]

Weigel confirms the point we have already made, that the crisis is what he calls "a metaphor for the entire post-Vatican II Catholic situation."[16] The sex abuse among clergy has its origins in the post-Vatican II period, he argues, when a "culture of dissent" was born.[17] Weigel calls this a period of so-called "faithful dissent" initiated by the successful revolt of many bishops, priests, and nuns against *Humanae Vitae.*[18] The dissent was "affirmed as an appropriate response to authoritative teaching" with the publication of the CTSA's *Human Sexuality* report, whose impact upon seminaries was "profound, and in some cases shattering."[19] Weigel characterizes this movement of dissent as "Catholic Lite," by which he means "Catholicism's transformation into a kind of high-church, politically correct American 'denomination,'"[20] a "soft Catholicism, understanding and sympathetic" that poses little "countercultural challenge to the spirit of the age," and whose project is rather "to surrender to modernity" rather than "to convert it," as John Paul tried to do.[21] It is the effects of that period that are "now on display, in clerical sexual scandals and irresponsible episcopal leadership." But, says Weigel, the "game is over."[22]

In spite of all the harm that has been done, Weigel sees a good aspect to the crisis: It embodies "catastrophe and opportunity,"[23] the two-fold meaning of crisis as found in the Bible: catastrophe, because of the "widespread clerical sexual misconduct" that was "immeasurably intensified" by "some bishops' inept and irresponsible response to grave sins and crimes"; opportunity, because it calls for a deepening of the "reforms" begun by Vatican II.[24]

"Reform" is the leitmotif of Weigel's work, by which he means "a return to the Church's roots . . . retrieving, renewing, and developing

[15] Ibid., 22, 174, 34.

[16] Ibid., 219.

[17] Ibid., 71.

[18] Ibid., 83–86. Charles Curran has recently written a book characterizing his life of major rejection of the moral teaching of the Church by this expression.

[19] Ibid., 75.

[20] Ibid., 3. Weigel defines a "denomination" as "an institution whose form is typically defined by the will of its members," as opposed to "a Church—a community whose basic structure and boundaries are defined, once and for all, by the will of Christ" (p. 26). Denominations are usually bureaucratic and emphasize group-maintenance rather than doctrine, and the bishop becomes a manager rather than a leader (pp. 96–99).

[21] Ibid., 221–22.

[22] Ibid., 223.

[23] "George Weigel on the Church Crisis in U.S.," interview by Zenit News Agency, www.zenit.org, August 29, 1992, 1–4, at 4.

[24] Weigel, *Courage*, 2.

often-forgotten elements of the Church's tradition . . . in such a way as to create the possibility of a genuinely new future."[25] Reform is the heading for four of the nine chapters in Weigel's work in which he offers an "agenda for reform" in seminaries and novitiates, in the priesthood, among the bishops and at the Vatican, and as the process by which the Church returns to its essential nature by recovering "the truths" given it by Christ, including "moral truths about the ways in which human beings truly flourish."[26]

At bottom, Weigel sees the present crisis in the Church as similar to every Church crisis of the past: in other words, "a crisis of fidelity," all springing "from inadequate conversion to Christ."[27] Therefore the answer to the present crisis is a return to fidelity, meaning "a deeper conversion to Christ," and a return to a Church that "rediscovers the courage to be Catholic." This does not mean "deconstructing Catholic faith" or "surrendering to the decadence of the sexual revolution" as proposed in the CTSA publication of *Human Sexuality* in 1977, but a restoration of "fidelity to the fullness of Catholic faith":

> Classic Catholicism—a Catholicism with the courage to be countercultural, a Catholicism that has reclaimed the wisdom of the past in order to face the corruptions of the present and create a renewed future, a Catholicism that risks the high adventure of fidelity.[28]

Weigel argues that John Paul in April 2002 made it clear to the American hierarchy "that while the crisis had psychological, legal, and even political dimensions, it was, at root, a spiritual crisis—a crisis of fidelity." The Pope had himself identified in the crisis of the Church in America a "linkage between the impact of a thirty-five-year-old culture of dissent and the crisis in both its dimensions—clergy sexual abuse and episcopal misgovernance," and that correcting the crisis would call for "courageous leadership" from the American bishops.[29]

As a result, Weigel spells out "a comprehensive agenda of reform"[30] that covers every sector of life in the Church where the guiding principle is always a call for the overcoming of the culture of dissent by "fidelity to the fullness of Catholic faith." Regarding seminaries and novitiates, a "reform of all seminaries and novitiates is necessary," guided by John Paul's principle asserted in his 1992 apostolic exhortation *Pastores Dabo Vobis* ("Shepherds I Shall Give You") "of reliving the experience of formation which our

---

[25] Ibid., 3–4.
[26] Ibid., 220.
[27] Ibid., 60.
[28] Ibid., 6–8.
[29] Ibid., 145.
[30] Ibid., 146.

Lord provided for the Twelve."[31] Priority should be given to theology over psychology in the recruiting of seminarians, though attention to both is important. Screening should look for depth of faith, openness to the entrance of Christ into their lives, and their ability to communicate their faith to others. Orthodoxy should not be an obstacle to entrance, as it has often been, since those who were committed to the teaching of the Church were not the problem in the scandal.[32] Before ordination, candidates for the priesthood should have "a firm conviction about the truth of the Church's sexual ethic" and be committed to an ethic of "celibate chastity" as a "radical gift of self . . . destined for glorification in an eternity of perfect self-giving and receptivity."[33] The "answer to clerical indiscipline is . . . more fidelity, more radical giving of self to Christ."[34]

Regarding the priesthood, "the 'answer' to the scandal of clerical sexual abuse is fidelity—a deeper conversion of American priests to Christ."[35]

Being a priest is already a deepened experience of what it means to be a disciple of Christ, one "whose life is formed by the conviction that in looking on the cross of Christ one is looking at the central truth of human history—God's love for the world, which was so great that God gave his Son for its redemption." Commitment to that truth, which is "*the truth*" for the world and not simply for Christians, stamps the entire life of the priest as a man who dies to self in the service of others, of which his celibacy is "a powerful witness." As a "sign of contradiction" to much of what the world stands for, the priest shares in Christ's mission of sanctifying the Church and "through the Church, the world," calling all people to become "saints" who will share eternal life "in perfect communion with each other and with God." Once one accepts the "awesome truth" of this role as "a living icon of the eternal priesthood of Christ," no room is left for sexual abuse.[36]

Weigel ends by calling all Catholics truly concerned about genuine reform in the Church (as opposed to supporting the "culture of dissent's" understanding of reform as deconstruction) to recognize that mediocrity in one's life in the Church is no longer acceptable, that what is required now is "Christian excellence [and] deeper conformity to Christ." Reform for Weigel means not accommodating to the spirit of the modern world, but *ressourcement*—the recovering of the truths given the Church by Christ, recovering "the Church's essential 'form' " by returning to the wisdom of the Scriptures, the teachings of the early Church Fathers, and the great medieval

[31] Ibid., 147–48.
[32] Ibid., 151–55.
[33] Ibid., 158–59.
[34] Ibid., 165.
[35] Ibid., 191.
[36] Ibid., 175–77.

theologians: "There could be no *aggiornamento* [updating of the Church] without *ressourcement* [a return to the sources]—no reform without form."[37]

The deepest recesses of the present crisis for Weigel lie in the fact that we are experiencing a "crisis of humanism." Correcting the crisis means supplanting the debilitating atheistic humanisms of the twentieth century with a "*Christian* humanism" based on "the face of the merciful Father and the true meaning of our lives." Weigel agrees with John Paul that central to this humanism is a new awareness that the truth the Church teaches is not a relative one but the only "truth about the world's story," and a rediscovery of "the great adventure of fidelity and Church orthodoxy." This includes a purification of the entire Church as it recognizes that its passage through the present Good Friday is a new call to the holiness that is necessary to experience "the Easter glory."

For Weigel, the path to a restoration of the life of the Church and the attaining of the ultimate goal for the world must include a renewed dedication to Catholic orthodoxy—"thinking with the mind of the Church and living in service to others." It is in this sense that the heart of the crisis in the Church is the "crisis of fidelity," and only a renewed commitment of "everyone"—the entire community, including bishops, priests, and laity—to Catholic orthodoxy will lead to a renewed Church.[38]

Weigel's synthesis of the present situation of the Church is superb in its clarity of perception and profundity. He reduces the present crisis to its essential elements as infidelity to the Church and a failure of its leadership to confront that infidelity. Reform must then be based on a call to restore a commitment to Christ that is integrated into a life of fidelity to his Church, concretely manifested by acceptance of the teachings of the Church in matters of doctrine and morals.

Weigel rightly excoriates the "culture of dissent" for its destruction of the inner unity of the Church in setting out a disparate and unorthodox standard of what it means to be a Catholic. He rightly sees the aberrations of the '70s and '80s as dying with the passing of the elite intellectuals of that era and the aberrations they espoused. Any formula for a renewal of the Church must refocus on an understanding of the mission of the Church that includes the need to reestablish unity in the Church, a unity that necessarily includes communion with the pope and the hierarchy.

Eamon Duffy Dissents

Not all scholars and commentators of course agree with Weigel's solution to the crisis. We have already discussed Gibson's disagreements above. Perhaps

---

[37] Ibid., 219–20.
[38] Ibid., 221–31.

a more balanced assessment of Weigel's position may be found in the recent comments of Eamon Duffy, the Catholic British historian of Christianity, who has criticized Weigel's formula of reform for being too submissive to authority, too eager to overcome the "culture of dissent."

For Duffy, dissent is an integral part of tradition. Duffy agrees with Weigel that accepting tradition includes "thinking with the Church," but Duffy objects that Weigel understands tradition "essentially as a brake rather than an accelerator, a fixed body of unchanging information and prescription designed to limit and constrain dangerous freedom of thought." Such a view places Weigel "in stark opposition to notions of conflict, debate and dissent," which Duffy sees as important to the development of tradition.

Weigel's call for the appointment of bishops and seminary teachers in the mold of John Paul II who will be "unimpeachably orthodox" and "defenders of the Church and of the Pontificate" even when it concerns "the most bitterly contested teachings" is, according to Duffy, based on a "deeply misleading" understanding of "how traditions actually function in the real world." Weigel is asking, says Duffy, that future priests be "trained to accept the whole of the Catholic tradition without criticizing it." This is a too narrow understanding of tradition as "obedience to authority." Such an approach, Duffy feels, fails to take into account the fact that traditions "need and are nourished by some degree of self-scrutiny and debate," and are "not undermined by it: indeed, where they become fixed and immune from such self-scrutiny, they die. Tradition is not a weight holding us down, but a tool for fresh discovery." To reject "the necessary presence of conflict, debate, invention, and innovation" is not to "do justice to what is in fact a fundamental feature of all traditions whatever."[39]

So what better solution does Duffy offer in place of Weigel's unity of fidelity that rejects the "culture of dissent"? In fact, none.

Duffy's criticism of Weigel is not only unfair but inaccurate for at least three reasons. Weigel does not understand tradition as a "weight holding us down," nor does he speak of it as a "fixed body of unchanging information and prescription designed to limit and constrain dangerous freedom of thought."[40] On the contrary, Weigel understands tradition as "a living, developing thing," and theology as "a developing science."

But he also sees tradition as a "conversation" that is "conducted within authoritative boundaries."[41] Weigel is objecting to the fact that seminarians

---

[39] Eamon Duffy, "Tradition and Authority: The Cardinal Hume Memorial Lecture, Newcastle, 27 November 2003," in his *Faith of Our Fathers: Reflections on Catholic Traditions* (New York: Continuum, 2004), 169–72. Duffy is responding to Weigel, *Courage*, 166–71.

[40] Duffy, "Tradition and Authority," 171, 169.

[41] Weigel, *Courage*, 168, 170.

are taught to "deconstruct" the tradition even before they have learned it. How does such a process maintain tradition? He is rejecting the "modern thought" that misrepresents tradition as outdated "obfuscation." In Weigel's eyes, treating tradition as superseded by the latest fad does not lead to freedom of thought, but rather, "intellectual chaos and moral confusion."[42] Weigel is really rejecting a freedom of thought that sees tradition as something to be torn down and discarded rather than as a living witness to the life of the Church with which the seminarian must be engaged.

Secondly, Weigel does not ask, as Duffy claims, that the whole of the Catholic tradition be accepted "without criticizing it." In fact, Weigel states just the opposite: that seminarians should learn the tradition so that they can "fruitfully engage it critically."[43]

Thirdly, Weigel's real point is that criticism should be leveled against tradition from within a loving relationship with the Church, "within a determined conviction to 'think with the Church.'"[44] Duffy accepts as well that thinking with the Church is fundamental to any study of Catholic theology.[45] The problem is, what does he mean by that? He speaks of tradition as "a tool for fresh discovery" (whatever that means) having a "plurality of voices."[46] Such language provides no parameters for maintaining continuity with tradition or restraint on innovation, and makes discussion of tradition a free-for-all over debatable and conflicting ideas. Duffy's approach seems to rest on a hope that somehow clarity will rise from such unstructured discussion.

In this kind of openness to unstructured discussion that somehow will produce fruit, one can discern the weakness of Duffy's general approach to the modern crisis: like so many liberals, he doesn't want to take a position. He seeks neither to side with the more conservative wing of the Church nor with the liberal, rejecting on the one hand an approach he considers too constricting, that which abides by the teachings of the hierarchy—he argues that "there is no single voice of the tradition"—yet arguing on the other hand that tradition is not "a source of freedom" unless we "submit ourselves" to the "disciplines" that keep it "Catholic."[47] How can it be both?

Duffy seeks to take a middle-ground, nonideological approach to issues—which would be fine since no one is in favor of ideologies except ideologists—but in doing so, he ends with no workable proposal on how to resolve the modern conflict. "There are no quick fixes," he concludes, and

---

[42] Ibid., 167.
[43] Ibid.
[44] Ibid., 170.
[45] Duffy, 169.
[46] Ibid., 170, 172.
[47] Ibid., 185–86.

asks only for a "shared endeavour" over "a painful and constant process of re-education and rediscovery"[48]—all nice-sounding words which show little understanding of the human need for authoritative direction, and do little to resolve the current crisis in the Church. If Duffy rejects Weigel's solution of unity in fidelity to authoritative teaching, he ought to have a better alternative than "shared endeavour."

Weigel himself needed to do one more thing: stress that the present crisis includes a crisis of the laity. For too long the laity have comfortably lived in cultural somnambulism in the Church, allowing themselves to be victimized by a culture that accepts mediocrity as a tenable norm for being Catholic. For too long the laity have taken a pass on becoming integrated into the countercultural spirituality of the Church and educating themselves about its teachings. They have too long been assimilating their lives as Catholics into a world that lives by a culture of materialism and utilitarianism, and not been troubled by the contradictions that entails.

To establish a renewed clergy and hierarchy, as Weigel wishes to do, demands a renewed laity as well, that challenge their priests and bishops to be faithful to their mission as leaders and shepherds of Christ's Church. Too many of the laity have failed to demand this leadership in the past. A renewed direction from the hierarchy needs to be complemented by renewed direction from the rank-and-file members: a hierarchy challenged to be pastoral will respond pastorally to a laity that demands that their leaders be icons of Christ.

For too long the laity have not been eager to learn what it means to be disciples of Christ. Too often they are unwilling to make the sacrifices discipleship demands. If the Church's mission is to succeed in transforming the world already into an experience of life in the Kingdom of God, responsible membership will be demanded from all of God's children, including a laity of renewed children of God in Christ's Body the Church.

Letter to the Ephesians

If we look for scriptural texts to substantiate the importance of Church unity for the success of Christ's mission, we need look no further than to the Letter to the Ephesians and the Gospel of John.

It is uncanny what remarkable similarity exists between the teaching of the Letter of Ephesians and the Gospel regarding the theological and soteriological importance of unity in God's plan for humanity. Ephesians also emphasizes, as does John, the role of self-sacrificing love in establishing union with Christ as well as in creating community: "One of the characteristics defining Christians as members of God's household is love of

---

[48] Ibid.

neighbor, modeled on the love that the Son of God manifested in his sacrificial death."[49]

Ephesians has been called "the epistle of Christian unity" and of Christians' bonding together in "the one new humanity, the church."[50] The "focus of the mystery," hidden for all eternity but now revealed by the author, is "the union of Christ, the head, with his body, the church."[51] The revelation of the "mystery" also makes known that the universal Church of Christ realizes "God's foreordained plan of salvation, uniting Jew and Gentile in the body of the risen Christ."[52]

Redemption comes in a realized eschatology in Ephesians in that Christians, in "their special relationship to God, . . . belong to the exalted, heavenly Christ who is head of the body, a new creation of the perfect human. . . . with the risen Christ."[53] The Church is even now a "cosmic body of all the faithful united with its head."[54] Indeed, the Church, as the beneficiary of Christ's "lordship over all things and over all angelic powers," shares "in the dominion of the head" over all reality.[55] Salvation has been brought about by the Cross which led to reconciliation "to God in one body" (Eph 2:16) in an "exaltation above the heavens with the risen Christ,"[56] a unity of believers identified even now with the exalted Christ "through their incorporation into a visible community under his leadership."[57]

Joseph Grassi beautifully sums up the letter as the announcement of God's plan from all eternity of creating a new

> people of God, a new community of men uniting in Christ both Jew and Gentile and erasing the impenetrable social and religious barriers that had previously divided mankind. It is Paul's privilege to be a chosen herald of God, appointed to reveal to men this mystery of God's love. Paul then prays that his audience may experience God's great love for men that has made possible such a bond of unity of men in the Church, . . . [a] unity in the body of Christ, . . . a true renewal of life motivated by a loving concern for fellow members in Christ.[58]

---

[49] Paul J. Kobelski, "The Letter to the Ephesians," *NJBC*, 55:26.

[50] Joseph A. Grassi, M.M., "The Letter to the Ephesians," in *The Jerome Biblical Commentary* (*JBC*), Raymond E. Brown, S.S. et al., eds. (Englewood Cliffs, NJ: Prentice-Hall, 1968), 56:29; Kobelski, *NJBC*, 55:21.

[51] Pheme Perkins, "The Letter to the Ephesians," *The New Interpreter's Bible*, vol. 11 (Nashville, TN: Abingdon, 2000), 357.

[52] Ibid., 355.

[53] Ibid., 370.

[54] Ibid., 358.

[55] Kobelski, "Ephesians," *NJBC*, 55:19.

[56] Perkins, *Interpreter's Bible*, 391.

[57] Grassi, "Ephesians," *JBC*, 56:14.

[58] Ibid., 56:11.

The unity of believers in Christ is so closely identified with the unity in Christ's Church that in Ephesians 3:20–21, "to say 'in the Church' or 'in Christ Jesus' is the same thing. The Church and Christ are necessary complements of each other."[59] This is undoubtedly because "Christ is the head of the body, the church," or "the church—Christ's body" shares in the life of the head.[60] For Ephesians, the Church is "the culmination of God's plan for the entire universe" and "the new humanity that results" from responding to the Gospel and becoming "one with Christ."[61]

The hortatory section of the letter (Eph 4:1–16) invokes the virtues required of Christians if Christ's Body is to preserve its unity: "perfect humility, meekness, and patience, bearing with one another lovingly." The letter then launches into a "seven-part statement of the pervasiveness of the unity that must characterize Christian life,"[62] with the "Spirit as its origin and peace as its binding force" (Eph 4:3):

> There is but one body and one Spirit, just as there is but one hope given all of you by your call [v. 4]; there is one Lord, one faith, one baptism [v. 5]; one God and Father of all, who is over all, and works through all, and is in all [v. 6].

No finer, no clearer, no more compelling statement can be found in the Scriptures to emphasize how theologically significant the unity of the life of the Christian community is for the completion of the Father's plan of salvation for the human race: There is "one body," that is, "one external visible community,"[63] which all exegetes identify with the Church;[64] "one Spirit," "the pledge of the future unified community (1:14)";[65] there is "one Lord" and "one faith." This is a unity found in the belief in one Christ who is Lord of heaven and earth, a unity of belief that by now, in the "institutional Christianity" that "emerges in the postapostolic period," denotes "acceptance of an authoritative apostolic tradition" of "teachings to which all members of the church subscribe." The repeated emphasis in verse 6 on the "all" of the power and pervasiveness of the "one God"—he is "Father of all," "over all," "works through all," and is "in all"—indicates that, from the

---

59 Ibid., 56:28.

60 Kobelski, "Ephesians," *NJBC*, 55:19.

61 Perkins, *Interpreter's Bible*, 411.

62 Kobelski, "Ephesians," *NJBC*, 55:25. The seven parts are: one body, one spirit, one hope, one Lord, one faith, one baptism, and one God and Father of all.

63 Grassi, "Ephesians," *JBC*, 56:29.

64 Cf., e.g., Perkins, *Interpreter's Bible*, 424; Margaret Y. MacDonald, *Colossians and Ephesians*, Sacra Pagina 17 (Collegeville, MN: Liturgical, 2000), 288: "'The body' is clearly a reference to the universal church."

65 Grassi, "Ephesians," *JBC*, 56:29.

author's point of view, there is only one God who is the one Father of the human race, and only one way designed by God for attaining the final goal of integration into his divine life.[66]

The "one baptism" is crucial: it integrates all believers into a common life through a "formal initiation into the body."[67] "Baptism confers one Spirit, which works toward unity in building up the body of Christ," and as the Church of Christ, "extend[s] God's summons to the rest of the world."[68] The diversity of Church offices of "apostles, prophets, evangelists, pastors and teachers" (Eph 4:11) does not in any way divide the community, but rather serves to build up the one Body of Christ (v. 12) until the unity of faith and "the knowledge of God's Son" lead to the perfection of the "man who is Christ come to full stature" (v. 13). It is in the total integration of the community through baptism, faith, and these offices, professing "the truth in love" and freed from doctrinal "error," that the unity "builds itself up in love," and has as its goal the growth of the whole of humanity into the "full maturity of Christ the head" and unity with the one God in and through the one Son, Jesus Christ (vv. 14–16).

According to Perkins, this formula of unity in 4:4–6 "underscores the dilemma of religious pluralism. The phrases indicate that for Ephesians there can be only one true people of God. Those who are not part of the 'body of Christ,' whether Jews or Gentiles, are not included in salvation." The letter does not grapple with divisive conflicts that might arise in community, as Paul does in 1 Corinthians with the problems caused by factions, or in Romans 14–15 over scruples of faith, but suggests they serve no purpose, since "all growth to maturity in faith" comes "through sound teaching, speech that reflects love, mutual concern, and support of others."[69]

In Ephesians 2:4–10, especially verses 7 and 10, there is evocation, similar to that found in John 17:21–23, as we shall see later, of the fact that the life of love in community proves the authenticity of the mission Christ came to perform in the world:

> But God is rich in mercy; because of his great love for us [v. 4] he brought us to life with Christ when we were dead in sin. By this favor [Gk. χαρις, grace] you were saved [v. 5]. Both with and in Christ Jesus he raised us up and gave us a place in the heavens [v. 6], that in the ages to come he might display the great wealth of his favor, manifested by his kindness to us in Christ Jesus [v. 7]. . . . We are truly his handiwork, created in Christ Jesus to live the life of good deeds which God prepared for us in advance [v. 10].

66 Kobelski, "Ephesians," *NJBC*, 55:25.

67 Ibid.

68 Perkins, *Interpreter's Bible*, 404.

69 Ibid., 423.

God's love here is motivated by one reason: his great mercy or love for us (Eph 2:4). But the love is manifested in two ways: through the love of Christ, who offered himself up to death for our sake (Eph 5:2); and through the manifestation of God's power, in that he has resurrected us as a "glorious church" (v. 27) and given us a "place in the heavens" with Christ (Eph 2:6): "If 'all the love of God' is manifested in the resurrection of the dead, then the very heart of God is now revealed."[70]

The proof of all of this is what has been brought about since Christ's Resurrection. In our "resurrected" state, reborn by baptism and living in the power of the Spirit, we live a life

> of courageous witness to God's mighty deeds which is extensively described in Acts; of that gathering into a wondering, loving, suffering community which forms the church; of that gift of forgiveness, knowledge, patience, hope, steadfastness which marks a true Christian. It is the fact and willingness to be conformed to the image of the crucified and raised Son of God. . . . witnesses of peace for the benefit of the whole world . . . . The life given is a self-demonstration of God the creator.[71]

According to Barth, in Ephesians 2:7, "the function of the church" is to be "God's evidence and showpiece" by which he proves to the world "the riches of his grace." The Church is God's new creation (Eph 2:15: "one new man") whose purpose is not simply to share in God's own life, but to be a "shining light to signal the dawn of a new heaven and a new earth . . . for all the world."[72]

The gift of the Spirit that creates the new community and gives it access to the Father makes possible "an actual new behavior" as "a responsive partner of God's covenant,"[73] existing for no other purpose than "the glorification of God and the revelation of his presence in and for the salvation of the world."[74] That revelation does not simply bring knowledge: it always "transforms the total person and changes the whole life of its recipient—and not only him" but "all the nations and the whole world, are affected by it."[75]

---

70 Markus Barth, *Ephesians*, Anchor Bible 34 (Garden City, NY: Doubleday, 1974), 219. Christians are already resurrected in Ephesians, but according to Barth, this does not mean a bodily removal from the earth. Rather, to be "enthroned" with Christ means that "because the saints are assembled with God who has been and still is present in their midst, they are 'in the heavens.'" To be resurrected with Christ, then, is to share in God's power and saving action through Christ even now (p. 238).

71 Ibid., 235–36.

72 Ibid., 240, 243.

73 Ibid., 251.

74 Ibid., 321.

75 Ibid., 353.

Theological Significance of God's Oneness

Barth finds Paul's appeal for unity an ingredient essential to the life of the Church as described in Ephesians 4:1–16. It is especially stressed in 4:3, according to Barth's translation of the verse: "take pains to maintain the unity . . . " It is a unity that needs to be "maintained," not "attained." The unity "rests upon the oneness of God" rather than the efforts of the Church. It is based on the bonding power of love (Eph 4:2): the "love among the saints which bears testimony to God's and Christ's love."[76]

Verses 4–6 "demonstrate how essential is oneness to the very being and life of the church." According to Barth, Paul "seems to be aware of disrespect for authority in the church, and counters by describing Jesus Christ as an omnipotent king who appoints in person some ministers to be respected by all his servants."[77] Indeed 4:11–16 makes it clear that Christ himself appointed the leaders of the community to lead it, to "become one in faith and in the knowledge of God's Son" (vv. 11–13), to "profess the truth in love" (v. 15), and to keep it free from "human trickery and skill in proposing error" (v. 14).

But the unity of the Church in Ephesians is not an end in itself. While for some Ephesians' scholars, God's work establishing unity in the Church includes all the cosmos in its realm, unity according to Barth is "a necessary sign manifesting the will and work of God that transcends the church." God is ultimately at the purpose of establishing peace that goes beyond the Church and all humanity to include even the cosmos: "The saints and their mutual love are a sign and a servant of God's purpose for all the world."[78]

Thus, again in a way similar to that of John 17:21–23, Ephesians' ultimate argument for the need for the existence and the preservation of unity in the Church is mission-directed, as a vindication of the existence of the triune God as a God of love and peace, and of God's desire to lead all creation to a saving union with him in the love and peace of his Kingdom: "Beyond the church are God himself and all the men, the ages, the creatures whom the church is to serve."[79] The community "makes known or lets shine the light of God's goodness, wisdom, gospel to the powers of this world."[80] In all they say and do, the members of the community "bear testimony to the revealed secret, that is, the unity and peace created by Jesus Christ."[81]

Thus it is God who, through his will and power expressed in the Spirit, brings about and maintains the unity in peace. Oneness represents the cre-

[76] Ibid., 427–28.
[77] Ibid., 451, 452.
[78] Ibid., 462.
[79] Ibid., 497.
[80] Ibid., 479.
[81] Ibid., 513.

ative presence of the Father in the Son through the Spirit: "Oneness in Ephesians is a dynamic, comprehensive force rather than a static entity existing in splendid isolation and lacking any contact with, or influence upon, its environment."[82] Ephesians's purpose is to show that "unity on earth is totally dependent upon God's eternal oneness and unity. Unity on earth is the creation, the manifestation, the glorification of the divine. By its very existence the church confesses God's essence to the universe."

The one God who calls the community to unity is a triune God, a God of "unity in diversity." It is the God of such unity who causes the community to reflect analogously that unity in diversity: "God's own oneness and manifoldness determines the church's oneness and manifoldness. . . . The church cannot be one except when it attests to its God's given oneness by proving unity in diversity, and when it ventures to respect diversity in unity."

> God makes the decision, has the power, and performs the deed of making "one new man" out of a mankind divided in hostility. In this epistle God's oneness is directly, i.e. causatively, dynamically, effectively, but also epistemologically, related to the unity of the church. Because God is one, his people are one and are to live on the basis and in recognition of unity. Similarly in OT and Jewish writings the oneness of God is the ontic and noetic presupposition of statements about the oneness of the temple, the law, or the people of God.

God, who is one in his plurality, is

> the unity that permits diversity, the power that holds together, brings together, and guarantees community. Without being bound by the Father, Son, and Spirit, the church could never proclaim that God's own unity is the basis, the source, the energy, and the criterion of her own unity and that of her many members and ministries.[83]

It is thus essential to the mission of the Church in Ephesians, if the Church is to lead all humankind into the unity of life in the Trinity, that the unity of the community be preserved as a paramount value.

Gospel of John

The most explicit biblical teaching mandating the preservation of unity in the Church as essential to the success of Christ's mission is found in the Gospel of John. It escapes me how Christians can continue to ignore John 17:20–26 and the soteriological significance Jesus places upon the role of

---

[82] Ibid., 487.

[83] Ibid., 465–67.

unity in this passage. As far as I can determine, few Christians ever cite this passage or appreciate the urgency contained there as a matter of overriding concern for all who would dare to call themselves disciples of Christ. We cannot justify this omission.

Jesus indicates in John 17 that the hour has come for the Father to give the fullness of glory to his Son through his death and Resurrection so that the Son may in turn give glory to the Father (v. 1) by giving the fullness of eternal life to all those the Father has given him (v. 2). John then defines eternal life as knowing the Father, the only true God, and the one sent by him, Jesus Christ (v. 3). "Knowing" here of course does not simply mean awareness of the Father's existence; it here contains the fullness of the biblical meaning of "knowing," which often includes acceptance of God and his teaching and commitment of life to him. In other words, knowing includes a way of life of praise, love, honor, and obedience to the will of the Father.

Jesus has already given the Father glory on earth by fulfilling the work the Father gave him to do, namely, making his presence manifest in the world through the "signs" and "wonders" he performed, and drawing together a group of disciples committed to the Father and to furthering his mission of salvation. Jesus now asks the Father to give him the glory at his side that he had before the world began (vv. 4–5), in addition to the glory Jesus has also received through his own disciples' acceptance of him (v. 10).

Jesus goes on to say that he has made the Father known to the disciples the Father has given him from out of the world, that they have kept the Father's word (v. 6), and have recognized that all that Jesus has been given has come from the Father (v. 7). They have accepted in truth that Jesus was sent on mission by the Father, and they have accepted as well the "message" Jesus entrusted to them on behalf of the Father (v. 8).

Jesus now prays for his disciples. They belong to him as well as to the Father (vv. 9–10). As long as Jesus was with them, he protected them with the power contained in the Father's name, and none of them was lost except the one who was destined to be lost (v. 12). Now that Jesus is en route to the Father, he leaves his disciples behind in a world that opposes them. Jesus therefore asks the Father to bestow on them the protection that comes with their acceptance of the Father's name (v. 11). Jesus continues to ask the Father to guard his disciples while they are in a world to which they do not belong any more than Jesus does, and which is hostile to them because of their acceptance of the Father's word which Jesus gave them (vv. 14–16). The word they have accepted and to which they have been consecrated is the Father as "truth" (v. 17). Jesus prays that as he consecrates himself for their sakes, so may his disciples be "consecrated" to the Father "in truth" (v. 19).

It is then that Jesus prays not only for his immediate disciples but also for all those who will follow them as his disciples, and provides the reason for his prayer:

> [20] I do not pray for them alone.
> I pray also for those who will believe in me through their word,
> [21] that all may be one
> as you, Father, are in me, and I in you;
> I pray that they may be [one] in us,
> that the world may believe that you sent me.
> [22] I have given them the glory you gave me
> that they may be one, as we are one—
> [23] I living in them, you living in me—
> that their unity may be complete.
> So shall the world know that you sent me,
> and that you loved them as you loved me.
> [24] Father,
> all those you gave me
> I would have in my company
> where I am,
> to see this glory of mine
> which is your gift to me,
> because of the love you bore me before the world began.
> [25] Just Father,
> the world has not known you,
> but I have known you;
> and these men have known that you sent me.
> [26] To them I have revealed your name,
> and I will continue to reveal it
> so that your love for me may live in them,
> and I may live in them. (Jn 17:20–26)

The passage is so theologically laden that it is difficult to know where to begin to explicate its significance. But surely we can begin with the "glory" Jesus has given to his disciples. What is this glory? In the Old Testament, God's glory has two aspects: "It is a *visible* manifestation of His majesty in *acts of power*. While God is invisible, from time to time He manifests Himself to men by a striking action, and this is His *kābōd* or glory." Jesus is the perfect manifestation of God's glory: as "the incarnate Word of God, he is an embodiment of divine glory. The two elements of *kābōd* are present in him. He represents the visible divine presence exercising itself in mighty acts."[84]

---

[84] Raymond E. Brown, S.S., intro., trans., and notes, *The Gospel according to John (i–xii)*, Anchor Bible 29 (Garden City, NY: Doubleday, 1966), 503. Brown's two-volume study of the Gospel of John was helpful through much of this section.

Glory represents the presence of God in the world. The works that Jesus performed manifested the glory of God and thereby made him present. The glory that Jesus gave to his disciples is found, then, in the fact that they accepted Jesus as the Son of God, the Messiah, the presence of God in the world. This represents the source of the "power" that the disciples will have in accepting the Father's name: that knowledge, that acceptance means that the power of the Father has now become present in their lives.

That power, then, conveys to the disciples a sharing in the life of the Son, though in an analogous way: Just as the Son shares in the life of the Father by the indwelling of each in the life of the other, so now does the life of the Father and the Son dwell in the disciples inasmuch as they have "believed": They have accepted and committed themselves to the Father in their acceptance of Jesus as his Son, in view of the "signs" and "wonders" that he performed "through his Father's power" as manifestations of his union with the Father.[85]

That divine life now shared by all is known as "eternal life." When Jesus' "hour" comes—when he returns to the Father—"the fact that he and the Father possess the same divine glory will be visible to all believers" through "the gift of eternal life to believers" in the gift of the Spirit. That gift will complete what Jesus had already begun to do on earth by way of "sign": "In his glorification, Jesus will glorify the Father by the gift of eternal life, for this gift will beget for God new children who will honor Him as Father."[86]

But John 17 brings out an even deeper level of significance to the integration of the disciples in the life of the Father and the Son. For what precisely is that life with which the Father and the Son are identified? It is love. "There is a strong insistence on love: the Father's love for the disciples (v. 23), the Father's love for Jesus (vv. 23–24), the Father's love for Jesus and the disciples (v. 26). The Father's love is the supreme revelation of the Gospel. Jesus, the incarnate Word, speaks the Father in one word—LOVE."[87] The Father's name is really Love, as we know from 1 John 4:8: "The man without love has known nothing of God, for God is love," and it is that love that he has bestowed upon the Son, and that the Son in turn bestows on his disciples:

> Jesus the Word is pre-eminently the revelation of God's love. God's love is the motive of his sending the Son into the world. But more than a

[85] Neal M. Flanagan, O.S.M., *The Gospel according to John and the Johannine Epistles*, Collegeville Bible Commentary 4 (Collegeville, MN: Liturgical, 1983), 28. This work has been of immense value throughout this section.

[86] Raymond E. Brown, S.S., intro., trans., and notes, *The Gospel according to John (xiii–xxi)*, Anchor Bible 29A (Garden City, NY: Doubleday, 1970), 751.

[87] Flanagan, *John*, 79.

> motive, love is the revelation itself. Even as God himself is love (1 Jn 4:16), Jesus is the incarnation of the divine love for man, embodying in himself this relation willed by God. Thus we are continually reminded of the love of the Father for the Son (Jn 3:35; 10:17), a love that the Son in turn extends to his followers, not as his own love only, but also as the love of the Father (17:23–26).[88]

The revelation of God in Jesus "has as its purpose and goal the indwelling of Jesus in the Christian," which is parallel to "the presence of the love of God in the Christian," making Jesus' presence "dynamic, expressive of love and expressed in love."[89] So the disciples become the living visible presence of the Father and Son insofar as they continue to express the love of the Father and the Son in the world:[90] there is

> a remaining in one another that binds together Father, Son, and the Christian believer. We hear in John that just as the Son is in the Father, and the Father is in the Son (xiv 10–11), so is the Son to be in men, and men are to be in the Father and the Son. . . . There can be no doubt that the intimate indwelling of Father and Son is being transferred through the Son to the Christian. . . . What John says about the relationship and unity of the Father and the Son is always oriented toward men. The mutual indwelling of the Father and the Son is not a static but a dynamic relation.
>
> The fact that the relationship between Jesus and his disciples is patterned on the Father-Son relationship is also given expression in what John says about life and love. Indeed, common indwelling, life, and love are but different facets of the basic unity binding Father, Son, and believer (xvii 11, 21, 23). Divine indwelling is an intimate union that expresses itself in a way of life lived in love . . . [and] intimately associated with keeping the commandments in a spirit of love.[91]

But how precisely is that life of love expressed in the world? The prime norm for determining the nature of that love is found in the way it is expressed between the Father and the Son in their mutual self-giving: the Father gives the fullness of himself to the Son, which the Son reciprocates.[92]

---

88 Bruce Vawter, C.M., "Johannine Theology," *JBC*, 80:25.

89 Brown, *Gospel according to John*, 29A:781.

90 That the disciples' love for one another is revelatory of who the Father and the Son are is brought out in Jn 13:35: "This is how all will know you for my disciples: your love for one another."

91 Brown, *Gospel according to John*, 29: 510–12.

92 "In the Trinity every tendency and every yearning of love is fully satisfied by the eternal, perfect self-communication of the Godhead from Father to Son and from Father and Son to Holy Ghost, and by the ever active mutual flow of infinite love between the Divine Persons." George Smith, *Teaching of the Catholic Church* 1:190.

The will of the Son is to do the will of the Father in an action of total self-giving. That self-giving is then extended through Jesus into the world by the total dedication of his life to the salvation of his disciples and, through them, to the whole human race:

> The whole of creation, and in particular its human inhabitants, is the object of God's saving love. . . . God's love is the dynamic principle for world salvation. Jesus' God, John's God, our God is a God motivated by love so great that he has gifted the world with his own Son, not to condemn but to save.[93]
>
> As Jesus mentions his own self-giving (vv. 23–24), he joins to it that of his disciples. They are called to identical servant roles (vv. 25–26).[94]

Self-giving is then the representative form of love, expressed from the Father through the Son and through the power of the Holy Spirit through Jesus' disciples.

Jesus above all reveals to the world that the Father is a God of love in the act of love where "the Son freely lays down his life" on the Cross at the same time as he "returns to the glory that was his" by his exaltation on the Cross.[95] Jesus' death and exaltation on the Cross is thus the supreme hour when Jesus not only expresses his love to his disciples in total self-giving, but also manifests to the fullest the revelation of God's glory:

> The HOUR has come in which Jesus will be glorified, that is, in which God will manifest to the utmost his presence in his Son. But this hour entails death . . . . Life will be offered to the world *through* his death. . . . This being raised on a cross, is also Jesus' glorification (vv. 23, 28), the manifestation in him of his Father's presence, nowhere more evident than in Jesus' act of self-sacrificing love.[96]
>
> The model of love for all true discipleship is extreme, limitless; for it is Jesus himself who lays down his life for his friends. . . . Yet it is precisely for love like this that Jesus has chosen them. They will bring forth enduring fruit, their prayers will be answered, to the extent that they love one another (vv. 16–17).[97]
>
> For the love of God is boundless, and whoever has truly received this revelation of love must love boundlessly in turn—he must love not only God but also his brothers who have been the objects of this same divine love.[98]

---

93 Flanagan, *John*, 17.
94 Ibid., 61.
95 Francis J. Moloney, S.D.B., "Johannine Theology," *NJBC*, 83:38.
96 Flanagan, *John*, 60–61.
97 Ibid., 72.
98 Vawter, "Johannine Theology," *JBC*, 80:26.

Jesus dies on the Cross for the salvation of the human race. He totally donates himself for its well-being. Thus in this supreme moment of giving, Jesus manifests to his disciples and the world that love expressed as self-sacrifice for others is the nature of divine love and the love that Jesus' disciples are called to express in the world:[99]

[99] There are four words in Greek (the language of John's Gospel) for love: (1) ἔρως (erōs), which is love between a man and a woman and includes sexual passion. This word is rarely used in the Old Testament and not at all in the New Testament, which instead uses ἐπιθυμία (epithumia) (desire, longing); (2) φιλία (philia), the love of friendship, which is used in John's Gospel to express friendship between Jesus and his disciples (Jn 21:17); (3) στοργή (storgē), love or affection as parents love children and vice versa, used in the New Testament only in compounds; and (4) ἀγάπη (agapē). As a substantive, ἀγάπη "is almost completely lacking in pre-biblical Greek," but as a verb its meaning is "weak and variable." It often means "no more than 'to be satisfied with something,'" but "must often be translated 'to show love': it is a giving, active love on the other's behalf" (Kittel, 36–37, below). The Septuagint version of the Old Testament "almost always" renders אהב, the main word for "love" in the Hebrew text, by ἀγάπη or a variant of it (the substantive ἀγάπη occurs "some 20 times" in the Old Testament). Since אהב refers to various types of love "with reference to persons as well as things and actions," it follows that in the Septuagint, the meaning of ἀγάπη is very general. According to Kittel, "love in the OT is basically a spontaneous feeling which impels to self-giving or, in relation to things, to the seizure of the object which awakens the feeling, or to the performance of the action in which pleasure is taken" (Kittel, 22–23). It is only in the New Testament that ἀγάπη takes on its original and distinctive characteristic as self-sacrificing love. This is because its meaning is derived from the new experience of love that comes from Jesus' death on the Cross. Ἀγάπη is unlike the other three types of love where the experience includes love of oneself and what one gains from the relationship. With ἀγάπη, the focus is entirely on the other: the other is loved for the sake of the other and not for anything the subject would derive from the relationship. In John, God is love (1 Jn 4:8, 16), and the Father shows love for the Son (Jn 17:26) and for the world (i.e., human beings) through the Son (3:16; 14:21, 23; 17:23). Ἀγάπη is also present in the love of the Son for the Father (Jn 14:31) and for others (14:21). It is shown in the love of the disciples for God (1 Jn 5:2–3) and for Jesus (Jn 14:15, 21). This is the kind of love that Jesus' disciples are to show to one another that will reveal they are disciples of the Lord inasmuch as the love of the Son is living in them (Jn 13:34–35; 15:12). It is this love that allows the disciples to lay down their lives for one another just as the Son has done for them (Jn 15:13; 1 Jn 3:16). William Barclay expresses the nature of ἀγάπη Christians love so well: "The real meaning of agapē is unconquerable benevolence. If we regard a person with agapē, it means that nothing that he can do will make us seek anything but his highest good. Though he injure us and insult us, we will never feel anything but kindness towards him. . . . This agapē . . . is that quality of mind and heart which compels a Christian never to feel any bitterness, never to feel any desire for revenge, but always to seek the highest good of every man no matter what he may be" (Barclay, 139–40). See G. Abbott-Smith, *A Manual Greek Lexicon of the New Testament* (Edinburgh: T. and T. Clark, 1956 [1921]), 3–4; Gerhard Kittel, ed., *Theological Dictionary of the New Testament*, vol. 1, trans. and ed. Geoffrey W. Bromiley (Grand Rapids, MI: Eerdmans, 1964); William Barclay,

> Love itself is vital, active, the very essence of the living God who would assimilate men to himself. Just as Jesus' love brings him to the supreme sacrifice, the love that he has revealed and that has been received by men must find a comparable expression in their lives (13:1–20). Thus love is not only the sign, but the very essence of true discipleship, of what it means to be a Christian (13:35).[100]

The self-donation in love that is expressive in John of the unity of the disciples and thereby the unity of the Father and the Son is always a reference to unity of life within the developing Christian community. This we know by the fact that in John the Spirit whom Jesus sends to carry on his mission after his departure from this world maintains the life of the community chiefly through the sacraments, especially baptism and the Eucharist, represented in John by the "blood and water" that flow from the side of the crucified Christ (19:34). The Spirit also fosters unity by leading the community into life and truth as promised by Jesus to his disciples (Jn 16:13):

> The Spirit, that is to say, the Son and the Father in the Spirit, is the route by which man enters into the way, the truth, and the life proclaimed by Christ. Thus we are reminded that it is not by the words of the "historical" Jesus alone that we live, but by the words of Jesus as made known by the Church enlightened by the Spirit.[101]

Division's Destructive Impact upon Christ's Mission

It is essential that unity be present among the disciples if the community is to pursue a way of life consonant with Jesus' teachings and come to the truth to be made known through history by the Spirit. If so, any element of division, disunity, disruption, disintegration, or animosity that exists among Jesus' disciples is destructive of this unity and impairs the work of the Spirit. To put it simply, unity in community in the Spirit is incompatible with conflictual factionalism—they cannot coexist. Differences in themselves present no problem if they are not self-alienating. A problem arises when they are.

Divisions in the Church today are of two kinds. Not only are mutually incompatible sectarian Christian groups tearing asunder the unity Christ intended for his disciples, but also the doctrinal, moral, and spiritual divisions within the Catholic community are doing the same. To cater to such

---

The Letters to the Galatians and Ephesians, rev. ed., Daily Study Bible Series (Philadelphia: Westminster, 1976); Benedict XVI, *DCE* 3.

100 Vawter, "Johannine Theology," *JBC*, 80:26.

101 Ibid., 80:45.

divisions in either case, then, is to cater to disunity within the Christian community in exact violation of the teachings of Christ. The prospect of causing division within the community should in itself be more than enough to induce any Christian to reject fomenting factionalism of any kind. There is, however, an even more compelling reason for doing so: as John 17:20–26 makes clear, Christian disunity impedes the success of Christ's mission.

How that is possible depends upon our understanding of Christ's mission. But what was that mission?

As we have seen, Jesus makes the Father known by revealing that the Father is one with the Son in a life of self-donation that reaches its apex in the Son's self-sacrificial death for the human race. Jesus' mission was successful in that he made disciples of all those who accepted his word as the revelation of his Father. The life of the Father and the Son thereby became visible to the world through the way of life of his disciples. That style of life was manifested by their patterning the life of unity of the Father and the Son in self-donating love. The disciples believed in and accepted and lived by that unity. Thus there was only one Church among Jesus' disciples, and no division was acceptable that tore asunder that unity. Division that corrupts unity therefore has no place in Christ's Church.

Based on Christ's own words, however, it is clear that the success of his mission was not determined simply by the existence of unity among his most immediate disciples. It was a unity intended to endure through all generations. Christians of all the ages are therefore called to preserve that same unity if Christ's mission is to succeed. And what is that mission? To bring the entire world into a community of life with his disciples in mind, heart, and truth, so that the world might thereby be brought to a participation in the eternal life of the Father and the Son.

Jesus' words make it clear that this call to unity was not simply a desideratum on Jesus' part: it is a unity *essential* to the success of his mission. It is only in seeing the unity of love among Jesus' disciples that people will become aware of the unity of love that exists between the Father and the Son and be impelled to accept it into their own lives. Thus the unity of love of the community has an inherent dimension of mission: it exists simply for the participation of Jesus' disciples in the Trinity's own life. It exists for the success of the Trinity's mission of bringing the whole of the universe into an experience of the life of the Trinity. This is what salvation is in Jesus' teaching in John. And apparently this mission had considerable success in the early life of the Church. It seems to have been the reason for the statement spread abroad at that time that Jesus' disciples could be known by the fact that they lived a life of love—apparently unlike anything seen outside the Christian community.

That unity in community is essential to the success of Jesus' mission Flanagan makes exceedingly clear in his exegesis of John 17:21–24:

> For future disciples, Jesus prays for one central gift—unity. . . . It will be only through this evidence of loving unity that the mission to the world (v. 18) can be effective; for only if the loving union of disciples is apparent can the world believe (v. 21), can the world know (v. 23) that the Father has sent Jesus and that the Father's love can be found in the disciples as it can be found in Jesus himself (v. 23). Where this loving unity of disciples is found, there too will be found the company of Jesus (v. 24), the divine presence (v. 24), the power of the divine name, and the living love of both Father and Son (v. 26).[102]

Flanagan goes on to note that in verses 21 and 23 in Jesus' prayer for his present and future disciples, Jesus also prays for "Christian unity" with a purpose: so that "the world may *believe* and *know* that Jesus has been sent by a loving Father,"[103] indicating that the unity of love is necessary as a witness to the world of the love of the Father and Jesus for the world.

The biblical exegete Pheme Perkins rightly points out that there are "two dimensions" to the unity discussed in John: "The vertical dimension grounds unity in the relationship between Jesus and God," and the "horizontal dimension sees in the command to love one another the expression of that relationship among members of the community." It is Jesus who in the creation of that community "brings the disciples into community with God." In the community of love, Jesus' disciples see his glory as they are "filled with enduring love" (Jn 1:14), the culmination of which is to share in that glory fully when they follow Jesus' return to the Father. The creation of the horizontal unity of the community "poses a challenge to the world" for Perkins, in that it is freighted with the possibility of attaining either "salvation or judgment," depending on whether the world accepts or rejects the gospel message about the life of "mutual love" between Jesus and the Father made visible in that community.[104]

Perkins stresses how significant for the salvation of the world is the preservation of a unity of love among the disciples, since if that unity is defective or "incomplete," the challenge to the world to receive the revelation of God's love is clouded and the ability to make the correct choice rendered more difficult. In other words, Jesus' mission to bring the human race

102 Flanagan, *John*, 79. Notice that if the mission is achieved, the unity is "complete" (p. 23).

103 Ibid., 80.

104 Pheme Perkins, "The Gospel according to John," *NJBC*, 61:205. This is not unlike the saving activity won by "the nations" in their response to the needs of Jesus' disciples on mission in Matthew 25:31–46, as we exegeted the text in chapter 7.

into a life of communion with himself and the Father is historically conditioned by the disciples' living that life of communion among themselves.

It is reasonable to conclude that if that life in unity exists in any way at all, the mission is in progress, is underway. But Jesus makes it clear that the complete success of his mission depends upon the unity among his disciples being complete. Jesus' prayer to the Father is precisely that that unity "may be complete" (Jn 17:23) so that his mission may be realized. Thus, disunity among the disciples is not only against the will of the Father and the Son for the salvation of his disciples, but also an undermining of the Son's mission to bring salvation to the world.

Deus Caritas Est

Benedict's first encyclical, *Deus Caritas Est*, adds its own coda to John's thought. For Benedict, it is ultimately to our creative sharing in the power of God's love that we must turn for our salvation as a community.

Benedict finds the Song of Songs a unique expression, for both the Old and the New Testaments, of a love relationship between God and the human being. The Song expresses both God's love relationship with human beings and "the essence of biblical faith": that "man can indeed enter into union with God," a "unity which creates love, a unity in which both God and man remain themselves and yet become fully one" (*DCE* 10).

The supreme form of this love is *agape*, the love that "seeks the good of the beloved," that "becomes renunciation" and is "ready, and even willing, for sacrifice." It is the love that Jesus portrays in "his own sacrifice" on the Cross, where love "reaches fulfillment" in the piercing of Jesus' side (Jn 19:37), manifesting "the essence of love and indeed of human life itself" (*DCE* 6). Jesus' love is at the same time the expression of God's love: "a personal love," an "elective love," a love "with a view to healing the whole human race" (*DCE* 9).

The unity created in love becomes complete in the New Testament in the sharing in the Eucharist, which "draws us into Jesus' act of self-oblation." "Union with God" is now achieved "through sharing in Jesus' self-gift, sharing in his body and blood" (*DCE* 13). But this is a unity "social in character": I become one with the Lord in a "union with all those to whom he gives himself." The Eucharist "draws me out of myself towards him, and thus also towards unity with all Christians. We become 'one body,' completely joined in a single existence. Love of God and love of neighbor are now truly united" because "God incarnate draws us all to himself" (*DCE* 14).

It is because God incarnate has loved us first that we are able to love one another. Thus the "deeds" of the apostles and of Christians are acts that express God's love for others, flowing from the love of God already experienced by them: "He loves us, he makes us see and experience his love, and since he has 'loved us first,' love can also blossom as a response within us." The "love-story between God and man" leads to a universal union of "will" and "thought" and "sentiment" that increasingly makes our will and God's will "coincide": "God's will is no longer for me an alien will . . . but it is my own will, based on the realization that God is in fact more deeply present to me than I am to myself" (*DCE* 17). According to Benedict, "love is 'divine' because it comes from God and unites us to God," but "through this unifying process it makes us a 'we' which transcends our divisions and makes us one, until in the end God is 'all in all' (1 Cor. 15:28)" (*DCE* 18).

It is in our sharing in the Eucharist that the divisions that currently separate us will be overcome. At least that is our hope.

Final Reflections on the Role of Unity of Love in the Church

To cater to division within the Catholic/Christian community is not only to promote the breakdown of the unity of love in violation of God's plan of salvation for his disciples, but also to erode the success of Christ's mission plan toward the entire non-Christian world, including Jews, Muslims, and all nonbelievers. How can non-Christians be made to desire to participate in the life of the Trinity, as Jesus intended, if they do not have presented to them a visible manifestation of that life? Barring miraculous interventions by God, the only way that life becomes visible is through the life of Jesus' disciples. And how can we Christians and Catholics be impelled to share more deeply in the life of the Trinity if we do not see more evidence of the power of that unity in our own Christian communities?

The life of disunity among Jesus' disciples, therefore, constitutes the major scandal in the Christian community today. As one scholar writes, "The section of the creed that speaks of the church as one, holy, catholic, and apostolic demands an equal or even greater capacity to overcome the scandal of appearances. . . . The profession of the church as part of the necessary statement of Christian belief is, clearly, both a critical and a scandalous proposition."[105]

By God's design, the world is supposed to be able to look to the Church as "the model that the world can see and imitate as the basis for its own rebirth as God's creation."[106] What kind of a model of God's plan for history can a Church of sex abuse of youth provide for the world? The Church has

[105] Luke Timothy Johnson, *The Creed: What Christians Believe and Why It Matters* (New York: Doubleday, 2003), 255.

[106] Ibid., 256.

too often become "a large stumbling block to faith" and "the prime evidence" for doubting "the reality of God's rule through the resurrected Christ."[107]

I cannot help but believe that if Christians from time immemorial had been sufficiently cognizant of the mission-role unity plays in God's plan of salvation for the world, they would never have allowed the success of God's mission to be sacrificed for the rule of disunity. To take a major case in point: How could Martin Luther have permitted his difficulties with the Church to lead him to accept separation from its life—for any purpose whatsoever, however noble his cause may have been, however certain he might have been, that the Church had deviated from its relationship with Christ—rather than to work for its purification from within, if he had recognized the theological and soteriological significance of Christ's teaching on unity? It seems inconceivable.

And I throw out the same challenge to today's Christians: How can we continue to accept the separation of the Christian communities from each other and continue to claim to be disciples of Christ? The inherent contradiction makes such a claim impossible.

And finally—and this is most to the point of this publication—how can Catholics continue to call themselves Catholic if they promote division within the Catholic Church? On the basis of Christ's teaching, as we have understood it in the Gospel of John and the Letter to the Ephesians, no cause, no perception of the truth, no moral conviction, however noble or just, is so worth pursuing that it may be allowed to sunder the unity of Christ's Church. If we take Christ's words about the importance of his mission seriously, to sacrifice the goal of Christian unity for the sake of any other cause seems unworthy of a disciple of Jesus. All efforts, therefore, must be made to overcome division *within* the life of the Catholic Church. We have presented here what we hope is a useful formula for achieving that goal: a life of love in self-donation for others, in imitation of Christ's sacrifice for all humanity on the Cross, in a community whose commitment to Christ is expressed in a union of love and fidelity to his Church and his Vicar on earth.

To struggle within the Church, to whatever degree one chooses, in pursuit of one's cause is not only desirable but necessary to promote growth in the Church's understanding of the truth. Such efforts are noble and good. One may seriously question, however, whether the Christian community has come closer to the truth and furthered Christ's mission more than it otherwise would have by defections from the Catholic Church, or whether it would not have been more advantageous for all if defectors had found ways of working toward clearer conceptions of the truth from within.

[107] Ibid., 257.

Many theologians throughout the twentieth century did indeed do that very thing: de Lubac, Rahner, Murray, Chenu, Häring, Congar, to name but a few. I find it difficult to argue that Charles Davis did more to promote the life of the Christian community by severing his relationship with the Church than these six did by not doing so. By and large, the theologies they were promoting have come to prevail in the life of the Church. But they never allowed the line to be crossed that risked undermining the unity of the Church, and for this all Christians must be grateful. All creative theologians today should be drawn to pattern their lives on the struggle for truth exemplified by the lives of these thinkers.

Since Vatican II, many seem to consider it a duty to publish widely and accept national TV appearances to promote dissonance. Many give the impression that it is the Church that disagrees with them that is necessarily in error. In an age that downgrades the role of the Spirit guiding the life of the Church, such theologians seem to give no weight to the fact that the hierarchy has the guarantee that the power of the Holy Spirit is working through them. In any case, the teaching authority of the Church has greater assurance that the power of the Holy Spirit is working there than in the lives of simple theologians!

Disagreements with Church teaching have always been permissible when they did not risk undermining the unity in the Church. Until recent times, moral and dogmatic disagreements were usually waged in erudite theological journals away from the view of the crowd, and only when such battles appeared to get out of hand were theologians silenced. No one enjoys being silenced, but a greater good was at stake.

Today we often consider the silencing of a dissident theologian an outrage rather than accepting the fact that the unity of the Church may have been put in jeopardy. So many of us have become theologians of the Enlightenment and have abandoned the insights of faith over reason in furthering the rationale of our arguments. The purpose of Catholic theologians is not simply dedication to truth, as the Enlightenment mind would think. As *Ex Corde Ecclesiae* makes clear, it is dedication to truth within the community of the Church, as the Scriptures, Tradition, and the history of dogma lead the community through its authorized leaders, the magisterium, toward a greater recognition of that truth. That is the nature of Christ's Church as he is living in it today.

Such a perspective necessarily includes a respect for and sympathy with the purposes of the hierarchy, and especially the pope, the concrete manifestation of the unity of Christ's mission working itself out in the world. There is ultimately no getting around the role of the pope as this symbol. That is the reason why his role was established, and until a better force for unity in Christ's Church can be found, I suggest we live with what Christ has given us. If we truly believe in the teachings of the Gospel of John and the Letter to the Ephesians, we will be dedicated to preserving the unity of the Church at all costs. No better source for unity in the Church exists today, so far as I can tell, than the symbol of unity provided by the pope.

It would be hard to find statements more strictly defined and more doctrinally clear than those from Vatican I regarding the role of the pope in the life of the Church. He is the ultimate definer of truth regarding what Christians are to believe in matters of faith and morality; he is endowed with a power of infallibility in special cases and certain circumstances so that he may preserve the Church from error; he provides the path that Christians must follow to arrive at union with ultimate Truth, participation in divine life, and eternal salvation. Certainly the path that dissidents provide is not better.

The fact is that division has come about within the Christian community because we have not given priority to maintaining unity in the Church in love. There is reason to ponder seriously this failing, and to ask forgiveness of one another for all that we have done to undermine Christ's mission of salvation, and to seek to repair the damage, insofar as that is possible, for the effects of that damage have been humongous.

It is necessary now to try to turn around the deformations of society and culture that centuries of war, conflict, division, and disorder, both personal and collective, among Christians have produced. For many of the ideologies that have undermined the quality of life have flourished because of our scandalous disunity as Christians. Would there ever have been the Crusades, civil wars in the United States and Europe, Communism, Nazism, clashes between cultures, the breakdown of the psychological and emotional well-being of individuals, the disintegration of morals, and animosities between races, if the Christian religion had never deviated from its fidelity to the mission of Christ as his unified Church? We shall never know.

One must not forget the evils that result from original sin, which no Church in time could ever totally conquer. But the extent of the success the Church could have mustered against all the ideologies and forces of evil that have troubled our world would surely have been greater had the Church never allowed the breakdown of its unity of love. In a word, so great is the theological and moral role of unity in the life of Christ's Church that it is impossible to argue that something less than unity would have accomplished Christ's mission of salvation more effectively. What force could have been created that would have produced greater power to succeed? Shame on the Christian communities of 1054 and the sixteenth century that allowed such divisions to occur!

The human community has paid dearly for our self-centeredness, our myopia, and our ill-will. And yet it is never too late to reform. This is what we must do, as we now come to recognize more than ever the importance of restoring unity to the Christian community. Radical Islam is waiting perhaps more than any for that unity to happen, for it would inevitably undercut the cynicism of the Muslim view of the Western world.

The power of Christ's light must be made to shine throughout the world, and we must accept that the light that shines from Christ can achieve his goal of bringing unity to the human family. We cannot accept that there are other ways to union with God except through Jesus Christ. Christ's teaching as presented to us in the Scriptures and the Christian tradition does not allow Christians to conclude otherwise, in spite of today's romance with diversity.

If Christians restore unity among themselves, they have every reason to believe that unity will set off a force of transformation that will overcome the evils of the world, and lead to a unity in peace and equality of life among all peoples. We must not underestimate the power of the love, peace, and reconciliation contained in the Word of Christ—to do otherwise is indefensible, in view of what Christ taught us. We must believe that there is no limit to the power to reconcile contained in the Word of Christ.

Let us Christians then focus on what we have in common: fidelity to Christ and his teaching. Let us unite under the banner of Christ's Cross as the way to overcome the evils of division and hatred in our world. We have to conclude that if we restore unity to Christ's Church, that he will attain within and through us his goal of unity of the human race with the Trinity. We have no choice but to begin this undertaking at once—for the good of his Church and the salvation of the human race depend upon it.

Is unity to Christ's Church—is total reconciliation among Christians—just a pipe-dream? Not really. In fact, it has already begun. As one writer put it:

> Various Episcopal priests and laity have been turning their spiritual eyes to Rome seeking answers for a unified Catholic Christendom that can only come through reconciliation and reunification with the Great Latin Church of the West in fulfillment of Christ's own priestly Gospel prayer in the Book of John that His Church may be one even as He and the Father are One.[108]

"Anglican Use" is the name of the new group of individual and group Anglicans who have been integrated into the Roman Catholic Church while retaining certain elements of Anglican identity in their liturgy. This is rooted in the Vatican's Pastoral Provision approved by John Paul II in 1980, which allowed Anglican priests to renounce their Anglican orders and be "sacra-

---

[108] Mary Ann Mueller, "Houston, TX: Anglican Use Conference: Three Days of Grace," VirtueOnline.org News, June 15, 2009, www.virtueonline.org/portal/article.php?storyid=10643.

mentally retrained for the Catholic priesthood and then re-ordained as a Roman Catholic priest." Intact congregations could also become Anglican Use parish churches in full communion with Roman Catholicism, and be cared for by a Pastoral Provision priest "with faculties to celebrate the Anglican Use liturgy."[109]

Several Anglican Use parishes have recently been established, but only in the United States, especially in Texas. The Anglican Use Conference of June 11–13, 2009, was held in Houston, TX, with Cardinal Daniel N. DiNardo of Galveston-Houston as the keynote speaker. DiNardo spoke regarding the Pastoral Provision approved by the Vatican in 1980. According to Catholic News Service:

> In his address Cardinal DiNardo said that the gift of Catholic unity is sometimes taken for granted by those in the Catholic Church, but this cohesiveness is not lost on those seeking communion.
>
> The cardinal observed the eventual reconciliation of church communities was anticipated by the Second Vatican Council, but he acknowledged that Christian unity "may not be realized in our own time."
>
> In the meantime, the church is "necessarily dependent on the personal and individual model to further the vision of Catholic unity," he explained.[110]

More recently, an opening to greater unity between Anglicans and Roman Catholics that one would never have dreamed of was created by Benedict with his brief apostolic constitution *Anglicanorum Coetibus.*[111]

Leaders of the worldwide Traditional Anglican Communion, which has about four hundred thousand members, had petitioned the Vatican on October 5, 2007, for full unity with the Catholic Church. They declared their willingness to adhere to the totality of Catholic doctrine while desiring to retain some of their distinct Anglican traditions. The Sacred Congregation of the Doctrine of the Faith responded favorably to the request in July 2008. On October 20, 2009, Cardinal William Levada, the prefect of the congregation, announced that Benedict would soon set up a structure to comply with the Anglican wishes. On November 9, 2009, *Anglicanorum Coetibus* was published.[112]

---

109 Ibid.

110 Teresita Johnson, "Cardinal Says Catholics Humbled by Anglicans' Decision to Join Church," CNS, June 22, 2009, www.thecatholicspirit.com.

111 Benedict XVI, "Apostolic Constitution *Anglicanorum Coetibus* (Groups of Anglicans): Providing for Personal Ordinariates for Anglicans Entering into Full Communion with the Catholic Church," dated November 4, 2009, www.vatican.va.

112 Zenit News Agency, "Canadian Anglicans Ask for Catholic Ordinariate," March 15, 2010.

Since then, according to Zenit, the House of Bishops of the Anglican Church in America of the Traditional Anglican Communion announced on March 3, 2010, their decision to request the implementation of the apostolic constitution in the United States for their 5,200 members in 100 congregations.[113] And on March 12, 2010, the College of Bishops of the Anglican Catholic Church of Canada petitioned the Sacred Congregation for the Doctrine of the Faith for full communion as well. In the petition, they expressed their wish to "seek a communal and ecclesial way of being Anglican Catholics in communion with the Holy See."[114]

In *Anglicanorum Coetibus*, Benedict states that, as one who has been "mandated by the Lord Jesus to guarantee the unity of the episcopate and to preside over and safeguard the universal communion of all the Churches," he could not fail to respond to the repeated requests of "groups of Anglicans" for "full Catholic communion."

Benedict continues most eloquently to describe the reason why the Church was "instituted by our Lord Jesus Christ": to be a "people gathered into the unity of the Father, the Son and the Holy Spirit [*LG* 4; *UR* 2] . . . as 'a sacrament—a sign and instrument, that is, of communion with God and of unity among all people' " [*LG* 1]. He then describes the damage that division in the Church has caused:

> Every division among the baptized in Jesus Christ wounds that which the Church is and that for which the Church exists; in fact, "such division openly contradicts the will of Christ, scandalizes the world, and damages that most holy cause, the preaching the Gospel to every creature" [*UR*, 1]. Precisely for this reason, before shedding his blood for the salvation of the world, the Lord Jesus prayed to the Father for the unity of his disciples [cf. Jn 17:20–21; *UR*, 2].[115]

That is the unity which we have seen is the goal of human history and the plan of salvation, as designed by God, which division in the Church has repeatedly attempted to thwart.

Full communion with the Catholic Church is not a pipe-dream, but a dream that is already coming to pass and that, God willing, will be realized in the future with other Christian communities. It is only a matter of time, God's will, and Christian initiative.

---

[113] Zenit News Agency, "US Anglicans to Request Catholic Ordinariate: 5,200 Expected to Enter Communion with Church," March 4, 2010, www.zenit.org.

[114] Ibid.

[115] Benedict XVI, *Anglicanorum Coetibus*, opening paragraphs.

Bibliography

Abbott, Walter M., S.J., gen. ed. *The Documents of Vatican II*. New York: Guild, 1966. See Paul VI.

Abbott-Smith, G. *A Manual Greek Lexicon of the New Testament*. Edinburgh: T. and T. Clark, 1956 [1921].

ABC News/*Washington Post* poll, July 18, 20–21, 2007. www.pollingreport.com.

Abernethy, Bob. "Bob Abernethy Interview with Princeton University Professor Peter Singer." *Religion & Ethics Newsweekly*, September 12, 1999, 1–13. www.pbs.org.

AbortionTV.com. "Abortion Statistics." www.abortiontv.com/Misc/Abortion Statisticshtm#UnitedStates.

Albright, William F., and C. S. Mann, eds. *Matthew*. Anchor Bible 26. Garden City, NY: Doubleday, 1971.

Allen, John L., Jr. "Evangelical Strength in Latin America Is Homegrown." *National Catholic Reporter*, August 25, 2006. ncronline.org.

American Association of University Professors (AAUP). *1940 Statement of Principles on Academic Freedom and Tenure*. www.aaup.org/AAUP/pubsres/policydocs/contents/1940statement.htm.

American Association of University Women (AAUW). *Hostile Hallways: The AAUW Survey on Sexual Harassment in America's Schools*. Washington, DC: AAUW, 2001.

Americans United for Life. "History of FOCA." April 23, 2010. http://www.aul.org/2010/04/history-of-the-freedom-of-choice-act/.

Appleby, R. Scott. "*Church and Age Unite*!" *The Modernist Impulse in American Catholicism*. Notre Dame, IN: University of Notre Dame, 1992.

Associated Press. "Age, Religion Factors in Ariz. Marriage Vote." November 5, 2008. www.azcentral.com.

———. "Poll: New Pope Should Push for Change: Most Americans Want Priests to Be Able to Marry, AP Survey Finds." April 4, 2005. www.msnbc.msn.com.

———. "Top Court Upholds Abortion Ban." April 18, 2007. www.msnbc.msn.com.

———. "10 Holy Cross Priests Object to Obama Notre Dame Invite." April 8, 2009. www.foxnews.com.

Association of Catholic Colleges and Universities (ACCU). Newsletter. *Update* 35 (Summer 2009). www.accunet.org.

Astin, Alexander W., and Helen S. Astin, co-principal investigators. *The Spiritual Life of College Students: A National Study of College Students' Search for Meaning and Purpose.* Los Angeles: HERI, University of California, Los Angeles (Fall 2004).

———, Helen S. Astin, and Jennifer A. Lindholm. *Cultivating the Spirit: How College Can Enhance Students' Inner Lives.* San Francisco: Jossey-Ball, 2011.

Baklinski, Thaddeus M. "Quest to Have Chimps Declared Persons Rejected by Austrian Supreme Court." May 23, 2008. www.lifesitenews.com.

Baldwin, Lou. "Archdiocese Takes Roll." *Catholic Standard and Times*, July 9, 1998.

Banerjee, Neela. "U.S. Bishops Adopt Guidelines on Gays." *New York Times*, November 15, 2006. www.nytimes.com.

Barclay, William. *The Letters to the Galatians and Ephesians.* Rev. ed. [Galatians, 1954; Ephesians, 1956]. Daily Study Bible Series. Philadelphia: Westminster, 1976.

Barna Group. "Americans Reveal Their Top Priority in Life." Barna Update. March 6, 2006. www.barna.org.

———. "Spirituality May Be Hot in America, But 76 Million Adults Never Attend Church." Barna Update. March 20, 2006. www.barna.org.

———. *State of the Church: 2006.* April 2006.

———. "Survey Reveals the Life Christians Desire." Barna Update. July 21, 2008. www.barna.org.

———. "Young Adults and Liberals Struggle with Morality." Barna Update. August 25, 2008. www.barna.org.

Barth, Markus. *Ephesians.* Anchor Bible 34. Garden City, NY: Doubleday, 1974.

Bashir, Martin. "Kirk Cameron, From Sitcom Star to Evangelist." March 17, 2006. abcnews.go.com/Nightline.

Baylor Institute for Studies of Religion. *American Piety in the 21st Century: New Insights to the Depth and Complexity of Religion in the US.* Waco, TX: Baylor Institute for Studies of Religion, 2006. www.isreligion.org.

Benedict XVI (See also Ratzinger, Joseph Cardinal). "Apostolic Constitution Anglicanorum Coetibus (Groups of Anglicans): Providing for Personal Ordinariates for Anglicans Entering into Full Communion with the Catholic Church." November 4, 2009. www.vatican.va.

———. *God Is Love: Deus Caritas Est; Encyclical Letter.* Washington, DC: U.S. Conference of Catholic Bishops, 2006.

———. "Lecture of the Holy Father: Faith, Reason and the University; Memories and Reflections." University of Regensburg, September 12, 2006. www.vatican.va.

Bénéton, Philippe. "True and False Tolerance." *Crisis* 14 (April 1996): 34–37.

Berry, Jason, and Gerald Renner. *Vows of Silence: The Abuse of Power in the Papacy of John Paul II.* New York: Free, 2004.

Black, Justice. See *Everson.*

Blanch, Stuart. *Way of Blessedness.* New York: Ballantine, 1985.

Bleichner, Howard P., S.S. *View from the Altar: Reflections on the Rapidly Changing Catholic Priesthood.* New York: Crossroad, 2004.

Bloom, Allan. *The Closing of the American Mind: How Higher Education Has Failed Democracy and Impoverished the Souls of Today's Students.* New York: Simon and Schuster, 1987.

Boff, Leonardo, O.F.M. *Faith on the Edge: Religion and Marginalized Existence.* Translated by Robert R. Barr. New York: Harper & Row, 1989 [1978 and 1980].

Boff, Leonardo, O.F.M. and Clodovis Boff, O.S.M. *Introducing Liberation Theology.* Translated by Paul Burns. Maryknoll, NY: Orbis, 1987 [1986].

Boniface VIII. *Unam Sanctam* (1302). In Clarkson, *Church Teaches.*

Bonnard, Pierre. *L'Évangile selon Saint Matthieu.* Cited in Gutiérrez, *Theology of Liberation.*

Brady, I. C. "Medieval Philosophy." In *New Catholic Encyclopedia,* 11:289–92.

———. "Scholasticism." In *New Catholic Encyclopedia,* 12:757–62.

Brennan, Justice. See *Grand Rapids School District.*

Brown, Raymond E., S.S. *Biblical Reflections on Crises Facing the Church.* New York: Paulist, 1975.

———, intro., trans., and notes. *The Gospel according to John (i–xii).* Anchor Bible 29. Garden City, NY: Doubleday, 1966.

———, intro., trans., and notes. *The Gospel according to John (xiii–xxi).* Anchor Bible 29A. Garden City, NY: Doubleday, 1970.

———. *An Introduction to the New Testament.* New York: Doubleday, 1997.

———, ed. *The New Jerome Biblical Commentary* (*NJBC*). Englewood Cliffs, NJ: Prentice Hall, 1990 [1968].

Brown, Raymond E., S.S., Joseph A. Fitzmyer, S.J., and Roland E. Murphy, O.Carm., eds. *The Jerome Biblical Commentary.* Englewood Cliffs, NJ: Prentice Hall, 1968.

Buckley, Michael J., S.J. *At the Origins of Modern Atheism.* New Haven, CT: Yale, 1987.

Burke, Archbishop Raymond, Prefect of the Apostolic Signature, Vatican City. "The Teachings of the Catholic Church: Archbishop Burke's Keynote Address from Friday's National Catholic Prayer." May 8, 2009. www.lifesitenews.com.

Burtchaell, James Tunstead, C.S.C. *The Dying of the Light: The Disengagement of Colleges and Universities from Their Christian Churches.* Grand Rapids, MI: Eerdmans, 1998.

Bushinski, L. A. "Loisy, Alfred." In *New Catholic Encyclopedia,* 8:765–66.

Butler, Christopher. *Post-Modernism: A Very Short Introduction.* Oxford: Oxford University Press, 2002.

Calvez, J. Y., S.J., and T. Massaro, S.J. "Social Justice." In *New Catholic Encyclopedia,* 13:242–44.

Cardinal Newman Society. "U.S. Bishops Praise Bishop D'Arcy in Wake of Notre Dame Scandal." June 22, 2009. www.cardinalnewmansociety.org.

Carlin, David. *The Decline and Fall of the Catholic Church in America.* Manchester, NH: Sophia Institute, 2003.

Carroll, Colleen. *The New Faithful: Why Young Adults Are Embracing Christian Orthodoxy*. Chicago: Loyola, 2002.

Carroll, Joseph. "Gallup Poll Assesses Views of Young Americans." Gallup Poll. November 5, 2003. www.gallup.com.

Casey, Eileen. "Survey Shows Young Catholics' Political Views Mirror Those of Peers." Catholic News Service. October 14, 2008. www.catholicnews.com.

Catholic League for Religious and Civil Rights. "Media Ignore Sexual Abuse in the Schools." *Catalyst Online*. December 2007. www.catholicleague.org/printer.php?p=Catalyst&id=2351.

Catholic News Agency. "25,000 Attend West Coast Walk for Life, Event Continues to Grow." January 20, 2008. www.catholicnewsagency.com.

CatholicCulture.org. "Catholics Split on Notre Dame Invitation to Obama, Poll Shows." May 1, 2009. www.catholicculture.org/news/headlines/index.cfm?storyid=2792.

Catholic World News. "Archdiocese Removes College's Catholic Designation." April 29, 2005. www.catholicculture.org/news/.

CBS News poll. "Abortion and Birth Control." www.pollingreport.com.

Center for Applied Research in the Apostolate (CARA). *Sacraments Today: Belief and Practice among U.S. Catholics*. Washington, DC: Georgetown University, April 2008.

———. "Self-reported Mass Attendance of U.S. Catholics Unchanged during Last Five Years." January 2005.

Center for Bio-Ethical Reform. "Abortion Facts." abortionno.org.

Centers for Disease Control (CDC). National Center for Health Statistics. www.cdc.gov/nchs/.

———. "Abortion Surveillance—United States, 2007." Morbidity and Morality Weekly Report (MMWR).

Chadwick, H. "Justin Martyr." *National Catholic Encyclopedia* 8:94.

Chaput, Charles, Archbishop of Denver. "Archbishop Chaput on Notre Dame and the Issues That Remain." May 18, 2009. www.archden.org.

Chaves, Mark, and James C. Cavendish. "More Evidence on U.S. Catholic Church Attendance." *Journal for the Scientific Study of Religion* 33, no. 4 (1994): 376–81.

Cherry, Conrad, Betty A. DeBerg, and Amanda Porterfield. *Religion on Campus*. Chapel Hill, NC: University of North Carolina, 2001.

Clarke, Norris, S.J. "John Paul II: The Complementarity of Faith and Philosophy in the Search for Truth." *Communio: International Catholic Review* 26 (Fall 1999): 557–70.

Clarkson, John F., S.J., et al., eds. and trans. *The Church Teaches: Documents of the Church in English Translation*. St. Louis, MO: Herder, 1962 [1955].

Clayton, Mark. "Sex Abuse Spans Spectrum of Churches." *Christian Science Monitor*, April 5, 2002. www.csmonitor.com.

CNN.com. "Corruption Named as Key Issue by Voters in Exit Polls." November 7, 2006. www.cnn.com.

———. "Edison-Mitofsky Exit Poll." November 10, 2004. www.cnn.com.

CNN.com Politics. Election Center 2008. www.cnn.com.

"College Students Once Again Spend Break Helping Others." *America* 184 (April 2, 2001): 4.

Commission on Global Governance. *Our Global Neighbourhood.* Oxford: Oxford University Press, 1995.

Congregation for the Doctrine of the Faith (CDF). "Instruction on Certain Aspects of the 'Theology of Liberation.'" *Origins* 14 (September 13, 1984): 193, 195–204.

———. "Instruction on Christian Freedom and Liberation." *Origins* 15 (April 17, 1986): 713, 715–28.

———. *Inter Insigniores* (Declaration of the Question of Admission of Women to the Ministerial Priesthood). October 15, 1976.

———. "Response to 'Dubium.'" *Origins* 25 (November 30, 1995): 401, 403.

Copleston, Frederick, S.J. *A History of Philosophy.* Vol. 2, pt. 1, *Mediaeval Philosophy: Augustine to Bonaventure.* Garden City, NY: Doubleday Image, 1962 [1950].

———. *A History of Philosophy.* Vol. 3, *Ockham to Suárez.* Westminster, MD: Newman, 1953.

———. *A History of Philosophy.* Vol. 3, pt. 2, *Late Mediaeval and Renaissance Philosophy: The Revival of Platonism to Suárez.* Garden City, NY: Doubleday Image, 1963 [1953].

———. *A History of Philosophy.* Vol. 4, *Descartes to Leibniz.* Westminster, MD: Newman, 1961.

———. *A History of Philosophy.* Vol. 5, *Hobbes to Hume.* Westminster, MD: Newman, 1959.

———. *A History of Philosophy.* Vol. 6, *Wolff to Kant.* Westminster, MD: Newman, 1960.

———. *A History of Philosophy.* Vol. 9, pt. 2, *Bergson to Sartre.* Garden City, NY: Doubleday Image, 1977 [1974].

Cord, Robert L. *Separation of Church and State: Historical Fact and Current Fiction.* New York: Lambeth, 1982.

Corporation for National & Community Service (CNCS). *College Students Helping America.* CNCS Report. Washington, DC: CNCS, October 2006. www.nationalservice.gov.

Council of Florence (1438–1445). See Clarkson, *Church Teaches.*

Cozzens, Donald. *Sacred Silence: Denial and the Crisis in the Church.* Collegeville, MN: Liturgical, 2002.

Crilly, W. J. "Scholastic Philosophy." In *New Catholic Encyclopedia,* 12:749–50.

Crossan, D. M. "Justice of Men: In the Bible." In *New Catholic Encyclopedia,* 8:73–74.

Crossan, D. M., and T. G. Weinandy. "Justice of God: In the Bible." In *New Catholic Encyclopedia,* 8:70–71.

Crouse, Janice Shaw. "Sexual Misconduct in Schools." July 26, 2004. www.townhall.com.

Current Issues in Catholic Higher Education 20 (Fall 1999).

Currie, Duncan. "First-Time Voters for Life: What a Pace Poll Suggests about New Registrants and Abortion Rights." *Weekly Standard,* August 20, 2004. www.weeklystandard.com.

Cyprian, St. *De orat. Dom.* Cited in Paul VI, *Lumen Gentium.*

D'Antonio, William V. "The American Catholic Laity in 1999." *National Catholic Reporter*, October 29, 1999.

———. "Generational Differences." Table 9. *National Catholic Reporter*, October 29, 1999.

———. "Trends in U.S. Roman Catholic Attitudes, Beliefs, Behavior." *National Catholic Reporter*, October 29, 1999.

D'Antonio, William V., James D. Davidson, Dean R. Hoge, and Katherine Meyer. *American Catholics: Gender, Generation, and Commitment.* Walnut Creek, CA: AltaMira, 2001.

D' Antonio, William V., James D. Davidson, Dean R. Hoge, and Ruth A. Wallace. *American Catholic Laity in a Changing Church.* Kansas City, MO: Sheed and Ward, 1989.

———. *Laity American and Catholic: Transforming the Church.* Kansas City, MO: Sheed and Ward, 1996.

D'Arcy, John M., Bishop of Fort Wayne–South Bend Diocese. "Concerning President Barack Obama Speaking at Notre Dame Graduation, Receiving Honorary Law Degree." March 29, 2009. www.diocesefwsb.org.

———. "Concerning the 'Vagina Monologues.'" February 2006. www.diocesefwsb.org.

———. "Statement on Vagina Monologues." April 5, 2006. www.diocesefwsb.org.

Darroch, Jacqueline E., and Susheela Singh. "Why Is Teenage Pregnancy Declining? The Roles of Abstinence, Sexual Activity and Contraceptive Use." December 1999. www.guttmacher.org.

Davidson, James D. "Belief in Church as Mediator Slips," *National Catholic Reporter*, September 30, 2005.

———. "Challenging Assumptions about Young Catholics." *National Catholic Reporter*, September 30, 2005.

———. "Generations Have Different Views of the Church." *National Catholic Reporter*, October 29, 1999.

———. "What Catholics Believe about Abortion and the Death Penalty." *National Catholic Reporter*, September 30, 2005.

Davison, James D., and Dean R. Hoge. "Catholics After the Scandal." *Commonweal* 131 (November 19, 2004): 13–19.

Davidson, James D., et al. *The Search for Common Ground: What Unites and Divides Catholic Americans.* Huntington, IN: Our Sunday Visitor, 1997.

Decree for the Jacobites. Council of Florence (1438–1445). In Clarkson, *Church Teaches.*

De Lubac, Henri, S.J. "The Church in Crisis." *Theology Digest* 17 (Winter 1969): 312–25.

Dillenberger, John, and Claude Welch. *Protestant Christianity: Interpreted through Its Development.* New York: Scribner's Sons, 1954.

Dinges, William, Dean R. Hoge, Mary Johnson, and Juan L. Gonzales, Jr. "A Faith Loosely Held: The Institutional Allegiance of Young Catholics." *Commonweal* 125 (July 17, 1998): 13–18.

Dolan, Jay P. *The American Catholic Experience: A History from Colonial Times to the Present.* Notre Dame, IN: University of Notre Dame Press, 1992 [1985].

Donnelly, Brian. "Pedophilia: Abnormality or Alternate Lifestyle?" *Our Sunday Visitor*, August 15, 1999.

Donohue, William A. "Catholic League's Survey of American Catholics." *Catalyst* 22 (June 1995): 4–11.

Dreisbach, Daniel L. *Thomas Jefferson and the Wall of Separation between Church and State*. New York: New York University Press, 2002.

Duffy, Eamon. "Tradition and Authority: The Cardinal Hume Memorial Lecture, Newcastle, 27 November 2003." In Eamon Duffy, *Faith of Our Fathers: Reflections on Catholic Traditions*, 168–87. New York: Continuum, 2004.

Dulles, Avery Cardinal, S.J. "The Contemporary Magisterium." *Theology Digest* 17 (Winter 1969): 299–311.

———. "Faith and Reason: From Vatican I to John Paul II." In Foster and Koterski, *Two Wings of Catholic Thought*.

———. *The Resilient Church*. Garden City, NY: Doubleday, 1977.

Dupré, Louis. *The Enlightenment and the Intellectual Foundations of Modern Culture*. New Haven, CT: Yale, 2004.

Echevarria, Laura. "Barack Obama before Planned Parenthood Action Fund, July 17, 2007." www.lauraechevarria.com.

Ellis, John Tracy. "American Catholics and the Intellectual Life." *Thought* 30 (Autumn 1955).

Eminyan, M./eds. "Salvation, Necessity of the Church for." In *New Catholic Encyclopedia*, 12:624–26.

Everson v. Board of Education of the Township of Ewing et al., 330 U.S. 1 (1947). www.FindLaw.com.

Fabro, C. "Participation." In *New Catholic Encyclopedia*, 10:905–10.

Faith in Public Life. *The Young and the Faithful*. The Faith and American Politics Survey. October 2008. faithinpubliclife.org/content/faps/.

Feeney, Joseph J., S.J. "Can a Worldview Be Healed? Students and Postmodernism." *America* 177 (November 15, 1997): 12–16.

Fennell, Desmond. "A Fragile World: Post-Western Civilization." *Studies* 86 (Autumn 1997): 225–37.

Fennell, Francis L. "Respondents." Response to Joseph A. O'Hare, S.J. In Tripole, *Jesuit Education 21*: 444–47.

Fettmann, Eric. "The Page-Stalker That Dems Lionized." *New York Post*, October 17, 2006. www.nypost.com.

Fichter, Joseph H., S.J. "Foreword." In McNamara, *Conscience First*.

Filteau, Jerry. "Theologians Back Notre Dame Honoring Obama." *NCR Today*, May 14, 2009. ncronline.org.

Finer, Lawrence B., Lori F. Frohwirth, Lindsay A. Dauphinee, Susheela Singh and Ann M. Moore. "Reasons U.S. Women Have Abortions: Quantitative and Qualitative Perspectives." *Perspectives on Sexual and Reproductive Health*, 37 (2005): 110–18. www.guttmacher.org/pubs/psrh/full/3711005.pdf.

Finer, Lawrence B., and Stanley K. Henshaw. "Estimates of U.S. Abortion Incidence in 2001 and 2002." May 18, 2005. www.guttmacher.org.

Finn, Robert W., Bishop of Kansas City-St. Joseph Diocese. "Kansas City Bishop to Pro-Lifers: 'We Are at War!' " *National Catholic Reporter*, April 28, 2009. ncronline.org.

Fitzgerald, Valpy. "The Economics of Liberation Theology." In Rowland, *Liberation Theology*, 218–34.

Fitzmyer, Joseph A., S.J. "What Do the Scriptures Say About Justice?" In Tripole, *Jesuit Education 21*: 99–112.

Flanagan, Neal M., O.S.M. *The Gospel according to John and the Johannine Epistles*. Collegeville Bible Commentary 4. Collegeville, MN: Liturgical, 1983.

Foster, David Ruel, and Joseph W. Koterski, S.J. *The Two Wings of Catholic Thought: Essays on Fides et ratio*. Washington, DC: Catholic University of America, 2003.

Fourth Council of Constantinople (869–870). See Clarkson, *Church Teaches*.

Foust, Michael. "Tragic: U.S. Passed 47 Million Mark for Abortions in 2005." *Baptist Press News*, January 20, 2005. www.bpnews.net.

Franz, Wanda, Ph.D. "Public Opinion and the Morality of Abortion." January 28, 2006. www.nrlc.org.

Fraser, Barbara, and Paul Jeffrey. "Latin America: Search for a Future." *National Catholic Reporter*, May 14, 2004. ncronline.org.

Friedland, Lewis A., and Shauna Morimoto. *CIRCLE Working Paper 40: The Changing Lifeworld of Young People: Risk, Resume-Padding, and Civic Engagement*. Center for Information and Research on Civic Learning and Engagement, University of Wisconsin-Madison, September 2005. www.civicyouth.org.

Froehle, Bryan T., and Mary L. Gautier. *Catholicism USA: A Portrait of the Catholic Church in the United States*. Maryknoll, NY: Orbis, 2000.

Frost, S. E., Jr. *Basic Teachings of the Great Philosophers: A Survey of Their Basic Ideas*. New and enlarged ed. Garden City: Doubleday Dolphin, 1962 [1942].

Fulgentius of Ruspe. *De Fide ad Petrum*. Cited in Decree for the Jacobites.

Fuller, Robert C. *Spiritual, But Not Religious: Understanding Unchurched America*. New York: Oxford University Press, 2001.

Gallin, Alice, O.S.U. *Independence and a New Partnership in Catholic Higher Education*. Notre Dame, IN: University of Notre Dame, 1996.

———, ed. "Land O'Lakes Statement: The Nature of the Contemporary Catholic University," 7–12, and "Rome Statement: The Catholic University and the Aggiornamento," 17–36. In *American Catholic Higher Education: Essential Documents, 1967–1990*. Notre Dame, IN: University of Notre Dame, 1992.

Gallup, George H., Jr. "Catholics Trail Protestants in Church Attendance." Gallup Poll. December 16, 2003. www.gallup.com.

———, ed. *The Gallup Poll: Public Opinion 1972–77*. Wilmington, DE: Scholarly Resources, 1978.

———, ed. *The Gallup Poll: Public Opinion 1979*. Wilmington, DE: Scholarly Resources, 1980.

———, ed. *The Gallup Poll: Public Opinion 1991*. Wilmington, DE: Scholarly Resources, 1992.

———, ed. *The Gallup Poll: Public Opinion 1998*. Wilmington, DE: Scholarly Resources, 1999.

———. "Religion and Values." Gallup Tuesday Briefing. February 19, 2002. www.gallup.com.

———. *Religion in America 1996*. Princeton: Princeton Religion Research Center, 1996.

———. *Religion in America 2002.* Princeton: Princeton Religion Research Center, n.d.

———. "The Religiosity Cycle." Gallup Poll. June 4, 2002. www.gallup.com.

———. *The Spiritual Life of Young Americans: Approaching the Year 2000.* Princeton, NJ: George H. Gallup International Institute, 1999.

———. " 'Unchurched' on the Rise?" Gallup Tuesday Briefing. March 26, 2002. www.gallup.com.

Gallup, George H., Jr., and D. Michael Lindsay. *Surveying the Religious Landscape: Trends in U.S. Beliefs.* Harrisburg, PA: Morehouse, 1999.

Gallup, George H., Jr., and Jim Castelli. *The American Catholic People: Their Beliefs, Practices, and Values.* Garden City, NY: Doubleday, 1987.

Gallup, George H., Jr., and Jim Castelli. *The People's Religion: American Faith in the 90's.* New York: Macmillan, 1989.

Gallup Organization. "Abortion." January 26, 2006. www.gallup.com/poll/1576/abortion.aspx.

Gautier, Mary L. "Does Catholic Education Make a Difference?" *National Catholic Reporter*, September 30, 2005.

———. "Lay Catholics Firmly Committed to Parish Life." *National Catholic Reporter.* September 30, 2005.

Geiger, L.-B. "Christian Philosophy." In *New Catholic Encyclopedia*, 3:538–42.

Geis, Sonya. "Latino Catholics Increasingly Drawn to Pentecostalism." *Washington Post*, April 30, 2006.

Gibson, David. *The Coming Catholic Church: How the Faithful Are Shaping a New American Catholicism.* New York: HarperSanFrancisco, 2003.

Gilbert, Kathleen. "San Francisco Abp. Emeritus Issues Letter of Support to Obama amid ND Scandal." May 15, 2009. www.lifesitenews.com.

Gleason, Philip. *Contending with Modernity: Catholic Higher Education in the Twentieth Century.* New York: Oxford, 1995.

Gonzales v. Carhart et al. Slip Opinion, No. 05-380. October Term 2006. April 18, 2007. www.FindLaw.com.

Goodnough, Abby. "New Hampshire Legalizes Same-Sex Marriage." *New York Times*, June 3, 2009. www.nytimes.com.

Goodstein, Laurie. "Decades of Damage; Trail of Pain in Church Crisis Leads to Nearly Every Diocese." *New York Times*, January 12, 2003.

Grand Rapids School District v. Ball, 473 U.S. 373 (1985). www.FindLaw.com

Grassi, Joseph A., M.M. "The Letter to the Ephesians." In Brown, *Jerome Biblical Commentary.*

Greeley, Andrew M. "After the Synod." America 125 (November 20, 1971): 424–26.

———. *American Catholics Since the Council: An Unauthorized Report.* Chicago: Thomas More, 1985.

———. *The Catholic Myth: The Behavior and Beliefs of American Catholics.* New York: Scribner's, 1990.

———. "The Crisis in American Catholicism." *Courier-Journal*, April 7, 14, 21, 28, and May 5, 1976.

———. *Crisis in the Church.* Chicago: Thomas More, 1979.

———. *Sex: The Catholic Experience.* Chicago: Thomas More, 1994.
———. "Sex and the Single Catholic: The Decline of an Ethic." *America* 167 (November 7, 1992): 342–47, 358–59.
Gregory XVI. "Encyclical Letter *Mirari Nos Arbitramur* (1832)." In Neuner and Dupuis, *Christian Faith.*
Grenz, Stanley J. *A Primer on Postmodernism.* Grand Rapids, MI: Eerdmans, 1996.
Gutiérrez, Gustavo. *Gustavo Gutiérrez: Essential Writings.* Edited and with introduction by James B. Nickoloff. Maryknoll, NY: Orbis, 1996.
———. "Option for the Poor: Review and Challenges." *Promotio Justitiae* 57 (September 1994): 11–18.
———. "The Power and the Poor in History" (1979). In *Gustavo Gutiérrez: Essential Writings.*
———. "The Task and Content of Liberation Theology" (1999). Translated by Judith Condor. In Rowland, *Liberation Theology*, 19–38.
———. *A Theology of Liberation: History, Politics, and Salvation.* Rev. ed. Translated and edited by Sr. Caridad Inda and John Eagleson. Maryknoll, NY: Orbis, 1988 [1971].
———. "Toward a Theology of Liberation" (July 1968). In Hennelly, *Liberation Theology.*
Guttmacher Institute. "Facts on Induced Abortion in the United States." July 2008. www.guttmacher.org.
———. *40 Years, 4 Defining Achievements: Advancing Sexual and Reproductive Health Worldwide through Research, Policy Analysis and Public Education.* 2007 Annual Report. www.guttmacher.org.
Hadaway, C. Kirk, Penny Long Marler, and Mark Chaves. "What the Polls Don't Show: A Closer Look at U.S. Church Attendance." *American Sociological Review* 58 (December 1993): 741–52.
Hamburger, Philip. "Against Separation." *Public Interest* 155 (Spring 2004): 177–92.
———. *Separation of Church and State.* Cambridge, MA: Harvard University Press, 2002.
Hamilton College National Youth Polls. "Hot Button Issues Poll: Guns, Gays and Abortion." January 2006. www.hamilton.edu/news/polls/HotButtonFinalReport.pdf.
Häring, Bernard, C.S.S.R. "Justice." In *New Catholic Encyclopedia*, 8:64–69.
Harrington, Edward F. "The Metaphorical Wall." *America* 192 (January 17–24, 2005): 10–13.
Harris Poll. "Abortion and Birth Control." Accessed May 31, 2009. www.pollingreport.com.
Harvanek, R. V. "Patristic Philosophy." In *New Catholic Encyclopedia*, 10:957–62.
Hatfield, Gary. "Reason." In Kors, *Encyclopedia of the Enlightenment*, 3:404–9.
Haughey, John C., S.J. *Should Anyone Say Forever? On Making, Keeping, and Breaking Commitments.* Garden City, NY: Doubleday, 1975.
Heaney, J. J. "Modernism, Oath Against." In *New Catholic Encyclopedia*, 9:757–58.
Hebblethwaite, Peter with C. Rowland. "Liberation Theology and the Roman Catholic Church" (1994–1999). In Rowland, *Liberation Theology*, 179–98.
Hegel, E. "Enlightenment." In *New Catholic Encyclopedia*, 5:254–55.

Hegy, Pierre. "'End of American Catholicism?'—Another Look." *America* 168 (May 1, 1993): 4–9.

Hemmerle, Klaus. Citations from *Thesen zu einer trinitarischen Ontologie*. In Körner, *Thinking Beyond the Reef.*

Hemming, Laurence Paul, and Susan Frank Parsons. *Restoring Faith in Reason: A New Translation of the Encyclical Letter "Faith and Reason" of Pope John Paul II together with a Commentary and Discussion.* Notre Dame, IN: University of Notre Dame, 2002.

Hennelly, Alfred T., S.J., ed. and trans. *Liberation Theology: A Documentary History*. Maryknoll, NY: Orbis, 1990.

Herr, Edward C. "The Catholic Priesthood." *Overview* 19, August 1985.

———. "The State of the Church." *Overview*, May 1985.

Hiesberger, Jean Marie, gen. ed. The Catholic Bible. Personal Study Edition of the New American Bible. New York: Oxford University Press, 1991.

Higher Education Research Institute (HERI). "Spiritual Changes in Students during the Undergraduate Years: New Longitudinal Study Shows Growth in Spiritual Qualities from Freshman to Junior Years." Spirituality in Higher Education. Los Angeles: Graduate School of Education & Information Studies, UCLA, December 18, 2007. www.spirituality.ucla.edu.

———. *The Spiritual Life of College Students: A National Study of College Students' Search for Meaning and Purpose.* Los Angeles: HERI, Graduate School of Education & Information Studies, UCLA, Fall 2004. www.spirituality.ucla.edu.

———. *Spirituality in Higher Education: A National Study of College Students' Search for Meaning and Purpose: Summary of Selected Findings (2000–2003).* Spirituality in Higher Education. Los Angeles: Graduate School of Education & Information Studies, UCLA, October 2004. www.spirituality.ucla.edu.

———. Spirituality in Higher Education brochure. Los Angeles: Graduate School of Education & Information Studies, UCLA. Accessed March 21, 2011, www.spirituality.ucla.edu/docs/spirituality-brochure.pdf.

———. "Students Experience Spiritual Growth during College: UCLA Study Reveals Significant Changes in Undergraduates' Values & Beliefs." Spirituality in Higher Education. Los Angeles: Graduate School of Education & Information Studies, UCLA, December 18, 2007. www.spirituality.ucla.edu.

———. "What is Spirituality?" Spirituality in Higher Education. Los Angeles: Graduate School of Education & Information Studies, UCLA, December 18, 2007. www.spirituality.ucla.edu.

Hitchcock, James. *The Decline and Fall of Radical Catholicism.* Garden City, NY: Doubleday Image, 1972 [1971].

———. *The Supreme Court and Religion in American Life.* Vol. 1, *The Odyssey of the Religion Clauses.* Princeton, NJ: Princeton University Press, 2004.

———. *The Supreme Court and Religion in American Life.* Vol. 2, *From "Higher Law" to "Sectarian Scruples."* Princeton, NJ: Princeton University Press, 2004.

Hoge, Dean R. "Attitudes of Catholics Highly Committed to the Church." *National Catholic Reporter*, September 30, 2005.

———. "Catholic Generations Polarized on Gender and Sex." *America* 179 (November 21, 1998): 16–18.

———. "Center of Catholic Identity." *National Catholic Reporter*, September 30, 2005.

Hoge, Dean R., William D. Dinges, Mary Johnson, S.N.D. de N., and Juan L. Gonzales, Jr. *Young Adult Catholics: Religion in the Culture of Choice*. Notre Dame, IN: University of Notre Dame, 2001.

Holusha, John, and Neela Banerjee. "Evangelical Leader Says He Bought Drugs." *New York Times*, November 3, 2006. www.nytimes.com.

Horowitz, Juliana. "Winds of Political Change Haven't Shifted Public's Ideology Balance." November 25, 2008. pewresearch.org

Hout, Michael, and Andrew M. Greeley. "The Center Doesn't Hold: Church Attendance in the United States, 1940–1984." *American Sociological Review* 52 (June 1987): 325–45.

Hsuan, Amy, Melissa Navas, and Bill Graves. "Schools Cut Secret Deals with Abusive Teachers." *The Oregonian*, February 18, 2008. www.oregonlive.com.

———. "Schools Let Sex Abuse Cases Slide." *The Oregonian*, February 17, 2008. www.oregonlive.com.

Hyman, Gavin. *The Predicament of Postmodern Theology: Radical Orthodoxy or Nihilist Textualism?* Louisville: Westminster John Knox, 2001.

Institute of Politics, Harvard University. "Redefining Political Attitudes and Activism: A Poll by Harvard's Institute of Politics." April 11, 2006. www.iop.harvard.edu.

Irvine, Martha, and Robert Tanner. "Sexual Misconduct Plagues U.S. Schools." StatesmanJournal.com (Salem, OR). October 21, 2007. www.statesman journal.com.

Janssen, Sarah, ed. "Number, Ratio, and Rate of Legal Abortions in the U.S., 1970–2006." *World Almanac and Book of Facts 2011*. New York: World Almanac Books, 2011.

Jenkins, John I., C.S.C. "Closing Statement on Academic Freedom and Catholic Character." April 4, 2006. newsinfo.nd.edu/news/8155-father-jenkins-issues-closing-statement-on-notre-damersquos-academic-freedom-catholic-character/.

———. "Text of Speech by Notre Dame President Rev. John I. Jenkins." May 17, 2009. www.southbendtribune.com.

John Jay College of Criminal Justice. *The Nature and Scope of Sexual Abuse of Minors by Catholic Priests and Deacons in the United States 1950–2002.* Washington, DC: United States Conference of Catholic Bishops, 2004.

John Paul I. "Catechetical Lesson on the Theological Virtue of Hope." September 20, 1978. In Hennelly, *Liberation Theology*.

John Paul II. "The Beatitude of the Poor: Christmas Message of John Paul II." *Origins* 14 (January 10, 1985): 496–98.

———. *Dives in Misericordia* ("Rich in Mercy"). Encyclical on the Mercy of God. Washington, DC: United States Catholic Conference, 1981.

———. *Ecclesia de Eucharistia* ("Church of the Eucharist"). Encyclical on the Eucharist. In *Origins* 32 (May 1, 2003): 753, 755–68.

———. "*Ex Corde Ecclesiae*: The Apostolic Constitution on Catholic Universities." *Origins* 20 (October 4, 1990): 265, 267–76.

———. *Fides et Ratio*. Encyclical on Faith and Reason. In *Origins* 28 (October 22, 1998): 317, 319–47.

———. *Mulieris Dignitatem* (On the Dignity and Vocation of Women). August 15, 1976.

———. "Opening Address at the Puebla Conference." In John Eagleson and Philip Scharper, eds. *Puebla and Beyond: Documentation and Commentary*. Translated by John Drury. Maryknoll, NY: Orbis, 1979.

———. *Ordinatio Sacerdotalis*. Apostolic Letter on Ordination and Women. In *Origins* 24 (June 9, 1994): 49, 51–52.

———. "Pope John Paul II, Selections from 'Opening Address at the Puebla Conference' (January 28, 1979)." In Hennelly, *Liberation Theology*, 225–32.

———. *Ut Unum Sint* ("That All May Be One"). Encyclical on Commitment to Ecumenism. In *Origins* 25 (June 8, 1985): 49, 51–72.

———. *Veritatis Splendor*. Encyclical on the Splendor of Truth. In *Origins* 23 (October 14, 1993): 297, 299–334.

John Paul II and Dimitrios I, Ecumenical Patriarch. Joint Declaration. December 7, 1987. *Acta Apostolicae Sedis* 80 (1988). Cited in John Paul II, *Ut Unum Sint*.

Johnson, Benton, Dean R. Hoge, and Donald A. Luidens. "Mainline Churches: The Real Reason for Decline." *First Things* 31 (March 1993): 13–18.

Johnson, Luke Timothy. *The Creed: What Christians Believe and Why It Matters*. New York: Doubleday, 2003.

Johnson, Mary, et al. "Young Adult Catholics: Conservative? Alienated? Suspicious?" *America* 180 (March 27, 1999): 9–13.

Johnson, Robert. *NFPC* (National Federation of Priests' Council) *News Notes*. March 1984. Cited in "The Catholic Priesthood," *Overview*.

Johnson, Teresita. "Cardinal Says Catholics Humbled by Anglicans' Decision to Join Church." Catholic News Service. June 22, 2009. www.thecatholicspirit.com.

Jones, Jeffrey M. "Majority of Americans Continue to Oppose Gay Marriage." May 27, 2009. www.gallup.com.

———. "Obama Approval Rating Stable, Polarized." April 7, 2009. www.gallup.com.

Jones, Kenneth C. *Index of Leading Catholic Indicators: The Church Since Vatican II*. St. Louis, MO: Oriens, 2003.

Kant, Immanuel. "What Is Enlightenment?" In Immanuel Kant, *Critique of Practical Reason: And Other Writings in Moral Philosophy*, 286–92. Translated and edited by Lewis White Beck. Chicago: University of Chicago, 1949 (Original: in *Berlinische Monatsschrift* 4 [1784]: 481–94).

Katz, Wilber G. "The Case for Religious Liberty." In John Cogley, ed. *Religion in America*. New York: Meridian, 1958.

Kelly, James R. "Abortion: What Americans *Really* Think and the Catholic Challenge." *America* 165 (November 2, 1991): 310–16.

Kinsey, A. C., et al. *Sexual Behavior in the Human Female*. Philadelphia, 1953.

———. *Sexual Behavior in the Human Male*. Philadelphia, 1948.

Kittel, Gerhard, ed. *Theological Dictionary of the New Testament* 1. Translated and edited by Geoffrey W. Bromiley. Grand Rapids, MI: Eerdmans, 1964.

Klocker, H. R. "Ockhamism." In *New Catholic Encyclopedia*, 10:535–37.

Kmiec, Douglas. "Finding Common Ground on Life Issues." *National Catholic Reporter*, June 1, 2009. ncronline.org.

———. "Obama at Notre Dame: Incomplete Eloquence." *National Catholic Reporter*. Accessed May 26, 2009. ncronline.org.

Knights of Columbus/Marist College Institute for Public Opinion Poll. *Moral Issues and Catholic Values.* October 2008. www.kofc.org/un/cmf/resources/Communications/documents/moralissues.pdf

Kobelski, Paul J. "The Letter to the Ephesians." In Brown, *New Jerome Biblical Commentary.*

Kohut, Andrew. "Post-Election Perspectives." November 13, 2008. pewresearch.org.

———. "Young Voters in the 2008 Election." November 12, 2008. pewresearch.org.

Körner, Bernhard. "Thinking Beyond the Reef: The Cross, Faith, and Reason in the *Trinitarian Ontology* of Klaus Hemmerle." *Communio* 26 (Fall 1999): 662–81.

Kors, Alan Charles, ed. *Encyclopedia of the Enlightenment.* Oxford: Oxford University Press, 2003.

Kosmin, Barry A., and Ariela Keysar. *American Religious Identification Survey 2008* (*ARIS 2008*): *Summary Report.* Hartford, CT: Trinity College, March 2009. www.americanreligionsurvey-aris.org.

Kosmin, Barry A., and Seymour P. Lachman. *One Nation Under God: Religion in Contemporary American Society.* New York: Harmony, 1993.

Kosnik, Anthony, William Carroll, Agnes Cunningham, Ronald Modras, and James Schulte. *Human Sexuality: New Directions in American Catholic Thought.* Commissioned by Catholic Theological Society of America. New York: Paulist, 1977.

Kreeft, Peter. *A Refutation of Moral Relativism: Interviews with an Absolutist.* San Francisco: Ignatius, 1999.

Lakeland, Paul. *The Liberation of the Laity: In Search of an Accountable Church.* New York: Continuum, 2002.

———. *Postmodernity: Christian Identity in a Fragmented Age.* Minneapolis: Fortress, 1997.

Lauer, R. Z. "Enlightenment, Philosophy of." In *New Catholic Encyclopedia,* 5:259–64.

Lawler, Philip F. "A Principle Rejected." *Catholic World Report* 7 (March 1997): 44–50.

Leege, David C., and Msgr. Joseph Gremillion. "Notre Dame Study of Catholic Parish Life: Pastors and People; Viewpoints on Church Policies and Positions." *Origins* 15 (April 24, 1986): 733–44.

Lemon v. Kurtzman, 403 U.S. 602 (1971). www.FindLaw.com.

"Letter of the Holy Office to the Archbishop of Boston (1949)." In Neuner and Dupuis, *Christian Faith.*

Levine, Judith. *Harmful to Minors: The Perils of Protecting Children from Sex.* Cited in Robert F. Worth, "Renegade View on Child Sex Causes a Storm." *New York Times,* April 13, 2002. www.nytimes.com.

LifeSiteNews.com. "Catholics Overwhelmingly Oppose Notre Dame Honor to Obama: Ramussen [*sic*] Poll." May 9, 2009. www.lifesitenews.com.

———. "List of Bishops Opposing the Notre Dame Invitation and Award to President Obama." May 6, 2009. www.lifesitenews.com.

———. "Notre Dame Alumni Confirm $13.9 Million in Withheld Donations." May 15, 2009. www.lifesitenews.com.

Livingston, James C. *Modern Christian Thought*. Vol. 1, *The Enlightenment and the Nineteenth Century*. 2nd ed. Upper Saddle River, NJ: Prentice Hall, 1997 [1988].

Livingston, James C. and Francis Schüssler Fiorenza. *Modern Christian Thought*. Vol. 2, *The Twentieth Century*. 2nd ed. Upper Saddle River, NJ: Prentice Hall, 2000 [1997].

Lynch v. Donnelly, 465 U.S. 38 (1984). www.*FindLaw*.com.

Lyons, Linda. "Protestants vs. Catholics: Who's Got Religion? Catholics Lag behind Protestants." Gallup Poll. January 25, 2005. www.gallup.com.

———. "Religiosity Measure Shows Stalled Recovery." January 11, 2005. www.gallup.com.

MacCulloch, Diarmaid. *The Reformation*. New York: Viking Penguin, 2003.

MacDonald, Margaret Y. *Colossians and Ephesians*. Sacra Pagina 17. Collegeville, MN: Liturgical, 2000.

Magister, Sandro. "The Church in Spain Is Sick, but It's Not Zapatero's Fault." July 28, 2006. www.chiesa.espressonline.it.

Malone, James. "Vatican II and the Postconciliar Era in the U.S. Church." Origins 15 (September 26, 1985): 225–33.

Marcovitz, Hal. *Teens & Gay Issues*. Broomall, PA: Mason Crest, 2005.

———. *Teens & Sex*. Broomall, PA: Mason Crest, 2004.

Marion, Jean-Luc. *God without Being*. Translated by Thomas A. Carlson. Chicago: University of Chicago Press, 1991 [1982].

Marks, Helen M., and Susan Robb Jones. "Community Service in Transition: Shifts and Continuities in Participation from High School to College." *Journal of Higher Education* 75/3 (May/June 2004): 307–39.

Masci, David. "Catholic Church in the U.S." *CQ Researcher* 5 (September 8, 1995): 777, 779–95.

"Massive Crowd Marches." *National Catholic Register*, February 8, 2009. www.ncregister.com.

Masters, W. H., and V. E. Johnson. *Human Sexual Response*. Boston, 1966.

Mathewes-Green, Frederica. "Embryonic Trend: How Do We Explain the Drop in Abortions?" *Policy Review* 73 (Summer 1995). www.policyreview.org.

Matthews, Chris. "Hardball." MSNBC. April 18, 2005. www.msnbc.msn.com.

Maziarz, E. A. "Philosophy." In *New Catholic Encyclopedia*, 11:275–81.

Mazzuca, Josephine. "Current Teen Views on Abortion." Gallup Poll. March 11, 2003. www.gallup.com.

McAvoy, T. T. "Americanism." In *New Catholic Encyclopedia*, 1:354–56.

McBrien, Richard P. *The Church: The Evolution of Catholicism*. New York: HarperOne, 2008.

———. "More on the Leadership Crisis." *National Catholic Reporter*, June 1, 2009. ncronline.org.

———. *The Remaking of the Church: An Agenda for Reform*. New York: Harper & Row, 1973.

———. "The Silence of the Presidents." *National Catholic Reporter*, June 8, 2009. ncronline.org.

McCready, William C., and Andrew M. Greeley. "The End of American Catholicism?" *America* 127 (October 28, 1972): 334–38.

McEvoy, James. "Commentary." In Hemming and Parsons, *Restoring Faith*, 175–98.

McNamara, Patrick H. *Conscience First, Tradition Second: A Study of Young American Catholics.* Albany, NY: State University of New York, 1992.

McNeil, Donald G., Jr. "When Human Rights Extend to Nonhumans." *New York Times*, June 13, 2008. www.nytimes.com.

Meacham, Jon. "The End of Christian America." *Newsweek*, April 13, 2009, 34–38.

Mead, Sidney E. *The Lively Experiment: The Shaping of Christianity in America.* Harper & Row, 1973.

Meek v. Pittinger, 421 U.S. 349 (1975). www.FindLaw.com.

Meier, John P. "Jesus among the Theologians: Sobrino and Segundo." In John P. Meier. *The Mission of Christ and His Church: Studies in Christology and Ecclesiology*, 49–69. Good News Studies 30. Wilmington, DE: Glazier, 1990.

———. *A Marginal Jew: Rethinking the Historical Jesus.* Vol. 1, *The Roots of the Problem and the Person.* New York: Doubleday, 1991.

Mejia, Jorge Julio, S.J. "Headline articles: Latin America: All Coherence Gone." Jesuits and Partners together for Justice. www.sjweb.info/sjs/headlines/news Show/cfm?PubTextID-2731.

Metzger, Bruce M., and Roland E. Murphy, gen. eds. The New Oxford Annotated Bible. New York: Oxford University Press, 1991.

Miller, Madeleine S., and J. Lane Miller, eds. *Harper's Encyclopedia of Bible Life.* 3rd rev. ed. San Francisco: Harper & Row, 1982.

Moloney, Francis J., S.D.B. "Johannine Theology." In Brown, *New Jerome Biblical Commentary*, no. 83.

Moody, Ernest A. "William of Ockham." In Paul Edwards, ed. *Encyclopedia of Philosophy* 8:306–17. New York: Macmillan and Free Press, 1967.

Mooney, Christopher F., S.J. *Religion and the American Dream: The Search for Freedom Under God.* Philadelphia: Westminster, 1977.

Morey, Melanie M., and John J. Piderit, S.J. *Catholic Higher Education: A Culture in Crisis.* New York: Oxford University Press, 2006.

Mott, S. C. "The Use of the New Testament for Social Ethics." *Journal of Religious Ethics* 15 (Fall 1987): 225–60.

Moynihan, Robert, ed. *Let God's Light Shine Forth: The Spiritual Vision of Pope Benedict XVI.* New York: Doubleday, 2005.

Mueller, Mary Ann. "Houston, TX: Anglican Use Conference: Three Days of Grace." VirtueOnline.org News. June 15, 2009. www.virtueonline.org.

Mühlen, Heribert. *Esprit dans l'Église.* Cited in Gutiérrez, *Theology of Liberation.*

Murphy, F. X. "Patristic Theology." In *New Catholic Encyclopedia*, 10:964–69.

Murphy, Jarret. "Abortion Battles at the Crossroads." January 22, 2003. www.cbsnews.com.

Murphy-O'Connor, Cormac Cardinal. "Christianity Almost Defeated in Britain, Cardinal Says." Zenit News Agency. September 6, 2001. www.zenit.org.

Murray, Mark. "Obama on Judges, Supreme Court." July 17, 2007. www.firstread.msnbc.msn.com.

Muth, Chaz. "Bad Economy Seen as Cause for Reports of Increased Abortion." Catholic News Service. April 6, 2009. www.americancatholic.org/News/news2print/newsreport.aspx?id=926.

National Center for Health Statistics. "Pregnancy Rate Drops for U.S. Women Under Age 25." Centers for Disease Control and Prevention. April 14, 2008. www.cdc.gov.

———. "Teen Birth Rate Rises for First Time in 15 Years." Centers for Disease Control and Prevention. December 5, 2007. www.cdc.gov/nchs/pressroom/07newsreleases/teenbirth.htm.

National Opinion Research Center (NORC) General Social Survey (GSS). Cumulative Data File, 1972–2004. Roper Center for Public Opinion Research, University of Connecticut. CD-ROM.

———. General Social Survey (GSS) Cumulative Data File, 1972–2008. Survey Documentation and Analysis Program, University of California, Berkeley. sda.berkeley.edu/archive.htm.

National Right to Life. "Abortion in the United States: Statistics and Trends." www.nrlc.org.

———. "A Closer Look: Factors Involved in Abortion Decline." January 2008. www.nrlc.org.

———. "The Presidential Record on Life: President Barack Obama 2009–Present." Accessed June 2009. www.nrlc.org.

Nealy, F. D. "Ignorance." In *New Catholic Encyclopedia*, 7:314–15.

Neuhaus, Richard John. "The Public Square: A Continuing Survey of Religion and Public Life: Scandal Time (Continued)." *First Things* 124 (June/July 2002): 75–83.

———. "Public Square: Scandal Time III." *First Things* 125 (August/September 2002): 85–93.

Neumayr, George. "*Ex Corde Ecclesiae* and the Notre Dame Affair." Editorial. *Catholic World Report*, May 2009.

Neuner, J., S.J., and J. Dupuis, S.J., eds. *The Christian Faith in the Doctrinal Documents of the Catholic Church*. 6th rev. and enlarged ed. New York: Alba House, 1996 [1973].

New American Bible (NAB). Personal Size Edition. New York: Catholic, 1992.

New Catholic Encyclopedia. 2nd rev. ed. Detroit: Gale, 2003 [1967].

Newport, Frank. "Americans Remain Very Religious, But Not Necessarily in Conventional Ways." Gallup Poll. December 24, 1999. www.gallup.com.

———. "Catholics Similar to Mainstream on Abortion, Stem Cells: Catholics Actually More Liberal on Some Issues." March 30, 2009. www.gallup.com.

———. "Estimating Americans' Worship Behavior: Survey-based Estimates Have Value." Gallup Poll. January 3, 2006. www.gallup.com.

———. "Mormons, Evangelical Protestants, Baptists Top Church Attendance List: Jews and Episcopalians Least Likely to Attend on Regular Basis." Gallup Poll. April 14, 2006. www.gallup.com.

———. "Religion Most Important to Blacks, Women, and Older Americans." Gallup Poll. November 29, 2006. www.gallup.com/poll/25585.

———. "This Easter, Smaller Percentage of Americans Are Christian." Gallup Poll. April 10, 2009. www.gallup.com.

———. "Update: Americans and Religion." Gallup Poll. December 23, 2004. www.gallup.com.

———. "U.S. Catholics Vary Widely on Moral Issues." April 8, 2005. www.gallup.com.

Newport, Frank and Lydia Saad. "Religion, Politics Inform Americans' Views on Abortion: Churchgoing Frequency Is Associated with Strength of Anti-abortion Views." Gallup Poll News Service, April 3, 2006. www.gallup.com.

NewsMax.com. "Democrats Narrow Gap in Religious Vote." November 19, 2006. www.newsmax.com.

Nickoloff, James B. See Gutiérrez, Gustavo.

Novak, Michael. "Defining Social Justice." *First Things* 108 (December 2000): 11–13.

———. "Liberation Theology and the Pope." In Hennelly, *Liberation Theology*, 272–81. Originally published in the June 1979 issue of *Commentary*.

———. *On Two Wings: Humble Faith and Common Sense at the American Founding*. San Francisco: Encounter, 2002.

———. *Will It Liberate? Questions about Liberation Theology*. New York: Paulist Press, 1986.

O'Bannon, Randall K. "Support for Pro-Life Policies and Legislation Growing." www.nrlc.org/news/1998.

O'Brien, David J. "American Catholics in an Age of Crisis." *New City* (November 1967).

———. "The Land O'Lakes Statement." *Boston College Magazine* 58 (Winter 1998): 38–45.

———. *The Renewal of American Catholicism*. New York: Oxford University Press, 1972.

O'Brien, George Dennis. *The Idea of a Catholic University*. Chicago: University of Chicago Press, 2002.

O'Hare, Joseph A., S.J. "What Are the Odds of Jesuit Higher Education Surviving in America?" In Tripole, *Jesuit Education* 21: 434–43.

O'Malley, John W., S.J. "Barack Obama and Vatican II." *America*, May 25, 2009. www.americamagazine.org.

O'Reilly, David. "A Faith in Flux." June 4, 2006. www.philly.com.

Orsy, Ladislaus, S.J. "The Congregation's 'Response': Its Authority and Meaning." America 173 (December 9, 1995): 4–5.

Oscar-Empokae, Osaui. "History of the Freedom of Choice Act." April 23, 2010. www.aul.org/2010/04/history-of-the-freedom-of-choice-act/.

Ostling, Richard N. "Protestant Sex-Abuse Data Murky." *Oakland Tribune*, February 23, 2004. www.findarticles.com.

Ott, Ludwig. *Fundamentals of Catholic Dogma*. Translated by Patrick Lynch. St. Louis: Herder, 1964 [1952].

Padover, Saul K., ed. *The Complete Jefferson*. Duell, Sloan & Pearce, 1943.

Page, Susan. "Survey Reveals Affection, Respect for John Paul." April 3, 2005. www.usatoday.com.

Parker, Star. "Moral Relativism and Obama at Notre Dame." May 17, 2009. town hall.com.

Paul VI. *Ad Gentes* (Decree on the Church's Missionary Activity). December 7, 1965. In Abbott, *Vatican II*.

———. *Apostolicam Actuositatem* (Decree on the Apostolate of the Laity). November 18, 1965. In Abbott, *Vatican II.*

———. *Christus Dominus* (Decree on the Bishops' Pastoral Office in the Church). October 28, 1965. In Abbott, *Vatican II.*

———. *Dei Verbum* (Dogmatic Constitution on Divine Revelation). November 18, 1965. In Abbott, *Vatican II.*

———. *Dignitatis Humanae* (Decree on Religious Freedom). December 7, 1965. In Abbott, *Vatican II.*

———. *Evangelii Nuntiandi* (Apostolic Exhortation on Evangelization in the Modern World). December 8, 1975. Washington, DC: United States Catholic Conference, 1976.

———. *Gaudium et Spes* (Pastoral Constitution on the Church in the Modern World). December 7, 1965. In Abbott, *Vatican II.*

———. *Humanae Vitae* (Encyclical Letter on Human Life). July 25, 1968.

———. *Lumen Gentium* (Dogmatic Constitution on the Church). November 21, 1964. In Abbott, *Vatican II.*

———. *Nostra Aetate* (Declaration on the Relationship of the Church to Non-Christian Religions). October 28, 1965. In Abbott, *Vatican II.*

———. *Populorum Progressio* (Encyclical on the Development of Peoples). March 26, 1967. Boston: Daughters of St. Paul, n.d.

———. *Sacrosanctum Concilium* (Constitution on the Sacred Liturgy). December 4, 1963. In Abbott, *Vatican II.*

———. *Unitatis Redintegratio* (Decree on Ecumenism). November 21, 1964. In Abbott, *Vatican II.*

Pennsylvania Pro-Life Federation. "2005 Abortion Polls Show Americans Support Abortion Restrictions!" *LifeLines* 25 (Winter 2006).

Perkins, Pheme. "The Letter to the Ephesians." The New Interpreter's Bible 11. Nashville, TN: Abingdon, 2000.

Pew Forum on Religion & Public Life. "Attitudes Toward Homosexuality in African Countries." November 14, 2006. pewresearch.org.

———. *Faith in Flux: Changes in Religious Affiliation in the U.S.* April 2009. www.pewforum.org.

———. "How the Faithful Voted." November 10, 2008. www.pewforum.org.

———. "Pragmatic Americans Liberal and Conservative on Social Issues." August 3, 2006. www.pewforum.org.

———. "Religion & Public Life: A Faith-Based Partisan Divide." Washington, DC: Pew Forum on Religion & Public Life, 2005. www.pewforum.org.

———. "States with Voter-Approved Constitutional Bans on Same-Sex-Marriage, 1998–2008." November 13, 2008. www.pewforum.org/Gay-Marriage-and-Homosexuality/States-with-Voter-Approved-Constitutional-Bans-on-Same-Sex-Marriage-1998-2008.aspx.

———. "Support for Civil Unions vs. Gay Marriage." Accessed November 15, 2006. pewresearch.org.

———. *U.S. Religious Landscape Survey [Report 1]: Religious Affliation; Diverse and Dynamic.* Washington, DC: Pew Research Center, February 2008. www.religions.pewforum.org.

———. *U.S. Religious Landscape Survey [Report 2]: Religious Beliefs and Practices; Diverse and Politically Relevant.* Washington, DC: Pew Research Center, June 2008. www.religions.pewforum.org.

Pew Research Center. "Election '06: Big Changes in Some Key Groups." November 16, 2006. pewresearch.org.

———. "Sex, Drugs and the 1040: A Barometer of Modern Morals." March 28, 2006. pewresearch.org.

Pew Research Center for the People & the Press. "Abortion, the Court and the Public." October 3, 2005. people-press.org/commentary/?analysisid=119.

———. "Less Opposition to Gay Marriage, Adoption and Military Service." March 22, 2006. www.people-press.org.

———. "Public Takes Conservative Turn on Gun Control, Abortion." April 30, 2009. pewresearch.org.

Pinckaers, Servais, O.P. *The Sources of Christian Ethics.* Washington, DC: Catholic University Press, 1995.

Pittau, Archbishop Giuseppe, S.J. "Nature and Mission of the Catholic Colleges and Universities." In Tripole *Jesuit Education 21*: 365–68.

Pius IX. *Quanto Conficiamur Moerore* (1863). In Clarkson, *Church Teaches.*

Pius XI. *Divini Redemptoris* (Of the Divine Redeemer). March 19, 1937. *Acta Apostolicae Sedis* 29. Cited in Calvez, "Social Justice."

PollingReport.com. "Abortion and Birth Control." *Los Angeles Times*/Bloomberg Poll. www.pollingreport.com/abortion.htm and www.pollingreport.com/abortion2.htm.

Porter, Roy S. "England." In Kors, *Enlightenment,* 1:409–15.

Potkay, Adam. "Happiness." In Kors, *Enlightenment,* 2:181–83.

Pryor, John H., Sylvia Hurtado, Victor B. Saenz, José Luis Santos, and William S. Korn. *The American Freshman: Forty Year Trends, 1966–2006.* Los Angeles: HERI, University of California, Los Angeles. April 2007.

Pryor, John L., Sylvia Hurtado, Linda DeAngelo, Laura Paluki Blake, and Serge Tran. *The American Freshman: National Norms Fall 2009.* Los Angeles: HERI, University of California, Los Angeles, 2009.

______. *The American Freshman: National Norms Fall 2010.* Los Angeles: HERI, University of California, Los Angeles, 2010.

Pryor, John H., Sylvia Hurtado, Linda DeAngelo, Jessica Sharkness, Laura C. Romero, William S. Korn, and Serge Tran. *The American Freshman: National Norms for Fall 2008.* Los Angeles: HERI, University of California, Los Angeles, 2008.

Public Policy Institute of California. "Just the Facts: Support of Proposition 8 Strongly Tied to Religion." December 2008. www.ppic.org/content/pubs/jtf/JTF_Prop8JTF.pdf.

Quinn, David. "Too Little, Too Late, Again." *The Tablet* 26 (February 27, 2010): 8–9.

Quinnipiac University Polling Institute. "Notre Dame Should Not Disinvite Obama." Release detail. May 14, 2009. www.quinnipiac.edu.

Ratzinger, Joseph Cardinal (See also Benedict XVI). "Faith, Philosophy and Theology." Address delivered at College of Saint Thomas, St. Paul, MN, 1984. In Joseph Cardinal Ratzinger, *The Nature and Mission of Theology: Essays to Orient Theology in Today's Debates*. Translated by Adrian Walker. San Francisco: Ignatius, 1995 [1993].

———. "Future Pope's Homily for Conclave's Opening." *Origins* 34 (April 28, 2005): 719–20.

———. *God and the World: Believing and Living in Our Time*. Conversation with Peter Seewald. Translated by Henry Taylor. San Francisco: Ignatius, 2002 [2000].

———. *Introduction to Christianity*. Translated by J. R. Foster. New York: Herder, 1971 [1968].

———. "Relativism: The Central Problem for Faith Today." Address to Presidents of the Doctrinal Commissions of the Bishops' Conferences of Latin America, Guadalajara, Mexico, May 1996. www.ewtn.com.

———. *Salt of the Earth: Christianity and the Catholic Church at the End of the Millennium*. Interview with Peter Seewald. Translated by Adrian Walker. San Francisco: Ignatius, 1997 [1996].

———. *Truth and Tolerance: Christian Belief and World Religions*. Translated by Henry Taylor. San Francisco: Ignatius, 2004 [2003].

Ratzinger, Joseph Cardinal, with Vittorio Messori. *The Ratzinger Report: An Exclusive Interview on the State of the Church*. Translated by Salvator Attanasio and Graham Harrison. San Francisco: Ignatius, 1985.

Reese, Thomas J., S.J. "The Bishops' Dispirited Agenda." Georgetown/On Faith: This Catholic's View, June 16, 2009. www.washingtonpost.com/blogs/georgetown-on-faith/.

———. "Memo to Bishops: Most Catholics Aren't Listening." Georgetown/On Faith: This Catholic's View, May 5, 2009. www.washingtonpost.com/blogs/georgetown-on-faith/.

———. "Notre Dame—Opinion: With One of Their Own under Fire, University Presidents Stood Silent." *National Catholic Reporter*. Accessed June 26, 2009. ncronline.org.

Reeves, Linda. "Catholics play major role in passage of marraige amendment," November 11, 2008, www.thefloridacatholic.org/iv/catholics-play-major-role-in-passage-of-marriage-amendment?searchPhrase=amendment2'sapproval aidedbyCatholic. *Wallace v. Jaffee*, 472 US 38 (1985). www.FindLaw.com

Reill, Peter Hanns, and Ellen Judy Wilson. *Encyclopedia of the Enlightenment*. New York: Facts on File, 1996.

Reilly, Patrick J. "Are Catholic Colleges Leading Students Astray?" *Catholic World Report* 13 (March 2003): 38–46. cns.winxweb.com/Portals/0/docs/UCLA Study.pdf

Richardson, Herbert W. *Toward an American Theology*. New York: Harper & Row, 1967.

Riley, Naomi Schaefer. *God on the Quad: How Religious Colleges and the Missionary Generation Are Changing America*. New York: St. Martin's, 2005.

Roberts, Tom. "Jesuit Educators Back Obama Notre Dame Invitation." *National Catholic Reporter*. Accessed April 13, 2009. ncronline.org.

Robinson, B. A. "Abortion Statistics: U.S. Abortion Ratio by Year." Ontario Consultants on Religious Tolerance. Accessed December 3, 2010. www.religioustolerance.org/abo_decr3.htm.

Rowland, Christopher, ed. *The Cambridge Companion to Liberation Theology*. Cambridge, UK: Cambridge University Press, 1999.

———. "Introduction: The Theology of Liberation." In Rowland, *Liberation Theology*, 1–16.

Russell, R. P. "Augustinianism." In *New Catholic Encyclopedia* 1:875–82.

Rutledge, Justice. See in *Everson*.

Saad, Lydia. "Abortion Views Reviewed as Alito Vote Nears." January 20, 2006. www.gallup.com.

———. "Americans Agree with Banning 'Partial-Birth Abortion.'" Gallup Poll, November 6, 2003. www.gallup.com.

———. "Americans at Odds Over Gay Rights." Gallup Poll. May 31, 2006. www.gallup.com.

———. "Americans Still Oppose Gay Marriage." Gallup Poll. May 22, 2006. www.gallup.com.

———. "More Americans 'Pro-Life' Than 'Pro-Choice' for First Time." May 15, 2009. www.gallup.com.

Samuel, Stephanie. "West Coast Pro-Life March Draws 40,000 in San Francisco," www.christianpost.com/news/west-coast-pro-life-march-draws-40000-in-san-francisco-48619/.

Schepers, M. B. "Liberalism, Theological." In *New Catholic Encyclopedia* 8:542–43.

Schepers, M. B./eds. "Lutheranism." In New Catholic Encyclopedia 8:887–96.

Schindler, David L. "God and the End of Intelligence: Knowledge as Relationship." *Communio* 26 (Fall 1999): 510–40.

Schultenover, David G., S.J. *A View from Rome: On the Eve of the Modernist Crisis*. New York: Fordham University Press, 1993.

Scola, Angelo. "The Integrity of Human Experience: Cultural Dimensions and Implications of the Encyclical *Fides et ratio*." In Hemming and Parsons, *Restoring Faith*, 256–76.

Second Council of Lyons (1274). See Clarkson, *Church Teaches*.

Second General Conference of Latin American Bishops. Bogotá and Medellín, Columbia, August 24–September 6, 1968. "Document on Justice." In Hennelly, *Liberation Theology*.

Senior, Donald, gen. ed. The Catholic Study Bible. New York: Oxford University Press, 1990.

Shakeshaft, Charol. "Educator Sexual Misconduct: A Synthesis of Existing Literature." Office of the Under Secretary, U.S. Department of Education. Washington, DC, June 2004, #2004-09.

Shaw, Russell. "Error of Americanism." *Our Sunday Visitor*, May 3, 2009.

———. "Obama Addresses Abortion at Notre Dame Commencement." Accessed May 31, 2009. www.osv.com.

Shorto, Russell. "Contra-Contraception." *New York Times Magazine*, May 7, 2006. www.nytimes.com.

Singer, Peter. "Animal Liberation at 30." *New York Review of Books* 50 (May 15, 2003): 23–26.

———. Letter posted on online magazine *Slate*, June 2001. Quoted in McGovern, Celeste, "Human Rights for Apes?" *National Catholic Register*, July 8, 2001.

Smith, Christian, with Melinda Lundquist Denton. *Soul Searching: The Religious and Spiritual Lives of American Teenagers*. New York: Oxford University Press, 2005.

Smith, Christian, Melinda Lundquist Denton, Robert Faris, and Mark Regnerus. "Mapping American Adolescent Religious Participation." *Journal for the Scientific Study of Religion* 41 (2002): 597–612.

Smith, George D., D.D. *The Teaching of the Catholic Church: A Summary of Catholic Doctrine*. 2 vols. New York: MacMillan, 1952.

SNAP (Survivors Network of those Abused by Priests) press statement, June 14, 2006. www.snapnetwork.org.

Soergel, P. and W. S. Barron, Jr. "Reformation, Protestant (on the Continent)." In *New Catholic Encyclopedia* 12:11–12.

Solomon, David. "A President's Retreat." *Wall Street Journal*. April 14, 2006. www.opinionjournal.com.

Soskice, Janet Martin. "*Fides et ratio*: The Post-Modern Pope." In Hemming and Parsons, *Recovering Faith*, 292–96.

Spanish Bishops Conference. "Theology and Secularization in Spain, Forty Years after the End of Vatican Council II." Pastoral Instruction. March 30, 2006.

Stark, Rodney. *What Americans Really Believe: New Findings from the Baylor Surveys of Religion*. Waco, TX: Baylor University Press, 2008.

Steinfels, Peter. *A People Adrift: The Crisis of the Roman Catholic Church in America*. New York: Simon & Schuster, 2003.

Sullivan, Francis A., S.J. "Guideposts from Catholic Tradition." *America* 173 (December 9, 1995): 5–6.

"Supreme Court Rules on Pennsylvania Abortion Control Act." *Origins* 22 (July 9, 1992): 113, 115–42.

Sweeney, Michael. "The Medievalism of *Fides et ratio*." In Foster and Koterski, *Two Wings of Catholic Thought*, 163–76.

Sweetser, Thomas P., S.J. "The Parish: What Has Changed, What Remains?" *America* 174 (February 17, 1996): 6–7.

Synod of Bishops, Second Extraordinary (November 24–December 8, 1985). "A Message to the People of God," "The Final Report," and "An Ecumenical Service: The Pope's Address." *Origins* 15 (December 19, 1985): 441, 443–44; 444–50; 453–54.

Synod of Bishops, Second General Assembly (September 30–November 6, 1971). "Justice in the World." (November 30, 1971): 513–29. In Joseph Gremillion, *The Gospel of Peace and Justice: Catholic Social Teaching since Pope John*. Maryknoll, NY: Orbis, 1976.

Teske, R. J. "Augustine, St." In *New Catholic Encyclopedia*, 1:850–68.

Third General Conference of Latin American Bishops. Puebla de los Angeles, Mexico. January 27–February 13, 1979. "Base-Level Ecclesial Communities (CEBs), the Parish, and the Local Church." In Hennelly, *Liberation Theology*.

———. "Document on the Poverty of the Church." In Hennelly, *Liberation Theology*, 116.

———. "Message to the Peoples of Latin America." In Hennelly, *Liberation Theology*, 93.

———. "Puebla Final Document: 'Preferential Option for the Poor.'" In Hennelly, *Liberation Theology*.

Thiselton, Anthony C. *Interpreting God and the Postmodern Self: On Meaning, Manipulation, and Promise*. Grand Rapids, MI: Eerdmans, 1995.

"Religion: To Save a Bankrupt." *Time*, February 21, 1972. www.Time.com.

Tripole, Martin R., S.J. "The American Church in Jeopardy." *America* 175 (September 28, 1996): 9–15.

———. "*Ex Corde Ecclesiae*: A History from Land O'Lakes to Now." *Review for Religious* 59 (September–October 2000): 454–70.

———. *Faith Beyond Justice: Widening the Perspective*. St. Louis: Institute of Jesuit Sources, 1994.

———, ed. *Jesuit Education 21: Conference Proceedings on the Future of Jesuit Higher Education, 25–29 June 1999*. Philadelphia: Saint Joseph's University Press, 2000.

———. "Religion and the First Amendment: How the Supreme Court Has Misinterpreted the Constitution." *Christianity in Crisis* 5 (June 1987): 12–20.

United Nations Development Program. "Report on Democracy in Latin America: Overview." April 21, 2004. www.undp.org.

———. "The Report on the Development of Democracy in Latin America, Brief to the Secretary General of the United Nations, February 2004." April 21, 2004. www.undp.org.

United States Catholic Conference. *Catechism of the Catholic Church*. 2nd rev. ed. Washington, DC: USCC, 1997.

United States Census Bureau. "Live Births, Deaths, Marriages, and Divorces: 1960 to 1007." 2011 Statistical Abstract, Table 78. www.census.gov/compendia/statab/2011/tables/.

United States Conference of Catholic Bishops (USCCB). "Catholics in Political Life." June 2004. usccb.org/bishops.

———. "*Ex Corde Ecclesiae*: An Application to the United States." *Origins* 30 (June 15, 2000): 68–75.

———. "U.S. Bishops Express Support for Bishop D'arcy [*sic*] and His Pastoral Concern for the University of Notre Dame." June 22, 2009. www.usccb.org.

University of California, Berkeley. "Quick Table: GSS 1972–2006 Cumulative Datafile." sda.berkeley.edu/.

Vatican Council I (1869–1870). In Clarkson, *Church Teaches*.

Vatican Council II (1962–1965). See Abbott, Walter.

Vawter, Bruce, C. M. "Johannine Theology." In Brown, *Jerome Biblical Commentary*.

Vidler, Alec. R. *The Church in an Age of Revolution: 1789 to the Present Day*. New York: Penguin, 1990 [1961; rev. ed. 1974].

———. *A Variety of Catholic Modernists*. Cambridge: Cambridge University Press, 1970.

Viviano, Benedict T., O.P. "The Gospel according to Matthew." In Brown, *New Jerome Biblical Commentary.*

Wagner, Steven. "Behaviors and Beliefs of Current and Recent Studies at U.S. Catholic Colleges." *Studies in Catholic Higher Education.* Cardinal Newman Society, Center for the Study of Catholic Higher Education, October 2008. www.CatholicHigherEd.org.

Wald, Kenneth D. *Religion and Politics in the United States.* 4th ed. Lanham, MD: Rowman & Littlefield, 2003.

Wallace v. Jaffree, 472 U.S. 38 (1985). Justice Rehnquist, dissenting. www.FindLaw.com.

Wallis, Jim. *God's Politics: Why the Right Gets It Wrong and the Left Doesn't Get It.* San Francisco: Harper, 2005.

Walz v. Tax Commission, 397 U.S. 664 (1970). www.Findlaw.com.

Weigel, George. *The Courage to Be Catholic: Crisis, Reform, and the Future of the Church.* New York: Basic, 2002.

———. *The Cube and the Cathedral: Europe, America, and Politics without God.* New York: Basic, 2005.

———. "George Weigel on the Church Crisis in U.S." Interview by Zenit News Agency. August 29, 1992. www.zenit.org.

———. "Obama and the 'Real' Catholics." May 18, 2009. www.nationalreview.com.

Westen, John-Henry. "Princeton Professor Singer: And I Repeat, I Would Kill Disabled Infants." September 12, 2006. www.lifesitenews.com.

———. "400,000 March for Life in DC with Great Joy," January 26, 2011, www.lifesitenews.com/home/print_article/news/28200/.

Williams, Raymond. "Letter from London: The Catholic Crisis." *The Nation* 205 (July 17, 1967): 51–52.

World Almanac and Book of Facts, "Number, Ratio, and Ratae of Legal Abortions in the U.S., 1970–2006."

Younis, Mohamed. "Muslim Americans Exemplify Diversity, Potential." March 2, 2009. www.muslimwestfacts.com.

Zenit News Agency. "Britain Is a Pagan Country, Says Cardinal Murphy-O'Connor." January 20, 2003. www.zenit.org.

———. "Canadian Anglicans Ask for Catholic Ordinariate." March 15, 2010. www.zenit.org.

———. "Christianity Almost Defeated in Britain, Cardinal Says." September 6, 2001. www.zenit.org

———. "European Parliament Recommends Recognition of Homosexual Couples." March 17, 2000. www.zenit.org.

———. "Generation X and the Turn to Christian Orthodoxy: Journalist Colleen Carroll on a Surprising Trend." April 29, 2003. www.zenit.org.

———. "US Anglicans to Request Catholic Ordinariate: 5,200 Expected to Enter Communion with Church." March 4, 2010. www.zenit.org.

Zinnbauer, Brian J., Kenneth I. Pargament, et al. "Religion and Spirituality: Unfuzzying the Fuzzy." *Journal for the Scientific Study of Religion* 36 (December 1997): 549–64.

Zogby International. "Majority of Catholics Approve of Same-Sex Civil Unions but Not Same-Sex Marriage." May 11, 2005. www.zogby.com/news/ReadNews.cfm?ID=992.

———. "National Survey of Catholic Adults." March 2006. www.philly.com/mld/inquirer/news/special_packages/catholic/14727180.htm?template.

———. "Support for Abortion in Sharp Decline." Interactive Poll. January 23, 2006. www.zogby.com.

About the Author

MARTIN R. TRIPOLE, S.J., is professor emeritus of theology, Saint Joseph's University, Philadelphia, Pennsylvania. Father Tripole has edited two volumes of essays on Jesuit education: *Jesuit Education 21: Conference Proceedings on the Future of Jesuit Higher Education* (Saint Joseph's University Press, 2000) and *Promise Renewed: Jesuit Higher Education for a New Millennium* (Loyola Press, 1999); written a study on Jesuit spirituality: *Faith Beyond Justice: Widening the Perspective* (Institute of Jesuit Sources, 1994); and a work on Christology: *The Jesus Event and Our Response* (Alba House, 1980). He has published numerous essays and book reviews on theology, spirituality, and education, in various Catholic publications, such as *Theological Studies* and *Review for Religious*, and has also taught at Marquette University in Milwaukee, Wisconsin, and at Le Moyne College and Syracuse University in Syracuse, New York. He has an S.T.D. from the Institut Catholique in Paris, France.

Index

CPSIA information can be obtained at www.ICGtesting.com
Printed in the USA
BVOW011252270312

286121BV00006B/5/P